W9-CAB-176

MAGILL'S
LITERARY ANNUAL
2006

MAGILL'S
LITERARY ANNUAL
2006

Essay-Reviews of 200 Outstanding Books
Published in the United States During 2005

With an Annotated List of Titles

Volume One
A-L

Edited by
JOHN D. WILSON
STEVEN G. KELLMAN

SALEM PRESS
Pasadena, California   Hackensack, New Jersey

LIBRARY OF CONGRESS CATALOG CARD NO. 77-99209
ISBN 1-58765-280-3 (set)
ISBN 1-58765-310-9 (vol. 1)
ISBN 978-1-58765-280-6 (set)
ISBN 978-1-58765-310-0 (vol. 1)

FIRST PRINTING

PRINTED IN CANADA

028.1
M1945
2006
v. 1

CONTENTS

Publisher's Note ix
Complete Annotated List of Titles xi
Contributing Reviewers xxxv

Active Liberty: Interpreting Our Democratic Constitution—
    Stephen G. Breyer 1
Acts of Faith—*Philip Caputo* 5
The American Classics: A Personal Essay—*Denis Donoghue* 8
American Ghosts: A Memoir—*David Plante* 13
American Prometheus: The Triumph and Tragedy of J. Robert
    Oppenheimer—*Kai Bird* and *Martin J. Sherwin* 17
America's Constitution: A Biography—*Akhil Reed Amar* 22
The Angel of Forgetfulness—*Steve Stern* 27
The Assassins' Gate: America in Iraq—*George Packer* 32
At Day's Close: Night in Times Past—*A. Roger Ekirch* 37

The Beatles: The Biography—*Bob Spitz* 41
Becoming Justice Blackmun: Harry Blackmun's Supreme Court
    Journey—*Linda Greenhouse* 45
Before the Frost—*Henning Mankell* 49
The Best Day the Worst Day: Life with Jane Kenyon—*Donald Hall* 54
Black Maria—*Kevin Young* 58
Blinding Light—*Paul Theroux* 62
Blink: The Power of Thinking Without Thinking—*Malcolm Gladwell* 66
The Bomb: A Life—*Gerard J. DeGroot* 70
Borges and the Eternal Orangutans—*Luis Fernando Verissimo* 74
Born Losers: A History of Failure in America—*Scott A. Sandage* 79
Boss Tweed: The Rise and Fall of the Corrupt Pol Who Conceived the
    Soul of Modern New York—*Kenneth D. Ackerman* 84
Bound for Canaan: The Underground Railroad and the War for
    the Soul of America—*Fergus M. Bordewich* 89
Break, Blow, Burn: Camille Paglia Reads Forty-three of the
    World's Best Poems—*Camille Paglia* 94
Budget Travel Through Space and Time—*Albert Goldbarth* 99
Bury the Chains: Prophets and Rebels in the Fight to Free
    an Empire's Slaves—*Adam Hochschild* 103

Campo Santo—*W. G. Sebald* 107
Carnivore Diet—*Julia Slavin* 111
A Changed Man—*Francine Prose* 115
Christ the Lord: Out of Egypt—*Anne Rice* 119
The Chrysanthemum Palace—*Bruce Wagner* 123
The Cigar Roller—*Pablo Medina* 127
The City: A Global History—*Joel Kotkin* 132
Classical Music in America: A History of Its Rise and Fall—
    Joseph Horowitz 137
Collapse: How Societies Choose to Fail or Succeed—
    Jared Diamond 142
Collected Poems—*Jane Kenyon* 147
The Collected Poems of Kenneth Koch—*Kenneth Koch* 151
Collected Stories—*Carol Shields* 155
The Command of the Ocean: A Naval History of Britain,
    1649-1815—*N. A. M. Rodger* 159
A Crack in the Edge of the World: America and the Great
    California Earthquake of 1906—*Simon Winchester* 164
The Cube and the Cathedral: Europe, America, and
    Politics Without God—*George Weigel* 168

The Dark Genius of Wall Street: The Misunderstood Life of Jay Gould,
    King of the Robber Barons—*Edward J. Renehan, Jr.* 173
Defining the World: The Extraordinary Story of Dr. Johnson's
    Dictionary—*Henry Hitchings* 177
Dictionary Days: A Defining Passion—*Ilan Stavans* 181
DisneyWar—*James B. Stewart* 186
The Dominion of War: Empire and Liberty in North America,
    1500-2000—*Fred Anderson* and *Andrew Cayton* 191

The Earth and Sky of Jacques Dorme—*Andreï Makine* 196
Edmund Wilson: A Life in Literature—*Lewis M. Dabney* 200
The End of Poverty: Economic Possibilities for Our Time—
    Jeffrey D. Sachs 204
Equiano, the African: Biography of a Self-Made Man—
    Vincent Carretta 209
Eudora Welty: A Biography—*Suzanne Marrs* 214
Europe Central—*William T. Vollmann* 219
Extremely Loud and Incredibly Close—*Jonathan Safran Foer* 224

Faculty Towers: The Academic Novel and Its Discontents—
    Elaine Showalter 229
The Failure of the Founding Fathers: Jefferson, Marshall,
    and the Rise of Presidential Democracy—*Bruce Ackerman* 234

CONTENTS

Faith at War: A Journey on the Frontlines of Islam, from
    Baghdad to Timbuktu—*Yaroslav Trofimov* 239
Fallen—*David Maine* 243
February House—*Sherill Tippins*. 247
Finding George Orwell in Burma—*Emma Larkin* 251
The First Poets: Lives of the Ancient Greek Poets—*Michael Schmidt* 255
Five Families: The Rise, Decline, and Resurgence of America's
    Most Powerful Mafia Empires—*Selwyn Raab* 260
Fledgling—*Octavia E. Butler* 265
Fleshmarket Alley—*Ian Rankin* 270
Follies: New Stories—*Ann Beattie* 275
Foucault and the Iranian Revolution: Gender and the Seductions
    of Islamism—*Janet Afary* and *Kevin B. Anderson* 279
The Founders on Religion: A Book of Quotations—
    James H. Hutson, Editor 284
1491: New Revelations of the Americas Before Columbus—
    Charles C. Mann 288
Freakonomics: A Rogue Economist Explores the Hidden Side
    of Everything—*Steven D. Levitt* and *Stephen J. Dubner* 292

The Glass Castle—*Jeannette Walls* 296
God's Gym—*John Edgar Wideman* 301
The Golden West: Hollywood Stories—*Daniel Fuchs* 305
The Good Wife—*Stewart O'Nan* 309
A Great Improvisation: Franklin, France, and the Birth of
    America—*Stacy Schiff* 313

The Ha-Ha—*Dave King* 318
Harry Potter and the Half-Blood Prince—*J. K. Rowling* 322
Henry Adams and the Making of America—*Garry Wills* 327
The Historian—*Elizabeth Kostova* 332
The History of Love—*Nicole Krauss* 336
The Hot Kid—*Elmore Leonard* 340
The Hummingbird's Daughter—*Luis Alberto Urrea* 344
The Hungry Tide—*Amitav Ghosh* 349

The Icarus Girl—*Helen Oyeyemi* 354
The Ice Queen—*Alice Hoffman* 358
If This Be Treason: Translation and Its Dyscontents: A Memoir—
    Gregory Rabassa 362
Imagined Cities: Urban Experience and the Language of
    the Novel—*Robert Alter* 365
Imperial Grunts: The American Military on the Ground—
    Robert D. Kaplan 370

In a Fine Frenzy: Poets Respond to Shakespeare—*David Starkey* and
    Paul J. Willis, Editors 374
In the Company of Cheerful Ladies—*Alexander McCall Smith* 378
In the Province of Saints—*Thomas O'Malley* 382
Istanbul: Memories and the City—*Orhan Pamuk* 387
Ivan the Terrible: First Tsar of Russia—*Isabel de Madariaga* 392

John Kenneth Galbraith: His Life, His Politics, His Economics—
    Richard Parker 397
Joseph Smith: Rough Stone Rolling—*Richard Lyman Bushman* 402
The Journals, Vol. I: 1949-1965—*John Fowles* 408
Juiced: Wild Times, Rampant 'Roids, Smash Hits, and How Baseball
    Got Big—*José Canseco* 412
Juicing the Game: Drugs, Power, and the Fight for the Soul of
    Major League Baseball—*Howard Bryant* 416

K.—*Roberto Calasso* 420
Kafka on the Shore—*Haruki Murakami* 424
Kremlin Rising: Vladimir Putin's Russia and the End of
    Revolution—*Peter Baker* and *Susan Glasser* 429

Last Call for Blackford Oakes—*William F. Buckley, Jr.* 434
Last Night—*James Salter* 439
The Last Titan: A Life of Theodore Dreiser—*Jerome Loving* 443
Lee Miller: A Life—*Carolyn Burke* 447

PUBLISHER'S NOTE

Magill's Literary Annual, 2006, is the fifty-third publication in a series that began in 1954. Critical essays for the first twenty-two years were collected and published in the twelve-volume *Survey of Contemporary Literature* in 1977; since then, yearly sets have been published. Each year, *Magill's Literary Annual* seeks to evaluate critically 200 major examples of serious literature, both fiction and nonfiction, published during the previous calendar year. The philosophy behind our selection process is to cover works that are likely to be of interest to general readers, that reflect publishing trends, that add to the careers of authors being taught and researched in literature programs, and that will stand the test of time. By filtering the thousands of books published every year down to 200 notable titles, the editors have provided the busy librarian with an excellent reader's advisory tool and patrons with fodder for book discussion groups and a guide for choosing worthwhile reading material. The essay-reviews in the *Annual* provide a more academic, "reference" review of a work than is typically found in newspapers and other periodical sources.

The reviews in the two-volume *Magill's Literary Annual, 2006*, are arranged alphabetically by title. At the beginning of each volume is a complete alphabetical list of all covered books that provides readers with the title, author, and a brief description of each work. Every essay is approximately four pages in length. Each one begins with a block of reference information in a standard order:

- Full book title, including any subtitle
- *Author:* name, with birth and death years
- *First published:* Original foreign-language title, with year and country, when pertinent
- Original language and translator name, when pertinent
- Introduction, Foreword, etc., with writer's name, when pertinent
- *Publisher:* company name and city, number of pages, retail price

Anthropology	Essays	Literary criticism
Archaeology	Ethics	Literary history
Autobiography	Film	Literary theory
Biography	Fine arts	Media
Current affairs	History	Medicine
Diary	History of science	Memoir
Drama	Language	Miscellaneous
Economics	Law	Music
Education	Letters	Natural history
Environment	Literary biography	Nature

Novel	Psychology	Sociology
Novella	Religion	Technology
Philosophy	Science	Travel
Poetry	Short fiction	Women's issues

- *Type of work:* chosen from standard categories
- *Time:* period represented, when pertinent
- *Locale:* location represented, when pertinent
- Capsule description of the work
- *Principal characters* [for novels, short fiction] or *Principal personages* [for biographies, history]: list of people, with brief descriptions

The text of each essay-review analyzes and presents the focus, intent, and relative success of the author, as well as the makeup and point of view of the work under discussion. To assist the reader further, essays are supplemented by a list of additional "Review Sources" for further study in a bibliographic format. Every essay includes a sidebar offering a brief biography of the author or authors. Thumbnail photographs of the book covers and the authors are included as available.

Four indexes can be found at the end of volume 2:

- Biographical Works by Subject: Arranged by subject, rather than by author or title. Readers can locate easily reviews of biographical works—memoirs, diaries, and letters in addition to biographies and autobiographies—by looking up the name of the person covered.
- Category Index: Groups all titles into subject areas such as current affairs and social issues, ethics and law, history, literary biography, philosophy and religion, psychology, and women's issues.
- Title Index: Lists all works reviewed in alphabetical order, with any relevant cross references.
- Author Index: Lists books covered in the annual by each author's name.

A searchable cumulative index, listing all books reviewed in *Magill's Literary Annual* between 1977 and 2006, as well as in *Magill's History Annual* (1983) and *Magill's Literary Annual, History and Biography* (1984 and 1985), can be found at our Web site, **www.salempress.com**, on the page for *Magill's Literary Annual, 2006*.

Our special thanks go to the editors for their expert and insightful selections: John Wilson is the editor of *Books and Culture* for *Christianity Today*, and Steven G. Kellman is a professor at the University of Texas at San Antonio and a member of the National Book Critics Circle. We also owe our gratitude to the outstanding writers who lend their time and knowledge to this project every year. The names of all contributing reviewers are listed in the front of volume 1, as well as at the end of their individual reviews.

COMPLETE ANNOTATED LIST OF TITLES

VOLUME 1

Active Liberty: Interpreting Our Democratic Constitution—
Stephen G. Breyer 1
A U.S. Supreme Court justice lays out his philosophy of constitutional interpretation, providing a diverse array of examples from recent history

Acts of Faith—*Philip Caputo* 5
In a civil-war setting Caputo portrays various combatants, all with deep stakes in the conflict's outcome and all trapped in the ambiguities of good intentions

The American Classics: A Personal Essay—*Denis Donoghue* 8
Donoghue examines the roots, themes, and ideologies of American literature by analyzing critical reaction to five works which have traditionally been regarded as classics

American Ghosts: A Memoir—*David Plante* 13
A writer examines the tangled strands of his religious, ethnic, and sexual identities

American Prometheus: The Triumph and Tragedy of J. Robert
Oppenheimer—*Kai Bird* and *Martin J. Sherwin* 17
This biography of J. Robert Oppenheimer provides the facts of his life and makes his personality come alive but does not analyze the meaning of his complex life

America's Constitution: A Biography—*Akhil Reed Amar* 22
This scholarly analysis of the formation and development of the U.S. Constitution includes its twenty-seven amendments, with an emphasis on the meanings of the component parts within their historical contexts

The Angel of Forgetfulness—*Steve Stern* 27
In the best tradition of Jewish American literature, this complex Bildungsroman *tells three separate stories that merge into one*

The Assassins' Gate: America in Iraq—*George Packer* 32
A journalist comments on various aspects of the Iraq War, including the causes of the conflict and how the war proceeded, considering both American and Iraqi viewpoints

At Day's Close: Night in Times Past—*A. Roger Ekirch* 37
Ekrich explores the nighttime activities of preindustrial people in Western Europe and colonial America

The Beatles: The Biography—*Bob Spitz* 41
This massive biography chronicles the most influential rock band in the history of popular music

Becoming Justice Blackmun: Harry Blackmun's Supreme Court
    Journey—*Linda Greenhouse* 45
This history of the career of Supreme Court Justice Blackmun, the author of the Roe v. Wade *decision, is based on his archives and his public and private papers*

Before the Frost—*Henning Mankell* 49
This novel inspired by the terrorist attacks on New York and Washington, D.C., on September 11, 2001, centers on an apocalyptic Christian cult

The Best Day the Worst Day: Life with Jane Kenyon—*Donald Hall* 54
Hall recalls his wife, Kenyon, her battle with cancer, and their twenty years together at Eagle Pond Farm in rural New Hampshire

Black Maria—*Kevin Young* 58
Young, known for his use of jazz in poetry, in Black Maria *appropriates the conventions and devices of film noir to produce a disjointed but startlingly original detective story which unrolls in a sequence of poems*

Blinding Light—*Paul Theroux* 62
Theroux explores the nature of the creative process through the life of a writer whose use of mind-altering drugs causes temporary blindness but provides him special insight

Blink: The Power of Thinking Without Thinking—*Malcolm Gladwell* 66
Gladwell examines the positive and negative aspects of rapid cognition in daily life

The Bomb: A Life—*Gerard J. DeGroot* 70
In his history of fission and fusion bombs, often tartly written, DeGroot addresses how they work and their destructive power as well as the politics impelling their development and their political and social consequences

Borges and the Eternal Orangutans—*Luis Fernando Verissimo* 74
A middle-aged scholar named Volgelstein and the literary genius Jorge Luis Borges tackle a murder mystery

Born Losers: A History of Failure in America—*Scott A. Sandage* 79
   Sandage considers the history and roots of failure in the United States from Herman Melville's Bartleby to Chic Young's Dagwood Bumstead to Arthur Miller's Willie Loman

Boss Tweed: The Rise and Fall of the Corrupt Pol Who Conceived the
   Soul of Modern New York—*Kenneth D. Ackerman* 84
   Ackerman presents an engaging study of William Tweed who, as "boss" of Tammany Hall, ruled and robbed New York City for years before his spectacular fall

Bound for Canaan: The Underground Railroad and the War for
   the Soul of America—*Fergus M. Bordewich* 89
   Bordewich provides a comprehensive account of the persons, slave and free, responsible for the origins and growth of the escape routes and networks known metaphorically as the Underground Railroad, through which slaves in the United States fled their bondage in the years prior to the Civil War

Break, Blow, Burn: Camille Paglia Reads Forty-three of the
   World's Best Poems—*Camille Paglia* 94
   The controversial cultural critic examines an idiosyncratic selection of poems

Budget Travel Through Space and Time—*Albert Goldbarth* 99
   This dazzling and challenging volume of poetry explores a vast array of topics

Bury the Chains: Prophets and Rebels in the Fight to Free
   an Empire's Slaves—*Adam Hochschild* 103
   The movement to end the slave trade in the British Empire grew from the efforts of a small group of people

Campo Santo—*W. G. Sebald* 107
   This posthumous volume of essays collects excerpts from a larger work on Corsica as well as pieces on literary figures, book reviews, and literary and cultural criticism

Carnivore Diet—*Julia Slavin* 111
   Slavin's first novel is the wildly inventive tale of the Dunleavy family and a mythical carnivorous beast called the chagwa who stalks the suburbs of Washington, D.C., looking for prey

A Changed Man—*Francine Prose* 115
   This comedy of manners focuses on a neo-Nazi skinhead who wants to change his life, a Holocaust survivor who decides to help him, and a single mother whose life is changed by the two of them

Christ the Lord: Out of Egypt—*Anne Rice* 119
    Using the seven-year-old Jesus as narrator, Rice tells the story of a boy discovering, through isolated comments and unexplained miracles, that he is Christ the Lord who is sent to redeem the world

The Chrysanthemum Palace—*Bruce Wagner* 123
    A tale of promise and poignancy, drugs, drinking, and death, this short novel explores in detail the lifestyles of three children of the Hollywood rich and famous

The Cigar Roller—*Pablo Medina* 127
    A paralyzed stroke victim, once a big man with big appetites, spends his last years in a nursing home mulling over his misdeeds and misspent life

The City: A Global History—*Joel Kotkin* 132
    Global in scope and sweeping in history, Kotkin's concise but insightful book considers the character of the human city and its special problems from its inception to the present day

Classical Music in America: A History of Its Rise and Fall—
    Joseph Horowitz 137
    This history of classical music in the United States focuses on institutions for performance, performers, and impresarios

Collapse: How Societies Choose to Fail or Succeed—
    Jared Diamond 142
    Diamond examines the reasons past societies have destroyed themselves and how modern humans can avoid their mistakes

Collected Poems—*Jane Kenyon* 147
    Kenyon's poems of daily life and of her struggle with depression continue to move readers

The Collected Poems of Kenneth Koch—*Kenneth Koch* 151
    This collection brings together Koch's shorter poems written over a period of forty years, from 1950 to the poet's death in 2002, and highlights his reputation as one the great experimenters and humorists in American poetry

Collected Stories—*Carol Shields* 155
    This tribute collection of Shields's three volumes of short stories includes a chapter of a novel she was working on when she died

The Command of the Ocean: A Naval History of Britain,
    1649-1815—*N. A. M. Rodger* 159
    This original analysis of Britain's Royal Navy and how it came to rule the seas is exhaustive

A Crack in the Edge of the World: America and the Great
    California Earthquake of 1906—*Simon Winchester* 164
    This work examines the geological science of plate tectonics and its influence on civilization, with particular focus on the San Francisco earthquake of 1906

The Cube and the Cathedral: Europe, America, and
    Politics Without God—*George Weigel* 168
    Weigel traces the cultural and philosophical causes of modern European secularism, which is portrayed as a profound betrayal of the religious origins of European civilization

The Dark Genius of Wall Street: The Misunderstood Life of Jay Gould,
    King of the Robber Barons—*Edward J. Renehan, Jr.* 173
    This revisionist biography of the notorious nineteenth century robber baron, resulting in a partial rehabilitation of the man and of his business practices, is vivid and impeccably researched

Defining the World: The Extraordinary Story of Dr. Johnson's
    Dictionary—*Henry Hitchings* 177
    This work recounts the story of Samuel Johnson's creation of the first great English dictionary

Dictionary Days: A Defining Passion—*Ilan Stavans* 181
    A multilingual scholar and writer reflects on words and their meanings and on his love of dictionaries, especially the Oxford English Dictionary

DisneyWar—*James B. Stewart* 186
    Michael Eisner's twenty-year tenure as head of the Walt Disney Company was initially successful, but his inability to delegate responsibility, establish clear lines of authority, and maintain a reputation for honesty cost the company millions in profits, lawsuits, and contract buyouts, eventually leading to his resignation as chairman

The Dominion of War: Empire and Liberty in North America,
    1500-2000—*Fred Anderson* and *Andrew Cayton* 191
    War has affected American concepts of liberty and democracy since the seventeenth century

The Earth and Sky of Jacques Dorme—*Andreï Makine* 196
Concluding the trilogy that documented the life of World War II pilot Jacques Dorme, this novel follows a war orphan on his mission to learn more about the mysterious Dorme, the pilgrimage he takes to Dorme's final resting place, and the quest the young boy embarks upon to develop a sense of self and family belonging where none exist

Edmund Wilson: A Life in Literature—*Lewis M. Dabney* 200
This biography of Wilson provides a great deal of material on the life of the noted American literary critic and cultural commentator, but it is confusingly written and often hard to understand

The End of Poverty: Economic Possibilities for Our Time—
    Jeffrey D. Sachs 204
Basing his conclusions on a variety of case studies, a maverick economist presents his plan to end extreme poverty worldwide by the year 2025

Equiano, the African: Biography of a Self-Made Man—
    Vincent Carretta 209
Carretta carefully documents his contention that Olaudah Equiano's first-person description of traveling via the Middle Passage from Africa to the New World, where he was sold into slavery, was fabricated and that Equiano was born in South Carolina

Eudora Welty: A Biography—*Suzanne Marrs* 214
Welty becomes three-dimensional in this comprehensive biography written by her close friend, who also authored the standard critical study of Welty's work

Europe Central—*William T. Vollmann* 219
European political and military turmoil of the 1930's and 1940's is examined through the lives of several Germans and Russians

Extremely Loud and Incredibly Close—*Jonathan Safran Foer* 224
A precocious nine-year-old boy wanders New York City hoping to unlock a mystery surrounding his father's violent death at the World Trade Center

Faculty Towers: The Academic Novel and Its Discontents—
    Elaine Showalter 229
Academic novels illustrate the dominant trends in higher education in Britain and America decade by decade

COMPLETE ANNOTATED LIST OF TITLES

The Failure of the Founding Fathers: Jefferson, Marshall,
     and the Rise of Presidential Democracy—*Bruce Ackerman* 234
     Ackerman claims that the rise of political parties and emergence of a popularly elected president in 1801 transformed the American Constitution in ways unanticipated by members of the 1787 Constitutional Convention

Faith at War: A Journey on the Frontlines of Islam, from
     Baghdad to Timbuktu—*Yaroslav Trofimov* 239
     An experienced reporter travels through nine majority-Muslim countries, describing his observations and experiences in an effort to illuminate the culture gap between Islam and the West

Fallen—*David Maine* 243
     This wry retelling of the biblical story of Cain and Abel, Adam and Eve focuses primarily on the characters as real but clearly flawed human beings

February House—*Sherill Tippins*. 247
     W. H. Auden, Carson McCullers, Jane and Paul Bowles, Benjamin Britten, and Gypsy Rose Lee are among the inhabitants of a commune in wartime Brooklyn

Finding George Orwell in Burma—*Emma Larkin* 251
     Larkin's quest to learn about Orwell's experience in 1920's Burma acquaints her with the brutal repression of the current government of Myanmar, whose ruthless conduct reminds her of Orwell's antiutopian novels

The First Poets: Lives of the Ancient Greek Poets—*Michael Schmidt* 255
     A renowned English poet and scholar brings learning, insight, and enthusiasm to the study of early Greek poets, whose influence extends to the present time

Five Families: The Rise, Decline, and Resurgence of America's
     Most Powerful Mafia Empires—*Selwyn Raab* 260
     This well-researched study of the creation and expansion of the New York Mafia includes an excellent description of how the FBI and federal prosecutors worked together to convict leading members of the five New York City Mafia families between 1980 and 2004

Fledgling—*Octavia E. Butler* 265
     This novel concerns an entire race of ancient people, the Ina, who have their own history, customs, and traditions; stronger, with heightened senses, they are more advanced than humans but rely entirely upon the human population for survival, as they survive by drinking human blood

Fleshmarket Alley—*Ian Rankin* 270
Scotland's best-known policeman confronts new challenges following the murder of an asylum seeker

Follies: New Stories—*Ann Beattie* 275
In a novella and nine stories, the spokeswoman for the passive and uncommitted takes a largely comic look at baby boomers growing older

Foucault and the Iranian Revolution: Gender and the Seductions
of Islamism—*Janet Afary* and *Kevin B. Anderson* 279
This critical analysis of French philosopher Michel Foucault's journalistic writings on the Iranian Revolution connects them to his better-known philosophical works

The Founders on Religion: A Book of Quotations—
James H. Hutson, Editor 284
These quotations on more than seventy topics, organized alphabetically, express the religious views of seventeen members of the founding generation of the American republic

1491: New Revelations of the Americas Before Columbus—
Charles C. Mann 288
Archaelogical and paleontological discoveries in the last centuries changed theories of Native American life in the pre-Columbian Americas. Evidence discovered in the last few decades have produced even more radically altered theories of American populations, culture, and practices prior to European contact

Freakonomics: A Rogue Economist Explores the Hidden Side
of Everything—*Steven D. Levitt* and *Stephen J. Dubner* 292
An award-winning economist explores topics usually considered outside the realm of his specialty, presenting theories regarding issues that often are considered moral rather than economic or scientific

The Glass Castle—*Jeannette Walls* 296
Walls describes growing up with an alcoholic father and a blithely negligent mother, her family's struggle to survive after moving to West Virginia, and her eventual escape to New York City and a successful life

God's Gym—*John Edgar Wideman* 301
These ten new stories examine race, family, spiritual fathers, and the relationship between fiction and reality

The Golden West: Hollywood Stories—*Daniel Fuchs* 305
Fuchs sympathetically describes the Hollywood milieu in which he worked as a screenwriter, and his fiction concerns the fates of his Hollywood characters

The Good Wife—*Stewart O'Nan* 309
An account of spousal love in the face of betrayal, hardship, and the exigencies of life for a woman faithful for nearly thirty years to a husband in jail for murder

A Great Improvisation: Franklin, France, and the Birth of
    America—*Stacy Schiff* 313
This biography narrates Benjamin Franklin's successful mission to secure a French alliance and French money for the newly proclaimed United States of America and describes his contributions when negotiating the 1783 peace treaty with Great Britain

The Ha-Ha—*Dave King* 318
A veteran, rendered speechless in the Vietnam War, struggles to reconnect with life through his relationship with a nine-year-old boy

Harry Potter and the Half-Blood Prince—*J. K. Rowling* 322
In the sixth novel in Rowling's best-selling series, the wizarding community is thrown into chaos as Harry's archenemy, Lord Voldemort, steps up his evil campaign to eliminate Harry and rule the world

Henry Adams and the Making of America—*Garry Wills* 327
Wills examines Adams's History of the United States of America *(1889-1891), sometimes subtitled* During the Administrations of Presidents Thomas Jefferson and James Madison, *as a misunderstood masterpiece*

The Historian—*Elizabeth Kostova* 332
After finding a mysterious book and reading a series of letters dating from the 1930's, a sixteen-year-old girl joins her family's terrible quest to kill Dracula

The History of Love—*Nicole Krauss* 336
Krauss's sophomore novel concerns survivors of the Holocaust and the impact of a book about true love on the lives of people connected beyond time and space

The Hot Kid—*Elmore Leonard* 340
A United States marshal and a bank robber, both sons of rich fathers, clash in Depression-era Oklahoma

The Hummingbird's Daughter—*Luis Alberto Urrea* 344
This novel is based on the life of the author's great-aunt Teresita, who was believed by the people of Mexico to be a saint and was believed by the corrupt government of Mexico's dictator, President Porfirio Díaz, to be a dangerous revolutionary

The Hungry Tide—*Amitav Ghosh* 349
In a beautiful but hostile island world, three people from very different backgrounds share adventures, learn to love, and make discoveries about the past and about themselves

The Icarus Girl—*Helen Oyeyemi* 354
A young girl of mixed race struggles with depression and loneliness until she encounters an unusual playmate who may not be real

The Ice Queen—*Alice Hoffman* 358
A woman, after wishing bad things in anger, experiences setbacks such as being struck by lightning—and then suffers years of confusion and guilt

If This Be Treason: Translation and Its Dyscontents: A Memoir—
    Gregory Rabassa. 362
Scholar Rabassa, writing in his eighty-third year, offers a cool-headed and humorous defense of translation

Imagined Cities: Urban Experience and the Language of
    the Novel—*Robert Alter* 365
Alter argues that the unprecedented expansion of European cities during the late nineteenth and early twentieth centuries affected the development of the contemporary novel in specific ways, including its alterations in modes of human perception

Imperial Grunts: The American Military on the Ground—
    Robert D. Kaplan 370
Kaplan explores the role of the common soldier in helping to establish an American presence and represent American values in countries where political instability is seen as a threat to U.S. democracy

In a Fine Frenzy: Poets Respond to Shakespeare—*David Starkey* and
    Paul J. Willis, Editors 374
The poems in this collection respond to, comment upon, or are influenced by the works of William Shakespeare

In the Company of Cheerful Ladies—*Alexander McCall Smith* 378
The sixth novel in Alexander McCall Smith's No. 1 Ladies' Detective Agency series tells the story of Mma Ramotswe and the various problems and adventures encountered in her daily life

In the Province of Saints—*Thomas O'Malley* 382
Nine-year-old Michael McDonagh comes of age in a rural Irish village, uncovering rumors and secrets about his family and himself that alter his life forever

Istanbul: Memories and the City—*Orhan Pamuk* 387
Turkey's most famous modern writer mingles recollections of his childhood and youth with reflections on the past and present of his beloved Istanbul

Ivan the Terrible: First Tsar of Russia—*Isabel de Madariaga* 392
The life, accomplishments, and brutalities of Russia's first czar are skillfully reconstructed from published sources and historical works

John Kenneth Galbraith: His Life, His Politics, His Economics—
Richard Parker 397
This biography of economist Galbraith describes his ideas and his history of political involvement as well as the events in his life

Joseph Smith: Rough Stone Rolling—*Richard Lyman Bushman* 402
This biography of the founder of the Church of Jesus Christ of Latter-day Saints, by a distinguished professional historian who is also a practicing member of that church, is detailed and massively documented

The Journals, Vol. I: 1949-1965—*John Fowles* 408
Fowles records his emotional and intellectual life, his reading, travels, loves, and friendships, from his last undergraduate days through his development as a teacher, husband, and writer

Juiced: Wild Times, Rampant 'Roids, Smash Hits, and How Baseball
Got Big—*José Canseco* 412
This unflinching tell-all by a controversial former professional athlete recounts the impact of steroids on Major League Baseball during the 1980's and 1990's

Juicing the Game: Drugs, Power, and the Fight for the Soul of
Major League Baseball—*Howard Bryant* 416
Sportswriter Howard Bryant takes a deep look at how steroids crept into baseball and why they went unchecked for a decade

K.—*Roberto Calasso* 420
Franz Kafka's stories and novels, like his letters and diaries, were studies in alienation and "foreignness," creating for readers the experience of being a stranger in a world that is strangely familiar

Kafka on the Shore—*Haruki Murakami* 424
    A teenage boy and an elderly man go on separate odysseys to discover their destinies

Kremlin Rising: Vladimir Putin's Russia and the End of
    Revolution—*Peter Baker* and *Susan Glasser* 429
    The reemergence of authoritarian rule in Russia discourages committed democrats even as the public accepts it

Last Call for Blackford Oakes—*William F. Buckley, Jr.* 434
    In the eleventh and final novel of Buckley's Blackford Oakes Cold War spy series, old hatreds end new loves as Oakes matches wits with his old nemesis, master spy Kim Philby, in a final deadly game

Last Night—*James Salter* 439
    These ten stories of modern American life focus upon the intense, flawed inner lives of the characters

The Last Titan: A Life of Theodore Dreiser—*Jerome Loving* 443
    This biographical study of Dreiser traces the sources of many of his plots and demonstrates how he incorporated details from his early life into much of his fiction

Lee Miller: A Life—*Carolyn Burke* 447
    This carefully researched and ruminative life of the important twentieth century photographer was written with the full cooperation of her family

VOLUME 2

Legends of Modernity: Essays and Letters from Occupied Poland,
    1942-1943—*Czesław Miłosz* 451
    In these essays, written during the Nazi occupation of Poland, Miłosz explores the roots of twentieth century literature and art and how certain aspects of modernism led to the horrors of fascism and Stalinism

The Letters of Robert Lowell—*Robert Lowell* 456
    Saskia Hamilton presents 711 of Lowell's letters, arranged chronologically and annotated

Light from Heaven—*Jan Karon* 460
In this seventh volume of the Mitford series, Father Tim starts to rebuild a small, rural church, unused for many years, and becomes involved in the lives of his parishioners

The Lighthouse—*P. D. James* 464
When Scotland Yard Inspector Adam Dalgliesh investigates a suspicious death on a private island off the English coast, he uncovers a complexity of intrigues among the island's residents as well as its closely screened visitors and is confronted with a double murder case

Lighthousekeeping—*Jeanette Winterson* 469
Two characters living a century apart both find that only love gives meaning to existence

Like a Fiery Elephant: The Story of B. S. Johnson—*Jonathan Coe* 473
This first-person account of the experimental British novelist who took his own life at the age of forty is unconventional and engaging

Like a Rolling Stone: Bob Dylan at the Crossroads—*Greil Marcus* 477
While at times disjointed and rambling, Marcus's book is a stunning portrait of Dylan's song "Like a Rolling Stone" and how its release changed the face of popular music

The Lives of Agnes Smedley—*Ruth Price* 481
Price has written a detailed study of a writer who was near the center of several of the most important political and cultural movements of the twentieth century

Living with Polio: The Epidemic and Its Survivors—
Daniel J. Wilson 485
Prior to development of the polio vaccines in the 1950's, tens of thousands of children contracted polio each year; using interviews with survivors, the author, himself a survivor, relates their stories

A Long Way Down—*Nick Hornby* 490
This comic novel brings together four would-be suicides

Lost in the Forest—*Sue Miller* 494
The sudden death of a beloved husband, father, and stepfather dramatically alters the dynamics of a Napa Valley family

Lunar Park—*Bret Easton Ellis* 498
Ellis includes himself as the central character in a metafictional horror novel

A Mannered Grace: The Life of Laura (Riding) Jackson—
    Elizabeth Friedmann 503
    Friedmann compiles a detailed record of the American writer who was one of the
earliest modernists and who lived nearly half a century after she renounced poetry

Mao: The Unknown Story—*Jung Chang* and *Jon Halliday* 507
    Through meticulous research, the authors demonstrate the evil, quintessentially
selfish, brutal, and power-hungry nature of Mao Zedong, the man who united China
under communism and whose climb to power and twenty-seven years of rule caused
the deaths of more than seventy million Chinese

The March—*E. L. Doctorow* 512
    Doctorow fictionalizes General Sherman's famous march to the sea and its effects
upon the Confederacy and the South's newly freed slaves

Mark Twain: A Life—*Ron Powers* 516
    Powers's massively documented historical biography is based on new archival
material, which should place it among the standard lives of Twain

Marriage, a History: From Obedience to Intimacy: Or, How
    Love Conquered Marriage—*Stephanie Coontz* 521
    An extensive and detailed look at marriage since the Stone Age and how the con-
cept of marriage has changed dramatically in the past two hundred years, making
matrimony both more satisfying and more fragile

Matisse the Master: A Life of Henri Matisse: The Conquest of
    Colour, 1909-1954—*Hilary Spurling* 526
    The second volume of this massive biography of Matisse analyzes his artistic con-
tributions and provides fascinating details about his personal relationships and his
unique contributions to modern art

A Matter of Opinion—*Victor S. Navasky* 530
    This account of the author's educational background and professional life as an
editor and publisher of The Nation *is accompanied by his thoughts on the importance*
to a functioning democracy of journals of opinion

Melville: His World and Work—*Andrew Delbanco* 535
    This modestly proportioned but authoritative biography of one of the greatest
American writers interprets his life and work in the context of the significant events of
his time

Memories of My Melancholy Whores—*Gabriel García Márquez* 540
    On his ninetieth birthday, a Colombian newspaper columnist arranges to go to
bed with a young virgin; for a year he visits her chastely and falls in love with her

COMPLETE ANNOTATED LIST OF TITLES

The Men Who Stare at Goats—*Jon Ronson* 544
As part of a strange and apparently ongoing history of the United States military's fascination and experimentation with psychic and supernatural ideas, this work describes the attempts of certain military figures to train psychic soldiers, as revealed through interviews with current and past participants

Methodism: Empire of the Spirit—*David Hempton* 549
In this brief, formidable volume, Hempton analyzes the rise and decline of Methodism in the British Isles, America, and throughout the world, within social contexts that both influenced and were influenced by the movement

Migration: New and Selected Poems—*W. S. Merwin* 554
This generous selection of poetry spans more than fifty years in the career of one of America's most respected poets

Monologue of a Dog—*Wisława Szymborska* 558
This collection of new poems by Szymborska further refines the spare, lean style of the poetry she has written since winning the Nobel Prize

My Name Is Legion—*A. N. Wilson* 563
A corrupt newspaper propels a dazzling array of characters toward their individual fates in a horrifying, postmodern London

My Noiseless Entourage—*Charles Simic* 568
In this collection, Simic revisits some familiar (albeit surreal) landscapes familiar to readers of his earlier work, and he enters some new territories using American settings and a less detached voice

Mysteries of My Father: An Irish-American Memoir—*Thomas Fleming* 572
A son looks into his family's history, illuminating the experiences of Irish Americans in the early twentieth century and the political machines that helped shape their lives

The Mysterious Flame of Queen Loana—*Umberto Eco* 576
Eco's fifth novel tells the story of a bookish man who rediscovers his identity by reading the books he loved as a child

The Narnian: The Life and Imagination of C. S. Lewis—*Alan Jacobs* 580
This work analyzes the intellectual, particularly the imaginative, development of writer Lewis

The Neutral: Lecture Course at the Collège de France, 1977-1978—
Roland Barthes. 585
Barthes explores a previously neglected area of literary theory in arguing that
Western civilization's reliance on binary oppositions (good/evil, true/false) as struc-
tures of thought is usefully amended and enhanced by consideration of the role of
"the Neutral" in producing cultural meaning

Never Let Me Go—*Kazuo Ishiguro* 589
As a young woman reviews her school days, she explores the realization that she
and her fellow students were cloned for purposes of organ donation and will not live
out their normal life spans

New York Burning: Liberty, Slavery, and Conspiracy in
Eighteenth-Century Manhattan—*Jill Lepore* 594
This study of a series of fires in colonial Manhattan is based on primary records of
the trials, convictions, and, in many cases, executions of the alleged conspirators,
mainly members of the city's free and slave African American population

The Niagara River—*Kay Ryan*. 598
The short, pithy poems in this collection reveal Ryan's attitudes about life's
"givens," the limits people place upon themselves, the blighting of nature, and the
hope that enables people to come to terms with their problems

No Country for Old Men—*Cormac McCarthy* 602
A young man out hunting antelope finds the gory tableau of an ill-fated drug deal;
on impulse he takes a satchel with millions in cash and goes on the run from both drug
kingpins and law enforcement

The Noodle Maker—*Ma Jian* 607
Through his protagonist's observations of city life, Ma offers a view of everyday
absurdities in China during the year following the bloody suppression of demonstra-
tors at Tiananmen Square

Ogden Nash: The Life and Work of America's Laureate of
Light Verse—*Douglas M. Parker* 612
Drawing on Nash's papers as well as interviews with his family and friends,
Parker has written a fast-paced, readable biography of the man he calls "America's
laureate of light verse"

The Old Ball Game: How John McGraw, Christy Mathewson, and
The New York Giants Created Modern Baseball—*Frank Deford* 617
Two baseball luminaries from sharply contrasting backgrounds forge a close per-
sonal relationship while making the New York Giants an early twentieth century suc-
cess

COMPLETE ANNOTATED LIST OF TITLES

On Beauty—*Zadie Smith* 622
In this Booker Prize finalist, a middle-aged liberal white professor and his mixed-race family interact with a conservative black public intellectual and his family in London and on the campus of an American liberal arts college

Ordinary Heroes—*Scott Turow* 627
A man discovers the nature of his father's involvement in political and military intrigue during the last days of World War II and tries to unravel what happened

The Peabody Sisters: Three Women Who Ignited American
    Romanticism—*Megan Marshall* 631
Marshall breaks new ground in her biography of three dynamic sisters who each made important contributions to the nineteenth century American Renaissance

Pearl—*Mary Gordon* 636
On Christmas, 1998, Maria Meyers receives a telephone call informing her that her daughter has chained herself to a flagpole outside the American Embassy in Dublin and is starving herself over the death of a young Irish boy

The People's Tycoon: Henry Ford and the American Century—
    Steven Watts 640
Watts's biography of the man who pioneered mass production and put America on wheels will stand as one of the best books written about Henry Ford

A Perfect Red: Empire, Espionage, and the Quest for the Color of
    Desire—*Amy Butler Greenfield* 644
The history of the red dye cochineal is traced from its discovery in Mexico to the spread of its use in Europe

The Perfectionist: Life and Death in Haute Cuisine—
    Rudolph Chelminski 649
Chef Bernard Loiseau's hotel-restaurant in the French countryside reached the pinnacle of three Michelin stars before Loiseau committed suicide

The Planets—*Dava Sobel* 654
Sobel surveys traditional views and modern theories of the planets and the solar system as a whole

Pol Pot: Anatomy of a Nightmare—*Philip Short* 659
Short analyzes how Pol Pot rose from obscurity to lead the Khmer Rouge regime that committed many of the twentieth century's worst crimes against humanity

Prince of Fire—*Daniel Silva* 664
Gabriel Allon, art restorer and terrorist hunter, tracks down the organizer of a Palestinian attack on the Israeli embassy in Rome

The Prince of the City: Giuliani, New York, and the Genius of
    American Life—*Fred Siegel*, with *Harry Siegel* 669
    This political history of Mayor Rudolph Giuliani focuses on New York City's twentieth century decline and subsequent rise

The Prophet of Zongo Street—*Mohammed Naseehu Ali* 673
    In ten narratives that sometimes feature the fantastic or the supernatural, sometimes focus on extraordinary events in ordinary life, Ali tells the stories of his Ghanian characters

Redemption: The Life of Henry Roth—*Steven G. Kellman* 677
    The first full-length biography of the author of Call It Sleep *(1934) uncovers the mystery of Roth's sixty-year silence, as well as the guilt and suffering that lay behind his fragmented career*

Return to Wild America: A Yearlong Search for the Continent's
    Natural Soul—*Scott Weidensaul* 681
    Weidensaul follows the pioneering route across North America that Roger Tory Peterson and James Fisher took in 1953 and records the environmental gains and losses in the half century since the publication of their best seller Wild America *(1955)*

The Road to Reality: A Complete Guide to the Laws of the
    Universe—*Roger Penrose* 685
    This comprehensive narrative elucidates how scientists have used mathematical principles in such revolutionary theories as relativity and quantum mechanics to understand the matter and movements of the universe's contents, from subatomic particles to galaxies

Rules for Old Men Waiting—*Peter Pouncey* 691
    Pouncey's novel about the ways that aging Scottish professor of history Robert MacIver devises to spend his last days

Salonica, City of Ghosts: Christians, Muslims, and Jews, 1430-1950—
    Mark Mazower 695
    This historical portrait examines the northern Greek port city of Salonica from the end of the Byzantine era through the city's reconstruction following World War II

Saturday—*Ian McEwan* 700
    This novel follows a day in the life of a London neurosurgeon and his family as they encounter the anxieties and realities presented by the terrorist attacks of September 11, 2001

School of the Arts—*Mark Doty* 705
This finely textured, meditative collection of poetry examines how it is possible for individuals to come to terms with both desire and loss

Seize the Fire: Heroism, Duty, and the Battle of Trafalgar—
    Adam Nicolson 709
Nicolson explores the nature and appeal of heroism and its ties to violence through an examination of Lord Horatio Nelson's great victory at Trafalgar on October 21, 1805

1776—*David McCullough* 714
Pulitzer Prize-winner McCullough reconstructs the year when thirteen British colonies became the United States of America, tracing the course of the Revolutionary War and those who shaped it, especially George Washington, William Howe, Henry Knox, and Nathanael Greene

The Seventh Beggar—*Pearl Abraham* 719
This novel sheds light on the ultra-Orthodox, almost mystical Hasidic world and establishes it firmly as part of mainstream America

Shakespeare: The Biography—*Peter Ackroyd* 723
Drawing on contemporary documents and later legends, Ackroyd situates William Shakespeare within the history, geography, and stagecraft of Elizabethan and Jacobean England

Shalimar the Clown—*Salman Rushdie* 727
This novel tells the story of a love triangle and bloody personal revenge in the global village, specifically within the context of Kashmir conflicts and worldwide Islamic terrorism

A Short History of Tractors in Ukrainian—*Marina Lewycka* 732
In 1990's England, two estranged sisters of a Ukrainian family join forces to rescue their elderly father from a sexy new Ukrainian refugee

The Singularity Is Near: When Humans Transcend Biology—
    Ray Kurzweil 736
The exponential growth of technologies, especially artificial intelligence, Kurzweil says, will lead to a pivotal event, the Singularity, when human intelligence will merge with vastly superior machine intelligence, a union that will allow solutions to problems ranging from pollution and poverty to human mortality

Slow Man—*J. M. Coetzee* 742
Following a bicycling accident that costs him a leg, a retired photographer falls in love with his nurse and is visited by an intrusive novelist

Small Island—*Andrea Levy* 746
  The lives of a middle-class English couple and a pair of Jamaican immigrants become enmeshed in London after World War II

Snakes and Earrings—*Hitomi Kanehara* 751
  A self-destructive young woman drifts into a nihilistic youth culture and dangerous love triangle

Søren Kierkegaard: A Biography—*Joakim Garff* 755
  This account of the life and work of Denmark's most distinguished philosopher-theologian includes the controversies that swirled around him all of his life

Specimen Days—*Michael Cunningham* 760
  Cunningham's three loosely interlocked stories of the hard side of life in New York City in the past, the near present, and the future create a fable for the present time

Spring Forward: The Annual Madness of Daylight Saving Time—
  Michael Downing 764
  The history of Daylight Saving Time legislation in the United States is related together with the political, practical, and nonsensical reasons behind it

Stalin: A Biography—*Robert Service* 769
  This scholarly synthesis acknowledges positive aspects of Joseph Stalin's personality and accomplishments while emphasizing his lust for power, his cruel indifference toward human suffering, and his stubborn commitment to Marxist-Leninist ideology

Star Dust—*Frank Bidart* 774
  This collection combines a chapbook published in 2002, Music Like Dirt, *with a long poem to explore the necessary relationship between creation and destruction*

Still Looking: Essays on American Art—*John Updike* 778
  One of America's most distinguished writers provides commentary on the works of major American artists whose careers have been highlighted in major exhibitions during the period from 1990 to 2004

The Successor—*Ismail Kadare* 783
  An investigation into the mysterious death of the successor to Albania's communist dictator builds to an exposure of the dark realities of modern totalitarianism

COMPLETE ANNOTATED LIST OF TITLES

The Summer He Didn't Die—*Jim Harrison* 788
The three novellas in this collection are all about people in search of happiness and meaning whimsical Upper Peninsula backwoods logger Brown Dog, three wives of well-respected men who have affairs with the same man, and the author himself

Sweetness and Light: The Mysterious History of the Honeybee—
    Hattie Ellis 792
Ellis explores the history of the working relationship honeybees and humans have shared over thousands of years

The Tender Bar: A Memoir—*J. R. Moehringer* 796
In this coming-of-age memoir, a fatherless boy is guided to manhood by a rough collection of neighborhood bar patrons

Testosterone Dreams: Rejuvenation, Aphrodisia, Doping—
    John Hoberman 801
Hoberman examines the history of human testosterone enhancement and its impact on modern American society

Them: A Memoir of Parents—*Francine du Plessix Gray* 805
This brutally candid yet loving account describes two eccentric, strong-willed, narcissistic Russian-born immigrants who became giants in America's postwar fashion industry and New York City's social scene but whose parenting skills left much to be desired

This I Believe: An A to Z of a Life—*Carlos Fuentes* 810
A finely wrought collection of short personal and political essays, presented alphabetically, on Fuentes's musings about everything from Amor to Zurich

This Is a Voice from Your Past: New and Selected Stories—
    Merrill Joan Gerber 815
Thirteen stories tell of middle-class life, focusing primarily on family and relationships, all narrated from a female point of view

Tooth and Claw, and Other Stories—*T. Coraghessan Boyle*. 819
Most of the fourteen stories in this collection continue Boyle's darkly humorous exploration of contemporary American life, especially the reckless loves and addictions of klutzy young men, but a few stories venture wildly off into time, space, and other species

Trawler: A Journey Through the North Atlantic—*Redmond O'Hanlon* 823
A middle-aged writer risks his life in order to fulfill a lifelong dream—shipping aboard a trawler in the North Atlantic in the hurricane season

The Trouble with Poetry, and Other Poems—*Billy Collins* 827
Collins's poems celebrate the world and all of its beauties, including poetry, jazz, and daily life, while they recognize mortality

Truth and Consequences—*Alison Lurie* 831
The novel chronicles the disintegration of a marriage, illustrating the destructiveness of chronic pain on both the sufferer and the caregiver

Understanding Iraq: The Whole Sweep of Iraqi History, from Genghis
    Khan's Mongols to the Ottoman Turks to the British Mandate
    to the American Occupation—*William R. Polk* 835
A brief history of Iraq, concentrating on the twentieth and early twenty-first centuries, particularly America's involvement with that nation

V. S. Pritchett: A Working Life—*Jeremy Treglown* 840
This study chronicles the life and work of Pritchett, explores his many travels and how he transformed them into articles and books, follows the development of his fiction, and surveys his extensive output of literary reviewing and essays

Vindication: A Life of Mary Wollstonecraft—*Lyndall Gordon* 845
This extensively detailed biography of Wollstonecraft's life as a woman living in eighteenth century England and Europe covers her struggle to overcome adversity and rise to notoriety

A War Like No Other: How the Athenians and Spartans Fought the
    Peloponnesian War—*Victor Davis Hanson* 849
This history describes how various aspects of the catastrophic Peloponnesian War of the fifth century B.C.E. brought to an end the golden age of Greece

The Watcher in the Pine—*Rebecca Pawel* 854
Carlos Tejada and Elena Fernandez, newlyweds, leave their metropolitan lifestyle to live in rural Potes, where they find themselves facing not only the challenges of assimilation but also a murder mystery

White Gold: The Extraordinary Story of Thomas Pellow
    and Islam's One Million White Slaves—*Giles Milton* 859
Milton uses the memoir of Thomas Pellow, an English boy kidnapped by Muslim corsairs in 1716, to explore the little-known story of the million Europeans held as slaves in North Africa in the seventeenth and eighteenth centuries

Who She Was: My Search for My Mother's Life—
 Samuel G. Freedman 864
 This intimate biography of Freedman's mother captures a young Jewish woman's experience of family, her East Bronx neighborhood, and World War II from the 1930's to the 1950's

Why Birds Sing: A Journey into the Mystery of Bird Song—
 David Rothenberg 869
 Rothenberg examines various hypotheses explaining birdsong, from the mechanistic view that song is communication between birds seeking mates to the possibility that birds enjoy singing and find their own songs beautiful

Wickett's Remedy—*Myla Goldberg* 873
 This multidimensional tale re-creates the Boston of the early twentieth century— one locus of the flu epidemic that killed more than half a million Americans

A Wild Perfection: The Selected Letters of James Wright—
 James Wright 878
 This selection of Wright's letters includes conversations on the craft of poetry with major poets of the second half of the twentieth century

William Empson, Vol. I: Among the Mandarins—*John Haffenden* 882
 The first in what will be a two-volume biography of one of the twentieth century's foremost literary critics covers the years from his birth in 1906 through the beginning stages of World War II in 1939-1940

The World Republic of Letters—*Pascale Casanova* 887
 Casanova examines inequalities in a global literary realm that exists independently of political and economic realms

Wounded—*Percival Everett* 892
 Tentatively reconnecting with other people after a period of self-imposed isolation, one man learns a bitter lesson about the abiding intolerance toward minorities in modern America

The Year of Magical Thinking—*Joan Didion* 897
 Didion is unsparingly candid in this account of her coming to terms with the sudden death of her husband, the grave illness of her daughter, and the grief attached to both

CONTRIBUTING REVIEWERS

Michael Adams
*City University of New York
Graduate Center*

Richard Adler
*University of Michigan-
Dearborn*

Emily Alward
*Henderson, Nevada, District
Libraries*

Andrew J. Angyal
Elon University

Dean Baldwin
*Penn State University Erie,
The Behrend College*

Carl L. Bankston III
Tulane University

Milton Berman
University of Rochester

Cynthia A. Bily
Adrian College

Margaret Boe Birns
New York University

Pegge Bochynski
Salem State College

Steve D. Boilard
*California Legislative
Analysts' Office*

Kevin Boyle
Elon University

Harold Branam
Independent Scholar

C. K. Breckenridge
Independent Scholar

Jeffrey L. Buller
Mary Baldwin College

Thomas J. Campbell
Pacific Lutheran University

Edmund J. Campion
University of Tennessee

Mary LeDonne Cassidy
*South Carolina State
University*

Dolores L. Christie
*Catholic Theological Society
of America (CTSA)
John Carroll University*

C. L. Chua
*California State University,
Fresno*

John J. Conlon
*University of Massachusetts,
Boston*

Richard Hauer Costa
Texas A&M University

Mary Virginia Davis
*University of California,
Davis*

Frank Day
Clemson University

Francine Dempsey
College of Saint Rose

M. Casey Diana
*University of Illinois, Urbana-
Champaign*

Margaret A. Dodson
Independent Scholar

Robert P. Ellis
Independent Scholar

Thomas L. Erskine
Salisbury University

Rebecca Hendrick Flannagan
Francis Marion University

Roy C. Flannagan
*South Carolina Governor's
School for Science and
Mathematics*

Robert J. Forman
*St. John's University, New
York*

Scott Fremin
Nicholls State University

Raymond Frey
*Centenary College, New
Jersey*

Jean C. Fulton
Landmark College

Ann D. Garbett
Averett University

Sheldon Goldfarb
University of British Columbia

Karen Gould
Independent Scholar

Lewis L. Gould
University of Texas, Austin

Hans G. Graetzer
South Dakota State University

Diane Andrews Henningfeld
Adrian College

Nika Hoffman
*Crossroads School for Arts
and Sciences*

John R. Holmes
*Franciscan University of
Steubenville*

William L. Howard
Chicago State University

Jeffry Jensen
Independent Scholar

Fiona Kelleghan
University of Miami

Steven G. Kellman
*University of Texas, San
Antonio*

James B. Lane
Indiana University Northwest

Eugene Larson
Los Angeles Pierce College

William Laskowski
Jamestown College

Leon Lewis
Appalachian State University

Thomas Tandy Lewis
St. Cloud State University

R. C. Lutz
CII Group

Janet McCann
Texas A&M University

Joanne McCarthy
Independent Scholar

Gina Macdonald
Nicholls State University

S. Thomas Mack
*University of South Carolina-
Aiken*

David W. Madden
*California State University,
Sacramento*

Lois A. Marchino
University of Texas at El Paso

Patricia Masserman
Microsoft Learning

Mira N. Mataric
University of Belgrade

Charles E. May
*California State University,
Long Beach*

Laurence W. Mazzeno
Alvernia College

Michael R. Meyers
Pfeiffer University

Robert A. Morace
Daemen College

Daniel P. Murphy
Hanover College

John Nizalowski
Mesa State College

Robert J. Paradowski
*Rochester Institute of
Technology*

David Peck
*California State University,
Long Beach*

Cliff Prewencki
Independent Scholar

Maureen J. Puffer-Rothenberg
Valdosta State University

Edna B. Quinn
Salisbury University

Thomas Rankin
Independent Scholar

R. Kent Rasmussen
Independent Scholar

Rosemary M. Canfield
Reisman
*Charleston Southern
University*

Bernard F. Rodgers, Jr.
Simon's Rock College of Bard

Carl Rollyson
*City University of New York,
Baruch College*

Joseph Rosenblum
*University of North Carolina,
Greensboro*

John K. Roth
Claremont McKenna College

Irene Struthers Rush
Independent Scholar

Carroll Dale Short
Independent Scholar

R. Baird Shuman
*University of Illinois, Urbana-
Champaign*

Thomas J. Sienkewicz
Monmouth College

Charles L. P. Silet
Iowa State University

Roger Smith
Independent Scholar

Ira Smolensky
Monmouth College

A. J. Sobczak
Independent Scholar

George Soule
Carleton College

August W. Staub
University of Georgia

Gerald H. Strauss
Bloomsburg University

Paul Stuewe
Green Mountain College

Susan E. Thomas
*Indiana University, South
Bend*

Evelyn Toft
Fort Hays State University

Jack Trotter
Trident College

William L. Urban
Monmouth College

Sara Vidar
Independent Scholar

Barbara Wiedemann
*Auburn University,
Montgomery*

Thomas Willard
University of Arizona

John Wilson
Independent Scholar

Eric A. Wolfe
University of North Dakota

Scott D. Yarbrough
*Charleston Southern
University*

MAGILL'S
LITERARY ANNUAL
2006

ACTIVE LIBERTY
Interpreting Our Democratic Constitution

Author: Stephen G. Breyer (1938-   )
Publisher: Alfred A. Knopf (New York). 161 pp. $21.00
Type of work: Current affairs and law

A U.S. Supreme Court justice lays out his philosophy of constitutional interpretation, providing a diverse array of examples from recent history

In *Active Liberty*, U.S. Supreme Court Justice Stephen G. Breyer outlines his judicial philosophy. In doing so, he consciously attempts to derive a compelling alternative to "originalism," an approach which dictates that constitutional (and statutory) provisions be narrowly interpreted in the light of the Constitution's text, augmented, when necessary, by the intent of their legislative authors. Originalism, along with other forms of self-proclaimed "judicial restraint," have been on the rise in recent years, backed by President George W. Bush and fronted by colorful spokespeople such as Antonin Scalia, also a Supreme Court justice. *Active Liberty* has caught the attention of many readers because it is seen as presenting a potential counterbalance to this growing trend.

Active Liberty is based on the Tanner Lecture series delivered by Breyer at Harvard University in November, 2004. The book opens with an exposition on "modern" and "ancient" notions of liberty as conceptualized by Swiss political philosopher Benjamin Constant (1767-1830). According to Constant, modern liberty is the freedom of individuals from any unnecessary government control (and Constant did not think very much government control was truly necessary). Ancient (or "public") liberty to Constant, or as Breyer refers to it, "active liberty," involves the freedom of the people as a whole to exercise self-government.

While Breyer thinks it is necessary to balance both forms of liberty to ensure a healthy republic, his purpose in the book is to promote active liberty as a beacon to constitutional interpretation. To Breyer, the U.S. Constitution is to be understood not just in the light of its specific provisions and the narrow intent of its authors but also in terms of the document's overall purpose, which is to provide for effective self-government. This does not mean that, to Breyer, judges are free to democratize the Constitution any way they see fit. Often enough though, cases arise where the law is not black and white, and there is room for interpretation. Breyer believes such interpretation should attach itself to the broader end of enhancing and refining a system of popular rule. Breyer does not present this as an easy task, but he does make clear that he thinks such interpretation can be done with restraint—especially as the inclination is to reinforce legislative government—and that it is fully consistent with the previous history of the living Constitution.

After explaining what is meant by "active liberty" and why it should serve as a source of constitutional interpretation, Breyer goes on to apply the concept to a number of modern constitutional issues, including free speech, affirmative action, and pri-

~

Stephen G. Breyer has been an associate justice of the U.S. Supreme Court since he was appointed by President Bill Clinton in 1994. Breyer received his law degree from Harvard University in 1964. He served in 1964-1965 as law clerk for Supreme Court Justice Arthur Goldberg, in 1965-1967 for the Justice Department's antitrust division, and as counsel for the Senate Judiciary Committee in 1974-1975 and 1979-1980. Breyer also taught law on and off before being named a federal appeals court judge in 1980.

~

vacy. Based on the primacy of active liberty, Breyer expresses dismay that his fellow Supreme Court justices have failed to recognize the privileged place of political speech, which is central to the system of popular rule in the United States. Instead, the Court has treated political speech as one among many protected forms. This has led to what Breyer sees as a judicially constructed barrier around commercial speech (essentially, the right to advertise) that has unduly impeded legislative authority.

Likewise, Breyer defends the right of legislatures to utilize affirmative action (within clear limits) in order to bring political equality to disadvantaged segments of the citizenry. This is a crucial part of the book, because it clarifies the difference, for Breyer, between active liberty and simple majoritarianism. Active liberty does not merely empower the privileged majority, acting through its elected representatives. It is also to be understood as an aspiration for enhanced democracy. Thus affirmative action and active liberty both are concepts that recognize U.S. government to be a work in progress. In addition, such progress must take place in a context of rapid social and technological change.

Thus, with regard to privacy, Breyer argues that, given the rise of new communication technologies, legislatures should be given some leeway in adapting to new challenges and situations likely to arise in a globally interconnected world. All in all, Breyer's applications are marked by his judicious respect for legislative authority. He also gives clear acknowledgment that caution should be used in order to avoid inappropriate intrusions into public policy by the judiciary.

In the third section of his book, Breyer returns to theoretical issues of constitutional interpretation, directly confronting Scalia and others likely to cast doubt on the salience of active liberty as a guiding principle. In his defense, Breyer asserts the legitimacy of looking at "purposes" and "consequences" when interpreting constitutional and statutory laws, rather than merely looking at the language and time-bound, narrow intent of their authors. Indeed, Breyer goes so far as to question the legal and historical basis for originalism, particularly if it is to be understood as the sole legitimate approach to constitutional interpretation.

Neither the text of the Constitution nor the stated intent of the Founders establishes originalism as the prescribed means of interpretation. Then, too, Breyer argues that interpreting the Constitution in the light of active liberty will not lead to arbitrary judicial decision making, as feared by originalists, given the presence of other checks and balances in the system. Indeed, among the "consequences" to be taken into consideration by jurists are the possible discontinuities that might arise from decisions that too readily ignore precedents or other revered parameters of law.

Thus, as conceived by Breyer, constitutional interpretation according to the purpose of active liberty includes a self-inhibiting factor, as well-founded rule of law is itself a pillar of effective democracy. As in the previous sections of the book, Breyer conveys a sense of modesty in promoting his views and refuting those of the opposition. He does not argue his case with even the slightest hint of ire, sarcasm, or bitterness, nor does he engage in personal attacks. Throughout the book, Breyer exemplifies the ideal of polite discourse.

Breyer's book drew notable response from commentators in the popular and scholarly media. His ideas were summarized and critiqued in various book reviews and opinion pieces. While Breyer has both supporters and detractors, he has generally been treated as a serious and at least somewhat original constitutional thinker, even by those who represent far different schools of thought. Nevertheless, a number of supposed flaws were pointed out. For advocates of "originalism" or other forms of judicial conservatism, Breyer is a throwback to the late Chief Justice Earl Warren and others on the Warren Court who, in the eyes of their critics, legislated from the bench instead of staying within the bounds of strictly interpreting the Constitution. These critics point out that the concept of "active liberty" is open to broad interpretation, leaving too much wiggle room for arbitrary judges to impose their values rather than the law.

Interestingly enough, some Breyer sympathizers partly agree. While advocating a judicial philosophy that is open to changing conditions and broader concerns of individual rights, social justice, and enhanced democracy, they see Breyer's notion of "active liberty" as too vague to offer clear guidance, especially in situations where majorities may or may not be the most enlightened segments of society. It has also been pointed out that Breyer, as a newcomer to the more esoteric issues of constitutional interpretation, fails to put his ideas into the context of previous scholarship on the subject, thus, perhaps, needlessly reinventing the wheel, or, worse still, drawing attention away from more compelling alternatives to originalism.

None of these criticisms is necessarily decisive. While originalists claim judicial high ground, there is, as Breyer suggests, no textual or contextual basis for their claim that theirs is the one way in which the Constitution should be interpreted. The Constitution itself includes no standards or rules for interpretation, nor are such laid out in any authoritative commentary by the Founders. Indeed, the very establishment of "judicial review" (the power of the court to strike down unconstitutional laws) by Chief Justice John Marshall in 1803 can be interpreted as precedent for massive judicial activism, and therefore a firm historical rebuke to judicial conservatives.

In addition, Breyer's cautious tone throughout this book, as well as his well-tempered definition of active liberty, makes it clear that he, too, is a practitioner of judicial restraint, albeit not in the form his conservative detractors wish. Indeed, reading this book might make one consider whether "judicial activism" has not, in reality, been much more than a convenient straw man for opponents of social and political change. As for the charge that "active liberty," though correctly inclined, is too vague to serve as a clear judicial guide, two things must also be pointed out. First, a well-accepted alternative principle is not in place at the moment. Second, it is not altogether clear that any useful guide to judicial interpretation can ever be as crystal clear as some people would like.

This said, the truth is that, for those who want to find in Breyer a champion to confront his fellow Supreme Court justice Anthony Scalia and other flamboyantly articulate originalists, this book, and its author, will be a disappointment. Rhetorical battles are not necessarily won by reason. Style points count as well, indeed, sometimes more than substance. In this regard, Breyer seems hardly able to carry the standard for judicial liberals. While his book, like his personal style, is admirably clear and unpretentious, he is never going to get as many points as Scalia for entertaining his audience or ridiculing his opponents. Given the current nature of American society, that probably means that Breyer's ideas will remain in the background unless championed in more vocal form by an advocate with greater stage presence. That said, *Active Liberty* is well worth reading, for both its style and its substance. Whether it will have a significant impact is another question entirely.

Ira Smolensky

Review Sources

Booklist 102, no. 6 (November 15, 2005): 9.
Library Journal 130, no. 15 (September 19, 2005): 77.
The New Republic 233, no. 12 (September 19, 2005): 29-34.
The New York Times 155 (September 26, 2005): A16.
Newsweek 146, no. 13 (September 26, 2005): 72.
Publishers Weekly 252, no. 30 (August 22, 2005): 48.
The Wall Street Journal 246, no. 37 (August 23, 2005): B1-B4.

ACTS OF FAITH

Author: Philip Caputo (1941-   )
Publisher: Alfred A. Knopf (New York). 669 pp.
    $27.00
Type of work: Novel
Time: The 1990's, at the height of the civil war in Sudan
Locale: Mostly in the hills of Central Sudan among the
    Nubas, one of the country's two largest non-Arab
    groups, with many scenes at or near an airstrip in
    Lokichokio, Kenya

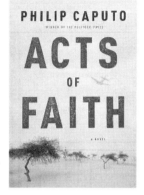

In a civil-war setting Caputo portrays various combatants, all with deep stakes in the conflict's outcome and all trapped in the ambiguities of good intentions

> *Principal characters:*
> DOUGLAS BRAITHWAITE, an American aviator and executive of Knight
>   Air Services, an independent airline flying aid into Sudan
> WESLEY DARE, a veteran Texas-born mercenary and bush pilot,
>   Douglas's partner in Knight Air
> MARY ENGLISH, Dare's copilot for Knight Air
> QUINETTE HARDIN, an evangelical Christian employee of a human rights
>   group that redeems black slaves captured by Arab raiders
> IBRAHIM IDRIS, a warlord commanding a detachment of *murahaleen*,
>   irregular Arab cavalry used as raiders by the Khartoum government
> FITZHUGH MARTIN, a mixed-race Kenyan and former United Nations
>   relief worker
> MICHAEL ARCHANGELO GORAENDE, commander of the Nuban rebel
>   forces

In the opening chapter of *A Rumor of War* (1977), a compelling memoir of combat in Vietnam, Philip Caputo writes of enlisting in the U.S. Marines immediately after finishing college. By his account, he survived the Vietnam War even though rendered "a moral casualty" and, at age twenty-six, faced the future with no skills other than those associated with killing. *Acts of Faith*, Caputo's epic fifth novel—this one about civil war in Sudan—highlights what he learned as a line officer and on journey by foot and camel across the deserts of Sudan in the 1970's. His return to sub-Saharan Africa in 2000-2001 is also reflected in a novel which, while far too long, offers its attractions.

For the reader who relies on being able to follow a clear plot line or the evolution of characters, finishing *Acts of Faith* will not be easy. However, Caputo provides two signposts in order to point a way through his jungle: a graded list of characters at the start and a tallying of the damage in the last one hundred pages. The six hundred middle pages often offer a morass. This book's backdrop is terra incognita for most Americans; its foreground is a complex of ethnic interconnections. *Acts of Faith* mounts the romantic and interpersonal gamesplay of a cast of Westerners and exotics

Philip Caputo worked nine years for the Chicago Tribune *and shared a Pulitzer Prize in 1972 for his reporting on election fraud in Chicago. He is the author of six other works of fiction and two memoirs, including* A Rumor of War *(1977), about his service in Vietnam. He divides his time between Connecticut and Arizona.*

performing in the darkening throes of Sudan's crisis. The action unfolds amid civil war, which reached a peak in Sudan in the 1990's when the Khartoum-backed Muslim government bombed parts of the Christian or non-Arab south, including animist tribes such as the Nubans, on whose agony Caputo focuses.

Although the Sudan has not yet become the setting for an American military adventure, this book mounts a fictional invasion by a vivid assemblage of insiders and outsiders. This very long work contains long passages about such planes as Beechcrafts, Gulfstreams, Hawkers, and Antonovs; stilted dialogue which often distracts more than it informs; and descriptions of a desolate landscape which come alive only when the narrative is airborne. As one reviewer puts it, "The psychology of young Islamic soldiers marching happily to martyrdom or raping and looting villagers is rendered as matter-of-factly as that of the fundamentalist Christians willing to murder their rivals or accommodate their religious doctrine to their private passions."

Caputo recently acknowledged to an interviewer that, although he occasionally feels a longing to try to transform the ordinary such as one finds in the fiction of Alice Munro and John Cheever, he is always drawn back to on-the-edge situations in exotic locales.

The character with whom he seems most at home is a legally bigamist Sudanese rebel commander with the musical name of Michael Archangelo Goraende. Like him, Caputo knows the crises of leadership under fire. The character who comes closest to reflecting Caputo's ambivalence about war is Fitzhugh Martin, the wise Kenyan who falls in love with a white Anglo-Kenyan much older than he. Well-traveled and well-read, Martin is the one character capable of an idealism that stems from love of Africa, but he can also grasp the folly of what Caputo calls "the recolonization of Africa by the imperialism of good intentions."

Less able and willing to ask questions such as what is enough intervention and what visitation rights Westerners should assume around the world are two Americans who have come to Sudan to create new lives for themselves. Their avowed mission is to bring aid to the starving rebels, but their real agenda is more personal and self-serving.

Doug Braithwaite, who arrives with dubious credentials of fighter-pilot heroism in the Persian Gulf War, is also armed with magnetic charm. At first, his takeover of Knight Air impresses even Fitzhugh Martin and a seasoned Texan, Wesley Dare, who becomes Doug's pilot-partner. Braithwaite's apparent altruism does a fictionally implausible quick-change into greed and zeal.

Quinette Hardin, a young evangelical Christian who works for a human rights group which buys back slaves captured by Arab raiders, sees herself as doing God's work and regards that work as a way to distinguish herself from the people she grew up with in Iowa. It's a way, reviewer Michiko Kakutani declares, to play the role of heroine in an action-packed drama of her own writing. One memorable sequence defines her well. "In Sudan," Quinette is advised by Colonel Goraende, the book's one Sudanese who should know, "the choice is never between the right thing and the wrong thing but between what is necessary and what isn't." Armed by a conviction of "divine approval," she deems it necessary to rescue four hundred Nuban captives from slavery. How she manages to save them—how she sweet-talks Goraende and the transport plane pilot who will receive the going rate of fifty dollars a head, promises American rockets and guns to the rebels and food and clothing for 410 chosen refugees who will take part in her ruse—provides both a thematic touchstone and that rarity in this book, an intended consequence.

Acts of Faith abounds in unintended consequences which often arise from the plot's various romantic complications. Wes Dare, four times married and divorced, falls in love with a much younger copilot, Mary English, and she—quite to his surprise—falls in love with him. Quinette eventually falls in love with "a big man with big ideas"—none other than Goraende.

Because Doug Braithwaite's desperate zeal undoes the idealism—unexamined as it is—of the others' "cause," many critics have paired him with the do-gooder known only as "Pyle," the title character of Graham Greene's *The Quiet American* (1955). Pyle, however, perished—still a true believer—and his portrait was far more fascinating than Doug's, in part, at least, because he cuckolded Fowler, Greene's stand-in. It is also an oversimplification to compare this African novel with the writings of Joseph Conrad. The book most like *Acts of Faith* is Norman Mailer's thousand-page *Harlot's Ghost* (1991), which revealed the perfidies of the Central Intelligence Agency worldwide. They are both ambitious books beyond the reach of most American novelists, but both suffer from the defects of their virtues, oversaturation. However, *Acts of Faith* may be the best novel on Africa by an American.

Richard Hauer Costa

Review Sources

Booklist 101, no. 11, (February 1, 2005): 916-917.
The Economist 375 (May 7, 2005): 78.
Entertainment Weekly, no. 819 (May 13, 2005): 91.
Kirkus Reviews 73, no. 4 (February 15, 2005): 189.
Library Journal 130, no. 3 (February 15, 2005): 114.
The New York Times 154 (May 3, 2005): B1-B8.
The New York Times Book Review 154 (June 19, 2005): 13.
The New Yorker 81, no. 15 (May 30, 2005): 91.
Publishers Weekly 252, no. 9 (February 28, 2005): 39.

THE AMERICAN CLASSICS
A Personal Essay

Author: Denis Donoghue (1928-   )
Publisher: Yale University Press (New Haven, Conn.). 304 pp. $27.00
Type of work: Literary criticism
Time: 1800-1900
Locale: The United States

Donoghue examines the roots, themes, and ideologies of American literature by analyzing critical reaction to five works which have traditionally been regarded as classics

> *Principal personages:*
> RALPH WALDO EMERSON, a philosopher and essayist
> HERMAN MELVILLE, a novelist
> NATHANIEL HAWTHORNE, a novelist
> HENRY DAVID THOREAU, an essayist
> WALT WHITMAN, a poet
> MARK TWAIN (born SAMUEL LANGHORNE CLEMENS), a novelist

Denis Donoghue, an Irishman who has spent a good part of his academic career in American universities, has been writing about literature for more than four decades, dividing his attention between British and American authors and critics. He has produced more than thirty books and editions on figures such as Jonathan Swift, T. S. Eliot, and William Butler Yeats, and on topics such as the relationship of literature and religion. He has been the subject of a book-length study, *Uncommon Readers* by Christopher J. Knight (2003), in which his critical principles are compared with those of other distinguished scholars, Frank Kermode and George Steiner. Trained during the years when New Criticism was in vogue, Donoghue has made his reputation by providing close readings of poetry, fiction, and drama and excellent assessments of the state of literary studies on both sides of the Atlantic Ocean. In *The American Classics: A Personal Essay* Donoghue offers some observations on works by nineteenth century American writers that he dubs classics.

The American Classics is in many respects a retrospective look at works about which Donoghue has previously written. The essays in this volume attempt to explain why five particular books, all but one written within a decade of one another in the mid-nineteenth century, deserve the title "classic." The selections are predictable: Nathaniel Hawthorne's *The Scarlet Letter* (1850), Herman Melville's *Moby Dick* (1851), Henry David Thoreau's *Walden* (1854), Walt Whitman's *Leaves of Grass* (1855), and Mark Twain's *Adventures of Huckleberry Finn* (1885). What Donoghue has to say about the "classic" status of these works, however, and about the status of American literature and culture, is not so predictable at all.

Donoghue explains that he was inspired to write *The American Classics* as a result of a course he taught to graduate students at New York University. He had thought his students would appreciate rereading five works that had, for a century, been staples in American high school and college English classes. He discovered, much to his amazement, only one student had read them all—and many had read only selections from any of them. Nevertheless, all the students could identify the five books as "the classics" of their literary heritage. This conundrum, Donoghue says, led him to ask several questions: What is a classic? Why are these books given that title? How have these texts been interpreted by generations of critics? How have they been used to shape American values?

Denis Donoghue, a native of Ireland, is professor of English and American literature at New York University. He is the author of a number of influential works of literary criticism, including The Practice of Reading *(1998) and* Words Alone: The Poet T. S. Eliot *(2000).*

To initiate his inquiry, Donoghue turns to the most influential critic of the twentieth century, T. S. Eliot, whose 1944 address to the Virgil Society titled "What is a Classic?" offers a definition of the term. Eliot sets a high standard: In his view, only Vergil's *Aeneid* (c. 29-19 B.C.E.; English translation, 1553) and Dante's *La divina commedia* (c. 1320, 3 volumes; *The Divine Comedy*, 1802) deserve the title, displaying concurrently the maturity of the writer, of his civilization, and of the language in which the work is composed. Donoghue immediately repudiates the possibility that any American work could rise to the status of "classic" under this definition, because in his view neither American culture nor American language has matured sufficiently to provide the framework for any writer who might be individually mature enough to produce such a work. That does not discourage Donoghue, however, from being more liberal than Eliot and allowing, provisionally at least, the possibility that some American writings could be given that sobriquet in a qualified sense. He argues that the five works he has selected, while not being "self-evidently" the best American literature has to offer the world, deserve to be read as classics for two important reasons. First, they provide readers "a shared cultural experience, something in which American society is otherwise impoverished." More important for him, perhaps, is the second reason: All of these works "put in question the otherwise facile ideology of individualism on which American culture complacently prides itself."

This introductory material is important not simply for the sake of Donoghue's formal argument but also to illustrate the tone he takes toward American literature in general and these five works in particular. Like most literary historians, Donoghue situates the birth of a truly American literature in the writings of Ralph Waldo Emerson, devoting a chapter to the New England writer's ideas which he claims permeate the five books chosen as classics. Donoghue reviews essays such as "The American Scholar" and "Experience" to identify the key to Emerson's argument—that American character will be distinguished by the degree of rugged individualism a person exhibits. He follows his assessment of Emerson with individual chapters on each of the classics he had identified. These books all demonstrate, in one way or another, how the spirit of individualism and nonconformity with the rules of older civilizations has made the United States a distinctive nation—and what price Americans have paid for adopting such an ideology.

In Donoghue's reading *Moby Dick*, in which Ahab's brand of individualism leads to massive destruction, exemplifies this trait quite well. Donoghue finds Thoreau the quintessential individualist, exhibiting disturbing traits of antisocial behavior and attitudes which clash with celebrations of him as a champion of the common person. Hawthorne's characters Hester Prynne and Arthur Dimmesdale are described as rebels against convention, rather than sinners against an angry God. Whitman is categorized as the optimistic singer of a new age committed to democratic values—ones that Donoghue finds uncomfortable. Finally, Huck Finn is the young romantic whose heart triumphs over a conscience misformed by conventional ideas about society carried over from a bankrupt European tradition.

This central argument must be extracted from Donoghue's rambling discussions of individual works. In fact, one might argue that Donoghue is less interested in offering his own interpretations of these five classics than he is in examining the ways other critics have responded to them. Acknowledging throughout *The American Classics* his own debt to scholars of an earlier age such as I. A. Richard, R. P. Blackmur, and William Empson, Donoghue takes every opportunity he can to test his readings against the ideas about literature expounded by his mentors. He is also prone to look at what he considers influential interpretations by his contemporaries, and he is not shy in challenging those assessments when he thinks them wrongheaded. He seems dismissive of theorists who would reduce these works (and others as well) to exercises in semiotics. He is especially critical of those who extract from any of these books some simple slogan or paragraph that seems to provide justification for a political movement. Donoghue finds serious fault with environmentalists and civil libertarians who have appropriated Thoreau by selectively excerpting passages that suit their ideology while ignoring the major argument of *Walden*, which Donoghue says promotes a kind of laissez-faire attitude toward nature and a disdain for civics.

The effect of Donoghue's retrospective examination of the critics from whom he learned the tools of his profession is nowhere more evident than in his commentary on the American scholar F. O. Matthiessen, whose 1941 study *American Renaissance: Art and Expression in the Age of Emerson and Whitman* established the canon of nineteenth century American literature. This monumental work "largely governed the direction of American studies" for the following half-century, Donoghue says. The criticism of the next generation's most influential critics—Lionel Trilling, Richard Chase, Richard Sewall, even the iconoclastic Leslie Fiedler—is little more than commentary on Matthiessen. Donoghue notes, however, that Matthiessen's approach was hardly free from ideology. As a young student, Donoghue says, he knew he was learning from Matthiessen what to read and what to think about the major works of American literature. What he and his fellow students did not know, though, was that "we were implicated, however marginally, in the propaganda of the Cold War." More recently, scholars such as Jonathan Arac and Donald Pease have pointed out how Matthiessen "turned *Moby Dick* and other classic books into Cold War texts." Donoghue is happy to join the list of critics eager to point out not only the error of Matthiessen's readings in American literature but also his simplistic judgment regarding the value of American democracy as the only alternative to fascism, communism, and the totalitarian state.

As one might expect, a book as idiosyncratic and judgmental as *The American Classics* is bound to provoke controversy. Some will object that no twentieth century works or authors are included. Others will be especially annoyed that Donoghue has included no women and no works by people of color. Some may be appalled at his judgments regarding the ideology of optimism about America that permeates so many writings by the figures he studies. The most likely critics, however, will be those who treat American authors and works with a special reverence—people who engage in the kind of chauvinism Donoghue excoriates throughout his study. One example serves as an apt illustration of his attitude. "What Whitman believed as an editor," Donoghue writes at the conclusion of his discussion of *Leaves of Grass*, "a propagandist, a post-Emersonian chauvinist is not, in my view, worth believing. It is mostly a pestilence." In this comment, and throughout *The American Classics*, there is an underlying message beneath Donoghue's literary analysis: Americans—authors, readers, and everyone else in the United States—have a misguided sense of their own importance and their own righteousness. The kind of ideology spawned by Emerson and his followers is responsible for what Donoghue believes is a dangerous, misguided sense of manifest destiny epitomized in President George W. Bush.

At numerous points in his narrative, Donoghue extends his discussion far beyond the bounds of literary analysis to explain how works such as *Moby Dick* and *Walden* promote wrongheaded thinking about the inherent rectitude of Bush's approach to handling both domestic and international issues. As an example: Donoghue's most direct attack on proponents of Emerson's ideas about democracy comes in his assessment of two distinguished critics of Emerson, Stanley Cavell and George Kateb. "Cavell and, much more blatantly, Kateb are notably complacent about the American character of the democracy they enjoy. They have apparently forgotten that the regime of George W. Bush and John Ashcroft contrive not only to interpret the USA Patriot Act illiberally but to keep an American citizen, José Padilla, indefinitely in solitary confinement without charge. Not to speak of the use to which the Bush administration has put Guantánamo Bay." Statements such as these seem to have strayed far from the aesthetic principals espoused by New Critics from whom Donoghue learned his craft. They are, however, emblematic of the far-reaching analysis he brings to bear on five classics of American literature. While one might not agree with his analysis, it is hard to deny the power of his argument. (Padilla was indicted on terrorism-related charges late in 2005.) As a result, *The American Classics* is a provocative, thoughtful study not only of five important American literary texts but also of the American culture these works represent.

Laurence W. Mazzeno

Review Sources

American Scholar 74, no. 3 (Summer, 2005): 131-133.
Library Journal 130, no. 10 (June 1, 2005): 128.
The New York Review of Books 52, no. 14 (September 22, 2005): 65-67.
Publishers Weekly 252, no. 17 (April 25, 2005): 51.
The Times Literary Supplement, September 9, 2005, p. 24.
Weekly Standard 10, no. 43 (August 1, 2005): 36-38.

AMERICAN GHOSTS
A Memoir

Author: David Plante (1940-   )
Publisher: Beacon Press (Boston). 288 pp. $24.00
Type of work: Memoir
Time: The 1940's to 2005
Locale: The United States, Canada, and Europe

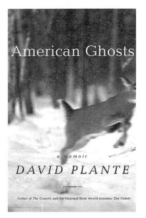

A writer examines the tangled strands of his religious, ethnic, and sexual identities

> *Principal personages:*
> DAVID PLANTE, an American writer
> ANACLET and ALBINA PLANTE, his parents
> NIKOS STANGOS, his life partner
> OCI, his first lover
> MARY GORDON, his friend, a Catholic writer

Beginning in the 1970's, David Plante established himself as a writer singularly occupied with the complicated and competing claims of spiritual and physical influences on human lives. In his novels, especially the widely praised Francoeur trilogy—*The Family* (1978), *The Country* (1981), *The Woods* (1982)—he explores the intersections of the visible and invisible, charting the interplay of faith and the body, seeking images that capture the moment when finite material opens up to reveal an infinite reality. The books constitute a sustained quest for wholeness in a fragmented world and for unity in a work of art. (Plante uses this kind of language.) Certainly *American Ghosts* is yet another attempt, this time stripped of the veil of fiction, to describe how history, ethnicity, religion, and sexuality connect to shape the spiritual life of a writer and his work.

This work irritates as often as it illuminates, feeling willed and protracted, the product of real struggle over many years. While the payoff for the reader is the exhilaration of transcending that struggle, in the text remain too many signs suggesting just how tortuous the path to resolution was—signs detectible in the syntax itself. Few pages unfold with fluency. Sentences, sometimes whole paragraphs, read as if they were literal translations from the German, with curious word order, awkward repetition, extended length, or a turgidity that can momentarily cloud meaning. However, such contorted and ruffled textures coexist with phrases of high lyricism and radiant ease as well. The memoir's contradictory quality may be unavoidable, even necessary, given that the story Plante has to tell is one of conflict, ambivalence, and paradox punctuated by moments of serene clarity and relaxation of spirit. Balked desire gives way to satisfaction and understanding, which then seizes up in knots of frustration.

Less a traditional memoir than a diary of a spiritual and artistic quest, *American Ghosts* has that characteristic feel of daily writing, the same unvarnished directness, the detailed but often obsessive, repetitive recording of moment-to-moment experience. Plante admits to being a compulsive diarist, the sort of person for whom events

~

David Plante is well known for his thirteen novels, particularly the Francoeur trilogy, one volume of which was nominated for the National Book Award. His work has appeared in The New Yorker *and* The Paris Review. *He holds citizenship in both Great Britain and the United States and teaches writing at Columbia University.*

~

take on reality after they have taken on language. He also confesses (rather late in the book, when readers will already have discovered this for themselves) to being "a totally humorless, unironical Canuck," someone who needs to hold things in, to be silent, to protect himself from revelation and possible embarrassment. Does Plante appreciate the irony of being such a person and yet having written this book, a book that holds very little in and risks embarrassment by letting it all out? There is no sign of this; a thoroughgoing earnestness pervades the memoir from start to finish. Still, the risks of not remaining silent seem largely to have been worth his taking. This traditional quest narrative—in many ways a cliché—is saved from portentous self-regard and given a spiky originality by a writer who brings the full weight of his sober, "unironical" personality to bear on it.

It should be said right away that the "ghosts" of the title are no idle metaphors. Ghosts of Plante's past abound, real, insistent presences which shoulder their ways into his writing and demand attention and space. Plante is one genuinely haunted individual: by his American Indian heritage, his French Canadian background, and, most profoundly, his Catholic upbringing in a Catholic, French-speaking neighborhood of Providence, Rhode Island. Added to this mix is the specter of his homosexuality, which he refuses to confront until it, like the rest, intrudes and forces itself upon him, adding to the complicated set of identities he tries to harmonize and embrace.

As a memoir, *American Ghosts* is very selective about what it remembers. Unlike many such personal accounts which cobble together colorful vignettes and cluster zesty personalities and anecdotes around the writer, Plante's is an underdramatized, underpopulated affair. For a narrative covering so many years, it boasts a relatively small cast of characters—a few family members, a few friends—and these are mostly supporting players brought on to cast further light on Plante's spiritual education. One is reminded of similar projects (William Wordsworth's 1850 volume *The Prelude*, perhaps) that, no matter what else they do, make it their principal business to record the growth of the poet's mind. In Plante's work, the reader is left with a depiction of the writer's metaphysical struggle to find meaning in life and make meaning in art. Other characters may provide counterpoint arguments in this contest between faith and doubt—friends such as Mary Gordon, stout Catholic apologist, and Sonia Orwell, heroically entrenched atheist—but the focus is fixed on Plante and the development of his writer's consciousness, from beginning to end.

As for the beginning: Plante grew up in "Le Petite Canada," a Rhode Island enclave steeped in nostalgic sentiment for "Le Grande Canada," the lost French continent and its lost culture. From the start, then, there is this sense of longing for something that seems real and is powerful but which is not actually visible. His father, part Blackfoot Indian, is a dark presence who will not share his Indian culture, and so David remains outside it. It is lost to him. His mother, French Canadian, shares only her intense desire to get out—of her house, of her parish, of her country. David is as trapped as she, in the dark about who he is. Such confusion leads, when Plante is fourteen, to his passionate enchantment with God, a being he sees as beyond this life yet aware of everything about it. The young boy grows excessively devout, inspired by empty spaces, death, and darkness—especially darkness, and by the images that grow out of the darkness. He begins to record the images, writing in English—his first attempts to make the invisible visible, to make it palpably real in order that he might possess it. He fails. The invisible remains beyond his grasp, but he realizes he can possess the visible, all of it, every sight, sound, smell, texture, taste. He can—it increasingly seems he must—catch these experiences of the senses and cast them in language. In many ways, the writer's agenda taking shape in this pietistic adolescent was the agenda Plante would embrace as an adult.

After a high school education with the Christian Brothers (all Petite Canadian darkness expunged by a bright, twentieth century American deity), Plante reaches Boston College, where, feeling an outsider among Irish Catholics, he loses the sense of things being possible for him. His struggle with the dark God of his parents and his shadowy heritage has worn him out. In that spirit of fatigue and unrest he goes, at age nineteen, to Europe. Only away from his family and culture can he say for the first time, "There is no God," and actually begin to acknowledge the existence and claim of the material world. As is often the case, however, for those newly emancipated from orthodoxy's tyranny, spiritual troubles persist: The god may die, but the need for the enlightenment, the coherence, the connection which that god promised remains very much alive. So it is for Plante. In Paris, he loses more of his provincialism and more of his province's God but now feels himself a divided being, part lawless, part lawful, caught in perpetual and maddening conflict. Therefore, reconciliation becomes his goal. This emerges most powerfully in his first homosexual experience, the complicated relationship with Oci, an elusive young Turk Plante meets in Spain.

It is Plante's first love affair, and as he describes it, this is not only romantic but Romantic: the act of lovemaking an act of completion, of uniting with everything beyond himself. It is his pathway to seeing himself and the world as one, to overcoming separateness and establishing connection, his way of including everything and making it mean everything. The spirit of William Blake hovers over this part of the narrative, and like that great Romantic visionary before him, Plante saw for the first time that this experience of totality was possible only outside of traditional religion. It was possible in sex. So, not surprisingly, he kept looking for it there; and, not surprisingly, he failed to find it. He sums up five years in New York in what amounts to parentheses: sex without love, sex without enlightenment. Whatever enlightenment he does discover comes through his writing, through identifying the writer's desire to find the secret that touches on all things. If he can find the right images, he feels, he can say everything. This insight he credits to Henry James, yet another of the "ghosts" he wrestles with in these years, as his first novel, *The Ghost of Henry James* (1970), makes clear.

Returning to England, he meets Nikos Stangos, the man who would become his life partner. A Greek Orthodox Christian whose God was a God of life and light not darkness, Nikos is a force urging Plante to engage with the world. In order to do that, he must engage the ghosts of his past. He travels to Canada to trace his father's people back ten generations and writes a series of richly imagined histories of each generation, determined to place himself within a seamless, comprehensible chronicle. He goes back to France to trace his mother's side of the family but realizes at last that he has come to free himself from his ancestry, not link himself to it. He will not discover his identity by means of these journeys back in time; he will not be made whole by conjuring up these ghosts. In the church where his father was baptized, he has one of his final moments of vision:

> I was more aware than I had ever been of the split in me (which is the split of this book): the split and the pull between the secular and the religious, between the definite and the vague, between what can be said and what cannot be said, between law and freedom, state and self, politics and poetry, between light and darkness, between life and death, between my mother and my father.

The great Romantic quest for wholeness has failed; oppositions have not been resolved. Division remains. Longing remains. As ultimate revelation—whether about the nature of the world or the nature of the self—this can all seem obvious or at least unexceptionable. The universe contains multitudes, and each person is many things, one person housing many diverse and contradictory desires, personalities, allegiances. Yet Plante longs for these diversities to be harmonized, to be connected. Tracing his ancestry, filling in the gaps, was a way to get at these primal connections. Finally, however, Plante abandons this quest for a unifying transcendence and settles for a sense of the connectedness of all things in the moment that he regards them. If there is no Divine Being, there is yet divinity, this "divinity of awareness." Christ is a "Canuck son" who personifies longing which will never be realized, and God is a darkness; yet humankind can still see, and in the act of truly seeing, experience the only deity available, the only wholeness one has or needs. Thus the memoir closes with Plante's hard-won accommodation to the puzzles and paradoxes of human aspiration, his embrace of attentive daily living.

Thomas J. Campbell

Review Sources

America 192, no. 12 (April 4, 2005): 30-31.
Booklist 101, no. 5 (November 1, 2004): 454-455.
Commonweal 132, no. 2 (January 28, 2005): 36-38.
Kirkus Reviews 72, no. 19 (October 1, 2004): 951.
Lambda Book Report 13, nos. 9/10 (April/May, 2005): 6-8.
Library Journal 129, no. 13 (August 15, 2005): 80.
The New York Times Book Review 154 (January 16, 2005): 6.
Publishers Weekly 251, no. 29 (July 19, 2004): 151.
The Times Literary Supplement, December 9, 2005, p. 11.

AMERICAN PROMETHEUS
The Triumph and Tragedy of J. Robert Oppenheimer

Authors: Kai Bird (1951-   ) and Martin J. Sherwin
    (1957-   )
Publisher: Alfred A. Knopf (New York). 721 pp. $35.00
Type of work: Biography and history of science
Time: 1904-1967
Locale: New York City; Harvard University; Cambridge
    University; the University of Göttingen (Germany); the
    California Institute of Technology; the University of
    California at Berkeley; Los Alamos, New Mexico;
    Princeton University; Washington, D.C.; and St. John
    Island in the U.S. Virgin Islands

*This biography of J. Robert Oppenheimer provides the
facts of his life and makes his personality come alive but
does not analyze the meaning of his complex life*

Principal personages:
J. (JULIUS) ROBERT OPPENHEIMER, a physicist
JULIUS OPPENHEIMER, his father
ELLA FRIEDMAN OPPENHEIMER, his mother
FRANK OPPENHEIMER, his brother, also a physicist
KITTY HARRISON OPPENHEIMER, his wife
JEAN TATLOCK, his first girlfriend
HAAKON CHEVALIER, a friend embroiled in the espionage incident
LEWIS STRAUSS, chairman of the Atomic Energy Commission and
    Oppenheimer's political enemy
LESLIE GROVES, the general in charge of the Los Alamos project
HARRY S. TRUMAN, the U.S. president, 1945-1953
EDWARD TELLER, a rival physicist, developer of the hydrogen bomb

Though he died at a relatively young age, J. Robert Oppenheimer, "the father of
the atomic bomb," lived long enough to see a play based on his life, *In der Sache
J. Robert Oppenheimer* (pr. 1964, pb. 1966; *In the Matter of J. Robert Oppenheimer*,
1967), by the German playwright Heinar Kipphardt. It focused on the investigation of
Oppenheimer as a suspected security risk during the Joseph McCarthy era. Though
the play mesmerized audiences in the 1960's, Oppenheimer himself was disgusted
with it, saying that it "turned the whole damn farce into a tragedy."

Kai Bird and Martin J. Sherwin recount his reaction at the end of *American Prometheus*, their Pulitzer Prize-winning biography of Oppenheimer. That they have
subtitled their book *The Triumph and Tragedy of J. Robert Oppenheimer* leads one to
wonder: Was Oppenheimer's life the stuff of triumph or tragedy? It is the sort of thing
that one might expect the authors to discuss in a conclusion, but none appears in this

*Kai Bird is a contributing editor
to* The Nation *magazine and has
written books on Hiroshima and
the nature of the American
establishment. Martin J. Sherwin,
the Walter S. Dickson Professor
of English and American History
at Tufts University, has written a
book on Hiroshima and has
worked on film documentaries on
nuclear weapons and nuclear
war.*

otherwise fine biography. An epilogue briefly recounts what happened to Oppenheimer's wife and children after his premature death from throat cancer in 1967, but there is no measured evaluation of the meaning of Oppenheimer's life by the two writers who might be best qualified to supply it.

Perhaps this is because there was so much ambiguity in Oppenheimer's life. Indeed, it is the lack of ambiguity in the Kipphardt play that the authors say explains Oppenheimer's disgust with it. Still, they might at least have tried to provide a summing-up, a statement of what Oppenheimer's life meant in the end, the life of a man who both facilitated the creation of the atomic bomb and warned against its dangers, a man who seemed devoted to physics and yet hardly worked in the field during his last two decades. Oppenheimer at times seemed fearless in defending unorthodox views and at other times gave way to the views of the orthodox or even embraced them. His is a confusing story.

However, the facts are all there in the account presented by Bird and Sherwin. They have mastered a vast array of sources, from Federal Bureau of Investigation files to published books to private letters, and also conducted dozens of interviews with people who knew Oppenheimer. Rather than overwhelming the reader with raw excerpts from this material, they have thoroughly digested it and are able to provide a flowing narrative which has a ring of truth about it.

Perhaps the best part of this book is the first section, with its account of Oppenheimer's childhood and prolonged adolescence. Bird and Sherwin present a detailed picture of a young boy who was precocious intellectually but slow to develop socially and emotionally. At the age of twelve Oppenheimer was so advanced in his study of rocks and minerals that he was made a member of the New York Mineralogical Club and was invited to give a lecture. The club's officials, who had been in touch with him only by letter, had no idea he was only twelve, and members were astonished and amused when he showed up to give his talk.

On the other hand, he had few friends, was painfully shy, and was a target for bullies. One time he was locked in an icehouse overnight. He had no romantic life until he was well into his twenties and no serious girlfriend until he reached his thirties.

The problem with his being successful in mainly one area of life, the intellectual, was that when things suddenly went bad in that sphere, Oppenheimer was devastated. He suffered upon arriving at graduate school at Cambridge University in the mid-1920's. After exploring various fields of study, Oppenheimer had settled on physics as the subject he most enjoyed, and he did well in his undergraduate studies at Harvard University. It was theoretical physics he was best at, but when he went to Cambridge he was expected to perform hands-on experimental work in the laboratory. Faced with his inadequacy in this aspect of physics, he became depressed and even violent at times toward others. There is even a strange story, not entirely confirmed by the biographers, about Oppenhiemer's attempting to poison his superviser with a doctored apple.

Oppenheimer was sent to several psychiatrists and was visited by his parents, who arrived from the United States with a young woman who they hoped could provide their son with a little romance. None of these efforts helped. Only when Oppenheimer was able to return to theoretical physics at the University of Göttingen, in Germany, did he come out of his depression. Indeed, he began to flourish and within a decade was publishing papers on theoretical physics and establishing a reputation for himself.

What he exactly was discovering in physics is a little unclear from this biography. Neither of the authors is a scientist, and the book is lacking somewhat on the technical side. Apparently Oppenheimer made discoveries in both astrophysics (predicting the existence of black holes) and nuclear physics (predicting the existence of positrons).

Oppenheimer never won a Nobel Prize, though several of his students did. The biographers suggest this is because Oppenheimer was more a man of many insights, provoking others into big discoveries. He would flit from problem to problem or project to project, coming up with original ideas which other physicists fine-tuned, tested, and presented in final form. Then they were the ones who won the prizes.

The exception to this way of working was the one big project of Oppenheimer's life, the creation of the atomic bomb. In its development, he persisted with the project in an almost compulsive way, intent on building the bomb before the Nazis built one of their own during World War II. Even in this case, though, he tended more to flit among tasks than to work persistently on one. He gathered together a large team of scientists and engineers and oversaw and inspired all of them on the various aspects of the larger project.

If there was any project for which Oppenheimer might have won the Nobel Prize, it would have been the creation of the bomb. Although creating the bomb was a staggering scientific accomplishment, it did raise troubling moral issues, issues on which Oppenheimer would reflect throughout the rest of his life.

After the war, he said that in creating the atomic bomb, "the physicists have known sin." However, at another point he argued that physicists had to create the bomb because it is the job of science to pursue knowledge wherever it leads. These are interesting, albeit conflicting, ideas which Oppenheimer did not reconcile in his lifetime. The conflict speaks to the ambiguity the biographers see in him.

Another ambiguity concerns his relationship with government. At times Oppenheimer seemed able to take an unpopular, antigovernment stand without backing down. For instance, he continually argued for openness about nuclear bombs, saying all nuclear information should be made available to everyone, including the United States' new adversary, the Soviet Union. Only through openness and international regulation, he said, could war be averted. He also opposed development of the hydrogen bomb—and yet he would not come out publicly against it. Nor would he sign a petition for international control of nuclear power, his own idea, after the government announced that it was pursuing a different approach.

Sometimes Oppenheimer seemed frightened of the government and the powers that be, perhaps with reason. The late 1940's and 1950's were a time of anticommunist hysteria in the United States in which anyone with left-wing connections, past or present, might face penalties. Oppenheimer had such connections. He had joined many so-called communist front organizations in the 1930's during the Depression, and many of his friends were members of the Communist Party.

It seems that Oppenheimer himself was not a communist. The biographers repeatedly examine this issue and often seem to be taking on the role of defense lawyers defending Oppenheimer against the charge. It is a minor lapse in judgment and proportion on their part, which leads the biography away from Oppenheimer the man, reducing him to the status of an unfairly accused victim of witch-hunts. In trying so hard to establish whether Oppenheimer was or was not a communist, the biographers for the moment forget that ambiguity was Oppenheimer's defining feature. Here they try to eliminate ambiguity, and the result is an awkward heavy-handedness and a one-sided portrayal of Oppenheimer's chief prosecutor, Lewis Strauss.

Strauss managed to have Oppenheimer's security clearance revoked on the grounds that Oppenheimer had communist associates who might have engaged in espionage for the Soviet Union during World War II. The result was to destroy Oppenheimer's influence in government circles, influence that had grown in the wake of his fame as the moving force behind the atomic bomb.

One irony is that Oppenheimer lost this battle with the forces of anticommunism despite his attempts to curry favor with them. Before his own investigation, Oppenheimer had cooperated with government and congressional investigations of several other physicists with left-wing connections. He had even provided names to the House Committee on Un-American Activities, presumably hoping that collaborating with the bullies would save him from them. Unfortunately, he was wrong.

The last years of Oppenheimer's life just seem to peter out in this biography. He spent much of his time on a Caribbean island and did little or no scientific work. Perhaps this is the tragedy Bird and Sherwin have in mind. Perhaps they are suggesting that McCarthyism killed Oppenheimer's creativity, though they do not quite say so.

However, Oppenheimer really gave up any serious physics work even before the hearing that removed him from public life. The very fact that he was in public life, on an advisory committee to the Atomic Energy Commission, and in frequent contact with influential politicians in Washington, shows that his focus from at least the end of the war was no longer on science. Even during the war, during the project to develop the atomic bomb, the biographers sometimes seem to be suggesting that Oppenheimer was working less as a scientist than as an administrator. One wonders why. Do many physicists do their best work young? If so, the fact that Oppenheimer after the age of forty did little scientific work hardly seems like a tragedy. Perhaps the tragedy is that such a renowned scientific figure could be hounded out of public life. Did he stop doing physics because he was so troubled at what his work in physics had produced: the first weapon of mass destruction? It is an interesting question, which unfortunately this biography does not address.

Sheldon Goldfarb

Review Sources

America 192, no. 20 (June 6, 2005): 27-28.
Booklist 101, no. 13 (March 1, 2005): 1100.
Discover 27, no. 1 (January, 2006): 73-74.
Kirkus Reviews 73, no. 4 (February 15, 2005): 205.
Library Journal 130, no. 7 (April 15, 2005): 115.
Los Angeles Times, April 10, 2005, p. R3.
The New Republic 233, no. 16 (October 17, 2005): 35-41.
The New York Times 154 (April 21, 2005): E1-E8.
The New York Times Book Review 154 (May 15, 2005): 7-8.
The New Yorker 81, no. 21 (July 25, 2005): 97.
Publishers Weekly 252, no. 10 (March 7, 2005): 63-64.
Time 165, no. 19 (May 9, 2005): 58-59.
The Washington Post Book World, April 10, 2005, p. 3.

AMERICA'S CONSTITUTION
A Biography

Author: Akhil Reed Amar (1958-   )
Publisher: Random House (New York). 657 pp. $30.00
Type of work: History and law
Time: 1787-2005
Locale: The United States

This scholarly analysis of the formation and development of the U.S. Constitution includes its twenty-seven amendments, with an emphasis on the meanings of the component parts within their historical contexts

Principal personages:
JAMES MADISON, called the father of the Constitution because of his many contributions to that document
THOMAS JEFFERSON, the author of the Declaration of Independence and Madison's colleague
GEORGE WASHINGTON, the first president of the United States, 1789-1797
JAMES WILSON, a participant in the Constitutional Convention and member of the Supreme Court
JOHN MARSHALL, called the great chief justice of the United States, 1801-1835
ROGER TANEY, pro-slavery chief justice of the United States, 1836-1864
ABRAHAM LINCOLN, the president of the United States, 1861-1865
JOHN BINGHAM, the primary drafter of the Fourteenth Amendment
EARL WARREN, a liberal chief justice of the United States, 1953-1969

Akhil Reed Amar writes that the purpose of his latest book, *America's Constitution: A Biography*, is to present a comprehensive account that will introduce readers "both to the legal text (and its consequences) and to the political deeds that gave rise to that text." He further explains that the word "biography" denotes his attempt "to illuminate a landmark text much as a standard biographer might shed light on the life of some prominent person" by examining the document's "external impact and internal structure"—its personality. In several places he mentions that he wants to illuminate both the letter and the spirit of the Constitution.

Amar examines all the separate parts of the written Constitution of the United States. He analyses how and why each part was written as well as its various meanings during and shortly after enactment. Although he makes numerous references to later interpretations by the Supreme Court, he does not attempt to present a comprehensive account of the later history. The subtitle *A Biography*, therefore, is something of a misnomer, for it would seem to suggest a narration of the entire life of the Constitution, including the aging process. The reader who desires a more complete story of the

Supreme Court's interpretation of the Constitution should look to other books, such as *A March of Liberty: A Constitutional History of the United States* (1988), by Melvin Urofsky.

In the U.S. political system, the courts, especially the Supreme Court, have long exercised significant social and political power as a result of their established authority to declare legislative or executive acts to be unconstitutional—a practice called judicial review. In a polarized political climate, therefore, one should not be surprised that conservatives and liberals strongly disagree about the methods

Akhil Reed Amar served as a clerk for Justice Stephen G. Breyer and became a member of the faculty of Yale Law School in 1985. His previous books include The Constitution and Criminal Justice: First Principles *(1997) and* The Bill of Rights: Creation and Reconstruction *(1998). He has also published scores of articles aimed at both scholarly and popular audiences.*

and theoretical approaches that should be used in interpreting the Constitution. Many conservatives decry the practice of "judicial activism," and they sometimes argue that judges and justices should take "strict constructionist" approaches to the constitutional text. Conservatives also tend to advocate exegesis based on the text's "original meaning." Liberals usually disagree and advocate the notion of a "Living Constitution," which most often means that judges should be allowed to make broad interpretations that promote liberal principles of equality, human rights, and natural justice.

Such debates about hermeneutics (or interpretative theory) become intense because they are relevant to judicial decisions about issues such as affirmative action, property rights, states' rights, abortion rights, criminal procedures, and capital punishment.

Amar uses a combination of interpretative approaches. While referring to himself as a constitutional textualist, he argues that it is necessary "to understand precisely what the document did and did not mean to those who enacted and amended it." Amar takes very broad views of both textual analysis and the search for original understandings. In the first place, he tries to discern the "meaning inherent in the basic acts" of the writing and ratification processes, so that he considers that these actions reflect understandings that are part of the very essence of the Constitution. Secondly, Amar's analysis gives special heed to how the constitutional texts were interpreted in the period following the ratification process. He insists that this is especially appropriate in the precedent-making acts of George Washington after 1789, even though a critic might object that framers and ratifiers did not indicate a desire to give Washington a carte blanche of unlimited prerogatives. In the case of the Fourteenth Amendment, Amar is more persuasive when arguing that the Reconstruction Congress signaled its intentions with implementing legislation.

Amar's emphasis on originalism does not mean that he is opposed to the Living Constitution perspective. Indeed, he argues that "at key points the text itself seems to gesture outward" toward the recognition of "unenumerated rights above and beyond the textually enumerated ones." This and other statements seem to imply that Amar would endorse an expansive reading of the Constitution to include the controversial right to privacy, which provides the theoretical justification for women to have abortions. It is unlikely, on the other hand, that he would give much attention to arguments in favor of legal rights for prenatal life.

Although Amar is highly critical of many provisions in the Constitution, especially on the issue of slavery, he acknowledges that his ideas are rather "Whiggish," for he views the Constitution as moving toward ever-expanding democracy, equality, and human rights. He even argues that the original document of 1787, despite its many defects and limitations, was based on a democratic vision that was fundamentally different from the monarchical and aristocratic ideals that were dominant almost everywhere in the civilized Western world at the time. Thus, he vigorously disagrees with those who perceive the Constitution as a conservative and antidemocratic backlash against the presumably more liberal principles of the Revolution, as expressed in the Declaration of Independence and similar documents.

According to Amar, the preamble is worded in such a way to suggest that the Constitution was a democratic contract to be voluntarily accepted or rejected by the citizens. He describes the ratification process as "the most democratic deed the world had ever seen." The process, of course, must be considered an example of representative democracy rather than direct democracy, because the Constitution was ratified by elected delegates to conventions rather than by direct popular votes. While cynics have inferred that the Framers, in rejecting the option of a direct vote, demonstrated a distrust of the population. Amar argues that the issues were so complex that "conventions offered the promise of democratic deliberation that direct statewide popular votes would have lacked."

Critics of the Constitution will certainly object that more than half of the population—all women, all slaves, and many men without property—were not permitted to vote for delegates to the state conventions. While conceding that the ratification process would be considered undemocratic according to twenty-first century criteria, Amar writes: "Never before had so many ordinary people been invited to deliberate and vote on the supreme law." Eight of the states, moreover, reduced the standard property qualifications for free adult males, two states had standing rules that extended the ballot to almost all taxpaying adult male citizens, while New York, "for the first time in history, invited all free adult male citizens to vote." One must not forget that this was at a time when "democratic self-government existed almost nowhere on earth."

In the early twenty-first century, intellectuals commonly assert that the Constitution established a republican form of government that was not meant to be democratic. Amar answers, however, that the primary distinction of the late eighteenth century was not between a republic and a democracy but between a republic/democracy on one hand and a monarchy or aristocracy on the other. In the eighteenth century the terms "republic" and "democracy" were often confounded with each other, and the terminology of "representative democracy" was extremely rare. Some Framers, nevertheless, did not hesitate to describe the Constitution as democratic in nature. James Wilson, for example, declared that "all authority, of every kind, is derived by representation from the people, and the democratic principle is carried into every part of the government."

Amar convincingly demonstrates that, as a whole, *The Federalist* essays of 1788 "linked republican government with various aspects of popular sovereignty" and majority rule. Although James Madison did recognize a contrast between a democracy and a republic, he wrote in *The Federalist* no. 52 that a widespread right to suffrage was a "fundamental article of republican government." In no. 57, moreover, he emphasized that the Constitution did not include any voting qualifications based on wealth, birth, profession, or religion, and that the electors of federal representatives "are to be of the great body of the People of the United States." Based on the eighteenth century concepts of a republic, Amar thinks that the Reconstruction Congress was entirely justified in making an expansive interpretation of the Republican-Guarantee Clause of Article IV. He describes the clause as a sleeping giant that eventually awoke to provide at least a few democratic rights to the oppressed freedmen of the South.

When Madison and other eighteenth century southerners spoke of government deriving from "the people," they clearly intended to exclude slaves. Amar writes: "Slavery was the original sin in the New World garden, and the Constitution did more to feed the serpent than to crush it." The constitutional framers particularly violated republican principles by allowing a slave without civil rights to be represented in Congress as three-fifths of a free citizen. As the three-fifths clause expanded the political clout of the slave states, it contributed to "an expanding rot at the base of America's system of representation." Despite its "slavocratic" aspects, Amar denies that the Constitution was one-sidedly pro-slavery. The Fugitive Slave Clause, for instance, did require the free states to extradite slaves who had escaped, but it did not obligate the states to return former slaves to masters who had voluntarily taken them to a free state. Like almost all scholars who have studied the topic, Amar finds that Chief Justice Roger Taney and his colleagues, in the infamous case *Dred Scott v. Sandford* (1857), had no textual or historical justification for ruling that Congress lacked the authority to prohibit the movement of slaves into the territories.

Amar presents a particularly interesting discussion about whether the Constitution originally provided the states with a right of secession. Under the Articles of Confederation, he argues that the thirteen states had operated as sovereign countries, but that after ratifying the Constitution, they "merged to form the sovereign people of the United States." He marshals a great deal of evidence to demonstrate that the ratifying conventions were conscious that they were ceding their state sovereignty, and that no region or state would have henceforth any right unilaterally to withdraw from the union. The American people "as a whole," certainly, would always retain the "the inalienable right to alter or abolish" the union, but only if this were approved by the majority of the national population.

Amar's discussion of the three Civil War Amendments is also excellent. The Reconstruction Congress, in his view, was entirely justified in promoting the rights of the freedmen and in countering the Southern states' "long history of slaveocratic contempt for core republican freedoms." In discussing the Fourteenth Amendment, Amar makes a strong case for the idea that the Framers intended to "incorporate" the provisions of the Bill of Rights as part of the "privileges or immunities of citizens" that the states were required to recognize. Like other scholars, he is highly critical of the way in which the Supreme Court chose to incorporate substantive freedoms, like those of the First Amendment, by means of the doctrine of substantive due process, a concept that "verges on oxymoron." While not a fan of the Second Amendment, he nevertheless concedes that the Framers of the Fourteenth Amendment wanted to protect the personal right of gun ownership for purposes of self-defense.

America's Constitution: A Biography is a serious work of scholarship which includes unexpected insights, fascinating anecdotes, and serious discussions of historical and legal debates. It is written with clarity and in an engaging style. Students of constitutional history will find that the 128 pages of endnotes are extremely helpful. Even though the publisher has attempted to market the book as a general audience book, it can only be recommended to readers who have some knowledge and considerable interest in constitutional history and theory. While energetic readers, no doubt, will enjoy reading the book from cover to cover, for many people it will be primarily valuable as a reference tool. Whenever one wants to know about the historical background and original understanding of a particular statement in the Constitution, it would impossible to find a better source.

Thomas Tandy Lewis

Review Sources

Booklist 102, no. 2 (September 1, 2005): 27.
Commentary 120, no. 2 (September 1, 2005): 90-92.
The Economist 376 (September 10, 2005): 80.
Kirkus Reviews 73, no. 14 (July 15, 2005): 771.
Library Journal 130, no. 13 (August 15, 2005): 104.
The Nation 281, no. 21 (December 19, 2005): 36-39.
National Review 57, no. 20 (November 7, 2005): 53-54.
The New York Times Book Review 155 (November 6, 2005): 35.
Publishers Weekly 252, no. 25 (June 20, 2005): 68.
The Washington Post Book World, September 25, 2005, p. TO3.

THE ANGEL OF FORGETFULNESS

Author: Steve Stern (1947-   )
Publisher: Viking (New York). 404 pp. $25.00
Type of work: Novel
Time: 1910 and 1969
Locale: New York City

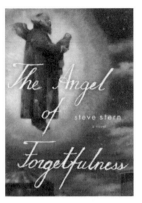

In the best tradition of Jewish American literature, this
complex Bildungsroman *tells three separate stories that*
merge into one

Principal characters:
  SAUL BOZOFF, a young Jewish student, the
    narrator
  KENI SHENDELDECKER, his dying aunt, who
    entrusts a manuscript to him
  NATHAN HART, Keni's late husband, who wrote the manuscript sixty
    years earlier
  MOCKY, the Angel of Forgetfulness, who watches over his half-human
    son on earth
  NACHMAN OPGEKUMENER, Mocky's half-angelic, half-human son
  RIVKA BUBITSCH, an actress with whom Nachman is infatuated

Some observers have called into question the future of Jewish American literature. Where, they wonder, are the worthy successors to Isaac Bashevis Singer and Bernard Malamud, who brought *yiddishkayt*—the culture of the Eastern European Diaspora—into American life, offering fable, melancholy humor, and quirky syntax as a vehicle for serious contemplation of human existence.

Some have even called into the question the viability of the Yiddish culture that underlies much of Jewish American literature. In 2004 Janet Hadda, retired professor of Yiddish at the University of California, Los Angeles, voiced doubt that Jews could "connect to a culture that doesn't really exist anymore authentically, which was the culture of Ashkenaz in Eastern Europe. It . . . existed in tremendous vibrancy before World War II and existed in remnants afterward through immigration, but is now gone."

A year earlier, however, in the magazine *Pakn Treger*, Hadda identified the one force she expects to bear the torch of Yiddish literary tradition into the twenty-first century: contemporary American Jewish novelists who write in English but whose themes are in keeping with the Yiddish literary tradition. "Through their work," she predicted, "the culture—and with it, the soul—of Ashkenaz, of Jewish Eastern Europe, will continue to breathe fire and light."

Hadda, along with other critics, has singled out Jewish American novelist Steve Stern as an exceptional bearer of that light. In a review of Stern's 1986 story collection *Lazar Malkin Enters Heaven*, Hadda described the work as luminous, remark-

~

Steve Stern has published several short-story collections, including Isaac and the Undertaker's Daughter *(1983), winner of a Pushcart Writer's Choice Award and an O. Henry Prize;* Lazar Malkin Enters Heaven *(1986), winner of the Edward Lewis Wallant Award for Jewish American fiction; and* The Wedding Jester *(1999), winner of the National Jewish Book Award. He has also written three novels and two books for children. A former Rhodes Scholar with Distinction, he teaches creative writing at Skidmore College in Saratoga Springs, New York.*

~

able, and filled with "dreamy brilliance." Calling Stern's work "a new link in the chain of Jewish fiction," she has likened him to such renowned Jewish writers as Moyshe Kulbak and I. J. Schwartz. She hastens to add that Stern's work is not derivative but original within the Jewish literary tradition. About his newest offering, *The Jewish Reader* magazine weighed in with enthusiasm: "Steve Stern's *The Angel of Forgetfulness* is proof positive that it is possible to write a 'Yiddish novel in English'—one that doesn't derive its yidishkayt from phony oy's or imagined shtetls, but from a profound knowledge of Yiddish literature, with all its intellectual and imaginative powers."

Indeed, Stern displays a skill with language and a knowledge of Yiddish literature rivaling that of Singer or Malamud. He tells his tale with all the verbal razzmatazz, inverted syntax, and fanciful naming one expected from the past golden era of Jewish American literature. Stern's lower East Side—the principal setting for *The Angel of Forgetfulness*—abounds with underworld characters (some of them historic) sporting names such as Big Jack Zelig, Lighthouse Freddy, and Gyp the Blood. Here is a typical locution from one of the lower East Side characters engaged in intellectual debate: "Don't give me no more your so-called Jewish Gothic. . . . Enough already with the characters that from the trees, which they sway like daveners under a sky like a wedding canopy, are all the time hanging themselves with their prayer shawls."

Here is a scene witnessed by one immigrant character on his first job in 1910 New York, "lugging piecework from the garment factories west of Broadway to the downtown sweatshops":

> Along the way he got an eyeful of the Golden Land. His route might take him through the Hester Street market, where men in gory aprons sank their cleavers into meat seething with blue fly larvae. Rail-thin women fingered the entrails of hanging fowl to determine their kosherness, haggled with merchants who alternated between deference and poisonous invective. There were streets like Allen, known as 'the street of perpetual shadow,' lousy with pickpockets and strutting pimps.

Though Stern's name is not a household word, *The Angel of Forgetfulness* seems likely to bring him wider notice among Jewish and non-Jewish readers alike. This ambitious novel presents a complicated plot, actually three stories in one, which may remind readers of nesting boxes. The "outer box" is the story of young Saul Bozoff, from Memphis, who has begun a directionless college career at New York University. The year is 1969, but Saul finds himself out of step with his fellow students' quest for sex, drugs, and rock 'n' roll. Instead, on lonely impulse, he goes to pay respects to his elderly Aunt Keni in New York's lower East Side, once a teeming center of Yiddish American culture and now a hub of protest happenings. After an awkward and slightly abrasive beginning, Keni recruits Saul to escort her to medical appointments that become a pretext for nostalgic walking tours of her neighborhood. Seeing past modern storefronts and crash pads to landmarks more than half a century old, and expounding on their significance to her nephew, Keni soon reveals herself as a kind of archeological prodigy.

Inevitably, the aging Keni's dependence on Saul increases, especially when infirmity makes her bedridden. He becomes her caretaker after quickly mastering the skills of a live-in nurse. Now, deprived of her memory-laden walks, Keni turns to another source of remembrance: a manuscript by her first husband, Nathan Hart, written to woo her sixty years earlier.

The story of Nathan is the second of Stern's nesting boxes. Like Saul, Nathan is a lost and lonely Jewish youth but living in the lower East Side of 1910. A new immigrant from Eastern Europe, Nathan almost accidentally lands a job as a proofreader at *The Jewish Daily Forward* newspaper. He also meets and falls in love with the young Keni, who scorns him at first but becomes intrigued when, to keep her from walking away, he desperately improvises a tale of an angel who descends to earth and falls in love with a mortal woman. The circumstances of Nathan's and Keni's meeting illustrate Stern's flair for comic absurdity: Their first encounter takes place in a shop where he has gone to return a pair of defective long underwear.

The story spoken, and later written, by Nathan—the manuscript that Keni entrusts to Saul—is the novel's third and innermost nesting box, and it is the source of Stern's title. The Angel of Forgetfulness, and the hero of Nathan's tale, is Mocky, who, though not explicitly named in the Talmud, is said by that sacred book to tap children beneath their noses just before birth, making them forget their experience of Heaven. (Remembering would cause them to balk at earthly existence.) One day, performing his angelic duties in Russia of the 1640's, Mocky hangs back and spies a mortal woman with whom he falls in love, to the neglect of his divine task. He pretends to be human so he can marry the woman, and together they have a child, half-angel and half-mortal. This is an age of pogrom in Russia; Mocky's wife is killed in an attack on their village, and he realizes that "earth was no place to raise a kid." He sneaks the baby into Heaven, but, with his worldly taint, the boy—Nachman Opgekumener ("the one who came down")—may not remain in paradise. The earth he returns to is the lower East Side of 1910. Mocky follows him there—partly from a wish to guard his son, partly from a realization that he, too, has ceased to belong in Heaven.

For a time on earth, Mocky forgets his heavenly nature altogether and becomes a vile, petty criminal. He is brought back to his senses when he realizes Nachman, too, has become excessively attached to earth through an infatuation with a schmaltzy actress. In a crucial scene, the angel unfurls his wings, straining to pull his son out of a lower East Side theater and back up to Heaven while gangsters below struggle to keep the young man on earth. The fight prompts Nachman to murmur, "Papa, in heaven they wouldn't believe it what goes on down here."

The tug-of-war serves as a symbol for the action of the entire novel, whose characters are torn between a sense of mission and capitulation to random but seductive circumstance. The action also rotates among the three stories, whose connection seems tenuous at first but becomes increasingly clear as the novel progresses. Each character, too, comes full circle. Early on, for example, the dying Keni hands Saul the dilapidated manuscript and enjoins him to complete the unfinished tale. Despite his promise, Saul hides the manuscript in a hollow tree and rushes off to embrace a life he formerly eschewed: the 1960's quest for sex, drugs, and rock 'n' roll. By a strange path, Saul ends up in communist Prague, where in the darkened attic of a medieval synagogue he ingests the dust of a golem—which proves hallucinogenic.

This seeming coincidence is just one of the ingenious ways in which Stern rotates his narratives of Saul, Nathan, Mocky, and Nachman before fusing them in the novel's momentous conclusion. Stern has said that *"The Angel of Forgetfulness* is in large part about the act of story-telling itself." Clearly, for him this is a high calling. He speaks of "an echo effect, with each of the three narratives resonating the others, so that the time and space between them was at least figuratively dissolved." These tales of three separate worlds are closely linked or, as Stern describes, each of them is married to the others, "one fictive ménàge a trois."

This was Stern's response to censure—somewhat alloying the critical praise for *The Angel of Forgetfulness*—for what was perceived as its circular narrative. To view this circularity as merely a flaw in the storyteller's art is in large degree to miss what Stern is trying to accomplish in literature. Indeed, Saul's evasion of his promise to finish the manuscript takes him on a circular journey in which the farther he flees from his fate, the nearer he approaches it. One thinks of Oedipus trying to escape the fate that decrees he will slay his father and marry his mother. Again, says Stern, "Like Jonah making a detour through the belly of a whale before returning to God's mandate, Saul is compelled to flee from a fear that ultimately chases him back to himself."

The novel's epigraph is a saying attributed to Abraham Abulafia, a fourteenth century kabbalist: "The end of forgetfulness is the beginning of remembrance." This declaration applies to all the stories in the novel. Each character has striven, unsuccessfully, to evade some inherent part in his nature: Mocky his angelic birth; Nachmann his father; Nathan and Saul their human identities. The angel of the title not only induces forgetfulness in children but suffers it himself. In the end, each individual has at least a prospect of being "repaired," as does the estrangement between Heaven and earth, so that the original state of perfection may be restored.

It is likely this hope that has induced critics such as Hadda and the editors of *The Jewish Reader* to view Stern as a bearer of Yiddish cultural light. Stern believes that a story should be "kosher," functioning as "a kind of cosmic template." The story "stirs the inanimate," which "rises up and walks abroad like a golem aspiring to humanity." Ultimately he is speaking of the kabbalistic concept of *Tikkun*, the reparation of the rift between Heaven and earth. In the Zohar, a classic book of Jewish mysticism, the world is repaired through *mitzvot* (good deeds), which must be performed continually so the world will return to its original state of perfection. To be recovered, however, that state must be remembered, and when it is one becomes painfully conscious of not having already attained it. Hence the curse/blessing that one character bestows on another: "*Zolstu krenkn un gedenken.* May you sicken and remember."

Until that recollection, until that reconciliation, all of the novel's heroes are (as Saul describes them) alienated from their true selves, destined to keep wandering, though their understanding may grow. For as long as they wander, each one's tale will have to be told by storytellers of high purpose. One suspects that a statement of Mocky's may apply not only to himself but also to Stern: "If the story sounds familiar, it's because I've been sentenced to repeat it until Nachman's soul comes home again."

Thomas Rankin

Review Sources

Booklist 101, no. 11 (February 1, 2005): 942.
Kirkus Reviews 72, no. 24 (December 15, 2004): 1163.
The New York Times Book Review 154 (March 20, 2005): 21.
The Washington Post Book World, April 3, 2005, p. 15.

THE ASSASSINS' GATE
America in Iraq

Author: George Packer (1960-   )
Publisher: Farrar, Straus and Giroux (New York).
   467 pp. $26.00
Type of work: Current affairs
Time: From the 1990's to 2005
Locale: Iraq

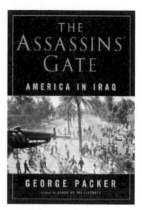

   A journalist comments on various aspects of the Iraq War, including the causes of the conflict and how the war proceeded, considering both American and Iraqi viewpoints

Principal personages:
   GEORGE PACKER, an American journalist
   KANAN MAKIYA, an Iraqi author in exile
   PAUL WOLFOWITZ, a neoconservative American policy maker
   GEORGE W. BUSH, the president of the United States
   RICHARD B. CHENEY, the vice president of the United States
   DONALD RUMSFELD, the U.S. secretary of defense
   CAPTAIN JOHN PRIOR, a United States Army captain
   PRIVATE KURT FROSHEISER, a United States Army private
   CHRIS FROSHEISER, Kurt's father

   George Packer's *The Assassins' Gate* is a narrative of the causes and consequences of American involvement in Iraq in the early twenty-first century. A self-described liberal, the author had supported the Iraq War at its inception, but as years went by and the quest for security and order made little progress, Packer's confidence in the outcome has waned considerably.

   When Packer first glimpsed Baghdad's so-called Assassins' Gate in 2003, he believed that it was an ancient gate which had guarded the city during the era of the Ottoman caliphs. Like much else in Iraq, views could be misleading, for the country's deposed dictator, Saddam Hussein, had constructed the gate. American troops nicknamed the structure, which leads to the former dictator's palace at the center of the Green Zone, the "assassins' gate." From the Green Zone, the American-controlled Coalition Provisional Authority (CPA) governed the country, and Iraqis assembled at the gate, requesting assistance and demanding redress, as under the caliphs of old.

   The author's interest in Iraq goes back to the first Gulf War. In the early 1990's, Packer became acquainted with Kanan Makiya, an idealistic Iraqi exile who envisioned an Iraq committed to Western concepts of natural rights. Others also had plans for Iraq, including members of the George H. W. Bush administration (1989-1993). In the aftermath of the Cold War, some foreign policy planners, known as neoconservatives, advocated an American foreign policy based upon United States

power, unfettered by either allies or international
organizations such as the United Nations. For
many neoconservatives such as Paul Wolfowitz,
the justification for such a policy was not merely
that American power should lead the world but
also that the world should be remodeled on the
American paradigm of democratic capitalism. In
1997, several future members of the George W.
Bush administration, including Wolfowitz and
Donald Rumsfeld, founded the Project for the
New American Century (PNAC), which was committed to regime change in Iraq.

*Journalist and novelist George
Packer is the author of several
works, including* Blood of the
Liberals *(2000), which received the
Robert F. Kennedy Award. A writer
for* The New Yorker *and* Mother
Jones, *he was among the five
finalists for the 2005 Michael Kelly
Award, and for his Iraq reporting
he was the recipient of an Overseas
Press Club award.*

Like many liberals remembering the Vietnam
imbroglio, Packer had opposed the Gulf War,
but images of Kuwaitis embracing American troops converted some liberals such as
him into believing that American military power could be a force for establishing and
protecting human rights. Genocides in Bosnia and Rwanda seemed to prove that the
United Nations was unable to cope with such disasters and that Security Council reso-
lutions were ineffective, as many conservatives had argued.

The terrorist attacks on U.S. soil of September 11, 2001, changed everything.
Many in the Bush administration immediately assumed that Osama bin Laden had enjoyed the support of Iraq's Hussein in carrying out the attack. Before September 11,
the president showed little interest in regime change in Iraq; after September 11 it became the focus of his foreign policy. Vice President Dick Cheney and Secretary of
Defense Rumsfeld were committed more to toppling Hussein than to establishing a
democratic Iraq. By early 2002, the administration had decided upon another Iraq
war.

Packer likens the question of why the war was begun to the Japanese film
Rashomon (1950), the different interpretations of which depend upon the viewer.
Some argued that Hussein had given support to al-Qaeda. Others asserted that the
Arab Muslim world had failed as a society and needed to be modernized by the West.
The specific justification for the war was the claim that Hussein had weapons of mass
destruction (WMDs). Only later, when no WMDs were discovered in Iraq, did Bush
justify the war as a means to make Iraq safe for democracy.

While Rumsfeld and Cheney prepared for war, the State Department established
the Future of Iraq Project, where Kanan Makiya became a major ideological force in
his advocacy of a democratic Iraq that transcended ethnic and religious differences.
Rumsfeld and Cheney assumed that the war would be quick, as it was, and that a re-
formed Iraq security force would quickly replace American troops, allowing an early
United States exit. There were no concerted plans for a long-term occupation. Packer
only briefly, and unsympathetically, discusses the opposition to the Iraq War. He
notes its essentially moral base, which he claims would merely enforce the status quo
in Iraq, leaving Hussein in power. Arguing that the antiwar movement was more ori-
ented toward what Americans wanted rather than what Iraqis might want, Packer

notes that many Iraqis desired to be free of Hussein's repression, even at the cost of war.

While much of *The Assassins' Gate* discusses the events leading up to the Iraq War, the work becomes riveting when the focus turns to Iraq itself. Packer first traveled there in the spring of 2003, shortly after the American invasion. In Iraq, he became acquainted with and interviewed a number of individuals, including American soldiers and the coalition's civilian officials. Most were sincerely committed to building a democratic Iraq, but Packer notes that many of them were young and inexperienced—the "fifth team," as one official commented—often lacking relevant information or even sufficient staff. Many suffered from burnout, and the frequent turnover of personnel reduced continuity and experience levels. When Paul Bremer assumed control of the CPA in May, 2003, he acted quickly, dissolving the Iraqi army, excluding former Baathists from the government and bringing to an end the possibility of creating an interim Iraqi government, actions that were controversial then and since. Were those decisions necessary, even inevitable, or did they make the situation worse? Packer eventually concluded, "a weak, feuding, and corrupt Iraqi government might be better than an isolated, illegitimate American one."

Army Captain John Prior's unit is exemplary of those involved in some of the early insurgency actions. Enjoying a ground level or "worm's eye" view, Prior was among those who understood the insurgency threat and the unanticipated guerrilla war sooner than those higher up, as well as the opportunities that had been lost in winning the hearts and minds of civilian Iraqis. Winning the military battle against Hussein's army paled in the face of Iraqi poverty and the absence of such amenities as electric power and a modern sewage system. Hussein's regime had failed to maintain the nation's infrastructure, in part because of the cost of the 1980's Iran-Iraq war and in part because of the international sanctions imposed on Iraq in the 1990's.

Iraqi responses to the war and the subsequent occupation vary widely. Among those whom Packer interviewed, Dr. Basher Butti from a Baghdad psychiatric hospital claimed that the fall of Hussein had created widespread post-traumatic stress disorder, a condition that had also existed under the old regime. Sheikh Emad al-Din al-Awadi saw the Americans neither as occupiers or liberators but a reality, a force that might be put to good uses or bad. While Kanan Makiya returned from exile, committed to establishing a Memory Foundation, a memorial to the years of Hussein's Baathist rule, in the summer of 2003 Packer was not convinced that Makiya's hope of civil society and democratic government stood much of a chance amid the violent chaos. Dr. Bashir Shaker represented a different Iraq. A forensic scientist at the Baghdad morgue, Shaker had witnessed the terror and brutality of the old regime, but because of the anarchy and insecurities that had come in the wake of the occupation, felt increasingly drawn toward Islam and Islamic law as the solution, rather than to Western democracy and natural rights. Another memorable Iraqi was Emad Hamadi, a Sunni, whom Packer hired as a bodyguard as journalists increasingly became targets of the insurgency. Previously, Emad had served as a bodyguard for Saddam Hussein and his despicable son Uday. Emad admitted that he knew of the thousands of victims of the old regime but denied that he had personally been involved. Packer sardonically writes, "In my dozens of conversations with servants of the old regime in Iraq, none of them ever admitted to having harmed a soul."

Packer contends that by the spring of 2004 no one, either in Washington or in Bremer's CPA, was making realistic decisions regarding the insurgency and restoring normality to Iraq. It was both a failure of planning and a failure of execution. It was also the failure to learn from history. "Iraq" was born an artificial state, created in the aftermath of the collapse of the Ottoman Empire in World War I, becoming a League of Nations mandate ruled by Great Britain. The British commissioner found a fractured state divided among Kurds, Sunnis, and Shias, with little Iraqi national consciousness. Packer does not believe it is inevitable that Iraq will be dismembered. However, in his discussion of the northern Kurds he admits that, for more than a decade, the Kurds have had little connection to Iraq, the result of the no-fly zone established by the Allies after the Gulf War. In the city of Kirkuk, Hussein had replaced the Kurds with Arabs. With Hussein's fall, the Kurds returned to Kirkuk, expelling the Arabs. Packer optimistically hopes that a more peacefully integrated Iraq will emerge.

It will, however, emerge at a cost. Packer relates the story of Private Kurt Frosheiser, who was killed by an improvised explosive device (IED) in November, 2003, and the impact his death has had on his family, particularly his father, Chris. Chris, a liberal Democrat, in 2004 feared that Democratic presidential candidate John Kerry would succumb to antiwar activists and abandon Iraq, thus making his son's death meaningless. Although some commentators see the Iraq War and the Vietnam War as similar events, Packer does not. The Iraq War, always controversial, became more so as the administration's justification for it—Iraqi WMDs—proved fictional. The conflict, however, still did not divide the United States in the same way the Vietnam War did. Packer claims that the disputes in Washington were less about the Iraq War than a reflection of the decade-long poisoned political atmosphere between the two parties. The events of September 11 failed to depolarize the United States, in part because of the leadership failures of George W. Bush, who was politically partisan and removed from decisions regarding the war.

By the beginning of 2005, the strongest elements in Iraqi society were the religious extremists and their militias. Secular Iraqis hoped to escape the dark shadow of Hussein's repression and enter the modern world, but for many religious Iraqis, freedom from Hussein's rule meant the opportunity to establish an Islamic society. For most Iraqis, the major issue was security, not democracy in the abstract. Changes were occurring in the Middle East: The Syrians reluctantly withdrew from Lebanon, and democratic elections of a sort took place in Egypt, but the relationship between these events and the American invasion of Iraq was uncertain. It might be decades, Packer admits, before the costs and benefits of the Iraq war can be known, both for Iraqis and for Americans.

The Assassins' Gate is an important work, in part because Packer, a former novelist, has an eye for the apt detail and an ear for the revealing phrase. It is also valuable because Packer is not a political partisan or an ideologue, and his insights catch the nuances of the events of the war as well as the hopes and fears of all the participants.

He claims that as of 2005, the cause is still winnable, but the book ends with Makiya saying that it was "said of me that I embody the triumph of hope over experience"—a quote that might be equally applied to the author.

Eugene Larson

Review Sources

The American Prospect 16 (November, 2005): 31.
Booklist 102 (September 15, 2005): 22.
Commonweal 132, no. 19 (November 4, 2005): 20-22.
The Economist 377 (October 15, 2005): 89.
Foreign Affairs 85, no. 1 (January/February, 2006): 129-134.
Kirkus Reviews 73, no. 15 (August 1, 2005): 834.
Library Journal 130, no. 14 (September 1, 2005): 158-159.
The New York Times Book Review 155 (October 30, 2005): 10-11.
Publishers Weekly 252, no. 23 (June 6, 2005): 50.
The Spectator 299 (November 12, 2005): 48.
Washington Monthly 37, no. 9 (September, 2005): 38-41.

AT DAY'S CLOSE
Night in Times Past

Author: A. Roger Ekirch (1950-   )
Publisher: W. W. Norton (New York). 447 pp. $26.00
Type of work: History
Time: The late Middle Ages to the early nineteenth century, primarily 1500-1750
Locale: Western Europe, from Scandinavia to the Mediterranean region; colonial America

Ekrich explores the nighttime activities of preindustrial people in Western Europe and colonial America

A historian of the fringes of American colonial society, A. Roger Ekirch began *At Day's Close* as an exploration of nightlife in the American colonies. Over some twenty years of research, Ekirch became more interested in nighttime activities of Western Europeans during the sixteenth through the mid-eighteenth centuries. *At Day's Close* focuses on European customs and beliefs with occasional references to Colonial America, describing in some detail a rich and varied culture involving a wide range of after-dark activities in both rural and urban neighborhoods, and involving all social strata from European aristocrats to colonial plantation slaves.

Ekirch was familiar with scholarly studies of early modern crime and the practice of witchcraft (occupations often pursued under cover of darkness) but found little research addressing the more common nighttime activities of preindustrial people. He drew upon more than one thousand primary resources including personal documents such as letters, memoirs, and diaries; books of proverbs; glossaries; literature, including novels, plays, and poetry as well as extant versions of popular fables and ballads; legal documents and court records; journals and autobiographies; newspapers; sermons; and advice books. Ekirch's research also extended to the visual arts; *At Day's Close* includes more than seventy examples of drawings, paintings, woodcuts, and cartoons illustrating nighttime activities.

These documents revealed that preindustrial people did not simply go to sleep at night but were involved in myriad after-dark activities. The nighttime had its own customs, rituals, and beliefs, forming a rich culture apart from that of the day. Social encounters, social events, work habits, and even morality changed after dark.

At Day's Close is organized into twelve chapters arranged by topic rather than chronology or geography. The first part, "In the Shadow of Death," discusses the many physical and spiritual dangers preindustrial people faced after sundown. Although educated people at the end of the Middle Ages knew darkness occurred in the absence of sunlight, many still believed that darkness descended like a cloud falling from the sky, and felt threatened by darkness and night air. Without artificial light, people perceived themselves to be surrounded and engulfed by impenetrable darkness.

~

A. Roger Ekirch is a historian of colonial America and professor of early American history at Virginia Polytechnic Institute and State University. He is the author of two previous books: "Poor Carolina": Politics and Society in Colonial North Carolina, 1729-1776 *(1981) and* Bound for America: the Transportation of British Convicts to the Colonies, 1718-1775 *(1987).*

~

The air itself was thought to have toxic effects on the body, with the potential for causing disease and even death. Women were thought to be especially susceptible to the dangers of breathing night air. People may have actually been more likely to sicken and die in the nighttime than in daytime because of customs based on erroneous beliefs—such as preventing air from circulating in sleeping chambers to avoid contamination, thereby preventing the healthful circulation of fresh air.

In preindustrial Europe, darkness was also a reminder of the darkness of Hell or the absence of God's light. Astronomical phenomena in the night sky—comets, meteors, and eclipses—were often interpreted as portents of doom sent from God. Preindustrial people believed strongly in Satan as an actual entity who came to torment them with illness or death. Misfortune could also come from the Devil's many minions—lesser devils, hobgoblins, ghosts, and witches.

People also feared the burglars and thieves for whom darkness provided cover. Households managed their own protection from crime; most families owned weapons and made sure to shut and bolt doors and windows at dusk. Ekirch provides many examples of the techniques employed by burglars as well as their typical modes of dress, colloquial expressions, and the methods they used for avoiding light (often simply waiting until the moon's light was lessened or obscured).

Law enforcement was provided by night watchmen in many cities, who were expected to prevent arson as well as lesser crimes, but watchmen tended to be boisterous and morally corrupt, more often an annoyance than a help. They were disparaged by the general populace and frequently subjected to verbal and physical abuse. Watchmen checked doors of houses to make sure they were locked. (Seventeenth century diarist Samuel Pepys noted that watchmen woke him up one night to let him know his back door was unlocked.) A contemporary cartoon showed the watchmen as buffoons with the faces of monkeys.

Fire, whether accidental or deliberately set, presented great danger. The use of candles, oil lamps, and fireplaces for light and warmth during night hours increased the likelihood of fires starting and then spreading throughout entire neighborhoods. Household materials and furnishings were highly combustible. Roofs were thatched. Lamps and candles were often left forgotten and could be tipped over by mice and rats. In addition, threats of arson were common, and the fear of arson so great that a perpetrator captured might be put to death.

The loss of visual cues in the darkness left people vulnerable to physical harm. Landmarks were obscured or invisible in the dark, as were hazards built into the terrain. In addition, people and social situations could not be visually assessed in darkness. European society was notably violent in the early seventeenth century, with a murder rate five to ten times higher than that in the United States in the twenty-first century. Drunkenness was common and contributed to the perils of maneuvering at night. Young, upper-class gentlemen often attended formal parties but more often vandalized property, consorted with prostitutes, gave beatings to both women and men found on the street, drank to excess, and fought among themselves. In the seventeenth and eighteenth centuries young aristocrats formed gangs whose nighttime activities were shockingly brutal; the Italian painter Caravaggio was a member of one such gang and went into exile from Rome after killing a rival gang member.

Despite the crime rate, the difficulties of traveling in darkness, supernatural dangers, and the possibility of fire, people remained very active during the night. Ekirch notes that although both secular and religious authorities tried to control society and protect its citizens, people from all social classes exercised increased freedom after sundown. Many people worked late into the night, or overnight: servants were often required to be on call or to perform housework during late hours; artisans worked late to fill orders; millers, bakers, and brewers typically worked during night hours; professions requiring sources of great heat (such as glass blowing and iron smelting) worked all night to maintain their fires. Women often performed piecework, spinning or knitting at home, and sometimes choosing to perform tasks after dark that they could have completed during the day. Cities hired groups of men to perform the dirtiest jobs at night, including emptying cesspools and disposing of the dead.

Ekirch found diaries of farmers who arose in early morning or worked late into the night—often relying on the moon alone for light—brewing beer, chopping wood, and irrigating fields. Livestock and crops were at risk from wild animals and thieves; farmers, hired hands, and plantation slaves often stayed awake working in fields, guarding animals, or patrolling to protect their crops throughout the night. Harvested crops were often hauled into storage after dark so they would not be stolen overnight.

In spite of common fears of night air, some advantages were seen to working at night. Water used to irrigate fields would not evaporate as quickly, and during warmer months it was naturally more comfortable to work outside in the cooler evenings. Many laborers worked their own small plots of land or at other home-based occupations after their day's work for an employer was done. On colonial plantations slaves sometimes hunted after dark; occasionally they were given small plots of farmland or a few animals of their own, to which they would tend in the night.

Laborers found that work performed after dark could be communal and sociable. Families and neighbors worked side-by-side to conserve resources or simply to enjoy having company, as work parties could be occasions for gossiping, telling stories, and pursuing romance. Women frequently gathered to spin or knit in groups, allowing them social support and freedom away from men. Nonetheless, some night shift workers were aware of the unnatural effects they suffered from struggling against the body's natural rhythms. In the cities, bakers in particular were known to be irritable and even violent; their outbursts were attributed to the stress of working in the bakeries all night.

In a final section Ekirch looks at sleep, including typical bedtime behaviors and rituals, interpretation of dreams, and a further variety of nighttime activities. Ekirch discovered that preindustrial people experienced first and second periods of sleep each night, usually waking up for an interval between the two. While awake between the first and second sleep, people might visit their neighbors, engage in sexual activity, smoke, or quietly reflect on their dreams or emotions. Ekirch argues that the nighttime period of introspection gave people a better sense of their own nature. The habit of sleeping twice became less common as artificial light increased the length of the working day and led people to sleep longer once in bed.

Ekirch's style is encyclopedic, reflecting his exhaustive research and command of a vast number and variety of contemporary writings. The topical arrangement forces abrupt shifts in time; in a single paragraph Ekirch might quote from a play, a personal diary, a folk tale, and a treatise on philosophy, each dating from a different century. While the facts presented are engaging and often even comical, the numerous quotations used to illustrate each point dry out Ekirch's prose, giving it a scattershot quality and sometimes the effect of a book of lists. Some of Ekirch's assertions would seem obvious; perhaps it need not be argued that crimes are more likely to be committed at night because darkness allows criminals to operate without being seen or recognized, or that romantic or sexual liaisons are more easily pursued at night. The author frequently relies on proverbs to support his descriptions of common activities, taking didactic sayings of the period as descriptive of what people actually did, rather than expressions of paradigms or ideals.

An epilogue, "Cock-Crow," looks at how darkness became less frightening and mysterious as the widespread use of artificial lighting became more common. In his final chapter Ekirch argues that artificial light and the increasing ability to eliminate darkness have changed the natural rhythms of day and night and of human society itself, to the detriment of the environment and humankind.

Maureen Puffer-Rothenberg

Review Sources

Booklist 101, no. 18 (May 15, 2005): 1621.
Harper's Magazine 310 (June, 2005): 81.
Kirkus Reviews 73, no. 6 (March 15, 2005): 330.
The Nation 281, no. 6 (August 29, 2005): 38-40.
The New York Times 154 (July 24, 2005): 18.
The New Yorker 81, no. 15 (May 30, 2005): 86-90.
Publishers Weekly 252, no. 14 (April 4, 2005): 52.
Spectator 298 (July 16, 2005): 36-37.

THE BEATLES
The Biography

Author: Bob Spitz (1950-   )
Publisher: Little, Brown (New York). 983 pp. $30.00
Type of work: Biography
Time: Primarily from the late 1950's until 1970
Locale: England, the United States, and various other
world locations

*This massive biography chronicles the most influential
rock band in the history of popular music*

Principal personages:
>
> JOHN LENNON, a songwriter and principal
> vocalist of the Beatles
>
> PAUL MCCARTNEY, a songwriter and prin-
> cipal vocalist
>
> GEORGE HARRISON, the lead guitarist,
> vocalist, and songwriter
>
> RINGO STARR, the drummer and vocalist
>
> BRIAN EPSTEIN, their manager
>
> GEORGE MARTIN, their record producer
>
> PETE BEST, the Beatles' original drummer
>
> STUART SUTCLIFFE, the Beatles' original bass player, who died
>
> CYNTHIA POWELL LENNON, John Lennon's first wife
>
> YOKO ONO, Lennon's second wife

With hundreds of books about the Beatles already in print, it could be either a bold or a foolish author who believes that he can uncover a fresh perspective, reveal a aspect of the band's story that so far had been overlooked. In just the last few years there has been a number of fascinating books published about the Beatles, including *Meet the Beatles: A Cultural History of the Band That Shook Youth, Gender, and the World* (2005) by Steven D. Stark, *Magical Mystery Tours: My Life with the Beatles* (2005) by Tony Bramwell, *The Beatles: Ten Years That Shook the World* (2004) edited by Paul Trynks, and *Ticket to Ride: Inside the Beatles' 1964 Tour That Changed the World* (2003) by Larry Kane. The author of several books, including a controversial biography of musician Bob Dylan, Bob Spitz decided that he would devote however long was necessary to research his subject completely. As the author of *Dylan: A Biography* (1989), Spitz knew well the pitfalls of taking a near legend as his subject. In the decades since the Beatles first became a phenomenon, and since the band's breakup in 1970, the mythology that surrounds the group has grown larger.

In popular music, the Beatles are the gold standard. Every band that gains both critical and public acclaim inevitably is compared to the Beatles. Spitz set out to write the definitive biography of the band, which took him almost eight years to complete. As first presented to the publisher, the work was more than 2,700 pages long. Because of

～
*Bob Spitz has managed musicians
Bruce Springsteen and Elton
John and is the author of* Making
of Superstars: Artists and
Executives of the Rock Music
Business *(1978),* Barefoot in
Babylon: The Creation of the
Woodstock Music Festival, 1969
(1979), Dylan: A Biography
(1989), and Shoot Out the Lights:
The Amazing, Improbable,
Exhilarating Saga of the 1969-
1970 New York Knicks *(1995).*
～

its length, the manuscript had to be trimmed dramatically. In what remains Spitz still has a rich story to tell, and he includes more than eighty pages of notes, a bibliography, a discography, and a detailed index.

Researching the book took two years. The author, working methodically, began by traveling to Liverpool, England, and interviewing everyone available who had been involved with the Beatles there. For Spitz, it was necessary to fill in the background first, to get a feel for what life was like in Liverpool after World War II. Initially, he made the conscious decision not to talk to the three Beatles who were alive at the outset of his research. At all costs, he wanted to avoid writing the "same story," the standard responses that have been perpetuated for decades. Among the more than six hundred individuals Spitz spoke with, many had never previously told their stories for public record. The author also was privileged to read the diaries of the Beatles' manager Brian Epstein. Amazingly, no one had secured access to these journals prior to Spitz. Spitz was shocked by what he read in the diaries, which cover the years from 1949 until Epstein's death in 1966. Epstein is revealed to be a man of "large vision." It was Epstein who believed that his Beatles would become "bigger than Elvis." After gathering all the facts, after piecing together all the elements of the vast puzzle, Spitz understood that the story that was in front of him was as large as history itself. As great historical figures deserve biographies large enough to do them justice, so too do the Beatles deserve such a work.

After Spitz had done his homework, he felt confident enough to approach the Beatles themselves. Of the three who were living, Spitz gained access to two, George Harrison—before his death from cancer in 2001—and Paul McCartney. Out of his conversations with both McCartney and Harrison, a more down-to-earth, gritty portrayal of the band began to take shape. As the book is only about one-third as long as was originally written, it is hoped that sometime in the future Spitz's excised prose will see the light of day. In *The Beatles: The Biography*, Spitz is at his very best describing how the four lads from Liverpool became the Beatles. Some readers may become impatient with the author for dwelling so much on the early days when these awkward teenagers grappled with making their mark on the music scene. Spitz, however, intended for the first few hundred pages of his biography to illuminate how these particular individuals made it through the maze of postwar English society and emerged as a force of nature in their own right.

Except for McCartney, none of the Beatles performed very well in school and were uninterested in doing what the system required of them. Although McCartney had lost his mother to cancer at the age of fourteen, he had a loyal and devoted father who cared for him and his younger brother, Mike. Of the band members, it was John Lennon who had the most dysfunctional family life. Since his father, Freddie Lennon, had left the family when John was a young child, and his mother, Julia Lennon, was not mentally stable, he was reared by his Aunt Mimi. His troubled childhood would haunt him for the rest of his life. In 1958, Julia Lennon was fatally struck by a car as she crossed Liverpool's Menlove Avenue. The automobile was driven by an off-duty policeman. The teenage Lennon's despair was monumental. Out of this tragedy, a special bond was established between McCartney and Lennon. While this connection may have been an unspoken one, the two friends now had something in addition to music that linked them.

The date July 6, 1957, is considered one of the most important in the annals of rock music: the day that McCartney and Lennon first met. Out of this encounter, these two restless souls would become close friends. They were both enamored with the rock-and-roll that was coming out of America at the time. While Elvis Presley was looked upon as almost a savior of sorts, these two Liverpool teenagers also were impressed by such performers as Gene Vincent, Eddie Cochran, the Everly Brothers, Buddy Holly, Chuck Berry, and Little Richard. Liverpool was looked upon as a suffocating place, a place where most youth saw very little chance of a better life. The dream of making music brought the youthful Lennon and McCartney together. With gripping detail, Spitz takes the reader on the musical journey that formed the Quarry Men, then the Silver Beetles, and—eventually—the Beatles. Each of these incarnations tested musical and cultural boundaries until the Beatles broke loose and went forth to conquer the world.

It is obvious throughout the book that Spitz has a burning passion for what the Beatles were, are, and continue to be for new generations of listeners. He coverage is vast in scope. There is a touching and painful description of an immature George Harrison following Lennon and his girlfriend, Cynthia Powell, around in the hope of joining them when they went to the cinema. Spitz captures the momentum as well as the serendipity of events that pushed the band's formation forward. Such figures as Stuart Sutcliffe, Pete Best, Brian Epstein, and George Martin all play their parts in the story. Sutcliffe could not play the bass guitar, but his talent as an artist and his ability to strike a pose helped to shape the group's sound and image. Best was a drummer who had the right look, but he was fired when Lennon and McCartney determined that he was not good enough for a band that had visions of going places. With the firing of Best, the lovable Ringo Starr was invited to join the Beatles. Brian Epstein, a man of wealth, was gay and frequently suffered from bouts of insecurity. At his best, though, he was a brilliant promoter of the Beatles, confident that they would reach uncharted heights. Producer George Martin has been called the "fifth Beatle" for his ability to bring out the musicians' best work in the recording studio. Finally, because none of the Beatles could read music, it fell on Martin's shoulders to translate their musical visions into songs.

The Beatles became the top band in England in 1963. They would conquer the U.S. musical scene one year later. On the surface, "Beatlemania" looks to be a magical experience. Spitz does not deny the magic quality of what was happening, but he points out how hard and—at times—dangerous it was to be in the maelstrom that was the Beatles' machine. As previous biographers have shown, their clean-cut image was more a public relations creation than a reality. Women and drugs were never in short supply for a band as big as the Beatles.

By the mid-1960's, the Beatles were growing tired of their "mop-top" public image. Additionally, growing personal tensions between the band members made it difficult for them to be around one another. Lennon and Harrison were frustrated by McCartney's perfectionism in the studio and his constant willingness to turn on the charm in public. Harrison was becoming a more accomplished songwriter in his own right, but no more than a couple of his songs were included on any Beatles album. The mental torment that always had been a facet of Lennon's personality became aggravated by his increasing use of LSD and other drugs. Spitz is extremely critical of Lennon in this regard. Even with all these personal aberrations, the Beatles consistently released groundbreaking albums. Their music remained vital all the way to the end of the their career together as a band.

As such extraordinary personalities grew apart, there was no easy way for them to make a clean break. As Spitz sees it, Lennon became attracted to Yoko Ono because she was unconventional and did not care about the Beatles. Lennon could, therefore, use her to extricate himself from his marriage to Cynthia Lennon and his marriage to the Beatles.

Of the many insightful books published about the Beatles, *The Beatles: The Biography* comes the closest to deserving the term "definitive." By showing the human side of the Beatles, Spitz has made their impact on cultural history seem all the more remarkable and impossible to duplicate.

Jeffry Jensen

Review Sources

Booklist 102, no. 2 (September 15, 2005): 5.
Chicago Tribune, December 11, 2005, p. 7.
Hollywood Reporter 391, no. 36 (November 7, 2005): 20.
Kirkus Reviews 73, no. 18 (September 15, 2005): 1016.
Library Journal 130, no. 15 (September 15, 2005): 67.
Los Angeles Times Book Review, December 4, 2005, p. 12.
The New York Times 155 (October 20, 2005): E9.
The New York Times Book Review 155 (November 27, 2005): 23.
Publishers Weekly 252, no. 39 (October 3, 2005): 64.
Time 166, no. 19 (November 7, 2005): 119.

BECOMING JUSTICE BLACKMUN
Harry Blackmun's Supreme Court Journey

Author: Linda Greenhouse (1947-   )
Publisher: Times Books (New York). 268 pp. $25.00
Type of work: Biography, history, and law
Time: 1908-1999
Locale: St. Paul, Minnesota, and Washington, D.C.

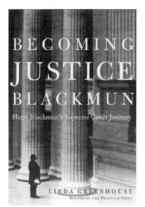

This history of the career of Supreme Court Justice Blackmun, the author of the Roe v. Wade *decision, is based on his archives and his public and private papers*

Principal personages:
HARRY BLACKMUN, associate justice of the
U.S. Supreme Court (1970-1994)
DOROTHY "DOTTIE" CLARK BLACKMUN,
his wife
WILLIAM J. BRENNAN, JR., associate justice of the Supreme Court (1970-1994)
WARREN E. BURGER, chief justice of the United States (1969-1986), Blackmun's lifelong friend
WILLIAM O. DOUGLAS, associate justice of the Supreme Court (1970-1994)
THURGOOD MARSHALL, associate justice of the Supreme Court (1970-1994)
WILLIAM H. REHNQUIST, chief justice of the United States (1986-2005)
BYRON R. WHITE, associate justice of the Supreme Court (1970-1994)

The workings of the United States Supreme Court are as mysterious as they are fascinating and important. Nine justices do their work largely in secret, deciding without public explanation which cases they will hear, discussing and voting on each accepted case in closed-door conference without even clerks in attendance. The Court has resisted all pressure to allow cameras—even still photographers—into its chambers. For this reason, books that offer more than speculation about the workings of the Court, including *The Brethren: Inside the Supreme Court* (1979) by Scott Armstrong and Bob Woodward and Linda Greenhouse's *Becoming Justice Blackmun: Harry Blackmun's Supreme Court Journey*, are eagerly read. While the selection of justices has become increasingly politicized, the information obtained about a prospective justice's opinions before joining the Court is rarely matched by an understanding of what he or she thinks and does once confirmed.

Becoming Justice Blackmun grew out of an extraordinary opportunity: Blackmun stipulated in his will that his personal and official papers be given to the Library of Congress and made public five years after his death. Public access became available in March, 2004. Greenhouse, presumably on the strength of her two decades of reporting on the Supreme Court for *The New York Times*, was allowed by the Blackmun

~

*Linda Greenhouse began covering
the U.S. Supreme Court for* The New
York Times *in 1978 and won the
Pulitzer Prize for beat reporting in
1998 for her "consistently
illuminating" coverage. A regular
panelist on the PBS program*
Washington Week, *she holds a
degree from Yale Law School.*

~

family to have access to the papers two months before anyone else. The resulting book is a distillation of more than half a million pages of diaries, marginalia, letters, official documents, and a list of every book Blackmun ever read into less than three hundred pages, pulled together in mere months. As Greenhouse reports, she "did not interview family members of former law clerks" and "made only minimal use of secondary sources." The book, then, offers a priceless glimpse into one of the greatest legal minds of a generation but only a glimpse. It will fall to future biographers and historians to examine the life that is not recorded in the archives, and to evaluate how Blackmun's sense of his own career aligns with that of others.

The book, which runs mostly chronologically, begins with Blackmun's diary, started in 1919 when he was eleven years old and continuing nearly to the end of his life in 1999. The story looks backward to Harry's birth in Illinois and to his childhood in St. Paul, Minnesota, where in kindergarten he met a boy who would become a lifelong friend, Warren Burger. The boys lived just six blocks apart, and they played sports and worked as summer camp counselors together even when they were attending separate high schools. Through college and law school, again at different schools, the two men maintained a warm correspondence, congratulating and encouraging each other. Blackmun was best man at Burger's wedding.

Like many friends, the two were very different. Burger, for example, always desired to reach the top of his profession, and he eagerly accepted his nomination as chief justice of the United States in 1969. For his part, Blackmun "was, frankly and self-consciously, risk-averse," and he did not seek out high-profile positions. In the mid 1930's he twice turned down chances to work in the Franklin D. Roosevelt administration, choosing instead to stay in Minnesota. There he married Dottie Clark and had three children with her before becoming, in 1949, the first resident counsel for the Mayo Clinic in Rochester, Minnesota. Blackmun's nine years with the Mayo Clinic, "the happiest of his professional life," gave him an insight into the challenges facing the medical profession, on which he would draw in drafting his most visible Supreme Court opinion.

From his first day on the Court, Blackmun found the job intimidating. He had been nominated to replace the retiring Abe Fortas and was confirmed after a hearing that lasted a mere four hours. Sworn in on June 9, 1970, Blackmun was immediately sent the paperwork for twenty-two cases that were in progress. For most of them, his vote would be the deciding one. In the three weeks before the Court's summer recess, he did his best to catch up with his colleagues' understanding of the cases. Adding to the pressure was the fact that the chief justice was none other than Warren Burger. Blackmun worried that working together would damage their friendship, and he worried also that the public—and Burger himself—would expect the two friends, dubbed the "Minnesota Twins," to vote in tandem.

Among Blackmun's first decisions was *New York Times v. United States*, the Pentagon Papers case. Burger and Blackmun were two of three justices voting that the government had the right to suppress classified documents on the history of American involvement in Vietnam. Blackmun's vote seemed to confirm the public's impression of him as a conservative who would follow Burger's lead. Blackmun's growing independence, running parallel to his increasingly liberal positions on such matters as birth control, abortion rights, and capital punishment, form one of the main threads of the book. Supreme Court justices tend to have long careers on the bench, and Blackmun's career is a demonstration of how ideas and opinions can evolve over time.

The core of *Becoming Justice Blackmun*, and nearly a third of its length, is devoted to the 1973 case on which Blackmun's legacy rests: the *Roe v. Wade* decision, which for the first time made abortion on demand legal in the United States. In Blackmun's mind, the case was not so much about a woman's right to choose whether or not to carry a child as it was about a physician's right to make medical determinations for a patient. After all, the prevailing laws of the time did not condemn women for obtaining abortions; the laws made it a crime for doctors to perform them unless the mother's life was at stake. Blackmun spent a week in July, 1972, in the library of his old employer the Mayo Clinic, "where the staff had set aside a place for him to work and compiled a stack of books and articles on the history and practice of abortion." He spent months reading, discussing, and arguing with his colleagues on the bench and considering his vote on the matter. It took him more than five months to draft and revise the 7-2 majority opinion.

In the end, as Greenhouse makes clear, the decision in *Roe v. Wade* enabled one of the most far-ranging social changes of the twentieth century, but by many accounts it was not good law. Some legal scholars, then and since, argued that the decision drove, rather than reflected, public opinion—that in rendering the opinion the Court took power for itself that properly belonged to Congress. Blackmun, who was personally opposed to abortion but judged that the Constitution supported it, was castigated and received death threats. Nevertheless, he remained proud of his decision and the changes it made in women's lives. He defended the decision throughout his tenure on the Court, though he never accepted the public perception that he was the man behind abortion rights and the right to privacy. As Greenhouse sums the matter up, "he locked *Roe* in a tight embrace and never let it go."

Greenhouse's breadth and depth of knowledge is evident in her ability to sort through great amounts of information to pull out the pieces that tell the story. A strength of the book is the clarity of its language; Greenhouse makes it possible for even a novice to understand the broader implications of habeus corpus, *certiorari*, and *stare decisis* as they apply to *Roe v. Wade* and to *Darden v. Wainwright*, an important 1986 death penalty case in which Blackmun, writing for the minority, expressed his growing discomfort with capital punishment.

Less successful is Greenhouse's attempt to tell the story of the erosion of the lifelong friendship between Blackmun and Burger. Like other weaknesses in the book, this deficiency comes largely from the limitations of working only with a one-sided paper record. In the first fifty years of their lives, when the two men send cards and letters back and forth, there is ample evidence of the warmth between them. Toward the end, however, there is less writing to analyze, and Greenhouse seems to be led more by impressions gathered from her years covering the Court than by the documents before her. An estrangement can be deduced from the fact that by 1986 "The letters and cards had petered out," but the adverbs seem forced in comments such as "'WEB announces retirement,' Blackmun recorded laconically" or "'WEB dies,' Blackmun noted tersely." The fact is, each of the quoted entries in the "chronology" Blackmun kept for several decades is only a few words long, and Greenhouse cites no examples in her book of entries that reveal emotion. The friendship undoubtedly was strained, even dissolved, by the men's conflicts on the Court, but the secrets of their hearts cannot be read clearly in their professional correspondence.

Becoming Justice Blackman is, as the subtitle suggests, the story of a journey, or of many journeys: from working-class boy to Supreme Court justice, from the Midwest to Washington, D.C., from conservative to liberal, from impressionable follower to confident equal. Blackmun's changing views of hot-button issues including abortion rights and capital punishment suggest something that twenty-first century conflicts over Supreme Court nominations often overlooks: that opinions can evolve over time, but a probing, intelligent, and fair-minded person—like Harry Blackmun—is likely to remain one. Through more than thirty-eight hundred Supreme Court rulings, Blackmun "performed in ways that neither he nor others would have predicted," and left behind a solid record of humble and dedicated service.

Cynthia A. Bily

Review Sources

The American Prospect 16 (September, 2005): 38-39.
Booklist 101, no. 18 (May 15, 2005): 1619.
The Christian Science Monitor, May 3, 2005: 15.
Commentary 120, no. 1 (July/August, 2005): 69-72.
Kirkus Reviews 73, no. 6 (March 15, 2005): 333.
Library Journal 130, no. 7 (April 15, 2005): 104-105.
Ms. 15, no. 2 (Summer, 2005): 35.
National Review 57, no. 14 (August 8, 2005): 47-48.
The New Republic 232, no. 24 (June 27, 2005): 36-41.
The New York Times Book Review 154 (May 8, 2005): 9.
Publishers Weekly 252, no. 15 (April 11, 2005): 45-46.
The Times Literary Supplement, September 23, 2005, p. 11.
Washington Monthly 37, nos. 7/8 (July/August, 2005): 58-60.
The Washington Post Book World 35 (May 8, 2005): 3.
The Wilson Quarterly 29, no. 3 (Summer 2005): 125-127.

BEFORE THE FROST

Author: Henning Mankell (1948-   )
First published: Innan frosten, 2002, in Sweden
Translated from the Swedish by Ebba Segerberg
Publisher: New Press (New York). 383 pp. $25.00
Type of work: Novel
Time: 1978 and 2001
Locale: Guyana and Sweden

This novel inspired by the terrorist attacks on New York and Washington, D.C., on September 11, 2001, centers on an apocalyptic Christian cult

Principal characters:
KURT WALLANDER, a veteran police inspector in Ystad, Sweden
LINDA WALLANDER, his daughter, who has just joined the police force
ERIK WESTIN, leader of an apocalyptic Christian cult
ANNA WESTIN, Erik's daughter, Linda's friend
STEFAN LINDMAN, a young detective recently transferred to Ystad

A number of articles published in 2005 noted the flourishing of a new subgenre: novels inspired by the September 11, 2001, terrorist attacks in New York and Washington, D.C. Some of these books make explicit reference to those events and their aftermath; in others, the link is implicit. Widely cited examples from 2005 include Jonathan Safran Foer's *Extremely Loud and Incredibly Close* and Ian McEwan's *Saturday.*

One such novel that was missed in many surveys of this trend is Henning Mankell's *Before the Frost.* For many years, Mankell has divided his time between his native Sweden and Africa, where he is a theater director in Maputo, Mozambique. Mankell has published in many genres including plays, novels, fiction for children and young adults. He has also compiled a "book of memories" from Africans dying of acquired immunodeficiency syndrome (AIDS), mainly for their children to read when they are older.

Mankell, however, is best known for a series of books featuring police inspector Kurt Wallander. Based in the town of Ystad, in the southernmost region of Sweden, the series began with the novel *Mördare utan ansikte* (1991; *Faceless Killers,* 1997). Altogether, the series consists of eight novels and a collection of stories. To the frustration of American readers, the books have not been translated in the order in which they originally appeared. The last of the novels to be translated into English, *Mannen som log,* published in Sweden in 1994, is chronologically the fourth book in the series. It appeared in Great Britain in the fall of 2005 as *The Man Who Smiled* and was slated for release in the United States in 2006. Only the collection of the stories remains to be translated.

*Henning Mankell is a theater
director and playwright as well
as a novelist, dividing his time
between Africa and Sweden, his
homeland. His books featuring
police inspector Kurt Wallander
have been adapted for television
and films in Sweden and have
been translated into many
languages.*

In many ways, Kurt Wallander could be called a typical protagonist of police and detective fiction. Like many of his British and American counterparts today (but in marked contrast to the typical fictional detectives of an earlier era), Wallander ages from book to book; his character develops over time. Divorced, a bit overweight, prone to drink too much and imperfect in many other ways, he is also an extraordinarily resourceful investigator and a compassionate, deeply sympathetic man. While he is typical of his fictional generation, Wallandar is also distinctive enough, individual enough, to appeal in a way few characters do. He seems to live outside the pages of books.

Although the character of Wallander is central to the appeal of the series, Mankell places a good deal of emphasis on the team of investigators who are Wallander's colleagues, and on his relations with his superiors, so that the books have some of the flavor of the classic police procedural. Several of Wallander's colleagues are gradually filled out as characters, and the give-and-take among these various personalities is of greater interest to Mankell than the details of forensic science (though the author has taken care to do his forensic homework).

Mankell also uses the detective novel to dramatize and reflect on contemporary issues in Sweden—for instance, the tension provoked by immigration to what has heretofore been an exceptionally homogenous society. The larger context of such conflicts is the self-assessment that Sweden has been forced to undertake as bigger and bigger cracks have emerged in the nation's carefully managed facade of enlightened prosperity.

In Sweden, the Wallander series has been enormously popular, spawning television series and film adaptations. The books have been translated into many languages and have been particularly popular in Germany. After nine Wallander books, however, Mankell decided to make a departure. He created a new detective character, Stefan Lindman, a younger policeman in another region of Sweden. Lindman was introduced in a novel titled *Danslärarens återkomst* (2001; *The Return of the Dancing Master*, 2004).

With *Before the Frost*, Mankell returns to Wallander's stomping grounds but adds a couple of twists. Like many of his fictional contemporaries, Wallander is shown over the course of the series relating to various people in his life: his former wife, his aging father, his daughter. While the detective plays an important role in *Before the Frost*, the focus is on his daughter Linda, who in an earlier book had expressed her desire to enter the police force. Wallander's relationship with Linda has been difficult, in part because they are more similar to each other than either one is willing to acknowledge. In the story's August, 2001, setting, Linda has completed her police training. She is poised to begin working in Ystad, in the same police station her father has occupied for decades. The story's other twist is that Stefan Lindman has just been transferred to Ystad, and he and Linda are quickly attracted to each other.

Before the main action of the novel begins, there is a brief but crucial prologue, set in Guyana in 1978. The scene takes the reader inside the consciousness of a survivor of Jonestown, where the members of the cult led by renegade pastor Jim Jones committed suicide or—if their resolve faltered—were killed by Jones and his most trusted followers, who then ended their own lives. The final death toll exceeded nine hundred.

After the enigmatic opening, the main action begins in August, 2001. The setting is a lake in the south of Sweden. A man who has made careful preparations attracts a group of swans with bits of bread, waits until they are occupied with their feeding, sprays them with gasoline, and sets them afire. The image of the "burning, screeching" birds and their "hissing, smoking wings" as they plunge into the water creates one of the striking tableaux characteristic of Mankell's fiction.

From its beginning, there are clear signs that this story will have a religious dimension. The prologue recalls a horrific instance in which misguided faith led to cruel death—including the death of children whose parents gave them a cyanide-laced grape drink. The man who sets the swans on fire thinks about "the animals he would soon be sacrificing." Gradually the reader begins to realize that the subtext of the novel is the terrorist attacks of September 11, committed by extremist Muslims. Mankell sets out to create a smaller, fictional counterpart to al-Qaeda—a kind of microcosm of religiously inspired terrorism. By creating an apocalyptic Christian cult, rather than a "foreign" group, Mankell seeks to show that terrorism is not alien to the West, that it cannot be seen simply as a byproduct of Islam.

The reader will soon be able to deduce the connection between the prologue and the burning swans: The unnamed survivor who escaped from Jonestown into the jungle is the same man who stands on the lake shore preparing for a sacrifice. His name is Erik Westin. Twenty-four years before that day with the swans, he deserted his wife and young daughter in Sweden and disappeared—to the United States, it turns out, where he fell under the spell of Jim Jones. Now he is back in Sweden, heading a cult of his own. Westin has revealed his presence to his wife, Henrietta, a composer, and his daughter, Anna. He has recruited Anna, whom he is grooming to succeed him, though he is not entirely sure of her commitment to the cause.

Linda Wallander, who has not yet officially started her police job, is drawn into the action through her coincidental friendship with Anna and another young woman, Zeba, an immigrant from Iran. Both women are friends from Linda's school days. Linda is killing time, impatient to begin her new career, and she is glad to be reunited with her friends. Not long after they have reestablished contact, however, Anna disappears. When Linda tells her father about her friend's disappearance and her sense that something is wrong, Wallander is dismissive. Linda is already involved in her father's investigation of a seemingly unrelated case, the brutal murder of a woman who was exploring an old path in the woods. Linda's status—as not quite on the force, but present, and as Wallander's daughter—makes her father defensive. At the same time, he values her insights. Ultimately a decision is made to let her start work officially ahead of time.

The odd case of the burning swans—phoned in to the police by the perpetrator but ignored as a prank call—is followed by another case of animal "sacrifice." This gives Wallander his first inkling that the incidents are not conventional crimes but religiously motivated acts of "cleansing." In fact, Westin plans a series of sacrifices—the next is to be a ritual execution of a woman who is a member of the cult—intended to culminate in a orgy of destruction, in which suicide bombers will destroy cathedrals all over Sweden, a deadly reproach to a kind of Christianity that has grown lukewarm and become too comfortable in a corrupt world. At one point, Westin muses that Christians seem to have forgotten about the great tradition of martyrdom; in his mind, "martyrdom" seems to be synonymous with suicide bombing.

As the novel proceeds toward its climax, in which the climactic destruction is averted at the last minute, Linda sees the pattern that allows the police to grasp the nature of the criminal plot. A conversation with Anna and Zeba, in which Anna reacts strongly to Zeba's revelation that she had an abortion when she was fifteen years old, is the catalyst for Linda's perception. The American cult member chosen for sacrifice, it turns out, had two abortions. Given this pattern, Wallander and his colleagues begin to see that a notion of violent atonement for sin is driving Westin's plot. (It is not clear whether Mankell intends to suggest that a passionate moral objection to abortion rights is ipso facto fanatical; certainly some of his readers will take him to be saying that.) A couple of days after the plan is thwarted, Linda walks to the Ystad police station to begin officially at last. The day is September 11, and soon she and her father and the others are gathered somberly around a television.

Like Mankell's earlier books, *Before the Frost* is not merely an intriguing story with compelling characters and a bearing on current events—though that alone would be fodder enough for many writers. Mankell's fiction is at once immediately accessible and richly textured. For example, the relationship between Wallander and Linda both parallels and contrasts with the relationship between Westin and his daughter, Anna. To follow the main line of the book and recognize its pertinence to September 11, it is not necessary to reflect on these two father/daughter pairs, but the reader who does so will be rewarded.

There are also many touches in the book, beginning with the title, that hint at a fairy-tale atmosphere. When Wallander and Linda examine the hut where the savage murder of the hiker has transpired, the hut is described "like something out of fairy tale, the house of a witch." Without compromising the surface plausibility of the story and its use of the familiar conventions of the police-detective genre, these fairy-tale motifs give the book an added depth, a haunting suggestiveness, and at the same time signal to the reader how the story as a whole is to be taken, as a kind of parable of faith gone terribly wrong.

John Wilson

Review Sources

Booklist 101, nos. 9/10 (January 1-15, 2005): 828.
The Economist 372 (October 2, 2004): 84.
Kirkus Reviews 72, no. 24 (December 15, 2004): 1168.
Library Journal 130, no. 3 (February 15, 2005): 124.
New Statesman 133 (September 6, 2004): 54-55.
The New York Times Book Review 154 (January 23, 2005): 21.
Publishers Weekly 252, no. 5 (January 31, 2005): 52.
The Times Literary Supplement, October 29, 2004, p. 24.

THE BEST DAY THE WORST DAY
Life with Jane Kenyon

Author: Donald Hall (1928-   )
Publisher: Houghton Mifflin (New York). 258 pp. $23.00
Type of work: Memoir
Time: 1969-1995
Locale: Eagle Pond Farm, New Hampshire

Hall recalls his wife, Kenyon, her battle with cancer, and their twenty years together at Eagle Pond Farm in rural New Hampshire

> *Principal personages:*
> DONALD HALL, a poet
> JANE KENYON, his wife, a poet
> LUCY HALL, Hall's mother
> POLLY KENYON, Kenyon's mother

The Best Day the Worst Day opens with the matter-of-fact statement, "Jane Kenyon died of leukemia at 7:57 in the morning, April 22, 1995," setting the tone for the pages to follow. Although describing both the most devastating and the most sublime moments of his life, poet Donald Hall maintains this straightforward tone throughout his memoir, creating an emotional impact stronger than the most dramatic prose could achieve. For example, Hall describes the excruciating sequence of events, painfully familiar to anyone who has buried a loved one, that immediately follows a death by a simple listing of necessary tasks: deciding upon the time and place of the funeral, arranging for the obituary, choosing a casket, informing friends and family of the death, arranging for pall bearers, and finding room in the refrigerator for all the donated casseroles. This stark, unadorned accumulation of details evokes an incredibly affecting portrait of Hall's emotional state, while setting the stage for the chronicle of his life with poet Jane Kenyon to follow.

Kenyon first met Hall in 1969 when she was one of 140 students in his "Introduction to Poetry for Non-English Majors" course at the University of Michigan. She found him intimidating, and he did not even know who she was. Later that year he accepted her as a student in his poetry writing seminar, where Kenyon was a good, but not outstanding, student. Although friendly, the two did not go out until 1971, when he took her out to dinner to console her on a breakup with her boyfriend. Hall was recovering from a divorce, and both were wary of forming a new relationship, so they progressed slowly, with once-a-week meetings, gradually increasing them to two, three, and then four times a week. By 1972, although worried about the nineteen-year age difference between them (he was forty-seven, she was twenty-eight), they decided to marry.

Three years after their wedding the couple resolved to take time off from their academic life in Ann Arbor to spend a year at the Hall family's Eagle Pond Farm, near

Wilmot, New Hampshire. Although they lived in the 1803 farmhouse through the coldest winter in one hundred years with no heat other than a wood stove, no insulation, and no storm windows, the couple fell in love with rural life and decided to make the farm their permanent residence. Hall quit his job at the university, hoping to make a living through free-lance writing. With one child in college and one headed there in two years, it was a risky decision to give up an annual income, medical insurance, and retirement pension. He took every writing job he could get—including essays, short stories, poems, book reviews, children's books, and even a book of riddles.

Donald Hall was appointed to the faculty of the University of Michigan at Ann Arbor in 1957 and taught there until he left in 1975 to work as a freelance writer and live at Eagle Pond Farm with the poet Jane Kenyon, his second wife. Hall has authored fourteen books of poetry and twenty-two books of prose, including children's stories, biographies, memoirs, sports journalism, and textbooks.

Although their happiness was tempered by Hall's two bouts with cancer and Kenyon's battle with bipolar disorder, the two poets lived an often idyllic life at Eagle Pond Farm for many years. They reveled in small-town life, and both became active in the church. (Hall ended up playing Santa in the Christmas pageant every year and both became deacons.) They doted upon their three cats and their beloved dog Gus, and Kenyon became an avid gardener, forming elaborate plans during the long winters, and planting in the spring. They enjoyed competitive ping pong games, walks with the dog, coffee in bed, reading, and most of all, their writing.

Hall credits much of the success of his marriage to what he calls "the third thing," something separate from the couple which strongly interests them both. He believed that "Third things are essential to marriages, objects or practices or habits or arts or institutions or games or human beings that provide a site of joint rapture or contentment. Each member of a couple is separate; the two come together in double attention." For many couples, this "third thing" is, of course, their children. Although Hall and Kenyon had many third things, including their pets, grandchildren, poet John Keats, summer afternoons at the pond, the church, literature, and ping pong, the third thing that brought them together and became the center of their lives was their shared love of poetry. They were each other's readers and critics and often presented joint poetry readings.

This idyllic way of life came to an unexpected and sudden halt in 1994, when a nosebleed and flulike symptoms sent Kenyon to her doctor, who immediately checked her into the hospital with a diagnosis of acute lymphoblastic leukemia. Kenyon began receiving chemotherapy as Hall moved into the nearby Days Inn and Kenyon's mother moved to Eagle Pond Farm to house-sit. For the next fifteen months life took on a new shape for the couple: "Leukemia was a dreary continuous landscape of drips, injections, and pills; sleeplessness and long sleep; nausea until there was nothing more to vomit. We sat in a small room with a big window, and we became ourselves a small room bounded by a door and a window, obsessed to remain together in life."

With a bone marrow transplant the only hope of a cure, Kenyon and Donald moved to Seattle, Washington, for four months so that Kenyon could receive treatment at the Fred Hutchinson Cancer Research Center. While there, they "lived in an apartment on a street of the city but our only address was leukemia. We woke and ate breakfast and showered in leukemia. We walked around the block, keeping up strength, in leukemia's neighborhood. We slept in leukemia all night, tossing and turning with unsettling dreams." Kenyon was isolated in a sterile cocoon to receive total body irradiation to prepare her bones to receive the new donor marrow. She and Hall were able to talk only by telephone from each side of the plastic wall that encased her. Her condition necessitated intravenous feeding and drug infusions, which Hall learned to perform. The countless drugs all had side effects, which in turn required more drugs.

Finally, on February 24, the bone marrow transplant complete, Kenyon was strong enough to go back to New Hampshire. Upon their return Hall recalls that "the happiness we felt that night was the greatest we ever felt." By March 13, the best and worst day of the book's title, Kenyon was strong enough to take a walk with their dog Gus, followed by a drive in the country and a stop at the Dairy Queen for ice cream. After this welcome, though tentative, resumption of normal activities, however, Kenyon checked into the hospital with severe abdominal pain and by April 11 learned that the leukemia had returned, and there was no hope of survival. She died eleven days later, at the age of forty-seven.

Hall omits nothing from his depiction of Kenyon's battle with leukemia—his prose is densely packed, and once again the sheer accumulation of detail presented heightens the horror of the situation. He does not shirk from presenting the most distasteful details, following with such speed, one upon the other, that the reader feels the full impact of the horror of the disease as well as of its treatment. The indignities and pain suffered by Kenyon, the loss of hair (accompanied by the growth of long hairs on her face, a side effect of one of her many drugs), incontinence and constipation, horrible mouth pain, nausea, clinical depression, herpes, shingles, and lung failure is almost too much to imagine, but Hall manages to make the unimaginable all too real, and nearly unbearable.

This memoir is as much about Hall's role as caregiver and grieving husband as it is about Kenyon. His insights into his own emotions during this period should strike familiar chords with readers who have been in his situation. One day in Seattle, for example, Hall is momentarily tempted to throw himself into the path of an oncoming bus. Later, he dreams he pursues Kenyon in a Honda through Vermont and Connecticut after she has attacked him with acid, and he awakens as he is about to strangle her. After her death, he feels adrift and dislocated: "I visited the new Concord Wal-Mart. I pushed a cart around and bought nothing. '*Who am I and what am I doing here?*' When I turned the cart into one aisle I suddenly wept."

The true power of this memoir lies in Hall's brilliant juxtaposition of life and death, health and illness. Hall alternates chapters describing the history and nature of his relationship with Kenyon with chapters describing her fifteen-month battle with leukemia. The opening chapter describes the immediate aftermath of Kenyon's death, followed by a chapter on the couple's life-changing decision to leave academia for rural life in New Hampshire. The succeeding chapters alternate between describing the couple's relationship and Kenyon's illness, effectively contrasting the mundane joys of life with the horror of serious illness. These alternating chapters, following simultaneously the progress of love and the approach of death, permit the reader to appreciate more fully the delightful minutiae of everyday life. The daily joys of Kenyon's routine—her garden, her pets, her grandchildren, her friends—are heightened in contrast to her illness, and from these joys emerges a vivid portrait of a life fully lived.

Mary Virginia Davis

Review Sources

Kirkus Reviews 73, no. 6 (March 15, 2005): 334.
The New York Times Book Review 155 (November 20, 2005): 20.
Poetry 186, no. 2 (May, 2005): 161-164.
Publishers Weekly 252, no. 10 (March 7, 2005): 57.

BLACK MARIA

Author: Kevin Young (1970-   )
Publisher: Alfred A. Knopf/Borzoi Books (New York).
  240 pp. $25.00
Type of work: Poetry

Young, known for his use of jazz in poetry, in Black
Maria *appropriates the conventions and devices of film
noir to produce a disjointed but startlingly original detective story which unrolls in a sequence of poems*

Principal characters:
  A.K.A. JONES, a film-noir sort of private
    investigator
  DELILAH REDBONE, a lovely southern
    nightclub singer

Kevin Young's *Black Maria* is a strange treat—it is a film noir in poems. As
Young explains, "Black Maria" means both hearse and paddy wagon, and this story
tells a tale of both. It creates the world of a detective story with the private investigator
(PI), A.K.A. Jones, and a dangerous heroine, Delilah Redbone, who has come from
the South to make her way in the city. The narrative is disjointed and creepy, marked
by the turns and betrayals which are common to the detective films of the 1940's. The
poems appropriate all the clichés of dialogue and action common to the genre the
book follows, but they have odd lyrical twists and riffs that keep the reader's attention
focused.

The cover indicates that the book was "Produced and directed by Kevin Young"
and features a black jacket over a cover picture of a moll with stocking seams, red
high heels and a gun; the hole in the cover reveals only her skirt hem, a glimpse of leg,
and the gun. Thus the reader is made complicit by being invited to "look in," and this
sense of complicity, of looking through rather than at, is present throughout the collection. One is invited to look through the keyhole into the noir world, where the only
thing one can count on is betrayal. The artistically designed book provides illustrated
scene-division pages with brief hints about the action, and there is a film-noir feel to
the book as an object.

There is a kind of freshness of snappy dialogue; the clichés are rebuilt to provide a
continuous state of surprise. The clichés of detective novels and films of the 1940's
and 1950's are deftly exploited, and a constant feature of the sequence is the clever
wordplay that uses the language of the films and plays with it and distorts it, producing the effect of a performance. The book, in fact, seems to be a performance; it
is a polyvocal recitation. The collection is divided into five parts or "reels," each
of which is introduced by a "voiceover" which summarizes the action, comments
on the characters, and poses the question of the "reel." The first sets the scene:
"Aliases and ambushes. Throughout, a hint of a crime, or at least a world in which ev-

eryone is a suspect." The noir world is maintained with consistency and wit throughout the
collection.

The story involves the detective A.K.A. Jones,
the femme fatale Delilah Redbone, and the other
characters, who are identified by characteristics
rather than names and who populate Shadowtown, the dim city where the mysterious events
take place. The characters are not intended to be
realistic, exactly, but are more like figures in a
dark allegory. A.K.A. Jones is drawn toward
Redbone despite repeated treachery; she is drawn
toward money. "The Gang" surrounds the main
characters and keeps the action flowing, com-

*Born in 1970 in Lincoln, Nebraska,
Kevin Young began writing early.
An only child, he moved around the
United States frequently as his
parents changed employment. His
previous poetry collections include*
Most Way Home *(1995),* To Repel
Ghosts *(2001), and* Jelly Roll: A
Blues *(2003). He has been
appointed Ruth Lilly Professor of
Poetry at Indiana University.*

prising "The Killer," "The Boss," "The Goon," "The Gunsel," "The Snitch," and
"The Champ," otherwise nameless characters who move through the bars and al-
leys of Shadowtown, creating an atmosphere of violence and fear. The pleasure of
this book, as is often the case with Young's poems, is largely in the sound of it—the
spare interior monologues filled with topsy-turvy clichés and riffs and street language. The element of music is strong, even though this collection is not directly
based on music.

The action begins with the meeting of Jones and Delilah and the beginning of his
fatal attraction to her. The rest of the plot follows the reel titles: "Honeymoon Rain,"
"Stone Angels," "Low Noon," "Alibi Saloon," and "Hemlock Lane." The PI, true to
form, puts away a lot of scotch between attractions and betrayals. Redbone uses him
repeatedly, and he is constantly put in debt to hoodlums. He takes part in a heist and is
chased by both cops and robbers. If there is a message in the story, it is a cynical one—
bad and good are hopelessly mixed and indistinguishable from each other; a person's
script is written, he or she does not write it. Any money Jones acquires comes with
threats to his freedom or even his life, but he is addicted to Redbone and always turns
the money over to her. She has a few scruples about using him, but she overcomes
them.

The minor characters are sketched with swift strokes—"The Boss," mysterious
underworld don; "The Gunsel," hit man who lets the hero walk once:

> Don't know why
>
> That hired fist let me
> walk, a head start, while
>
> He & the night watched—
>
> Just spat his shoes
> till they shone

Like exclamation points,
said *See youse*

& wished me dead
& luck.

This scene is one of the quieter rhythms; most are noisier, some a headlong rush. The clichés are fun: Jones does a lot of "drinking/ about his thinking problem" and the detective gets started because "Snake oil sales/ were slow. So I hung/ out my shingle on/ a shadow." Comic and tragic balance on a knifepoint in the unreal, surreal world of Shadowtown.

Young's previous book, *Jelly Roll: A Blues* (2003) was a finalist in two major poetry competitions and won the Paterson Poetry Prize. It uses jazz rhythms to propel and interrupt its lines. The brief, witty poems are the equivalent of a musical performance. They catch the feel of blues, boogie-woogie, even opera, although their dominant note is blues. There is here, too, a trace narrative, an underlying story of love and loss, but the narrative is less important in *Jelly Roll* than it seems to be in *Black Maria*. *Jelly Roll* contains performance pieces, performing themselves on the page, and the reader is pulled into the soundstorms, the fractured syntax, the music. Often the poems are very short, a couple of lines, but a beat is implied to "fill out" the page.

Young's strongest appeal throughout his work may be his use of music in all senses. Even his first book has the effect of rhythm and blues; Lucille Clifton said of *Most Way Home* (1995), which she selected as winner of the National Poetry Series Award, "This poet's gift of storytelling and understanding of the music inherent in the oral tradition of language recreates for us an inner history which is compelling and authentic and American." The book also won the John C. Zacharis First Book Award, offered by *Ploughshares* and Emerson College. *Most Way Home* tells of the African American myth of home in spare, lyrical verse, and is based in part on tales of Young's Louisiana relatives.

Black Maria has its music too, although it is a little harder to enter than *Jelly Roll* despite the fact that its poems are often simpler, as the film noir conventions are more readily translated to words than those of jazz. There is a film noir language, of course, and this book speaks it, twisting and distorting it at the same time, so that the reader gets a sense of doubleness—of parody and straight narrative at once. Once again, many of the poems dance, using the poet's well-known run-on, short-lined style to create suggestive, incomplete, dark images, elliptical narration. What is intriguing is the way it does provide a sense of performance poetry on the page, as in *Jelly Roll*; one cannot imagine that *Black Maria* would be more effective if read aloud, for the spare lines and the subtleties emphasized by the line breaks and the white space on the page might well be lost in an actual physical performance. The book is a complete work; it needs nothing further to achieve its effect. It is, indeed, produced and directed by its creator, as it says on the cover.

The story itself is not easy to follow. Despite the careful character descriptions and the closeups of scene and action, despite the summary voiceovers at the beginning of the sections, the narrative does not quite come clear. The book really should be read at a sitting, to keep track of the events and threads, but poetry does not lend itself to such reading. These are finally poems; some have been published separately—*Black Maria* is not fully a novel in verse like Les A. Murray's *Fredy Neptune* (1998) or Vikram Seth's *The Golden Gate* (1986).

Some of the events of the outcome seem to be so subtly implied that the reader may not be sure what happens, or must bring knowledge of the typical ending of film noir to fill in the apparent blanks. The reels run out to the end, the last scene called "credits," leaving the reader amused, bemused, and vaguely troubled—and unsure as to what actually happened. The shifts in voice—most poems from Jones's point of view but not all—may also confuse. Still, the collection has a powerful stylistic unity to it, and the individual poems as well as the whole "script" command attention for their wit and wordplay, and for the bleak cityscape they evoke. This book is a welcome experiment, a strange exploration of the subterranean that demonstrates another way Young can use music.

Janet McCann

Review Sources

Black Issues Book Review 7, no. 2 (March/April, 2005): 34.
Booklist 101, no. 11 (February 1, 2005): 936.
Library Journal 130, no. 3 (February 15, 2005): 135.
The Nation 280, no. 18 (May 9, 2005): 28-32.
The New York Times Book Review 154 (May 1, 2005): 8.
Publishers Weekly 251, no. 51 (December 20, 2004): 52.

BLINDING LIGHT

Author: Paul Theroux (1941-   )
Publisher: Houghton Mifflin (New York). 438 pp.
  $26.00
Type of work: Novel
Time: The 1990's
Locale: The United States

Theroux explores the nature of the creative process through the life of a writer whose use of mind-altering drugs causes temporary blindness but provides him special insight

Principal characters:
  SLADE STEADMAN, a writer
  AVA KATSINA, a physician
  MANFRED STEIGER, a journalist

In *Blinding Light*, author Paul Theroux combines three recurring interests which have distinguished his work for decades: travel, sex, and the nature of creativity. Theroux's experience as a travel writer is evident in his twenty-sixth novel. The work is filled with vivid descriptions of such lush hideaways as the jungles of Ecuador and the Massachusetts resort community at Martha's Vineyard. His facility for description carries over, too, in the graphic depictions of sexual activity which highlight pleasure without exploring its moral dimensions. Nevertheless, *Blinding Light* is more than simply another attempt by a prolific writer to top the best-seller lists. Like many novels written during the postmodern period, *Blinding Light* is about self-consciousness and the nature of the creative process. Theroux deals with large questions: What does it mean to have imagination? What is the nature of the artist's vision of reality? What is the cost to the artist for producing his work? What makes this novel different from many that deal with these same issues, however, is Theroux's interesting and provocative narrative, which obliquely asks and answers these questions in a story that, despite its comic overtones, is a tragedy.

Theroux's hero, Slade Steadman, is a middle-aged writer who has lived for nearly two decades on the proceeds of a highly successful travel book titled *Trespassing*. Written when he was a young man, the book has remained widely popular, and licensing rights for television and various forms of logo merchandise have made Steadman rich. In the years immediately following the publication of *Trespassing*, he had enjoyed celebrity status, but unfortunately for him, he had never been able to write another book. Now fifty and living the life of a recluse, Steadman decides to travel incognito to Ecuador to seek out a group of shamans who are said to possess powerful, consciousness-enhancing drugs. Traveling with Steadman is his longtime companion Dr. Ava Katsina. Also along for the experience are four rich American tourists, for whom the trip is but one more adventure fraught with inconvenience and poor accommodations. Rounding out the group is Manfred Steiger, a German journalist who is not exactly forthcoming in describing his reasons for being on the journey. Ironically, while the four Americans carry "Trespassing" travel gear and use Steadman's book as a kind of guide for their journey, they do not realize that they are traveling with the author of the famous travelogue. Only Steiger recognizes Steadman, and a testy relationship develops between the two men. Steadman takes pleasure in ridiculing the German, calling him a Nazi and poking fun at his antisocial tendencies.

After a lengthy boat ride into the heart of the jungle, Steadman and others in the group partake of the drug they had come to sample. The advertised drug proves less potent than Steadman had anticipated, but Steiger tells him of another, more powerful substance, datura, which may be available from the Ecuadorians. Steadman agrees eagerly to try some. In a ritual resembling a voodoo ceremony, he imbibes the liquid

Paul Theroux is the author of numerous works of fiction, including the novels The Mosquito Coast *(1981) and* My Secret History *(1989) and more than a dozen travelogues, such as* The Old Patagonian Express *(1979) and* Dark Star Safari *(2002).*

containing the potent hallucinogen, and the experience is life-transforming. Made temporarily blind, he experiences a searing light inside his brain which illuminates his past and allows him to see into the future. Instantly addicted, he sets out to purchase a supply of the plant containing the drug. Unable to convince the shamans to sell it to him, he is almost ready to give up when Steiger appears with a curious basket woven from the dried plant from which the miraculous datura is made. After he purchases the basket from Steiger, however, Steadman continues to humiliate him, eventually accusing him of stealing from the group. The two men depart Ecuador on bad terms.

When Steadman and Katsina return to his estate on Martha's Vineyard, Katsina becomes the writer's caretaker and amanuensis, forgoing her own medical career to tend him during his spells of blindness and transcribe the novel he begins to write. The rich and famous inhabitants of Martha's Vineyard find Steadman to be a curiosity. He is invited to various social functions, and women repeatedly come on to him. Steadman astounds people by sensing their innermost thoughts and getting about quite capably despite his blindness. Katsina, who knows the truth about Steadman's disability, continually criticizes him for taking advantage of his situation. She convinces him to see an oculist in Boston, but there Steadman simply mocks the doctor who attempts to discern the source of his blindness. Later, at a party on Martha's Vineyard, Steadman meets the president of the United States; the two strike up a special friendship. When the president is pilloried by the press and the American public for his affair with a White House intern, Steadman sympathizes with him. The writer realizes that both he and the president are lying to the public, although Steadman admits that the stakes for the president are much greater.

Steadman continues to administer the datura to himself because he finds that his temporary blindness stimulates his creative powers. These he uses to dictate a novel he titles *The Book of Revelation*, a semiautobiographical fiction which is really a sexual memoir. Not satisfied simply to remember past experiences, Steadman encourages Katsina to perform new sexual acts with him, which he details in his prose. The publication of the novel, however, turns out to be anticlimactic. Initially a best seller, the book receives mixed reviews. Steadman ends up on a book tour during which interviewers and the public seem more interested in his disability than his novel. At the same time, the blindness which had initially been self-induced through use of the drug begins to take hold permanently. No longer prescient, Steadman ends up becoming dependent on others for his very survival.

His situation is exacerbated when Katsina decides to distance herself from him, apparently taking up a lesbian lover who inhabits Steadman's house and occasionally participates in ménage à trois during which the writer becomes the object of the women's fantasies. Retreating once again from the public eye, Steadman becomes genuinely paranoid. At this point Steiger reappears to take vengeance on the writer for spurning his efforts at friendship and collaboration. Almost killed by his encounter with the journalist, Steadman decides to return to Ecuador to see if he can be purged of his reliance on the drug. The final scene leaves readers wondering if Steadman, under the influence of the shaman once again, has been cured or is dying.

As the title implies, *Blinding Light* is filled with irony. The central image, a searing white light which seems to illuminate everything for Steadman, at the same time makes him blind. In his blindness, however, Steadman is able to see past, present, and even the future with exceptional clarity. He is like the classical blind seer Tiresias, who serves Odysseus well in his wanderings back to Ithaca in Homer's *Odyssey* (c. 725 B.C.E.). Theroux obviously wants readers to make this connection, as he has the writer William Styron, a resident of Martha's Vineyard, call Steadman "Our own Tiresias." The title of Steadman's books act in similar fashion: *Trespassing* describes the young writer's method of travel around the world, but it also suggests that his success has been achieved by trespassing on others' privacy. *The Book of Revelation*, produced while Steadman is in a drug-induced blind state, recalls the final book of the Christian Bible (also alleged to be the product of visions) but also highlights the contrast between its author's physical state and his ability to expose the inner workings of the human psyche.

There is irony in the plotting, too. As the novel opens, readers learn that Steadman and Katsina are traveling together only as a matter of convenience. Their affair had ended, but the trip to Ecuador had been planned before the breakup, so they had decided not to lose the money already paid for the excursion. When they return to the United States, however, Katsina gives up all of her own activities to remain with the novelist. Near the end of the book Steadman discovers, much to his chagrin, that the blindness which he could induce or eliminate is no longer under his control. Theroux takes opportunities to point out other ironies as well. For example, Steadman seems to take special pleasure in recalling that the worldwide headlines announcing the death of John F. Kennedy on November 22, 1963, drove into oblivion the fact that the novelist Aldous Huxley died the same day.

The irony is carried out in the examination of the novel's principal theme, the exploration of the creative process. Like the Argentinean novelist Jorge Luis Borges, to whom he refers by name, Steadman has traded the ability to see the external world for the ability to see into the hearts of others—and into himself. Throughout the novel, distinctions are made between sight and vision, playing on the multiple meanings of the latter term. For example, when the president of the United States expresses sympathy for Steadman's blindness, the writer tells him, "My vision is excellent. . . . It's my eyesight that's a little faulty." Similarly, when he is visiting a specialist bent on uncovering the cause of his blindness, Steadman tells her, "My reader's and writer's sight is gone," but he observes immediately that, "There are all sorts of vision, not all of them measurable." The question that begs to be answered, of course, is: Is the value of attaining this vision worth the cost one must pay?

Theroux's answer seems to be "no." Steadman has struck a deal with the devil, mortgaging his "soul"—or at least, his ability to interact with humankind—in exchange for the notoriety of the successful novelist. Hints of this Satanic bargain are present in his exchanges with the German Steiger, who is described by one of the tourists in Ecuador as "Mephisto," and from whom Steadman obtains the magical drug. Unfortunately, the visions Steadman experiences as a result of taking the datura are translated into a novel that is little more than an overnight curiosity. The work brings him money, to be certain, but it does nothing to achieve the ambitious goal he sets out for himself in *The Book of Revelation*: to explain the real nature of human happiness. His novel is dismissed as self-centered, slightly pornographic, and—worst of all—not particularly original. As he learns all too well, his own happiness never materializes. It is a sobering lesson for readers as well.

Laurence W. Mazzeno

Review Sources

Booklist 101, no. 13 (March 1, 2005): 1103.
Kirkus Reviews 73, no. 5 (March 1, 2005): 258.
Library Journal 130, no. 6 (April 1, 2005): 89.
New York 38, no. 21 (June 13, 2005): 113.
The New York Times Book Review 154 (June 5, 2005): 22.
Publishers Weekly 252, no. 12 (March 21, 2005): 35.
The Spectator 298 (July 16, 2005): 35.
The Times Literary Supplement, July 15, 2005, p. 19.
The Wall Street Journal 245, no. 99 (May 20, 2005): W10.

BLINK
The Power of Thinking Without Thinking

Author: Malcolm Gladwell (1963-   )
Publisher: Little, Brown (New York). 277 pp. $26.00
Type of work: Psychology

Gladwell examines the positive and negative aspects of rapid cognition in daily life

Every day, often without even realizing it, people "blink"—that is, make quick decisions, snap judgments, or follow their intuition. Indeed, it would be impossible to drive a car, cross a street, or engage in myriad other daily activities without accessing such rapid and usually unconscious thought processes. *Blink: The Power of Thinking Without Thinking* examines and celebrates this seemingly mundane mode of cognition.

Oddly, as Malcolm Gladwell, the best-selling author of *The Tipping Point* (2000), points out, despite the ubiquity of these moments of "rapid cognition," individuals are suspicious of them for several reasons. For one thing, Gladwell rightly states that people assume that "the quality of a decision is directly related to the time and effort that went into making it." For another thing, individuals do not know how they arrive at these quick decisions, which just seem to come, almost unbidden. They are fleeting and evanescent. In sum, "we really only trust conscious decision making."

In his introduction, Gladwell sets out three purposes of this book. The first is to demonstrate that these quick, unconscious decisions are good, valid, and, in some cases, superior in quality to decisions reached by more methodical deliberation. The second purpose is to acknowledge the reverse proposition. Sometimes these quick decisions turn out to be bad or erroneous. Gladwell believes that when the latter outcome occurs, consistent, specific reasons are operating. By identifying such reasons, people can, in turn, learn from the mistakes. This process of analysis and education about the patterns of failures in rapid cognition leads to the author's third purpose, which is to show that "our snap judgments and first impressions can be educated and controlled." The body of this intriguing and fascinating book elucidates each of these three key points.

To illustrate his first point about the value of quick decisions and following intuition, Gladwell introduces several pertinent anecdotes and examples. He begins the book with the well-known case of an ancient Greek statue known as a kouros which the J. Paul Getty Museum seriously considered buying to add to its prestigious art collection. Experts in a number of fields studied the statue from many scientific standpoints and found the piece to be authentic. Several respected art historians, however, reached the opposite conclusion. At first glance, each one of these scholars "knew" that the statue was a forgery, as it turned out in fact to be.

On another subject, the author discusses the work of a psychologist, John Gottman, who has spent years studying the interaction of couples in his "love lab." His extensive research shows that if a person knows what to look for, it is possible to predict the success or failure of a relationship based on just minutes of observing the couple. This technique is called "thin-slicing," which Gladwell defines as "the ability of our unconscious to find patterns and situations and behavior based on very narrow slices of experience."

In the second chapter, titled "The Locked Door: The Secret Life of Snap Decisions," Gladwell discusses the unconscious nature of the process. He uses examples of people such as Vic Braden, a tennis professional and coach who, as a tennis player is about to serve, can determine whether that player will double-fault. However hard Braden tries, he cannot explain how he reaches this rapid conclusion. Gladwell speaks of this situation as the locked door, and he asserts that an advantage exists to leaving this rapid cognition process behind that door. The effectiveness of these quick judgments seems to depend on not subjecting them to analysis.

Malcolm Gladwell has been a science and business reporter for The Washington Post *and is currently a writer for* The New Yorker. *He is the author of* The Tipping Point *(2000).*

However, just as the reader is primed to accept the value of rapid cognition and thin-slicing as well as its unconscious and unfathomable nature, Gladwell turns the tables by pointing to occasions when this kind of quick decision making fails and can produce serious or even disastrous results. Some failures of this kind stem from the interference or layering of stereotypes and prejudices that can cloud judgment. Racial and gender prejudices are good examples of how unconscious attitudes, those "immediate, automatic associations," can interfere with and hijack conscious, chosen beliefs. So, even if individuals choose to believe in racial or gender equality, tests measuring spontaneous attitudes toward race or gender often reveal that the person, in fact, has not shaken off those underlying unconscious stereotypes.

Another kind of error comes from making decisions under extreme stress. Gladwell introduces several examples of law enforcement officers who have killed an innocent suspect because, under intense pressure, the officers "begin shutting down so many sources of information" that they "become useless." They may suffer from "momentary autism."

At this point, it seems that Gladwell has come to an impasse. On one hand, he has described many instances when rapid cognition has been beneficial and when quick judgments have worked and been correct, even more so than decisions produced by careful deliberation. On the other hand, he has shown an equal number of cases in which rapid cognition has produced important errors in judgment. Some of these failures have been costly and fatal. Furthermore, Gladwell has asserted that the process of rapid cognition is unconscious and that the locked door of the unconscious cannot, and indeed should not, be opened lest the effectiveness of rapid cognition be lost.

So, how does Gladwell address his third point, that this process of rapid cognition can be educated and controlled? The thesis and purpose of *Blink* hinge on this third point, as most readers want to know how they can educate, control, and ultimately improve their own abilities for rapid cognition. Because of the structure and presentation of Gladwell's book, however, he does not address this third crucial point fully. *Blink* never abandons its relentless barrage of anecdotal examples for extended analysis. Even the conclusion, where readers might expect to find a summation and an analytical discussion of ways in which to make rapid cognition work to their benefit, is presented as yet another anecdote.

Scattered throughout the book, tucked here and there among the parade of examples, the careful reader might be able to discern some points about how to educate and control rapid decision making. One theme that recurs in many different types of examples is the crucial value of expertise. A substantial number of cases that Gladwell cites of good instantaneous decisions and judgments are drawn from people who have extensive training and experience in a particular field. The art historians who instantly recognized that the purported ancient Greek statue was a forgery, the gamblers who get sweaty palms, the successful car salespeople, and the professional food tasters, among many others, have cultivated the ability to use and trust thin-slicing and rapid cognition.

In some cases—the car salespeople, the food tasters, and the gamblers—these people have developed their expertise on their own. In other cases, the expertise comes from extended periods of specialized study and training. Art historians and medical doctors are examples of professionals who have spent years studying and earned advanced degrees in their fields. Gladwell cites the training program for police officers in Dade County, Florida, which is designed to instill in the officers appropriate actions to follow before they come face-to-face with a suspect and thus reach a moment of crisis.

With these varied types of training and expertise, one key in making rapid decisions is knowing what to look for and how to edit down large amounts of information. For example, in Gottman's research on the interactions of couples, he was able to simplify the process of prediction. Of about twenty categories of emotion, one in particular, the presence or absence of contempt, is the strongest and most reliable predictor of a couple's chances for success or failure of a relationship. As Gladwell says: "This is the gift of training and expertise—the ability to extract an enormous amount of information from the very thinnest slice of experience."

A related approach is to identify the components in a situation that are the most important for thin-slicing and then, using those components, create a structure within which rapid decision making can function. One example is the procedure for evaluating heart patients who are admitted to the emergency room at Cook County Hospital in Chicago. After extensive study, doctors isolated four crucial factors in determining the severity of symptoms reported by heart patients. A procedure was formulated based on these four key factors. This structure then allowed doctors to respond more spontaneously because they could identify patterns without becoming overwhelmed with extraneous information in the stress of the moment. They could operate more freely because they were working within the framework of what Gladwell calls "the structure of spontaneity."

Another way in which to improve the quality of rapid cognition is to take steps toward changing unconscious attitudes which may interfere with intuitive abilities. Gladwell explains that such unconscious attitudes come from "our experiences and our environment." Experiences and environment can be controlled in order to change attitudes. Unconscious racial prejudice, for instance, requires a person to make active, conscious efforts to know people of different races and to enter into the environments they inhabit.

In the conclusion, Gladwell focuses on how symphony orchestras now hold blind auditions, in which prospective musicians play behind a screen for a jury. In this way, the applicants are judged solely on the basis of their musicianship. This change in audition policy eliminates unconscious gender or racial prejudices and allows pure sound to be the determining factor. As Julie Landsman, principal French horn player for the orchestra of the Metropolitan Opera in New York, says: "The only true way to listen is with your ears and your heart." This kind of problem solving is what Gladwell espouses. It demonstrates how a constructive change in circumstances, procedures, or environment enables people to gain some control over the process of rapid cognition. Gladwell emphasizes that "if we can control the environment in which rapid cognition takes place, then we can control rapid cognition."

In the end, however, all these approaches to educating and controlling rapid cognition are difficult. They require extensive research and training as well as the willingness to make changes. They all belie and, to a certain extent, contradict Gladwell's assertion that rapid cognition is something that remains behind the locked door of the unconscious. In fact, in various ways that involve conscious attention to rapid cognition, individuals can achieve "a much better understanding of what goes on behind the locked door." *Blink* is a useful book for drawing attention to rapid cognition. However, by keeping the discourse primarily on the level of anecdotal example and eschewing analysis, Gladwell limits the work's usefulness for doing what he advocates: making rapid cognition an instrument for creating "a different and better world."

Karen Gould

Review Sources

Booklist 101, no. 1 (September 1, 2004): 2.
Maclean's 118, no. 5 (January 31, 2005): 56.
The New Republic 232, no. 2 (January 24, 2005): 27-30.
New Statesman 134 (February 14, 2005): 51-52.
The New York Review of Books 52, no. 7 (April 28, 2005): 19-21.
The New York Times 154 (January 6, 2005): E1-E10.
Publishers Weekly 251, no. 44 (November 1, 2004): 52.
Time 165, no. 2 (January 10, 2005): 57.
U.S. News & World Report 138, no. 7 (February 28, 2005): 52-61.

THE BOMB
A Life

Author: Gerard J. DeGroot (1955-   )
Publisher: Harvard University Press (Cambridge,
    Mass.). 397 pp. $28.00
Type of work: History and history of science
Time: The 1930's to 2005
Locale: North America, Eurasia, and the South
    Pacific

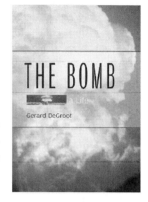

*In his history of fission and fusion bombs, often tartly
written, DeGroot addresses how they work and their destructive power as well as the politics impelling their development and their political and social consequences*

Gerard J. DeGroot's *The Bomb: A Life* is a political his-
tory of nuclear weaponry which is likely to delight readers who disapprove of the
bomb and its masters, the United States government in particular. For the same reason
DeGroot's tone, bitingly witty upon occasion, may disaffect defenders of these weapons. In both cases the effect would be unfortunately diverting. Even though the Cold
War and its rationale for nuclear deterrence are history, the bomb remains an appall-
ing threat deserving of sober consideration. DeGroot recognizes this and discusses
the dangers, past and present, generally with insight and balance. The passages in
which he lets his indignation burst forth as sarcasm and name-calling distract from his
argument.

DeGroot persuasively answers some very intriguing questions. Did the atomic
bomb need to be developed? Did nuclear policy in the United States and the Soviet
Union avert a major war? Did the members of the "nuclear club" really need so many
nuclear weapons during the Cold War? What were the costs?

The costs are worth bearing in mind as the reader progresses through the book.
There are many, but aside from political consequences the principal costs are psychological, medical, environmental, and economic. DeGroot's well-documented discussions of these alone make the book worth reading. Take the economic toll, for example. Near the end of the last chapter he cites a Brookings Institution estimate of the
monetary cost to the United States since the bomb's birth: $5.8 trillion. The figure is
breathtaking, overwhelming, but by that point in the narrative readers will probably
have become so thoroughly shocked by the other costs as to be desensitized to the
money—and how it might have been used for other purposes.

Among the psychological costs is damage to the reputation of scientists. Before
World War II, physicists and chemists, DeGroot points out, were as little likely to
change the world as medieval historians. That altered during the 1930's, and scientists
lost their political innocence. Leading physicists, such as Enrico Fermi and Otto
Hahn, came to realize that the atom could be split and in the process a great amount of

energy released. German scientists working under the Nazi government took the lead in exploring the possibility.

That they might succeed so worried physicists Leo Szilard and Edward Teller that they
visited Albert Einstein in 1939 and urged him to
write a letter of warning to President Franklin
Roosevelt. Einstein did so, and his prestige as the
world's greatest physicist nudged the U.S. government into action; it launched its own atomic
bomb program, the Manhattan Project. From the
start some scientists had misgivings about plac-

*Professor of modern history at the
University of St. Andrews in
Scotland, Gerard J. DeGroot has
written eight books about military
history and consults for the United
Nations. His books include* The
First World War *(2000) and* A
Noble Cause? America and the
Vietnam War *(2000).*

ing a super-powerful weapon in the hands of the military, but they put qualms aside as
World War II initially went badly for the Allies, and rumors suggested the German
bomb program was well advanced.

By the time intelligence reports proved that the German program had fizzled in
1943, the Manhattan project was not only under way; it was also the biggest scientific
research effort ever created, and its momentum carried it beyond the initial motivation to beat the Germans to the bomb. Moreover, DeGroot establishes that from the
very beginning the bomb was meant to be used. It was never intended as a symbol or
deterrent. Politicians thought of it as just another weapon, despite the dire warnings of
scientists, many of whom believed it would end the war early.

When decision time came after the successful test in New Mexico in 1945, President Harry Truman did not hesitate. He ordered atomic bombs dropped on Japan in
hopes of scaring the imperial military into surrender and thereby avoiding an invasion, which was expected to kill tens of thousands on both sides. Military leaders supported Truman's reasoning, although some were more interested in revenge for Pearl
Harbor and the Bataan death march. Afterward Robert Oppenheimer, director of the
Manhattan Project, and many of his fellow scientists felt both pride at their achievement and horror at its destructive power. Concurrently, the world recognized that scientific genius was a profoundly mixed blessing; the desire to participate in cutting-
edge research could lure scientists into moral dilemmas.

According to DeGroot, however, ending World War II quickly was not Truman's
only motivation. He also wanted a weapon that would frighten the Soviet Union after
the war and thereby influence its behavior. At that point the atomic bomb became a
weapon of intimidation and terror. Advisers, disdainful of Soviet science and industry, assured Truman it would take the Russians twenty years to develop a bomb of
their own, and so the United States would have an unanswerable advantage. Their ar-
rogance blinded them and set the United States on a dangerous path. The Soviets,
thanks to information from spies, were able to test their first atomic device in 1949,
and the Cold War and its arms race began.

From that point until the late 1980's the United States and the Soviet Union competed to gain an atomic advantage in order to deter an attack: more bombs, more
powerful bombs, bombs of new types such as the fusion bomb (or hydrogen bomb,

H-bomb, or thermonuclear bomb), better methods of putting them on targets, and defenses against them. Paranoia drove both superpowers to a better-safe-than-sorry policy, which meant that, no matter which side started a nuclear war, both would be devastated—a doctrine called mutual assured destruction (MAD) in the United States.

DeGroot's account of these developments makes for engrossing and terrifying reading. It is especially disturbing as he argues that the arms race might have been avoided had the Truman administration not bungled its dealing with the Soviets, that several incidents nearly escalated to nuclear war (the Cuban Missile Crisis of 1962, above all), and that both sides regularly misread the intentions and capabilities of the other.

As great as the psychological damage was to average people from this brinksmanship (as it was once called), the damage to health was more immediate. DeGroot discusses the increase in cancer rates in communities near American, British, and Russian nuclear facilities and test sites, the reckless exposure of soldiers during tests, the ineffective relocation of populations (as of Polynesians from islands obliterated by test detonations), the initial naïveté about the danger of radioactivity, and denials of problems from governments—a disgraceful story all around. The damage to the environment is as frightening. Large tracts of land in Russia, the United States, and the South Seas will not be habitable for thousands of years, if ever, and radioactive materials have seeped into watercourses and aquifers, endangering life even further away.

Was the bomb worth these titanic costs? On this subject DeGroot treads carefully. He points out that nuclear weaponry, expensive as it is, is still cheaper than maintaining large armed forces to ensure national security. He also recognizes that weapons research and development spawned an entirely new, vastly profitable industry which not only attracted young people to careers in science but also had peaceful spin-offs in, for instance, medicine and power production. These are, however, side arguments. To the big question—did the bomb prevent major warfare?—DeGroot answers yes. The United States, Russia, China, Great Britain, and France did not turn the Cold War into World War III. So, the doctrine of deterrence succeeded. To the related question—did deterrence require so many weapons of such destructive power?—DeGroot answers no. The nuclear powers, especially the Soviet Union and the United States, went to hysterical excesses driven by ideology, chauvinism, and fear.

It is in his discussion of the bomb's development and Cold War politics that DeGroot vents his disdain for many of the scientists and politicians involved. He writes, "In the race to build the bomb, scientists trampled over their moral doubts and muddied the noble traditions of their profession." He calls Werner Heisenberg, leader of the Nazi bomb effort, a worm. Edward Teller, one of the creators of American's fusion bomb, is "CEO of Bombs R US," and DeGroot's reaction to the decision of Hans Bethe to stay in bomb research because he might yet be a force for disarmament is "and pigs might fly." He refers to strategists at the Rand Corporation think tank as eggheads and twice repeats a contemporary writer's characterization of Harry Truman being like a boy hurtling downhill on a sled without knowing what to do about it.

DeGroot's greatest scorn appears to be for the American people. He finds them complacent about the threat of nuclear warfare, gullible about their government's misinformation and futile programs for civil defense, self-righteous in their belief that the United States is a positive force in the world, and silly. There is no denying the silliness. From the very beginning of the atomic age, the peculiar American gift for converting everything and anything into a consumer fad had its effect: parties to watch atomic bomb tests from Las Vegas casinos, beauty contests for Miss Atomic Bomb, businesses and goods bearing the word "atomic" in their names, and motion pictures with irresponsibly ill-informed plots based on atomic power and radiation.

DeGroot's charge of gullibility and complacency, however, seems hasty. Historical hindsight makes it tempting to be high-handed—a temptation DeGroot admits but does not entirely resist. During the Cold War, most Americans had faith in their government, faith that if an administration could not be counted on to act with great wisdom, at least it would not do anything truly stupid. Perhaps that faith was misplaced, but faith, misplaced or otherwise, is not the same as complacency. Moreover, DeGroot misses an essential component of the American mentality: The Manhattan Project encouraged people to believe that, given enough resources, scientists could produce miraculous advantages in national prestige and security. This belief was later reinforced by the Apollo voyages to the moon.

During the 1950's and early 1960's, America's public schools held federally supported drills which taught children how to protect themselves from an atomic bomb blast: "drop and cover." Readers who recall absurdities such as that during the very real Cold-War fear of nuclear war will find that *The Bomb: A Life* evokes the confusion of the times powerfully.

The danger is hardly gone, DeGroot reminds readers. He describes how easy it was during the 1990's to steal bomb-grade uranium from laboratories in the Russian Federation, how its scientists, desperate for money, could be tempted to sell nuclear secrets, how much bomb-making material is unaccounted for, the slowness of the United States to adapt its strategic doctrine after the Cold War, and the reckless hatred that could move terrorists to build and use atomic bombs. DeGroot presents the history of the bomb, he writes in the book's preface, so that readers will understand its civilization-crippling deadliness and ubiquity, still. That is an invaluable reminder.

Roger Smith

Review Sources

Booklist 101, no. 14 (March 15, 2005): 1253.
Discover 26, no. 5 (May, 2005): 80.
Kirkus Reviews 73, no. 1 (January 1, 2005): 31.
Library Journal 130, no. 1 (January, 2005): 127.
Publishers Weekly 252, no. 1 (January 3, 2005): 46.
Science News 167, no. 20 (May 14, 2005): 319.

BORGES AND THE ETERNAL ORANGUTANS

Author: Luis Fernando Verissimo (1936-   )
First published: Borges e os orangotangos eternos, 2000, in Brazil
Translated from the Portuguese by Margaret Jull Costa
Publisher: New Directions (New York). 135 pp. Paperback $14.00
Type of work: Novel
Time: 1985
Locale: Buenos Aires

A middle-aged scholar named Volgelstein and the literary genius Jorge Luis Borges tackle a murder mystery

Principal characters:
 ANGELA, the organizer of the Israfel Society conference
 JORGE LUIS BORGES, a brilliant Argentinean writer
 CUERVO, a criminologist, Edgar Allan Poe scholar, and friend of Borges
 JOACHIM ROTKOPF, an unpleasant German Poe scholar who becomes a murder victim
 OLIVER JOHNSON, an American with a motive to kill Rotkopf
 VOGELSTEIN, a middle-aged Brazilian writer who idolizes Jorge Luis Borges and who has translated Borges's stories into Portuguese
 PROFESSOR XAVIER URQUIZA, an Argentinean Poe scholar with a motive to kill Rotkopf

In *Borges and the Eternal Orangutans,* Brazilian writer Luis Fernando Verissimo offers a brilliant literary tour de force: The novel is at once an homage to the great Argentinean writer Jorge Luis Borges; a classic detective story; a study of conspiracy theory; a philosophical treatise on geography and coincidence; and a send-up of all of the above. Verissimo uses a style reminiscent of Borges's detective stories, mixing facts from Borges's life with fictional details created for the book and drawing on many of Borges's favorite themes.

The narrator of the book is Vogelstein, a fifty-year old scholar of the works of Edgar Allan Poe. Vogelstein structures his tale as a letter to Borges. He writes the book, he says, to remember the events that took place at the 1985 meeting of the Israfel Society, a group devoted to the study of Poe, in Buenos Aires. (Fittingly, Borges, the writer of stories such as "Borges and I," is doubled in the book: He is both the party to whom the book is addressed and a main character in the action of the story.)

"Geography is destiny," Vogelstein begins, and geography and coincidence play major roles in the story. The Israfel Society has invited the aged Borges to speak at the society's first meeting held outside the Northern Hemisphere. For Vogelstein, this is a happy coincidence. Not only does he belong to the society, he also idolizes Borges, and the meeting is sufficiently close to his home in Brazil to allow him to attend the conference. In addition, his cat Aleph (named after a Borges short story) has died, and Vogelstein has placed his Aunt Sophie in a nursing home, leaving him free to travel. "I did not see that I was being subtly summoned or that this story needed me in order to be written," Vogelstein writes. "I did not see that I was being plunged headfirst into the plot, like a pen into an inkwell."

∽

Luis Fernando Verissimo is a well-known Brazilian writer who works in journalism and advertising. According to Verissimo, he is "not a graduate of anything." He also plays the saxophone in a jazz band.

∽

Vogelstein further relates that years earlier, he translated a short story by Borges and committed the nearly unpardonable sin of changing the text by adding a "tail," an ending other than the one written by Borges. In the intervening years, Vogelstein repeatedly attempted to apologize to Borges for this presumption, but the Argentinean never replied to his letters. With time, Vogelstein developed an obsession with Borges, fully identifying himself with the "master." As he describes himself, Vogelstein uses Borges's images and language: "I am fifty years old. I have led a cloistered life, 'without adventures or surprises', as you put it in your poem. Like you, master. A sheltered life spent among books, and into which only rarely did the unexpected enter like a tiger." Borges, blind for much of his life, wrote often of libraries, labyrinths, and tigers.

Before he even arrives in Buenos Aires, Vogelstein knows that the Poe scholars are a contentious group, their sniping and feuds carried out in the pages of the Israfel Society's journal, *The Gold-bug*. The most arrogant of them, a German named Rotkopf, has tricked one of the scholars into committing an academic faux pas, and Rotkopf now threatens to expose him. Furthermore, Rotkopf had traded insults with yet another Poe scholar at a previous meeting of the Israfel Society. The three men hate one another deeply; yet through another coincidence, all three are staying at the same hotel, along with Vogelstein.

At the conference's opening reception, Vogelstein meets these three as well as the criminologist Cuervo (whose name means Raven, another reference to Poe). Vogelstein also has his first meeting with Borges. He is in rapture: "Jorge Luis Borges! I was standing next to Jorge Louis Borges! You were smiling at me and holding out your hand to be shaken. Your hand was real; yes, the hand of Jorge Luis Borges, which I was incredulously shaking, was made of flesh and blood!" The reception, furthermore, is the site of an antagonistic meeting between Rotkopf and the two scholars who have reasons to wish him dead. In addition, Rotkopf carelessly bowls over a Japanese professor—not once but twice—during the course of the evening.

When the reception ends, Vogelstein finds himself returning to the hotel in a car with Rotkopf because no one else will ride with the ill-tempered and boorish man. When he leaves Rotkopf at his room, Vogelstein warns the German to lock his door, as Vogelstein believes there are many who would like to see him dead.

Later that night, Vogelstein receives a call from Rotkopf, who appears to be in trouble. When Vogelstein rushes to his room, he finds the door locked, and Rotkopf does not answer his knock. Vogelstein calls the hotel porter for help, and when the door is opened, Rotkopf is found to be dead on the floor, in front of a mirror.

Here is where the mystery begins: How could a murder be committed within a room whose door is bolted and chained, with no sign of the murderer inside? For such a murder to be committed at a conference of Poe scholars is no coincidence; Poe's story "The Murders at the Rue Morgue," widely regarded as the first detective story, features just such a murder, something that every participant at the conference and every Poe reader will recognize. (Poe aficionados will probably also remember that an orangutan plays an important role in that story as well.)

Cuervo takes Vogelstein to Borges's library, where the three men contemplate the murder and try to solve the crime, based on Vogelstein's memory of the murder scene. As the group compiles their information, they find they have no shortage of clues, suspects, potential murder weapons, and motives. Both American Oliver Johnson and Argentinean Xavier Urquiza have motives and opportunities, as does the Japanese scholar, who is angry that the conference location has been shifted. It is the latter who was knocked over, twice, by Rotkopf.

During the subsequent days, Borges and Vogelstein construct hypothesis upon hypothesis. One theory suggests that Rotkopf had to be killed because he was about to reveal that the *Necronomicon*, an imaginary work described by writer H. P. Lovecraft, existed in reality and that Poe also knew of the book. Another hypothesis argued that the murder had to do with the kabbalistic idea that the secret name of God could destroy the world. Each theory draws on the amazing detail and esoteric knowledge attributed to Borges. Several of the theories even include orangutans.

Vogelstein does not make the process of solving the mystery easy, however. Each time he recalls the scene, he remembers it differently. At first he recalls Rotkopf lying in a V-shape in front of the mirror; then he remembers that, with the mirror, the body makes an X. After narrating two pages on possible theories involving the letter X, Vogelstein recalls that "in Poe's story, a newspaper editor with a mania for using the letter O in his texts discovers that, because the letter O is missing from the newspaper's typecase, it has been replaced by an X in one of his articles. . . . The X formed by Rotkopf's V-shaped body . . . represent[s] an O."

Later, Vogelstein decides that the combination of the body and the mirror actually makes an M, or a W. With each development, Borges and Vogelstein tap into a new set of arcane facts and theories. Borges suggests, finally, that "perhaps the real target of this whole complicated conspiracy . . . was me. Apart from Poe and Lovecraft, I have written more literature with apparently hidden meanings—always so tempting to unhinged interpreters—than anyone."

Ultimately, Vogelstein turns over his memoir to Borges, who ostensibly writes the final chapter, revealing the name of the murderer and solving the mystery. The chapter is remarkable, both in its ingenuity and in the careful replication of a Borgesian voice. Indeed, the final postscript of the letter that makes up this chapter is a masterpiece in itself, infinitely multiplying the possible solutions.

In his story, "Borges and I," Borges separates himself into two characters, one the "real" Borges and the other the public persona created by his fame. Of course, even the "real" Borges of the story is not the blood-and-bones person but a literary fiction, serving as an example of the layers Borges sets down in his stories and Verissimo replicates in his novel. Indeed, "Borges and I" closes with the words, "I do not know which of us has written this page." This line could serve as the motif for the final chapter.

There are more allusions in *Borges and the Eternal Orangutans* than one could imagine possible in a 131-page book. For example, the testing of one wrong hypothesis after another is reminiscent of Borges's story "Death and the Compass." The eternal orangutan of the title refers to a creation of sixteenth century scholar John Dees, who theorized that if an orangutan were given a good pen, an inexhaustible source of ink, and eternity, it would inevitably write all the books of the universe. The continuing references to mirrors are a Borgesian device. Nevertheless, while some knowledge of Borges, Poe, Lovecraft, Dees, the *Necronomicon*, and secret societies might add to the reader's appreciation of the novel, such knowledge is not necessary for one's sheer fun in working through the convoluted mystery. Indeed, the story holds together on its own quite nicely, in spite of being a text thick with references to other texts.

Finally, what distinguishes *Borges and the Eternal Orangutans* from other mysteries involving secret codes is that it not only refers to other texts but also is subtly self-referential. The mystery is so compelling that readers forget it is not Vogelstein who is writing the book but Verissimo. The last chapter, then, although supposedly written by Borges and relayed by Vogelstein, is really written by Verissimo, just as the rest of the novel is his creation.

Verissimo sprinkles clues throughout the novel that this work comprises a game he is playing with readers. Thus, when Vogelstein writes, "Someone or something is using me to untangle the tangled plot over whose direction I have as little influence as the pen has over the poets who wield it, or man over the gods who manipulate him, or the knife over the murderer," he is unwittingly uttering a true statement. As a fictional character, Vogelstein's every word, every action is determined by Verissimo.

Borges and the Eternal Orangutans is Verissimo's second book to be translated into English; the first, *O clube dos Anjos* (1998; *The Club of Angels*, 2001), comprises a pair of novellas. Both books speak to Verissimo's remarkable talent, and it seems likely that more of his earlier work will be translated in the future. Until then, readers will have to satisfy themselves with *Borges and the Eternal Orangutans*, each rereading of which offering yet more labyrinthine layers, more fodder for thought about fiction and reality.

Diane Andrews Henningfeld

Review Sources

Booklist 101 (June 1, 2005): 1757.
Kirkus Reviews 73, no. 6 (March 15, 2005): 316.
Library Journal, July 15, 2005, p. 71.
The New York Times, August 28. 2005, section 7, p. 18.
Publishers Weekly 252, no. 15 (April 11, 2005): 32.
The Seattle Times, August 14, 2005, p. K7.
The Washington Post Book World, July 17, 2005, p. T02.

BORN LOSERS
A History of Failure in America

Author: Scott A. Sandage (1964-   )
Publisher: Harvard University Press (Cambridge, Mass.).
    Illustrated. 362 pp. $35.00.
Type of work: Economics and sociology
Time: The early nineteenth century to the late twentieth
    century
Locale: The United States generally but mostly the north-
eastern and midwestern United States

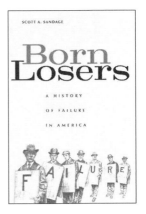

*Sandage considers the history and roots of failure in the
United States from Herman Melville's Bartleby to Chic
Young's Dagwood Bumstead to Arthur Miller's Willie
Loman*

Principal personages:
    HENRY DAVID THOREAU, an author and philosopher
    RALPH WALDO EMERSON, an author and transcendental philosopher
    SAMUEL LANGHORNE CLEMENS (pen name MARK TWAIN), a humorist
    EUGENE O'NEILL, a playwright
    TENNESSEE WILLIAMS, a playwright
    ARTHUR MILLER, a playwright

In *Born Losers*, a comprehensive anatomy of failure in the United States, Scott A. Sandage focuses on the nineteenth century and on America's move from an agrarian to an industrial society. He chronicles the painful adjustments this switch required, referring not only to the growth of such behemoths as Standard Oil and America's railroads but also honing in on what this growth presaged for the masses caught in the intersection between small, independent enterprise and the corporate giants which made it difficult for small businessmen to maintain their identities and their financial integrity.

Sandage writes about a notably male chauvinist, patriarchal society in which men's manhood depended on how well they provided for their families. Raised with the conviction that honesty, hard work, and reliability would assure financial independence and a modicum of success, hundreds of disillusioned businessmen were sucked into the vortex of an economic whirlpool which relentlessly drew them down. Such events as the financial panics of 1819, 1837, 1857, 1873, and 1893 brought about a reshaping of the American economy and resulted in widespread suicides by honorable men, many past middle-age, whose financial independence and ability to provide for their families suddenly evaporated.

Most of those who had no safety net on which to rely through the great depressions that recurred during the nineteenth century faced total ruin when circumstances destroyed the small businesses they depended on for their sustenance. The United States

Scott A. Sandage is a member of the Department of History at Carnegie Mellon University. Born Losers, based on his doctoral dissertation produced at Rutgers University in 1995, was awarded the Thomas J. Wilson Prize by the Board of Syndics of the Harvard University Press as the best first book accepted by the press in 2004.

Bankruptcy Acts of 1800, 1841, and 1867 offered some respite for those who faced financial annihilation, but the very nature of bankruptcy ran counter to the spirit of independence and responsibility that had long been trademarks of reputable American businessmen. Society often equated financial failure with moral failure. Many ruined businessmen viewed suicide as preferable to bearing the stigma of filing for bankruptcy, which they considered a public admission of failure, both economic and moral.

Although most women in this era were stay-at-home wives and mothers, many of them were forced to exert their resourcefulness to find means of survival, resorting to such measures as growing their own vegetables, making clothing for themselves and their families, taking in boarders, and, as Sandage well illustrates, writing begging letters to the captains of industry. These letters, on which Sandage comments with admirable insight and sensitivity, exist in large numbers in the archives he explored in preparing this book. He devotes a great deal of time to discussing both the structure and the contents of such letters, using them essentially as case studies.

The letters are remarkably similar structurally. They usually began with an apology for intruding on the recipient, then proceed both to outline their cases and extol the virtues of their ruined spouses, and finally ask the recipient to give such spouses an opportunity for employment, which would, in their eyes, be of mutual benefit. Most of these letters reflected the pride and self-respect of those who sent them. Almost none directly request financial assistance. They almost uniformly ask only that the men on whose behalf they write be afforded opportunities to work.

Sandage identifies born losers as those who are misfits of the capitalist societies which nineteenth century industrialism spawned. Early in his book, he focuses on the funeral of Henry David Thoreau, whose eulogy is delivered by his friend and neighbor Ralph Waldo Emerson. Although Emerson respected Thoreau and valued his ideals, he had to admit that, judged by the prevailing measures of success in the United States during the nineteenth century, Thoreau was far from being successful. Emerson identified him as "the captain of a huckleberry-party" and went on to enumerate the pursuits that Thoreau tried but to which he did not give his continued attention: "teacher, surveyor, pencilmaker, housepainter, mason, farmer, gardener." Thoreau's interests were eclectic; captains of industry are often single-minded in their pursuits.

Obviously, such successes of the nineteenth and early twentieth centuries as John D. Rockefeller, J. P. Morgan, and Andrew Carnegie were judged in their own time by their material achievements more than by the sorts of contributions to society that people such as Thoreau or Samuel Langhorne Clemens or Abraham Lincoln made. Clemens and Lincoln both experienced business failures and never claimed material successes comparable to those of the great captains of American enterprises.

Clearly America's industrial leaders, who often were shamelessly ruthless in building their corporations, eventually made huge contributions to society. They usually did this, however, through creating charitable foundations, some of which flourish to the present day but were established long after they had firmly secured their places in the growing industrial complex which, during the late nineteenth and early twentieth centuries, defined American society socioeconomically.

Sandage, whose work grew out of the doctoral dissertation he completed at Rutgers University in 1995, spent a decade expanding and polishing his original study. The result is a comprehensive consideration written with such exemplary literary style that it is a model of how effectively expressed a study such as this one can be. Besides writing extraordinarily well, Sandage consistently reveals his full mastery of the socioeconomic conditions of the nineteenth century which have helped shape contemporary conceptions of what constitutes both success and failure.

If the mind of this study resides in the historical details which inform it, its heart is clearly in the moving, sensitively presented accounts of ruined businessmen revealed in the begging letters Sandage explored. Among these is the story of J. W. Bomgardner. In 1860, when Bomgardner was thirty years old, a little-known grain merchant in Ohio proposed becoming a partner with him. Bomgardner declined the offer and instead bought a grain mill in Indiana. He made a decent living from this mill until he was ruined financially during the Panic of 1873.

To survive, Bomgardner headed west, to the "land of opportunity" which many people in similar situations viewed as a means of salvation in difficult times. He touched down in Illinois, first in Decatur, then in Springfield, and eventually in Quincy. Illinois, however, was not the promised land he had envisioned. He soon relocated to Iowa, where he spent two years before moving on to Kansas to work as a grain dealer. Throughout these wanderings, he endured severely reduced income, earning barely enough to keep his family from going under financially. He complained that companies with large capital were systematically squeezing small businessmen such as himself out of the market.

Finally, in 1890, at age sixty, Bomgardner overcame his pride sufficiently to write to the man who invited him to become his partner thirty years earlier, John D. Rockefeller. His letter was self-effacing. It expressed the hope that Rockefeller would remember him after three decades and told of the interest and admiration with which he had followed Rockefeller's career. He also expressed his regret at not having teamed with Rockefeller when presented with the opportunity.

Bomgardner hoped that Rockefeller would be willing to employ him, convinced that he could be an asset to this oil mogul if placed in a job where his talents could best be used. Although Rockefeller seldom answered the begging letters which arrived for him at the rate of several hundreds each week, he responded to Bomgardner, saying that he, indeed, remembered him and that he was pleased to hear from him again. He sent Bomgardner his good wishes but nothing more.

Humiliated by Rockefeller's noncommittal response, Bomgardner wrote again, this time emphasizing that in writing to him, he was not asking Rockefeller for charity but was, rather, offering his services to fill some appropriate position in Rockefeller's vast enterprises where he could serve Rockefeller productively while simultaneously reestablishing himself as a worthwhile businessman. Presumably, Rockefeller did not respond to this second letter.

Sandage comments in regard to Bomgardner's request, "A man who could neither support a family nor pay his debts violated the contracts of both rational economics and sentimental conduct." In this observation, Sandage gets to the heart of what failure portended for those being crushed beneath the irresistible weight of huge industries and runaway capitalism. Those who succeed as captains of big industry succeed so grandly that their success defies the imagination. The paths they traverse in achieving their successes, however, are littered with the bodies of countless thousands who have fallen by the wayside and been destroyed, mowed down and pushed aside by the mechanisms of a relentless, brutally competitive capitalism.

Sandage takes his study into the twentieth century by noting the onslaught of failure in such literary resources as Eugene O'Neill's *The Iceman Cometh* (pr. 1946) and *Long Day's Journey into Night* (pr. 1956); in Tennessee's Williams's *A Streetcar Named Desire* (pr. 1947), in which the figure doomed to failure is, uncharacteristically, a woman, Blanche DuBois; and most notably in Arthur Miller's *Death of a Salesman* (pr. 1949), whose protagonist, Willy Loman, represents the cult of personality that pervaded the business community of the first half of the twentieth century and proved to be phony.

In the end, Willy, unemployed, with no hope of a future, like so many of the men ruined by the earlier economic panics of the nineteenth century, resorted to his only viable out: suicide. Commenting on Willy's death, Sandage, writes, "This was the legacy of the nineteenth century: failure is an imputed deficiency of self." He calls the play a "visceral portrait of the success [Willy was a good shoe salesman] that is failure." He notes how society had moved from its admiration of the Horatio Alger myth to the cult of personality touted by Dale Carnegie in his enormously popular book, *How to Win Friends and Influence People* (1936), during the depths of the Great Depression.

The epilogue of Sandage's study is subtitled "Attention Must Be Paid," the statement Willy Loman's widow, Linda, makes about Willy to his two sons. Sandage points to the optimism of Russell Conwell's "Acres of Diamonds" speech, delivered over six thousand times by 1925, but it is Willy Loman's uncritical acceptance of such unaccountable optimism that leads him inexorably to his disillusionment and to his tragic end. His widow's statement, which Sandage notes for its passivity in both its grammatical voice and content, speaks volumes about what Willy and many like him were: mere passive recipients of an industrial society's indifference and inhumanity.

The American Dream, as it was called, was a dream of success and independence, one of self-worth and accomplishment recognized and rewarded. Sandage demonstrates convincingly how this dream soured as the underpinnings of a patriarchal society were eroded to the point of collapse by the inroads that a new society, one grounded in big business and capitalism, made upon those who were unable to resist the forces of a new, efficient economy and of a society that had become increasingly depersonalized.

R. Baird Shuman

Review Sources

The Atlantic Monthly 295 (January/February, 2005): 159-160.
The Economist 374 (February 26, 2005): 34.
Esquire 143, no. 2 (February, 2005): 38.
Kirkus Reviews 72, no. 20 (October 15, 2004): 996-997.
Library Journal 129, no. 16 (October 1, 2004): 95-96.
National Journal 36, nos. 47/48 (November 20, 2004): 3549.
The New Republic 233, no. 6 (August 8, 2005): 32-35.
Publishers Weekly 251, no. 44 (November 1, 2004): 52.
The Washington Post Book World 35 (January 30, 2005): 12.

BOSS TWEED
The Rise and Fall of the Corrupt Pol Who Conceived the
Soul of Modern New York

Author: Kenneth D. Ackerman (1951-   )
Publisher: Carroll & Graf (New York). Illustrated.
  437 pp. $27.00
Type of work: Biography
Time: 1823-1878
Locale: New York City

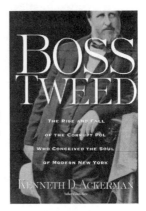

Ackerman presents an engaging study of William Tweed who, as "boss" of Tammany Hall, ruled and robbed New York City for years before his spectacular fall

Principal personages:
  WILLIAM MARCY TWEED, a politician, the
    "boss" of Tammany Hall
  THOMAS NAST, a political cartoonist
  SAMUEL TILDEN, a politician and reformer

Kenneth Ackerman's *Boss Tweed: The Rise and Fall of the Corrupt Pol Who Conceived the Soul of Modern New York* is a richly colored tale of ambition, greed, and skullduggery in Gilded Age America. Perhaps because of his experiences working in Washington in the last decades of the twentieth century, Ackerman has been drawn to the history of the Gilded Age, the raucous and flamboyant period in American history between the end of the Civil War and the Progressive era. Many commentators of the late twentieth century wondered if the gaudily prosperous years dominated by the likes of President Ronald Reagan were not another age of excess. One can easily imagine businessmen Michael Milken, Donald Trump, and Bill Gates all thriving in the industrialized society of the century before their own. Certainly the scandals, crashes, and bubbles of the 1980's and 1990's would have been familiar to the tycoons and Wall Street operatives of the 1880's and 1890's.

The Gilded Age marked the real emergence of modern America. The period received its name from a novel by Mark Twain and Charles Dudley Warner which famously criticized the political and economic corruption which sprang up in the years following the Civil War. The triumphant Republican Party, heir to the "American System" of Henry Clay and the economic nationalism of Alexander Hamilton, felt no compunctions about using the power of the national government to spur economic development, through the Homestead Act, subsidizing railroads, or enacting a high protective tariff. The Civil War and the nationalist perspective it fostered also changed the scale of the political and economic environments in which Americans operated. Farmers, laborers, and business owners all found themselves beholden to forces outside local control. The unprecedented mobilization of men and material for the conflict accustomed Americans to political and economic projects that dwarfed antebellum dreams.

The Civil War, as so many wars do, also ushered in a period of ethical laxity, a reaction perhaps to the sacrifices and heightened passions of the conflict. Corruption became noticeable during the war as profiteers grew rich selling the government goods that were often overpriced and substandard. Ackerman notes that even the distinguished firm of Brooks Brothers clothiers sold the Union Army twelve thousand uniforms made of "shoddy," ground-up rags, which disintegrated in a good rain. The moral and legal laissez-faire of the war years paved the way for the rise of the "robber barons," businesspeople who

Kenneth D. Ackerman is a writer well equipped to unravel a scandal involving money and politics. He brings to his writing a wealth of practical experience: He spent twenty-five years working in a variety of positions on Capitol Hill and in the executive branch of the federal government. Among his assignments were investigating the 1979-1980 silver corner and the 1987 stock market crash. He practices law in Washington, D.C.

would make ruthless use of the favorable political climate in order to accumulate enormous fortunes. At the same time, they would foster an extraordinary industrial revolution in America.

In 1890, the United States would be the leading industrial power in the world. By the end of this messy era, the modern United States had come into being. Thomas Jefferson's agrarian republic was a memory. The future belonged to the cities. More and more Americans were working in factories and offices instead of on farms. The economy was increasingly being shaped by the ebb and flow of consumer demand. A vibrant popular culture had emerged, nurtured by mass media. In 1896, William McKinley's famous victory over William Jennings Bryan, the last great spokesman for rural America, would ratify a social and economic fait accompli.

Ackerman has explored this historical ground in two previous books. In the first, *The Gold Ring* (1988), he detailed the attempt by the notorious Wall Street manipulators Jay Gould and Jim Fisk to illicitly corner the gold market in 1869. In the second, *Dark Horse* (2003), he described the election and subsequent assassination of President James Garfield. A study of William Marcy Tweed is a natural subject for Ackerman. The story of Boss Tweed combines in highly dramatic form the themes of politics, money, and corruption. Tweed dominated New York City at a time when it was becoming America's regnant metropolis. He was a great builder. During his years in power, millions were spent on Central Park, sewers were laid and streets paved. An expensive new courthouse went up, and the Brooklyn Bridge began to span the East River.

All this was constructed at a cost—a huge cost which has never fully been documented in graft and fraud. Tweed was more than a civic visionary; he was the head of one of the first great urban political machines. He was a master of vote fraud and manipulation. He "bought" individual politicians and on one occasion was accused of buying the state legislature. His mighty political organization was fueled by kickbacks and cost overruns on his vast building program. For a time Tweed's massive

Ponzi scheme worked magnificently. When it crashed with his political downfall, New York City's finances were crippled for a generation.

Tweed was born in New York City in 1823. He grew up in modest circumstances. His father was a chair maker who owned a small shop. Seeing promise in his son, William's father scrimped enough money to send him off for a year's course in mathematics and accounting. Most of William Tweed's education, however, would come from the public schools and on the streets, where he was known to be good with his fists. Outgoing as well as bright, Tweed came to lead a gang of local boys. Then he joined the local volunteer fire company. Here he won such popularity that he was elected foreman. The seventy-five men of this company would become the germ of Tweed's political organization. He also prospered in business, launching a brush-making shop with his father and doing well enough to marry at the age of twenty-one. Tammany Hall, the powerful Democratic political club in New York City, marked Tweed as a young man of promise. Tammany introduced him to the gritty world of urban politics. In 1852 Tweed was elected alderman. In 1853 he was sent to Washington as a congressman. National politics held little interest for Tweed, however. His heart was in his native city. After one term in Congress, he returned home. Tweed spent the ensuing years working his way up the Tammany organization, learning the intricacies of city management and machine politics.

Tammany Hall was the most powerful and enduring urban political machine in American history. It was founded in 1786 as a patriotic society. It was named for a legendary Indian chief, and into Tweed's day and beyond, its officers were called "sachems," its members "warriors," and its headquarters "the wigwam." Aaron Burr had helped convert Tammany Hall into a political organization that played a pivotal role in New York politics. By the mid-nineteenth century, it dominated the Democratic Party in New York City. National, as well as state and local, Democrats had to factor Tammany Hall into their political calculations. William Tweed would carry Tammany Hall to new heights of influence and notoriety.

Tweed held a succession of jobs after he returned from Washington which, to an observer, might have seemed a letdown after a term in Congress. He served as a member of a school commission, as a county supervisor, and as a deputy street commissioner. In fact, Tweed was paying his dues, immersing himself in the Tammany system. He set up a law office which operated as a front for his real vocation, acting as a political fixer for hire. In January, 1863, Tweed's hard work for Tammany Hall was rewarded with his election as chairman of the organization's general committee. William Tweed was becoming "Boss" Tweed to his contemporaries. He soon showed his political worth. In early 1863, the Civil War seemed stalemated. The federal government desperately needed more men at the front. Congress accordingly passed a Conscription Act that favored the wealthy by allowing them to purchase exemptions. In response, working men in New York City, many of them Irish immigrants, went on a riotous rampage in June. The New York Draft Riots were forcibly quelled by federal troops. Tweed did all that he could to calm his fellow New Yorkers during the riots. Afterward he worked out a political solution to the problem, establishing a public fund that allowed poor draftees to hire substitutes.

Tweed's power grew in the years following the Civil War. The expanding nation was booming, New York City was booming, and Tweed saw his opportunities and took them. In 1868 he was elected to the state legislature. There Tweed passed a law which gave greater power to the local offices that he and his Tammany associates held. This made possible the infamous Tweed ring. Tweed as commissioner of public works; Peter Sweeny, the city chamberlain; Richard Connolly, the city comptroller; and A. Oakey Hall, the mayor, together controlled patronage and public contracts in the city. They used this power to amass huge fortunes. Estimates of the sums that they skimmed from the city range from thirty million to two hundred million dollars. Tweed was able to get away with this epic robbery for years because he delivered new public works and services to the city, because he was generous with his money, giving freely to charity, and because he maintained the loyalty of his immigrant political constituency, providing them with jobs, assistance, and, above all, with respect at a time when newcomers were regarded with suspicion and disdain by more established citizens.

William Tweed was first challenged by the new mass media. Thomas Nast, the brilliant cartoonist at *Harper's Weekly*, despised Tweed for his corruption and for the support that he gave to Catholic Irish immigrants. Nast began a relentless campaign against Tweed in 1870-1871, indelibly caricaturing him as the archetypal bearded, bloated "boss." *The New York Times* joined in the attack, hoping to build circulation. At first, Tweed's enemies had no facts with which to substantiate their charges. Only when former members of Tweed's organization leaked information did the campaign gain purchase. Then Samuel Tilden, a rich lawyer and state Democratic Party official, acted. Ambitious for higher office, Tilden gathered crucial evidence suggesting Tweed's wrongdoing. Under pressure, other members of the Tweed ring crumbled.

Tweed found himself isolated and alone. After surviving one trial in 1872, he was convicted on corruption charges in 1873. Tweed was released from jail a year later, but he was a political albatross. Tilden had won the New York governorship on the strength of his reputation as a crusader for good government. He did not want Tweed loose. So Tweed was promptly rearrested on new charges. Ackerman makes clear that Tweed was caught in a nightmarish trap. By fair means or foul, his opponents were determined to keep him behind bars. His money evaporating, his health deteriorating, Tweed escaped from prison. He made it to Spain before being recaptured and returned to prison. He made a long confession of all of his misdeeds in return for a promise of release. The authorities reneged on this promise, and Tweed died in jail in 1878. William Tweed was a colorful rogue, a quintessential Gilded Age character. As Ackerman makes clear, for all of his faults, Tweed played a pivotal role in the history of New York City, through both his building projects and his bold contribution to its jaunty and expansive spirit. Tammany Hall, the machine that Tweed made notorious, would survive its greatest boss by many decades, helping shape the politics of the city, the state, and the nation.

Daniel P. Murphy

Review Sources

Booklist 101, no. 12 (February 15, 2005): 1054.
Campaigns and Elections 26, no. 3 (April, 2005): 46.
Kirkus Reviews 73, no. 6 (March 15, 2005): 323.
Library Journal 130, no. 3 (February 15, 2005): 138.
The New York Review of Books 52, no. 19 (December 1, 2005): 52-55.
The New York Times Book Review 154 (March 27, 2005): 5-6.
Policy Review, August/September, 2005, pp. 82-86.

BOUND FOR CANAAN
The Underground Railroad and the War for the Soul of America

Author: Fergus M. Bordewich
Publisher: Amistad (New York). 540 pp. $28.00
Type of work: History
Time: From the American Revolution through the Civil
War
Locale: The United States and Canada

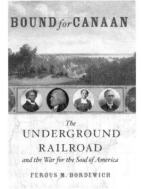

Bordewich provides a comprehensive account of the persons, slave and free, responsible for the origins and growth of the escape routes and networks known metaphorically as the Underground Railroad, through which slaves in the United States fled their bondage in the years prior to the Civil War

The Underground Railroad was a pre-Civil War movement which combined clandestine action to aid men and women fleeing slavery with political efforts to make enslavement of human beings illegal throughout the United States. Taking advantage of increasingly available primary and secondary materials on the Underground Railroad and its role in the abolition movement, Fergus M. Bordewich in *Bound for Canaan* chronicles the numerous routes by which African American slaves fled their masters and credits numerous persons who made the system work.

Bordewich takes the title for his history of the Underground Railroad from the words of Frederick Douglass, former slave and fervent abolitionist:

> We [slaves] were at times remarkably buoyant, singing hymns, and making joyous exclamations, almost as triumphant in their tone as if we had reached a land of freedom and safety. A keen observer might have detected in our repeated singing of
>
> > *O Canaan, sweet Canaan*
> > *I am bound for the land of Canaan,*
>
> something more than a hope of reaching heaven. We meant to reach the *North*, and the North was our Canaan.

Bordewich's title also seems a deliberate echo of that of Kate Larsen's acclaimed *Bound for the Promised Land* (2003), a biography of Underground Railroad heroine Harriet Tubman.

This study of the Underground Railroad is important because Bordewich brings together in one comprehensive narrative the myriad and diverse strands of a complex and significant historic movement. He acknowledges earlier studies important in his

Fergus M. Bordewich's earlier historical works are Killing the White Man's Indian: The Reinvention of Native Americans at the End of the Twentieth Century *(1999) and* Cathay: A Journey in Search of Old China *(2001). He has also published articles in* The New York Times, Smithsonian, American Heritage, *and* The Atlantic Monthly.

work, including Wilbur H. Seibert's *The Underground Railroad from Slavery to Freedom* (1898) and Larry Gara's *The Liberty Line: The Legend of the Underground Railroad* (1961). The former is the first comprehensive study of the Underground Railroad; the latter is important for disproving a prevailing "myth . . . that overemphasized the role of white Northerners" in the movement. Gara argues, and Bordewich substantiates Gara's view, that "the central figures in the history of the underground were the fugitive slaves themselves."

Bordewich's study also relies on numerous local histories of the Underground movement and biographies of heretofore unknown heroes and heroines of the movement, most published in the last decades of the twentieth century A final important antecedent to Bordewich's book is Julie Ray Jeffrey's *The Great Silent Army of Abolitionism: Ordinary Women in the Anti-Slavery Movement* (1998). Feeding and clothing fugitive slaves in the middle of the night were regular tasks for which Bordewich gives appropriate attribution in his effort to make his account of the Underground Railroad truly inclusive of all who contributed to the work of aiding fugitive slaves. Finally, Bordewich's extensive travels and research add to his broad and deep study. A bibliography acknowledges all sources.

The overall narrative is structured in two basic patterns, geographical and chronological. First, the text moves from slaveholding Southern states and territories to nonslaveholding Northern states and territories and Canada. Four maps accompany Bordewich's narrative. These are necessary tools for following the Underground Railroad's wide and ever-growing range of starting and ending points across settled areas of the United States and in Canada. A full-page map covers all geographic regions covered by the Underground Railroad from 1800 to 1850. Smaller maps detail areas of highest activity: the Philadelphia region, sites of African American settlements in Canada, and the intersecting border regions of northern Kentucky and Virginia and southern Indiana and Ohio. Second, the narrative moves chronologically, from 1800 through the Civil War, tracing the growth of the Underground Railroad against the rapid changes of a fast-growing and spreading people moving from agriculture to commerce and industrial revolution. The text records an ever-increasing numbers of slaves fleeing bondage after 1830 via the Underground Railroad as well as the heightening political debate and violent exchanges between pro- and anti-slavery advocates. There is no doubt that the Underground Railroad was a major cause of the growth in abolitionist sentiment which culminated in John Brown's violent attack at Harpers Ferry, Virginia, and the American Civil War.

Tying an exact original date and site of the Underground Railroad to facts is impossible because it was a secret system, not founded or planned in any formal way, and one which lacked corporate headquarters and leadership. The Underground Railroad was a networking system which emerged because it was needed, because slaves chose to flee their bondage and free men and women chose to help them. When did the movement take on the name Underground Railroad? No one knows. The first American railroad ran in the 1830's, three decades after the fugitive slave line began to take shape. Bordewich's best guess is that Emmor Kimber and Elijah Pennypacker, who worked on both the metaphorical and the actual railroads in the Philadelphia area, created the terminology. It was, says Bordewich, an apt metaphor with the iron railroad's "exotic new idiom" of trains, engines, lines, stations, and, of course, passengers.

Bordewich's well-written narrative interweaves historical facts with biographies of heroic participants. Some figures are familiar ones: Frederick Douglass, William Lloyd Garrison, John Brown, and Harriet Tubman. Others introduce less-known heroes: Carrit Smith, Levi and Catherine Coffin, Jermain Loguen, William Still, Josiah Hensen, Margaret Garner, Harriet Jacobs, Alexander Hensley, and more. Some are European Americans, some African Americans. All sacrificed for the sake of others, but those who did the most and risked the most were the African Americans, always in danger of capture or death. Bordewich includes stories of fugitives who were recaptured or died failing to reach the promised land of freedom, so that they and their "countless thousands" of unknown brothers and sisters "are not forgotten." Biographical materials enrich the reader's grasp of this original civil rights chapter in American history.

While providing this comprehensive study of the Underground Railroad, Bordewich reveals irony and paradox in the history of the United States in the pre-Civil War era. Irony appears in the subtitle's phrase, "the War for the Soul of America." Slavery was a troubling topic to the Founding Fathers who framed the United States Constitution in 1787. Influenced by the Enlightenment, their debate about slavery turned on moral and political arguments for liberty and equality for all. Pro-slavery forces prevailed, and if some hoped that slavery would die a natural death, post-Revolution changes proved them wrong. Eli Whitney's 1792 invention of the cotton gin and the great demand for cotton by England's factories increased the American South's demand for fresh shipments of slaves and the continuation of slavery.

Men and women who after 1800 helped fleeing slaves and founded abolitionist societies were devout Christians who read their Scripture as a mandate to act from a belief in the "equality of all souls before God." Quakers in North Carolina and Pennsylvania, whose founder, George Fox, had in the pre-Revolutionary seventeenth century urged his followers to free their slaves, were the first to work together to move fleeing slaves to freedom. Quakers endorsed nonviolence, and this spirit prevailed among the Methodists and Baptists who also became strong antislavery voices and actors in antebellum America. In an evangelical spirit these men and women declared slavery a sin against God and humanity. Zealous Christian preachers traveled from town to town, sometimes facing violent resistance, and urged their followers to join in the battle against this great evil flourishing in their midst. Converts meant new, local, religion-based antislavery societies in more and more northern locales, urban and rural. These preachers and their converts practiced their religion by providing more hands to assist fugitives from slavery running north on the Underground Railroad.

Thus the irony that shortly after the birth of the first country governed on the principle of equality, in the first nation to embrace political liberty, not these principles but religious virtue motivated post-1800 antislavery cause. While Southern slaveholders used their political strength in the nation's capital to keep northern lawmakers' hands off slavery, their opponents created the Underground Railroad as an act of righteousness, a religiously justified act of civil disobedience.

Paradox, however, complicates the religious motivation of European American workers on the Underground Railroad. Participation in the Underground Railroad was dangerous. All workers endured one or more of the following: attacks on their families and homes, assassination attempts, long nights in inclement weather waiting for the arrival of a slave fleeing over land or by water, imprisonment, and even death. Still, the majority of European Americans who aided fleeing African American slaves were racist in their view of African Americans. Although in its networking the Underground Railroad was a "model of cooperation across racial and class lines," it was not a force against racially based prejudice in America. Social equality, especially miscegenation, was opposed by most fighting for abolition; their aim for freed slaves was either separate black settlements in the United States and its territories or the slaves' return to Africa. Slavery, treating human beings as property, was a sin for Christians and wrong for African Americans or anyone; however, social separation of the races was not wrong. Bordewich takes pains to point out the rare exceptions to those who believed this. For example, European American Jonathan Walker, a heroic figure who suffered violent attacks, imprisonment, and even branding for his abolitionist activities, was not racist in his attitude toward African Americans.

Even in the free states and territories fugitives enjoyed little protection from law, lived in constant fear of recapture, with its inevitable suffering, and were oppressed by racist barriers to both economic and educational opportunities. The paradox of the oppression of even free African Americans living in such a climate explains the number of pages in the text about the many ex-slaves' choice to make the dangerous journey over Lake Erie to West Canada. Alexander Hensley escaped slavery and settled for a number of years in New Jersey. Eventually recaptured, and then freed again, he finally found his Canaan in Canada. He wrote: "When I reached English territory, I had a comfort in the law. . . . that [in Canada] a man was a man by law." The financial and educational accomplishments of African Canadian citizens surpassed any achieved by fugitive slaves in the United States. Josiah Henson, an escaped slave whose flight from Kentucky was long and difficult, finally reached Canada. A successful preacher, writer, and property owner, he founded a settlement, Dawn, for runaway slaves. Recognizing from his own struggles the importance of even basic education for free men and women, he organized and set up an educational institution which benefited many. Bordewich asserts that the fruits of the Underground Railroad were best experienced by the at least twelve thousand fugitives who settled in Canada, where, with rare exceptions, they experienced real political freedom and, if they chose, educational and economic opportunity.

The Underground Railroad's achievements make up an extraordinary chapter in American history and deserve the careful study Bordwich provides. However, by documenting also the shadow that the United States' racism casts on those achievements, he has made an invaluable contribution to an understanding of the United States in the past and in the present.

Francine Dempsey

Review Sources

American Heritage 56, no. 2 (May, 2005): 20.
Booklist 101, no. 11 (February 1, 2005): 933.
Kirkus Reviews 73, no. 2 (January 15, 2005): 94-95.
Library Journal 130, no. 2 (February 1, 2005): 95.
The Nation 280, no. 20 (May 23, 2005): 46-49.
The New Yorker 81, no. 15 (May 30, 2005): 91.
Publishers Weekly 252, no. 5 (January 31, 2005): 56.
The Wall Street Journal 245, no. 61 (March 29, 2005): D6.

BREAK, BLOW, BURN
Camille Paglia Reads Forty-three of the World's Best Poems

Author: Camille Paglia (1947-   )
Publisher: Pantheon Books (New York). 256 pp. $20.00
Type of work: Literary criticism

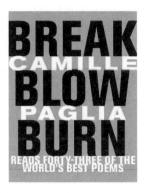

The controversial cultural critic examines an idiosyncratic selection of poems

Camille Paglia's penchant for flamboyant observations, penetrating and provocative insights, and frequent contemptuous dismissals of rival positions has resulted in her reputation as a maverick intellectual determinedly self-exiled from nearly any kind of communal school or group. In her introduction to *Break, Blow, Burn*, Paglia rails at "cliques and coteries in book and magazine publishing" and defiantly proclaims "I have no such friendships and am a propagandist for no poet or group of poets."

While she has relished this position and employed it effectively to distinguish herself among critics and commentators, it has also led to the kind of derisive response shown by Lee Siegel in his review of Paglia's reading of "Forty-three of the World's Best Poems": After acknowledging that her "polemical tome *Sexual Personae*" (1991) effectively "attacked the stale orthodoxies of both left and right," Siegel stated that "her once-gratifying affirmations of individuality, imagination and incalculable experience began to sound like playground shouts of Look at Me." In addition to his contention that her style has grown stale, her observations shrill, and her personae obnoxious, Siegel felt that the subject of her new book amounts to having "exhumed a dead herring."

This objection is at the heart of Paglia's enterprise. While Siegel regards Paglia's concerns as "alarmist" and her prospective audience a "small, rarefied group of devotees who write and/or avidly read poetry," Paglia is determined to revive what she regards as a vital human activity and reclaim for it a wider audience than Siegel identifies. In this, her dispute with Siegel is more a matter of emphasis than substance. More to the point is Siegel's description of Paglia's work as "an elementary, and exceedingly banal, primer on how to read a handful of poems from the distant and recent past."

The sneering tone of Siegel's dismissal is meant as a counterbalance to Paglia's extravagant assertions, such as her characteristic diatribe against all the faults of the critics operating under the pernicious influence that she reduces to the term "European poststructuralism" and which she castigates for its "clotted jargon, circular reasoning, and smug, debunking cynicism." However, once beyond Paglia's often entertaining but not necessarily enlightening verbal assaults on various villains, a heartfelt and seriously prepared argument emerges, initially in Paglia's explanation of how her interests and methods developed and then, most crucially, in the actual dis-

cussions of the poems that she has chosen for inclusion.

    Alternating somewhat uneasily with the at-
tacks, Paglia has presented a passionate brief for
the poems that have moved her from her earliest
days as a student through her graduate education
with esteemed authorities such as Harold Bloom,
whom she proudly claims as a mentor and then
colleague. Her introduction shifts abruptly in
tone from wrath to supplication, alternately suspicious and defensive and then open and imploring. This blend of the intimately personal and the
determinedly dialectical is an integral element of
Paglia's approach and will probably have much to do with a reader's interest in and
response to her readings. The often overwrought rhetoric that Paglia employs, like a
habit or addiction surfacing almost unbidden, gradually recedes as she builds a case
for the poems that she insists are timeless contributions to human endeavor.

    *Camille Paglia, described by her
publisher as "America's premier
intellectual provocateur," is the
author of* Sexual Personae: Art and
Decadence from Nefertiti to Emily
Dickinson *(1991) and* Vamps and
Tramps: New Essays *(1994). She is
a professor of humanities and media
studies at the University of the Arts
in Philadelphia.*

    Although Paglia is generally thought of as an ultra-contemporary observer of post-
modern phenomena—the competitor who claimed in *Vamps and Tramps* (1994) that
she had surpassed Susan Sontag as the premier "tough-cookie feminist" ("I've been
chasing that bitch for twenty-five years, and I've finally passed her.")—she has mixed
this mode with a kind of offhand semimodesty, countering what Daniel Harris called
her "racy personae as a scandalous Jezebel" with claims that for years in the 1990's
she was "just an old nun." While this might seem like a cunning strategy to disarm
some of her detractors, the introduction to *Break, Blow, Burn* reveals a previously
concealed sentimental side which Paglia has kept under wraps. Here, she is ready to
risk a sincerity unprotected by irony, confident that her position is secure enough to
withstand scrutiny—or, at least, that many of the poems which she champions are so
centered in the cultural consciousness of her readers that they will be sufficient to support her claims about and for them.

    When Paglia states in the first paragraph that her goal is "to write commentaries on
poetry that illuminate the text but also give pleasure in themselves as pieces of writing," she is placing herself within the classical tradition of commentary epitomized by
Aristotle's well-known injunction in *De poetica* (c. 334-323 B.C.E.; *Poetics*, 1705) "to
instruct and delight." When she describes her technique as a "close reading, or what
used to be called 'explication of text,'" and explains it as a "superb instrument" with
which one can "focus the mind, sharpen perception, and refine emotion," she is using
the rhetoric of the Augustan age.

    Characteristically, though, after acknowledging that this instrument is based on
the analytical methods of the New Critics of the mid-twentieth century, she asserts
that she had become impatient with their "prim evasion of the sex and aggression in
artistic creativity." As a corrective to the increasingly academic bent of the New Criticism, she cites such counterculture figures as Marshall McLuhan and Leslie Fiedler
as models of the dissident academic, respectful and aware of a tradition that now re-

quires bold and inventive strategies to remain relevant. She sees herself, a professor of humanities and media studies at the University of the Arts in Philadelphia, as a proud advocate for and practitioner of this position, prepared to reinstate the primacy of "humanistic principles and honest practical criticism" which has been supplanted in major universities by a "vain, showy professoriat" who advocate a "pretentious 'theory'—which claims to analyze language but atrociously abuses language."

In contrast to these wrong-headed professors, Paglia offers as an ideal Milton Kessler, a poet with whom she studied at Harpur College and who himself had been a student of Theodore Roethke. She fondly recalls Kessler's classes, where "emotional directness and amplitude in art" were encouraged. Even though this "intense way of reading poetry was definitely not the norm in graduate school" at Yale, the next stage in the development of her aesthetic took place there when Bloom, learning about the doctoral thesis that eventually became *Sexual Personae*, summoned her and insisted that he was "the *only* one who can direct that dissertation." Thus anointed, Paglia was prepared to bring together the diverse elements that coalesce in *Break, Blow, Burn*, including her family background with romance languages, her fascination with American vernacular speech and its connections to pop culture, the performance art and poetry slams emerging in the 1990's, and the rhythms of rock music.

To support her claims, Paglia offers a quick summary of the poetry that excited her as a student, mentioning first many of the traditional British poets whom she discusses, then noting mid-twentieth century American poets such as William Carlos Williams, Robert Lowell, and Sylvia Plath, whose poems "stunned and bewitched me when I first read them." With loving nostalgia, Paglia also evokes the halcyon days of the 1960's when she claims that "Poetry was at the height of its prestige," illustrated by a diverse litany ranging across the poetic spectrum, including Donald Justice, Robert Creeley, Richard Hugo, Muriel Rukeyser, Isabella Stewart Gardner, Adrienne Rich, and John Berryman, later Robert Lowell and Elizabeth Bishop, and then Allen Ginsberg and Gregory Corso at Yale Law School "in an event significantly not sponsored by the English Department." This personal history will undoubtedly resonate with many of Paglia's prospective readers, and her immersion in the ethos of the era is a convincing inducement to follow her as she reads the forty-three poems chosen for discussion, an odd number perhaps determined by the conspicuous singularity that Paglia prefers.

In explaining some of the reasons for her choices, Paglia says that the "canonical poems from the Renaissance through Romanticism" in the first half of the book were those that "proved most successful for me in the classroom." This reliance on the familiar is one of the reasons that Siegel defines the volume as akin to an archeological excavation. Paglia's decision to include more modern poems based on a "long search through library collections and bookstores," seems to counter her accounts of the readings that she attended, suggesting a canvassing of approved anthologies rather than a purely personal, instinctive reaction. In concluding her extensive prefatory remarks, Paglia counsels the reader to "let the poem speak," a logical result of her emphasis on sound and her pleasure at performance but a contradiction of sorts to an earlier assertion that "it's poetry on the page—a *visual* construct—that lasts." The tension between what seem to be opposite modes, though, is an aspect of the dynamic, the "ceaseless, darting energy" which Paglia finds in the poetry that "develops the imagination and feeds the soul." This is the ultimate criterion for her selections.

She begins with William Shakespeare's Sonnet 73, which Paglia offers as an example of a very traditional form still vital for the contemporary reader—not that easy an argument to make. Paglia discusses three poems by Shakespeare, three by John Donne (whose "Holy Sonnet XIV" provides the powerful title for the book), three by George Herbert, Andrew Marvell's well-known "To His Coy Mistress," two by William Blake, two by William Wordsworth, and two other often anthologized Romantic poems, Percy Bysshe Shelley's "Ozymandias" and Samuel Taylor Coleridge's "Kubla Khan," before shifting across the Atlantic to examine works by American poets Walt Whitman and Emily Dickinson. In a kind of reversion to the classical, Paglia returns to England for three poems by W. B. Yeats and then back to the United States for two by Wallace Stevens before moving toward the modern with two of William Carlos Williams's distinctly American poems, "The Red Wheelbarrow" and "This Is Just to Say."

In effect, the book is clearly divided between the curriculum that Paglia accepted and now endorses as a fundamental basis for poetic appreciation and an inevitably much more personal anthology designed to support and express the principles established by the older poems in the most engaging current forms of speech, subject, and style. In essence, this plan approximates the desire of many truly serious teachers of literature, who feel constrained by even the best anthologies and are eager to blend the poems from the distant past that make up the formation of their own poetic discourse with more recent poems that fire their spirit and enliven their minds. As such, an individual reader's response is going to depend to a considerable extent on personal preference and previous pleasure. Paglia's laudable goal of bringing relatively unfamiliar work to the reader's attention in the second section is admirable, but it is more likely that many readers will be more interested in how she handles the poets and poems that they already know. This is also likely to be the point where the most contentious responses to her critiques will occur.

For instance, both Siegel and Clive James, who found many things to praise among the essays, are disturbed that W. H. Auden is (in Siegel's words) "inexcusably absent from this slim selection." While James calls Plath's "Daddy" an "agonized masterpiece by which Paglia is driven to a stretch of critical writing that stands out for its richness even in a rich book," Siegel dismisses Paglia's essay, a highly charged and intense effort, by lumping it in a group that he criticizes for comparing poems to films. As Paglia may use but does not depend on cross-cultural comparisons, this is not a really useful way to regard her work.

A more instructive key to her method is her dense inclusion of myriad allusions drawn from her extensive, and frequently informative, grasp of a multiera intellectual history. With the canonical poems, this approach works especially well, providing a substantial context which places a poem within the conditions of its time, even as Paglia concentrates in close readings on the specific words and images of the poem. Her work with Donne's "The Flea" is a fine example, noting the resistance of Donne's wife's family to the poet's Catholicism, the theological dimensions of the Metaphysical poets, the implications of a flea as pest common to medieval life, and the connotations of the insect in intimate circumstances as a sexual surrogate. Paglia's reading of the poem as Donne's "ingenious indictment of the perennial double standard" successfully carries a work concurrent with Shakespeare's time to the present without losing its intricate exposition of its own era.

With more modern poems such as Williams's two tight lyrics, the range of allusion tends to add more weight than the poems can bear, the comparison of "The Flea" to "This Is Just to Say" a reach not required, the use of a metaphysical conceit ("the icebox is analogous to a book or poem") a distraction. Yet even in these poems, even when Paglia overreads "glazed with rain" from "The Red Wheelbarrow," expanding the terse simplicity by rephrasing it "as if sprinkled with diamonds or iced like a cake in a fairy tale," her controlling sense that the poem is about "the art of *focus*, the effort to see clearly" is sufficient to make her discussion viable.

One of the most appealing facets of the book is the way in which essay after essay provides similar insights and assertions that bring the reader to the poem and to Paglia's interpretations, declarations, and suggestions, creating an active dialogue that succeeds in keeping an ancient art alive. Whether one is delighted or infuriated (or both) by Paglia's unbridled expressions and perceptions, the book, like the author, will not go quietly to the back shelf.

Leon Lewis

Review Sources

Booklist 101, no. 11 (February 1, 2005): 916.
Commentary 120, no. 1 (July/August, 2005): 72-75.
Kirkus Reviews 73, no. 2 (January 15, 2005): 107-108.
Library Journal 130, no. 5 (March 15, 2005): 86.
The Nation 280, no. 23 (June 13, 2005): 48-52.
National Review 57, no. 8 (May 9, 2005): 43-44.
The New Leader 88, no. 2 (March/April, 2005): 33-35.
The New York Times Book Review 154 (March 27, 2005): 8-10.
Poetry 187, no. 1 (October, 2005): 47-52.
Publishers Weekly 252, no. 8 (February 21, 2005): 168.

BUDGET TRAVEL THROUGH SPACE AND TIME

Author: Albert Goldbarth (1948-   )
Publisher: Graywolf Press (St. Paul, Minn.). 162 pp.
   $14.00
Type of work: Poetry

   This dazzling and challenging volume of poetry explores a vast array of topics

   Albert Goldbarth looks at life as a complex maze, something not easily reduced. As a poet, he has thrived on the contradictions of life. Goldbarth is fascinated by the common human quest to establish connections with some people and to break connections with others. He is amused by the need to find a structure to life. In his poetry, Goldbarth throws together myriad images, facts, anecdotes, and historical perspectives. It is an understatement that Goldbarth is a challenging poet. He has a knack of gathering together obscure details in order to fill out his universe. The uninitiated reader may scratch his or her head and puzzle over where the poetic journey may lead.

   Goldbarth is the author of more than twenty volumes of poetry and several collections of essays. Two of his previous volumes have won the National Book Critics Circle Award for poetry. His poetic approach has been called postmodernist. Some of his poems can be best described as puzzles, as labyrinths for the curious and diligent reader. Every subject is fair game for Goldbarth, worth adding to the mix.

   Educated at the University of Illinois and the University of Iowa, Goldbarth published his first full-length poetry collection, *Coprolites*, in 1973. Since then, he has amazed the literary community with his output. He has stated that he strives for "a kind of shared wisdom or power" to exist "between my poems operating at their best and the best reading that can be brought to them." Goldbarth clearly recognizes the special bond that can be established between reader and poet. Any truth that can be culled from a poem becomes possible only when the "good reader" and the poem that was "so well written" intersect. Goldbarth believes intensely in the "integrity to the written word." The good reader must be able to absorb what is on the page.

   Goldbarth searches for connections in odd places, between strange items, things that are in seemingly unrelated orbits but in the end are linked by the human condition. For him, "the universe is nothing but incomprehensible multilayers." He can be looked at as an archaeologist or a private detective, a sleuth for the ages. A Goldbarth creation is packed with details. For him, individuals are "all a thousand things at once." People and the universe are "multiplicitous." It is as if he has plucked elements out of the air like a magician, has unearthed a lost civilization like a dedicated scientist. A Goldbarth reader must love becoming immersed in the surroundings. There is no fast in and out, poem understood, point made. If Goldbarth can dig, collect, gather together, then his readers must be willing to do the same.

~

*Albert Goldbarth has won numerous
literary awards, including the
National Book Critics Circle Award
for poetry on two occasions. He is
the author of more than twenty
volumes of poetry, a number of
collections of essays, and a novel.*

~

Over his career, Goldbarth has been extraordinarily productive. *Budget Travel Through Space and Time* is his twenty-third volume of poetry, and it is no less complex than all of his previous volumes. It is divided into nine sections. Most of the sections contain four or five poems. Three of the sections, the first, fifth, and ninth, are named "Space and Time." Sections 4 and 7 are titled "Through History on Pennies a Day," with 4 subtitled "1" and 7 subtitled "2." The collection opens with the poem "Budget Travel Through the Universe." As Goldbarth's poetry primarily is written for the peruser, the casual reader may immediately recoil and seek refuge elsewhere. The first line of the title poem makes the bold statement "We can rig a supernova in a single laptop jiffy." This certainly is an intriguing concept, and the curious reader will continue down the page with eager anticipation of what comes next. Toward the end of the second stanza, the poet lets the reader understand that "It turns out we can travel assuredly through time/ by simply sitting in our chairs or on the floor/ and making lazy conversation. Just by having/ a metabolism, we can voyage into the future." By the end of the poem, the poet is left breathless by the journey, "changed for a moment" and "beached on a foreign shore."

The second section of the collection appropriately is titled "A Trip to the Country of Crazy, and Back." It always has been Goldbarth's approach to take the reader on a journey to somewhere far beyond the ordinary, beyond any semblance of normalcy. The images in this section can be startling, as is the following from the poem "A Knife Through the Head (Your Distresses and Mine)":

> One man, in a stellarscape of novas and cankered planets,
> displays his asshole as if it's a ring on a white silk pillow:
> eyes spew out. One woman is nothing but a red penny-sized dot.

The poem ends with "it's only one more/ room in the world of a thousand selves of the one self." In a sense, this is a precise way to describe Goldbarth himself. He is at least a thousand selves wrapped into one, but this is something he would say is true for everyone. Humans, the universe, everything has too many faces to count, but Goldbarth will not go away without giving the exercise a brilliant attempt. As a poet he is also philosopher, scientist, historian, explorer, inventor, and more. Always seeming to relish the telling of a good yarn or tall tale, as long as something can be learned by its telling, the poet uncovers truth wherever it may hide. Goldbarth is certainly of the viewpoint that someone can learn just as much from an everyday experience as from some lofty profound one.

As the poet sees it, good ideas can be found under every proverbial rock. Over the years, though, some critics have taken issue with Goldbarth's approach to poetry. It has been argued by some that his poetry really is nothing more than a bunch of lists and that all the dazzling wordplay adds up to very little. The idea of everything being interconnected, therefore, becomes nothing more than an elaborate smokescreen.

Goldbarth is one of America's most learned and prolific poets. It can be argued that he has been prolific and learned to a fault. He is a poet who needs to be revisited, to be savored, and yet he continues to produce volume after volume. In sheer output, he has been compared to the amazingly prolific American novelist Joyce Carol Oates. For some in the literary community, the comparison is more a complaint then a compliment. The critics seem to be asking Goldbarth to better manage his literary career, to not oversaturate the market. In reality, writers cannot think this way. For more than thirty years, Goldbarth has felt inspired to write long poems, to sew together his multilayered visions of the world. It is unlikely that he will be giving up his quest to make sense of what is around him anytime soon.

The last section of *Budget Travel Through Space and Time* opens with the poem "Three Days: Three Sections." In the first stanza, Goldbarth lets the reader know that "It's a thousand years after the last real city" and that "Humanity is nomadic again, is scattered bands/ with collapsible tents." The nomads come across "the remains/ of a cloverleafed freeway." With this remarkable discovery, the nomads hope that by following the route of the freeway that it will be possible for the glorious past to be "regained." By the end of the stanza, it is revealed that "For now, their chosen task is preparedness." Goldbarth emphasizes the necessity for patience, for being prepared for every eventuality. The last stanza informs the reader that waiting "is what this poem is about" and that there is beauty in the very act of waiting. The poet is not about to promise instant gratification. If anything is to be gained by reading poetry, it only will come through the methodical, line-by-line reading of what has been put on the page.

A Goldbarth poem can be as exhausting as it is exhilarating. Although similarities can be found in each Goldbarth collection, he does not look back at what came before, instead blazing a new trail. Within each new collection, he constructs unique labyrinths that stimulate him as well as those who make up the family of his devoted readers. Goldbarth believes in the "power of books to save some individual life out there." It is obvious that he will not give up his attempt to connect with the good readers of the world. While Goldbarth is not naïve enough to think that a book alone can have a major impact on culture at large, he still remains a poet who strives to make a difference in one person's life.

Budget Travel Through Space and Time is one of Goldbarth's most challenging collections. The reader will be introduced to William Herschel constructing a telescope out of horse manure in the eighteenth century, to the migratory patterns of Arctic terns, to American colonial history, to the Paleolithic era, and much more. The collection can be thought of as an 162-page jigsaw puzzle. Goldbarth once again has done his part to write with extraordinary fervor and can only hope now that this collection will be picked up and closely read by one good reader, and from one good reader the collection will be shared with an ever-expanding number of devotees who are willing to take the journey through space and time.

Jeffry Jensen

Review Sources

Booklist 101, no. 12 (February 15, 2005): 1053.
Library Journal 130, no. 3 (February 15, 2005): 134-135.
Poetry 186 (June, 2005): 260.
Publishers Weekly 252, no. 10 (March 7, 2005): 66.

BURY THE CHAINS
Prophets and Rebels in the Fight to Free an Empire's Slaves

Author: Adam Hochschild (1942-   )
Publisher: Houghton Mifflin (New York). 468 pp. $26.95
Type of work: History
Time: About 1740 to 1838
Locale: England, Africa, the Caribbean region, and the
    Atlantic Ocean

The movement to end the slave trade in the British Em-
pire grew from the efforts of a small group of people

> *Principal personages:*
> JOHN NEWTON (1725-1807), a seaman and
>   English slave ship captain, who wrote the
>   hymn "Amazing Grace"
> OLAUDAH EQUIANO (c. 1745-1797), a for-
>   mer slave, antislavery activist, and author
> GRANVILLE SHARP (1735-1813), an early British abolitionist and
>   cofounder of the movement to abolish the British slave trade
> THOMAS CLARKSON (1760-1845), a crusader against slavery who
>   brought the influential William Wilberforce into the antislavery
>   movement
> WILLIAM WILBERFORCE (1759-1833), a member of the British Parlia-
>   ment who devoted much of his career to abolishing the slave trade and
>   slavery
> JAMES STEPHEN (1758-1832), a lawyer and later member of the British
>   Parliament who spent his youth in the Caribbean region and became
>   an important strategist for the movement against slavery

Slavery, Adam Hochschild observes at the beginning of *Bury the Chains*, was a normal and accepted condition around the world at the middle of the eighteenth century. Many civilizations, from the beginning of history, had held slaves. The African slave trade, moreover, had become a huge business for Europeans over the previous three centuries. Profits from the trade built many of the elegant buildings in London and elsewhere in England. Even the Church of England was deeply involved in a business that depended on violently seizing innocent people, imprisoning them in horrific conditions on ships, and condemning them to short lifetimes of forced labor.

Hochschild illustrates just how normal slavery was considered by most people in eighteenth century England by weaving the biography of John Newton through the story of the struggle against the slave trade. As a young man, Newton had been seized by a naval press gang in his era's version of the military draft. After managing to get out of service with the Royal Navy by being exchanged in a swap of seamen with a slave ship, Newton entered years of involvement with African slavery. Wild and rambunctious as a youth, he later experienced a religious conversion. Christianity did not

⌇

Adam Hochschild has written for numerous major newspapers and magazines, and he was one of the cofounders of the magazine Mother Jones. *He has published five previous books, including* King Leopold's Ghost: A Story of Greed, Terror, and Heroism in Colonial Africa *(1999). Hochschild teaches writing in the Graduate School of Journalism at the University of California at Berkeley.*

⌇

turn him away from dealing in human beings any more than it did the Church of England, though, and when he became the captain of a slave ship, Newton would gather his crew for prayer daily while delivering slaves to America. Only near the end of his life, in 1788, twenty-four years after becoming ordained as an Anglican Evangelical deacon and after gaining fame as an evangelical preacher did Newton publicly denounce the immorality and the brutality of slavery. This belated recognition of evil was sixteen years after Newton wrote one of the most famous hymns of the English language, "Amazing Grace."

Newton's second conversion, to opposition to the slave trade, came as part of the rise of an antislavery campaign which had begun with the meeting of a dozen men on May 22, 1787. Granville Sharp, an eccentric musician and pamphleteer, had already become known as the chief legal defender of black people claiming their freedom in London. Thomas Clarkson, a young recent Cambridge scholar, had taken up the cause of abolition after writing a prize-winning Latin essay on slavery two years earlier. At the meeting in 1787, Sharp, Clarkson, and another Anglican joined together with a committee of nine Quakers to begin the long fight to end the buying and selling of humans on British territory.

Hochschild acknowledges the importance of the Quakers to the antislavery movement. Their unyielding insistence on their own religious guidelines, however, prevented Quakers from engaging in such ordinary social practices as removing their hats in greeting, addressing nobles as "my lord," and using names of days of the week derived from pagan gods. This prevented them from working effectively with authorities. Therefore, they took on non-Quaker spokesmen such as Clarkson and Sharp. The relative anonymity of the Quakers has led Hochschild to give relatively little close scrutiny to their work and to concentrate on the personalities and efforts of the spokesmen. This is understandable but unfortunate because the movement probably could not have progressed at all without the Quakers.

One of the central actors who was not at the meeting was an African who became known as Olaudah Equiano. This impressive individual had learned to read and write as a slave and had earned the money to purchase his own freedom. He became a public speaker and a writer, giving lectures and publishing newspaper articles against slavery. In 1786, a year before the meeting, he had published his autobiography. Claiming to have been born in Africa, Equiano gave white readers one of the first inside views of the lives of slaves, and helped the English public see enslaved people of African ancestry as human beings. Equiano, like the later Frederick Douglass, offered undeniable evidence that brilliance, and not just humanity, could be packaged in any shade of skin.

Another activist who did not attend the meeting was James Stephen, a lawyer who had lived in the Caribbean region and seen firsthand the deadly brutality of life on sugar plantations. Later, as an attorney in London and an adviser to members of Parliament, Stephen helped to develop strategies that would bring British lawmakers gradually behind legislation that would limit the slave trade. One of the members of Parliament with whom Stephen worked closely was a man whose name became almost synonymous with the fight against slavery, William Wilberforce. Wilberforce, an intensely religious and socially conservative member of Parliament, was recruited for the fight against slavery by Clarkson in the spring of 1787. For years, Wilberforce would introduce legislation against the slave trade. As a result, he made the deepest mark on historical memory. One of the virtues of Hochschild's book is that he reminds the reader that Wilberforce was not the sole or even the most important of the early British antislavery activists.

The fight against the slave trade did have its strange events. One of these was the founding of a colony for freed black people in Africa's Sierra Leone, a project in which Granville Sharp was deeply involved. Slaves who had fought for the British against the American war for independence were settled there, and Sharp and others saw the colonization of Africa by freed slaves as a possible answer to the question of what to do with the newly freed people. The colony was plagued by constant troubles, and today it seems troublesome that those opposed to slavery would feel the need to send black people anywhere. Still, Hochschild sees some positive implications even in this attempt. As the colony was to involve black people in their own governance, in spite of oversight by white people, it was a recognition that black people were capable of running their own affairs.

After Parliament defeated one of the abolition bills, in 1791, the program of the small committee that had met just a few years earlier became a mass movement. More than three hundred thousand people joined in a boycott of sugar grown by slaves, despite the dependance of the British on sugar to sweeten their other relatively recent addiction, tea. Other committees against slavery began to spring up at this time. Hochschild makes a convincing argument that the British were acting against their own economic interests, as well as against their own tastes in consumption, in joining together to end dealing in slaves. The effort against slavery was based on moral grounds, he maintains, and it gained momentum through the energies and strategies of those with moral convictions. It was not, in his view, simply a matter of ideology reflecting economic interests.

With the war against France from the end of the eighteenth century through the first fifteen years of the nineteenth, the antislave-trade movement experienced setbacks as radical, and even liberal ideas, became suspect. Many of those who supported freedom for slaves also supported greater political freedom for white Europeans and this led some, such as Clarkson, to be early supporters of the French Revolution. As France became the enemy, French ideas became widely seen as dangerous and subversive. Still, some of the antislavery activists managed to find ways to further their cause by identifying with British patriotism. In 1806, James Stephen masterminded the Foreign Slave Trade Act, which banned British subjects from engaging in the slave trade to colonies of France or French allies. As Stephen knew, many of the slave ships flying under the American flag were actually owned and manned by Britons, and his bill quietly cut off two thirds of the British slave trade.

Slave uprisings in the West Indies contributed to popular discontent with slavery. By 1807, Parliament passed a law banning the slave trade. Although slavery would continue on British soil, no new slaves would be legally imported. A year later, the United States also banned the importation of slaves. However, after it had become illegal to bring slaves into virtually all the English-speaking world, slavery itself continued to exist. The men who met in 1787 had been appalled by the brutality of the shipping of slaves, but they had never seen stopping the trade as the ultimate goal. Instead, ending the forced migration of men and women from Africa to the Americas was only a first step toward their ultimate goal, the abolition of slavery.

The ultimate goal seemed to be achieved when Parliament passed an emancipation bill in 1833. While Parliament set up steps for freeing slaves in British territory, though, it did so in terms that were much more generous to the slave owners than to the slaves themselves. Slave owners received monetary compensation for their lost property, much of which ended up in the hands of London bankers who held mortgages on Caribbean plantations. The slaves themselves were to become unpaid apprentices to their former owners and would only gain freedom after several years. British slavery did not ultimately end until August 1, 1838. By then, Clarkson was the only one of the antislavery activists still alive.

Hochschild provides a fascinating history of the origins and spread of the antislavery movement in Britain. He draws vivid portraits of the main actors and conveys the often complex historical events of the movement with clarity. While some social historians may be skeptical of the type of personality-driven history offered here, the concentration on individuals helps to make the narrative engaging and to show the human side of history. Hochschild may occasionally be a little anachronistic in connecting the fight against slavery to contemporary social justice movements. Nevertheless, he makes a compelling argument for the view that wide-scale social action can begin with the convictions of a few people. He also gives readers an understanding of how both West Indian slave uprisings and political reform in England combined with social action to bring an end to British slavery.

Carl L. Bankston III

Review Sources

Booklist 101, no. 1 (September 1, 2004): 2.
The Christian Science Monitor 97 (January 11, 2005): 15-16.
The Economist 374 (February 5, 2005): 76-77.
Kirkus Reviews 72, no. 21 (November 1, 2004): 1038-1039.
Library Journal 129, no. 19 (November 15, 2004): 70-71.
The Nation 280, no. 6 (February 14, 2005): 23-29.
The New York Times Book Review 154 (January 9, 2005): 1-11.
Publishers Weekly 252, no. 1 (January 3, 2005): 48.

CAMPO SANTO

Author: W. G. Sebald (1944-2001)
Translated from the German by Anthea Bell
Publisher: Random House (New York). 220 pp. $25.00
Type of work: Essays
Time: 1975-2001
Locale: Germany, Corsica, Great Britain

This posthumous volume of essays collects excerpts from a larger work on Corsica as well as pieces on literary figures, book reviews, and literary and cultural criticism

Winfried Georg Maximilian Sebald was born in Allgäu in the southern region of Bavaria in Germany. He grew up in Wertach, a Alpine village which was predominately Roman Catholic. His father, Georg Sebald was a professional soldier, having joined the army prior to 1933 when Adolf Hitler took power. Because of his military profession he was away from home a great deal, fought in World War II, and was interned in France for some time after the war. He rejoined the military when the new German army was established in 1953. In later years Sebald said that his maternal grandfather, Josef Engelhofer, largely brought him up.

Sebald went to school in Immenstadt and Obersdorf and attended the University of Freiburg, where he concentrated on German literature and earned a Licence des Lettres in 1966. Also, he studied French literature in Switzerland. He later taught both subjects. Following his graduation from Freiburg he accepted a position at the University of Manchester in England, beginning his long residence in the United Kingdom. For a year, after receiving a master's degree in German literature in 1968, he taught elementary school in St. Gallen in Switzerland. In 1969 he returned to Manchester, and, except for a year at the Goethe Institute in Munich in 1975 to 1976, he remained in England for the rest of his life, teaching French and German literature at the University of East Anglia in Norwich, where he became a professor in 1987.

Although he eventually became best known as a novelist and essayist, his literary career began with the prose poem *Nach der Natur: Ein Elementargedicht* (1988; *After Nature*, 2002), published in Germany. The poem won the Fedor-Malchow Prize for lyric poetry in 1991 and established Sebald's literary reputation. Although he spent most of his adult life living and working in England, Sebald wrote his literary works in German, and they were subsequently translated into English. His first novel, *Schwindel: Gefühle* (1990; *Vertigo*, 1999) was also well received and was followed during the next ten years by three more. His final novel, *Austerlitz* (2001), won a number of literary prizes both in England and in the United States. He also continued to write poetry. His last collection, *For Years Now*, a book of twenty-three poems in English, was published in 2001.

～

W. G. Sebald was born in Germany and studied German literature and language in Germany, Switzerland, and England. For thirty years he taught at the University of East Anglia in Norwich, England. From 1989 to 1994, he was the first director of the British Centre for Literary Translation. His works won a number of awards, including the National Book Critics Circle Award, the Los Angeles Times Book Award, the Berlin Literature Prize, and the Literature Nord Prize. He was also a member of the Collegium of the German Academy. He died in December, 2001.

～

Although Sebald became an accomplished novelist and poet, his first published work was a critical study of a German writer, *Carl Sternheim: Kritiker und Opfer der Wilhelminischen Ära* (Carl Sternheim: critic and victim of the Wilhelminian era) in 1969. Sebald went on to write or edit six more books of literary and social essays.

Sebald's reputation has been largely confined to the literary privileged. Although he did gain a wider audience as his works were translated into English, they have remained an acquired taste. However, his place in modern letters is a substantial one, and the critics have uniformly praised him as one of the masters of contemporary prose. His novels are now seen as reflecting a major development in European literature, and he has been credited with the invention of what has been described as a field of "documentary fiction." His critical works are landmark efforts in experimental prose.

Sebald's writing has been praised for his scope of cultural and historical knowledge, for his exacting power of its description, for his skill at unifying multiple narrative threads, and for his ability to relate the subjective expression with objective representation. Among his more prominent themes are the human struggle with nature, the burden of personal depression, the relationship between individual talent and society, and the unreliable and autonomous nature of memory. He has developed these ideas by crossing the boundaries in his prose among various types of writing, documentary, fiction, dream diaries, historical record, travelogue, elegy, and case studies. His writing frequently is organized around a series of oppositions: the surreal and the realistic, the melancholy and the hopeful, and the beautiful and the destructive. This all leads to a style that is both disquieting and reassuring.

Sebald's writing comes out of his experience in postwar Germany, a country devastated by the war and wracked by guilt, although often unacknowledged, over the havoc originating from the expansionist and racial policies of National Socialism. Sebald left his native country because of its failure to come to grips with its responsibility for the suffering—including its own—caused by World War II and its destruction of European civilization which caused the deaths of millions. The effects of this experience are evident in his writings in the intertwining of the past and present, the interplay of memory, and the autumnal and elegiac tone of much of his work.

Campo Santo is a posthumous collection of essays, chronologically arranged, including several pieces that had been previously published in a larger work on the island of Corsica. The second part of the collection includes critical pieces primarily on literary topics. The earliest is on Peter Handke's play *Kaspar* (1968) from 1975, which is followed by essays from the 1990's on Ernst Herbeck, Vladimir Nabokov,

Franz Kafka, Jan Peter Tripp, and Bruce Chatwin. There are two speeches on the opening of the Munich Opera Festival and on the Stuttgart House of Literature. Finally, there is also the speech Sebald gave accepting membership in the German Academy for Language and Literature.

The first section of the book contains four essays from Sebald's unfinished work on Corsica: "A Little Excursion to Ajaccio," "Campo Santo," "The Alps in the Sea," and "*La cour de l'ancienne école.*" In one way or another, all these essays compare the island's past with its present. Ajaccio was the birthplace of the emperor Napoleon, and Sebald visited the town and the Musée Fesch. Joseph Fesch was Napoleon's stepuncle, an ecclesiastic, and art collector. The museum contains both his art collection and some Napoleon mementos. Finally, Sebald went to the Casa Napoleon. The essay provides an occasion for Sebald to reflect not only on Napoleon and on Gustave Flaubert, who wrote about his visit to Corsica, but also to reflect on history itself.

"Campo Santo" details his meditations on death and the effects it has on the survivors during his walk through one of the island's cemeteries. "The Alps in the Sea" is a reflective piece on the once-forested hills of Corsica and the hunting that took place there, both now much diminished by time and human destruction. The final essay contains a brief discourse on a photo of an old school of Porto Vecchio sent to Sebald by one of his correspondents from a previous stay on Corsica.

The second part of *Campo Santo* contains a dozen essays mostly on literary figures who have interested Sebald or influenced him in various ways. "Strangeness, Integration, and Crisis" is on Handke's play *Kaspar* and about human communication and the function of language in the definition of self. Sebald was interested in the effects of World War II on the German people, and his themes of destruction, memory, and mourning arose largely from this interest. "Between History and Natural History: On the Literary Description of Total Destruction" offers a good summary of these ideas through his analysis of the writers, Hans Erich Nossack, Hermann Kasack, and Alexander Kluge, the postwar Germans who most forcefully addressed, in different ways, what Sebald calls the murder of memory experienced after the war.

"Constructs of Mourning" continues this examination through a discussion of Alexander and Margarete Mitscherlich's theory of the inability to mourn and the writers Heinrich Böll and Günther Grass. Sebald writes movingly in this essay about the issues of guilt, responsibility, and conscience. Ernst Herbeck spent most of his life in a mental hospital writing strange poetry which Sebald found especially evocative of the times. "*Das Häschens Kind, der kleine Has* (The Little Hare, Child of the Hare)" contains his meditations on this odd poet's work.

There are two essays on modernist writer Franz Kafka: "To the Brothel by Way of Switzerland" and "Kafka Goes to the Movies." The former is on a trip Kafka made with his friend and literary executor, Max Brod, from Prague to Paris via Switzerland and northern Italy during August and September, 1911. The latter essay is a book review of and commentary on Hanns Zischler's *Kafka geht ins Kino* (1996; *Kafka Goes to the Movies*, 2003), a study of the influence of films on Kafka's work. Sebald describes most academic criticism of Kafka as tedious and unhelpful to understanding the work and the man. Zischler's book is an exception. Rather than a plodding study of literary theorists, *Kafka Goes to the Movies* is well written and engagingly speculative about Kafka's interest in, and literary debt to, films.

Sebald's chapter "Dream Textures" discusses Nabokov's autobiography *Speak, Memory* (1966) and provides Sebald an occasion to talk about Nabokov's style and his position as an exile from his native Russia. Exile became one of Sebald's often recurring themes, one that he felt keenly, being an exile himself. The literary essays are rounded out by a short piece on the photographs of Jan Peter Tripp, "*Scomber scombrus*, or the Common Mackerel" which contains two pictures by Tripp, which Sebald dissects. The use of illustrative material often is featured in Sebald's writing, and he used such material as a jumping-off point for his speculations on a variety of issues.

"The Mystery of the Red-Brown Skin," subtitled "An Approach to Bruce Chatwin," explores an author who appealed to Sebald's fascination with unconventional prose writing, especially that which combines the autobiographical with the historical in new and startling ways. In Chatwin's writing Sebald found a kindred soul, a writer who traveled widely, made copious use of his own biography, and experimented in his prose.

Campo Santo is rounded out with three short occasional speeches: "*Moments musicaux*" on the opening of the Munich Opera Festival, "An Attempt at Restitution" written for the opening of the Stuttgart House of Literature, and "Acceptance Speech to the Collegium of the German Academy," occasioned by Sebald's joining that institution.

Sebald is not well known in the United States, and this collection of his essays, speeches, and excerpts from his work on Corsica offers a good introduction. Most of his recurring themes are presented here: his sense of exile, his conflicting feelings about his native country and its amnesia about its recent past, his interest in language and its uses, and his preoccupation with memory and history as filtered through the writer's autobiography. Here, too, is a fine selection from which to glean something of Sebald's lucid but challenging style as an essayist. For readers unfamiliar with his work, *Campo Santo* is a good place to start.

Charles L. P. Silet

Review Sources

Booklist 101, no. 11 (February 1, 2005): 931.
The Economist 374 (March 5, 2005): 81-82.
Kirkus Reviews 73, no. 1 (January 1, 2005): 44.
Library Journal 130, no. 3 (February 15, 2005): 130.
The New Republic 233, no. 4 (July 25, 2005): 32-37.
The New York Review of Books 52, no. 13 (August 11, 2005): 30-32.
The New York Times Book Review 154 (April 3, 2005): 12.
Publishers Weekly 252, no. 7 (February 14, 2005): 68.
The Spectator 297 (February 26, 2005): 40-42.
The Wilson Quarterly 29, no. 2 (Spring, 2005): 120.

CARNIVORE DIET

Author: Julia Slavin
Publisher: W. W. Norton (New York). 299 pp. $24.00
Type of work: Novel
Time: 2005
Locale: Washington, D.C.

Slavin's first novel is the wildly inventive tale of the Dunleavy family and a mythical carnivorous beast called the chagwa who stalks the suburbs of Washington, D.C., looking for prey

Principal characters:
> DYLAN DUNLEAVY, a fourteen-year-old boy who for the previous three years has been the voice of the most popular cartoon figure in the United States
>
> HARLAN, a postapocalyptic rodent cartoon character played by Dylan
>
> WENDY DUNLEAVY, Dylan's mother
>
> MATT DUNLEAVY, Dylan's father, a U.S. congressman serving time in prison for bribery
>
> BEN SOTTERBERG, a hyperliberal political activist who breaks women's hearts
>
> THE HARLANS, a group of young men who played Harlan in the past before their voices changed
>
> BILLY, a sadistic former Harlan charged with driving Dylan from his home to the studio
>
> PETER ALLINGHAM, Wendy's former lover, who renounces modern life
>
> RAHIM WILSON, a star basketball player
>
> THE CHAGWA, a mythical carnivorous beast that roams the streets of suburban Washington, D.C., looking for prey

Author Julia Slavin switched careers in 1992 when she left New York City where she had been working as a television producer, moved to Washington, D.C., and reinvented herself as a writer of fiction. In 1999 she published her first book, a collection of stories with the unlikely title *The Woman Who Cut Off Her Leg at the Maidstone Club.* The book was well received, earning for Slavin a following among readers who appreciated her hip, quirky tales of love in the postmodern age. Those readers who have been impatiently waiting for Slavin's second book will not be disappointed in her novel *Carnivore Diet.*

Slavin sets the novel in suburban Washington, D.C., in something like the present day; however, the world of *Carnivore Diet* is slightly askew, a surreal parallel present in which a senator holds a funeral for his amputated leg, most of the population is addicted to a tranquilizer called Solisan, the hospital is called Our Lady of Incumbency, and a dangerous beast wanders the streets. While Slavin's factual details about the locale are accurate and realistic, there is nonetheless an aura of the magical and mythical in the

Julia Slavin is the author of The
Woman Who Cut Off Her Leg at
the Maidstone Club *(1999), a*
New York Times *Notable Book.
She has won numerous
prestigious literary awards for
her short fiction.* Carnivore Diet
*is her first novel. She lives with
her family in Washington, D.C.*

writing. Indeed, it is hard definitively to label this
book; part parody, part allegory, part slick comedy,
and part family drama, the magically real *Carnivore Diet* defies classification. It is both drop-dead
funny and deeply troubling, often at the same time.

The novel opens with a prologue describing the
birth of the mythological creature known as the
Chagawanadon, created from the pearl of a dragon
and the ambition of a human. Next, the novel
moves to a narration from the point of view of
Dylan Dunleavy, a fourteen-year-old on the brink of
puberty whose incipient voice change will quickly
end his career as the voice of the United States'
most-watched cartoon character, Harlan, a "post
apocalyptic rodent of questionable phylum." Ironically, Harlan's life is more secure and happier than
is the life of Dylan Dunleavy. Dylan has much to
worry him: His father, a congressman from Can-
ton, Ohio, is serving a term in a federal prison for
bribery. His mother, Wendy, is addicted to tranquilizers. He is being terrorized by a former voice
of Harlan, Billy, who now serves as his driver. As
if all of this is not enough, bodies have been found in Ruth Bay, Dylan's neighborhood, their torsos missing, their faces fixed in expressions of abject terror.

Sitting on the front porch with his head in his mother's lap, Dylan first spies the
chagwa: the beast has "black eyes the size of softballs, the two sides of his face not
even vaguely similar, gashes of stripes on one side, bludgeons of spots on the other, a
nose triangular on one side, smashed on the other. . . . He was bigger and more horrible than I could have imagined, a five-hundred pound knife with paws." Oddly,
although the beast approaches closely enough to take Dylan's hand in its mouth,
Wendy does not notice him.

Wendy, who narrates the next section of the novel, has her own set of problems.
With the imprisonment of her husband, Matt, she finds it difficult to find the money to
provide food for herself and Dylan. She finds it even more difficult to keep herself
supplied with tranquilizers made necessary by the terror she endures because of the
chagwa's fascination with her son. Her gynecologist will only supply prescriptions if
she participates in demonstrations for animal rights and women's issues. In addition,
her lover Peter Allingham has renounced their affair, choosing to commit to the reality television show *Colonial World* with his wife. He goes to live in a settlement that
replicates colonial Jamestown, complete with a war with Indians. As Peter explains to
Wendy, "At first we got along. Then they began to resent us. They burned down the
commons two weeks ago and now we're on full-alert, twenty-four hour watch. . . .
Who can blame them? Gold Street cancels *Indian Territory* after five episodes and
builds Jamestown on top of the sacred ground."

Meanwhile, the chagwa terrorizes the Dunleavy home nightly, and Wendy must find raw meat to keep it from breaking into her house and eating Dylan. She even gives it a whole box of Omaha Steaks. Looking for help with her situation, Wendy finally turns to Ben Sotterberg, an ultraliberal political expert who is fascinated with the chagwa and who is followed by weeping women whose hearts he has broken. Ben tells Wendy about the Carnivore Diet, "an entire ground cow with some vitamins thrown in" as a way to satiate the beast at the door.

When Wendy mistakenly takes a handful of uppers instead of downers, she finds herself in a paranoid, hallucinatory state. She also finds herself committed to the psychiatric ward of Our Lady of Incumbency hospital, separated from the son she so desperately wants to protect.

The story returns to Dylan, who must now fend for himself. A crew of former Harlans joins him, as does the basketball star Rahim Wilson. When the boys are caught stealing a pony to feed to the chagwa, they are arrested. The Harlans get a boot-camp-like sentence, while Rahim gets hard time in jail. Meanwhile, the chagwa continues to menace the city. This part of the book seems deadly serious, in spite of odd and quirky moments. The letters that Dylan and his mother write to each other are particularly poignant as each tries to get around the rule about not writing anything sad or upsetting. In addition, Dylan, suffering an injury from the chagwa, continues to decline in health and morale. Underlying the entire novel, and nowhere more than here, is the anxiety of life in the present age, an age that is beset with problems, lies, and fear.

The book ends with a bang: All the characters (including Wendy, who has been released from her treatment program, and Matt, who is out of prison) meet in Washington, along with the entire United States military, bent on destroying the chagwa. Although they pulverize all the major monuments on the Mall, they do not succeed in killing the beast. The chagwa, injured, nevertheless works magic on Dylan, restoring him to health. Wendy follows the beast into the forest until she is lost, just as the book closes.

While at times, Slavin gets carried away by her own talent, sometimes veering off into silliness and sometimes into self-indulgent slickness, she is generally in control of her material. She has an ear for the inside-the-Beltway patois, providing her characters with dialogue both parodic and nuanced. Her powers of description are likewise on target. At a party, for example, Wendy sees someone she recognizes:

> From the center of the patio came the booming voice of Coleman Burke, former deputy undersecretary of Money. Sycophants hanging on every word surrounded him. A man with something to say and plenty of airtime to say it, he kept the crowd enthralled. His secret of attracting attention and respect by stating the obvious suddenly dawned on me.
>
> "With eaRRRly intervention," Coleman said, "we can arreSSSt problems befoRRRe they become cataSSStrophes."
>
> "Do you hear what he's doing?" I whispered to Nuke. "Listen. He annunciates his consonants. It's brilliant."

Although it would be easy to let her characters become one-dimensional tools for her Washington allegory, Slavin creates both Dylan and Wendy with surprising depth. Dylan is heartbreaking in his anguish over losing his job, his disappointment in his father, his love for Rahim, and his sympathy for his mother. This is a child any mother would want to take home. Wendy, although strung out on drugs and engaging in affairs with men, is nevertheless sympathetic. Her dogged determination to save her son from the chagwa speaks of a mother's unflinching courage. Further, Dylan's need for his mother's love and care while trying hard to be an adult is a touching portrait. In all, these characters exhibit some very real human concerns: How should people act in an age of uncertainty? How can people find and give love? How can they make human connections when everything else that has traditionally given meaning to life seems shaky?

While this novel is both funny and surreal, there is nonetheless a dark, brooding side to it as well. The chagwa's presence is always felt, even when the beast is not on the page. There is underlying tension in the book, created by the chagwa's mythic origins as well as its ability to sprout new eyes and change from male to female. It is a truly horrifying creature, unpredictable and deadly. Slavin's vision of American life is likewise troubling. Although she successfully satirizes life inside the Beltway, she also suggests that American leaders are neither wise nor compassionate. As Wendy reports, describing the time in which she lives,

> We were unable to go to the market without sedatives, unable to sleep without meds. . . .
> In our peripheral vision we saw [the chagwa] and the smallest sounds made us jump. . . .
> We developed facial tics and worry lines. We got our priorities straight. We fixed up our homes, renewed old connections, then remembered why we'd broken those connections and ended them again.

There is unlikely to be a neutral response to *Carnivore Diet*. Readers who want straightforward plot and characterization with a realistic setting will probably find this book to be a surreal nightmare. More adventurous readers will love the roller-coaster ride of Slavin's prose and luxuriate in her turn of phrase. Certainly, however, all readers will take from the book a sense of both the humor and the nightmare of modern life, the intuition of the chagwa lurking just outside the field of vision.

Diane Andrews Henningfeld

Review Sources

Booklist 101, nos. 19/20 (June 1, 2005): 1757.
Elle 20, no. 11 (July, 2005): 60.
Kirkus Reviews 73, no. 8 (April 15, 2005): 447.
Library Journal 130, no. 12 (July 1, 2005): 71.
The New York Times, August 28. 2005, section 7, p. 18.
The New York Times Book Review 154 (August 28, 2005): 18.
Publishers Weekly 252, no. 22 (May 30, 2005): 35.
The Seattle Times, August 14, 2005, p. K7.
The Washington Post Book World, July 17, 2005, p. T02.

A CHANGED MAN

Author: Francine Prose (1947-   )
Publisher: HarperCollins (New York). 421 pp. $25.00
Type of work: Novel
Time: Spring, 2001
Locale: New York

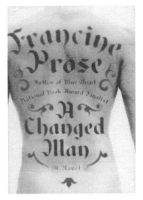

This comedy of manners focuses on a neo-Nazi skin-head who wants to change his life, a Holocaust survivor who decides to help him, and a single mother whose life is changed by the two of them

> *Principal characters:*
> VINCENT NOLAN, a skinhead who wants to change his life
> MEYER MASLOW, a famous Holocaust survivor and director of the World Brotherhood Watch foundation
> IRENE MASLOW, his wife
> BONNIE KALEN, the foundation's director of development
> MAX and DANNY KALEN, Bonnie's twelve- and sixteen-year-old sons
> RAYMOND, Vincent's neo-Nazi cousin

Writer F. Scott Fitzgerald could not have been more wrong when he said that there are no second acts in American lives. To begin anew is the oldest and most persistent of American dreams, having shaped the narrative of much of American literature and defined the character of American religion. In their current incarnations, stories of re-form and rebirth, second chances and second acts—ideally accompanied by revealing autobiography and heartfelt confession—are also staples of the celebrity-obsessed popular media.

In *A Changed Man*, one of American fiction's most consistently provocative comic novelists offers another variation on this perennial theme. In recent novels such as *Primitive People* (1992), *Hunters and Gatherers* (1995), *Guided Tours of Hell* (1997), and *Blue Angel* (2000), Francine Prose has created a series of fearless, funny, acerbic, and humane portraits of men, women, and children and the culture that sur-rounds and shapes them. She has never been afraid of being politically incorrect—in *Hunters and Gatherers* she mocked New Age feminism; in *Guided Tours of Hell* she examined the envious vanity of a minor writer and the character of a flawed Holo-caust survivor in a visit to Auschwitz; in *Blue Angel* she showed how charges of sex-ual harassment could be used as a weapon in the culture wars and a means of personal advancement. Prose has also been inclined to treat all of her characters with under-standing and affection: Though her tone is often satiric, there are no villains and few fools in her fiction.

The changed man of this novel is Vincent Nolan. A directionless, thirty-two-year-old man, he has been fired from minimum-wage jobs with a pool-cleaning company

*Francine Prose has written novels,
collections of short stories, and
works of nonfiction. Her novel*
Household Saints *(1981) was
adapted for film, and* Blue Angel
*(2000) was a finalist for the
National Book Award. Prose has
been awarded Guggenheim and
Fullbright Fellowships and served
as a director's fellow at the Center
for Scholars and Writers at the
New York Public Library.*

and a doughnut shop before finding himself homeless, working the night shift at a Quik-Mart and sleeping during the day in a nursing home bed. When his cousin Raymond offers him a couch to sleep on and a job at a tire shop, he moves in and—out of gratitude as much as anger at his life—joins Raymond and his friends in the Aryan Resistance Movement. The group mainly drinks, complains about minorities and the government, curses at news and talk shows on television, and attends rallies. During the time Vincent is with them, they never act on their beliefs. One night when Vincent is drunk, he gets two tattoos—a swastika and an *SS* lightning bolt.

Then, at a rave where he helps Raymond sell ecstasy, Vincent imbibes one of the little pills and experiences a revelation and a sense of love for all humankind: "Everyone. Black and white, Jewish, Christian, Communist, freaks, retarded, mutant, whatever."

During his lunch hours, Vincent has been sitting in his car, reading by himself. His reading has included *The Way of the Warrior* and *The Complete Pogo*, as well as two books by a Holocaust survivor named Meyer Maslow, *The Kindness of Strangers* and *Forgive, Not Forget*. The first line of *The Kindness of Strangers* ("This is a book about being taken in and saved by ordinary people of courage and conscience") and the description Vincent reads of Meyer's newest book, *One Heart at a Time* (about "changing one person, one heart, at a time"), inspires him to escape his dead-end life and start over by volunteering to work with Meyer's foundation, World Brotherhood Watch. One morning, Vincent steals the $1500 in drug money Raymond got at the rave, along with Raymond's Vicodin and Xanax prescriptions, his latest issue of *Soldier of Fortune* and his pickup truck, and heads off to Manhattan.

Meyer Maslow has devoted his adult life and the efforts of his foundation to promoting peace and understanding and helping oppressed people throughout the world. He is not without his weaknesses, including envy, vanity, a taste for luxury, and a willingness both to do good and to do well. In the words of Bonnie Kalen, his director of development, Meyer "insists on having it all at once: history, God, and expensive clothes. He demands his right to wear Armani while using a mystical tale from Rabbi Nachman to make a point about former Soviet bloc politics or hunger in Rwanda."

The moment Vincent arrives at the foundation headquarters turns out to be auspicious. Half the tickets for the foundation's upcoming fund-raising dinner are unsold, Meyer's latest book is not selling well, and a pot scandal the previous summer at the foundation's Pride and Prejudice friendship camp for teenagers ("Keep our pride!

Lose our prejudice!") has created some bad publicity. Meyer tells Bonnie he has a funny feeling that "Someone is coming. Something's going to happen."

That someone turns out to be Vincent, who gives Meyer and Bonnie a version of his life story minus the ecstasy and the thefts. The story "has two levels," he thinks. "One is the truth, which makes it easy to tell. The second level is not a lie so much as a highlight, drag, and delete." He has come to them, Vincent says in a sentence he has carefully rehearsed. "I want to help you guys save guys like me from becoming guys like me." Because Meyer sees the potential for an "outreach" initiative which could change the minds and hearts of other skinheads, and they are all also aware that a similar defection has recently been a publicity and fund-raising bonanza for the Simon Weisenthal Foundation, Meyer decides to offer Vincent shelter and a job. Because he is afraid that Vincent may change his mind and flee, and because he knows that Bonnie will do almost anything for him, Meyer asks her to let Vincent stay at her suburban home for a few days, until they can make more permanent arrangements for him.

Bonnie is still reeling from a recent divorce, she is frightened and lonely, and her two boys are beginning to worry her. The idealism she brings to her work at the foundation is the best thing in her life. Yet Bonnie suddenly finds herself crossing the Tappan Zee Bridge with a neo-Nazi skinhead in the passenger seat, trying to figure out how she has gotten into this situation and how she is going to introduce him to her sons. Danny, her angry, pot-smoking sixteen-year-old, wonders "What the hell is Mom thinking? Inviting some demented tweaker to stay here until one night, high on crystal meth, he figures out they're Satanists and that God needs him to hack them up and stash them in the freezer." Max, her gentle and confused twelve-year-old— Danny calls him "the middle-school Dalai Lama"—simply observes that "Mom's just trying to be a good person."

Over the next three months—which are highlighted by set pieces that include a dinner party at the Maslows' to see if Vincent can be trusted to mingle with the foundation's supporters, the fund-raising event at the Temple of Dendur in the Metropolitan Museum where Vincent is the featured speaker, the media frenzy that follows that event, and an appearance by Vincent and Meyer on the *Oprah*-like *Chandler* show— Vincent, Meyer, Bonnie, and Danny all have changes of heart. The story unfolds through alternating chapters of interior monologue by these four characters, each of which displays an eye for the absurd and an ear for the idioms of contemporary American speech that have long been Prose's hallmarks. Along the way, Prose presents an entertaining comedy of manners which skewers class, the culture of celebrity, the press, reality television and talk shows, pop psychology, self-help movements, cults, public high school administrators, philanthropy, fund-raising and public relations, pretentious restaurants, and a host of other targets.

At the same time, Prose is never cynical about her characters. By allowing readers access to the thoughts of Vincent, Meyer, Bonnie, and Danny, she lets each of these characters emerge as a complex human being with both high aspirations and baser motives. She even manages to make characters such as Bonnie's former husband Joel and Vincent's cousin Raymond more than caricatures. Parts of *A Changed Man* may remind readers of Raymond Carver country, of Tom Wolfe's dissections of contemporary mores, or of Jerzy Kosinski's *Being There* (1970). Through references to Charles Dickens's *Bleak House* (1852-1853) and George Eliot's *Middlemarch* (1871-1872), however, Prose both underlines some of the themes in *A Changed Man* and suggests that her comedy has larger ambitions.

In her own way, Prose means to write a comic novel which does what Dickens did: dissect social reality by examining believable characters who embody and are shaped by the contradictions of the time. Ultimately, the novel's epigraph from *Middlemarch* is the key to understanding Prose's attitude about, and sympathy for, her characters. "I have a belief on my own and it comforts me . . . That by desiring what is perfectly good, even when we don't quite know what it is and cannot do what we would, we are part of the divine power against evil—widening the skirts of light and making the struggle with darkness narrower." It is easy to imagine Meyer Maslow or Bonnie Kaden as part of that power, but it takes a novelist of Prose's talent and empathy to convince readers that Vincent Nolan might widen the skirts of light too.

Bernard F. Rodgers, Jr.

Review Sources

Booklist 101, no. 7 (December 1, 2004): 619.
Entertainment Weekly, March 11, 2005, p. 106.
Kirkus Reviews 73, no. 1 (January 1, 2005): 17.
Library Journal 130, no. 1 (January, 2005): 100.
The New Leader 88, no. 2 (March/April, 2005): 29-31.
New York 38, no. 8 (March 7, 2005): 72.
The New York Times 154 (March 14, 2005): E4.
The New York Times Book Review 154 (March 27, 2005): 14-15.
The New Yorker 81, no. 6 (March 28, 2005): 77.
People 63, no. 9 (March 7, 2005): 51.
Publishers Weekly 251, no. 51 (December 20, 2004): 34.

CHRIST THE LORD
Out of Egypt

Author: Anne Rice (1941-   )
Publisher: Alfred A. Knopf (New York). 322 pp. $26.00
Type of work: Novel
Time: The first decade C.E.
Locale: Egypt and the Ancient Holy Land

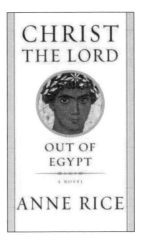

Using the seven-year-old Jesus as narrator, Rice tells the story of a boy discovering, through isolated comments and unexplained miracles, that he is Christ the Lord who is sent to redeem the world

Principal characters:
   The boy JESUS
   JAMES, his stepbrother
   MARY, his mother
   JOSEPH, Mary's husband
   CLEOPAS, ALPHAEUS, and SIMON, Jesus'
      uncles
   MARY, SALOME, and ESTHER, Jesus' aunts

There have been many works written about the life of Jesus, but none have ever presented him, as Anne Rice does in *Christ the Lord: Out of Egypt*, as a seven-year-old boy telling his story from a child's point of view. Rice's novel begins in Alexandria, Egypt, with a bully attacking the young Jesus, who wishes the other boy dead. Die the bully does. Jesus is immediately distraught that he has somehow caused the boy's death and wills him back to life. With this raising from the dead, the question of just what kind of being he is first enters the mind of the young Jesus. He then remembers being able to cause clay pigeons to fly, and more questions arise. The remainder of the novel is devoted to the year in Jesus' life during which he comes to understand exactly who he is and to deal with the intimations of what he must grow up to do.

On the day of the death and raising-up of the bully, Jesus also learns from Joseph that King Herod is dead and that it is time to return to Nazareth, the home they left for Bethlehem, from which they had fled. Before they leave, Jesus has a final visit with his Egyptian teachers, who wonder how Joseph knows Herod is dead, a question that also bemuses Jesus. Among the teachers to whom Jesus bids farewell is the philosopher Philo, a person not connected in any historical reports to Jesus but certainly an important Jewish intellectual in Alexandria and a thinker who had significant influence on Saint Paul and the writers of the Gospel of John by combining Jewish thought with Greek philosophy. Indeed, there are those who consider Philo the first Christian. While there is no evidence, it is entirely possible that Jesus had contact with Philo in Alexandria. The introduction of Philo in the story creates intellectual excitement for

Anne Rice is the author of twenty-seven books devoted to the stories of the vampire Lestat and other creatures of the night. She also wrote the screenplay for the 1994 film version of Interview with the Vampire *(1976). Rice has published additional work under the name Anne Rampling. A native of New Orleans who resided there for many years, she now lives in California.*

the knowledgeable reader and demonstrates the extensive research Rice did before undertaking her novel.

As Joseph's extended family prepares to leave for the Holy Land, Jesus is party to a family conversation about why they will settle in Nazareth and not Bethlehem, a conversation filled with innuendoes about wise men and shepherds and some sort of horrendous event. When Jesus asks about these things he is told gently but firmly that this is not the time to discuss such matters, which makes him feel more unsettled. He is further disturbed by his brother James telling him that Nazareth is a very small town and that he must never again exercise his powers to fell a bully. As Jesus contemplates the implications of James's instructions, the news arrives of Herod's death, and all in Alexandria are puzzled as to how Joseph knew beforehand. Without explanation, Joseph loads his extended family on a boat to the Holy Land. On the boat Jesus hears much conversation about how wicked the dead King Herod was, including a reference to a slaughter in the town of Bethlehem and some talk about Mary's being visited by an angel in Nazareth. Finally the ship docks, and the family is on its way to celebrate Passover in Jerusalem.

As they camp outside Jerusalem, Jesus' uncle Cleopas, now quite ill and feverish, decides to tell Jesus that he believes that an angel appeared to his thirteen-year-old sister, Mary, who was betrothed to Joseph. Jesus is working hard to understand, and Cleopas says that Jesus must endure growing to manhood just as King David had to spend his youth as a shepherd boy. Jesus now realizes that he is not Joseph's son, and Mary confirms for him that she has not ever been with a man.

With much on his mind, the boy Jesus arrives at Jerusalem with his family and is overwhelmed by the size and beauty of the great temple there. They have no time to enjoy it, for almost immediately a horde of soldiers comes thundering down upon the pilgrims arriving at the temple and begins to drive them away from Passover worship. When the crowd resists the soldiers, a massacre takes place, and a great civil war follows. Jesus is witness to a brutal murder of a man destroyed by a soldier's spear. Jesus begins to cry, and, indeed, Rice's description of this dreadful scene is so vivid and powerful that many a reader will no doubt be urged to tears as well.

The holy family leaves for a village outside Jerusalem where Mary's relative Elizabeth lives with her son, John. Elizabeth announces that she does not have long to live and that she has decided to send her son to the desert to live with his relatives among the Essenes. In a powerful scene, Rice has John staring long and hard at the boy Jesus, and the reader knows that John, later to be known as the Baptist, senses what will ultimately unfold. Joseph, Mary, and their family leave Elizabeth and head toward Nazareth. The young Jesus overhears more innuendoes about the past as well as hints about what might be the future. Jesus makes more and more effort to understand what he is and what he must become. One realizes how sensitive this seven-year-old is by the frequent tears that come to his eyes. One also realizes his power when he saves Cleopas from drowning in the River Jordan by curing him of his chronic illness with a touch of a hand.

The arrival in Nazareth brings relief and peace to all. Their house must be rebuilt and, while the town now seems deserted, there is every indication that its inhabitants will soon reappear. As the little town comes back to life, Joseph and the other men find much work as carpenters rebuilding Nazareth and villages nearby which have been destroyed by the civil conflict following the death of Herod. Rice provides many interesting details about the daily life of the Jews of Nazareth, including the rebuilding of such necessary family religious structures as the ritual bath, the Mikvah. Another puzzling moment takes place when the rabbi at the local synagogue refuses to allow Jesus entrance. After some discussion, Joseph claims him as his son, and Jesus enters with his male relatives. It is not long after this event that Jesus demonstrates to his new rabbi that he is gifted with a quick mind and a solid education based on the works of Philo of Egypt. Another unintentional miracle occurs when, during a rainstorm, Jesus wishes for the rain to stop and it does immediately.

In one of the most provocative episodes in the novel, Rice, in a manner reminiscent of her vampire tales, presents a dream had by Jesus as he lies in a fever with a flu-like illness. The dream begins with Jesus walking through a stately palace overlooking a lovely blue sea. Then appears a beautiful winged creature. The creature keeps asking Jesus who he is and even tempts Jesus with a crying fit, but Jesus recognizes the crocodile tears for what they are, mere deception. Then the winged creature shows him the beautiful palace being burned and destroyed as Romans and Jews fight with each other. Christ hides his eyes, and the winged one whispers in his ear that he is the Prince of Chaos and that Jesus can go on being a child if he wishes, but he had better decide what he intends to do in a world in which the Prince of Chaos rules. Not long after his dream, Jesus hears a man tell of terrible destruction in Jerusalem, and he realizes that he has seen it all in his dream of Satan. Now Jesus begins fully to appreciate who he is and what he is to become.

As the peaceful life of Nazareth brings comfort and stability to them, Jesus' family seems more willing to reveal to him the events surrounding his conception and birth. As Jesus approaches his eighth year, and Rice's story draws to an end, his stepbrother James has an important conversation with the child about to become more than man. James declares his love for Jesus and his understanding of what Jesus must grow to be, but he has an important confession to make. In a touching revelation James states that he has hated Jesus intensely even before he was born because, like any only child, he resented the attention given to the newborn but more important was the great attention given to one who was apparently beyond this world. Now, after almost eight years, he wishes Jesus to know that he loves him. James's pronouncement of love causes a great sweetness to come over Jesus.

In his eighth year Jesus now knows that he is Christ the Lord and is ready to accept his obligation and fate. He has yet one more difficult piece of information to receive. At the end of the novel he comes to learn that the reason the family fled from Bethlehem the night of his birth was on order of an angel to escape the terrible slaughter of the innocent children by Herod. Now Jesus is a man while still a child.

Rice, a gifted writer, is renowned for being an inventor of stories that have held the attention of countless readers for many years. In *Christ the Lord* she comes to a story often told and immediately displays her inventiveness by telling that tale from the viewpoint of a seven-year-old child, albeit a child possessed of considerable insight and intimations of immortality. Moreover, she keeps her readers' interest throughout the book by letting the boy glean bits of information about his past in much the same way most people learn their own pasts as they grow.

Rice weaves a rich background out of many details of ancient Jewish daily life, including the babble of four different languages—Hebrew, Greek, Latin, and Aramaic. She even renders Jesus' name in the preferred Aramaic: Yeshua. Even though one knows the ultimate outcome, the reader is occupied throughout the novel with the moods of the boy Jesus and the tensions brought to bear on a family as questions of the boy's legitimacy continually arise. Rice triumphs in telling an old story quite anew. Obviously, presenting so many details of daily life required considerable research, which she outlines in an interesting author's note appended to the novel. The author's note also contains a discussion of how and why Rice came to write *Christ the Lord*.

August W. Staub

Review Sources

Booklist 102, no. 5 (November 1, 2005): 5.
Entertainment Weekly, November 4, 2005, pp. 32-34.
Kirkus Reviews 73, no. 19 (October 1, 2005): 1050.
Library Journal 130, no. 18 (November 1, 2005): 70.
The New York Times 155 (November 3, 2005): E1-E9.
Newsweek 146, no. 18 (October 31, 2005): 54-55.
People 64, no. 20 (November 14, 2005): 52.
Publishers Weekly 252, no. 40 (October 10, 2005): 38.
School Library Journal 51, no. 12 (December, 2005): 178-180.

THE CHRYSANTHEMUM PALACE

Author: Bruce Wagner (1954-   )
Publisher: Simon & Schuster (New York). 210 pp.
  $23.00
Type of work: Novel
Time: 2005
Locale: Southern California, Hollywood, Martha's Vine-
  yard

*A tale of promise and poignancy, drugs, drinking, and
death, this short novel explores in detail the lifestyles of
three children of the Hollywood rich and famous*

Principal characters:
  BERTIE KROHN, a moderately successful
    actor trying to reinvent himself as a
    writer
  CLEA FREEMANTLE, his enduring friend, Thad's lover, daughter of a
    famous actress
  THAD MICHELET, Bertie's friend, son of larger-than-life literary icon
    "Black Jack" Michelet
  MIRIAM LEVINE, Thad's literary agent and cheerleader, Bertie's lover
  PERRY KROHN, Bertie's dad, the brilliant creator-producer of a long-
    running television series, *Starwatch*
  GITA KROHN, Bertie's mom, who is wheelchair-bound because of
    Parkinson's disease
  MORGANA MICHELET, Thad's mother, Black Jack's long-suffering and
    unpleasant wife

The Chrysanthemum Palace describes the giddy joys and private envies of the self-absorbed fast-track Hollywood crowd. Writer, actor, director, and producer Bruce Wagner's latest novel, a bit autobiographical, wallows happily in the domain of drugs, famous people and also-rans, and the tectonically moving culture of Hollywood's celebrity families. It offers a clip taken from the underachieving lives of three children of the rich and famous and their supporting cast of dysfunctional characters.

Bertram Valentine (an allusion to the hero of the 1961 novel *Stranger in a Strange Land* by Robert A. Heinlein) Krohn narrates the book. He is the thirty-eight-year-old son of a multitalented and megasuccessful television producer. The father's current series in production is the long-running *Starwatch: The Navigators*, an enterprise on which Bertie has long resisted sailing. His hope has been to become successful without resorting to nepotism. In the shadow of his larger-than-life dad, Bertie has come to realize that he will never achieve significant greatness as long as he continues to ply his trade as an actor. He revises his dream to a more manageable and possibly more attainable one: life as a writer. In the verisimilitude of fiction, *The Chrysanthemum Palace* is presented as the product of this new career direction. It is Bertie Krohn's work.

∼

Born in Madison, Wisconsin, Bruce Wagner grew up mostly in Beverly Hills. He dropped out of high school to work in a bookstore. In addition to writing fiction, he has been an actor, a screenwriter, a director, and a comic-strip artist. His novel I'll Let You Go *(2001) was nominated for the PEN/USA fiction award.*

∼

To support himself while he writes, he accepts an acting role in his father's television series and climbs aboard the starship *Demeter.* In the episodes currently being filmed, *Demeter* and its crew will be drawn into the political exigencies of an alien culture whose governmental structures resembling a circular white flower are deemed "Chrysanthemum Palaces." At least that is the image that Krohn's character sees.

The story is engaging, if somewhat predictable. The reader is introduced to a troika of friends. There is Bertie's longtime buddy and sometime lover, Clea Freemantle. Clea's advantaged youth has been compromised by the suicide of her mother, a famous actress. Clea engages in partying, extravagance, and over-the-top sex. The trajectory of her life seems pointed toward self-destruction. Nevertheless, like many of her star-crossed Hollywood contemporaries, she eventually stumbles into recovery and into the inevitable round of Alcoholics Anonymous meetings. It is at one of these gatherings that she becomes reacquainted with Bertie, whom she had not seen in years, since the death of a high school friend in a Pacific Coast Highway accident. During the intervening years Clea has been working as an actress and at an unsatisfying relationship with Thad Michelet.

Thad Michelet, like Clea and Bertie, is the child of a Hollywood legend. Perhaps he is related to the grandest and deadliest icon of them all. The overarching shadow of Thad's famous father, whose funeral is detailed in the book, seems more menacing than that of the others: "Black Jack Michelet who most definitely *didn't* end with a bang or a whimper but instead lingered in bodystink and agonized ill health so as to take pleasure in maiming and brutalizing whomsoever loved him." As the story unfolds, it comes to light that the elder Michelet has extended his abusive control of his son beyond the grave by placing a harsh stipulation in his will. Thad may inherit some of the millions from daddy's estate only if he can write a book that makes *The New York Times* best-seller list. This paternal goal seems out of reach. Nevertheless, the urgency of Thad's significant debt and the fact that he is being questioned by the Internal Revenue Service motivates him to try. Miriam Levine, his enterprising literary agent, has confidence in him—and a plan.

Thad is older than Bertie, perhaps not coincidentally the exact age of author Wagner as he writes *The Chrysanthemum Palace.* Thad is described as "gifted," "diminutive," and a "melancholy troll." He has achieved a greater level of success as an actor than has either Clea or Bertie. Thad is recognized in public, and his acting credits linger in the public mind. He is also a credible writer, although few would situate him in the same league as his famous father. The Olympian accomplishments of Black Jack stand as an apparently unreachable measure against which the son must be judged. Thad is plagued with migraine headaches, addictions to various substances, and severe mood swings. His endeavors consistently succeed but never satisfy. He is further haunted by the memory of a twin brother, Jeremy, who died on the Isle of Capri under rather murky circumstances. The gradual revelation of the circumstances of Jeremy's death allows the reader to understand, in part, why Thad's state of depression is much deeper than those of his friends.

What binds the trio together is their collective failure. They cannot match the level of success of their famous parents, and their attempts seem destined to end in tragedy. Among the tangle of connections is the detail that Bertie's dad is a collector of first editions of Jack Michelet's works. Perry Krohn owns the right to *Chrysanthemum*, Michelet's favorite among his own works. The story, as summed up by Thad in a drunken monologue, has a melancholy congruence with his own guilt-soaked past.

The central plot line of the book is that each of the three friends has landed an acting job on *Starwatch*. Clea plays a series of roles but is now an alien diplomat in full latex splendor. Compliant and camouflaged behind her makeup, she seems almost typecast in various secondary roles, much as she is in life. Bertie plays the "son of a legendary warrior," serving aboard the fictitious starship as commander Will Karp from Kansas City. To sustain himself financially while he pursues his writing, Bertie has succumbed to being a part of his father's fabricated world. The part he plays is art imitating life. The starring role belongs, appropriately, to Thad. He is the guest celebrity, featured in a two-part episode in a dual role. He is the unassuming Ensign Rattwell, encased in the understated uniform and overstated facial foam of a "Vorbalid" citizen. (Later it is revealed that the young ensign is really the Vorbalidian prince in exile.) Thad's other character is his twin brother, the evil Morloch, pretender to the Vorbalid throne. Echoes of Thad's real life are rendered loud and unavoidable.

Wagner's description of the *Starwatch* set, the costumed appearance and foibles of the cast, as well as the over-the-top action in the television drama is marvelously crafted. He constructs a splendid spoof of all memorable small-screen science-fiction series, from *Space Cadet* to *Star Trek*. Anyone who has been loyal to the genre will identify with the characters, the illusionary and sometimes low-budget sets as well as the quasi-scientific terminology which punctuates the grandeur of space on the small frontier of the living-room screen. This lighthearted interlude is a welcome relief for the reader from the intense navel-gazing of the principal characters. By adding this descriptive lampoon, Wagner has provided a needed contrast to the heaviness of the story. From time to time, he drops a whimsical footnote or the name of a real Hollywood personality among his fictional characters. These touches lighten the reader's load.

Spicing the narrative are occasional descriptions of the sexual encounters of the players: Clea and Thad, Clea and Bertie, Miriam and Bertie, and so on. Almost any location becomes a site for stolen moments of lovemaking. Meanwhile, Wagner continues to name-drop the "real people" who know and admire the fictional characters. The grand Martha's Vineyard funeral of Black Jack Michelet, for example, boasts attendees such as authors Norman Mailer and Kurt Vonnegut and actors Jim Belushi, Daryl Hannah, and Nicole Kidman. Actor Nick Nolte appears, as though in a cameo role, in a local bookstore. Secretary of State Donald Rumsfeld is known to watch *Starwatch*. It is clear that Wagner's characters travel in celebrity circles, even if they do not personally make the cut.

The book is tragic but captivating. Although it may take the reader awhile to engage in the plot, the story becomes compelling in a macabre way. It is clear that the ending will not be a happy one for the trio of friends, but the reader wants to embrace every sordid detail leading to that ending. Wagner is heavy-handed with his language and has an annoying tendency to alliterate incessantly—and to write badly. Is it possible that such is a device used by the author to underline the weaknesses of Bertie's writing? As the work proceeds, Wagner's superior ability to weave a tale takes over. Even with the literary device of having the title work be that of Krohn rather than of Wagner, the author manages to layer the plot lines in a way that is sometimes surprising in its sophistication and multiple meanings.

Ultimately, the story draws the reader into the sad and sullied world of privileged children whose lives never quite come together. While not a book packed with joy and good feeling, Wagner's novel is more than a weekend beach read. It chronicles, one has to assume accurately and effectively, lives of inherited privilege turned tragic.

Dolores L. Christie

Review Sources

Booklist 101, no. 8 (December 15, 2004): 709-710.
Kirkus Reviews 72, no. 22 (November 15, 2004): 1068.
The New York Times 154 (February 22, 2005): E1-E6.
The New York Times Book Review 154 (March 13, 2005): 27.
People 63, no. 9 (March 7, 2005): 51.
Publishers Weekly 252, no. 1 (January 3, 2005): 33-34.
Time 165, no. 6 (February 7, 2005): 75.

THE CIGAR ROLLER

Author: Pablo Medina (1948-   )
Publisher: Grove Press (New York). 178 pp. $21.00
Type of work: Novel
Time: The mid-nineteenth to the mid-twentieth century
Locale: Tampa, Florida; Pinar del Río and Havana, Cuba

*A paralyzed stroke victim, once a big man with big ap-
petites, spends his last years in a nursing home mulling
over his misdeeds and misspent life*

Principal characters:

AMADEO TERRA, a Cuban American cigar
  roller
JULIA GONZÁLEZ HERRERA TERRA, his
  wife
RUBÉN, PASTOR, and ALBERTICO TERRA, their sons
AMALIA, a young woman with whom Amadeo has an affair
SERGIO "CHANO" REINALDO RAMOS, Amadeo's mentor and friend in
  Tampa
ANA, a fourteen-year-old girl whom Amadeo seduces
AMADEO'S FATHER, a mean Canary Islander immigrant to Cuba
TAVITO, Amadeo's retarded brother
ELPIDIO, a Cuban man who teaches Amadeo to roll cigars
NURSE, Amadeo's main nursing-home attendant
NURSE II, another nursing-home attendant
ORDERLY, a nursing-home attendant who beats Amadeo
SOR DIMINUTA, a nun who visits Amadeo in the nursing home

Pablo Medina's *The Cigar Roller* is narrated throughout from the point of view of
its protagonist, Amadeo Terra, an old man who lies paralyzed and dying in a Tampa,
Florida, nursing home. His experiences in the nursing home intermingle with his
memories and flashbacks which gradually reveal his life story. Amadeo, a cigar
maker, fled with his family from Cuba to Tampa in the late nineteenth century when
he got into trouble with the Spanish authorities. Despite his brief association with the
Cuban independence movement, Amadeo is no hero. Instead, he is a self-centered,
antiheroic figure who is almost comic except for some of the awful things he has
done. Now, after suffering a stroke which leaves him paralyzed from the head
down—but apparently suffering no other brain damage—he has had nothing to do for
over four years in the nursing home except linger on and contemplate his condition,
his vices, his evil deeds, and his missed opportunities.

Amadeo's main vice is lust, which led him to consort with cabaret dancers and
prostitutes, to have an affair with a fourteen-year-old girl, and to abandon his long-
suffering wife, Julia, mother of his three sons, for a much younger woman, Amalia,
with whom he had a daughter. Amadeo loved Julia and at times seemed to dote on her:

Pablo Medina came from Cuba to the United States in 1960, when he was twelve. The author of a memoir, a translation, volumes of poetry, and novels, he teaches writing at New School University and Warren Wilson College.

She was his helpmate who followed him wherever he went and forgave him for most of the long years of their marriage. Amadeo even found Julia sexually exciting, at least for the first couple of years, but then he got bored with the routine of marriage. As Amadeo told Julia, a man has appetites his wife cannot satisfy, which might say something about the male sex and certainly says something about Amadeo. Amadeo's occupation as a cigar roller symbolically suggests his most outstanding vice.

Amadeo also had a fondness for food and drink. He recalls times when he consumed six helpings of paella for lunch and two steaks for dinner. It is not surprising that he once weighed three hundred pounds. He also went on drinking binges and came home ill, at which times Julia would revive him by feeding him rice and *vaca frita*. Amadeo's other vices included gambling and overspending, but for the most part his vices were the earthy vices of the flesh (as his name Terra suggests). For Amadeo's sensualist nature, the cigars he made and loved to smoke and savor are again an appropriate symbol. Amadeo's idea of supreme satisfaction was "to sit in the shade with a bottle of wine, a cigar, and a friend or two."

Amadeo's male relationships were mainly with role models or mentors. At the age of twelve Amadeo began learning cigar rolling from Elpidio, a mixed-race Cuban, and he moved in with Elpidio and his wife Lala for two years. Elpidio and the other men in the cigar factory taught Amadeo that it did not matter what else one was— cheater, abuser, thug, drunk, or some other lowlife—as long as one was a good cigar roller. This sentiment seems to have stuck with Amadeo. Elpidio also set an example for Amadeo in the realm of appetites: Elpidio shoveled in food, but Amadeo expanded on his teacher's example, just as he learned to roll better cigars.

Another mentor of Amadeo was Sergio Reinaldo Ramos, nicknamed Chano, a dapper wheeler-dealer who hung out in bodegas but presented himself as a gentleman intellectual. Chano met Amadeo as soon as Amadeo stepped off the boat in Tampa. He set Amadeo up with a low-ranking job in a local cigar factory and moved Amadeo and his family into a rundown house. Julia saw through Chano, but Amadeo accepted him at face value, felt obliged for the favors, and over the years became Chano's friend and student, imbibing knowledge of literature and philosophy from Chano's deep conversations over wine and cigars. Later in Amadeo's life, after Chano died, Chano's replacement seems to have been Giacobo Bombo, the local Mafia kingpin, with whom Amadeo regularly met and conversed in the Columbia Restaurant.

Amadeo's ability to absorb higher learning much as he inhaled cigars is rather implausible because he had little schooling and was no great reader, but perhaps his feat is a tribute to male bonding. Amadeo and his friends are all products of the macho male culture. The macho culture places value on surface qualities and appearances, so a little learning could go a long way, and the culture also values knowledge and behavior handed on from man to man. Homosexuals, whom Amadeo hates, do not fit this culture's definition of machismo, nor do poets (one of Amedeo's sons is a poet, and so is the novel's author).

Also typical of the macho culture are outbreaks of anger and violence, which in Amadeo's case allowed him to commit some terrible acts. The reasons for Amadeo's behavior are further complicated by his childhood relationship with his abusive father, who would come home angry or drunk (or both) and beat him. The father also beat Amadeo's brother, Tavito, who was developmentally disabled, possibly from the abuse. Amadeo could escape the beatings only by hiding in the mango orchard. Eventually he escaped, having grown much bigger than his father and leaving home. It is not surprising that Amadeo, abused as a child, should have problems with violence and with relating to people as an adult.

Still, whatever the causes of one's actions, one is responsible for them and must live with them. With the introduction of this theme *The Cigar Roller* gets richer and deeper and becomes more interesting. The novel is obviously a critique of macho behavior, but it can also be read as a commentary on any life lived too close to the surface, without reflection, self-indulgent and centered on oneself.

The pervasive irony of *The Cigar Roller* is that Amadeo, a macho man used to getting his way and indulging his appetites, is rendered helpless. As he is lying on the sidewalk immediately after his stroke, his first thought is "that just when he had it all—money, a comfortable house, a new car—somebody dropped an anvil on him." He surmises "that he would never move or speak again and that his life was, for all intents and purposes, over." He is partly wrong: Instead of his life being over, it is time for him to pay the proverbial piper. Payback begins when a street kid runs by and steals his watch. Then a crowd gathers around which includes some of Julia's old cronies, one of whom issues a malediction: "He finally got what he deserved."

During his four to five years in the nursing home, Amadeo, the man of fleshly appetites, suffers mortification of the flesh on a daily basis. His lust is reduced to fantasies about the nurse and nun who feed, bathe, and care for him. Since his teeth were pulled when he entered the nursing home, he is spoon-fed baby food. He also wears a diaper and has to be changed regularly, though sometimes he messes his bed, especially when he has diarrhea or an enema. Frequently he has to lie in his own filth, because he cannot move or speak to call assistance. He has to endure the idle chatter of people attending him, and once the nurse slaps him for drooling. Not long before he dies, an orderly gets mad, curses him, beats him across the belly with a belt, then jumps atop him and chokes him with the belt.

Amadeo's main punishment, however, consists of memories, longing, and remorse. These activities of his mind determine the novel's style and narrative technique. Reflecting Amadeo's personality, the style is generally self-indulgent and extravagant, mixing in a bit of Cuban Spanish, moving from the gross to the poetic (with some striking metaphors and similes), sometimes loading numerous details into long, strung-out sentences. Occasionally the catalogs of impressions and bored spot-on-the-wall broodings can become tedious, but they are usually functional, mirroring Amadeo's sensuality (like his catalog of women smells) or his significant past experiences (like his fear of spiders and his love of mangoes). Toward the end, Amadeo's obsessions with a dripping faucet and a repeating noise at the window signify time running out and the coming of death.

Also reflecting the movement of Amadeo's mind, the narrative technique, like the rolling or unrolling of a cigar, circles back to significant events in a recursive pattern, telling more each time and finally revealing his most repressed memories. The narrative technique, so to speak, ties Amadeo to the psychiatrist's couch. Among his recurring memories are those of his relationship with his father, his hiding in the mango grove, his nostalgia for Havana, his relationship with Julia and their sons, and his professional pride as a cigar roller. His obsessive remembrances become more painful over time, as he runs together past and present and grows slightly confused over what is reality, dream, or fantasy. Significantly, his minor confusion does not prevent him from coming to a few major realizations about his life.

Most important, he realizes that he alienated the people who loved him and whom he loved. Julia was the love of his life, but instead of telling her so, during their tender moments this sensitive fellow said things such as "you planted too much calabaza this year, you are gaining too much weight." Eventually Amadeo's actions drove her to religious occultism and finally back to Cuba, alone, for the last two years of her life. His jealous suspicions also drove away Amalia, with whom he had an otherwise happy affair and a daughter whom he never again saw. Now his two surviving sons pay his nursing home bills but do not come to visit. Neither do any of his old pals (most of whom perhaps are dead). Instead, Amadeo is left unloved and alone in a nursing-home scenario worthy of a drama of the absurd, where the people caring for him do not have names but are only called Nurse, Orderly, Doctor, and so forth. Amadeo is as forgotten as poor, lonely Chinese Lady, another patient, who slips into bed at night with Amadeo for a few weeks before she disappears.

A few other people in the impersonal nursing home are given names, some patients who are briefly mentioned and a couple of the religious figures who visit. An unnamed priest and another cleric who is a dwarf, Rigo, come by Amadeo's room; the astute priest uses Amadeo as a text to show Rigo he is not so bad off as this miserable paralyzed creature. The main religious visitor is Sor Diminuta, whose name, like the dwarf signifies the smallness and humility that Amadeo should feel before God. She and her unwashed smell only turn Amadeo on; luckily, her crucifix dangles on his chest and irritates him as did Julia's. (A crucifix is known to repel even vampires.)

The religious figures and the name of the nursing home, Santa Gertrudis, suggest a theological interpretation of *The Cigar Roller*. Amadeo's stay in the nursing home is like time spent in purgatory (though Amadeo thinks of it more like time in hell), giving him an opportunity to purge his sins and heal spiritually. If so, Amadeo's stay in the nursing home seems to fail, as he remains unregenerate, lustful, and atheistic. The author does not insist on this interpretation, however, and an existentialist interpretation may be a better fit. Toward the novel's end occurs a key realization: "Desire—for

women, for money, for work, for respect—has made Amadeo an exile from himself."
Amadeo dies seeing the faces of people he has known and loved, which gradually turn
into his own face.

Harold Branam

Review Sources

Booklist 101, nos. 9/10 (January 1-15, 2005): 820.
Hispanic 18 (May, 2005): 67.
Kirkus Reviews 72, no. 24 (December 15, 2004): 1160.
Library Journal 130, no. 1 (January, 2005): 99.
The New York Times Book Review 154 (March 13, 2005): 17.
Publishers Weekly 252, no. 5 (January 31, 2005): 48.

THE CITY
A Global History

Author: Joel Kotkin (1953-   )
Publisher: The Modern Library (New York). 218 pp.
  $22.00
Type of work: Environment, history, and sociology
Time: 5000 B.C.E.-2005 C.E.
Locale: Worldwide

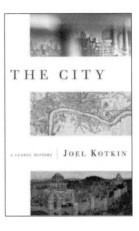

Global in scope and sweeping in history, Kotkin's concise but insightful book considers the character of the human city and its special problems from its inception to the present day

In *The City: A Global History* noted urban scholar Joel Kotkin considers humankind's unique and brilliant creation, the city, as this phenomenon has occurred throughout history and around the globe. Kotkin argues that, from its inception, the human city was based upon three fundamental concepts: The city is a place that is sacred, a place that is safe, and a place that is busy with commerce. Kotkin commences his study with the first known human cities, created about 5000 B.C.E. in the fertile crescent known to the Greeks as Mesopotamia. The oldest cities in this region were established in the valley between the Tigris and Euphrates Rivers. Each of these cities began as the location of a sacred place.

In Ur, the largest of the ancient Mesopotamian cities, the city center was the seventy-foot shrine to Nannar, the Moon god. This tower dominated the entire city. Little wonder, then, that the priestly class dominated the city's citizens. It was to protect the sacred place that Mesopotamian cities developed city walls. So protected was the sacred place that the court surrounding it became the central marketplace. This pattern of a city as a sacred space, dominated by priests and protecting the commerce at its center, was to spread across Mesopotamia and into Egypt. In the latter locale, the city was dominated by a single priest, the pharaoh, who ultimately claimed to be a god. Egypt's great pyramids are still reminders of the power of the sacred place. China and India also developed cities featuring a sacred place often dominated by a single priest or prophet. Even as far away as the Americas, which had no contact with the rest of the globe, great cities, following the same pattern of sacred place, safety and commerce, were erected in Mexico and Peru.

An important variation in the pattern of ancient cities took place in Babylon, which Kotkin describes as deliberately established by Sargon to be his imperial city. This variation provides protection for a large empire associated with the imperial city, and, under this protection, commerce expands from the central market and embraces the entire empire. In the Far East, cities in China, Japan, and Korea also became imperial capitals. By the eighth and ninth centuries C.E., Phoenician Tyre and Sidon had be-

come commercial giants, especially in trade involving shipping, and thus the power began to
shift from the priests to the commercial class.
Carthage, in North Africa, was the most powerful of such commercial cities. Cities built primarily for commerce were to fall to a new variant: the city designed for conquest.

Ancient Greek cities, on Crete as well as the
Greek mainland, were organized around sacred
places and supported large markets at their centers, but above all they were intended for conquest. The Athenian philosopher Plato was said
to observe that every city is constantly at war
with every other city. The greatest of these warrior cities was Athens, in which every male citizen was trained as a soldier. Famous for its center, which holds the sacred Acropolis, the Theater
of Dionysus (also a place of worship), and the
Agora or marketplace, Athens saw its natives
produce great architecture, poetry, drama, visual
art, and the creation of a governing democracy,
but its main function was always military.

Athens and the other Greek city-states, however, could never form a permanent confeder-

*Joel Kotkin, Irvine Senior Fellow
with the New America Foundation
in Washington, D.C., is the author
of several books. He lectures at
Branch College of the City
University of New York and at the
Southern California Institute of
Architecture. He is a frequent
contributor to* The Wall Street
Journal *and the* Los Angeles Times.

acy. Successful at joining together to turn back Persian imperialism, the Greek cities
finally destroyed one another, the crowning blow being the conquering of Athens by
Sparta. Weakened, the Greeks fell to Phillip of Macedonia, and it was his son Alexander who conquered the area from Greece to India. To rule over this vast empire, Alexander established in Egypt the grand Hellenistic city of Alexandria, which Kotkin labels the first cosmopolitan city. What characterizes the cosmopolitan attitude is that,
although the culture is dominated by a central ideal, all other cultures, religions, and
races are tolerated and even encouraged. The cosmopolitan ideal brings with it its
own demise, for certain subcultures will eventually insist upon their right to be independent. This insistence was typified by the Jews, who ultimately reestablished their
own independent state in Judaea. By 100 B.C.E. the Alexandrian empire had unrav-
eled, but not before it had spread the Greek cultural vision throughout Europe and the
Middle East.

Rome, was to inherit the Alexandrian ideal of cosmopolitanism. Kotkin classifies
Rome as the first great megacity, a type which would ultimately include such modern
urban monsters as New York, Tokyo, Los Angeles, London, and Mexico City. According to Kotkin, Rome was able to attain its great size and maintain its position of
dominance throughout the ancient world by blending two of the three essential aspects of a city: The Romans united religious conviction with organized military activity. It was Mars, the god of war and agriculture, whom the Romans worshiped. In-

deed, the Latin word *religio* means the citizens' obligation to the gods, the family, and civic duty. The most sacred concept was the *res publica*, the public thing. So powerful was this sense of civic love and duty that Rome was able to survive both public disasters and foreign invasions and ultimately become the master city of Europe, the Middle East, and Egypt. Much of its impetus to foreign conquest was as a means for Rome to feed, clothe, and house its enormous population.

Indeed, it was to support this teeming populace that Rome became an innovator in urban engineering, developing extraordinary skills in road building and inventing one of the great marvels of the ancient world: the system of fourteen aqueducts which carried water to all sections of the huge city. Not only were Romans splendid engineers, but they were also gifted with superior legal minds, which aided in the creation of legal structures and a governmental system that provides guidance to modern cultures. Above all, Kotkin argues, what made it possible for Rome to maintain its ascendancy for so many centuries was that Romans preserved peace by constantly preparing for war. Important also was the Roman view that all conquered territories were to be also considered Roman. It was this concept of Rome as a city extending across the entire breadth of the known world that would sustain the city for so long but would also ultimately be its downfall. As more and more slaves were imported, the elite abandoned Rome to live on suburban estates. The city soon became populated by slaves and the working class who were controlled not only by religion but also by ever-increasing entertainments, many of a savage quality such as gladiatorial contests and animal fights.

Ultimately Rome was to lose its best minds and talents and fall to barbarian attacks. Indeed, with the advent of Christianity from the East, the whole concept of an earthly city as sacred was finally replaced by what Saint Augustine would call "the city of God," a place not of this world. Rome succumbed in importance to Constantinople, but even that Western and Christian city would fall to the Turks in 1453 C.E. A new Eastern dominance would take place. Islam, the third of the Abrahamic religions, sought out Mecca as a sacred place to organize a city. Here Muhammad centered his new faith as an urban phenomenon dominated by the spires of the mosques. Soon Mecca was replaced by Damascus, Baghdad, and finally Cairo. Each of these centers of Islam was also characterized by important cultural institutions such as universities, libraries, and hospitals.

Most important for the health of these cities was their robust engagement in trade and commerce. Ultimately, Islamic commerce would extend from Spain to North Africa to the borders of China. It was in China that Islam encountered other great cities organized about a complex system of trade and commerce, a system which would so impress the Western adventurer Marco Polo. Kotkin observes that the brilliance and strength of the Eastern cities was overturned by the avarice of their ruling class, who destroyed the vigor of the urban entrepreneurs by excessive taxation and favoritism shown to the aristocrats. It was as these cities weakened that European cities regained ascendancy, and urbanity entered the modern era.

In the second half of his history, Kotkin examines the modern city from the Italian Renaissance to modern-day metropolises such as New York and London. First, there emerge in Italy a number of important city-states built upon new knowledge and research and the desire for profitable trade. The Italian entrepreneurs created beautiful new churches and lovely city centers with the profits from their commercial activity. Chief among such cities were Venice, Genoa, and Florence, all committed to Christianity but all sufficiently cosmopolitan to embrace other peoples and faiths. Florence also gave the world the Medicis: a new urban class now known as political bosses. To match the splendor of Italy, the ruling classes of Spain and Portugal, invigorated by their defeat of the Moors, created the grand capital cities of Lisbon and Madrid. The Iberians sponsored voyages by Christopher Columbus and other explorers to extend Christianity and expand trade.

The cities of Iberia, however, were no match for Paris, in Kotkin's mind. He sees Paris as the ultimate European capital city. Paris was unique in that it was the center of the richest European empire, and its function was to serve the bureaucrats, priests, students, and scholars who flocked there. Its merchant class flourished, supporting Paris as a spiritual and intellectual center. More outward-looking entrepreneurs were active in the cities of Northern Europe, such as Amsterdam, Antwerp, and London, whose emphasis on world trade ultimately dominated even Lisbon and Madrid. It was in the northern cities that culture was democratized and made available to all classes. This movement is typified by the availability of great works such as those of William Shakespeare in the public theaters. Ultimately, it was London that became the new capital city of Europe.

The next great shift in the history of the modern city was the industrialization of certain Anglo-American cities. With the rise of the industrial city comes modern culture. While Lancaster, England, was probably the birthplace of the industrial revolution, it was New York that epitomized the first great industrial complex. In order to house the teeming multitudes that came to work in its various industries, New York became the world's first vertical city. Moreover, because its huge population included persons of all religions and ethnicities, New York did not have a central sacred place. Rather, it substituted commercial and cultural structures and activities for the traditionally sacred ones. Hence, Times Square, the center of the commercial and theatrical district, became the city center.

Other major industrial cities such as Detroit, Chicago, and Liverpool followed the pattern set by New York. With great wealth and growth in population arrived dangerous elements as well, and security became a major concern of industrial cities. There were also problems caused by the destruction of air quality due to the release of smoke and other pollutants. The most affluent residents fled the problems of the central city, and this exodus was yet another force for transformation. The final change of the late twentieth century was the decentralization of the industrial city by the so-called information age. Now control of industry or commerce can as easily be accomplished from a suburb of Atlanta as from the center of Chicago.

Kotkin concludes his study by observing that half the world's population now lives in cities and that those cities have done good work lately in providing commerce and personal security. For Kotkin, the major threat is not from terrorism but from the loss of a sense of the sacredness of place. Urban dwellers must find a way to continue to believe in the uniqueness of locale of their city for those cities to survive.

August W. Staub

Review Sources

Booklist 101, no. 15 (April 1, 2005): 1328.
The Chronicle of Higher Education 51, no. 37 (May 20, 2005): B4.
Kirkus Reviews 73, no. 3 (February 1, 2005): 167.
Library Journal 130, no. 4 (March 1, 2005): 98.

CLASSICAL MUSIC IN AMERICA
A History of Its Rise and Fall

Author: Joseph Horowitz (1948-   )
Publisher: W. W. Norton (New York). 625 pp. $40.00
Type of work: History and music
Time: The mid-nineteenth century to 2005
Locale: The United States, especially New York, Boston,
    Philadelphia, and Chicago

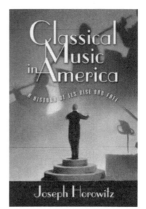

This history of classical music in the United States fo-
cuses on institutions for performance, performers, and im-
presarios

Principal personages:
HENRY LEE HIGGINSON, the founder and
    principal patron of the Boston Symphony
THEODORE THOMAS, a Gilded Age orchestra
    organizer and conductor in the United States
ARTURO TOSCANINI, an orchestra conductor in the United States and
    abroad
LEOPOLD STOKOWSKI, an orchestra conductor of the Philadelphia
    Symphony
DAVID SARNOFF, the head of the National Broadcasting Corporation
    (NBC) who championed classical music performances on the radio
ARTHUR JUDSON, the director of the New York Philharmonic and
    business manager for classical musicians
AARON COPLAND, an American twentieth century composer
LEONARD BERNSTEIN, an American twentieth century composer and
    conductor of the New York Philharmonic

The title of this book, *Classical Music in America*, is a good summation of its scope and purpose: "to excavate the saga of American classical music." Joseph Horowitz gives three reasons for writing this comprehensive history. First, no histories of classical music in the United States exist, and in histories of American music, the classical genre occupies a minor position. Second, Horowitz believes that classical music in America focuses on a culture of performance, not composition. The development of American institutions such as the symphony orchestra for performing classical music has received little attention from scholars.

At the same time, Horowitz admits that in this historical study of classical music in America, he was motivated by his conviction that classical music in the United States has not fulfilled its promise and is in danger of self-destructing. He turns to history to provide, if not answers, at least a crucial context for understanding the present dilemma.

The subtitle of his book conveys his message: *A History of Its Rise and Fall.* Horowitz sees a trajectory of classical music in America that begins with a period of education and growth in the second half of the nineteenth century. During the Gilded

~

Joseph Horowitz is a music critic, scholar, and arts administrator. He has published several books on classical music in the United States, including Understanding Toscanini *(1986) and* Wagner Nights *(1994).*

~

Age through the early twentieth century, Horowitz finds a peak characterized by a balance between performance and composition. Finally, after World War I he identifies a decline through the remainder of the twentieth century down to the present. This fall is driven by various aspects of the music business that came to dominate and overpower the creative energies of composition.

The author structures his narrative into two major sections. Book 1, titled "'Queen of the Arts': Birth and Growth," begins in the mid-nineteenth century when classical music began to put down roots in American soil. This section focuses on the two major cities where classical music was cultivated, Boston and New York. By the end of this first section, classical music in America has reached a peak in the Gilded Age and in the years before World War I. Growth and optimism are the predominant themes in this section, just as this spirit was reflected in other aspects of American culture at this historical period.

In book 2, "'Great Performances': Decline and Fall," the curve goes in the opposite direction—downward. This second major section covers most of the twentieth century. Horowitz identifies the "culture of performance" as the primary culprit. In book 2, he examines the interlinking components of the culture of performance: the "star" system of conductors and soloists, including famous opera singers, the "new" audience, demands of new media including radio, television, film, and recording, and the business managers of the classical music enterprise. In the author's view, this unwieldy composite of the classical music package pushed the invigorating creativity of composers and new music to the sidelines, leaving classical music in the United States to stagnate and inevitably decline.

This book has many strengths. One of its most significant features is its comprehensive treatment of the subject. The author brings together most of the major components of the experience of classical music in the United States. In addition, he integrates the place of classical music into other features of American culture.

This ability to cover so many diverse topics relating to classical music comes out of Horowitz's years of professional engagement with classical music in America. He was a music critic for *The New York Times*. He has published numerous books on more specific subjects that appear in this book including *Understanding Toscanini* (1986) and *Wagner Nights* (1994). He has also worked on the management side of classical music, having served as executive director and consultant to orchestras such as the Brooklyn Philharmonic Orchestra, the New Jersey Symphony, and the Pacific Symphony. All of his scholarly and administrative expertise is distilled in this book, a veritable magnum opus.

Another strength of *Classical Music in America* is its treatment of topics that have been relatively neglected in studies of classical music and of American music. The most outstanding example is the development of the symphony orchestra and how orchestras function as institutions. Horowitz argues that the creation of symphony orchestras as a primary vehicle for the performance of classical music was an American contribution. He uses the contrasting cases of the Boston Symphony and what eventually became the New York Philharmonic as key examples of how symphony orchestras were established and what features shaped their distinctive artistic and cultural characters. He also illuminates the development of symphony orchestras in other major cities including Chicago, Philadelphia, Minneapolis, Cincinnati, and San Francisco.

Horowitz demonstrates how in the twentieth century the orchestras came under the spell of star conductors such as Arturo Toscanini and Leopold Stokowski in Philadelphia. Solo performers, such as pianists Vladimir Horowitz and Van Cliburn and the violinist Jascha Heifetz, also became regular features of orchestral programming. Horowitz's discussion of how celebrity could outweigh the orchestral performance is well argued. His case could have been further strengthened by putting these stellar performers in the context of the growing cult of celebrity that has become a key feature of American culture.

Horowitz's discussion of "offstage participants" is equally compelling. One of these participants is the audience. Horowitz brings in much interesting material about attracting and educating audiences for classical music through various programs of music appreciation. He discusses in some depth the careers of important figures in the business of managing classical music. Arthur Judson, who served as manager of the New York Philharmonic and produced concerts, both live and on the radio, is a striking example.

In some ways, however, the comprehensive scope of this book and its wealth of detail can become a weakness. The book's density sometimes impedes the flow of the narrative and obscures the author's key points and arguments. In places, the reader is confronted with lengthy lists of performers or conductors. Even the author warns the reader that the path through the book is not linear: "Though the basic framework of my story is chronological, I frequently circle back, as to leitmotifs, to reconsider or replenish pivotal personalities, events, and ideas."

Although the author is writing a history, he brings a clear viewpoint. He believes that for classical music to thrive in a particular setting it needs "native works by native composers." He thinks that the downfall of classical music in America is that it remained too Eurocentric. What is missing is a "vital national repertoire." In his historical account, he includes the work of American composers of classical music. However, in every case, they fall short in some way. George Gershwin's music, even his opera *Porgy and Bess*, was too closely aligned with jazz and popular music. Aaron Copland went too far into the realm of folk music and native musical expressions, for example in his ballet score for *Billy the Kid*, and the same could be said of Leonard Bernstein. Other composers such as Charles Ives were too individualistic or avantgarde.

The problem that Horowitz does not fully confront is how to create and nurture a "vital national repertoire." What are the defining characteristics of "native works?" In the peak period that Horowitz sees around the turn of the twentieth century, these questions were being asked. The main solution was to import a "Eurocentric" classical composer, Antonín Dvořák, who composed "native works" using thematic elements from what he understood as American Indian music and African American spirituals. Yet, Horowitz seems reluctant to accept similar approaches from American-born composers. In addition, he acknowledges that the most vital expressions of American music have come from jazz and popular music. However, he does not consider these musical forms in any way "classical."

The question then arises about the definition of classical music. It *is* Eurocentric. It was developed in Western Europe. Classical music was then imported to America as part of the European heritage that still dominates the "high" culture of the United States. Throughout the book, it sometimes seems that Horowitz wants it both ways. He wants classical music that is inherently Eurocentric but at the same time he wants classical music that would be somehow distinctively American. Jazz and popular music may not be, strictly speaking, classical, but they are native and they are vital. They offer the possibility of infusing some of the missing vigor into a form of classical music that is American. In addition, one strength of American culture is that it is truly a "melting pot." Incorporating these various musical traditions would be one natural expression of classical music that is distinctively American, as opposed to Eurocentric.

In assessing the state of a "vital national repertoire," another consideration Horowitz does not fully engage is the phenomenon of cultural lag. Classical music is inherently challenging for the audience. Throughout the history of European classical music, few composers enjoyed popularity from the listening audience during their lifetimes. They struggled to have their compositions performed. That situation has magnified as twentieth century classical music charted new paths in terms of tonality and rhythm. Classical music audiences are in the process of adjusting to these new sounds. Viewed from the historical perspective, the burgeoning cadre of American composers also have had to contend with the demands that twentieth century classical music placed on the listening audience. As Copland put it: "The new musical audiences will have to have music that they can comprehend."

Considering these issues and others, Horowitz's thesis that American classical music has never quite found its stride has much validity. He locates the difficulty with the many facets of the "culture of performance" that have been a predominant feature of classical music in America from the origin of the large scale and permanent institutions, especially the symphony orchestra, for performing classical music. The sheer complexity of their organization and the vagaries of the economic forces with which these institutions of classical music performance must contend make them major forces in setting the agenda for classical music in the United States. The great value of this book is that it provides the historical background and perspective with which to assess the present and future of classical music in America. The reader may agree or disagree with some of Horowitz's ideas about the "fall" of classical music in America. However, with this book Horowitz has succeeded in providing the thorough historical grounding with which to understand how to meet what many consider "today's 'classical music crisis.'"

Karen Gould

Review Sources

America 192, no. 19 (May 30, 2005): 26-27.
Booklist 101, no. 13 (March 1, 2005): 1127.
Commentary 119, no. 4 (April, 2005): 71-74.
The Economist 376 (July 9, 2005): 74.
Kirkus Reviews 73, no. 1 (January 1, 2005): 34.
Library Journal 130, no. 1 (January, 2005): 114-115.
The Nation 281, no. 10 (October 3, 2005): 34-36.
The New York Times 154 (June 25, 2005): B17.
Publishers Weekly 252, no. 4 (January 24, 2005): 232.
Weekly Standard 11, no. 8 (November 7, 2005): 38-41.

COLLAPSE
How Societies Choose to Fail or Succeed

Author: Jared Diamond (1937-   )
Publisher: Viking Press (New York). 575 pp. $30.00
Type of work: Environment, history, and sociology
Time: Historical and modern
Locale: Global

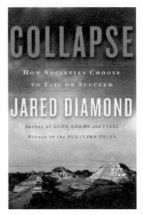

Diamond examines the reasons past societies have destroyed themselves and how modern humans can avoid their mistakes

History is littered with the ruins of past civilizations, great and small, whose fate stands as a cautionary warning to modern people. Is it possible to analyze scientifically the reasons complex civilizations collapse? Can the insights of science and history be combined to provide warnings about the risks facing technologically advanced cultures that overexploit their environments? Out of such analysis, is there a message for the modern Western culture of gas-guzzling cars, so-called McMansions, "big box" shopping centers, superhighways, suburban sprawl, and gridlocked cities? Can members of complex societies learn from their mistakes and modify their behaviors when threatened by collapse, or are they doomed to continue their unsustainable, environmentally destructive behavior? How aware were past societies of the impact of their behavior?

In *Collapse: How Societies Choose to Fail or Succeed*, Pulitzer Prize-winning author Jared Diamond likens the plan of his book to "a boa constructor that has swallowed two very large sheep"—case studies of past and present societies which have either succeeded or failed to resolve their environmental problems. After beginning with a discussion of the environmental problems of Montana, Diamond compares the disappearance of four past societies—the Easter Islanders, the Mayans, the Anasazi, and the Greenlanders—with the survival of others—the Icelanders, the New Guinea highlanders, and the Japanese—in order to identify the social and environmental factors leading to long-term survival or decline. Diamond next examines four modern societies—Rwanda, the Dominican Republic, China, and Australia—which have, in various degrees, met or failed to meet their environmental challenges. Finally, he concludes with some practical advice on corporate business practices, social values, globalization, and environmental decision making.

Diamond represents a new approach to environmental history which combines social and ecological factors to try to understand the interaction between human societies and their ecological environments. Traditional historical approaches have tended to explain the collapse of human societies primarily in terms of human factors—notably the "four horsemen" of war, famine, disease, and death—but Diamond believes that environmental factors are also important and that most societies eventually tend to deplete their natural resource base.

Humans are not very good about anticipating future environmental problems such as deforestation or soil depletion, or modifying their social behavior to avoid these kinds of problems. In the past, such environmental problems have been relatively localized, but now there is evidence of unprecedented problems of global proportions, and few mechanisms for global action to prevent them. The environmental mismanagement of one nation's resources, such as the Amazonian rainforest, or an ecological commons, such as the world's oceans, can affect the entire planet.

~

Jared Diamond is a geography professor at the University of California at Los Angeles and a member of the National Academy of Sciences, the American Academy of Arts and Sciences, and the American Philosophical Society. He has published more than two hundred articles, and his book Guns, Germs, and Steel *(1997) won the Pulitzer Prize.*

~

In his analysis of past and present societies' environmental collapse, Diamond identifies a framework of five contributing factors—environmental damage, climate change, hostile neighbors, friendly trade partners, and, most important, a society's responses to its environmental problems. Environmental damage can never alone cause social collapse; it is the response to those problems that is critical. Societies can choose to succeed or fail.

Diamond cites eight causes of ecocide (ecological suicide) in traditional societies: deforestation, habitat destruction, soil depletion, poor water management, overhunting, overfishing, introduction of nonnative species, human population growth, and increasing human consumption. To these he adds four modern problems: human-caused climate change, buildup of toxic chemicals in the environment, energy shortages, and human utilization of the earth's photosynthetic capability. All these problems point to the difficulty in achieving sustainability.

Not a single advanced industrial culture in the world today practices fully sustainable economic and ecological policies. The nonsustainable resource-extraction industries of mining, forestry, and petroleum production are particularly problematic. In such industries, nonsustainable environmental practices are encouraged by corrupt governments, weak regulations, the prevailing corporate business culture, and the desire for short-term profitability. Changes in consumer attitudes can bring about more sustainable business practices, however, if consumers demand that the products they purchase be produced sustainably.

The power of Diamond's arguments in *Collapse* stems from his thorough case studies and exhaustive details. In his prologue, "A Tale of Two Farms," he compares the practices of two dairy farms—one past and one present—in Norse Greenland and in modern Montana. Both are state-of-the-art, well-managed farms situated in ecologically and economically marginal areas for dairy farming. Each has a short summer growing season, is subject to climate change, is far from its market, and is subject to forces beyond its control. In the Garder colony of Greenland, the bishop's farm collapsed along with the rest of the colony five hundred years ago when the climate changed and the Greenlanders could not adapt to the new conditions. The Huls dairy farm in the Bitterroot Valley of Montana faces shrinking profit margins, suburban encroachment, and public environmental concerns that will force its owners to modernize or develop their farmland.

Diamond's thesis is that world society is currently on a nonsustainable course, with a series of environmental time bombs with fifty-year fuses which will explode during the next generation's lifetime. A nonsustainable course means that people are spending down environmental capital—forests, fisheries, soil, water, energy, and other resources. Despite the warnings of scientists, many governments persist in destructive policies, and businesses choose to maximize their profits by damaging the environment and hurting people. Diamond refutes the environmental skeptics by pointing out that a list of the fourteen most serious political trouble spots in the world—Afghanistan, Bangladesh, Burundi, Haiti, Indonesia, Iraq, Madagascar, Mongolia, Nepal, Pakistan, the Philippines, Rwanda, the Solomon Islands, and Somalia— is also a list of the most environmentally stressed nations in the world. People in these failed states—environmentally stressed, overpopulated, and unstable—tend to emigrate or turn to terrorism or violence.

Can a transition from the current unsustainable corporate-consumer culture to a more sustainable global culture be made without massive social dislocations and unrest? Can people anticipate future global problems and agree upon international solutions, or will short-term self-interest prevail? The examples of Rwanda and Haiti demonstrate that humans act desperately and irrationally when societies fail. Law and order disintegrate, economies collapse, and remaining resources are depleted as people fight over whatever is left. Anyone who thinks carefully about the world's present economic system must realize that a local and regional economy would be more sustainable from a transportation, energy, and resource perspective than the present transnational system.

Global economy is fueled by cheap, nonrenewable petroleum energy, but the age of cheap energy may be coming to an end. A statistical measure, the Hubbert curve, predicted that U.S. domestic oil production would peak about 1970, and now worldwide oil production is soon to peak. The future will bring increased worldwide demand for diminishing reserves. Global trade imbalances, especially in the United States, make economic adjustments difficult. The popular ideology of infinite economic growth and Americans' sense of entitlement make voluntary consumer restraints difficult. There are additional problems of global fresh water and food shortages, increasing competition for raw materials, and the threat of impending global pandemics. Democracies show little willingness or ability to make difficult long-term planning decisions, especially with a lack of credible political leadership on environmental issues such as global climate change, which are still not sufficiently understood. Unscrupulous leaders may try to distract their populations from looming environmental crises with war or religious conflict.

After his exhaustively researched and detailed analyses of comparative social collapse, Diamond's central question is: Why do some societies make such disastrous decisions? Building on Joseph Tainter's *The Collapse of Complex Societies* (1988), Diamond lists additional factors such as human lack of understanding or appreciation of ecological dynamics; inability to perceive gradual, long-term environmental degradation; rationally selfish short-term choices; destructive religious or social values; crowd psychology; and ignorance or denial. To the above list could be added the deliberate propaganda and corporate misinformation in American society that have left individuals so woefully misinformed about environmental issues.

Some societies avoid environmental collapse, either through enlightened political leadership or through determined grass-roots self-regulation. An example of the former is former president Joaquin Balaguer's environmental leadership of the Dominican Republic; an example of the latter is the stewardship of the New Guinea Highlanders. The magnitude of present environmental problems calls for unprecedented global cooperation and management of environmental "commons" such as the oceans and the atmosphere, but neither the means nor the will seems to be there yet, judging from the history of recent environmental treaties, especially the Kyoto Protocol. Are the preservation of clean air and the stability of the earth's climate more important than the individual's right to own a sport utility vehicle? How do societies make value decisions and distinguish between luxuries and necessities? Is it possible to find the social will to regulate nonessential uses of essential, finite natural resources? The key to survival seems to be to recognize which core social values to retain and which to discard.

Diamond offers a comparative analysis of the recent environmental records of five major extractive industries—oil, coal, hardrock mining, timber, and marine fisheries—and accounts for their varied records in terms of public pressure and differences in corporate culture. While some sectors of the oil industry have made major environmental progress, such as the Chevron oil fields in the Kutubu area of New Guinea, others such as the state-owned Pertamina oil company in Indonesia or Exxon Mobil have done less well, in part because of differences in management attitudes.

The hardrock mining industry has had an almost uniformly poor record, including resistance or noncompliance with environmental regulations and massive cleanup problems with abandoned copper or gold mines—mine tailings are dumped into rivers, and leach dams fail. Instead of taking responsibility for their actions, mining companies declare bankruptcy and walk away from the problems they have caused, leaving taxpayers with the cleanup burden. Considering the costs of environmental cleanup, Diamond questions whether hardrock mining can ever be considered profitable. The timber and marine fisheries industries have taken small steps toward sustainability, but much more needs to be done.

Some reviewers have objected that Diamond primarily discusses the decline of small and inconsequential societies, although he does discuss the role of periodic droughts and overpopulation in the collapse of Mayan culture. The purpose of the book, however, is to try to understand the interrelated cultural and environmental causes of social collapse and to learn from other cultures' mistakes. The magnitude of the present-day environmental problems is much greater than that of past cultures, whose fall had, at most, a regional impact. Modern societies are faced with the task of global sustainability.

Industrial cultures have weakened their ties to the natural world in order to take advantage of the economic efficiencies of industrial production, specialization, and mass markets. In the process, they have created consumer habits and expectations which will be difficult to change. Prevailing economic models assume unlimited growth in a finite world. Current levels of developed world consumption are unsustainable, but it will be difficult to persuade citizens to limit their consumption voluntarily and to conserve natural resources for the future. *Collapse* asks whether it is humankind's inevitable fate to overconsume its resource base, or whether people will be able to learn to live sustainably.

Andrew J. Angyal

Review Sources

America 192, no. 17 (May 16, 2005): 16-17.
Booklist 101, no. 5 (November 1, 2004): 442.
Commentary 119, no. 4 (April, 2005): 85-88.
Library Journal 130, no. 3 (February 15, 2005): 154.
Los Angeles Times, December 17, 2004, p. E1.
National Review 57, no. 6 (April 11, 2005): 43-44.
Nature 433 (January 6, 2005): 15-16.
New Statesman 135 (February 7, 2005): 50-51.
The New York Review of Books 52, no. 6 (April 7, 2005): 4-6.
The New York Times Book Review 154 (January 30, 2005): 10-11.
The New Yorker 80, no. 41 (January 3, 2005): 70-73.
Publishers Weekly 251, no. 46 (November 15, 2004): 48.
Time 165, no. 7 (February 14, 2005): 61.
The Wall Street Journal 245, no. 5 (January 7, 2005): W1-W4.

COLLECTED POEMS

Author: Jane Kenyon (1947-1995)
Publisher: Graywolf Press (St. Paul, Minn.). 357 pp.
  $26.00
Type of work: Poetry

*Kenyon's poems of daily life and of her struggle with
depression continue to move readers*

Jane Kenyon's *Collected Poems* assembles all of her
collections and adds her few uncollected poems. Published
at the tenth anniversary of her death, it is a handsome volume of poems which will continue to claim readers in the
future.

As a poet who died young and who was ill for some time before her death from leukemia in 1995, Kenyon is an appealing figure: One realizes that the photograph of her
on the book's back flap is a well-known one. Looking like an old child with streaks of
gray through her long hair, she sits, studious, and eyes downcast, in front of a typewriter. The image of the serious child is projected in the poetry—a sincere, serious,
direct tone maintained from first to last page. One might think that a full-length collection of such work would pall, as sometimes individual poems seem slight. This is
not the case, however. Although perspective remains the same throughout the decades of Kenyon's poetry, her subjects change; the angle of vision becomes more and
more clear to the reader as she looks at different aspects of experience.

Kenyon has many devoted admirers. She has had the same publisher, Graywolf
Press, from her first book, *From Room to Room*, published in 1978. She had four
books published before her death in 1995, and Graywolf has released two posthumous collections, *Otherwise: New and Selected Poems* (1996) and *A Hundred White
Daffodils: Essays, Interviews, the Akhmatova Translations, Newspaper Columns,
and One Poem* (1999), in addition to *Collected Poems. Collected Poems* contains all
of Kenyon's published poems, including those previously uncollected. The arrangement is chronological, except for the translations and uncollected poems, and so the
reader can follow the directions of the poet's life in her art.

The poems from *From Room to Room* are mostly short, observing New England
scenes and pondering the meaning of details of daily life. There is a lightness in the
texture of her free verse despite the sometimes heavy themes of the omnipresence
of sadness, death, loss—the lightness is the counterweight of nature's vulnerable
beauty. The natural scenes of New England in the early poems and the speaker's delight in her new experience of married life provide the surface of these poems: their
depths are shadows, glimpses of past and future losses, the constant realization that
youth and energy do not stay.

These poems narrate small events: cleaning the rooms of her new home, attending
a Baptist potluck dinner, enduring the felling of an eighty-year-old oak destroyed by a

Jane Kenyon was born to a jazz musician and a nightclub singer; her childhood was dominated by music and by the hard-line Christianity practiced by her grandmother. Kenyon received a B.A. and an M.A. from the University of Michigan, and she married poet Donald Hall in 1972. She won numerous awards for her work, including fellowships from the National Endowment for the Arts and the New Hampshire Commission on the Arts. She died of leukemia in 1995.

storm. The quiet of these poems is not equal to peace—there is a lot of anxiety in it. She looks for links to the past—in the feminist way of the 1970's, she seeks her place among the women of her family and her history, and yet her finding the links is not necessarily reas8suring, because it reminds her that she who is present will soon be part of the past. There is a lot of housewifery in this book—the trivial daily acts of a wife which acquire meaning, almost a sacramental meaning, through repetition.

The second section, from her 1986 book *The Boat of Quiet Hours*, moves more into concepts—the poet plays with philosophical ideas but always brings them down to earth, makes them concrete. Some of these poems make daring leaps from tenor to vehicle of a metaphor. A theme here seems to be simply perspective, what affects it, how it is changed by knowledge or position. The poems, mostly narratives, chronicle brief experiences which produce lasting or permanent changes. She also begins her travel poems, travel being another catalyst for change. More and more the poems are preoccupied with time, attempting to fix the moment; they are dominated by images of weather, elements of passing seasons and places.

The third section, from *Let Evening Come* (1990), has as its title poem the work that is seen in many anthologies—a poem that chronicles the events of an ordinary day, with its refrain, "Let evening come." Almost reminiscent of Margaret Wise Brown's 1947 children's classic *Goodnight, Moon*, its details emanate peace:

> Let dew collect on the hoe abandoned
> in long grass. Let the stars appear
> and the moon disclose her silver horn.

Its conclusion makes the jump from the particular to the absolute:

> Let it come, as it will, and don't
> be afraid. God does not leave us
> comfortless, so let evening come.

The feel of this poem characterizes the section—leaving the reader with a sense of true quietude. Too simple? For many readers, no. The sense of the ultimate rightness of things, however, does not predominate in the collection.

Constance (1993) has been called Kenyon's dark collection, as it describes her struggle with mental illness in vivid though sometimes strangely impersonal images. The reader does not get the sense of a Sylvia Plath or an Anne Sexton, though those women described similar experiences. Kenyon's poems are simple and direct. Moreover, they tend to focus on recovery as much as on the perceptions of illness.

"Having It Out with Melancholy" represents Kenyon's struggle with depression and her treatment for it; the doctors and medicines and the unfortunate though well-meant advice. Her visitor, depression, is described as an unholy ghost. The symptoms, as she describes them through images, will resonate with the reader who has encountered depression. The poem is especially persuasive in describing Kenyon's return to the world and her refreshed, renewed vision.

Other poems in this collection describe elements of her illness and others', and her sense of loss and fear. Her husband's illness is presented through odd detached details; illness and deaths of strangers preoccupy the poet. There are a lot of doctors and hospitals, details of illness, bandages, medicine. Oddments of ordinary conversation sound bizarre in clinical surroundings. There is frequently a rapid shift between beauty and loss, the ordinary and the catastrophic, so the reader has a sense of double vision and seems to see wholeness and health at the same time as fragmentation and illness. There is some spiritual consolation in the poetry, but it does not present itself as firm faith—rather as glimpses of light.

The two posthumous collections are combined in a section called *Last Poems*; they show Kenyon facing her final illness, interrogating God. These poems are filled with religious analogues and images as the poet tries to find coherence in her world.

Kenyon was a keen observer of small things, so sometimes her poems seem to evoke a whole era, and the decades merge into one another as the book progresses. The details of household activities and possessions are typical of the time period. Even the style seems fitted to the era. The first book, published in the 1970's has that decade's bluntness and tendency to brevity and closure. Kenyon's poems become more open and layered in later years. The tone, however, remains the same: direct, lucent, precise, someone describing a life from inside it, alert to all nuances.

A theme that surfaces and disappears like a dolphin throughout the book is the search for God. Conflicting, shifting attitudes toward the spiritual make this a poetry of spiritual searching, not quite in the muscular, almost God-stalking manner of Sexton but rather in a tentative way. The sacramental vision appears and disappears throughout Kenyon's work as she walks through foreign and familiar landscapes, almost always the observer but sometimes reaching out to partake or touch. Epiphany seems to be a sudden conjunction of planets, not to last, but for a moment satisfying the deep thirst for belief.

Her fundamentalist grandmother is a major figure in early poems, making her grandchild wonder how a person could be loving and yet so unyielding as to fill her grandchild's ears with tales of hellfire. Kenyon's response to spiritual bullying is withdrawal, of course, but she desires to define God for herself.

Kenyon's search for transcendence goes in a different direction, toward a transparent nature which reveals glimpses of its creator, but Grandmother surfaces now and then with her Protestant severity, and images of the catholic world begin to appear. At times a vocal Christian, resting secure in her faith, at times withdrawing from any kind of structured belief, Kenyon remained a God-seeker whose poems are spiritual explorations and perhaps experiments. The faith of them is most evident in the poems of mental illness and recovery. She said in an interview with Bill Moyers, when asked how she avoided attempting suicide when depressed, "My belief in God, such as it is, especially the idea that a believer is part of the body of Christ, has kept me from harming myself."

Her later poems, especially but not exclusively those written after the diagnosis of her fatal illness, took on the quality of a struggle with belief. In one poem, "With the Dog at Sunrise," she comments: "Searching for God is the first thing and the last,/ but in between such trouble, and such pain."

The appeal of Kenyon's books grows through the reading. The childlike directness of her vision is enhanced by her sudden and sometimes startling insights into the transcendence of nature and the reality of loss. The books are followed by a brief section of uncollected poems, on the same topics but slighter than those included in the books; the last poem of the last collection, "The Sick Wife," seems to dwarf them.

At the end of the book is a group of translations of Anna Akhmatova, preceded by a brief biography and discussion of that poet's work. The poems are free-verse translations, as Kenyon explained, because she had to sacrifice either form or image and chose to sacrifice form. The poems are odd, sounding halfway between Kenyon's work and Akhmatova's. So much of the Russian poet's meaning is in the sound that Kenyon's free-verse renditions seem more interpretations than translations. She has chosen mostly Akhmatova's less political poems about her experiences as a woman, some of them early works before Russian history caught her in its deadly entanglements. These poems sound pleasant and real, though not particularly Russian. They may appeal more to Kenyon's audience than to Akhmatova's. It is a little disappointing to find this section last, as readers might like to close the book on Kenyon's own words, although certainly the translations can be read into Kenyon's life.

One might expect that a full-length book of readily accessible poetry might be dull, but the freshness of vision and the directness of the observation make this one hard to put down and easy to come back to. The clear-eyed spiritual seeking and the refusal to compromise with the truth make this work particularly rewarding for readers who look for transcendence in literature but are unwilling to settle for the canned variety.

Janet McCann

Review Sources

Booklist 102, no. 1 (September 1, 2005): 43.
The New York Times Book Review 155 (November 20, 2005): 20.
The Washington Post Book World, October 9, 2005, p. 12.

THE COLLECTED POEMS OF KENNETH KOCH

Author: Kenneth Koch (1925-2002)
Publisher: Alfred A. Knopf (New York). 761 pp. $40.00
Type of work: Poetry

This collection brings together Koch's shorter poems written over a period of forty years, from 1950 to the poet's death in 2002, and highlights his reputation as one the great experimenters and humorists in American poetry

The Collected Poems of Kenneth Koch begins with his earliest poems written between 1952 and 1954 but not published until fifty years later in the 2002 collection *Sun Out*. Koch admitted that they were so different in style from what he wrote later that they never quite fit in any of his early collections, and the reader can quickly see how different, how strange the work seems. If readers are looking to poetry for a message, or some subtle argument about various themes, this collection will quickly put them off that hunt. Koch quotes the philosopher Ludwig Wittgenstein to help readers appreciate his philosophy in his earliest poems: "There are no subjects in the world. A subject is a limitation of the world." Indeed, a reader would be hard-pressed to determine any meaning, any theme or subject in the poems: They are experimental in nature, playful, whimsical, nonsensical in most senses of that word but they give pleasure if one gives in to the anarchic, antilogical, antirationalist world of the surreal.

One poem, titled "The Man," is cleverly organized into short speeches given by various parts of the body, from the penis to the thumbnail, with brief stops in the forehead and underarms, among other sites. A quick look at what these parts say will show that Koch's very rational and theatrical structure is being undermined. The tibia, for example, says, "When the foreleg is blue/ Covering the lanternslides with fluff country/ Panoramic Canada seventieth/ Catalogue white swans beer barrel publishing mouse ditch/ Wristwatch." The knee quickly adds a rejoinder: "With fennel pals the ranch./ The best nights in Arabia. Cotton punches. Rearward actions."

Where does this kind of nonsensical poetry come from? Certainly it derives, in part, from the experiments of the surrealists and Dadaists in Europe in the early part of the twentieth century. They introduced the idea of using chance, dreams, and random associations in the construction of literature and art. They also began the work of using nonnarrative techniques to subvert readers' desires for clear, easy-to-read texts. Koch, at least in this early stage of his career, embraces their ideals without hesitation.

In addition, Koch was working at the time in New York with a group of writers and painters who were opposed to works of art that emphasized linearity, rationality, logic, and sentimentality. This group, known as the New York School, included the poets Frank O'Hara, John Ashbery, and James Schuyler as well as the artists Jane

Freilicher and Larry Rivers. Although Koch would later go his own way, eventually making a truce with narrative and meaning, in his earliest works his complete immersion in the New York School of poetry is clear.

Koch's first published book, *Thank You, and Other Poems*, appeared in 1962. It included one of Koch's most famous poems, "Variations of a Theme by William Carlos Williams." It is a comic send-up of Williams's well-known 1934 poem "This Is Just to Say," which reads:

> I have eaten
> the plums
> that were in
> the icebox
>
> and which
> you were probably
> saving
> for breakfast
>
> Forgive me
> they were delicious
> so sweet
> and so cold

Koch makes four comic passes at Williams's original, keeping the logic of the petition for forgiveness after a transgression, but his transgressions and apologies are so extreme, and so funny. Here is one: "We laughed at the hollyhocks together/ and then I sprayed them with lye./ Forgive me. I simply do not know what I am doing." Clearly Koch is maintaining his anarchic vision of the world, demonstrated by his inability to let stand the more staid parts of the literary tradition, but he also shows that he is able to make sense, create comic logic.

Another example from this 1962 collection will demonstrate the kind of poetry that Koch grew into after his overly surreal period. "Desire for Spring" actually seems to be about a speaker's desire for spring—nothing anarchic there. He states clearly, "I want spring," and asks, again clearly, "When will there be a perfectly ordinary spring day?" He then ups the ante by contrasting his spring days of desire with his actual days, not of winter coldness, snow and drear, but "Calcium days, days when we feed our bones!/ Iron days, which enrich our blood!/ Saltwater days, which give us valuable iodine!" The language may be clear, the syntax appropriate and grammatical, but the peculiarity of the words to describe the days—calcium, iron, and saltwater—create the joyful playfulness readers associate with Koch's most successful poems.

In his 1969 collection, *The Pleasures of Peace*, Koch includes translations of poems by Latin American authors (who do not exist outside of Koch's imagination) as well as one of his signature poems, "Sleeping with Women," in which the phrase "sleeping with women" appears more than sixty-five times. It is a very sensual, quirky poem in which there are "lands sleeping with women, ants sleeping with women . . ./ Bees sleeping with women/ And tourists, sleeping with them/ Soap,

sleeping with women; beds sleeping with women/
The universe." The expansive closing line summarizes the poem's central theme: "Asleep and
sleeping with them, asleep and asleep, sleeping
with women, asleep and sleeping with them,
sleeping with women." The erotic and the comic
are, for some, strange bedfellows, but in this
poem they rest together comfortably.

In *New Addresses* (2002), Koch uses an old
technique of writing apostrophes—poems spoken directly to a person, usually—and in this
case he speaks to, among other things, buckets,
stammering, orgasms, scrimping, and "To Various Persons Talked To All at Once." There is
even one address to Koch's old addresses, his
old places of residence: "I am all right but I think
I will never find/ Sustenance as I found in you,
oh old addresses/ Numbers that sink into my soul/
Forty-eight, nineteen, twenty-three, o worlds in
which I was alive." In this case the comic idea of

*Kenneth Koch has won many
awards for his poetry, including the
Bollingen Prize (1995), the Rebekah
Johnson Bobbitt National Prize for
Poetry awarded by the Library of
Congress (1996), and the Phi Beta
Kappa Prize in Poetry (2001). He
taught at Columbia University and
published two seminal works on the
teaching of creative writing to
young children:* Wishes, Lies, and
Dreams *(1970) and* Rose, Where
Did You Get That Red? *(1973). A
fiction writer, essayist, dramatist,
and poet, he was elected to the
American Academy of Arts and
Letters in 1996.*

addressing an address, of speaking so glowingly of numbers, is linked with a nostalgic moment of seemingly genuine emotion. One of the many effective poems in this
winning collection is "To Jewishness." Here the addressee is Jewishness itself, not Ju-
daism the religion, and Koch mentions his desire to conceal his Jewish identity when
he discovers the virulence of anti-Semitism in the Army and his own desire for the
other, for women with "blonde/ Hair, blue eyes": For Koch, "Christianity (oddly
enough) had an/ Aphrodisiac effect." When Jewishness speaks in the poem, like
Yahweh, offering the cultural gifts of Gustav Mahler, Albert Einstein, and Sigmund
Freud, Koch balks, preferring the non-Jewish, the canonized icons of Percy Bysshe
Shelley, Lord Byron, John Keats, and William Shakespeare. By the end of the poem,
however, Koch acknowledges that he let the "flatness" of life capture his own concept
of Jewishness, and "I let it keep you/ And, perhaps, of all things known,/ That was
most ignorant."

Although Koch's poems, in general, are playfully inventive, free-verse romps, he
also was a formalist who enjoyed, specifically, writing in the verse structure of his
comic poetic hero, Lord Byron. Byron made ottava rima famous in his epic *Don Juan*
(1819-1824), and Koch uses the same eight-line stanza with its *ababababcc* rhyme
scheme in a number of his poems, including his long epics *Ko; or, A Season on Earth*
(1959) and *The Duplications* (1977), not included in this book. When his last collection, *A Possible World*, appeared in 2002, when Koch was seventy-seven, readers
were given one last glimpse of the formalist Koch in the opening poem, "Bel Canto."
Here he makes an inventory of his life, from his poetic theories, including his "Desire
of course not only to do old things/ But things unheard of yet by nuns," to his own life
as a man—both father and husband—rather than his life as a poet only:

How much I'd like to live the whole thing over,
But making some corrections as I go!
To be a better husband and a father,
Be with my babies on a sled in snow.

In "My Olivetti Speaks," a poem from *Straits* (1998), Koch writes that "poetry, which is written while no one is looking, is meant to be looked at for all time." For many readers, lines such as those describing his desire to be a better father, or be "with his babies on a sled in snow" may not have the power, or resonance, or attraction in them to be looked at for all time, or even briefly, but Koch's career can certainly not be decried simply because of a few flat lines. Koch achieved in his brilliant career what few poets have managed: He produced poems seemingly effortlessly and often; he experimented tirelessly with form, with technique, with genre classification; he influenced countless poets by his inventiveness and his openness to the comic, the sensual, the nonsensical, and the mundane; he lived a life devoted to art, both its creation and its promulgation, through such influential books as *Wishes, Lies, and Dreams* (1970), a guide for teaching young people how to write poetry; and he wrote more than thirty-five books of poetry, fiction, theater, and nonfiction—an amazing output.

For those enamored of his work, *The Collected Poems of Kenneth Koch*, when linked with his *Collected Long Poems*, will provide readers with the entire poetic career of this outrageous, energizing, wildly inventive American poet.

Kevin Boyle

Review Sources

Booklist 102, no. 6 (November 15, 2005): 15.
The Nation 282, no. 3 (January 23, 2006): 28-32.
Publishers Weekly 252, no. 42 (October 24, 2005): 38.
The Times Literary Supplement, November 25, 2005, p. 9.

COLLECTED STORIES

Author: Carol Shields (1935-2003)
Introduction by Margaret Atwood
Publisher: Fourth Estate (New York). 593 pp. $30.00
Type of work: Short fiction

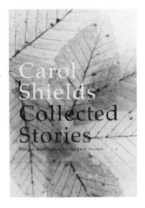

This tribute collection of Shields's three volumes of short stories includes a chapter of a novel she was working on when she died

Carol Shields is better known and more respected as a novelist than she is as a short-story writer, having established her reputation with her Pulitzer Prize-winning novel *The Stone Diaries* (1993). "Light and breezy" is a phrase often used to describe her short stories. Whereas Shields appears most interested in the realistic exploration of character in her novels, her stories seem primarily intent on examining ideas; these stories are frequently little "what if" concept pieces or considerations of common objects and phenomena. To call Shields's stories experimental, as many reviewers have, may be to dignify them with more weight than she intended to give them. One critic has described her witty fictional forays as "Borges-lite," but that, too, may connote more philosophical implications than many of her stories deserve. After all, the word "experimental" perhaps should not be confused with "fooling around" with little narrative essays on the metaphoric significance of such things as keys, or windows, or the weather.

Shields once told an interviewer that her earliest writing began with short stories. Although the form was not one that interested her much, she said that she did not think she could write a novel until she served some sort of apprenticeship in the shorter form. After writing several forgettable—as she termed them—short stories, she turned to poems, which she thought of as little toys one carries around in the head. Years later, after beginning to write novels, she returned to the short-story form when she got stuck in the middle of her novel *Swann* (1987) and decided to spend a year experimenting with different narrative approaches, having in mind about twenty short stories from various imaginative angles. The book that resulted from these experiments was *Various Miracles* (1985), and the year she spent on it she considered a sort of mini-sabbatical. This attitude suggests a crucial difference between the short stories of Shields and her Canadian colleague Alice Munro, who uses the short form to explore complex human interactions.

All of Shields's previously published short stories are included in *Collected Stories*. Her three collections span three decades. Typical of Shields's kind of story is the title piece of her first collection, *Various Miracles*, for it signals both her delight in coincidences and her interest in the intersection between fiction and reality. After listing several anecdotal coincidences, such as the time three strangers riding on a bus were reading the same novel, Shields narrates this longer anecdote: A writer takes her

Canadian author Carol Shields's
The Stone Diaries (1993) won the
Pulitzer Prize and the Governor
General's Award in 1995. Her
novel Larry's Party *(1997) won the*
National Book Critics Circle Award
and the Orange Prize. Shields died
of cancer in 2003.

manuscript to a publisher who had earlier expressed some reservations that the novel depended too heavily on coincidences. A gust of wind blows it out of her hands, and she has to retrieve the separate sheets which have landed all over the street, only to discover that one page is missing. Later, a woman in a red coat finds the missing page while buying zucchini in a grocery store. The first lines of the page describe a woman in a red coat buying zucchini in a grocery store.

"Scenes" has a similar feel to it. Various incidents from the life of a woman named Frances are described, ending with a conviction central to Shields's short stories, that scenes are what a life is made of, little keys on a chain that open nothing but simply exist for their beauty and the way they chime in her pocket.

Shields likes to create lists of objects as well as incidents. She uses such objects as metaphors for various aspects of the way she perceives the whimsical nature of reality. "Dolls, Dolls, Dolls, Dolls" describes a half-dozen different experiences one woman has with dolls. "Invitations" is about a series of five invitations a woman receives to parties, all for the same Saturday evening. When she begins to imagine that something is conspiring to consume a portion of her life by taking possession that particular evening, she decides to stay home. Some of these "list" stories are about little events of everyday life which achieve some sort of transcendent meaning. For example, "Taking the Train" is about one woman's experience of separate moments of unsharable significance, such as listening to a special song or finding a rare manuscript in a museum. "The Journal" is about a woman who keeps a diary on the travels she and her husband make, finally describing a rare moment of intimacy that she knows occurs only two or three times in one's life.

Only a few stories in *Various Miracles* are longer, more substantial examinations of character. For example, "Fragility" explores a man's point of view as he and his wife look for a home in a new area after the death of their son. "Others" is about a simple, friendly gesture which initiates a couple's yearly receipt of a Christmas card. Although Shields begins the story with a serendipitous event, as she usually does, the piece is really about the parallel development of two marriages, the distant one serving as a mirror template of the primary one.

Shields admitted that she was always compelled by the idea of transcendental moments in which one is occasionally able to glimpse a kind of pattern in the universe. She said that each of the stories in *Various Miracles* hangs on this faith and the question of what one is to do with such moments. She also said that she used the Emily

Dickinson quote "Tell the truth but tell it slant" as an epigraph to her first collection of short stories because she liked to use various angles of perspective. Her favorite means of writing was to set up a story conventionally and then turn it upside down. There is always a technical problem in writing, said Shields, and often a problem gave her something on which to hang the fiction. Sometimes a word or a phrase begins a story, a problem or a puzzle, something odd or surreal that does not quite fit in. Shields would begin with some point that interested her and then piece the story together, writing it over and over until it got longer and thicker.

Shields's second collection, *The Orange Fish* (1989), begins with a witty title story which sums up the nature of most of the collection's stories. Although there is more focus on character than in the first collection, these stories are short separate tales connected together rather than extended narratives. "Orange Fish" is about a couple who buys a lithograph of orange fish to hang in their home. The picture has an extraordinary effect on all those who see it, and it becomes a treasured piece, only finally to be copied endlessly and therefore cheapened and destined to fade into insignificance.

"Hazel" focuses on a woman who tries to make a life for herself and become independent after the death of her husband by demonstrating kitchen gadgets in department stores. Although she becomes very successful, she knows that all of her success is an accident, that things occur by happenstance and that such is the heart of life itself. Other more substantial character-based stories include "Hinterland," in which a middle-aged married couple go to Paris and are frightened by a bomb scare in 1986, and "Family Secrets," which takes the form of several separate stories which explore a young woman's coming to terms with the secret of her mother's mysterious illness.

Dressing Up for the Carnival (2000), Shields's final collection, seems to revert back to her original interest in "what if" concept stories, although here they become more fanciful, more self-conscious, and therefore more postmodern in their explorations of the interrelationship between fiction and reality. The title story is a parable about people in a town putting on costumes each day, illustrating that one cannot live without one's illusions. In "The Scarf," a story which was the basis for Shields's final novel, *Unless* (2002), a middle-aged writer wins a small literary prize for her first novel and must then embark on a modest promotional tour around the United States. She is bemused and a little embarrassed by the lack of interest in her work at her bookstore appearances.

"Weather" is a satirical parable about the weather ceasing to exist when the meteorologists go on strike. "Ilk" is an academic satire of postmodern jargonistic literary theory. Shields is more effective when her "what if" stories examine individual characters rather than abstract ideas. For example, there is a certain poignancy and truth in "Mirrors," about an aging couple who do not permit any mirrors or other reflective surfaces in their vacation home, thus enforcing a sort of vacation from focusing on the self.

Shields's playful experiments sometimes become tours de force of cleverness and ingenuity. For example, in "Absence," a writer discovers that a certain vowel key, denoting the very letter that signifies the "hungry self," no longer works on her typewriter. The dilemma she faces is how to write her story without a first-person pronoun, a problem she tackles as being similar to the limitations of the sonnet form. As one follows the struggles of the fictional writer, one only gradually becomes aware that Shields has written her entire three-and-a half-page story without a single "I," a feat that may make one smile with admiration but which, after all, is merely a highly skilled trick. Too many examples of the *jeu d'esprit* story in one collection can become tedious.

That many of the central characters in Shields's stories are artists should alert the reader to the fact that the author is using the short-story form to play literary games about the nature of the imagination. For example, "Invention" begins with Shields's examinations of seemingly trivial inventions, such as the steering wheel muff, but becomes a story about the invention of invention itself; that is, the discovery of how art itself comes into being. In it, a Greek shepherd boy makes the startling discovery that he can dream by day as well as by night. In "Windows," a window tax is imposed on the citizenry, making the economy-minded board up their sources of light. However, in a classic example of art triumphing over reality, a couple of painters paint a window over their boarded-up one, providing themselves not with real light but with the idea of light, which is even more alluring than light itself. The art window becomes ever better than a real window in its presentation of all that is ideal and desirable in the sensual world.

The only previously unpublished story in the volume is "Segue," written as the first chapter of a novel Shields was working on when she died. (Her daughter prepared the piece for publication.) About a sixty-seven-year-old woman who writes a sonnet every fourteen days, the work stands alone as an independent story about Shields's fascination with frozen moments of transcendence created within the seeming restrictions of literary form.

Charles E. May

Review Sources

Atlanta Journal and Constitution, February 13, 2005, p. 6L.
Booklist 101, no. 8 (December 15, 2004): 709.
Kirkus Reviews 73, no. 3 (February 1, 2005): 149.
Library Journal 130, no. 1 (January, 2005): 104.
Los Angeles Times, February 6, 2005, p. R8.
The New York Times Book Review 154 (February 6, 2005): 22.
Publishers Weekly 252 (January 24, 2005): 223.
The San Diego Union-Tribune, February 6, 2005, p. B1.
The Times Literary Supplement, July 23, 2004, p. 21.

THE COMMAND OF THE OCEAN
A Naval History of Britain, 1649-1815

Author: N. A. M. Rodger (1949-   )
Publisher: W. W. Norton (New York). 907 pp. $45.00
Type of work: History
Time: 1649-1815
Locale: Great Britain, the Caribbean, Denmark, Egypt,
France, the Netherlands, Spain, and the United States

*This original analysis of Britain's Royal Navy and how
it came to rule the seas is exhaustive*

Principal personages:
SAMUEL PEPYS, a diarist and administrator
who did much to improve the financing
of the British navy
LORD NELSON, a vice admiral whose victo-
ries in the Napoleonic Wars confirmed
Britain as the world's most feared naval
power

There is an enduring fascination with Britain and its performance during what has come to be known as the Napoleonic Wars, a period of continual conflict with France from 1793 through 1815. Such interest is hardly surprising when one considers that this was the first global conflict, one that ranged from Egypt to the Caribbean region, whose participants numbered in the millions. Keen interest among readers is reflected most notably in historical fiction, where a number of multivolume series have cele-brated British military prowess, from C. S. Forester's Horatio Hornblower of the Royal Navy to Bernard Cornwell's Richard Sharpe of the army.

Noteworthy among recent works in this genre are Patrick O'Brian's Aubrey/ Maturin novels, which have been highly praised for raising historical military fiction to a new level. The volumes in the series examine the fictional lives of Captain Jack Aubrey and naval surgeon Stephen Maturin against the backdrop of Napoleon Bonaparte's rule as emperor of France. For those who are familiar with the series— and its followers are legion—it is all too easy to accept what O'Brian posits in a work of fiction as an established historical fact. That he was a frequent visitor to the Na-tional Maritime Museum in London lends his writing even more authority. By com-bining an easy grasp of historical research with a perfect pitch for period dialogue, O'Brian—in the tradition of the best novelists—created a world more convincing than the thing itself. Let the reader beware. Every O'Brian aficionado knows that Ste-phen Maturin continually lambastes the Royal Navy regarding grog, the daily ration of diluted rum which the doctor believes is undermining the sailors' health. It is with some degree of shock, therefore, to learn that crewmen largely consumed beer or wine and that there are no references in the historical record to a rum ration until 1844. This

～

N. A. M. Rodger is the author of
numerous books, including The
Wooden World: An Anatomy of the
Georgian Navy *(1986) and* The
Safeguard of the Sea: A Naval
History of Britain, Volume 1, 660-
1649 *(1997). In addition to being a*
fellow of the British Academy, he
holds the title of professor of naval
history at Exeter University.

～

is just one of countless revelations, both large and small, in N. A. M. Rodger's book *The Command of the Ocean: A Naval History of Britain, 1649-1815.*

Most studies of maritime military history fall into two fairly distinct categories. There are those that concentrate on the sea battles and how the participants brought about victory or defeat and the consequences for combatants. The most common example, of course, is Lord Nelson's victory at Trafalgar, Spain, in 1805. Then there are the technical studies of the ships which describe their sailing qualities, their durability under fire, and their armament, complete with detailed line plans. Each of these approaches has its advantages: The deeds performed by sailors under the most adverse conditions are worth remembering, and one does need to understand how vessels of war perform the way they do.

Although these approaches can reveal much about the design and operation of the machines of war, the risk here is that of freezing a moment in time. One can learn much about late eighteenth century naval tactics from a study of the Battle of Trafalgar, but the action itself reveals little about the political and financial forces that led to the battle being fought at that place and time. Moreover, the British naval force that opposed Napoleon and his allies at Trafalgar was not the same entity that battled the Dutch in the seventeenth century. In other words, what is lacking is both breadth and depth. Happily, readers are well served by N. A. M. Rodger, whose highly lauded previous volume on the Royal Navy, *The Safeguard of the Sea* (1997), dealt with the period 660-1649. *The Command of the Ocean*, the second volume in the series, continues with the same high level of scholarship.

Clearly, Rodger has done his research, and he is nothing if not comprehensive. In addition to the thirty-six numbered chapters and the usual introduction and conclusion, the book includes some fine illustrations of common sailors as well as naval administrators, eighteen well-executed maps, eight appendixes ranging from a chronology of events to naval finance, and two extensive glossaries of terms. He even provides a brief note on the conventions used in dates and battle names—a considerate and welcome service for nonspecialists wading through this closely printed book. In spite of its density of detail and historical sweep, Rodger's book essentially answers some deceptively simple questions: What were the forces that shaped the Royal Navy from the mid-seventeenth century through the Napoleonic period? What enabled Britain to become the mightiest naval power by the time of Napoleon's defeat in 1815?

In shouldering this task, Rodger could have adopted the traditional date-by-date narrative, organizing his book in a straightforward chronological format or even by key battles in British naval history. The drawback of this method, again, is a certain shallowness. There is the potential for a multiplicity of narratives or perspectives even when dealing with a well-defined topic in a narrow time frame. From one vantage point, one might examine the political and financial forces that constituted the fleet during a particular decade. Other approaches might take that same period and examine fleet actions or shipboard life.

Of course, there is no single "correct" method in writing a book of history. Inevitably, one is faced with the fact that only a selection of the available information can be used, and even that reflects the prejudices of those who created the historical record and the person making the selections. What makes Rodger's method unusual—and ultimately successful—is that he engages his subject matter with a four-part approach. Each of the chapters is named, but each also bears one of four subtitles characterizing the type of subject matter in that particular chapter: "Operations," which comprises nineteen chapters in the book, describes the various naval engagements of the British navy; "Administration," constituting six chapters, addresses such essential matters as funding for the navy; nine chapters are devoted to "Social History," that is, the lives of the crew and officers; and finally, "Ships," two chapters that deal with the actual vessels.

The upshot of this method is a repeated examination of a given block of time from several different perspectives. This is evident in the opening chapters of Rodger's book. In the first two chapters, fleet operations against the Netherlands and Spain are described under the Commonwealth (1649-1654) and then the Protectorate—the period when Oliver Cromwell became military dictator (1654-1659). Rodger follows this with a detailed discussion of the same period (1649-1660) from the perspective of administration: how the government sought ways to fund and provision an expanding navy. Finally, in a chapter titled "The Melody of Experienced Saints," Rodger deals with the issues that vexed seamen in an organization stressed by change: shifting ranks, the chances for promotion, and the grim reality of unpaid wages. Both structurally and aesthetically, Rodger's method is a triumph, a grand symphony of British history that informs and delights the reader with its recurring themes.

What emerges from this veritable sea of nautical research is a picture of a nation endeavoring to fashion itself into world power while struggling with its own internal strife. That last item is not a small matter. With the notable exception of Ireland, the British domestic historical record is one of relative tranquility throughout the nineteenth and twentieth centuries. However, anyone reading Rodger's volume will be reminded that the British were shaken by political and religious temblors of great magnitude from the fifteenth through the eighteenth centuries. By 1649, Britain had deposed and beheaded Catholic monarch Charles I in a brutal civil war and had become a military dictatorship operated by Puritan oligarchs. At what must have been the lowest point in its history, Britain's fleet was divided between Royalist and Puritan elements, while French and Dutch naval forces dominated the seas. This is undoubtedly the most informative segment of Rodger's book, for in it one can perceive the seeds of the mighty fleet which would one day defeat Napoleon.

The Commonwealth government and the Protectorate somehow managed to crush Royalist forces, expand their own fleet, fend off the French in an undeclared naval war, and survive several engagements with the Dutch navy, then the world's largest.

Britain's survival was due in part to its isolation as an island and the simple fact that, unlike the Netherlands, it could feed itself. As Rodger makes clear, however, these early naval engagements set the pattern for the centuries to come. In response to large fleet actions, the British navy developed the classic line-of-battle strategy, which made more effective use of gunnery. As the navy acquired battle skills, it came to be identified by the public as the prime defender of an island nation whose land forces were quite small.

One of Rodger's wonderful insights is that the huge expansion of the navy during the interregnum, the period when Britain lacked a monarch, is what led to its rise as a sea power under subsequent rulers. Despite all the prose of military histories that laud the valor of heroes, Rodger makes it clear that what enabled a ship of war to be adequately armed and manned was just as important as the battle itself. While there was a succession of English governments throughout the seventeenth century—monarchy, military dictatorship, a restored monarchy in 1660, followed by a coup and the installation of a foreign monarch (William of Orange, from the Netherlands) in 1688—there was a distinct continuity in the structure of the naval administration throughout.

Even though the system was strained by continual changes in personnel, neither Cromwell nor the monarchy scrapped structure that ensured the building and maintenance of the fleet. Indeed, one of the key insights of *The Command of the Ocean* is that of the navy's funding. The decision of the Cromwell administration to finance the expansion of the navy through permanent taxation and the use of credit represented a major innovation. These changes enabled this deeply divided nation to provision large fleets so they could remain at sea for long periods, something that was necessary to protect growing colonial possessions and the commercial fleets that delivered their products. This was the repeated cycle that was essential to the economic/military growth curve: the better the Royal Navy protected its commercial sailing fleets, the more revenue the economy generated for the Crown and the navy.

This system of imperial expansion did not always succeed. Britain's best-known military failures, of course, were its two wars with the United States, the American Revolution and the War of 1812. *The Command of the Ocean* is worth reading for the author's manifestly British analysis of these two conflicts alone. Those who believe in American destiny might find their views shaken by Rodger's book. He convincingly argues that the loss of the American colonies was largely due to the ineptitude of Lord George Germain, the man responsible for their administration. While some regard the War of 1812 as a kind of second struggle for independence, Rodger makes a strong argument for viewing it as a tragic sideshow during the Napoleonic Wars. What finally enabled Britain to dominate other navies was a combination of administration (building, maintaining, and feeding the navy) and seamanship (years of blockading French ports). For those who wish to know how Britain's navy came to rule the seas in the Napoleonic period, *The Command of the Ocean* is, and will undoubtedly remain, the best work on the subject.

Cliff Prewencki

Review Sources

The Atlantic Monthly 295, no. 4 (May, 2005): 112-114.
Contemporary Review 286 (April, 2005): 249.
The Economist 373 (November 20, 2004): 88.
History Today 54, no. 12 (December, 2004): 55-56.
Library Journal 130, no. 2 (February 1, 2005): 99-100.
New Criterion 23, no. 9 (May, 2005): 86-88.
New Statesman 133 (October 11, 2004): 54.
Publishers Weekly 252, no. 7 (February 14, 2005): 63.
The Spectator 296 (October 23, 2004): 54.

A CRACK IN THE EDGE OF THE WORLD
America and the Great California Earthquake of 1906

Author: Simon Winchester (1944-   )
Publisher: HarperCollins (New York). 462 pp. $28.00
Type of work: Environment, history, natural history, and
 science
Time: April 18, 1906, and thousands of years into the past
Locale: San Francisco

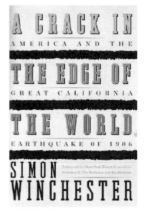

*This work examines the geological science of plate tec-
tonics and its influence on civilization, with particular focus on the San Francisco earthquake of 1906*

As indicated by its subtitle, *A Crack in the Edge of the
World* is focused on the earthquake of 1906, which destroyed much of the young city of San Francisco. That
earthquake is easily worthy of a book of this length (more
than 450 pages), both for the magnitude of destruction and for the human drama that
accompanied it. Indeed, there have been many books already published on the topic,
including memoirs of survivors, clinical accounts of the seismic causes, more lurid
semifictionalized accounts of suffering and heroism, collections of photographs, and
more engineering studies of how different types of structures fared. (This book lists
some of these books in an appendix of "suggestions for further reading.")

While this book uses the 1906 San Francisco earthquake as a focal point, its temporal and geographic scope is much broader, extending across millennia and continents. Indeed, the earthquake is not so much the reason for the book as it is the lens for
looking at the sometimes-dry and always-esoteric science of plate tectonics, which
concerns movements in the earth's crust. Introduced in the 1960's, the theory of plate
tectonics, now widely accepted, explains earthquakes and other seismic events as being caused by the movement of continent-sized segments of the earth's surface. These
"plates" are in constant (albeit gradual) motion, riding on the earth's mantle. The location where the edges of two plates meet is a fault line, along which slippage occurs
and, occasionally, earthquakes.

There are obvious advantages to understanding the behavior of these plates, most
important for the location and engineering of buildings and other structures. Clues
that help to illuminate plate behavior are found in all manner of geological forma-
tions: mountain ranges, rivers, volcanoes, rock outcroppings, soils, and so forth.
These point to past seismic events and may help in the prediction of future ones.
Though there is general acceptance of the concept of enormous fragments of the
earth's crust slowly drifting on the sea of molten rock that is the earth's mantle, the
science of earthquake prediction is still in its infancy. For the time being, scientists are
much better at explaining why and how an earthquake has occurred, than when or
how it will occur.

The author, Simon Winchester, leads the reader on a journey across the North American plate, which encompasses not only North America but also part of the Atlantic Ocean, the western end of Eurasia, and Greenland. Winchester uses this trip, which he actually took, as a rough guide for a travelogue that goes on for about one hundred pages. At various points along the way—such as Charleston, South Carolina, and Meers, Missouri—Winchester describes not just the local geography but how that geography and infrastructure and society were shaped in part by geological forces over time. These are not dispassionate history lectures but engaging stories of people, places, and societies, laced with a healthy dose of trivia and vignettes about such things as how place names were conferred, how simple lives were affected by the insuperable forces of nature, and how Winchester's car responded when the road inclined upward to pass over a mountain.

Simon Winchester obtained his geology degree from Oxford and is a former journalist. He has written more than a dozen books, including The Surgeon of Crowthorne *(1998),* The Professor and the Madman *(1999),* The Map That Changed the World *(2001), and* Krakatoa: The Day the World Exploded, August 27, 1883 *(2003).*

The result is a story that is not quite a stream of consciousness but a far cry from a linear narrative. Winchester's constant shifting of time, place, and focus are not disorienting, thanks to his comfortable grasp of storytelling. He is an engaging and skilled writer, effortlessly balancing his prose on the edge between authoritative explanation and entertaining description. In those rare cases in which he deems a detail too off-point for the flow of his story, Winchester employs a footnote. One seldom reads more than three or four pages without running into one of these. Overall, Winchester's approach works as a way to connect the social, cultural, physical, temporal, and geographical facets of North America in a way that could not be achieved with a more traditional, linear text.

What of San Francisco and 1906? After a twenty-two-page prologue that introduces several individuals who would awake to the earthquake in the early morning of April 18, Winchester largely puts the event aside until the second half of the book, devoting the first half to discussing other places and eras and topics. Then, beginning in chapter 9, the book returns to San Francisco on the evening before the great earthquake. Equipped with the geology lessons and historical context from the preceding chapters, the reader is better able to appreciate the significance of the 1906 quake. One has learned how and why the city of San Francisco appeared where and when it did. One has a sense of the aspirations and mores of the society. One better understands the lurking, unpredictable, but inevitable danger that the San Andreas fault posed for the city. Afer providing background information in this way, Winchester, clearly relishing the suspense, describes the setting for the earthquake with a dramatic buildup of detail. He tells of the evening temperature, the sunset, the promise of spring in the air. He explains that the famous tenor Enrico Caruso was preparing to sing the role of Don Jose in *Carmen*, taking care to describe the Pacific Hotel, which shortly would fall victim to earthquake-triggered fire. Winchester describes the earliest wakers in the city, baking bread and brewing coffee. Then, finally, the individuals described in the prologue are back, experiencing "the savage interruption" that arose just minutes before dawn on April 18.

The chaos, confusion, and destruction are described in poignant detail. Then, after fewer than twenty pages, Winchester makes another detour to describe how the Chinese in 200 C.E. created an early version of a seismometer (or "earthquake weathercock"). After tracing the subsequent improvements to the point of the modern seismic device, the book returns (briefly) to the scene in San Francisco on April 18. These pages are illustrated with maps and photographs of the devastation. As Winchester notes, the San Francisco earthquake was "the world's first major natural disaster to have been extensively photographed: It was the seismic equivalent of the Civil War."

Winchester moves from describing the shaking of the earth and the toppling of buildings to the efforts to save lives and property. The earthquake itself lasted only about a minute, but the fires it spawned (through downed electrical cables and ruptured gas lines) lasted for three days. The injured had to be tended, and the dead had to be buried (or, in some cases, burned). Buildings had to be salvaged or, most often, razed and rebuilt. Perhaps especially interesting in the immediate aftermath of the earthquake are the efforts to restore civil order. Military troops from the Presidio were dispatched to cordon off dangerous areas and keep away onlookers. Orders were given to shoot looters on the spot. Liquor sales were banned, as were bare candles and other items and practices deemed dangerous. Additional U.S. soldiers came from Army bases in other states as far away as Virginia.

The large question that loomed as order was eventually restored was whether San Francisco could (or should) be rebuilt. One bemusing anecdote related by Winchester concerns the effort by San Francisco civic leaders to combat a potential perception that their city was earthquake-prone. Evidently, they attempted to expunge the word "earthquake" from official descriptions of the tragedy, substituting the word "fire." Their discussions concerning whether or not to rebuild Chinatown are also illuminating. On a larger scale, decisions about reconstructing the city would determine the physical appearance and cultural image of San Francisco. Winchester describes how streets were planned, how the new city hall was designed, and how parks were laid out. For the most part, he describes these efforts as hasty. Winchester regrets that the unique opportunity to rebuild San Francisco as a grander, more beautiful, and more significant city was passed up, suggesting that San Francisco came to be eclipsed in many ways by the likes of Los Angeles. He makes a good case that much of what defines San Francisco today was decided in those first few years after the earthquake. Once again, it is the intersection of seismic events and societal development that is illuminated by the aftermath of the earthquake.

Looking forward, Winchester turns to the obvious question of whether San Francisco is destined for another great earthquake. He notes the 1989 Loma Prieta earthquake (centered a few dozen miles south of San Francisco) which, while causing damage to many buildings and bridges, came nowhere near ruining Bay Area cities, which presumably were safer thanks to rigorous building codes. It is popularly accepted that the Loma Prieta earthquake, though not as large as its 1906 predecessor (6.9 and 8.3 on the Richter scale, respectively), managed to relieve plate tectonic tension that, were it to build up over time, could make possible a much larger earthquake. Winchester, however, sees the Loma Prieta earthquake as a "worrisome" harbinger because the latter quake was not a result of a rupture along the San Andreas fault. Therefore, because of constant tectonic movement, the San Andreas fault has been building up tension (unrelieved by an earthquake) since 1906. According to Winchester, "this means that an unimaginably enormous amount of kinetic energy is currently stored in the rocks of the Bay Area; one day, and probably very soon, this energy will all be relieved, without warning."

On that ominous note, Winchester finishes with an epilogue about his May, 2004, travels in Alaska to see how the trans-Alaska oil pipeline survives the movements of the Denali fault, which it traverses. After observing how various technological features allow the pipeline to flex with the earth's movements, Winchester ends the book with a pronouncement about "the fragility of humankind [and] the evanescent nature of even our most impressive achievements."

Steve D. Boilard

Review Sources

Booklist 101, no. 22 (August 1, 2005): 1951.
Entertainment Weekly, October 7, 2005, pp. 80-82.
Kirkus Reviews 73, no. 15 (August 1, 2005): 841.
Library Journal 130, no. 15 (September 15, 2005): 76.
The New York Times Book Review 155 (October 9, 2005): 18.
Newsweek 146, no. 16 (October 17, 2005): 70.
People 64, no. 15 (October 10, 2005): 51.
Publishers Weekly 252, no. 28 (July 18, 2005): 195.
Science 310 (October 7, 2005): 55-56.

THE CUBE AND THE CATHEDRAL
Europe, America, and Politics Without God

Author: George Weigel (1951-   )
Publisher: Basic Books (New York). 202 pp. $23.00
Type of work: Current affairs, history, philosophy, and religion
Time: The nineteenth century to 2005
Locale: Europe

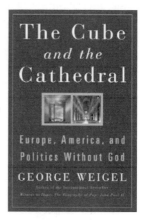

Weigel traces the cultural and philosophical causes of modern European secularism, which is portrayed as a profound betrayal of the religious origins of European civilization

Although he is frequently described as a Catholic theologian, George Weigel's best-known work is a biography of the late Karol Wojtyła, titled *Witness to Hope: The Biography of John Paul II* (1999). A senior fellow of the Ethics and Public Policy Center in Washington, D.C., Weigel has also written numerous articles and books best described as Catholic apologetics. Thus the present work, *The Cube and the Cathedral*, while ranging widely across the disciplines of history, current affairs, theology and philosophy, is essentially a defense of Christian civilization in Europe, and more particularly of the Roman Catholic patrimony upon which that civilization was built. What it lacks in originality, *The Cube and the Cathedral* more than makes up for in its incisive critique of Europe's post-World War II abandonment of that patrimony.

Weigel's book might better be described as an extended essay than an academic study of its subject. It does not progress systematically but rather by digressions and regressions. There are twenty-four titled chapters, though these are not numbered, nor is there a table of contents. Weigel cites a number of secondary sources, but these are not at all obtrusive and are documented in a brief set of endnotes. *The Cube and the Cathedral* is, therefore, intended for a broad audience of readers, especially those interested in the politics and history of modern Europe and the lessons its current "crisis of civilization" might hold for the United States.

A number of American writers (as well as some Europeans), even those with no particular religious position to defend, have regarded the rise of European secularism in the post-World War II era as symptomatic of a cultural malaise which threatens not only European identity but its very survival as a distinct civilization. Weigel enters the discussion with a memorable juxtaposition of symbolic images—the cube and the cathedral. The cube in question is the *Grande Arche de la Défense* in Paris, a colossal "human rights" monument completed in 1990 and intended to mark the bicentenary of the French Revolution. In fact, the *Grande Arche* is not so much an arch as an open cube of some forty stories faced in modernist glass and marble. Weigel notes that when he visited the *Grande Arche* in 1997, he was struck by the claim made in most of the Paris guidebooks that the *Grande Arche* is sufficiently gigantic to house within its cubic frame the entirety of the cathedral of Notre Dame. Indeed, in its grandiose geometrical purity, the *Grande Arche* is an aggressively secular symbol, one that seems to suggest that the age of faith represented by the cathedral of Notre Dame is now defunct.

Given the political and social symbolism of the *Grande Arche*, Weigel began to meditate upon the central question of *The Cube and the Cathedral*: "Which culture would more firmly secure the moral foundations of democracy? The culture that built this . . . essentially featureless cube? Or the culture that produced . . . the holy 'unsameness' of Notre-Dame and the other great Gothic cathedrals of Europe?" For Weigel, the *Grande Arche* represents a secularity now become the dominant motif of European culture and politics but is associated as well with the monolithic bureaucratic pretensions of the European Union, a potential superstate whose constitution omits any reference to the Christian origins of European civilization. Weigel's book assumes from the outset that the civilization that produced the *Grande Arche* is a civilization in a state of crisis.

The symptoms of "crisis" are manifold, at least from the American perspective. Dozens of articles and books have charted Europe's precipitately declining birthrates and noted its all but empty churches. Others have puzzled over Europe's flight from genuinely democratic political conflict into the safety of bureaucratic proceduralism and lamented its increasingly materialistic vision of social order. In seeking causes for these changes, Weigel considers a number of possible answers, only to reject them as superficial. It is not enough to point to the devastating demoralizing effects of two world wars; it is insufficient to look to the Holocaust as the definitive factor in the shaping of the postmodern European guilty conscience (and thus its failure of self-confidence). For him, a more satisfying answer to the problem must lie deeper.

Turning his attention to the early decades of the twentieth century, Weigel agrees with those historians who have seen World War I as the turning point in modern European history. It was, as he describes it in a chapter titled "The Trapgate of 1914," the "moment when European civilization began to destroy itself." In asking how the Great War could have happened, how the rage for self-mutilation could have started and continued for so long, Weigel turns to the nineteenth century philosopher Friedrich Nietszche (1844-1900), the "true prophet" of the age following upon his death. It was Nietszche's claim that all human moral systems are, in essence, fictions, that they are not grounded in any transcendental order and that when all such delusions are stripped away, the fundamental attribute of humanity is the "will to power." Weigel appears to see in the intense European nationalism of the second half of the nineteenth century, and in "the breakdown of the system of trust . . . that had been the

George Weigel is a Roman Catholic theologian and a senior fellow of the Ethics and Public Policy Center in Washington, D.C., as well as a consultant on Vatican affairs for NBC News. He has written numerous books, including The Courage to Be Catholic *(2002) and* Letters to a Young Catholic *(2004).*

human and moral glue of the European diplomacy in the preceding century," an underlying nihilism, one that was brought to full philosophical expression in the work of Nietszche.

In a key chapter, "Something New: The Drama of Atheistic Humanism," Weigel draws upon the work of the great Catholic theologian Henri de Lubac (1896-1991) to argue that Europe's twentieth century civilizational crisis is, in the last analysis, the product of the growth of what de Lubac called "atheistic humanism—the deliberate rejection of the God of . . . Abraham, Isaac, Jacob, and Jesus, in the name of authentic human liberation." While Weigel later traces the development of this atheistic humanism back to its origins in medieval nominalism, here he is concerned with the increasing tendency among nineteenth century thinkers to see the Christian moral order not as a liberating force (as it had traditionally been seen) but as a form of bondage. What is called authentic human freedom could only be achieved through liberation from the illusion of divine claims upon humankind.

Ironically, Weigel notes, the humanistic moral, political, and social orders conceived by the most influential of nineteenth century thinkers, such as Karl Marx (1818-1883), resulted in the construction of tyrannies greater than anything human society had known in the ages of faith. As Weigel writes, "At the heart of the darkness inside the great mid-twentieth century tyrannies—communism, fascism, Nazism—Father de Lubac discerned the lethal effects of the marriage between modern technology and the culture shaping ideas borne by atheistic humanism." Modern technology is, in itself, merely a tool, but a tool capable of producing in humans the illusion of autonomy from the transcendent order. When combined with purely human-centered philosophy, such a tool can become murderous. As Weigel eloquently argues, "ultramundane humanism is inevitably inhuman humanism. And . . . can neither sustain, nor nurture, nor defend the democratic project."

It is true, of course, that since 1989 and the collapse of the Soviet Union, any confidence among the European elite that the more radical utopian systems might produce a new millennium of social justice and world peace has waned. Nonetheless, the leaders of the new Europe remain wedded to a milder, liberal rather than radical, form of atheistic humanism. This relatively more benign vision of social order is most evident in the post-World War II formation of the European Union, several decades in the making but now an accomplished fact. Weigel focuses at some length on the recent debate over the European Constitution and its lack of any reference to the centrality of Christianity in the formation of European identity. For Weigel, this omission is a distressing indicator of a cultural amnesia which refuses to see anything of value in the centuries that preceded the Enlightenment and which may also reflect a widespread "Christophobia," not only among the elites but also within European society at large. Just as important, the omission of any specifically Christian reference in the constitution suggests a profound misconception about the purpose of constitutions. According to Weigel, constitutions have three functions: they organize the roles of the state and its various legislative, judicial, and legislative bodies; they define the relationship between the state and its citizens; and "they are the repository . . . of the values, symbols, and ideas that make a society." The framers of the European Constitution have ignored this third function, and in so doing "jeopardize, even abort, the entire constitutional process."

In the second half of *The Cube and the Cathedral*, Weigel returns to his original question: Is a wholly secular European society able to nourish and sustain democracy better than a society which recognizes the importance of its Christian foundations? His answer is, unequivocally, no. The problem for secular modernity is that its conception of the key democratic value, freedom, is flawed. The European elites, he says, look no further back than the eighteenth century Enlightenment for their understanding of freedom. Within this Enlightenment paradigm, freedom is understood only in negative terms; it is a freedom *from* rather than a freedom *for*. In other words, post-Enlightenment ideas of freedom presuppose that it is the possession of wholly autonomous individuals. What *telos*, or purpose, is this freedom supposed to serve? If this notion of freedom is severed from any traditional moral order, what is to prevent the autonomous individual from assuming the primacy of his or her own will, and thus shattering any lasting idea of the common good?

Weigel's alternative is the concept of freedom found in the theology of one of the most important Catholic thinkers of the Middle Ages, Thomas Aquinas (1225-1274). For Aquinas, freedom was not so much a condition granted by constitutions or states to their constituents but a habit of being. As Weigel puts it, "Freedom, on this understanding, is the means by which we act, through our intelligence and our will, on the natural longing for truth, goodness, and happiness." For Aquinas, the purpose of freedom is to develop the self in conformity with a transcendent moral order, not a license for self-indulgence or self-glorification. The unfettered, autonomous individual of the modern era has no place in this vision of freedom. Yet it is precisely an individualism run rampant which is threatening the common good and thus the democratic social order.

In one of the concluding chapters ("The Stakes for the States") of his book, Weigel asks just what the "Europe problem" has to do with Americans who, after all, are far from being the wholly secular society that Europe is. One answer is that a Europe uncertain of its identity, and lacking the self-confidence (and faith) to uphold the primacy of the traditional Christian moral order, is a Europe increasingly vulnerable to the influence of militant Islam. Already such nations as France and England are reeling from the effects of unprecedented Islamic immigration. It is, of course, possible that the Islamic immigrants will themselves eventually conform to the dominant secularism of European society, but early indications are that significant numbers will not. The Islamic tradition simply does not share the European (and American) understanding of a "civil society" existing separately from the state and the religious authorities, which is so essential for healthy democracy. Another reason Weigel believes that Americans should be concerned about the "Europe problem" is that many of the trends in Europe are at least tendencies in the United States. Even though church attendance and religious belief are still common, America is increasingly a secular society and one that shares the idea of freedom so common in Europe, which Weigel considers flawed.

In closing, one may with fairness say that Weigel has written an impressive introductory study of his subject. However, for the more serious student of the "Europe problem," *The Cube and the Cathedral* does not offer much that has not already been argued elsewhere and in greater detail. It might also be objected that Weigel never in this work defines precisely what he means by "democracy." There are many understandings of the term, and not all of them are compatible with the Christian tradition that Weigel so obviously values. Presumably he means to uphold an American-style democracy in which radically equalitarian claims of justice are constrained by the freedoms enshrined in the original Bill of Rights, but this is never clarified.

Jack Trotter

Review Sources

America 192, no. 21 (June 20, 2005): 25-26.
The American Spectator 38, no. 4 (May, 2005): 64-68.
Booklist 101, no. 14 (March 15, 2005): 1251.
Kirkus Reviews 73, no. 2 (January 15, 2005): 114.
Publishers Weekly 252, no. 10 (March 7, 2005): 62-63.
Weekly Standard 10, no. 30 (April 25, 2005): 39.

THE DARK GENIUS OF WALL STREET
The Misunderstood Life of Jay Gould, King of the Robber Barons

Author: Edward J. Renehan, Jr. (1956-   )
Publisher: Basic Books (New York). 352 pp. $30.00
Type of work: Biography
Time: 1836-1892
Locale: New York City

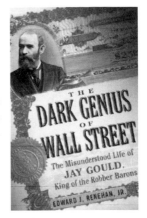

This revisionist biography of the notorious nineteenth century robber baron, resulting in a partial rehabilitation of the man and of his business practices, is vivid and impeccably researched

Principal personages:
JAY GOULD, a financier
JOHN GOULD, his father
JIM FISK, his business partner
DANIEL DREW, the chief (and unscrupulous) investor in the Erie
    Railroad
CORNELIUS VANDERBILT, a railroad tycoon, Gould's rival

Jay Gould was a "dark genius of Wall Street"—but not *the* dark genius, contends Edward J. Renehan, Jr. Plenty of other men—Cornelius Vanderbilt and Nelson Rockefeller, for example—engaged in cutthroat monopolistic practices. Gould was no inhuman engine of financial predation. He managed many of his businesses well and made good profits for his stockholders. He was well read, and he wrote well. He loved to garden, and flowers gave him a sense of exquisite joy. He was a family man, caring deeply for his children and devoted to his wife. He was charitable—often supporting good causes anonymously, and—other biographers notwithstanding—Renehan demonstrates that Gould was able to make and maintain many friendships. Even more impressive, he treated his workers well, although he had no tolerance for unions.

What accounts, then, for the legion of reporters and biographers who deemed Gould a fiend, the worst of the nineteenth century robber barons, the epitome of rapacious capitalism? Previous biographers, Renehan reveals, have not done their homework. Some of them, such as Edwin Hoyt, wrote nearly pure fiction, suggests Renehan, an avid researcher. His biography provides an eye-opening lesson in how a myth is fostered in order to further the biographer's biases and desire to entertain readers. Even contemporary newspapers invented copy about Gould when they could not find evidence to support a real story. *The New York Sun*, in fact, predicted divine retribution for Gould, a kind of editorializing no longer in fashion that the nineteenth century public craved when reading stories about robber barons—a phrase popularized by Gould's most famous, if not most accurate, biographer, Matthew Josephson.

Edward J. Renehan, Jr.'s books include The Kennedys at War, 1937-1945 *(2002),* The Lion's Pride: Theodore Roosevelt and His Family in Peace and War *(1998),* The Secret Six *(1995), and* John Burroughs: An American Naturalist *(1992). His writing has also appeared in* The Wall Street Journal *and* American Heritage. *He lives in Rhode Island.*

Surely Gould deserved infamy, the average reader might object. He did try to corner the gold market and drove the United States into a financial panic. He invented the sort of financial chicanery that the Securities and Exchange Commission was created to police. Renehan would not disagree. As he points out, Gould was a genius at identifying precisely that point in financial transactions where the most money was to be made. Early on, he made a small fortune in the leather trade, recognizing, as he wrote his father, that it was not the tanners but the merchants who commanded the true power of the industry. If Gould stood out from most other capitalists, it is because he was consistently innovative—sometimes acting in concert with his financial partners, sometimes cutting them out of the action when he saw an opportunity he must seize immediately.

Renehan does an excellent job of detailing Gould's financial schemes, but his most significant contribution is his portrait of the man himself. How did Gould feel about his own reputation? The well-read Gould quoted Niccolò Machiavelli to a friend: Better to be feared than loved. It was good business, in other words, to be perceived as the evil genius of Wall Street. In fact, Gould was not always successful. He made bad investments, his biographer shows—including those that resulted in tremendous losses when he attempted to corner the gold market.

Gould wanted the public to believe he was a Mephistopheles and that his businesses could not fail. Near the end of his life he did regret that he could not leave a better name for his progeny to bear. By then, however, he had become a captive of his myth. If he gave significant sums to charity anonymously, it was because on those occasions when his donations became public, Gould was ridiculed as attempting to salve his conscience (an odd accusation, actually, as the devil by definition does not feel guilt).

There is one point that Renehan might have emphasized even more than he does: Gould was a man in a hurry. He had a weak constitution, and several members of his family had died of tuberculosis. He did not expect to live long. Descriptions of him in his mid-forties emphasize premature aging. Given his immense labors and long hours at the office, it is surprising that he lived to age fifty-six, and he knew it. Perhaps Gould felt he did not have the time to be overly scrupulous.

Certain biographers, such as Renehan, balk at their genre's fragmentary nature and try to lend to their biographies the omniscience of fiction. For example, Renehan handles the fact that Jay Gould's father, John, outlived three wives by suggesting that John did not take a fourth wife because he felt he was cursed. This kind of idle speculation is unwarranted. Because of the state of medical science in the nineteenth century and especially the threat to women's health posed by puerperal fever, men tended to outlive their wives. Why would John feel especially cursed? Perhaps he was a doomsayer; perhaps not. "Perhaps" is the only word that rescues the biographer from falling entirely into the realm of fiction.

Fortunately, Renehan does not indulge in this kind of factitious filler often. Indeed, it is his mission to present Jay Gould's life by chiseling away at the encrusted myth that has elevated Gould as the cyclops of American capitalism, a monster who had an eye only for making money.

This work includes colorful portraits of "Diamond Jim" Fisk, Gould's business partner, and Daniel Drew, Gould's nemesis at the Erie Railroad. These rogues certainly rivaled Gould as cunning connivers, yet their outlandish personalities—especially Fisk's—drew more favorable press attention, because they seemed more human than Gould.

Reviewers have split on Renehan's revisionist biography, suggesting that his portrait of the young Gould learning about the tanning trade and how to survey land, as well as learning to be a conscientious railroad chief executive officer, are more persuasive than that of the later Gould who tried to dupe President Ulysses S. Grant into tightening the gold supply so that Gould could make an enormous profit. That Gould failed to hoodwink Grant may indicate he was not quite as clever as his legend suggests, but it obviously does not absolve him from the charge that he was a stock manipulator and schemer. Because of Gould's machinations, more than a dozen brokerage houses and banks went out of business. Roger K. Miller of the *Denver Post* thinks Renehan tries too hard to exonerate his subject. Miller notes that while Renehan claims that Gould only wanted to make money like his competitors, the biographer contradicts himself in showing that Gould corrupted the courts and the New York State legislature and worked with an already crooked Tammany Hall in New York City.

Renehan also provides a remarkably thorough social history of the post-Civil War period, often called the Gilded Age. It was a period rife with corruption—not merely in the business world but in politics as well. Scandals rocked President Grant's administration, and it was in this free-for-all atmosphere that Gould thrived, feeling that he had to protect himself from connivers and cutthroats who used physical force (even employing gangs) to corner their share of the market.

The rough-and-tumble of business in the nineteenth century United States is not entirely absent from today's world, suggests Joseph Nocero, in his *New York Times Book Review* assessment of Renehan's biography. Nocero compares Gould to Bernie Ebbers, the chief executive of WorldCom sent to jail for perpetrating a massive accounting fraud. Rogues such as Ebbers and Gould, Nocero suggests, may have hurt investors, but they also seem to have been indispensable in advancing technology. Whereas Gould pioneered a communications industry through his telegraph companies, Ebbers was responsible for the installation of many miles of fiber-optic cable.

In the end, though, it is Renehan's portrait of an exhausted Gould, the dedicated family man with surprisingly loyal friends—some of them dating back to his earliest, impoverished years—that sets this biographer's work apart from others. Gould used up every ounce of himself and yet never lost his humanity—a remarkable feat, in its own way, when so many of his contemporaries were as ruthless in their private lives as in their public careers.

Renehan scrupulously documents his sources, yet he never allows them to bog down his narrative. He writes with a zest and an intense curiosity which suits his subject, a man who deftly grasped the intricacies of any business or industry he wished to control. It should also be remembered that Gould operated in a largely unregulated financial world. The Securities and Exchange Commission was not instituted until the 1930's, after the stock market crash, so that many of the protections for investors that he would have been obliged to observe were not in place to act as a curb on excessive speculation. At the same time, recent scandals on Wall Street, and Renehan's deft tracking of Gould's maneuvers (legal and illegal), raise doubts as to whether, even in today's monitored financial climate, Gould would have been any less successful.

Carl Rollyson

Review Sources

The American Spectator 38, no. 7 (September, 2005): 73-76.
Booklist 101, nos. 19, 20 (June 1, 2005): 1729.
Forbes 175 (June, 2005): 111.
Library Journal 130, no. 12 (July 1, 2005): 94-95.
The New York Times 154 (July 17, 2005): 3.
The New York Times Book Review 154 (July 31, 2005): 6.
Publishers Weekly 252, no. 24 (June 13, 2005): 47-48.
The Spectator 299 (September 10, 2005): 43.
The Washington Post Book World, June 19, 2005, p. 9.

DEFINING THE WORLD
The Extraordinary Story of Dr. Johnson's Dictionary

Author: Henry Hitchings (1974-   )
Publisher: Farrar, Straus and Giroux (New York).
   292 pp. $14.00
Type of work: Biography and literary history
Time: The eighteenth century
Locale: England, mainly London

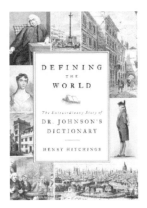

   This work recounts the story of Samuel Johnson's creation of the first great English dictionary

   Principal personages:
      SAMUEL JOHNSON (1709-1784), an English
         writer, critic, and lexicographer
      ROBERT DODSLEY (1703-1764), an English
         author, publisher, and bookseller
      LORD CHESTERFIELD (1694-1773), the supposed patron of Johnson,
         known for his maxims
      ELIZABETH PORTER JOHNSON (1689-1750), Johnson's wife

A cantankerous subject, Samuel Johnson appears in James Boswell's famous biography, *The Life of Samuel Johnson, LL.D.* (1791), as a great talker and wit, spending most of his time in conversation. This Johnson, though, evolved only after hard years spent on one of the great early monuments of the English language. His dictionary was not the first in English. There had been earlier attempts to create such a work, but these mostly listed difficult or specialized words, with inadequate definitions. By the 1740's a group of British booksellers, who were in that era also in the publishing business, decided that there would be a market for a truly comprehensive dictionary. The ambitious Johnson estimated that he could produce the work for them in three years. A decade later, in 1755, Johnson's *A Dictionary of the English Language: To Which Are Prefixed, a History of the Language, and an English Grammar* appeared, containing more than forty-two thousand entries.

   In *Defining the World*, Henry Hitchings gives both the story of Johnson's dictionary and the biography of the man. As Hitchings demonstrates, his subject's dictionary contained so much of Johnson that the two remain almost inseparable. The names of the chapters are taken from dictionary entries, alphabetically arranged from "Adventurous" to "Zootomy." It begins with Johnson's childhood in Lichfield, where he was friends with the great English actor David Garrick, with whom he moved to London when both were young men. Having left Oxford without a degree, the young Johnson sought to make his living as a writer in the rough-and-tumble literary world symbolized by Grub Street.

   Johnson may have been a moralist in Hitchings portrayal, but his life was not conventionally moralistic. He married Elizabeth Porter, who was some years older than

~

Born in 1974, Henry Hitchings studied at Oxford and London Universities. He wrote his Ph.D. dissertation on Samuel Johnson, which prepared him for Defining the World, *his first book. Hitchings works as a journalist in London, writing for newspapers and other periodicals.*

~

he and with whom he had a frequently difficult relationship. Observers both in Johnson's time and later have suggested that he was being opportunistic in his marriage. Hitchings argues, however, that Johnson genuinely loved Elizabeth and that she was more of a burden than a benefit to the struggling writer. Johnson also enjoyed the company of bohemian figures such as the poet Richard Savage, whose biography Johnson later wrote. The London of the time was an intensely competitive, dirty, and dangerous place, where everyone seemed to be scheming and crime was rampant and rarely policed. Only Johnson's great physical bulk enabled him to wander the streets at night. At the same time, London was an intensely vibrant place, the right location for a young man seeking to make a name in the world.

Although he struggled financially, Johnson did manage to gain some recognition in London's literary world. This put him into contact with the publisher and bookseller Robert Dodsley, who, with other booksellers, was searching for someone to compose a comprehensive and authoritative dictionary of the English language. In his proposal, Johnson seemed to know precisely how this should be done. At that time, according to Hitchings, Johnson was a "linguistic conservative." He believed that change was a corruption of language and that the purpose of a dictionary was to fix proper meanings, spellings, and usage. In this view, he was a child of his time. The eighteenth century was characterized by its passion for order and systematization. Hitchings argues, though, that as the years progressed Johnson moved away from this conservative view of language and began to appreciate that language was a living and evolving thing. He began to see his dictionary as a work to describe the language as it was and had been, not to prescribe how it should be for all time.

Part of the conservatism of Johnson's original plan for the dictionary may have been a result of his attempt to appeal to Lord Chesterfield as a patron. If so, Johnson was wasting his time. Chesterfield showed little interest in helping the writer through the difficult years of working on the dictionary. Only after it was finished did Chesterfield attempt to claim credit. Johnson's rebuke of Chesterfield, included in the dictionary in the bitter definition of the word "patron," has become legendary. Hitchings describes Johnson's resentment of Chesterfield without giving undue emphasis to this sideshow on the main drama of the work.

Many of Johnson's other definitions reflect his own opinions and prejudices. While this makes the definitions entertaining, it also undermines their accuracy. Johnson was also sometimes simply wrong in his definitions. More often, definitions are circular, such as defining a poet as someone who writes poems and poems as the writings of a poet. Frequently, Johnson's love of ornate, Latinate words led him to offer definitions of simple words that seemed to obscure rather than clarify their meanings. Some of these problems were the natural result of so massive an assignment in the hands of one man, with a variety of often eccentric helpers. Other problems were produced by the fact that the dictionary really was a projection of Johnson's personality, which pervades every page. Still, Hitchings argues for the dictionary's scholarly as well as literary value.

One of the most valuable contributions of the dictionary was its use of literary quotations to illustrate the meanings of words. This practice necessitated an extraordinary amount of reading on Johnson's part. He tended to concentrate on writers from the Elizabethan period, which he regarded as a golden age of English literature. He also had a conscious policy of avoiding citations from living writers, although he sometimes violated this policy. Johnson included quotations from more than five hundred authors, a testament to his wide and voracious reading. The selection of quotations, as much as the definitions, provide Hitchings with insights into Johnson's tastes and interests. Although many of Johnson's authors, such as William Shakespeare and John Milton, continue to be well-known, others are obscure to modern readers. Hitchings ascribes the selection of now-obscure authors partly to changes in literary fashion and partly to Johnson's preferences, which inclined him toward authors who offered moral lessons.

The descriptions of Johnson's approaches to literature and books are particularly interesting. The print explosion of Johnson's era had diminished the status of books as rare items to be handled with care and respect. Johnson seems to have seen books as sources to be mined, and often treated them with all the caution of a modern strip miner. His friends learned that lending books to Johnson could be risky, as the books tended to come back tattered and heavily annotated.

Johnson's choice of authors reflected his psychology as well as his literary tastes. Johnson, as Hitchings portrays him, was often given to gloom and melancholy. Many of the books he chose to quote deal with death and sadness. Hitchings identifies Robert Burton, the author of the celebrated *Anatomy of Melancholy* (1621), as one of Johnson's favorite writers. Oddly, though, as Hitchings mentions in a footnote, Johnson included relatively few passages from Burton in the dictionary.

Although the dictionary had its critics, it was well received and made its author's reputation. Sales did little to alleviate his financial difficulties, though. At one point after publication, Johnson was arrested for debt and was saved from debtors' prison only by a loan from his friend Samuel Richardson. The Johnson known from Boswell's book, free to spend time drinking and discoursing with friends, emerged only after he was granted a pension by the king in 1762. The dictionary also brought Johnson academic recognition. Having left Oxford without a degree, he managed to obtain a master of arts from the university just before his work's publication. A decade later, in 1765, Trinity College in Dublin granted him an honorary doctorate. Hitchings thus reminds readers that the man who became known to posterity as Doctor Johnson had no doctorate or even academic standing when he accomplished his most important work.

Samuel Johnson completed his dictionary as England was transforming itself from a small island to a global military and economic empire. Thus, Hitchings maintains, the work became an instrument of cultural imperialism, part of the spread of the English language around the world. Accustomed as the modern reader is to thinking of the Oxford English Dictionary (OED) as the language's fundamental work of lexicography, it comes as a little of a shock to be reminded that Johnson's dictionary was the essential one throughout the late eighteenth and most of the nineteenth century. All later dictionaries, including the OED, built on Johnson's work. Even Noah Webster's dictionary for American English was heavily influenced by Johnson.

In the next-to-last chapter, Hitchings illustrates the changing nature of language, a nature realized by the supposedly prescriptivist Johnson over the course of writing the dictionary. Among the words that have changed in meaning since Johnson's day are "fake," which meant for Johnson "a coil of rope"; "cruise," which meant "a small cup"; and "pompous," which meant "splendid." Some of the changes may take readers aback. A "urinator," for example, apparently referred to "a diver, one who searches under water" in the eighteenth century. A "fireman" was "a man of violent passions." If time travel ever becomes a reality, the travelers will clearly risk a great many awkward misunderstandings.

Defining the World is a worthy tribute to Samuel Johnson and his dictionary. It is witty and entertaining without treating its subject lightly. On occasions, it does make some questionable claims. Hitchings's suggestion that Johnson was something of a political progressive will likely raise eyebrows and would probably have enraged Johnson himself. It is true that being a conservative meant something different in the eighteenth century from what it does today, and that Johnson was a staunch and outspoken opponent of slavery. Nevertheless, he was an ardent traditionalist and a royalist as well as a critic of the American Revolution. Hitchings recognizes that Johnson's dictionary is the work of a man who preferred the past to the future and who was against all foreign influences, especially those from France.

Hitchings's book will inspire many readers to take up Johnson. In spite of the claims that the dictionary is a work of literature, few modern readers are likely to peruse it from beginning to end, as poet Robert Browning did in Hitchings's description. Probably, though, the book will lead many to try to find library copies to thumb through at random or in which to look up their favorite words. After this monument of the language has received so little attention for so many years, such a result should be welcomed by anyone with an interest in words or literature.

Carl L. Bankston III

Review Sources

Booklist 102, no. 4 (October 15, 2005): 12.
Kirkus Reviews 73, no. 16 (August 15, 2005): 897-898.
Library Journal 130, no. 15 (September 15, 2005): 66.
New Statesman 134 (May 16, 2005): 42-44.
The New York Times Book Review 155 (December 4, 2005): 48-49.
Publishers Weekly 252, no. 28 (July 18, 2005): 197-198.
San Francisco Chronicle, October 30, 2005, p. M2.
The Times Educational Supplement, April 1, 2005, p. 33.
The Times Literary Supplement, April 15, 2005, p. 10.
The Wall Street Journal 246, no. 76 (October 12, 2005): D13.

DICTIONARY DAYS
A Defining Passion

Author: Ilan Stavans (1961-   )
Publisher: Graywolf Press (St. Paul, Minn.). 228 pp.
$17.00
Type of work: Essays and memoir

A multilingual scholar and writer reflects on words and their meanings and on his love of dictionaries, especially the Oxford English Dictionary

> *Principal personages:*
> ILAN STAVANS, the author, a professor of
>   Hispanic and Latino cultures at Amherst
>   College
> ABRÉMELE STAVANS, his father
> ISAIAH and JOSHUA STAVANS, his young
>   sons, who converse with their father about words and their meanings
> SAMUEL JOHNSON, the author of *A Dictionary of the English Language*
>   (1755)
> RAMONA GLADYS PÉREZ LOZANO, a Salvadoran immigrant whom
>   Stavans tutors in English

Dictionary Days is best understood in the context of the author's life history. Born in Mexico of Jewish parents, Ilan Stavans nurtured in his youth a love for Yiddish and Hebrew as well as his native Spanish. Only in his adulthood did he come to appreciate the English language. In his autobiography, *On Borrowed Words* (2001), Stavans described this polyglot background and reflected on his own linguistic development. In *Dictionary Days* he places this multilingualism in the context of his great passion for words and his fascination with dictionaries of all sorts.

In the "Acknowledgements" in *Dictionary Days*, Stavans explains how this book came to be. After an academic symposium where he read a paper (which came to be the chapter called "Ink, Inc." in this book), Stavans was invited to write a book on words and his love of dictionaries. While initially apprehensive about such an undertaking, Stavans eventually agreed to this proposal; *Dictionary Days* is the result.

The essays in *Dictionary Days* are not just academic and theoretical. They are often also personal and autobiographical. In "Fictionary," Stavans reflects on his love of the word game of that name and explains his adolescent experiences as a writer. As he examines the meaning of the word "love" in the essay "Invention of Love," he tells the sad story of his childhood dog Coki, who abandoned his family. In "Gladys," he describes the efforts of an illegal immigrant to bring her daughter across the U.S. border. This tale of coyotes (Mexican border guides) and linguistic excitement provides a context for Stavans to reflect on his own crossing from Mexico into the United States. In "Gladys" he also moves from the linguistic problems of this Salvadoran im-

*Ilan Stavans, the Lewis Sebring
Professor of Latin American and
Latino Cultures at Amherst College,
is a prolific writer and scholar. His
publications, in both English and
Spanish, include fiction, nonfiction,
translations, anthologies, and
scholarly editions.*

migrant to attempts to create a universal language such as Esperanto, as well Stavans's own academic interest in Spanglish and other hybrid languages.

Stavans uses his own name in "Keeping My Name" to reflect on the meaning of monikers and identity. In "Land of Lost Words," the author transforms memories of his father's performance in a Mexican production of *Singin' in the Rain* into a stream-of-consciousness consideration of the multilingual layers of the production; Stavans identifies with his father in his Spanish performance of an English-language work. As a Mexican Jew writing in English, he calls himself a "tongue snatcher," a stealer of other people's words and languages, and reflects on his own relationship with Yiddish and the history of that language.

Stavans also takes his readers on a wide-ranging linguistic and geographic journey. He browses in an English-Arabic dictionary and observes some of the Americanisms in the Arabic language. He dreams about examining books in a Near Eastern market and suddenly finds himself in a dreamlike scene of trading with a Navajo girl in Arizona. He quotes a variety of authorities on dictionaries, including Ralph Waldo Emerson, Charles Dickens, W. H. Auden, and Samuel Johnson.

Lovers of words will enjoy the way in which definitions of words are woven into these essays. Some of the words that have caught Stavans's attention include "antipodes" and "quixotic." He talks about "nonce" (actually "nonsense") words such as "bardlatry" as well as archaic or "relic" words such as "maraud," "rodomontade," "terpsichorean," and "gaberlunzie." He also examines Yiddish words such as "dybbuk" and "Yiddishkeit" and Spanish words such as "rascuachismo."

Stavans demonstrates the challenges of definition by examining such words as "reading," "impossible," and "death." In "Invention of Love," he examines definitions of "love" in various language dictionaries. He notes how different cultural attitudes result in very different approaches to that word. While the German definition is based more on sacrifice and dedication, Italians emphasize affection. In the process he also considers the challenges of interlingual communication and the problems of mistranslation. For example, in Spanish the same word can be used to describe someone who is either "angry" or "upset." In "Keeping My Name" he uses dictionary definitions to contrast Spanish and English concepts of "honor." In "Gladys" he observes the communication problems of tourism and hypothesizes a dictionary of tourism dealing with linguistic gaffes such as the phrase "to drink a note" caused by the fact that the Spanish verb *tomar* means both "to take" and "to drink."

The subject of "Zebra and the Swear Word" is tergiversation, an archaic word which literally means "the act of turning one's back" and which also refers to equivocation and evasion. Here Stavans looks at animals in order to demonstrate the inaccuracy of many dictionary definitions. He asks, for example, whether zebras are white with black stripes, as described by some lexicographers, or whether they cannot also be described as "black with white stripes." Stavans suggests that lexicographers not only tergiversate but also leave out words they do not endorse, such as the four-letter words and scatological references which Stavans celebrates as "cacophonies."

Throughout *Dictionary Days* Stavans demonstrates his voracious and wide-ranging reading habit. He refers to the Russian Aleksandr Romanovich Luria in his discussion of memory and Alexis de Toqueville on culture. He cites Paul Celan's "Deathfugue" on the Holocaust and the end of poetry, T. S. Eliot's *Four Quartets* (1943) on getting the better of words, and Saint Augustine of Hippo's *Confessiones* (397-400; *Confessions*, 1620) on learning to speak through imitation. Also woven into the book are Ray Bradbury's *Fahrenheit 451* (1953), Denis Diderot's *Encyclopédie* (1751-1772), and Vladimir Nabokov's "Ode to the Dictionary."

In the first essay, "Heaven," Stavans describes a conversation with his son Isaiah, in which they consider whether words are alive and whether they die. In the process he talks about a dictionary as a museum, a depository or, even a heaven for words. In another essay, "Land of Lost Words," he has a conversation in a theater with another son, Joshua, about the Spanish word "mierda," used to wish actors good luck before a performance. In the final essay, "The Impossible," Stavans returns to the theme of heaven; contemplating his own eventual death, he hopes to be remembered for his "logotheism," his worship of words.

In "Sleeping with My OED," Stavans offers a description of his personal library, which is organized chaotically, except for his editions of Miguel de Cervantes's *Don Quixote de la Mancha* (1605, 1615) and his dictionaries, which are carefully arranged. Always eager to acquire a new dictionary, Stavans calls himself a dictionary hunter. Stavans writes lovingly about his own compact edition of the Oxford English Dictionary, in which he often browses late into the night. The OED is his bible. In fact, Stavans suggests that in its attempt to define all the words in the English language, the OED is, in a sense, defying God. (Some readers may be puzzled by Stavans's reference to God as "G-d," but this vowel-free spelling of the word reflects Jewish tradition in which writing the full name of God is avoided.) Stavans also notes his preference for a print dictionary over an electronic one and complains about the problems caused by a word processor's spellcheck, which treats "charming" and "chocolate box" as synonyms.

While acknowledging that dictionary definitions create character and authority, Stavans prefers a descriptive rather than normative role for dictionaries. Dictionaries should provide information about how words are used but not make usage rules. Referring to John Witherspoon's ridicule of American use of English in 1781, Stavans debunks the nostalgic view of language as better in the past. Instead he revels in the beauty of an ever-changing and evolving language.

In a chapter called "No-Kim-Bah" Stavans speaks of the aroma, color, and flavor of words such as "maelstrom." With the playful chapter title "Ink, Inc.," Stavans focuses on the sound of words, on their musicality, and on onomatopoeia. The two words "ink" and "inc." sound alike but have widely different word histories and meanings. The word "ink" represents chaos, disorder, and playful freedom, while "inc." implies agreement, responsibility, and unity of a group. For Stavans, "ink" represents the individual, while "inc." refers to capitalism.

Citing the Kabbalist Isaac Luria and linguists Ferdinand de Saussure and Noam Chomsky, Stavans asks whether language exists separate from sound and affirms that communication is the result of both thought and language, that language, like a Platonic form, does exist apart from sound.

In "Pride and Prejudice" Stavans suggests that dictionaries are like mirrors, that they reflect the culture of the people who create them as well as the language they speak. Here he takes the reader on a sweeping history of lexicography, beginning with the cuneiform writing of the Near East and moving to the first known dictionary written by Aristophanes of Byzantium c. 200 B.C.E. Emphasizing the importance of Arabic lexicography, he cites the tenth century Arab Abū Bakr ibn Duraid's plea for literacy and sophisticated lexicons.

He describes Ambrosius Calepinus's sixteenth century lexicon of eleven languages and notes that such multilingual lexicons were popular before monolingual ones. Finally, he acknowledges the contributions of Samuel Johnson in England and the French Encyclopedists such as Diderot, before noting the preference for specialized dictionaries in the twentieth and twenty-first centuries. He also compares and contrasts the lexicographic traditions of what he calls the Anglo-Protestant and Hispano-Catholic worlds. Some early English dictionaries reflect efforts to purify and preserve the language. One of the goals of Johnson's *A Dictionary of the English Language* (1755), for example, was to cleanse the language of Gallicisms. Generally, however, lexicographers of the English language have focused on organizing and documenting the language.

In contrast, the aim of Spanish lexicographers has always been to cleanse and purify the language. The goal of the first Spanish dictionary, published by Antonio de Nebrija in the momentous year 1492, was the removal of Arabic elements that had crept into the language during the Moorish period. By the time that Sebastián de Covarrubias's *Tesoro de la lengua castellana o española* (treasury of the Castillan or Spanish language) was published in 1611, Americanisms such as "canoa" ("canoe") had begun to appear in the language. However, Stavans especially examines Covarrubias's definition of the word "Jew" in order to demonstrate the strong Catholic bias of this dictionary.

For the most part, English dictionaries have developed without government support. Stavans objects to the role which the Real Academia Española and the Académie Française have played in Spanish and French lexicography. He holds the position that both language and dictionaries need to develop freely and without governmental, political, or religious influence.

The climax of *Dictionary Days* is an imaginary visit by Samuel Johnson to Stavans's house in Amherst. The author has a wide-ranging conversation with the En-

glish lexicographer. The two discuss the Katsura tree outside the house and the definitions of words such as "telephone" and "airport," which are foreign concepts for
Johnson. They argue about whether people think in images (Stavans) or words (Johnson). They talk about books in Stavans's library, the origins of eyeglasses and of language, cacophonies, and the eventual fate of the English language. Stavans imagines
that Johnson came to express his displeasure about Stavans's interest in Spanglish,
but that, by the end of the conversation, Johnson acknowledges that Stavans will not
take his criticisms to heart.

Binding together all these far-reaching essays is the OED in Stavans's library. This
book provides both inspiration and focus for *Dictionary Days*. Any reader sharing
Stavans's logotheism will find this book both alluring and enticing.

Thomas J. Sienkewicz

Review Sources

Booklist 101, no. 14 (March 15, 2005): 1252.
Kirkus Reviews 73, no. 3 (February 1, 2005): 171-172.
Library Journal 130, no. 8 (May 1, 2005): 85.
Publishers Weekly 252, no. 11 (March 14, 2005): 57.

DISNEYWAR

Author: James B. Stewart (1951-   )
Publisher: Simon & Schuster (New York). 573 pp. $30.00
Type of work: Film and media
Time: 1984-2004
Locale: Mainly New York and Los Angeles

Michael Eisner's twenty-year tenure as head of the Walt Disney Company was initially successful, but his inability to delegate responsibility, establish clear lines of authority, and maintain a reputation for honesty cost the company millions in profits, lawsuits, and contract buyouts, eventually leading to his resignation as chairman

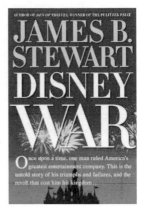

Principal personages:
WALT DISNEY (1901-1966), the founder of the Walt Disney Company
ROY E. DISNEY, his nephew, chairman of Walt Disney Feature Animation (1984-2004)
MICHAEL EISNER, the chief executive officer (1984-   ) and chairman (1984-2004) of Disney
FRANK WELLS, the president and chief operating officer of Disney (1984-1994)
JEFFREY KATZENBERG, the chairman of Walt Disney Studios (1984-1994)
MICHAEL OVITZ, the president of Disney (1995-1997)
ROBERT IGER, the president and chief operating officer of Disney (2000-   )
GEORGE MITCHELL, the former U.S. senator and chairman of the Disney board of directors (2004-   )

Many a baby boomer has a soft spot in his or her heart for Walt Disney and the entertainment company he founded. Millions grew up watching the various television programs he hosted (such as *The Wonderful World of Disney*) and produced (*The Mickey Mouse Club*), visiting the theme parks he built, and watching his classic films. His avuncular presence as television host was comforting and inspiring. Thus, after his death in 1966, the slow, steady decline in the quality of Disney animated feature films was observed with dismay.

Michael Eisner, a successful former executive at ABC, then Paramount, was brought to Disney to rejuvenate it artistically. He became head of the company in 1984. After he took over, the decline of animated features reversed, and the Walt Disney Company returned to its former eminence with animated films such as *The Little Mermaid* (1989), *Beauty and the Beast* (1991), *Aladdin* (1992), and *The Lion King* (1994). Later in the 1990's, Disney bought the ABC network, and Eisner began hosting Disney's new weekly show. His wooden, shallow cheeriness was a far cry from Walt's warmth and relaxed expertise. A gradual but unmistakable decline in the quality of traditionally animated Disney films was, in part, overshadowed by the spectacular rise of Disney's Pixar Studios, groundbreaking pioneers in computer animation.

Problems with Eisner's management style were revealed as former executives filed lawsuits after leaving the company. Disney's attempts to build theme parks around the world came to a crash with the financial insolvency of EuroDisney. When Pixar's contract with Disney ran out, negotiations over its renewal became bitter and acrimonious. Roy Disney, Walt's nephew, who because of his physical resemblance to Walt was a tangible reminder of the Disney legacy, was forced into resigning from the board of directors. All these elements contributed to a contentious shareholders' meeting in 2004, when a record-setting 43 percent of shareholders (many of them lifelong Disney fans) voted against Eisner's continuing as chairman of Disney. The complicated story of his rise and fall is masterfully told by James B. Stewart in *DisneyWar*.

James B. Stewart is a Pulitzer Prize-winning journalist and former editor of The Wall Street Journal. *He is Bloomberg Professor of Business and Economic Journalism at Columbia University. His previous books include* Den of Thieves *(1991) and* Heart of a Soldier: A Story of Love, Heroism and September 11th *(2002).*

"Complicated" might be too mild an adjective to apply to the Byzantine intricacy and depth of this saga. A list of "cast members" at the beginning of the book helps the inattentive reader, and in general Stewart keeps the protagonists and chief subsidiary characters and companies differentiated. Near the end, when the number of Disney acquisitions has ballooned, and Stewart is writing not only about Disney and its main branches but also the ABC network, ESPN, Miramax Pictures, Pixar, and Dreamworks SKG, even a conscientious reader can be forgiven for having to check occasionally who Angela Shapiro and Anne Sweeney are.

Throughout the work, however, the focus is on Eisner. His career before Disney is outlined. At ABC television, Eisner claimed responsibility for the hit shows *Taxi*, *Happy Days*, and *Laverne and Shirley*. At Paramount film studios, Eisner and studio head Barry Diller made *Saturday Night Fever* (1977), *Grease* (1978), and *Flashdance* (1983). Eisner himself came up with the concept for *Beverly Hills Cop* (1984). From Paramount, Eisner took with him to Disney his production mind-set, as well as his assistant, Jeffrey Katzenberg. Formerly, when the owner of Paramount had suggested firing Katzenberg, Eisner assured his assistant that they were "partners for life." This proved true, in the sense that people can be partnered in enmity as well as in amity.

Eisner's filmmaking philosophy was encapsulated in a famous 1982 memo in which he used a baseball analogy to declare that studios were better off not swinging for the fences with every film, looking for a gigantic hit on the order of *Star Wars* (1977), but producing a steady stream of "singles and doubles": more modest but nevertheless profitable motion pictures produced on economical budgets. The successful films would be "high concept" pictures, whose plot or point could be encapsulated in a few short sentences. For the most part, this is the strategy Eisner followed in his first years at Disney. He bragged that his order at Paramount to director James Brooks to stay on budget for his film *Terms of Endearment* (1983) made it, according to Brooks, a better picture. Eisner was not averse to supporting a few big-budget gambles, the sort of package deals of script, stars, and director that his friend mega-agent Michael Ovitz assembled. Eisner had backed, for instance, *Raiders of the Lost Ark* (1981) at Paramount. Most of Eisner's early hits at Disney, however, were modestly budgeted comedies and dramas such as *Down and Out in Beverly Hills* (1986), *Honey, I Shrunk the Kids* (1989), and *Dead Poets Society* (1989). Yet the main sources of Disney profit increases during this period were from higher ticket prices at the theme parks, increased revenues at their associated hotels, and the newly burgeoning home video market—not from live-action films.

Katzenberg involved himself mainly with the animated productions of the studio. An adaptation of a Hans Christian Andersen fairy tale, which Eisner had initially disparaged, received support from Katzenberg and Roy Disney and eventually became *The Little Mermaid*, the first of the Eisner-era animated mega-hits, films that were as artistically accomplished as they were financially successful. It was followed by *Beauty and the Beast* and *Aladdin*; all these films were immeasurably enriched by the music of Alan Menken and the lyrics of Howard Ashman and Tim Rice. Katzenberg himself came up with the idea for the next animated success, *The Lion King*, which he shepherded to the screen. In these four motion pictures, it seemed, the Disney legacy was reborn, and in some aspects, such as the joining of story, music, and lyrics, surpassed.

However, even though Katzenberg championed the animation division, he was not very well liked there: His chant of "bigger, better, faster, cheaper" was not welcome, and he did not get along well with Roy Disney. Nevertheless, this string of successes made a seemingly harmless clause in Katzenberg's contract become potentially disastrous: If he left, he would be entitled to 2 percent of any profits earned by any of his productions in any way—videos, merchandise, theme-park rides.

Frank Wells, the former head of Warner Brothers who became president and chief operating officer of Disney when Eisner became chief executive officer, was mainly in charge of financial matters. In several instances, such as the debacle of Euro Disneyland, Wells was able to ameliorate some of the problems Eisner had a hand in causing. After Wells died in a helicopter crash, many analysts, including Stewart, inferred that a restraining presence on Eisner had been removed. Well aware of Eisner's increasing dissatisfaction with him, Katzenberg resigned, without the 2 percent settlement finalized. Although Katzenberg would have settled his ensuing lawsuit for $90 million, he ended up with $280 million after battling it out in court.

Eisner brought in his close friend Michael Ovitz as president; within two years, again because of Eisner, Ovitz was gone, never having had Eisner's support. His separation agreement cost $140 million. Without Katzenberg, the quality of Disney's animated features slowly but steadily declined. Eisner's judgments about quality and appeal had never been stellar: He backed, as a potential big-budget blockbuster, Warren Beatty's overblown *Dick Tracy* (1990) and belittled Garry Marshall's less expensive yet popular *Pretty Woman* (1990). Eisner advocated the egregiously bad comedy *Cabin Boy* (1994). He did not support the executive who championed M. Night Shyamalan's *Sixth Sense* (1999); Disney consequently lost millions of dollars in profits. Eisner insisted on putting Edward Elgar's "Pomp and Circumstance" march in *Fantasia 2000* after hearing it at his son's graduation. He refused Harvey Weinstein's pleas to finance Peter Jackson's *The Lord of the Rings* (2001-2003). He enthusiastically hawked Michael Bay's tepid *Pearl Harbor* (2001). He reportedly disparaged Pixar's wondrous *Finding Nemo* (2003). He alienated the Weinstein brothers at Miramax and Steve Jobs and John Lasseter at Pixar. In spite of these decisions and actions, Eisner's compensation rose dramatically, to over $565 million a year at one point, and his compensation in stock made him one of Disney's largest stockholders.

In Eisner's defense, two decisions he made at the major organizational level were presciently successful. His vigorous resistance to a takeover attempt by AOL was proved correct when Time/Warner-AOL was crippled by the dot.com collapse. Eisner also promoted the acquisition of ABC by Disney, but here the results, although ultimately profitable, were also problematic as Eisner's judgment again proved skewed. Executives were shuffled and misassigned: Steve Boorstein, who had made ESPN so successful, for instance, was given the Augean and ultimately hopeless task of rescuing Disney's Internet gateway. Eisner dismissed potential television hits such as *CSI* and came up with a distasteful way to exploit the death of John Ritter, the star of ABC's *Eight Simple Rules*, during a ratings sweeps period. All these wrong-headed moves culminated in the ouster of Roy Disney, which led to the stockholders' rebellion and Eisner's relinquishing of his chairmanship to George Mitchell and his naming of Robert Iger as his successor. As Stewart hints at the end of the book, none of these setbacks portend the end of Michael Eisner's power at Disney.

Some critics maintain that Stewart relies too much in *DisneyWar* on the disgruntled testimony of former Disney executives. Even if that charge is true, the fact that there are so many of these executives thriving in powerful positions throughout the entertainment industry indicates that a fire probably existed somewhere at Disney. Also, Stewart is careful to present Eisner's views in Eisner's own words whenever possible. The problem is that so many of his statements, including the most damning, exist in the public record because of the court cases in which Eisner has been involved (including the infamous "little midget" remark about Katzenberg). On the whole, Stewart's portrait of Eisner seems fair; whenever a dispute arises as to what was said, Stewart presents both sides.

What is missing from Stewart's book are artistic judgments about the Disney works: He measures the worth of each in only financial terms. He calls Roy Disney's insistence on the primacy of creativity over profit "a sometimes romantic view." He relates that *Toy Story* (1995) was supposedly improved by Katzenberg's advice, but whether his suggestions actually made the film better is never settled, nor does Stewart seem to care. Stewart also seems insensitive to some of the subtleties involved in the works. He accurately talks about the financial success of Dreamworks's *Shrek* (2001) but fails to note how much of the film's content is an anti-Disney satire, which must have made its production exasperating to Eisner.

Eisner himself was the first to note the Shakespearean ramifications of his story, a theme that Stewart underscores throughout the book. *DisneyWar* is not Shakespearean in the sense that it is about rulers and ruled, or the perils of monarchy, but in the sense that it is about inheritance and legacy. Each of three main claimants to Walt Disney's artistic mantle—Eisner, Katzenberg, and Roy Disney—sees himself as Walt's true successor. That none could see the sense in which it was true for all of them, preventing them from working together and becoming a real Team Disney, is the true tragedy of *DisneyWar*.

William Laskowski

Review Sources

Business Week, February 28, 2005, pp. 24-25.
The Economist 374 (February 26, 2005): 83-84.
Fortune 151, no. 5 (March 7, 2005): 24.
New York 38, no. 7 (February 28, 2005): 72-73.
The New York Times 154 (February 10, 2005): E1-E9.
Publishers Weekly 252, no. 7 (February 14, 2005): 61.
Time 165, no. 8 (February 21, 2005): 39.
The Wall Street Journal 245, no. 39 (February 25, 2005): W1-W8.

THE DOMINION OF WAR
Empire and Liberty in North America, 1500-2000

Authors: Fred Anderson (1949-   ) and Andrew
   Cayton (1954-   )
Publisher: Viking Press (New York). 400 pp. $28.00
Type of work: History
Time: 1500-2000
Locale: North America

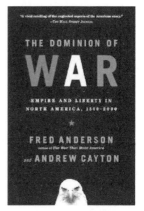

War has affected American concepts of liberty and de-mocracy since the seventeenth century

               Principal personages:
                    SAMUEL DE CHAMPLAIN, the French
                      explorer and founder of Canada
                    WILLIAM PENN, the Quaker founder of
                      Pennsylvania
GEORGE WASHINGTON, a combatant in the French and Indian war, com-
    mander of the Continental Army, and first president of the United
    States
ANDREW JACKSON, the victor of the battles of Horseshoe Bend and New
    Orleans, president of the United States
ANTONIO LÓPEZ DE SANTA ANNA, eleven times Mexican president,
    defeated at San Jacinto in 1836 and in the Mexican War
ULYSSES S. GRANT, a combatant in the Mexican War, commander of the
    Army of the Potomac in the Civil War, United States president
DOUGLAS MACARTHUR, a commander of the U.S. army forces in the
    Pacific theater in World War II, in occupied Japan, and in the Korean
    War
COLIN POWELL, the chairman of the Joint Chiefs of Staff during the Gulf
    War, former national security adviser, and secretary of state

    Three wars are most noted in American history—the American Revolution, the
Civil War, and World War II—but other conflicts have become part of the grand narrative of American culture—the French and Indian War, the War of 1812, the Mexican War, the Indian wars, and the Spanish-American War. The great conflicts were
fought for the cause of freedom and liberty, the minor ones for empire. Then came the
wars of intervention—Korea, Vietnam, Iraq—the unintended consequences of out-
sized imperial ambitions.
    The earliest moments of exploration and colonization were marked by war. When
Samuel de Champlain first came to Canada to foster trade and quiet missionary activity, his American Indian contacts insisted on his supporting their wars against the
Iroquois for control of the fur-trapping regions. In doing so, Champlain unwittingly
emulated the Spanish policy of freeing oppressed tribes from barbaric Aztec rule.
However, unlike Hernán Cortés, who replaced the Aztec empire with a Spanish one,

~

Fred Anderson is professor of history at the University of Colorado. He received the Francis Parkman Prize and the Mark Lynton History Prize in 2001 for Crucible of War: The Seven Years' War and the Fate of Empire in British North America, 1754-1766. *Andrew Cayton is a Distinguished Professor of History at Miami University in Oxford, Ohio. He has taught at Harvard University, Wellesley College, and Ball State University. His previous publications generally concern Ohio history.*

~

Champlain found himself the hostage of Indian policies. When his traders provided some tribes with hatches, knives, swords, and arrowheads, other tribes swiftly turned hostile. Then they turned to other Europeans.

When the Dutch began supplying the Iroquois Confederation with weapons, the entire balance of power was changed—the Iroquois swept west, destroying or displacing fifty-one tribes. Defeated tribes begged the French and English for help. Meanwhile, the British, French, and Dutch, having learned that they could not rely on Indians or on supply ships for food, had encouraged the immigration of farmers. Thereafter, the colonial powers had to protect those immigrants, who were not prepared for forest warfare. Often, however, the British left their colonials to their own devices, thus unintentionally fostering a sense of liberty and self-reliance.

The Iroquois had not been interested in furs alone but also in prisoners to replace tribesmen lost to disease, alcohol, and retaliatory attacks. The Iroquois rampage came to an end in 1664 when the British navy seized the Dutch colonies and imposed the pro-French policies of Charles II on the traders. Soon thereafter a French regiment was sent to Canada to assist the Hurons; this relatively small force routed the Iroquois, who appealed to the British for help. Within years the Iroquois Confederacy had been reduced to a fraction of its earlier size. It still dominated the frontier militarily but could do so only as long as the French and British did not disturb the status quo.

Into this situation came William Penn with the intent of creating a refuge where all cultures and religious beliefs could flourish. His colony succeeded beyond expectations, attracting not only dissenting Protestants but also many Native Americans. In fact, the pacifist Quaker state was sheltered by allied Indian tribes who relied on Pennsylvanians for weapons and ammunition. Meanwhile, the dynamics of tribal and colonial economics and politics were reorganizing the frontier. Native American tribal groups played one colonial power off against another, until at last the struggle for the depopulated hunting grounds of the upper Ohio River brought Native Americans against Native Americans, whites against whites.

The Pennsylvania tribes had not intended to move west into Ohio, much less seek French assistance in expelling the Iroquois, but the Penn family's infamously unfair purchase of land moved tribes away from their homes at the same time that the local deer population was overhunted. At no time were the Indians passive observers of their fate, but their options were limited. War was their only means of forcing settlers to abide by their understandings of treaties.

It was in this French and Indian War that George Washington rose to prominence. He had grown up in the Tidewater region of Virginia, where growing tobacco had enriched the planter class temporarily while impoverishing the soil. Far-thinking residents understood that the future lay inland, and that the wealthy landowners, such as Washington's friends the Fairfaxes, could thrive only by obtaining, then selling, lands there. In the course of Washington's life, the balance of power tipped, so that Americans could swarm into the Ohio and Tennessee Valleys. The Native Americans, without French backing, had no way of driving them out.

Washington had dreamed of a future in which American Indians eventually assimilated into the now-dominant culture, a future in which the Indian men would cross the gender gap within their own society to become farmers and artisans. In effect, Native Americans would vanish, becoming in time like other immigrants, a part of a free, prosperous, generally Protestant yeomanry. Native American men, however, were unwilling to do women's work and were even more hostile to the unmanly academic work necessary to becoming doctors and lawyers.

Some tribal leaders, usually of mixed ancestry, tried to persuade their fellows that the alternative to assimilation was destruction. However, young hotheads, especially the Red-Sticks of the Creeks, preferred to fight to the last. Andrew Jackson gave the southern civilized tribes a choice of assimilation or moving west. Some tribal leaders, seeing their members succumbing to drink and gambling, had already decided to put as much distance between themselves and white civilization as possible; Jackson sent many of the rest to join them. Jackson was the prototype of the new Southerner: a patriarch who took care of his women, his children, and his slaves—and Native Americans, too. Jackson was argumentative, dislikable, and ready to use violence to defend his honor. The South as a region, and America as a proud and expansive nation, reflected this new concept of manhood.

The Mexican War was the product of aggressive acquisitiveness justified by love of personal liberty and freedom—liberty and freedom won by depriving "lesser" races and cultures of theirs. In addition, there was a strong conservative desire to bring order out of chaos, and few areas were more chaotic than the Mexican Republic and its almost empty northern territories. Antonio López de Santa Anna shared many of the Southerners' attitudes and beliefs, but his interests began and ended with himself, not his nation. He was willing to sell as much Mexican soil as necessary to hold onto power. Northerners, who wanted land as much as Southerners, saw the growth of slave power as a threat to their own liberty.

The Civil War arose when Northerners insulted Southern concepts of patriarchy by saying that slavery was wrong and frustrating Southern wishes to expand. The war began as a struggle for power but became a moral crusade to abolish slavery. In its aftermath came the great disappointment—President Ulysses S. Grant chose neither to force racial equality on the South nor to guarantee it for Native Americans. He was content to protect civil rights, confident that assimilation would come in due time. Congressional limits on the size of the Army also affected what he could do in the South and in the West. Grant's naïve racist paternalism was doomed to fail.

By this time Americans had come to assume a close connection between liberty and empire, and while they refused to acknowledge that America was an imperialist state, they were willing to use force to impose liberty and democracy on people who were not ready for it or did not want it.

The Philippines were the unintended acquisition of a war fought for the noblest of motives, the end of Spanish tyranny in Cuba. The wisdom of allowing Cuba to go its own way was proven in the Philippines, where the United States found itself fighting a long colonial war. Cultural imperialism there was fully represented in the MacArthur family, where a father-son dynasty dominated politics and war for half a century. In *The Dominion of War*, Douglas MacArthur's many personal vanities and military mistakes are painted against a background of American popular culture—motion pictures and novels that demonstrate white America's view of itself and the world, a view which ignores racial minorities, dissenting opinions, and non-Protestant values and beliefs. Casual racism was an integral part of America's self-satisfied conceit that its social, economic, and political systems were models for the rest of the world.

This, and the chaos following World War II, required the United States to intervene abroad, first in Korea, then in Vietnam and elsewhere, usually in the name of protecting freedom from Soviet and Chinese Marxism but without an acknowledgment that the United States now possessed an empire that must be defended.

There were some who were open about America's military responsibilities—Douglas MacArthur, more than anyone. Others, such as Harry S. Truman, wanted foreigners to work out their destinies in their own ways. Even Truman, however, succumbed to political reality—if the United States did not take the lead in fighting communism, then who would?

Thus the United States became involved in a redefinition of its racial beliefs, a rethinking of taboos and prejudices which eventually led to the end of legal segregation, a breakdown of gender roles and a more tolerant view of foreigners. This process, marked by wars in Korea and Vietnam, has not been completed. The contradictions between believing in liberty and desiring to impose democracy on other peoples are still felt. Americans continue to see themselves as righteous and well-meaning, justified in the military interventions, even when faced by obvious resistance on the part of those who are supposed to benefit from American sacrifices. Wars are unpredictable, and many of its consequences cannot be foreseen.

The Powell Doctrine was a effort to put restraints on America's reformist and imperialist ambitions. Its tenets include, first, no war except as a last resort; second, no war without complete public support; and, third, the use of overwhelming force. Authors Fred Anderson and Andrew Cayton see the first Gulf War as the embodiment of this doctrine. They are noncommittal on the wars of 2002 and 2003, but they suggest that theses conflicts illustrate well the dilemma they have described, the importance of the interplay of concepts of liberty, of empire, and Americans' divided views about war and a strong military.

It is important for Americans to see that previous visions of the past—especially the struggles against the British Empire—are outdated. Wars have made the United States an imperial power. A strong American military is necessary, but there is no consensus on how to exercise its power legitimately and wisely. A proper understanding of American history is the first step to the development of such a consensus.

William L. Urban

Review Sources

Booklist 101, no. 6 (November 15, 2004): 547.
Foreign Affairs 84, no. 3 (May/June, 2005): 138.
Kirkus Reviews 72, no. 21 (November 1, 2004): 1033.
New Statesman 134 (July 25, 2005): 52-53.
Publishers Weekly 251, no. 47 (November 22, 1004): 52.
The Washington Post Book World, January 30, 2005, p. 5.

THE EARTH AND SKY OF JACQUES DORME

Author: Andreï Makine (1958-   )
First published: La Terre et le ciel de Jacques Dorme,
2003, in France
Translated from the French and with an introduction by
Geoffrey Strachan
Publisher: Arcade (New York). 206 pp. $23.00
Type of work: Novel
Time: 1942, the 1960's, and 2000
Locale: World War II Stalingrad, Russia in the 1960's,
and Paris in 2000

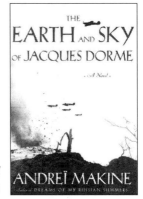

*Concluding the trilogy that documented the life of World
War II pilot Jacques Dorme, this novel follows a war orphan
on his mission to learn more about the mysterious Dorme,
the pilgrimage he takes to Dorme's final resting place, and the quest the young boy
embarks upon to develop a sense of self and family belonging where none exist*

> *Principal characters:*
> THE NARRATOR, an unnamed orphan
> ALEXANDRIA, also known as SHURA and SASCHA, the narrator's stand-in
> mother and lover of Jacques Dorme
> JAQUES DORME, a World War II French pilot who sympathizes with, and
> flies for, the Russians and becomes the subject of the narrator's curi-
> osity and fantasies
> BIG LEV, a geologist who accompanies the narrator on his mission to
> find Dorme's remains
> LITTLE LEV, the second geologist on the mission
> VALYA, the cook who tends the geologists' headquarters
> AIR CAPTAIN, the narrator's boyhood friend, a captain who flies the nar-
> rator to the Tundra Village
> WITOLD, Dorme's friend and fellow escapee from the German prisoner-
> of-war camp
> LI EN, Dorme's brother's wife

The Earth and Sky of Jacques Dorme is the final installment of Andreï Makine's
ambitious World War II trilogy which follows the events in the life of Jacques Dorme.
The trilogy begins with *Le Testament français* (1995; *Dreams of My Russian Summers*, 1997) which is followed by *Requiem pour l'Est* (2000; *Requiem for a Lost Empire*, 2001). The novels follow the lives and brief love affair between two French expatriates living in Russia during World War II. This last novel takes place decades
after the war has ended and is narrated by an unnamed orphan who, like so many others, is a product of the war. Upon learning of Jacques Dorme, the narrator seeks out all
information about the mysterious pilot, fulfilling his longing for a sense of belonging
and familial heritage.

Jumping from Stalingrad in 1942 to the Russian steppes in 1966 to Paris in the year 2000, Makine is able in the third volume to weave three stories seamlessly together in an experimental nonlinear fashion. Here the narrator befriends Alexandria, who claims to have been friends with his parents and now serves as a part-time "mother" for him. As such, the boy is allowed to leave the orphanage once a week to visit her. It is during these visits that he learns of Alexandria's past, and she teaches him her native language, French. She tells the boy that the only treasure she has to give to him is that of her mother tongue. He feels French is a covert code which only they share, and their secret language provides the sort of familial bond he has been yearning for his entire existence. The orphan absorbs the language and discovers under Alexandria's staircase a hidden library of Russian books translated into French. He surreptitiously reads them, absorbing their treasured vocabulary and history, and enjoys the feeling of belonging and security the language and the books offer, "the feeling of being home at last mingled imperceptibly with this foreign language [he] was learning."

Andreï Makine was born in Siberia in 1957 and moved to Paris in 1987 as a political exile. He has written novels in both Russian and French. Makine received both the Prix Goncourt and the Prix Medici in 1995 for his novel Le Testament français *(1995), translated into English as* Dreams of My Russian Summers *(1997), a feat which no French citizen had ever before accomplished.*

These visits also provide a source of hope for the young boy, who is raised in a Russian orphanage under deplorable conditions. Most of the other children in the home are war orphans, too, and they dream of their heroic fathers bursting into the classrooms or dormitories to rescue them from their miserable circumstances. Makine creates blatant parallels between the orphanage conditions and those of World War II prisoner of war camps. The orphaned children are forced to perform hard labor when not in the classroom or act as stand-ins to fill stadiums for countless ceremonies and war monument unveilings, serving as good citizens who are appreciative of the Soviet Republic. It is at one such ceremony that the protagonist becomes transfixed while witnessing a speech by General Charles de Gaulle presented in French, a language the boy presumed was dead and that only he and Alexandria still spoke. He is left in a state of awe with curiosity and hope.

During one of these outings, the children also learn that their orphanage is closing in the autumn, and they will be forced into the real world from which they have been relatively sheltered. Several make attempts to assimilate into the surrounding town, and a few run away. The narrator makes a failed attempt to blend into the townspeople by drinking at a local tavern. He witnesses a girl he knew from the orphanage being mistreated by a man twice her age. Filled with dread and a sense of failure, he returns to the orphanage afraid of what his future will offer. The narrator and other orphans continue to visit the town and during one outing are attacked by street hoodlums. During the attack, the narrator's only true friend from the orphanage, Village, is stabbed to death while trying to protect the others. The narrator realizes at Village's funeral that there is no one in the world to inform of Village's murder. He is once again filled with feelings of isolation, hopelessness, and dread. Alone and scared, the young narrator is allowed to stay with Alexandria for one week. Sensing his desperate loneliness and the need for familial roots, Alexandria shares a second treasure with the boy: her wartime experiences.

Alexandria tells the boy of her experiences during the war and the circumstances that brought her to Russia forty years earlier. In 1921, she came to Russia, a nurse engaged as part of a Red Cross humanitarian effort. Upon her arrival, she immediately fell in love with a Russian man. Shortly after their marriage, he was executed following a twenty-minute trial staged by the totalitarian government. Alexandria was sent into exile after the execution but emerged during World War II to serve once again as a nurse. During this service Alexandria met Jacques Dorme, a French pilot who sympathized with Russia's fight against the Nazis. The two spent one week together, out of which came a lifelong love affair.

She tells the story of Dorme's plane being shot down over Poland in a German dogfight, resulting in Dorme becoming a German prisoner of war. The boy learns of Dorme's escape with his Polish ally and fellow captive, Witold. The two are able to make their way out of Poland and find themselves roaming the Russian countryside until they are once again taken prisoner, this time by the Russians. During this second internment, Dorme witnesses Witold's execution without trial, but he himself is spared when the camp is attacked moments later in an air raid. Dorme is able to prove himself useful as a pilot by successfully flying an overloaded cargo plane on a test mission for his captors. He quickly becomes a sought-after pilot and is entrusted with the dangerous mission of flying American airplanes from Alaska across the Urals to Siberia, the 'Alsib' line, to help in the fight against the Germans.

Although he is a loyal sympathizer, with World War II coming to an end and the Cold War about to begin, many of the Russians continue to meet Dorme with suspicion, resentment, and at times hostility. When Dorme is told by a Russian superior to change his flight path because the one he had previously flown was less fuel-efficient, Dorme knows not to argue, even though the newly proposed path will almost certainly result in death. Dorme instructs the other pilots on the mission to fly the original plan, assuring them that he will take responsibility for the decision and disobedience. Dorme then flies the new path alone, and in doing so, sacrifices himself by flying into an icy mountainside. Makine artistically parallels Dorme's freezing isolation with the orphan's solitary life and sterile conditions.

Obsessed with the heroic tale and desperate to create a family history, the young orphan makes it his life's mission to find out everything he can about Jacques Dorme and tell the world of his story. Decades later, in 2000, the boy-turned-man finds himself a successful author and journalist living as an exile in France (a life and career not unlike Makine's). The narrator has written a fictionalized account of Jacques Dorme and Alexandria's experiences and has sent it to French publishing houses, with little success. In his never-ending quest to discover all he can about Jacques Dorme, the narrator tracks down and visits Dorme's brother and his wife, Li En. Although the brief visit grants the narrator a few stolen glimpses at family photos, the brother is not willing to speak about Dorme, other than to reveal that Dorme was a nickname based on Jacques's idol, World War I pilot Rene Dorme, whose plane was shot down during battle.

The narrator asks the brother for permission to use the life story of Jacques Dorme in a fictionalized biography, and the brother refuses. Meanwhile, the narrator has already received word from a Paris publishing house and signs a contract to publish the novel on the condition that he remove the pilot character from the book because the publisher sees the character as being too unbelievable. The Jacques Dorme pilot character is removed, the novel is published, and the promise to the brother is kept. After the brother reads the novel, he has mixed emotions. The brother is happy that the young author kept his promise and disappointed that Jacques Dorme's story will die with him.

The narrator returns to Russia with forged documents to find the crash site and the remains of Dorme's plane in the Tundra—the final piece in the puzzle he has spent his life trying to solve. With the help of two geologists and an accommodating, although reluctant captain, the narrator flies to the Tundra and eventually discoveries what he is seeking. He catches a glimpse of light reflecting on metal through the snow from the few rays of sun the hour and a half of daylight provides. The narrator is able to look at and reflect upon the wreckage only for minutes before he must leave or be left behind by the crew forever and contemplates "No thought speaks within me. No emotion. Not even joy at having achieved the goal. Only the certainty of experiencing the essence of what I had to understand."

In finding the wreckage and closing the last chapter of Jacques Dorme's life, the narrator also finds a connection to the past and a sense of belonging previously unknown. In doing so, he creates for himself the family he never knew and the personal history he had sought during his entire life. Through a simple yet powerful use of vocabulary, complemented by a sensitive and eloquent writing style, Makine is able to provide comfort and companionship for the two isolated characters by finally introducing them to each other, giving the narrator a family and ensuring that Jacques Dorme's legacy will live on.

Sara Vidar

Review Sources

Artforum 11, no. 5 (February/March, 2005): 41.
Kirkus Reviews 72, no. 24 (December 15, 2004): 1159.
Library Journal 130, no. 2 (February 1, 2005): 69.
Los Angeles Times, June 13, 2004, p. R5.
The New York Times, March 6, 2205, p. 17.
The New York Times Book Review 154 (March 6, 2005): 17.
Publishers Weekly 251, no. 51 (December 20, 2004): 34-35.
The Spectator 297 (April 16, 2005): 43.

EDMUND WILSON
A Life in Literature

Author: Lewis M. Dabney (1932-   )
Publisher: Farrar, Straus and Giroux (New York).
    642 pp. $35.00
Type of work: Literary biography
Time: 1895-1972
Locale: The eastern United States and the Vosges, France

This biography of Wilson provides a great deal of material on the life of the noted American literary critic and cultural commentator, but it is confusingly written and often hard to understand

Principal personages:
    EDMUND WILSON, a literary critic
    EDMUND WILSON, SR., his father
    HELEN WILSON, his mother
    F. SCOTT FITZGERALD, his friend, a writer
    VLADIMIR NABOKOV, his friend, a writer
    EDNA ST. VINCENT MILLAY, his lover, a poet
    MARY BLAIR, his first wife
    MARGARET CANBY, his second wife
    MARY MCCARTHY, his third wife, a writer
    ELENA MUMM WILSON, his fourth wife

One of the most interesting sections of Lewis Dabney's biography of literary critic and cultural commentator Edmund Wilson comes near the very end of the book, when Dabney discusses *Patriotic Gore* (1962), Wilson's study of the Civil War era. In this extended section, Dabney reveals just how interesting a thinker Wilson was. Rather than recycle conventional views on the evils of slavery and the heroism of U.S. president Abraham Lincoln, Wilson called Lincoln into question, expressing disquiet with how a large political unit (the North) imposed its will on a smaller and weaker one in a form of imperial expansion.

In a series of essays on various figures of the era, Wilson, according to Dabney's account, showed the complexity of human existence by having the heroes of one essay show up as the villains of another, depending on whose eyes through which he was portraying events. Wilson also provided a controversial introduction in which he generalized from the example of the Civil War to condemn all wars, suggesting that in all such conflicts it is much too easy to claim moral superiority, to claim to be fighting for a just cause and liberation. "Whenever we engage in a war or move in on some other country," Wilson wrote, "it is always to liberate somebody," suggesting that, in reality, wars are never for liberation.

These are highly provocative views with which many will disagree, but they show Wilson to be a stimulating thinker whose work would be interesting to read for the intellectual challenge he provides. Elsewhere in his biography, Dabney says that one of Wilson's main achievements was to bring various authors to the attention of the public, to popularize works and make people want to read them. In this section on *Patriotic Gore*, Dabney creates some of the same effect.

Lewis Dabney is the author of The Indians of Yoknapatawpha *(1974), a study of the American novelist* William Faulkner. *He has also edited two collections of Edmund Wilson's work:* The Portable Edmund Wilson *(1983) and* Edmund Wilson: Centennial Reflections *(1997). He also edited Wilson's last journal,* The Sixties *(1993). He teaches in the English department at the University of Wyoming.*

Unfortunately, this is one of the rare successful moments in Dabney's study, and even in this section the reader often has to puzzle out what Dabney is actually saying. Is he really saying Wilson criticized Lincoln? To be certain, it is necessary to consult an earlier biography of Wilson, a 1995 work by Jeffrey Meyers titled *Edmund Wilson: A Biography*.

Meyers's work is everything Dabney's is not: clear, crisp, coherent. Where Dabney puts sentences next to each other that do not seem to belong together, Meyers constructs paragraphs that stick to their topics and carry the discussion along in a clear direction. Dabney seems unable to do this. It is as if he has taken his twenty years' worth of notes on Wilson and just dumped them in the reader's lap, as if saying, Here, you figure out how all this fits together.

Sometimes Dabney does not seem able to grasp the significance of his own material. For instance, he reports on how Wilson saw his former lover, the poet Edna St. Vincent Millay, years after their love affair ended and found her looking "ruddy and overblown." Somehow, from this Dabney concludes that Wilson still loved her, though the evidence he has just presented would suggest the very opposite.

Other times his paragraphs ride off in all directions. In one he begins by making the interesting remark that Wilson's sober judgments in print on various authors and their works masked the disorder of his private life. An elaboration on this idea might have been quite illuminating; there does seem to have been a large gap between the public Wilson, the distinguished man of letters calmly presenting his views on a variety of topics, and the private Wilson, a difficult man with a drinking problem, a short temper, and a propensity for adultery.

Wilson married four times, and at times he seemed to be running away from his marriages, going off on assignments around the world, setting up a second house, having affairs. He seems in many ways to have been a lonely, isolated man. Dabney shows him to have been a shy boy, not taking part in sports, preferring the more solitary pursuits of magic tricks and, of course, reading.

At Princeton, Wilson felt out of place among the children of wealthy families who regarded him as too serious about his schoolwork. He had no romances until the age of twenty-five, when Millay became his first lover. His classmates had voted him most likely to remain a bachelor. They were wrong about that in a literal sense, but in the sense of making a true connection with another human being, they may not have been far off.

In his working life, Wilson never felt at ease in a classroom, so instead of becoming a teacher, he remained a full-time freelance writer, a solitary pursuit. Wilson's most famous theory, referred to usually as "the wound and the bow," describes how artists are shaped by their wounds and how their abilities are inseparable from their psychic problems, just as the ability of the mythical archer Philoctetes to fire arrows from his bow was inseparable from his horrible wound. In Wilson's case, the wound may have been his isolation and alienation from others, which was harmful to him personally but which allowed him to approach the study of culture and politics from an independent and interestingly unorthodox perspective.

This is the sort of argument, along the lines of the wound and the bow theory, that one might have expected Dabney to elaborate in a paragraph beginning with a comment on the difference between the public and the private Wilson. Instead, Dabney's paragraph shifts to discussing various attitudes Wilson had, for instance his view that it was important for artists to engage with society, an interesting view for such an alienated thinker as Wilson to adopt—perhaps it was some sort of compensation for his alienation—but Dabney does not explore this issue.

That same paragraph goes on to say Wilson commented on the importance of developing an American culture separate from the old culture of Europe, then mentions that Wilson at this point was writing on three major literary figures: T. S. Eliot, James Joyce, and Marcel Proust. Dabney does not say so, but these three figures were all associated with Europe rather than America (though Eliot was born in the United States), so it would be interesting to know how Wilson's emphasis on such European writers accorded with his call for an American culture. This is another point that Dabney does not explore.

He finally ends the paragraph by saying that Wilson liked to go out drinking with his friends and discussing politics. How that point connects to what went before it in the paragraph is unclear. Wilson, Dabney tells the reader, was noted for his ability to integrate the personal and the public in his essays on literary figures; Dabney's book demonstrates no such ability. The book contains a great deal, probably too much, on Wilson's personal life, along with extended discussions of his works, but there is little integration. It is left to the reader to puzzle out the connections.

Dabney's book is confusingly written throughout, not just because of its lack of order and development, but because the author's style is as convoluted as that of Henry James, though without James's delicate insights. In one section, however, the confusion has a certain aptness. Wilson, like so many of his contemporaries, was much taken with the Bolshevik Revolution in Russia, and as the Depression of the 1930's got under way, he moved further and further to the left, becoming quite drawn to Marxism.

However, he never joined the Communist Party, and a visit to the Soviet Union shook his new faith, a faith that seemed in part intended to replace his family's strict Presbyterianism, in which he no longer believed. At this point he was in the middle of writing one of his major works, *To the Finland Station* (1940), detailing the history of the development of socialism from a mostly pro-socialist point of view.

Wilson began the book in the grip of the notion of progress, seeing history advancing and culminating in the moment when the Russian revolutionary V. I. Lenin arrived back in Russia at the Finland railroad station in St. Petersburg. However, by the time he finished the book Wilson was no longer sure history was going in the right direction—he certainly disliked much of what he saw in the Soviet Union under Joseph Stalin—and yet he did not renounce communism altogether, maintaining an idealized vision of Lenin. Nor did he give up entirely on Karl Marx, though he lost faith in the dialectical theories of Marxism. He came to admire Marx more for his manner than for the content of his views. He saw him as a sort of Old Testament prophet railing against society, a position that must have appealed to Wilson, who in a way was doing the same thing.

The effect on *To the Finland Station*, however, was to make its attitudes seem contradictory and confused. In a way, as it emerges in Dabney's account, it is a book reflecting its author's journey away from a set of beliefs; it catches Wilson in the middle of losing his Marxist faith.

As Dabney tells it, Wilson spent much of the rest of his life seeking, but never finding, a new faith. He visited the Zuñi Indians in New Mexico, examined the Dead Sea Scrolls when they were discovered in Israel, and was drawn to Jewish writers and the Jewish intellectual tradition.

He was always exploring new ideas and new places, and Dabney makes him sound like an admirable intellectual, if perhaps not an entirely admirable human being, someone whose writings bear rereading. To the extent that Dabney succeeds in directing readers back to Wilson, his book can be said to be a success, however awkwardly and confusingly it is written.

Sheldon Goldfarb

Review Sources

America 194, no. 1 (January 2, 2006): 25-26.
American Scholar 74, no. 4 (Autumn, 2005): 131-134.
The Atlantic Monthly 296, no. 1 (July/August, 2005): 126-127.
Booklist 101, no. 22 (August 1, 2005): 1982.
Harper's Magazine 311 (September, 2005): 81-86.
Kirkus Reviews 73, no. 10 (May 15, 2005): 573.
Library Journal 130, no. 12 (July 1, 2005): 79-80.
New Criterion 24, no. 2 (October, 2005): 74-77.
New Republic 233, no. 13 (September 26, 2005): 23-32.
New York 38, no. 29 (August 22, 2005): 57-58.
The New York Review of Books 53, no. 1 (January 12, 2006): 31-33.
The New York Times Book Review 154 (September 4, 2005): 1-11.
Publishers Weekly 252, no. 24 (June 13, 2005): 44.

THE END OF POVERTY
Economic Possibilities for Our Time

Author: Jeffrey D. Sachs (1954-   )
Publisher: Penguin Press (New York). 397 pp. $28.00
Type of work: Current affairs and economics
Time: The late twentieth and early twenty-first centuries
Locale: The world

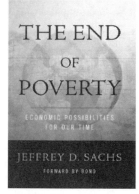

Basing his conclusions on a variety of case studies, a maverick economist presents his plan to end extreme poverty worldwide by the year 2025

In *The End of Poverty*, Jeffrey D. Sachs draws on his scholarly expertise and experience to argue that extreme global poverty can be eliminated by the year 2025, that is, if the wealthy nations of the world truly wish to do so. Sachs, a Harvard-educated economist, rejects the view of those who see globalization simply as a conspiracy to enable the rich and powerful to get richer and more powerful at the expense of the poor and powerless. For Sachs, globalization, in some form or other, is definitely the wave of the future. More to the point, globalization, if carried out in an enlightened way, can be a source of hope, even—and especially—for the poorest people.

On the other hand, Sachs does not believe that supercharged globalization will automatically end extreme forms of economic deprivation. In fact, if badly guided, globalization can exacerbate problems, causing more economic upheaval than is necessary, failing to alleviate the pain that often accompanies rapid economic change, and turning a blind eye to deep-rooted stagnation. The last issue is crucial to Sachs. In the absence of special measures, the most extreme poverty will surely remain resistant to conventional forms of market-driven global economic development. Thus, while Sachs embraces globalization, he is definitely not among those who offer unqualified applause for the rapidly globalizing economy. Globalization will either be kind or cruel to the worst-off, depending on the policies and values of those who are prosperous. If people's hearts are in the right places, Sachs says, and if they open their minds to what actually works (rather than clinging to dogmatic biases), there exists an unprecedented opportunity to end extreme poverty throughout the world. Indeed, there is no excuse not to do so.

In the opening chapters of the book, Sachs presents a historical overview of the world economy and introduces readers to the concept of clinical economics. Previous to the last few centuries, nearly the entire human race was poor by today's standards. True, most societies had a class structure of some sort, but there was not enough in the way of wealth or productivity for massive economic fortunes to be amassed. Put another way, even the economically privileged were badly off compared to a middle-class person in one of the today's rich nations. Thus, radical austerity and relative global equality were the rule. Over the last three centuries or so, however, global wealth has expanded exponentially. Driven by global trade, market forces, and capitalist zeal, the human race has amassed undreamed-of wealth. The problem is that this great economic expansion has been uneven, giving many millions of people cushy lives with ever-expanding expectations, leaving other millions of people at the tumultuous early stages of prosperity, and, finally, leaving still other millions of people in dire economic straits, where even the bare necessities of life are inadequately supplied, and the prospects for improvement are truly dim.

Jeffrey D. Sachs is an economist interested in global development. He earned his B.A. (1976), M.A. (1978), and Ph.D. (1980) in economics from Harvard University, where he was also a professor until 2002, when he became director of the Earth Institute at Columbia University and special adviser to U.N. Secretary-General Kofi Annan on the Millennium Development Goals. Sachs has advised many governments around the world and has become something of a global celebrity.

It is in his explanation of (and remedies for) the above inequalities where Sachs parts company with most cheerleaders for global capitalism. For one thing, though Sachs does not blame everything bad on colonialism, he is quite willing to admit its role in adding an element of naked exploitation to the spread of global capitalism. Even more than this, Sachs thinks uneven development and lingering poverty can be explained by the different economic, social, and political conditions—including, but not limited to colonialism—which have been and are currently faced by various nations and regions of the world. This is in direct opposition to those who see the world's poor populations as being substantially responsible for their own condition, due to sloth, moral backwardness, or other cultural weaknesses, including the wrongheaded failure to wholeheartedly embrace the ideology and policies of free-market capitalism. Not surprisingly, this divergence of explanations leads to divergent policy recommendations as well.

For conventional economists and the policymakers they advise, the task is simple. Economically distressed people must be thrown into the marketplace to compete and, as the cliché goes, pull themselves up by their own bootstraps. The job of wealthy nations (and the world banking and development system they control), therefore, is to employ a one-size-fits-all policy which encourages (and even compels) austerity, small government, and as close a condition as one can get to the abstract marketplace described in freshman economics courses. This is where Sachs's notion of clinical economics comes in. Drawing an analogy to the field of medicine, Sachs likens this conventional approach to nineteenth century doctoring when, no matter what the malady was, the treatment offered was likely to be a generous dose of bloodletting, often with the help of highly cooperative leeches. Given the primitiveness of medical science, this may have been understandable at the time, but it is certainly not today, because so much more is known about the nature and variability of diseases and also of individual patients.

Likewise, when it comes to global economic development, there is now far more detailed knowledge available about various economic maladies and the treatments that are likely to be successful in each case. Thus, for Sachs, the goal of development economists, and world leaders, should be to make modern, scientific diagnoses of economic maladies facing nations and regions, and then to prescribe and implement treatments based on ever-more refined experiences. In short, experts and power holders alike have to get beyond their academic and cultural biases in order to look at the world as it really is and can be.

Sachs goes on to demonstrate the notion of clinical economics by examining a number of case studies. Based on his own adventures as an economic development consultant to (in chronological order) Bolivia, Poland, Russia, China, India, and various nations in Africa, these case studies demonstrate the range and variability of development diagnoses and treatments. Sachs's opening revelation is how poorly his education in academic economics prepared him for the practical task of understanding and addressing real-life problems in economic development. Contrary to the conventional wisdom of times since the 1970's, Sachs found that particular cases varied; while it might be that no situation was entirely unique, nor were any two situations identical. Thus each experience called for careful observation and analysis and led to different policy solutions. While Sachs's central concern in this book is dire poverty, and, therefore, Africa and the poorest parts of Asia are the main focal points, the early consulting experience is crucial to his overall argument.

In addition to learning about the shortcomings of conventional wisdom and the variability of individual cases, he also concluded that economic development often requires a jump-start from the outside, most specifically in the form of debt relief. While forgiving debts may seem counterintuitive and morally slack, it is sometimes necessary to put nations on the track for success. Citing the Marshall Plan following World War II and personal bankruptcy as parallels, Sachs argues that, when used in the right way, debt relief becomes a very positive investment in the future. The point is crucial, because it lays the groundwork for the guts of the book, in which Sachs calls not only for the strategic employment of debt relief for the world's poorest nations but also for an unprecedented cash investment in these nations to put them on the first rung of the development ladder.

Sachs, in essence, is advocating that the world's rich nations graduate from the practice of offering gestures—grand or otherwise—to that of making a first-priority commitment to end poverty in its most extreme forms around the globe. In return, he shows that what he proposes is eminently affordable, offers a detailed plan (rather than vague generalities) for proceeding, directly addresses likely objections, and makes sensible arguments about why this is a good thing to do. What is needed to finance this campaign against extreme poverty is an allocation by rich nations of 0.7 percent of their gross national product (GNP). According to Sachs, this would raise aid to a scale where it actually could make a lasting impact, rather than merely raising false hopes. It would also be easily affordable, barely if at all affecting the living standards of the citizens in donor countries, especially if the burden within rich nations is placed primarily on those who are most rich.

While Sachs lauds private philanthropy on the part of the wealthy, he believes that governments will also have to ante up to raise funds adequate to the job. The aid would, in any case, have to be centrally administered, preferably by the United Nations, so that a coordinated effort could address basic health issues, education, infrastructure needs, and technological modernization on a country-by-country (and, where needed, regional) basis.

Sachs insists that, in order to succeed, all these areas of concern must be addressed in an aid "package" tailored to specific conditions and carefully monitored to ensure efficient implementation and ongoing effectiveness. From start to finish, the process must be informed by free-flowing discourse, both among experts, and between aid-givers and recipients. Sachs knows that there will be doubters. To those who believe that poor Africans, for example, lack the cultural sophistication to profit from such aid, he offers stories that indicate a readiness to adapt if given the conditions to succeed. To those who disparage the ineptitude of African governments, Sachs offers examples to the contrary and also argues that economic development is needed to provide a basis for better government. As to why the campaign to end poverty should be launched (and completed), Sachs eschews moral or religious arguments, instead focusing on practical self-interest. A world without dire poverty will be politically safer and offer more economic opportunity for everyone.

Needless to say, Sachs's book will not please everyone. Some observers reject his most basic premise altogether, denying that any obligation whatsoever exists for the rich nations to address global poverty. Others accept global poverty as a shared problem but believe Sachs's solution is misconceived. Many in the global financial establishment still believe that unfettered markets work better than government, no matter how well intentioned it may be.

Among his audience in the United States, Sachs also arouses suspicion because of his reliance on the U.N. to administer the effort to eradicate poverty as well as his critical attitude toward the Bush administration's tax cuts and the costly war in Iraq. On the other side of the fence, for some observers, Sachs is way too easy on colonialism. They see the causes of global poverty as clearly lying with the rich nations, and, subsequently, the aid Sachs calls for as a mere trickle rather than anything resembling just reparations. Then, too, to those with an egalitarian bent, Sachs is too accepting of global as well as domestic disparities between rich and poor. As Sachs makes clear, his proposal only seeks to eliminate the most extreme of economic circumstances. Even if his plan works, there will still be great disparities between rich and poor, with some people experiencing wealth beyond their dreams while others struggle to make ends meet. Meaningful inequalities exist even in the richest nations. Sachs does not directly address this issue in his book.

As indicated by the book's forward, written by celebrity philanthropist Bono (lead singer of the rock group U2), Sachs also has found substantial support for his ideas among world leaders, academics, and the more general public. After reading this book, one can easily see why. Sachs writes very clearly, anticipates opposing arguments, avoids knee-jerk platitudes, and marshals impressive arrays of evidence to support his position. The result is a work that is suitably complex, yet also remarkably accessible. It is also a work that tempers idealistic motives with a realistic assessment of what can be done, and how. As such, *The End of Poverty* is a book that may actually help to change the world.

Ira Smolensky

Review Sources

Booklist 101, no. 12 (February 15, 2005): 1043.
Business Week, April 11, 2005, p. 20.
Commentary 119, no. 6 (June, 2005): 71-72.
The Economist 374 (March 19, 2005): 87.
Foreign Affairs 84, no. 3 (May/June, 2005): 133-134.
Kirkus Reviews 73, no. 2 (January 15, 2005): 111.
National Review 57, no. 10 (June 6, 2005): 52-53.
New Statesman 134 (May 16, 2005): 47-49.
The New York Times Book Review 154 (April 24, 2005): 18.
The New Yorker 81, no. 8 (April 11, 2005): 72-77.
Publishers Weekly 252, no. 6 (February 7, 2005): 51.
The Wall Street Journal 245, no. 57 (March 23, 2005): D8.

EQUIANO, THE AFRICAN
Biography of a Self-Made Man

Author: Vincent Carretta (1945-   )
Publisher: University of Georgia Press (Athens). 376 pp.
   $30.00
Type of work: Biography and history
Time: The last half of the eighteenth century and 1995-
   2005
Locale: England, Essaka (now southeastern Nigeria), the
   West Indies, South Carolina, Virginia

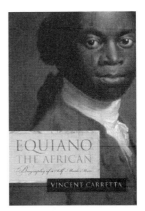

Carretta carefully documents his contention that Olau-
dah Equiano's first-person description of traveling via the
Middle Passage from Africa to the New World, where he
was sold into slavery, was fabricated and that Equiano was
born in South Carolina

Principal personages:
> OLAUDAH EQUIANO (1745-1797), a freed slave whose slave name was
> Gustavus Vassa
> MICHAEL HENRY PASCAL (fl. c. 1755), a British navy lieutenant who
> bought Equiano as his slave
> DR. CHARLES IRVING (fl. c. 1770), Equiano's former employer
> LOUIS HENRY GATES, JR., the director of Harvard University's African
> and African-American Studies department
> PHILIP D. MORGAN, a professor of history at Princeton University
> PAUL E. LOVEJOY, the director of the Harriet Tubman Resource Center
> at York University, Toronto, Canada
> ADAM HOCHSCHILD, a teacher of writing at the University of California
> at Berkeley

Vincent Carretta's *Equiano, the African: Biography of a Self-Made Man* has all
the ingredients of a sensational exposé. However, the author, who through exhaustive
scholarly research presents his case, has done all in his power to avoid the sensational.
When he first began to question the veracity of some elements in Olaudah Equiano's
renowned and supposedly autobiographical slave narrative, *The Interesting Narrative
of the Life of Olaudah Equiano: Or, Gustavus Vassa, the African, Written by Himself*
(1789), he accelerated his research efforts, which yielded interesting results and suggested that Equiano had never made the Middle Passage about which he wrote so dramatically and with such apparent authority.

Carretta first became aware of Equiano's narrative through reading *Classic Slave
Narratives* (1987), edited by Louis Henry Gates, Jr., director of Harvard University's
African and African-American Studies Department. Because there was little extant
writing by African Americans in eighteenth century Britain, Carretta decided to in-

∼

Vincent Carretta is professor of English at the University of Maryland, College Park. He is the editor of Unchained Voices: An Anthology of Black Authors in the English-Speaking World of the Eighteenth Century *(1996), the* Complete Writings *(2001) of Phillis Wheatley, and, with Philip Gould,* Genius in Bondage: Literature of the Early Black Atlantic *(2001). Carretta also wrote* George III and the Satirist from Hogarth to Byron *(1990).*

∼

clude Equiano's narrative in his course in eighteenth century British literature.

When the book elicited an encouraging response among his students, Carretta decided to edit *The Interesting Narrative* himself for Penguin Books. In preparing this edition, he expanded his research and, in so doing, found evidence suggesting that Equiano was not born in Africa, as Equiano had contended, but had been born in South Carolina in 1745.

Given the authority that had traditionally been ascribed to Equiano's narrative by those teaching African American literature and history throughout the United States and Canada, Carretta's suspicions were nothing short of revolutionary. Carretta, however, did not come forth with these suspicions in any spectacular way. Rather, he buried them in the footnotes of his edition and awaited the outcome. In actuality, readers failed to respond to his contentions, presumably because they read the narrative but skipped the footnotes. He described his startling revelation as a depth charge submerged in footnotes.

There was no doubt that Equiano had been a slave who, upon buying his freedom, had opted to settle in London, which he had previously visited while working as a seaman for his owner, Michael Henry Pascal, a British naval lieutenant who was also his friend. Equiano assumed that in time Pascal would emancipate him, but he was mistaken in his expectation that this would happen. After he had served his master as a seaman in the Seven Years' War, Pascal in 1763 sold Equiano in the West Indies, where he used his skills of self-promotion and business acumen to save the money he needed to buy his freedom, which he did in 1766 when he was twenty-one years old and still had much of his life before him. Although he settled in England after he gained his freedom, Equiano continued to work as a seaman, venturing to many Atlantic ports as well as into the Arctic Ocean.

Knowing what he did about the background of the former slave, Carretta began to dig for further information about him and was dismayed to find that no previous scholar had sought to verify the seemingly factual information Equiano presented in *The Interesting Narrative*. Carretta eventually secured the muster list of the HMS *Racehorse*, on which Equiano was known to have sailed. On this list, Equiano's birthplace is given as South Carolina. This information shocked Carretta, who now sought additional intelligence about Equiano's origins. In England, he obtained a baptismal record which, like the ship's muster list, indicated that Equiano's birthplace was South Carolina.

Equiano's tale of how at age eleven he was kidnapped by Africans from his idyllic home in an area called Essaka, in what is now southeastern Nigeria, is thoroughly engrossing. According to *The Interesting Narrative*, Equiano was turned over to white slave traders on Africa's west coast, shackled, and put aboard an overcrowded ship on which many people died during the voyage west. He offered convincing and heart-rending details about the ship's squalid conditions and about the moaning and shriek-ing of the shackled Africans who, if they survived the arduous ocean voyage, were conveyed to the slave markets of the West Indies and sold.

There Equiano, according to his narrative, was put up for sale at a slave auction. When he failed to attract any bids, he was transported to Virginia, where Michael Henry Pascal purchased him and taught him seamanship. Equiano served Pascal as a seaman in the Seven Years' War and, as a seaman, visited several venues outside the United States, including England.

The Africa that Equiano's narrative presents ran completely counter to the percep-tions most white people had of the dark continent. Equiano portrays Africa, especially the land of the Igbo, where he claimed to have been born and raised to age eleven, as a land in which members of small communities were genuinely concerned about one another. They were hardworking, creative, and, according to Equiano's account, a community of dancers, poets, and musicians.

This portrayal of Africa was completely contradictory to the most commonly held European and American notions of Africa, but many accepted Equiano's account as the true picture of Africa's hinterland. His narrative challenged completely the notion that Africa was inhabited by heathen savages. His was the sole source that presented seemingly authoritative information about the Igbo society of the eighteenth century.

One might ask whether it is really important to determine whether Equiano's nar-rative is a fiction. Certainly, even if it has marked fictional elements, a great deal of it is probably authentic. Carretta's students, on reading *The Interesting Narrative*, noted that the first three chapters read like an anthropological treatise, whereas the subse-quent chapters seem to be related in a different voice.

This suggests that Equiano, if indeed he was born in South Carolina as Carretta contends, might have encountered slaves from Essaka and gained from them the over-view of Igbo society which he presents in his book. Theoretically, once he had sketched in the anthropological details, he was free to create the gripping story of his abduction and subsequent life.

His was an unusual and fascinating life, tracing as it does his rise from involuntary servitude to freedom and to eventual wealth. Equiano has been called an African American Benjamin Franklin, parts of whose *Autobiography* had appeared before *The Interesting Narrative*, but the final version of which appeared in 1818, after Equiano published his narrative.

Be it fact or fiction, *The Interesting Narrative* had a considerable impact upon so-ciety on both sides of the Atlantic Ocean. In England, it was instrumental in bringing about heated debate about the selling of human beings into slavery. In 1807, largely because of the impact of Equiano's book, England legally abolished its slave trade, profitable though that trade had been. Abolitionists found in Equiano's work a great deal to support their opposition to slavery.

After Equiano gained his freedom in 1766, he chose to live in London, although his work as a seaman demanded that he be away for long periods of time. By 1774, he had undergone a religious conversion, becoming what would in modern parlance be termed a born-again Christian.

Despite his background as a slave, Equiano helped Dr. Charles Irving, who had previously employed him, to establish a profitable plantation in Central America which was staffed with slaves. Presumably, he helped Dr. Irving buy Igbo slaves with the understanding that they would eventually earn their freedom. Some scholars have viewed Equiano's association with Dr. Irving as an abolitionist move, inasmuch as he considered the slaves involved to be indentured servants who, after a stipulated time, would be free. In time, Equiano became an ardent and articulate abolitionist.

Shortly before he married a white woman in 1792, Equiano, ever an astute business man and a notorious self-promoter, published *The Interesting Narrative*. He not only published the book by himself and held the copyright, but he also garnered a long list of prominent people who agreed to buy copies, thereby guaranteeing that Equiano would at least recover the production costs involved in getting his narrative into print. This was an extraordinary thing for him to do because few books in that era went into second editions, and the first editions of many lay moldering unsold on printers' and publishers' shelves.

Before his death in 1797, Equiano's narrative had become a best-selling book in England and the United States, having gone into nine editions. As a result, he was a wealthy man, whose considerable fortune he left to one of his two daughters who outlived him. Even though England's abolition of the slave trade in 1809 led to reduced sales of *The Interesting Narrative*, the book had made a substantial impact upon readers, many of whom had been won over to the abolitionist cause after reading and discussing the book.

Carretta's investigations have resulted in a revolutionary reevaluation of this, perhaps the most significant slave narrative of the eighteenth century. If his contentions turn out to be valid, as many are convinced they will, the entire depiction of eighteenth century Africa, much of it based on this single source, will have to be reexamined, reconsidered, and thoroughly researched.

Hordes of Nigerians, particularly the Igbo, who have turned Equiano into a national hero, are deeply troubled by Carretta's contentions. Scholars will be forced to reevaluate much of the information they have accepted as sacrosanct in their teaching of African American literature and society. Although such prestigious scholars as Princeton University's Philip D. Morgan consider Carretta's research convincing, others are unwilling to accept it categorically.

Paul E. Lovejoy of Toronto's York University admits that everything scholars presently know about the Middle Passage depends upon Equiano's being born in Africa. Adam Hochschild of the University of California at Berkeley commends Carretta's careful and exhaustive scholarship as well as his doggedness in tracking down sources. Neither Lovejoy nor Hochschild, however, has abandoned his conviction that Equiano was born in Africa. They have found means of explaining away the two pieces of documentation on which Carretta's case depends.

Regardless of the outcome of the disputes that Carretta's research has engendered, it is clear that the revisionist history his theories have spawned will lead to continued fruitful investigations of sources that have been overlooked for more than two centuries. Carretta has rendered an invaluable service in bringing to light the questions that his investigation pose about Equiano's origins.

A word of praise must be reserved for the University of Georgia Press. It has produced this book in a beautiful and enticing format.

R. Baird Shuman

Review Sources

Booklist 102, no. 2 (September 15, 2005): 9.
The Chronicle of Higher Education 52 (September 9, 2005): A11-A15.
Kirkus Reviews 93, no. 16 (August 15, 2005): 892.
The Nation 281, no. 17 (November 21, 2005): 33-37.
The New York Review of Books 52, no. 16 (October 20, 2005): 27.
Publishers Weekly 252, no. 30 (August 1, 2005): 54.

EUDORA WELTY
A Biography

Author: Suzanne Marrs (1946-   )
Publisher: Harcourt (New York). 652 pp. $28.00
Type of work: Literary biography
Time: 1909-2001
Locale: Centered around Jackson, Mississippi; includes
   Welty's national and international travels

Welty becomes three-dimensional in this comprehensive biography written by her close friend, who also authored the standard critical study of Welty's work

Principal personages:
   EUDORA WELTY, a writer
   JOHN ROBINSON, her one-time lover and
      later friend
   V. S. PRITCHETT, her friend, a fellow writer
   CHESTINA WELTY, her mother

Eudora Welty, one of the most highly regarded American authors of the twentieth century, created works that are considered classics. She is best known for her short stories, mining deep veins of humanity to create characters who take up permanent residence in readers' hearts and minds. In addition, Welty wrote long fiction—*The Optimist's Daughter* (1972) was awarded the Pulitzer Prize in 1973—and nonfiction. She received many honors, including the Howells Medal for Fiction in 1955 and the Gold Medal for Fiction in 1972. In 1972, she was elected to membership in the American Academy of Arts and Letters. Welty received the Medal of Literature and Medal of Freedom in 1981 as well as the National Medal of the Arts in 1986. In 1996, she was elected to the French Legion of Honor. Two years later, she became the only living writer whose works were included in the distinguished Library of America series. Throughout her long life, Welty made herself accessible to reviewers and scholars, spoke at colleges and universities, appeared on television, supported worthy causes by her presence at fund-raising events, and even responded cordially to strangers who turned up at her home in Jackson.

Welty's private life, however, was just that. When she was asked questions of a personal nature, she deftly turned the conversation back to her work. An exception was her memorable autobiography *One Writer's Beginnings* (1984), and even there, the information about people, happenings, and influences in her early years was included to help the reader understand Eudora Welty, the writer. Readers who do not know details about a beloved author tend to imagine them, and—until the publication of *Eudora Welty: A Biography* by Suzanne Marrs—Welty has been generally painted in clichés: a gentile southerner tending her garden, perhaps inviting lady friends for tea and sandwiches; a woman of great imagination, able to pour it intuitively into fantastic and unusual characters and situations; a spinster content with her lot in life, living in the family homestead with her mother, devotedly caring for her in old age.

Anne Waldron's unauthorized bibliography *Eudora: A Writer's Life* (1998) was a source of misconceptions, according to Marrs. Waldron suggested that Welty compensated for lack of love and excitement in her life through her stories. Waldron also suggested that Welty was a proverbial ugly duckling, in Marrs's words, who "sought to overcome the liability of her appearance by being a dutiful daughter and a generous friend." Welty was both, Marrs explains, "but not by way of compensation." She calls it a blessing that Welty never read Waldron's book. By the time it was published, Welty's memory was failing, and she was unable to read anything longer than a *New York Times* article.

Shortly after Waldron's book appeared, Claudia Roth Pierpont published a lengthy article in *The New Yorker*. Whereas Waldron had focused on Welty's physical attributes, Marrs explains that Pierpont discussed politics, characterizing Welty as "a born outsider" who "wrote her way into acceptance," who—in later years—became "a perfect lady—a nearly Petrified Woman—with eyes averted and mouth set in a smile." Marrs refutes such charges, drawing both from her personal experience as Welty's close friend and from a massive collection of correspondence, manuscripts, date books, and photographs—some never before available—that Welty opened to Marrs. Even considering the more limited material that Waldron and Pierpont had to work with, Marrs finds their conclusions unjust.

Suzanne Marrs is the author of One Writer's Imagination: The Fiction of Eudora Welty. *She has served as Welty Scholar at the* Mississippi Department of Archives and History and received the Phoenix Award for Distinguished Welty Scholarship. Marrs is a professor of English at Millsaps College in Jackson, Mississippi.

Clichés and misconceptions aside, Marrs's portrait is likely to surprise, perhaps startle, even knowledgeable Welty fans. Although Jackson, Mississippi, was home to Welty virtually all of her life, she traveled extensively and lived for extended periods elsewhere, both in the United States and other countries. As a young woman, Welty journeyed with friends by car to Mexico. In 1944, she interned for several months at *The New York Times Book Review*, and New York City became her second home. Over the years, Welty visited frequently, sometimes staying in a hotel or sublet apartment, sometimes staying with friends, but always enchanted. The social life that Marrs details sounds grand—meeting friends for drinks, dinner, and the theater; welcoming friends of friends to town with parties; and dancing into the night. Welty had a knack for friendship, literary and otherwise; during the course of her ninety-two years, she kept in touch with close friends around the world and tended to maintain friendships for life.

In 1946-1947, Welty had two extended stays in San Francisco to be near John Robinson, an aspiring writer with whom she was in love. Over the following decade, she traveled three times to Europe, the first in October, 1949. Says Marrs, Welty set sail "as a woman of forty, an accomplished writer who was confident in her literary stature but not arrogant and certainly not blasé." Welty, who loved the freedom of traveling alone, "was already far, far from a sheltered provincial, but she did not relinquish a sense of wonder at all she had encountered. Neither an innocent nor a cosmopolitan exactly, she was an independent woman and an artist on whom nothing was lost." Welty continued to travel well into her later years, for example, visiting London by herself at eighty-one to see her dear friend the author V. S. Pritchett and his wife one last time.

In addition to tending her friendships, Welty maintained close family ties, and few personal details of her life escaped from that circle until this authorized biography was published. Welty had long opposed writers' biographies, being "tenacious" in her belief that "we don't need to know a writer's life in order to understand his work." She also objected to the way biographies were written because "reviewers say they're not any good unless they reveal all sorts of other things about the writer." Welty felt that it was good to know some details about a writer's background, "but only what pertains." She also did not want her friends imposed upon for interviews.

Marrs knew these views but nonetheless requested permission to write her account in 1998. By then, unbeknown to Marrs, Welty's opposition to biography was fading. She had already permitted friend and well-known author Reynolds Price to speak with the biographer of Kenneth Millar (known as detective novelist Ross Macdonald) about the close relationship Welty and Millar shared in the second half of her life that sustained them both. When Marrs asked to write the book, Welty quickly agreed. She only cautioned: "You may be getting into deeper water than you imagine." Marrs certainly does chart new territory in this biography, for example, quoting extensively from the Welty/Millar correspondence.

In this work, Marrs approaches Welty—whom she refers to as "Eudora"—from a privileged vantage point. Not only is Marrs a respected scholar who has focused her academic career around the life and works of Welty, but Marrs was also a close friend of Welty during the last eighteen years of her life. In 1975 Marrs was a university professor in upstate New York. She read *Losing Battles* (1970), an anthology of all Welty's work to date, and began to incorporate some of it into her classes. She also published essays about Welty's fiction. Eventually, Marrs wrote Welty, asking for an appointment but got no reply. In the summer of 1983, Marrs drove to Jackson anyway, intending to immerse herself in material at the Mississippi Department of Archives and History.

With another Welty scholar, Marrs eventually took her subject to lunch. In that first meeting, Marrs felt "a sense of connection, of ease, of the common sensibility that typifies friendship." The friendship deepened in 1985-1986, when Marrs worked with Welty to catalog her correspondence, photographs, and manuscripts. In 1988, Marrs joined the faculty of Millsaps College in Jackson and, by that time, was meeting with Welty several times each week to talk about fiction or watch the evening news or have drinks and dinner.

Marrs, then, is hardly a disinterested party here. She makes as much clear from the book's introduction, focusing not only on Welty's life but also on their innumerable conversations at home and their travels, often to conferences. Marrs also celebrated holidays and birthdays with Welty and entertained her visitors. It is clear the Marrs holds Welty in high regard. Some reviewers have commented on this book's pains-taking detail, some even suggesting that Marrs seems reluctant to leave out anything. Indeed, there are passages that read more like lists than prose—of what was eaten at dinner, or names of all who attended a party, or what was on the theater program—which even the most determined reader may find slow going. Worse may be the temp-tation to skim, thereby missing some of the factual gems and insights that Marrs em-beds. Some reviewers have also suggested that Marrs keeps her observations polite, wondering why she does not examine some issues more closely. These include Welty's relationship with her mother before the latter became ill and Welty had to tend to her full-time. Perhaps there are aspects of her life Welty did not want included, or Marrs may have decided not to include certain things.

At any rate, this biography is certainly a tribute to a friend. It also illuminates Welty's friendships with noted writers including Katherine Anne Porter, Pritchett, Price, Robert Penn Warren, Stephen Spender, Anne Tyler, and Elizabeth Bowen as well as editors such as Mary Lou Aswell, William Maxwell, and Welty's friend and agent, Diarmuid Russell—often quoting from voluminous correspondence. In addi-tion, the biography offers occasional insight for aspiring writers, especially through Welty's early letters to John Robinson. Theirs was a passionate relationship that waxed and waned over many years. After Robinson eventually determined he was gay, he and Welty maintained a lasting friendship, and the two stayed in touch until Robinson's death in Italy in 1989.

Most important, however, this biography is a gift to all Welty readers. It offers ex-panded understanding of her rich personality, providing clear correction to the stereo-typic image. Of special interest may be Welty's politics. As early as the 1940's, she had become increasingly unhappy with the slow pace of social progress in Mississippi and resolved to spend more time out of her home state. Marrs quotes from a 1948 let-ter to Robinson criticizing the state's main newspaper. "I feel like burning the *Clarion Ledger* every morning . . . And the Legislature a disgrace every day, and altogether Mississippi seems to get more hopeless all the time."

Over the years, in her own way, Welty continued to take her stand. For example, she demanded that her 1963 address to the Southern Literary Festival be open to an in-tegrated audience at Millsaps College. After delivering her remarks, Welty read "Powerhouse," her story of an African American pianist and his band playing at a seg-regated dance, which focuses on the white audience's concurrent fascination with and repulsion by the band leader, Powerhouse. This reading was seen as a risky political act, a choice "to proclaim the destructiveness of segregation and the emancipating ef-fect of imagining oneself into other and different lives."

This was not the first, or last, risk that Welty would take. In the 1988 presidential campaign, for example, Democratic candidate Michael Dukakis was sharply criti-cized by Republicans and many southern Democrats for his "liberal" leanings. Appalled by the pejorative connotations being attached to that word, Welty joined other distinguished citizens in signing a letter to that effect, which appeared in *The New York Times*. Anyone spotting Welty's car at that time would have also seen a Dukakis bumper sticker displayed. This kind of microscopic detail makes the biography unique and compelling.

Marrs has included sixteen pages of photographs, a Welty chronology, a list of her honorary degrees, and notes for each chapter's references. There is an exhaustive bibliography, and the book is indexed. Although some critics consider it Welty's definitive biography, others find it incomplete. All seem to agree that this valuable book will encourage Welty readers, critics, and the world at large to see Welty through a decidedly different lens, one probably only Marrs could provide.

Jean C. Fulton

Review Sources

America 193, no. 4 (August 15, 2005): 25-26.
Booklist 101, nos. 19/20 (June 1, 2005): 1742.
The Boston Globe, August 14, 2005, p. E8.
Kirkus Reviews 73, no. 11 (June 1, 2005): 626.
Library Journal 130, no. 14 (September 1, 2005): 141.
The New York Times Book Review 154 (August 14, 2005): 21.
People 64, no. 11 (September 12, 2005): 60.
Publishers Weekly 252, no. 24 (June 13, 2005): 42.
The Washington Post Book World, August 14, 2005, p. 2.
The Wilson Quarterly 29, no. 4 (Autumn, 2005): 109-112.

EUROPE CENTRAL

Author: William T. Vollmann (1959-   )
Publisher: Viking Press (New York). 811 pp. $40.00
Type of work: Novel
Time: 1914-1975
Locale: Soviet Union, Germany, Poland, Czechoslovakia, and New York City

European political and military turmoil of the 1930's and 1940's is examined through the lives of several Germans and Russians

Principal characters:
DIMITRI DIMINTRIYEVICH SHOSTAKOVICH, a
   Russian composer
NINA VASILYEVNA SHOSTAKOVICH, his
   wife, a physicist
ELENA EVSEYEVNA KONSTANTINOVSKAYA, the love of Shostakovich's
   life
ROMAN LAZAREVICH KARMEN, a Soviet filmmaker, one of Elena's
   husbands
ISAAK DAVIDOVICH GLICKMAN, Shostakovich's best friend
KURT GERSTEIN, an SS officer
FRIEDRICH PAULUS, a German general
ANDREI VASLOV, a Soviet general
ANNA ANDREYEVNA AKHMATOVA, a Russian poet
KÄTHE KOLLWITZ, a German lithographer
ADOLF HITLER, a German chancellor
VLADIMIR ILYICH LENIN, a Soviet leader
NADEZHDA KONSTANTINOVNA KRUPSKAYA, Lenin's wife
FANYA KAPLAN, the would-be assassin of Lenin
JOSEPH STALIN, a Soviet leader

William T. Vollmann's demanding postmodern fiction has tackled a number of subjects ranging from a war between insects and the inventors of electricity in *You Bright and Risen Angels: A Cartoon* (1987) to San Francisco prostitutes and drug addicts in *The Royal Family* (2000) to what he terms a "symbolic history" of North America in *Seven Dreams: A Book of North American Landscapes* (1990-2001). Vollmann offers another metahistorical fiction in *Europe Central*, a look at much of the twentieth century from German and Russian perspectives, with the emphasis on the events of World War II. A massive, ambitious, demanding work, *Europe Central* won the National Book Award but may put off some readers because of its bulk and its failure to adhere to a linear narrative. In addition to being a meditation upon war and totalitarianism, *Europe Central* is also, through several sections dealing with artists, about the transforming nature of art: "Art does not so much derive from

∼

*William T. Vollmann has worked
as a computer programmer and
founded CoTangent Press,
producing limited editions of his
works and those of other writers.
Vollmann received the Whiting
Writers' Award in 1988 for* You
Bright and Risen Angels: A Cartoon
*and the Shiva Naipaul Memorial
Prize in 1989 for an excerpt from*
Seven Dreams: A Book of North
American Landscapes. *He lives in
Sacramento, California.*

∼

life as actually change the perception and appreciation of it, casting itself across existence *like a shadow*."

Vollmann has said in his fiction he strives for a dreamlike effect. *Europe Central* resembles a slow-motion nightmare in which political conflict spins the lives of a large cast of characters out of control. Composed of thirty-seven stories, *Europe Central* looks at how artists, military leaders, and ordinary people struggle to understand the nature of evil. The central event, for which Vollmann has drawn a map, is Operation Barbarossa, the German advance into Russia in 1941, ending with the defeat of the invaders at Stalingrad. Vollmann employs both historical and fictional characters, all of whom exist at the petulant whims of Adolf Hitler and Joseph Stalin, who lurk in the background and occasionally make cameo appearances.

Europe Central is dedicated to Danilo Kiš, whose *A Tomb for Boris Davidovich* (1978) has a similar structure with interrelated stories, and for a 2001 edition of which Vollmann wrote an afterword. (Kiš is also cited within the novel.) Both books also deal with anti-Semitism and Stalin's purges within the Soviet Union. With one exception, the stories appear as contrasting pairs from German and Russian points of view.

The longest set of pairs, "Breakout" and "The Last Field-Marshal," presents Soviet General Andrei Vaslov's capture and formation of a Russian Liberation Army to oppose Stalin and the efforts of German General Friedrich Paulus to complete his initially successful invasion of the Soviet Union. Vaslov first fights against Paulus's forces, only to join with the enemy after his capture. Paulus is likewise captured and used for propaganda purposes by his enemy. Both are good men doing what they must, and both of their lives end badly. "Breakout" is the more effective story because Vollmann's Vaslov has greater psychological depth than does his Paulus. "The Last Field-Marshal" becomes bogged down a bit by the details of military maneuvering, one of several instances when Vollmann is seduced by his extensive research. He comes close to being a more literary version of James Michener who feels obligated to cram every bit of his research into the narrative.

One of the most affecting stories, "Clean Hands," tells of Kurt Gerstein's endeavors to alert the world to the horrors of the Holocaust. Beaten in 1936 and 1938 for opposing Nazi policies, Gerstein is a devout Christian whose beloved sister-in-law is killed by Nazis. Nevertheless, he becomes the SS officer responsible for supplying the toxic canisters used to exterminate Jews at Belzec and other concentration camps in Poland. He tries to sabotage his own efforts and get word to the Allies. While everyone around him, including his father, supports Hitler and hates Jews, Gerstein just grits his teeth. The less known about his true feelings, the more likely he will find some way to help his victims. Because he does not believe in what he is doing, Gerstein keeps telling himself that he has clean hands.

Most of Vollmann's characters are protagonists in only one story, but many also appear briefly or are mentioned in other stories, creating the sense that all the people and events in *Europe Central* are inextricably linked by their fates. One character haunted by Vaslov is Dimitri Dimintriyevich Shostakovich, the Russian composer who comes closest to being the novel's principal character, appearing in several stories. Like Vaslov and Gerstein, Shostakovich is a patriot shaken by his nation's policies. Vollmann devotes considerable attention to Soviet efforts, especially those of Stalin himself, to convince Shostakovich to join the Communist Party. The composer's refusal results in constant denunciations despite his increasing international fame.

The Shostakovich stories, however, center less on politics than on his complicated love life. In 1934-1935, the composer has a passionate affair with Elena Konstantinovskaya and remains obsessed by her throughout his unhappy marriage to the long-suffering Nina, two more marriages, and many affairs. Ironically, Shostakovich eventually becomes friends with Roman Karmen, Elena's first husband, and writes scores for his films. Despite his devotion to propaganda filmmaking, Karmen feels that his love for Elena "is the only thing that's genuine about me." In a note, "An Imaginary Love Triangle: Shostakovich, Karmen, Konstantinovskaya," Vollmann admits that he has fictionalized this trio's relationship because there is no evidence that Elena was the love of the composer's life.

If Shostakovich cannot be faithful to Nina, at least he is true to his musical genius, composing symphonies, quartets, and operas which party-controlled critics attack as belonging to "that secret world of chromatic dissonance which everybody called 'formalism.'" Vollmann strives to show how Shostakovich's music, the string quartet Opus 110 in particular, with its "swarm of sorrows," reflects his inner turmoil about his love life, the war, and the pressure to conform to a political ideology he abhors. The composer's love for Elena becomes a metaphor for his inability to resolve his demons, and Elena herself, as Vollmann says in his postscript, represents the unfathomable enigma that is Europe.

The volume's first story, "Steel in Motion," sets up the theme of the interconnectedness of things, of the search for the meaning of Europe. Events in Germany influence those in the Soviet Union, whose countermeasures lead to additional countermeasures, all affecting numerous other countries. The political climate of the twentieth century creates an almost perpetual climate of vagueness, uncertainty, and fear throughout the continent. Vollmann sees Europe less as a victim than a co-conspirator, full of self-delusions: "Europe's never burned a witch or laid hands on a Jew!"

Vollmann does not just tell several stories but also writes each in different styles, using relatively straightforward, chronological narratives, stream-of-consciousness, and a dense, postmodernist, often elliptical technique. Each story is divided into chapters of varying lengths. Vollmann will string together several chapters on a page or less, followed by a much longer one. There is only moderate dialogue, and several sentences go on for more than one hundred words, often interrupted by lengthy parenthetical remarks. Vollmann seems to be doing everything he can to engage his readers in the same sort of struggle for understanding his characters are experiencing as they face complex social, political, psychological, romantic, and moral quandaries for which simple solutions are impossible.

In the early stories, Vollmann also calls attention to style as the essence of his aesthetic by having Vladimir Ilyich Lenin proclaim about a dictionary, "The alphabetical arrangement of words creates such a refreshing sort of chaos." There are meditations, as well, on the meanings of letters, some of which take on almost human characteristics. Vollmann's self-conscious method becomes obvious when he writes, "Most literary critics agree that fiction cannot be reduced to mere falsehood . . . the pretense that life is what we want it to be may conceivably bring about the desired condition. . . . [I]f this story . . . crawls with reactionary supernaturalism, that might be because its author longs to see letters scuttling across ceilings, cautiously beginning to reify themselves into angels."

Although Vollmann provides fifty-four pages of notes from his research into the complex historical background of his novel, his narrators still resort to explanatory, often scholarly footnotes. Vollmann wanted to provide a chronology to help his readers sort out events, but his publisher made him "cut it, on account of the wartime paper shortage."

One of the most fascinating aspects of *Europe Central* is the identity of the narrator or narrators. A first-person narrator pops up periodically throughout the novel. The narrator of the Russian stories is a member of the secret service who arrests and interrogates some characters, while the German stories are told from the perspective of someone from the signal corps. While these two narrators might be said simply to be spokesmen for their national sensibilities, they are specific characters with families and foibles they readily admit.

The German narrator is berated by his wife in 1962: "We all suffered in the war, even me whom you left alone while you were off raping Polish girls and shooting Ukrainians in the ditches." The self-conscious Russian narrator begs the reader's pardon for a digression and promises to exit the story, only to announce paragraphs later his preference for André Previn's conducting of Shostakovich's Tenth Symphony to Herbert von Karajan's and to confess his love for Elena. Vollmann himself seems to be the narrator at times: "I'm writing in the year 2002." Adding to the confusion is Vollmann's omission of quotation marks in his dialogue so that "I" has numerous identities. Vollmann employs his narrators, who often use "we" as well as "I," as unreliable interpreters who see events only from a political perspective.

The critical response to *Europe Central* has been mixed. A surprising number of publications, including *Time*, *Newsweek*, *The New Yorker*, and *The New York Times* did not even review it. Not doing so did not keep *USA Today* from labeling the novel the year's most overrated. Michael Wood, in *The New York Review of Books*, wrote, "The book is always lucid, even as it hovers between the obvious and the recondite, and the under- and over-examined." In *The Village Voice*, Brandon Stosuy praised the work as "a visionary textbook on human suffering" but complained about the slack-

ness of Vollmann's "sentence-to-sentence care." Many sentences, passages, and entire chapters fail to add anything to the novel's overall effect and could easily have
been excised. Then there is the occasional sloppiness, as with misuses of "hopefully."

Yet the large themes, vivid characters, and frequently brilliant writing of *Europe
Central* overshadow such flaws. At their best, Vollmann's sinuous sentences evoke
both the complexity of the world that they describe and the human misery at its core:
"First the screaming of the enemy's Katyusha rockets, much shriller than the sirens of
Wolf's Lair; then the explosions, followed after an interval by the crystal-clear
cracklings of frozen rubble shivering to fragments, the cries of the survivors, each cry
utterly sincere and wrapped up in itself, as if its own pain were the first pain which had
ever come into this world."

Michael Adams

Review Sources

Booklist 101, nos. 9/10 (January 1-15, 2005): 784.
The Boston Globe, April 3, 2005, p. D7.
Los Angeles Times Book Review, March 20, 2005, p. 5.
The New York Review of Books 52 (December 15, 2005): 64.
The New York Times Book Review 154 (April 3, 2005): 16.
Publishers Weekly 252, no. 6 (February 7, 2005): 38.
Review of Contemporary Fiction 25, no. 2 (Summer, 2005): 137.
The Times Literary Supplement, April 1, 2005, p. 22.
The Village Voice, April 12, 2005, p. 86.
The Washington Post Book World, April 17, 2005, p. 7.

EXTREMELY LOUD AND INCREDIBLY CLOSE

Author: Jonathan Safran Foer (1977-   )
Publisher: Houghton Mifflin (Boston). 368 pp. $25.00
Type of work: Novel
Time: 2001-2003 and the 1940's
Locale: New York City and Dresden, Germany

A precocious nine-year-old boy wanders New York City hoping to unlock a mystery surrounding his father's violent death at the World Trade Center

Principal characters:
OSKAR SCHELL, a precocious, nine-year-old New Yorker
THOMAS SCHELL, his father, a jeweler who died in the World Trade Center terrorist attacks
THOMAS SCHELL, Oskar's grandfather, a sculptor who survived the Dresden firebombing
ANNA SCHMIDT, a young woman who died in Dresden
OSKAR'S GRANDMOTHER, an immigrant from Dresden who dotes on her grandson
OSKAR'S MOTHER, who copes in her own way with widowhood
A. R. BLACK, an elderly neighbor who accompanies Oskar during his quest

The publication of *Everything Is Illuminated* in 2002 marked one of the most dazzling American literary debuts in recent decades. The novel, an international bestseller, recounts a young man's search in Ukraine for the woman who saved his grandfather's life during the Holocaust. The young man happens to share the name of the book's remarkable author, Jonathan Safran Foer. A cultural celebrity at only twenty-five, Foer sold his second novel, *Extremely Loud and Incredibly Close*, to film producer Scott Rudin even before it appeared in print. It was published a few months before the release, in August, 2005, of the film version of *Everything Is Illuminated*, starring Elijah Wood as Foer.

Though Foer's early success created exalted expectations, few readers were disappointed by *Extremely Loud and Incredibly Close*. Whereas the plot of his first novel is generated by the worst atrocity of the twentieth century, the extermination of most of Europe's Jews, the brilliant new novel responds to an early twenty-first century atrocity, the terrorist attacks on the World Trade Center and the Pentagon on September 11, 2001.

Most of *Extremely Loud and Incredibly Close* is narrated by Oskar Schell. Schell's voice, while evoking some comparisons with that of J. D. Salinger's Holden Caulfield and Günther Grass's Oskar Matzerath, is not quite like any other in modern fiction. A nine-year-old with an erudite vocabulary and a penchant for bilingual puns, Oskar

summarizes his attributes in the calling card he
dispenses to new acquaintances:

INVENTOR, JEWELRY DESIGNER, JEWELRY FABRI-
CATOR, AMATEUR ENTOMOLOGIST, FRANCOPHILE,
VEGAN, ORGAMIST, PACIFIST, PERCUSSIONIST, AMA-
TEUR ASTRONOMER, COMPUTER CONSULTANT, AM-
ATEUR ARCHEOLOGIST, COLLECTOR OF: rare coins,
butterflies that died natural deaths, miniature cacti,
Beatles memorabilia, semiprecious stones, and
other things.

Oskar's favorite book, *A Brief History of Time*
(1988), daunts most adults, and he writes fan letters to its author, the physicist Stephen Hawking.
Alienated from children his own age, who do
not share his interests and talents, Oskar was unusually close—indeed, incredibly close—to his
father, a jeweler by trade but by inclination a
scholar whose daily diversion was ferreting out
mistakes in *The New York Times*.

*Jonathan Safran Foer was thrust
into literary prominence with the
publication of his first novel,
Everything Is Illuminated (2002). It
won several awards, became an
international best seller, and was
adapted into a film, Foer also edited
A Convergence of Birds (2001), an
anthology of writing inspired by the
bird boxes of Joseph Cornell;
collaborated with sculptor Richard
Serra and photographer Hiroshi
Sugimoto on the book Joe (2005);
and wrote the libretto to Seven
Attempted Escapes from Silence
(2005), an opera commissioned for
the German National Opera House.*

Thomas Schell happens to be in the World Trade Center on the morning that the
terrorists strike. Dismissed from school because of the emergency, Oskar arrives
home in time to hear the six final messages that his father, trapped in the collapsing
skyscraper, left on the family answering machine. Burdened by overwhelming grief,
what he calls "heavy boots," Oskar attempts throughout the novel to reconcile himself
to the sudden, violent death of the man whom he adored.

Father and son bonded not only over bedtime stories but over "Reconnaissance
Expeditions"—elaborate, esoteric scavenger hunts that Thomas devised for Oskar.
After September 11, Oskar embarks on the supreme Reconnaissance Expedition, an
arduous quest that will enable him to understand and accept the loss of his father.
Rummaging through Thomas's effects, Oskar discovers an envelope inside a vase.
The envelope contains a key, and the boy is convinced that, if only he can find the lock
the key fits, the mystery of why his father was in the World Trade Center at the moment of its destruction will be solved. Oskar calculates that there are about 162 million locks in New York City. A single word, "Black," is written on the envelope, and
he concludes that someone by that name will recognize the key and unlock the puzzle
of his father's death. Wearing the exclusively white clothing that is his trademark fe-
tish, Oskar sets about—on foot, because he has become terrified of public transportation—to track down all 472 people named Black living in the five boroughs of New
York.

One of the first Blacks Oskar interviews, a 103-year-old retired war correspondent
named A. R. Black, happens to be living one floor above the Schell apartment on the
Upper West Side of Manhattan. Mr. Black maintains a private biographical index—
the names of thousands of persons, famous and obscure, recorded on separate cards

and assigned a one-word epithet; Oskar's is "son." Though Mr. Black knows nothing about the enigmatic key, he agrees to accompany the boy on his continuing mission. During the course of their travels throughout the city, the two encounter scores of Blacks, rich and poor, of every race, with memorable stories of their own. One, for example, is a tour guide in the Empire State Building who has not been outside the famous skyscraper for decades. Another is a doorman from Russia. Two other Blacks are a couple who each maintain a museum of the other in adjacent rooms.

Trying to cope with her own loneliness as a sudden widow, Oskar's mother cannot provide her son with the emotional support he needs. He is closer to his grandmother, who lives across the street and is in constant, obsessive communication with him, in person and through a walkie-talkie. An immigrant from Germany, Oskar's grandmother has lived alone since her husband abruptly left her thirty-nine years ago, before the birth of her only son. Oskar has free access to his grandmother's apartment and begins to sense an invisible presence in it. His grandmother explains that a tenant, who always seems to be gone when Oskar visits, has taken up residence in one of her spare rooms. However, the boy eventually discovers that "the renter" is in fact his long-lost grandfather, named, like Oskar's father, Thomas Schell.

Woven throughout the account of Oskar's search for the lock to fit his father's key is the story of the elder Thomas Schell, a sculptor in his native Dresden who was passionately in love with a woman named Anna Schmidt. After Anna, pregnant with his child, is killed during the massive Allied firebombing of the city, Thomas turns mute. From then on, he communicates by writing on pads he carries about with him. The most basic thoughts are expressed manually; his left hand is tattooed with the word "YES" and his right hand with "NO." After emigrating to New York, Thomas encounters Anna's sister in a bakery. She had spied on her older sister's trysts with Thomas in Dresden, and, despite his misgivings, she prevails on him to marry her. However, Thomas, unable to cope with the fact that his wife is pregnant while he remains in love with the memory of Anna, retreats to Dresden. Over the years, he will write anguished, unsent letters to the son he never meets. When he learns that the younger Thomas Schell died in the September 11 attacks, he returns to New York.

While Oskar's grandfather has opted for silence, A. R. Black is voluntarily deaf, having turned his hearing aid off a long time ago. "I thought I'd save the batteries!" he explains, just before Oskar turns the hearing aid on again. At that moment, according to Oskar, "a flock of birds flew by the window, extremely fast and incredibly close." *Extremely Loud and Incredibly Close* examines the strategies people adopt to distance themselves from pain while trying not to estrange themselves from everything else. Oskar delivers a class report on the bombing of Hiroshima, which echoes against the intrusions of catastrophe at Dresden and the World Trade Center. Oskar, who plays Yorick—assertively, not just as a silent skull—in a school production of William Shakespeare's *Hamlet* (pr. 1600-1601), comes to learn that loss is universal and inevitable, but he never loses heart.

By telling his distressing tale largely through the perky voice of a wise-cracking prodigy, Foer risks trivializing or belittling the September 11 massacre. However, his novel is a spirited response to atrocity, a work whose vivacity defies misfortune and denies a separation between the tragic and the comic, as if the best way to deal with heavy boots is to be light on one's feet. Foer includes passages from the hundreds of unsent letters that Thomas Schell composes to his unseen son, but the decision to present most of the novel through the perspective of the sculptor's young grandson emphasizes human vulnerability as well as resiliency in the face of tribulation.

Oskar manages anxiety by imagining ingenious devices to make the world a better and safer place—a teakettle that recites Shakespeare, a birdseed shirt that allows its wearer to fly, windmills on the roofs of skyscrapers, intelligent ambulances which inform passersby that the injured party is not their loved one, a postage stamp whose back tastes like crème brûlée, dogs trained both to be seeing eyes for the blind and to sniff out bombs. Such ideas teem most abundantly through Oskar's brain when he is most distressed, and during the sleepless nights following his father's death the boy becomes a veritable Thomas Alva Edison of imaginary innovations.

Foer displays similar inventiveness, not only in the multitude of remarkable characters and incidents that he packs into the novel but also in the work's physical design. He complements the text with a variety of visual effects, including blank pages, an extended passage in numerical code, overwritten type, names in colored script, and words that are circled or crossed out. In addition, the book contains a number of disparate photographs, including a roller coaster, an elephant's eye, the Manhattan skyline, a key, a starry sky, Laurence Olivier playing Hamlet, turtles mating, and a human body falling from the World Trade Center.

Oskar's brilliance has the effect of antagonizing his denser classmates, and to some readers parts of *Extremely Loud and Incredibly Close* will seem superfluous. The novel, however, which begins and ends in a cemetery, is a bravura performance whose extravagant excess makes a point about how to reconcile oneself with mortality. Ultimately, Oskar's citywide quest for the lock that matches his father's key dwindles into insignificance. His experiences and acquaintances along the way justify the prolonged effort. The ancient lesson is that the journey itself is more valuable than any destination. While tramping throughout the five boroughs of New York, a city devastated by a terrorist assault, an extraordinary boy discards his heavy boots.

Steven G. Kellman

Review Sources

Artforum, April/May, 2005, p. 43.
Atlanta Journal and Constitution, April 3, 2005, p. L8.
The Boston Globe, April 3, 2005, p. D6.
Chicago Tribune, March 20, 2005, p. 1.
Commentary 119, no. 5 (May, 2005): 80-85.

Los Angeles Times, April 3, 2005, p. R7.
The Nation 280, no. 16 (April 25, 2005): 29-32.
The New York Times Book Review 154 (April 3, 2005): 1-12.
The New Yorker 81, no. 4 (March 14, 2005): 138-140.
Time 165, no. 11 (March 14, 2005): 59-62.
USA Today, March 31, 2005, p. D5.
The Washington Post, March 27, 2005, p. T03.

FACULTY TOWERS
The Academic Novel and Its Discontents

Author: Elaine Showalter (1941-   )
Publisher: University of Pennsylvania Press (Philadel-
phia). 144 pp. $25.00
Type of work: Literary criticism
Time: 1950-2004
Locale: England and the United States

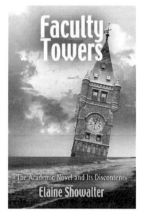

*Academic novels illustrate the dominant trends in higher
education in Britain and America decade by decade*

Principal personages:
GEORGE ELIOTT, the author of *Middlemarch*
    (1872)
C. P. SNOW, the author of *The Masters*
    (1951)
KINGSLEY AMIS, the author of *Lucky Jim*
    (1954)
MARY MCCARTHY, the author of *The Groves of Academe* (1952)
STANLEY FISH, a widely published figure in cultural studies
MALCOLM BRADBURY, the author of *The History Man* (1975)
DAVID LODGE, the author of *Changing Places* (1975)
CAROLYN HEILBRUN, the author of the Amanda Cross detective novels
PHILIP ROTH, the author of *The Human Stain* (2000)
SAUL BELLOW, the author of *Ravelstein* (2000)

This slim book is partly an intellectual memoir, the author's reflections on her own
past, on the people she has known, discussions she has had, thoughts she has shared
about life and literature. Elaine Showalter began her academic career not as a professor but as a faculty wife. This gave her insights into university life that a more conventional career would not have provided. It also contributed to her interests in feminism
and in literature illustrating the mores of the academic elite. Twice at least, characters
in academic novels have been based on Showalter—one a vamp, one a frump. (She
prefers to think of herself as the former.)

Half of the work's subtitle, *The Academic Novel and Its Discontents*, is slightly
misleading—*Faculty Towers* is not about "the" academic novel but about the ways in
which academic novels depict English departments—Showalter's specialty. The discontents accurately reflect a half-century of uncomfortable challenges and change.
Hers is not the popularly conceived image of a department that examines literature
and writing, but insiders will recognize it instantly. Still, Showalter deals gently with
her one-time colleagues, much more so than did the novelists.

Academic fiction begins with George Eliot's *Middlemarch* (1872), partly because
Eliot is widely considered the first woman to attempt to make a living in the literary
profession, partly because a major subplot concerns a young woman's ambition to

Elaine Showalter has been a teacher, feminist author and inventor of gynocriticism, and president of the Modern Language Association. She is currently professor emeritus at Princeton University. Her books include A Literature of Their Own: British Women Novelists from Brontë to Lessing *(1977) and* Inventing Herself: Claiming a Feminist Intellectual Heritage *(2001).*

share in the scholar's life, and partly because another character, Mr. Casaubon, is the embodiment of all that is sterile and unattractive in the dedicated and desiccated academic. He is the personification of death in a black robe, a humorless scholar who comes to realize that his life's work is worth nothing. Realizing the ultimate purposelessness of human existence, Showalter argues, is the scholar's worst nightmare—that a lifetime of incredible work and self-denial is all vanity, all for nothing, all useless.

Eliot's model was followed by Willa Cather in *The Professor's House* (1925), the protagonist suffering a mental breakdown after life loses its meaning. For Showalter, there is more to a professor's job than research, writing, and failure: Professors have to teach, sit on committees, counsel students, and negotiate budgets. Moreover, they interact with one another and with specialists at other universities and even on other continents. Showalter attempts to demonstrate that the academic novel illustrates how these various duties have been influenced by intellectual trends since World War II. This book is very much a study of the process of change in higher education over five tumultuous decades.

Showalter's first chapter is titled "The Fifties: Ivory Towers." During that decade one could still think of professors living in those proverbial places; at least, one could visualize that image when looking back at the prewar world. C. P. Snow (1905-1980), a writer of that era, produced his novel *The Masters* (1951) about novelist Anthony Trollope, who in 1857 had written about the internal politics in an Anglican Church, politics which can be easily visualized as the equivalent of Victorian academics seeking preferment. Snow's story takes place at a small college in 1937 Cambridge, where the impending death of a master set off an ever-so-subtle competition among his thirteen fellows to succeed him. The novel is widely considered the best of its kind. Although Cambridge scholars took pains to assure Showalter that Snow's plot was purely fictional, personal observations she made on her first visit to Cambridge told her that Snow had been spot-on.

Only three years later, Kingsley Amis's *Lucky Jim* (1954) broke with the traditions of gloom and self-abasement, providing both parody of the inbred intellectual world and hope for escape. Jim's revelation was that there was life out there beyond the university, and it included sex! Was a job, a very dull job, worth sacrificing one's humanity, he asks; was it worth marrying the wrong woman? Could he even get the right woman from her domineering boyfriend—a future "great man" at the university—

and his influential family? Recognizing that he was in a bizarre situation, Jim began to act bizarrely. The students loved his quirks, but not his colleagues. In the end Jim left the university, properly considering himself a very lucky man indeed.

In contrast, Mary McCarthy saw academic life as utterly normal and the university's connections to the real world very real. The central plot of her novel *The Groves of Academe* (1952) involved the communist scare in the 1950's United States. While many professors had flirted with communism in the 1930's, inquiries about their current beliefs were taken as a threat to academic freedom. In the present day McCarthy's book still presents powerful arguments against investigating what is taught in the classroom or discussed at cocktail parties. Political orientations, the role of women in the university, and even the existence of homosexuality drive the story line to the novel's surprising conclusions.

Showalter ends her discussion of the 1950's with Snow's observation of the two cultures—science and the humanities—facing one another, uncomprehendingly, in each faculty meeting. Future authors would model their work on *Lucky Jim*, not *The Groves of Academe*, choosing satire and irony when treating academe.

Showalter summarizes the 1960's as "Tribal Towers." Political protest and ideological rage were surprisingly absent on the campuses described by novelists, though there was anger and frustration aplenty—at stuffy patriarchs and bitchy feminists. The men are impotent, and their wives frustrated—ambitious, frustrated and angry. Universities had grown into mammoth institutions without losing their provincialism, and the Modern Language Association (MLA) had become a hotbed of radicalism. McCarthyism had shifted ground, from politics to the syllabus. The literary canon was challenged by interest groups, but it was not until the 1970's that anyone could see where this was leading.

The "Glass Towers" of the 1970's was a fragile institution rather than a fortress, but the innovations in teaching and scholarship made the university an exciting place to work. Malcolm Bradbury's *The History Man* (1975) caught the spirit of the new campus architecture and the new intellectual spaces. Bradbury's fictional University of Watermouth is filled with feminism, every leftish idea imaginable, and lots of sex: a Women's Lib Nude Encounter Group, a Marxist version of William Shakespeare's *King Lear* (pr. 1605-1606), and much more. It is a discouraging place, too: vandals deface the buildings, the revolution never comes, the wives lose their respected role in academic society without finding a new one. David Lodge's *Changing Places* (1975) is more positive, but barely. Lodge's protagonist, Morris Zapp, exchanges jobs with a professor in England for a semester. Zapp—a thinly disguised Stanley Fish, some think—is an academic hotshot on a Faustian roll, one of the great Jewish characters in a profession now filling with nontraditional arrivistes from the big cities of the United States. With Philip Roth the academic novel begins to merge into the Jewish novel, the outsider trying to make sense of dual identities.

The chapter on the 1980's, "Feminist Towers," examines the ultimate outsiders, those who are excluded by virtue of gender. While plenty of women taught at small liberal arts colleges (note the word "taught," meaning they were therefore not really professors), at the major universities the unspoken rule was, the better the institution, the fewer women on the faculty. Showalter was among the women breaking through the barriers.

The most important academic novel of the 1980's may be Carolyn Heilbrun's *Death in a Tenured Position* (1981). Heilbrun's protagonist hates Harvard University, its pretensions, and its competitiveness. None of her characters is based on anyone at Harvard, and none has any admirable characteristics, but in higher education, once one has met the narrow range of pompous male professors anywhere, one recognizes them everywhere.

The "Tenured Towers" of the 1990's are mean-spirited places, battlegrounds of political correctness, affirmative action, the culture wars, and the tragedies of tenure. The marketplace having become a buyer's paradise, untenured faculty are desperate to find a niche, to curry favor with hiring committees, and somehow land a permanent job at the right kind of place. The MLA is no longer a sexual bacchanal but deadly serious competition. One favorite niche is in critical theory, an arcane and rapidly evolving world disdained by literature.

The ground is thus prepared for the twenty-first century's "Tragic Towers." The free sex of the 1960's gives way to fear of sexual harassment charges or accusations of racism. Such are the central themes of Philip Roth's *The Human Stain* (2000). The protagonist, Coleman Silk, a dean of classics at Athena College, asks innocently if two students who have never attended class are "spooks"; the absentees turn out to be black, and the game is on. The controversy contributes to the death of Silk's wife and to his resignation. He still is given no peace—where the college leaves off the persecution, the community begins. When Silk takes up with a black cleaning woman, younger than he, a young feminist professor of French leads the attack. If Silk is an unattractive figure, his sexually repressed persecutor makes him positively sympathetic. It is eventually revealed that Silk is himself black but had sought to hide the fact.

Silk may know his ancient literature, but his own meaninglessly tragic fall takes him by surprise. Roth suggests that the world is more complex than anyone imagines, and that anyone who believes that they have figured anyone out is deluded. Roth's suggestions that Silk, as well as former president Bill Clinton, have been wrongly persecuted are obvious (the "human stain" on White House intern Monica Lewinsky's silk dress). The day of the seductive student out to destroy her mentor has arrived. The time is ready for Saul Bellow's fictional portrayal in *Ravelstein* (2000) of his friend Alan Bloom, author of *The Closing of the American Mind* (1987). Morality and Jewishness are the central themes; the setting just happens to be a university. The university has joined the rest of society.

Showalter is not greatly impressed by the typical academic novel. She feels that in it there is too much satire and too little tragedy, too much concern with intellectual fads and petty discrimination, too little that will stand the test of time. In it, students tend to vanish—their needs cannot compete with the lures of class, race, gender, multiculturalism and diversity. Fictional English professors seem to believe that they are the centers of the universe, or else that spot is occupied by their department or perhaps their university. In any case, theirs is a closed society, and it is not one that an intelligent person would want to spend much time in.

In contrast, Showalter loves university life. It may not be utopia, but there are people dedicated to ideas rather than ideology, to literature rather than just books, to teaching as well as scholarship, and who have friends, spouses, children, and even parents in their lives. It is refreshing that reality comes off better in her book than does its fictional counterpoint.

William L. Urban

Review Sources

The Boston Globe, March 27, 2005, p. K2.
New Statesman 134, no. 4759 (September 26, 2005): 85.
The Spectator 299, no. 9223 (September 10, 2005): 50.
The Times Literary Supplement, September 16, 2005, p. 24.
The Virginia Quarterly Review 81, no. 4 (Fall, 2005): 291-291.
Weekly Standard 10, no. 32 (May 9, 2005): 35-39.

THE FAILURE OF THE FOUNDING FATHERS
Jefferson, Marshall, and the Rise of Presidential Democracy

Author: Bruce Ackerman (1943-   )
Publisher: Harvard University Press (Cambridge, Mass.).
    384 pp. $30.00
Type of work: History
Time: 1787-1812
Locale: The United States

Ackerman claims that the rise of political parties and emergence of a popularly elected president in 1801 transformed the American Constitution in ways unanticipated by members of the 1787 Constitutional Convention

Principal personages:
> JOHN ADAMS (1735-1826), the second president of the United States, 1797-1801
> JAMES A. BAYARD (1767-1815), a congressman from Delaware, 1797-1803
> AARON BURR (1756-1836), the third vice president of the United States, 1801-1805
> SAMUEL CHASE (1741-1811), a Supreme Court justice, 1796-1811
> THOMAS JEFFERSON (1743-1826), the third president of the United States, 1801-1809
> CHARLES LEE (1758-1815), the attorney general of the United States, 1795-1801
> JAMES MADISON (1751-1836), secretary of state, 1802-1809; president, 1809-1817
> JOHN MARSHALL (1755-1835), the third chief justice of the United States, 1801-1835
> WILLIAM PATERSON (1745-1806), a Supreme Court justice, 1792-1806

In *The Failure of the Founding Fathers*, Bruce Ackerman rejects the notion of an unchanged "original understanding" of the American Constitution, arguing that the political crisis in 1801 led to profound changes in the constitutional role of the president that were unforeseen, indeed considered undesirable, by the Framers of the 1787 Constitution. Unlike many legal scholars, Ackerman does not hold the Founding Fathers in high esteem. "In designing the presidency," he asserts, "the Framers made blunder after blunder—some excusable, others not." Ackerman blames those blunders for bringing the nation to the brink of civil war in 1801.

Ackerman's criticism of members of the 1787 Constitutional Convention for not foreseeing the rise of political parties is unjustified. Delegates who remembered clashes with colonial governors thought of the executive as a threat to liberty, legislatures as the defenders of freedom. They equated parties with undesirable factionalism that advanced private interests over the public good. They could not have foreseen the emergence of a popularly elected president claiming a mandate for change.

The convention adopted a procedure designed to keep the people as far away as possible from choosing a president. Everyone knew George Washington would be unanimously elected. The problem they struggled with was, in a country as geographically and culturally diverse as the United States, how to discover who had the support of the greatest number of men of substance. To solve the problem, they set up an electoral college in which each member would have two votes. Assuming that one vote would normally be for a local worthy, they forced each elector to cast a second vote for a nonresident of his state. Because few, if any, were expected to achieve a majority, the electoral college served, in effect, as a nominating body, sending the House of Representatives the names of five Americans winning votes outside their own states. To reassure the small states, the convention agreed that the House would vote by states, a majority of states being necessary for election. If two candidates tied with the votes of more than half the number of electors, the decision again went to the House.

Bruce Ackerman is Sterling Professor of Law and Political Science at Yale Law School. He is writing a three-volume study of American constitutional development, We the People, *two volumes of which have been published:* Foundations *(1991) and* Transformations *(1998).*

In the late 1790's however, organized groupings appeared, passionately divided over foreign affairs. Those favoring revolutionary France called themselves Republicans; those favoring England supported the administration, calling themselves Federalists. In the 1800 election everyone knew that John Adams and Charles Cotesworth Pinckney were Federalist presidential and vice presidential candidates, respectively, while Thomas Jefferson and Aaron Burr were Republican contenders. When word of the electors' votes trickled back to Washington in December, Republicans discovered they had blundered. Unlike the Federalists, one of whose electors had scuttled Pinckney, putting Adams one vote ahead, all Republican electors had faithfully voted for both Jefferson and Burr, sending the election to the House of Representatives.

Republicans had a clear majority of states in the House elected in 1800, but the Founding Fathers assigned the decision to the lame-duck House chosen in 1798, where Republicans were one state short of victory. Federalists would decide who became president and, Ackerman remarks, ardent Federalists who abominated Jefferson were not disposed to award him the office just because he had won the election. The rules gave them the chance to find a more malleable candidate. When the House met on February 11, 1801, to decide the election, Federalists unanimously voted for Burr, even though he remained silent in Albany, earning the dislike of each party for not openly siding with them.

Extreme Federalists wanted to continue the deadlock through the rest of the session. In what Ackerman considers another original blunder—along with the double vote for electors and allowing a lame-duck House to decide the election—the Convention had failed to consider what happened if no one were chosen by inauguration day, March 4. The first Congress provided that the president pro tem of the Senate would be acting president when the president and vice president were incapacitated. Federalists were a majority in the Senate; perhaps, if the deadlock were maintained, they might make one of their own acting president.

A pamphlet by "Horatius" suggested that government officers, with the secretary of state first, would be better choices for acting president than senators. Ackerman argues on stylistic grounds that John Marshall, still secretary of state as well as chief justice, wrote the pamphlet, but this assertion is not convincing—only in the footnotes does Ackerman disclose that computer techniques fail to establish Marshall's authorship.

Threats of civil war circulated in Washington, based on rumors that Republican governors of Pennsylvania and Virginia would march their militia to the capital if Jefferson were not chosen. Over three days and thirty-five ballots, no one budged until moderate Federalist James Bayard decided that as sole congressman from Delaware he would singlehandedly decide the contest. On February 17, after assuring himself that Jefferson did not intend to carry out a purge of Federalist officeholders, Bayard announced he would absent himself on the thirty-sixth ballot, making the eight Republican states a majority of the remaining fifteen, electing Jefferson president.

Jefferson's tolerance of Federalist appointees did not extend to the judiciary. Ackerman is highly critical of Adams's behavior regarding judges. When the chief justice of the United States resigned, Adams, despite knowing he had lost the election, did not leave the choice of a replacement to his successor. He nominated John Marshall on January 20, 1801, while continuing him as secretary of state. Congress had been considering a bill to organize intermediate federal circuit courts, relieving Supreme Court justices of the task of riding circuit and presiding over trials with district judges. Ackerman and most scholars agree the change was desirable, but Congress waited until February to create sixteen new judgeships. Adams, with less than a month left in office, rushed to appoint reliable Federalists. Secretary of State Marshall labored until nine in the evening of March 3, signing and sealing their commissions, along with those of newly named justices of peace for Washington, D.C.

These "midnight judges" were a particular affront to the Republicans. Claiming a popular mandate for reform, Jefferson proposed two priority measures, which Congress quickly enacted, cutting taxes and repealing the Judiciary Act of 1801. Ackerman notices what most historians miss—repeal easily passed the Senate due to blunders by Adams and Marshall in including senators among the new judges, permitting governors to appoint enough Republican replacements to make them a majority. Extreme Federalists urged affected judges to ignore the law abolishing their office. Marshall, with the enthusiastic support of Justice Samuel Chase, considered having the Supreme Court refuse to go on circuit as required in the repeal act but was dissuaded from creating another constitutional crisis by more moderate justices led by William Paterson.

Jefferson explored using impeachment to remove objectionable federal judges. The first target was district judge John Pickering, who apparently had become mentally ill and incapable of holding court. Federalists objected that the Constitution provided for removal of judges only for high crimes and misdemeanors, which an insane man could not intentionally commit. Ackerman accepts the Federalist defense, ignoring the real reason the Federalists bitterly, if unsuccessfully, opposed removal—they wanted to prevent Jefferson from appointing a Republican judge, even if it meant keeping the federal court in New Hampshire inoperable.

The next target was Justice Chase, impeached for his behavior on circuit in cases involving Adams administration critics. He had prevented defense lawyers from presenting evidence and then directed juries to find defendants guilty. Chase had clearly committed gross judicial impropriety, but removing a Supreme Court judge was a serious matter. As the Constitutional Convention planned, the Senate acted as a brake on an impetuous House. The majority voted to convict Chase, nineteen to fifteen, but six Republicans joined nine Federalists keeping the tally four votes short of the necessary two-thirds majority. Marshall felt relief, believing he would be next if Chase were convicted.

Ackerman is not an admirer of the great chief justice, nor does he rate Marshall's decision in *Marbury v. Madison* (1803) as highly as do most constitutional historians. Ackerman wryly comments that Marshall was more properly a witness rather than an adjudicator in the case, which arose because Marshall, as secretary of state hurrying to sign and seal commissions of the midnight judges, failed to give William Marbury his certificate. Marbury petitioned the Court to issue a writ of mandamus ordering James Madison, the new secretary of state, to deliver the document. Marshall did not recuse himself but wrote a lengthy opinion lecturing Jefferson and Madison on their duty to uphold the law and the Constitution by delivering Marbury's commission. However, he ruled the provision for mandamus in the Judiciary Act of 1789 (passed by the first Congress in which many former members of the Constitutional Convention sat) was unconstitutional because it was not a power specifically assigned to the Court in the Constitution. Therefore, the Court could not grant Marbury's petition.

The decision has been celebrated for asserting the power of the Court to rule acts of Congress unconstitutional. However Ackerman asserts that in the context of the struggle between Jefferson and Marshall, it was a confession of weakness, as it carefully avoided setting up a confrontation that the Court would certainly lose. Ackerman sees it as part of the Court's accommodation to the Jeffersonian triumph and places even more stress on a less well known decision a week later, *Stuart v. Laird*, in which the Court directly validated the repeal act.

When the fifth circuit court met at Richmond on December 2, 1802, with John Marshall presiding, Charles Lee, former attorney general of the United States and lawyer for the defendant in *Stuart v. Laird*, challenged the legitimacy of the court. He alleged that Congress did not have the power to remove judges installed by the Judiciary Act of 1801 and that Supreme Court justices had no authority under the Constitution to sit as circuit court judges. When Marshall rejected both claims, Lee appealed the issue to the Supreme Court, where he argued that the same logic that in *Marbury* invalidated a section of the 1789 Act applied here—the Constitution did not assign circuit court duties to Supreme Court judges any more that it granted power to issue mandamus writs, therefore the 1802 repeal act was unconstitutional. Marshall recused himself. In the only decision among the first twenty-four issued during his time on the Court that Marshall did not write, Justice Paterson rejected the argument on the grounds that Supreme Court justices had ridden circuit all through the 1790's, creating a powerful precedent that could not be ignored. Ackerman points out that Marshall ignored appeals to precedent in his *Marbury* decision.

Ackerman asserts that by accepting the validity of the 1801 Judiciary Act repeal in its *Stuart* decision, the Supreme Court began a process of accommodation to the changing constitutional position of the presidency resulting from Jefferson's claim to have a mandate for reform. Ackerman points out that this was accomplished without changing a word of the Constitution, as the Twelfth Amendment merely established separate votes for president and vice president, leaving the rest of the original system formally in place.

Ackerman objects that "legal scholars have been flooding the journals with competing versions of the 'original understanding' of the presidency, barely noticing that the American people repudiated these understandings after a brief decade of democratic experience." Not every assertion in this detailed, iconoclastic book will win immediate acceptance, but readers will find it challenges preconceptions and stimulates rethinking constitutional history.

Milton Berman

Review Sources

Library Journal 130, no. 15 (September 15, 2005): 75.
The New Republic 233, no. 19 (November 7, 2005): 32-37.
Publishers Weekly 252, no. 30 (August 1, 2005): 54-55.
The Wilson Quarterly 29 (Autumn, 2005): 124-125.

FAITH AT WAR
A Journey on the Frontlines of Islam, from Baghdad to Timbuktu

Author: Yaroslav Trofimov (1969-   )
Publisher: Henry Holt (New York). Maps. 312 pp.
   $25.00
Type of work: Current affairs, history, and religion
Time: 2001-2004
Locale: Saudi Arabia, Tunisia, Iraq, Afghanistan, Yemen,
   Kuwait, Lebanon, Bosnia, and Mali

An experienced reporter travels through nine majority-
Muslim countries, describing his observations and experi-
ences in an effort to illuminate the culture gap between Is-
lam and the West

With the catastrophic attacks on the Pentagon and New
York City's Twin Towers on September 11, 2001, Ameri-
cans suddenly realized that Islamic extremism was a force with enormous potential
effect upon world affairs. Among the effects of this recognition was a renewed interest in the Middle East and Islam. Few Westerners, either within the educated public or
the government, knew much about the Islamic faith or the countries to whose life it is
central. One Westerner who does is Yaroslav Trofimov. Fluent in Arabic, he had for
ten years prior to the attacks traveled the Middle East, reporting for Bloomberg News
and *The Wall Street Journal.* After 2001, he decided to revisit various Muslim countries, to see how the terrorist attacks and their aftermath of Western responses have
changed conditions in the Middle East. The resulting project is titled *Faith at War.* A
personal, unofficial account of what Trofimov found, in form it resembles a percep-
tive, highly literate travelogue. Often, however, it reads like a travelogue through a
nightmare landscape.

Islam has over one billion adherents worldwide. Fittingly, the book opens with a
view of Saudi Arabia, the birthplace of Islam. The richest and most influential Muslim country, the Saudis fund schools, mosques, and "reformist" religious movements
across the globe. Because of the country's importance to the Muslim world, Trofimov
underwent considerable difficulty to obtain a visa. The Saudis, notoriously reluctant
to grant entrance to tourists, are even more reluctant to grant entrance to foreign writers. Once in Saudi Arabia, despite the country's superficial signs of modernity,
Trofimov found an utterly alien place. The two chapters on the country are packed
with information little known beyond its borders.

The stark Wahhabi sect, which Arabia is trying to export, originated there in the
late eighteenth century. Like adherents of many religious movements, the Wahhabis
sought to "purify" the faith and restore it to its—real or imagined—state at the time of
the Prophet Mohammed. Few Westerners have realized that, while the Saudi regime
controls the oil, all the wells are concentrated in the Eastern Province, a majority-

～

*For ten years, Yaroslav Trofimov
worked as a freelance journalist,
reporting from a variety of countries.
While based in Jerusalem, he
learned Arabic and Hebrew. In
1999, he became affiliated with* The
Wall Street Journal, *specializing in
Middle Eastern coverage.* Faith at
War *is his first book.*

～

Shiite area whose inhabitants receive little benefit from "their" oil. Saudi authorities keep a close enough watch on the territory to hamper any organized independence movement. Some elders among the Eastern Province's Shiites met with Trofimov and told him of their oppression and the way their lands had been taken from them. They realize that a different arrangement could only come with outside intervention. Because of the West's dependence upon Saudi oil, successive American governments have turned a blind eye to oppressive Saudi practices.

In contrast to Saudi Arabia, Tunisia takes pride in its achievement of secularism. Habib Bourguiba, president when the country won independence in 1956, tirelessly pursued modernization. His aggressive secularism has become government policy. Trofimov met with various government ministers, each of whom proudly described the Tunisian brand of Islam, which is almost 180 degrees different from that of the Saudis. Their way of life is maintained against the influence of extreme Islamists by extreme measures. Force and imprisonment have been used here since the early 1990's. Since the "war on terror" escalated, Western governments have stopped pressuring Tunisia about human rights, allowing such repression to be extended to secular dissidents as well. Tunisia, with its dictatorship and torture, was very disappointing to Trofimov, despite the regime's successes. In its defense, maintaining an egalitarian legal code and a thriving tourism-based economy in a Muslim country is no small achievement.

Trofimov next begins his series of chapters on Iraq. He traveled there several times, and the four resulting chapters are in many ways the heart of the book. The author has an eye for revealing incidents; he uses vignettes to reveal larger problems within specific areas. To the Westerner who has followed the so-called war on terror on the news, there are few surprises. What was first hailed—at least in many quarters—as a war of liberation has turned into an aftermath of sullen and often bloody resistance.

Trofimov went into Iraq during the 2003 invasion as a "unilateral." Not embedded with any military unit, he was on his own in finding transportation and protection. Besides being dangerous, this was surely one of the most confusing ways to brave the fog of battle. He and a colleague kept circling back to a cloverleaf where British troops were lining up prisoners, with other wounded Iraqis streaming in. An Iraqi soldier took the opportunity to surrender to them; apparently reporters were less terrifying than the "Tommies." Eventually Trofimov, along with two French reporters, made his way to Baghdad. From there, he could see Iraqi supplicants turning into demonstrators even as the occupation settled in.

Trofimov talked with many ordinary Iraqis and with American soldiers. For example, he visited a region in Anbar, west of Baghdad, held by a Florida National Guard battalion. The unit's commander, Lieutenant Colonel Hector Mirabile, is a Miami po-

lice officer in civilian life. Older and with more life experience than the young soldiers in charge in many areas, he made it his first priority to get his troops home alive,
which he did. The province is among the most violence-wracked in Iraq, and casualties did occur, but Mirabile's policies minimized them: He educated himself about
Iraqi culture and decided to let the local sheikhs manage their tribes as long as they did
not incite trouble. Such strategy made a difference.

In the book, some important aspects of the Iraq situation are neglected. There is
no coverage of the 2005 election and almost none of the Kurdish provinces, where
different conditions prevail. Nor does the author offer any estimate of how deeply the
Shiite-Sunni divide cuts, although several attacks stemming from this divide are described.

From Iraq, the focus turns to Afghanistan. Here Trofimov's outlook differs from
that of many Americans who see the Afghanistan incursion as a success (and a justified war) in contrast to that of Iraq, where events seem to have gone from bad to
worse. The writer reminds one that, relative to the number of troops posted, as high a
percentage of American soldiers have been killed in Afghanistan as in Iraq. He does
admit that the aftermath in Afghanistan appears relatively more peaceful. He attributes this to the presence of a truly multinational force in Afghanistan and to the wisdom of appointing an Afghan American who understands the culture as ambassador.

Trofimov accompanied a U.S. Army company as they investigated villages in a remote mountain region. Their stated purpose was to find Taliban guerrillas, or failing
that, signs of Taliban influence. Naturally, the villagers whose homes they raided
were terrified. None admitted to seeing any Taliban, although Taliban were known to
control the mountainous region. Even though the situation was fraught with the potential for tragic misunderstanding or misfires, the only actual casualties of the raid
were two donkeys whom the troops commandeered.

The raid coverage notwithstanding, Trofimov's treatment of Afghanistan tends to
be more lighthearted than is the Iraq account. If his experiences do not quite make the
case for the Taliban having rebounded, they do not disprove it either. One fascinating
vignette describes a former brandy factory and its ups and downs under various past
regimes. The director hopes to start producing its famous raisin-based brandy again
someday. No one in officialdom could offer him any encouragement about this in
still-Muslim postwar Afghanistan. Meanwhile he makes alcohol, officially for industrial and medical uses, and tries to prevent constant pilfering.

Trofimov also visited Yemen, Kuwait, Lebanon, and Bosnia. Beyond the unique
histories and customs of each country, his interviews reveal some common threads.
Few people show their true feelings to the casual questioner, but distrust of and disdain for Western ways is widespread—and growing. Books produced by Wahhabis
dominate the bookstores and libraries in most Islamic countries, presenting a picture
of the West scarcely recognizable to most Westerners. It is hardly a situation conducive to democracy or peace.

Lest this be the last word, though, the author also recounts his trip to Mali. This remote African nation—best known as the site of Timbuktu—manages to combine Islam with a robust democracy. Local elections took place during Trofimov's visit.

They were straightforward and spirited, with campaign promises and pretty women singing in support of the parties. Malians attribute their democracy to their African heritage. "We're not Arabs here. We're Africans," said one, whose attitude appears almost universal in Mali. Vendors sell gris-gris charms right outside the mosque. Such "witchcraft" would bring beheading in Saudi Arabia, but Mali's clerics take it in stride. Although Mali's political independence is recent, its independent take on Islam goes back to the fourteenth century. Religion is separate from politics, too, and the Malians like it that way.

Faith at War is, of necessity, a personal account. Trofimov avoids theorizing, but his experiences and impressions are bound to be subjective to a certain extent. That said, the book is an invaluable guide to the important—and often puzzling—segment of the world shaped most strongly by Islam. The maps of each country he visited and the glossary at the book's end are helpful additional resources. Excellent reportage such as Trofimov's is a big help to readers seeking to cut through the official "lines" of all parties to the Western-Muslim culture clash, and to understand what is going on behind the headlines.

Emily Alward

Review Sources

Kirkus Reviews 73, no. 6 (March 15, 2005): 345.
Library Journal 130, no. 6 (April 1, 2005): 112.
The New York Times Book Review 154 (July 17, 2005): 11.
Publishers Weekly 252, no. 16 (April 18, 2005): 56.
The Washington Post Book World, May 29, 2005, p. 3.

FALLEN

Author: David Maine (1963-   )
Publisher: St. Martin's Press (New York). 244 pp.
   $24.00
Type of work: Novel
Time: A few years after the creation of Adam and Eve
Locale: East of Eden

This wry retelling of the biblical story of Cain and Abel, Adam and Eve focuses primarily on the characters as real but clearly flawed human beings

> Principal characters:
> ADAM, the first man
> EVE, the first woman, his wife
> CAIN, their oldest son, a moody farmer
> ABEL, Cain's younger brother, a shepherd
> ZORU, Cain's wife
> HENOCH, Cain's loyal son, a builder
> GOD, the author of it all

Fallen, the title of David Maine's second novel, obviously refers to humanity's first parents, Adam and Eve, and their unfortunate offspring Cain and Abel. Although the account in the biblical book of Genesis is straightforward, Maine presents its events in reverse order, through the perceptions of his four major characters, while everyone grows younger. In this respect, the book is reminiscent of Nobel Prize-winner Harold Pinter's play *Betrayal* (pr. 1978), which likewise begins with short scenes from the unhappy present and works backward to a more idyllic time.

Maine begins with the imminent death of the fratricidal Cain as an old man, moves back through his youthful murder of his brother, Abel (which is covered in a single sentence), and ends with Adam and Eve's expulsion from the Garden of Eden. God is almost an afterthought, manifesting himself occasionally "in the form of a gray-bellied cloud" or rock and speaking cryptically in italics.

The novel is composed of four sections and forty short chapters, several with identical titles to signal a shift in viewpoint. Because the events are familiar, there is little suspense. Instead, the delight comes in Maine's witty, unorthodox version, which is replete with irony. This First Family represents a multitude of races. Father Adam is bandy-legged and dark-skinned, with black, kinky hair; copper-haired Eve is pale and gray-eyed, with a propensity to give birth to twins; slender Abel has olive skin, brown curls, and green eyes. The recalcitrant Cain is, ironically, the blue-eyed, fair-haired boy.

The sons appear first. At the beginning, Cain is seen as an old man dying in a wet climate, crippled and dogged by a murderer's guilt. He recalls a time early in his wandering when he began to recognize the full ramifications of his actions, after he en-

David Maine attended Oberlin College and the University of Arizona; he has taught English in Morocco and Pakistan. An American, he has lived in Lahore, Pakistan, since 1998. His first novel, The Preservationist, *was published in 2004.*

countered a teenager who had stoned a man to death for "stuff I wanted" and who told Cain admiringly, "You were the, the, inspiration." Currently, Cain is shunned by all, even his own grandchildren. Only his loyal son Henoch, builder of a mighty city that Cain himself designed, cares for him, even though as a child Henoch nearly died at the hands of his angry father. Cain's wife Zoru, the only woman who never feared him, was older than he and no beauty, yet he still grieves her absence these many years after her death from plague. The ghost of his brother visits him frequently for intense discussions. When Cain impulsively asks for forgiveness, Abel does not answer.

Cain is the rebel figure, angry and scornful. As a teenager, he shrugs repeatedly, infuriating his father. He argues with Adam against making a burnt offering of food when they have precious little for themselves, because it makes no sense. When he brings stale food as his reluctant offering to God, he is scolded, yet at the same time the shepherd Abel is permitted to sacrifice two decrepit sheep, rather than healthy young ones. Cain's problems intensify in a few years when God, with choking smoke, famously refuses his hard-earned offering of a bountiful harvest, while Abel's offering of sheep is accepted, enriching him fortyfold. After Cain angrily challenges God's response, Adam warns him not to curse God and banishes him when he persists. Abel tries to mediate; Eve stays quiet.

There is a double standard working against Cain. His parents, and God, seem to favor Abel, who in turn notes that Cain and his father are very much alike, proud and stubborn. Eve is leery of her firstborn because she witnessed his twin brother born dead, with bruises and tiny handprints on his body. She believes that Cain killed him in her womb.

Abel is a lovely boy with a sunny disposition, but he is not much brighter than the troublesome ewe he calls Rockhead. He is placid, good-natured, and hopeless with numbers, as he is the first to admit. To his mother he is a perfect child, her joy. Abel reminds her of Eden, her home, but Cain's blue eyes remind her that the blue skies of the garden are lost forever, and she cannot forget it. Cain in turn resents Abel's "bland joyous righteous infuriating face" because he is always eager to give their younger siblings (and Cain) advice, even when it is not good; his two favorite words appear to be "should" and "shouldn't." Abel is essentially a peacemaker, attempting to maintain harmony within the family. Adam sometimes views him, less kindly, as a busybody.

Abel, however, is unquestioningly kind. Missing Cain after Adam sends him away, Abel determines to visit him at the winter solstice. He plans to leave his own warm shawl, woven by their little sister, with Cain, who will need it more than he will. Two years later he will journey to share his brother's exile and keep him company, but by then Cain will have other plans for him.

As Adam grows increasingly stiff, he seems to have developed arthritis. He realizes he must be getting old—but how old is old? No one knows, because no one is older than Adam. In fact, Adam and Eve have had to face the unique problem of being the first to experience everything. In Eden everything was furnished for them, but once they were expelled they had to fend for themselves, and their children share that experience. All of them become inventors by virtue of necessity. Early on, Adam accidentally bakes mud into clay, then learns to make sun-dried bricks to build a hut. In exile, Cain's first tiny house is carefully built of stones, snug but dark.

Eve is by far the most ingenious: She fashions clay pots, weaves baskets from reeds, invents the hand loom and the fishing net. She discovers how to make yogurt, cheese, and olive oil. By watching the moon, she develops a method of measuring time. Their oldest daughter invents a better loom and becomes an accomplished weaver. Another daughter is a natural storyteller, and the oldest twins invent and play musical instruments.

Adam possesses a rough exterior but his speech is cultured, and he worries a great deal. Quick-tempered like his eldest son, he is nevertheless paralyzed by indecision, but when he finally makes up his mind, he will not be swayed. He and Eve have produced fourteen children in sixteen years and wonder when they should stop. He is torn by two contradictory concerns: God's commandment to be fruitful and multiply, and Eve's diminishing health. Adam proposes a harvest offering as thanks that Eve is not pregnant again. (There will be at least one more child, Seth, the one conceived to take Abel's place.)

Adam has an endearing quality—he used to be afraid of all animals, especially rabbits because of their big teeth. Within his family, he is the most respectful to God and holds to tradition: praying, resting on the Sabbath, making regular offerings. When he and Eve awake that first morning after their exile from the Garden, Adam is passive, stunned by their punishment. Eve refuses to give up. Adam thinks they should offer their scanty food to God; Eve wants to eat it. He has faith, but she has common sense.

If Adam is certain, Eve is not. She has been a largely tangential figure in the story until the final section, in which she is more clearly revealed. Occasionally she will lift a roguish eyebrow, an act that turns Adam to jelly. She questions silently, seldom speaks, and generally keeps her own counsel. She is determined and surprisingly practical. After finding a pregnant cat, then kittens, and then their bodies, she is no longer confident of God's protection or mercy.

Just as Eve does not trust God, neither does Cain. These two ask the "big" theological questions. Eve examines her decision to taste the forbidden apple in the Garden. She recognizes that she chose to disobey God, and she fears that her son Cain will make similar choices. Is she evil, she wonders, and if so, why did God make her imperfect? Is God truly good? She prays, finally, for forgetfulness because she is so troubled.

Cain, the belligerent teenager, questions his father: What would have happened if Eve alone had sinned? What will the children do when their parents die? The two engage in a familiar debate: "God rejects you," the boy says, "but you cling to him tighter than ever. . . . It's confusing." Adam responds with certainty: "God's will is done, always. Accept it and be free, or fight it and remain a prisoner of your own limited understanding." Cain will not be deterred: "Why are you so afraid to *talk* about anything? . . . we don't *discuss* things." Adam finally admits he does not comprehend God, but God in turn is not forthcoming with answers.

A key conversation between Adam and his sons introduces the boys to an ambiguous world: "They see trees and low distant mountains and the river unspooling from them, like a thread. Or slithering toward them, like a threat." With great reluctance, Adam reveals the history of the expulsion from Eden and how he and Eve wandered for years. The uncertainty of their present life sets up an obvious dichotomy: Although Adam understands the story literally, Cain thinks that his father's account of his creation, when God breathed on dust and water, is a metaphor. Abel, as usual, is confused.

One might ask why God, the prime mover of this story and appropriately unknowable, is so removed from their lives. God does seem capricious. Cain, the cynic or the voice of reason, poses the same question again and again: "Why would God create a perfect place and then allow the Devil in it, just to trick you? Why tell you not to do something when He could have just removed the tree?"

The novel contains multiple ironies, beginning with its dust jacket, on which two cherubs on a black background appear to be playing; upon closer inspection, they are fighting. Adam, whose disobedience is the source of Original Sin, rejects the idea that human beings are born evil. He promises the young Cain, "I would never send you away." (He does.) Shortly before Abel's death, even as he announces to his brother that the world now contains other people, he echoes the complaint of some biblical scholars: "To be honest I don't understand where [the others] come from. . . . It's confusing, to tell the truth." Abel's ghost materializes as Cain is defecating, to question him somewhat peevishly about their youngest brother, Seth. The loss of Eden is signaled by a mosquito bite.

Maine has an engaging narrative voice, through which he presents a new perspective on a well-known story. *Fallen* is neither religious nor antireligious. Instead, Maine is adding a new dimension to his fully fleshed character studies. (In a charming aside, the reader learns that Cain habitually sleeps on his stomach.) These four individuals are doing the very best they can: questioning, resisting, accepting, with or without faith. They are very human figures.

Joanne McCarthy

Review Sources

Booklist 101, no. 22 (August, 2005): 1993.
Kirkus Reviews 73, no. 14 (July 15, 2005): 759.
The New York Times 154 (September 8, 2005): E9.
The New York Times Book Review 154 (October 30, 2005): 25.
People 64, no. 15 (October 10, 2005): 53.
Publishers Weekly 252, no. 28 (July 18, 2005): 179.
The Washington Post, October 2, 2005, p. T4.

FEBRUARY HOUSE

Author: Sherill Tippins (1955-   )
Publisher: Houghton Mifflin (Boston). 317 pp. $24.00
Type of work: Literary history
Time: June, 1940, to December, 1941
Locale: Brooklyn, New York

W. H. Auden, Carson McCullers, Jane and Paul Bowles, Benjamin Britten, and Gypsy Rose Lee are among the inhabitants of a commune in wartime Brooklyn

> *Principal personages:*
> W. H. AUDEN, a prizewinning poet and
>   playwright
> CARSON MCCULLERS, a novelist, essayist,
>   and short-story writer
> JANE BOWLES, a novelist
> PAUL BOWLES, a novelist and musician
> BENJAMIN BRITTEN, a British composer
> GYPSY ROSE LEE, a mystery writer and entertainer
> KLAUS MANN, a German-born journalist and publisher

Just before the United States' entrance into World War II, a group of young writers and musicians experimented with communal living in a house at 7 Middagh Street in Brooklyn, New York. *February House* is the story of that experiment and the awesomely creative group of artists who lived there. The title is the name which Anaïs Nin, diarist and novelist, gave to the house because so many of the residents were born in February. Although the communal arrangement was fraught with tension and many disagreements, the outcome was an extraordinary outpouring of creative work. It was here that W. H. Auden first worked out his philosophical and religious beliefs and wrote many of his finest poems, as well as the words for his collaborative effort with Benjamin Britten, the opera *Paul Bunyan*, and the words to his oratorio, *For the Time Being*. Here Auden also first met the man who would be his life partner, Chester Kallman. It was the house in which Carson McCullers conceived the ideas for her novel *A Member of the Wedding* (1946) and the novella *The Ballad of the Sad Café* (1951). The house on Middagh Street is where Gypsy Rose Lee first learned to write mystery novels, and where many other transients found new inspiration for their art.

To tell the history of this collective living experiment, author Sherill Tippins divides the story of the house into three chronological periods: Part 1 is "The House on the Hill, June-November 1940"; part 2 is "The Bawdy House, December 1940-February 1941"; and part 3 is "The House of Genius, March-December 1941." In an epilogue, she summarizes the stories of the various artists in the years following 1941, as well as the people who would occupy the house until it was torn down to make room for a highway.

∽

Sherill Tippins has worked as an
associate television producer. She
has coauthored a travel guidebook,
Frommer's Irreverent Guide:
Manhattan *(1996), and several*
parenting handbooks.

∽

Tippins begins with an introduction tracing her interest in the house on Middagh Street, then proceeds in part 1 to relate chronologically the origin of the communal idea, the dream of the house, its renovation and furnishing, and the gathering of the artists. George Davis, a talented editor at *Harper's Bazaar* magazine in the 1930's, first encountered the house in a dream, then went to Brooklyn to find it. He was superb at recognizing talent but terribly disorganized and quite willing to ignore corporate rules and regulations. Having been fired, he still wanted literary surroundings and figured that he could secure them without the job.

Once he located the house, he approached McCullers, with whom he had worked on her novel *The Heart Is a Lonely Hunter* (1940). McCullers's marriage was on the rocks, and she also wanted to expand her circle. Then Davis contacted Auden, who had been struggling financially as well as artistically, and invited him to join in the venture, luring him into the house with the promise of low rent and a top-floor view of the Brooklyn Bridge. The British poet signed onto the project on the condition that he could bring Britten and Britten's partner, Peter Pears, along. Auden and Christopher Isherwood, perhaps most famous as the author of *The Berlin Diaries* which was the source for the musical *Cabaret*, were struggling to survive in New York City, while at the same time dealing with the guilt of not being in Britain at the start of Hitler's attacks. Auden accepted the offer, and the renovations and struggles for funding began, not to cease until the house was demolished.

The house on Middagh Street was home to an eclectic, constantly changing group of creative people who moved in and out of projects and relationships and who were often at odds with one another. To bring order to this chaos, Tippins focuses on individuals or couples for a portion of each chapter, approaching them biographically, which helps the reader to follow the events in their lives during the years at the house. Thus Tippins describes the creative, emotional, and physical upheavals in McCullers's life as she moves to the house, leaving her husband, Reeves, behind, develops passions for various men and women, works on what at the time she was calling "The Bride and Her Brother" but which became *A Member of the Wedding*, sips from her thermos of sherry, falls ill, returns to her home in Georgia, goes back to New York, and so on. Adding to the instability of the communal arrangement was the fact that several of the men and women living there at one time or another would go to the bars at nearby docks and pick up sailors to bring back with them.

Ironically, the artists who were most creative, such as Auden, discovered in the bohemian ferment of February House just what the great poet realized; that the

fundamental premise on which bohemianism was based—the idea that 'good' equals what the bourgeoisie do not do—was self-evidently false. Regular meals and quiet work hours were required for efficiency in every realm.

So those who benefited most from the communal arrangement were artists who were capable of imposing discipline upon themselves in the midst of creative chaos and the outsiders who swarmed to Brooklyn to experience the avant garde at first hand.

In part 2, with the provocative title of "The Bawdy House," Tippins discusses the early period of the house when guest flocked to drink cocktails with the notorious Gypsy Rose Lee, to discuss literature with poets and novelists, to listen to music with composers and musicians, and to dance with the founder of the American Ballet Company, George Balanchine. Those who came also included pimps and piano players, soldiers and sailors, publishers and playwrights. During this period, Auden was collaborating with Britten on their musical *Paul Bunyan*, and McCullers was creating Miss Amelia, the Amazon from Brooklyn who falls in love with a dwarf, Cousin Lyman, who in turn falls in love with Miss Amelia's former husband in that masterpiece of unrequited love, *The Ballad of the Sad Café*. It was also a time when each of the inhabitants of the house, barring perhaps the stripper Gypsy Rose Lee, were exploring their sexuality and discovering love, just as Miss Amelia does. During these months Auden met Chester Kallman, a very young Jewish man, eighteen years old, with whom he was to spend the rest of his life, although he would not be the only, nor even at times the central, love in Kallman's life. For Auden, perhaps the most important part of the relationship was that the great and often demanding, sometimes thwarted, love he felt for the young man led him on a spiritual quest which would bring him back to Christianity in a most profound and meaningful way, which in turn inspired some of his greatest poems and poetic sequences.

For February House it was an unsettled, somewhat crazy time, as Davis taught Lee to write a mystery novel, her famous *The G-string Murders* (1941), Salvador Dali and his wife brought Surrealism into the mix, along with circus performers and their animals, chimpanzees included, and Paul and Jane Bowles arrived with their utterly dysfunctional marriage, wild sexual games, and cruel fights. It was not the best of times for any of the residents, as too much was unstructured and uncontrolled. Auden finally recruited some servants and imposed some order upon the house, at which point it could become "The House of Genius."

During the spring and on through the winter of 1941, as the world became more deeply consumed by war, the people of Middagh Street struggled to find a way to move forward. Part 3 explores this period and the soul-searching, philosophizing, and hard work that geniuses within the house put forth. The artists in residence recognized that there was little they could do about the war pounding Europe and the Far East but, led by Auden, they could at least try to make a safe and productive haven for the people, especially the "geniuses,"who had left Europe. It was also a way that the expatriate British citizens, Auden, Isherwood, Britten, and others, could ease their consciences about deciding not to return to endure the bombing of Britain.

This was probably the most creative time in the house. Klaus Mann, the son of author Thomas Mann, launched his magazine *Decision*, which helped to disseminate the ideas the February House inhabitants were exploring. Auden particularly was struggling to define for himself the role of the artist in wartime. If one would be a truly incompetent warrior, did it make sense to simply volunteer to be cannon fodder in order to prove one's patriotism, or was there another role that the artist could or should play in wartime? The consensus of the expatriates, who were receiving a constant barrage of angry denunciations from the homeland, was that the artist's role was to preserve and move forward civilization wherever that was possible.

This is a highly readable history of one of the most interesting groups of writers, artists, and musicians working both together and, at times, at odds with one another in mid-twentieth century America. They formed an alliance similar to the famous British Bloomsbury group, which included writers such as Virginia Woolf and Lytton Strachey and painters such as Augustus John. Another excellent feature of *February House* is a delightful collection of photographs which allows the reader to picture the artists and writers as they were at the time of Middagh Street and the surroundings in which they lived.

It is unfortunate that Tippins chooses to end her study with the start of America's involvement with World War II, because at least one of the most interesting and gifted of the residents, the great African American author Richard Wright, came to live there the following year. Wright brought with him his white wife, which caused a great deal more consternation in the neighborhood than the goings-on of Davis and his crowd. including their steady recruitment of casual sexual partners of various types. American racism—in a time when American soldiers were fighting to defeat the proponent of a "master race"—would finally make the house uninhabitable.

Mary LeDonne Cassidy

Review Sources

Booklist 101, nos. 9/10 (January 1-15, 2005): 803.
Kirkus Reviews 72, no. 23 (December 1, 2004): 1140-1141.
Library Journal 130, no. 2 (February 1, 2005): 80.
New Criterion 23, no. 10 (June, 2005): 74-78.
New Statesman 134, no. 4760 (October 3, 2005): 51-53.
The New York Times Book Review 154 (February 6, 2005): 8.
The New Yorker 81, no. 3 (March 7, 2005): 81.
The Spectator 299 (November 26, 2005): 44.
The Washington Post, February 13, 2005, p. T4.

FINDING GEORGE ORWELL IN BURMA

Author: Emma Larkin
Publisher: Penguin Press (New York). 294 pp. $23.00
Type of work: Biography, current affairs, history, literary
   history, and travel
Time: 1995-2003
Locale: Burma, officially known as Myanmar

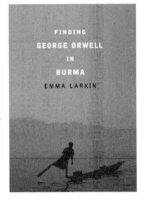

*Larkin's quest to learn about Orwell's experience in
1920's Burma acquaints her with the brutal repression of
the current government of Myanmar, whose ruthless conduct reminds her of Orwell's antiutopian novels*

Something happened to a young English policeman in
1920's Burma that transformed him from Eric Blair, a rep-
resentative of the British Empire, into the writer George Orwell (1903-1950). In *Finding George Orwell in Burma*, American journalist Emma Larkin recounts her attempt
to discover it. Between 1995 and the spring of 2003, she traveled several times in
Burma, now called Myanmar, conducting interviews, tracking down records, sightseeing, and observing the culture of that nation. The results of her quest to learn about
Orwell's transformation were inconclusive, but she reached a disquieting conclusion
about the ruling military junta in Myanmar: It behaves like the single-party dictator-
ships described in Orwell's satirical fable *Animal Farm* (1945) and dystopian novel
Nineteen Eighty-Four (1949). A mixture of anecdote, history, reportage, and literary
sleuthing, her presentation is at times impressionistic and tangential yet nonetheless is
effective in portraying Myanmar as a brutally repressed nation.

"Emma Larkin" is a nom de plume, and for good reason. The Myanmar government dislikes international attention. Tourists are welcome; journalists are not. Larkin
pretends to be sightseeing. Just being a foreigner there automatically brings one under
suspicion, especially if, like Larkin, one does not participate in a government-
approved tour program. She was followed and harassed by the police and military intelligence. Worse, any Burmese people detected talking openly with a foreigner are
risking their freedom. Larkin's pen name is an attempt to protect her in-country
sources from government reprisal.

These sources—among them guides, students, officials, small business owners,
writers, housewives, retirees, book dealers, professionals, waiters, clergy, grounds-
keepers—were almost universally hesitant to speak. Many finally did, a testament to
Larkin's talent for drawing out people. In listening to their stories, she heard an astonishing mixture of insight, fear, confession, and bitter humor. For example, upon asking a prominent academic about Orwell, he replied, "You mean the prophet!" Another
joked, darkly, that in Burma Orwell's books *Burmese Days* (1934), *Animal Farm*, and
Nineteen Eighty-Four are considered a trilogy that depicts the Burma's pre- and post-
World War II history.

∽
*Emma Larkin is the pseudonym
for an Asian-born American
journalist who lives in Bangkok,
Thailand, and writes about Asia.
She studied Burmese at the School
of Oriental and African Studies in
London and has been visiting
Burma since the mid-1990's.*
∽

Larkin takes the trilogy joke seriously. Throughout her book she compares the policies and actions of the Myanmar government to passages in the novels. Such comparison is, of course, selective and polemical when applied to the last two novels. For *Burmese Days* it is historically appropriate: Based upon Orwell's experience as a district policeman from 1922 to 1927, it tells a story of British racism, control of the Burmese, and decline while the colonial administration ruled—that is, before the Japanese invasion.

Animal Farm, on the other hand, satirizes the 1917 Bolshevik Revolution in Russia; *Nineteen Eighty-Four* concerns the individuality-crushing power of single-party tyrannies in general. To see Burmese history in these last two novels is entirely a matter of applied literary interpretation. Still, one cannot help admiring the Orwellian reversal of Larkin's approach: She goes looking for Orwell in Burma, and finds Burma in Orwell. The irony does not achieve the caliber of "Freedom is Slavery" (*Nineteen Eighty-Four*), but it will do.

In modern Burma, freedom *is* slavery, in the sense that "slavery" is unquestioned obedience to the military junta's rule, which provides the "freedom." Myanmar's record of human rights abuses is among the most dismal in the world. Larkin makes clear the tools of enslavement on which the military relies: the distortion and haphazard application of laws (the "rubber band" is what Burmese call their law code); pervasive, unexplained censorship; outlawing or harassment of opposition parties; torture and jailing of political prisoners on the slightest pretext; forced unpaid public labor, including that by children; staged military-friendly demonstrations by government employees; the rewriting of history; systemic discrimination against nonparty members; a network of informers and stooges belonging to a state-supported "social organization"; "Bermaization" of ethnic minorities, a euphemism for cultural genocide; thuggery, intimidation, and murder by the military or its hirelings; displacement of villages supporting dissenters and wholesale burning of property; confiscations; an army that consumes nearly half of the state's official budget; and defense against feigned internal and external enemies used as a pretext for repression.

Larkin's account of the historical developments leading to this despotism is sketchy but adequate, and in any case the general outlines are all too familiar to Western readers: a colony forceably assembled from diverse, antagonistic chiefdoms and kingdoms, post-World War II independence, budding democracy under the guidance of freedom fighters, infighting among them and assassinations, reactionary parties on one side or the other of the Cold War struggle between Sino-Soviet communism and Western capitalist democracy, separatist militias, coups, economic deterioration, squelched dissent, and autocracy. Add to these its shadow economy of black marketeering and narcotrafficking and the economic aid from China that increasingly is making Myanmar a client state, and the picture is reasonably clear about how ordinary Burmese citizens live.

The Burmese military is unlikely to relinquish power willingly. It has much blood on its hands, by all accounts, and the generals surely realize what their fates would be if citizen rule returned. Then again, as Larkin points out, power becomes its own justification under authoritarianism, even for those autocrats who started out as idealists and freedom fighters. Apparently Orwell came to this conclusion about the colonial administration that he served and became disillusioned. In this regard Larkin quotes a famous passage from his essay "Shooting an Elephant" (1936): "when the white man turns tyrant it is his own freedom that he destroys . . . he wears a mask, and his face grows to fit it."

Apparently, too, Orwell was unpopular among his fellow English in Burma, came to loathe his job, and sympathized with the Burmese, at least in principle. Larkin cites another essay as perhaps the very turning point in his experience for which she was searching. In "A Hanging" (1931) Orwell describes accompanying a Burmese prisoner to the gallows. When the man unexpectedly sidesteps a puddle, this simple movement shocks Orwell into seeing the prisoner as another human being, rather than just as a member of a subject citizenry.

If the incidents of the elephant hunt and the hanging represent the "something happened" that Larkin set out to discover, then her discovery is far from original. After all, Orwell himself wrote of them. Larkin, however, provides more, some small but tantalizing literary scoops. Orwell's father was an official in Burma, and his mother was born there. In searching for their various residences, Larkin learns that Orwell had Anglo-Burmese cousins, a fact she had not found in any of his biographies or his own writings. Furthermore, if Orwell did not keep a Burmese mistress (a common practice), he at least appreciated the local women and had sexual liaisons. Did the aroused passions for the "natives" in a puritanical young Englishman and his mixed-blood relatives influence his change of mind in Burma? Larkin implies so, but the evidence, apart from its value as simply new, is tenuous. An aside to this is Larkin's treatment of "Shooting an Elephant" and "A Hanging." There has long been controversy about whether these are essays or short stories, fact or fiction. Larkin takes them as factual and provides some evidence from the Burmese to support it.

At one point in her travels a new acquaintance asked Larkin, "What exactly are you doing in Burma?" It was a dreaded question for her; she could never be sure that the person asking was not a spy for the government, and a truthful answer might have resulted in her expulsion, or even physical danger. She usually answered vaguely, at first—that she was interested in colonial architecture or in Orwell's family. These answers probably did not satisfy the Burmese authorities, and even her stated purpose of uncovering what "happened" to Orwell may not satisfy readers of her book. The motivation for it sounds muddled, as if Orwell was simply an excuse for her daring travels through Burma.

As a thematic center for the book it suffices, more or less, but again and again Larkin includes descriptive passages that, while often lovely in their own right, are of murky relevance. Perhaps these passages are merely intended to set a tone or show her to be a sensitive observer, but their effect is to juxtapose vivid images—for example, between imperial splendor and its degenerate relics under the present rulers, or between the country's astonishing natural beauty and abundant resources and the government's tawdry, exploitative self-aggrandizement.

Intended or not, such contrasts constitute a form of slanting. In fact, her bias is never in doubt. She makes little attempt to take the viewpoint of the military junta, even for the purpose of refutation, other than to repeat their farcical claims that theirs is a successful governance for prosperity and happiness. Instead, she relates the army's weird behavior, for instance its bizarre machinations to prevent citizens from watching the military parade on Armed Forces Day (the biggest national holiday), or the rumor that Myanmar's strongman, Senior General Than Shwe, regularly consults astrologers, or the government's intimidation campaign against Nobel Peace Prize winner Aung San Suu Kyi, who leads the National League for Democracy. The party won the last election (1990) but was prevented from taking power by the military.

Probably no one of conscience can write on any subject about Burma without eventually, somehow, segueing to the wretched state of affairs there. In all events, as with Orwell, something happened to Larkin there that inspired her risky investigative journey. Whatever her deepest motivation for writing *Finding George Orwell in Burma*, through it she offers readers a glimpse into present-day Myanmar that is rare in the popular press, whose attention is largely turned elsewhere in the world. It is a regime that knows it can bully its populace in order to maintain power precisely because the world is not watching and does not much care to. There is yet a darker theme. The British Empire gave Burma a push down the path to becoming Myanmar by making it a nation, implanting Western institutions and economy, and then largely abandoning it after independence. It is an example of what happens when a superpower, for whatever reasons, forcibly meddles in the affairs of a distant region. Portraying Myanmar's rapacious, repressive government as Orwellian is all very well, but that gives it a literary flavor. Such regimes as Myanmar's were not Orwellian to Orwell. They were the enemy.

Roger Smith

Review Sources

Booklist 101, no. 18 (May 15, 2005): 1631.
Foreign Affairs 84, no. 3 (May/June, 2005): 150.
Kirkus Reviews 73, no. 7 (April 1, 2005): 403.
Library Journal 130, no. 11 (June 15, 2005): 88.
The New Leader 88, no. 3 (May/June, 2005): 46-47.
The New York Times Book Review 154 (July 17, 2005): 14.
Newsweek 146, no. 1 (July 4, 2005): 53.
Outside 30, no. 9 (September, 2005): 36.
Policy Review, August/September, 2005, pp. 86-92.
Publishers Weekly 252, no. 15 (April 11, 2005): 41-42.
The Times Literary Supplement, September 17, 2004, p. 30.

THE FIRST POETS
Lives of the Ancient Greek Poets

Author: Michael Schmidt (1947-   )
Publisher: Alfred A. Knopf (New York). 410 pp. $30.00
Type of work: Literary history

A renowned English poet and scholar brings learning, insight, and enthusiasm to the study of early Greek poets, whose influence extends to the present time

In 1999, Michael Schmidt published a book titled, like Samuel Johnson's famous work, *Lives of the Poets*, covering the development of English poetry and language from Geoffrey Chaucer to Thom Gunn. Ambitious as that undertaking was, at least the existence of its subjects could be proved. Not so with Schmidt's *The First Poets: Lives of the Ancient Greek Poets*. The subtitle must not be taken literally, considering how little is known about the preclassical Greek poets, including, in some cases, whether they lived at all.

Undaunted, Schmidt presents verifiable facts when he can, drawing on varied sources, ancient and modern—poets, historians, philosophers, critics, linguists, and archaeologists. While he duly reports on the scientific underpinnings of modern knowledge about ancient literature, he is clearly more interested in people's beliefs about the past than in what science can prove. He declares, "I wanted to write a book that instructs and entertains, to suggest some of the theoretical and critical issues of the present and earlier ages, but primarily to honour ancient patterns of belief." Schmidt, himself a poet as well as a scholar, succeeds in that aim by balancing established fact with informed, sometimes inspired, conjecture.

Schmidt seems to be aiming at a general audience, though academic specialists will be interested in his scholarly notes at the book's end. Before introducing particular "first poets," the author establishes, for lay readers, the general framework of Greek poetry. First he accounts for the paucity of knowledge about the actual content of the earliest Greek poems: Some of them, such as the work of Stesichorus, survive only as brief passages from long poems, assorted lines or phrases, single words, or sometimes just parts of words. In an introductory section titled "Materials," Schmidt offers a key explanation as he describes the surviving texts—and the materials on which they are written, such as clay and papyrus—from which modern society draws whatever direct knowledge it has of early Greek poetry.

Modern scholars know much more about ancient Babylonian culture (predating the Greeks by as much as a millennium), which preserved laws and literature on clay, than about the earliest Greek culture, whose poems were transcribed onto papyrus from centuries-old oral tradition. "Without such papyri," Schmidt notes, "we would have no Greek texts at all. By the middle of the fifth century BC, 'all civilised people'

~

Since 1969, Michael Schmidt has been managing editor of Carcanet Press, a literary publisher in Manchester, England. He is also editor of the PN Review, *as well as a poet, novelist, and lecturer at the University of Manchester. His scholarly works include* Lives of the Poets *(1999) and* Twentieth Century Poetry *(1999). He has declared a goal "to set poetry and criticism back into the mainstream of cultural concern."*

~

wrote on papyrus scrolls." Papyrus scrolls, therefore, represent a more recent period of poetry than do clay tablets, but papyrus is more fragile: The last great library of ancient scrolls burned in Istanbul in 1204 C.E. It is the oldest poetry which has survived the best—having been inscribed in clay, which is durable to begin with and which hardens during a fire, unlike papyrus. Schmidt also reports that almost all Babylonians were required to be literate, while relatively few Greek men were allowed the privilege. From such observations, the lay reader may learn many new things, while even specialists may be introduced to new insights into familiar facts.

Still laying the foundation for his main subject, Schmidt distinguishes "hot" cultures, in which poetry was always recited and never written down, from "cold" cultures with printed literature. His readers learn that, centuries before they were first written down, epics took poetic form partly because they had to be memorized and recited, and mnemonic devices such as rhythm, meter, and alliteration were conducive to this task. These devices were reinforced by dancing and playing music in time to the recited poetry.

Oral tradition allowed for little or no variation in the words of the epics. In a predominantly Greek culture, illiteracy kept the long-established versions intact. A time then came when, to be preserved in a non-Greek culture, Greek poetry had to be written down in an "official" version. Schmidt notes, "When it reaches Alexandria, poetry comes in out of the sun, it retires to the library, becomes one with its medium, language. And so it survives in a world where the vulgar tongue is not Greek."

At length, change in the common language brought a change in poetic form. Schmidt describes the difference between quantitative poetic meter, a feature of Greek and Latin verse, and stress meter, characteristic of English-language poetry. (He recommends some good books on meter for the reader who does not speak Greek, though he asserts that, to understand Greek poetic meter fully, one must learn the language.) Quantitative meter works in a vocalic language such as Greek, in which the pronunciation of a long vowel takes about twice as much time as a short vowel. The English Renaissance, with its revival of classical learning, ushered in a vogue for quantitative verse in English, which attracted not only such preeminent poets as Edmund Spenser but also Queen Elizabeth I. As late as the twentieth century, Robert Bridges made the attempt. Schmidt says the quantitative experiment in stress-based English was doomed. He does not mention the work of A. C. Swinburne or Gerard Manley Hopkins although, arguably, both succeed in English quantitative verse. Hopkins, especially, seems to control the length of vowels by increasing or reducing consonant clusters that follow them—a quantitative technique not readily imaginable in the vocalic Greek.

Language is just one difference between ancient and modern poetry. "For the ancients, poetry socialized people; for the moderns, it reflects or promotes alienation," Schmidt argues. The preference born of his Greek studies is abundantly evident in the chapter on Orpheus, "father of poetry, of music and, some say, of the art of writing itself. . . . If I start with Orpheus, it is to make it clear from the outset that this is a history in something other than the modern sense of the word."

Schmidt acknowledges that "we cannot point to a single line of verse or prose that is undeniably by Orpheus," even though poems attributed to Orpheus were common in Greece as late as the sixth and fifth centuries B.C.E. A major contention of this book, however, is that, despite the dearth of verifiable information about Orpheus and other early poets, there is "a wealth of stories, and they are worth telling, whether their truths are literal . . . or indicative. Biblical scholars and theologians argue that, when a tale in the Bible is implausible, or is disproved by archaeology, it may nonetheless contain a higher truth or impart a truth of another order than the truth of fact." (Still, the author disclaims any notion that in the case of Orpheus, "we are dealing with holy writ or prophesy.") To drive his point home, he charges that modern "critics and scholars tiptoe about, fearing to assert too much."

Orpheus, then, is a "first poet" of whose poetry—if he actually lived and composed—nothing may survive; he is a possibly fictive poet who inspired later "real" poets. Similarly, while "the most famous Greek hymns are those attributed to Homer," modern scholars cannot prove that he wrote any of them. Yet the hymns attributed to Homer have inspired many poets, notably Pindar and Callimachus, whose work does survive. While acknowledging the confusion of successive eras about both Orpheus the man and his work, Schmidt declares, "From our point of view, he is at least the *first* poet."

More familiar to the modern reader is Homer, presumed author of the *Iliad* (c. 750 B.C.E.; English translation, 1611) and the *Odyssey* (c. 725 B.C.E.; English translation, 1614). Three chapters on Homer, his epics, and his apocryphal poems take up fully one-sixth of *The First Poets*. Yet this poet is only a bit less elusive than Orpheus. Schmidt whimsically describes the difficulty of knowing the man: "Over time Homer, 'the blind poet with seven birthplaces,' has appeared, multiplied identities, then vanished like the Cat"—the Cheshire Cat of Lewis Carroll's *Alice's Adventures in Wonderland* (1865). The reference to "seven birthplaces"—the towns that claimed Homer as their native son—is from Ford Madox Ford.

For Schmidt, it is again a question of poetic versus literal truth. "Why," he asks, "are readers so very eager to find out who Homer was, so reluctant to consider the possibility that the epics assigned to his name were not 'composed' as other poems are?" He is equally harsh on the opposite view, which holds that it is futile to pursue Homer's identity because it cannot be known: "Such categorical purism—we cannot know and therefore we waste time in considering—impoverishes our reading in another sense. Each life of Homer tells us something about the changing attitudes to the poet and the poems." Again Schmidt sounds his book's inventive premise with an observation about the historical Homer: "We know nothing, but there is a considerable amount of nothing that we know."

Schmidt is at his best when contemplating Homer's epics. First he considers the poems' objectivity. "Whatever the brutality of the deeds recounted in the poems, what marks them both is their balance . . . an absence of partisanship, a reluctance to moralise . . . What feelings are expressed belong to the characters and their situations, and the poem reports without colluding in them."

Next Schmidt turns to the profound differences between the *Iliad* and the *Odyssey*, leading him and other scholars to doubt that the same poet is responsible for both.

> Any ten people reading the *Iliad* closely, or hearing it recited, will have a more or less common sense of what the poem is saying and doing. The *Odyssey* is different, more "open" and susceptible to different readings, at literal, psychological, political, allegorical and other levels. . . . This certainly does not make it a *better* poem. Plato in the *Hippias* declared that the *Iliad* excels the *Odyssey* as much as Achilles excels Odysseus. . . . Two *types* of man, then, and two models of action.

Schmidt sums up with a gnomic statement: "Despite all the action of the *Iliad*, it is in the *Odyssey* that we find adventure."

Many general readers have studied Homer in school, but few have even heard of such poets as Stesichorus, whom the Pythagoreans considered a reincarnation of Homer "because in scale and theme his work was Homeric." For hundreds of years after his death, Stesichorus exerted a seminal influence on ancient poetry. He is credited with originating the formal structure of Greek song, which according to Schmidt "leads directly into the Pindaric tradition and, in another form, into the drama: *strophe*, turn; *antistrophe*, counterturn; and *epodos*, after-song."

In presenting other poets less known in modern times, Schmidt focuses on the flourishing poetic era of the seventh and sixth centuries B.C.E. before ending with the literate Hellenistic period represented by Callimachus, Apollonius, and Theocritus. This provides scope to introduce Greek concepts such as *moira* (destiny), *kleos* (glory), *phua* (inborn character), and *dike* (roughly translated as "justice"). Frequently he reminds the reader that nearly always a given poet's work survives in mere fragments, though sites such as the refuse dump at Oxyrhynchus in Egypt are still yielding "reliques of ancient poesy."

The poets are referred to not just by their given names but also by the places they hailed from: Stesichorus of Himera, Sappho of Eressus, Apollonius of Rhodes. Schmidt offers a conjecture on the connection between birthplaces and the origin of poetic diction itself. In ancient times, people's place of origin was an important key not only to their politics and religion but also to the dialect of Greek they spoke. Dialect, in turn, would be the key to how they handled meter. In time a dialect of poetry evolved, transcending place of origin and thus a place's politics—the deeds of local heroes could be recognized, in poetry, as heroic regardless of locale.

In the same vein, Schmidt describes how a sixth century B.C.E. poem (now lost) by Stesichorus about the fall of Troy became the basis for a poem by Theodorus (465-398 B.C.E.) which in turn was inscribed on the first century C.E. Tabula Iliaca, now displayed in Rome's Capitoline Museum. "It's how poetry works; nothing need ever be quite lost, even when it passes out of memory."

Schmidt has shown that ancient poetry still has significance for the modern world, and that the spirit of it, if not always the letter, seems destined to reach the modern world through obstacles.

Thomas Rankin

Review Sources

Kirkus Reviews 72, no. 24 (December 15, 2004): 1192.
The New Republic 233, no. 1 (July 4, 2005): 38-41.
The New York Times Book Review 154 (August 28, 2005): 10-11.
Poetry 187, no. 1 (October, 2005): 53-63.
The Spectator 295 (June 19, 2004): 35.
The Times Higher Education Supplement, April 22, 2005, p. 25.
The Times Literary Supplement, June 3, 2005, p. 10.

FIVE FAMILIES
The Rise, Decline, and Resurgence of America's Most Powerful Mafia Empires

Author: Selwyn Raab (1934-   )
Publisher: St. Martin's Press (New York). 765 pp.
  $30.00
Type of work: History
Time: The early twentieth century to 2004
Locale: New York City

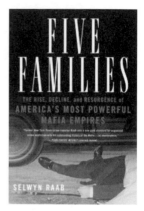

This well-researched study of the creation and expansion of the New York Mafia includes an excellent description of how the FBI and federal prosecutors worked together to convict leading members of the five New York City Mafia families between 1980 and 2004

Principal personages:
> G. ROBERT BLAKEY, the author of the 1970 Racketeer Influenced and Corrupt Organizations (RICO) Act who persuaded Rudolph Giuliani to use this act in order to convict leading members of Mafia families
> JOE BONNANO, the head of the Bonnano Mafia family
> PAUL CASTELLANO, the head of the Gambino Mafia family
> VINCENT GIGANTE, the head of the Luciano/Genovese Mafia family
> JOHN GOTTI, the successor to Paul Castellano as the head of the Gambino Mafia family
> RUDOLPH GIULIANI, a federal prosecutor in the Southern District of New York and later the mayor of New York City (1993-2001)
> ANTHONY CASSO, the head of the Lucchese Mafia family
> CHARLES LUCIANO, the founder of the Genovese Mafia family
> CARMINE PERSICO, the head of the Profaci/Colombo Mafia family

Many people have an unrealistic view of American gangsters. Motion pictures such as *The Godfather* (1972) and popular television series such as *The Sopranos* do portray the violence committed by gangsters against other gangsters, but such works of fiction do not convey to viewers the terrible damage to American society as a whole and the destruction of entire neighborhoods as a result of organized crime. In the excellent history *Five Families*, Selwyn Raab describes quite well the unglamorous criminality of amoral Mafia gangsters who caused so much avoidable suffering during the last eight decades of the twentieth century.

In 1931, Charles "Lucky" Luciano and heads of other criminal "families" created a national "commission" that settled matters of national interest to Mafia leaders and strove to lessen competition between different Mafia families so that all the gangsters could profit from criminal activities such as loan-sharking, gambling, protection rackets, manipulation of labor unions, drug trafficking, prostitution, political

corruption, stealing cargo, and manipulation of
certain essential industries such as garbage pick-
up, construction, and shipping. Each Mafia family was organized into a specific structure, designed to protect each level from prosecution for
crimes committed by gangsters at a lower level
in the chain of command. At the head of each
family was the head, or godfather; below him
were his "underbosses," and below them were
the "capos," or captains, who implemented the
head's wishes and controlled the "soldiers" who
actually committed the crimes or murders for
their bosses. The tradition of *omerta*, or silence,
required all gangsters not to cooperate with police and prosecutors.

*For more than twenty-five years,
Selwyn Raab was an investigative
reporter for* The New York Times.
*More recently, he has written
extensively on the corruptive
influence of the Mafia on the quality
of life in New York City.*

From the 1920's until well into the 1970's,
this system worked effectively for the criminal
organization that has often been referred to as the
Mafia or La Cosa Nostra. Police officers would
regularly arrest Mafia soldiers for specific crimes,
but it was almost impossible to convict the capos and godfathers who received shares
of the profits from each crime. In the 1960's, the Federal Bureau of Investigation
(FBI) received the authority to tap the telephone wires of suspected criminals, but
wire tapping was not entirely effective because the information acquired that way
could be used against only those who actually spoke on recorded intercepts and unwittingly admitted the commission of specific crimes.

In 1970, an attorney named G. Robert Blakey, who had worked in the Justice Department investigating the activities of organized criminal syndicates, served as the
chief counsel to the Senate Subcommittee on Criminal Laws and Procedures whose
chairman was Senator John L. McClellan. Blakey and McClellan shepherded through
Congress the Organized Crime Control Act of 1970 that contains an important provision which has come to be known as RICO, for Racketeer Influenced and Corrupt Organizations section. The RICO provisions authorize prosecutors to indict those at all
levels of a criminal syndicate if the prosecutors can prove both a pattern of criminal
activity and the existence of a criminal enterprise.

Raab explains quite clearly that in the 1970's neither prosecutors nor criminals understood the breadth of the RICO provisions. Prosecutors were hesitant to bring a
RICO indictment because of serious questions about the constitutionality of the RICO
provisions. Mafia bosses, underbosses, and capos did not take seriously the RICO
provisions, thinking they amounted to an empty threat that would never be used
against them. They thought themselves to be insulated from criminal convictions because of the multitiered nature of their criminal enterprises. Traditionally, each criminal in a Mafia organization would claim to have no connection with other criminals,
and if a Mafia soldier was indicted for a specific crime, his or her Mafia family would

pay for his legal representation at his trial, and his wife and children would have their financial needs met if the soldier had the misfortune to be convicted and sent to prison.

Throughout the 1970's, Blakey tried unsuccessfully to persuade the FBI and the Department of Justice to use RICO in order to attack the very highest levels of Mafia families. At first he was ignored, but things slowly began to change after 1978, with the appointment of former federal judge William Webster as the FBI director. Webster very much wanted the FBI to go after the Mafia, and he instructed Neil Welch, then the special agent in charge of the FBI's New York field office, to meet with Blakey to learn how RICO could be used against the Mafia. Blakey explained to Welch and to several high-ranking special agents that RICO granted extraordinary powers to the FBI and federal prosecutors. RICO made it easier for federal judges to approve requests for wire taps, permitted the seizure of property acquired as a result of criminal activity, and authorized life sentences without the possibility of parole for those who were convicted of involvement in a criminal enterprise. Under the RICO provisions, Mafia bosses, underbosses, and capos could all be convicted for crimes committed by the soldiers in their criminal enterprise.

With the support of Director Webster, agents in the FBI's New York field office began obtaining court orders for wire taps, and information obtained from initial wire taps was then used to obtain court approval for wire taps against higher ranking members in all five of New York's Mafia families.

Slowly FBI agents began to acquire proof of the existence of the five New York Mafia families and detailed information about the chain of command and specific types of crimes carried out by the various families. The appointment of Rudolph Giuliani in 1983 as the federal prosecutor for the Southern District of New York, which includes Manhattan, the Bronx, and the counties just north of New York City, had a profound impact on the prosecution of high-ranking Mafia gangsters. As an Italian American, Giuliani despised the Mafia, as did many law-abiding Italian Americans who were ashamed of the way the Mafia's criminal activities dishonored their ethnic heritage. Five of Giuliani's uncles had served in the New York Police Department, and his cousin had been killed in the line of duty as a NYC police officer. Giuliani enthusiastically cooperated with the FBI's New York field office. He used the information acquired through years of wire tapping by the FBI's New York field office to indict leading members of all five New York Mafia families on a RICO indictment in 1995, and the subsequent trial resulted in the conviction of all those accused on all charges. This trial has come to be known as the commission case, and the lead prosecutor was Michael Chertoff. As Blakey had hoped, this was just the first of many RICO indictments against members of the national Mafia.

Federal prosecutors and FBI agents understood all too well that the successful conclusion of the commission case did not destroy the Mafia, because new criminals simply took the places of those who had been sent to federal prison for life. Prosecutors realized very quickly that the Mafia would do anything in order to retain its power. Murders of witnesses and jury tampering occurred with great frequency.

Federal prosecutors recognized the need to hide the true identities of jurors at RICO trials, and extensive use was made of the witness protection program to keep safe from Mafia assassins those who testified against gangsters. Overt attempts at jury manipulation were thwarted when federal judges prevented lawyers such as Lloyd Cutler, John Gotti's lawyer, from making disparaging remarks about witnesses by threatening to hold such Mafia lawyers in contempt of court. Cutler was even excluded from representing Gotti at a 1992 trial when federal prosecutors proved that Cutler was involved in a criminal conspiracy with Gotti and therefore could not represent him at trial. At this trial, Gotti's new lawyer, Albert Krieger, was not allowed to intimidate or disparage witnesses. After Gotti's conviction, he was sent to the maximum-security federal prison in Marion, Illinois. He died in prison in 2002. By then his criminal empire had been almost destroyed. His fellow thugs were either dead or serving long prison terms.

Raab describes quite well how successfully FBI agents and federal prosecutors have continued to pursue organized crime since Gotti's conviction in 1992. In a separate 1992 trial, Vittorio Amuso, head of the Lucchese Mafia family, was sentenced to life in prison, and his successor Anthony Casso was also sentenced to life in prison. Both Amuso and Casso were convicted under the RICO provisions. Juries found them guilty of participation in a criminal enterprise and that the crimes committed under their orders demonstrated a pattern of criminal activity, the two requirements for conviction under RICO.

In his final chapters, Raab describes the positive changes that have occurred as a result of all the RICO convictions. Mafia families have lost their control over unions, and union members are no longer being exploited by corrupt leaders who enrich themselves and Mafia leaders at the expense of innocent union members. The price of concrete and construction materials in New York City is no longer under gangster control, making it less expensive to construct buildings there. The cost of garbage removal has decreased significantly in New York City because there is now fair competition among private waste removal companies.

In his concluding chapter, Raab expresses the concern that, should the FBI and federal prosecutors relent in their pursuit of organized crime, criminal enterprises such as the Mafia or new gangs such as the Russian Mafia may once again be able to threaten and exploit law-abiding citizens. Raab notes that the terrorist attacks of September 11, 2001, have caused the FBI to devote a great amount of its resources to preventing further terrorist attacks against the United States and its allies. This is an understandable concern, but the need for the FBI to investigate organized terrorist cells and organizations should not prevent the bureau from continuing to pursue organized crime. It is notable that Michael Chertoff, who was the lead federal prosecutor in the 1986 commission case in the Southern District of New York, became in 2005 secretary of the Department of Homeland Security. Chertoff and FBI leaders understand that terrorists and organized gangsters both represent serious threats to the security of the United States.

Edmund J. Campion

Review Sources

Booklist 102, no. 2 (September 15, 2005): 12.
Entertainment Weekly, September 16, 2005, p. 95.
Kirkus Reviews 73, no. 12 (June 15, 2005): 674.
Library Journal 125, no. 14 (September 1, 2005): 162.
The New York Times Book Review 154 (September 11, 2005): 9.
Publishers Weekly 252, no. 22 (May 30, 2005): 48.

FLEDGLING

Author: Octavia E. Butler (1947-2006)
Publisher: Seven Stories Press (New York). 316 pp. $24.95
Type of work: Novel
Time: The early twenty-first century
Locale: Seattle and Northern California

This novel concerns an entire race of ancient people, the Ina, who have their own history, customs, and traditions; stronger, with heightened senses, they are more advanced than humans but rely entirely upon the human population for survival, as they survive by drinking human blood

Principal characters:
> SHORI MATTHEWS, the protagonist, who learns the ways of the Ina
> WRIGHT HAMLIN, her first symbiont
> THEODORA HARDEN, her second symbiont
> RALEIGH CURTIS, a guard of the burned village
> IOSIF PETRESCU, Shori's father
> STEFAN PETRESCU, Shori's brother
> BROOKE, a former symbiont of Iosif
> CELIA, Brooke's daughter and Stefan's former symbiont
> THE GORDONS, the Ina family that takes in Shori and her symbionts
> DANIEL GORDON, the Gordon with whom Shori agrees to mate when she matures
> VICTOR COLON, an attacker sent by the Silks to kill Shori
> MILO SILK, the patriarch of the Silk family
> JACK ROAN, Katherine Silk's symbiont, who kills Theodora

In her final novel, Octavia E. Butler took the romantic and supernatural notion of vampires and created an engaging, entertaining tale which serves as a commentary on race and societal workings. *Fledgling* offers a vampire that is not paranormal, does not harm its human victims, and, despite high intelligence and knowledge, is susceptible to flaws that commonly plague societies, such as bigotry, racism, and ignorance.

Fledgling begins with a young, confused, and hungry Shori Matthews awakening in a pitch-black cave, badly injured and blinded. As she regains consciousness, she finds she has no idea who or where she is, and that she is starving. Alone and desperately hungry, she captures what she thinks is an animal (later discovering it was a man), kills it with her bare hands, and eats it raw, beginning her healing process and her first step toward regaining her identity and discovering what she is.

When Shori is able to walk, she unwittingly returns to a burned-out village. Unaware of where she is or why she walked there, she begins to sift through the rub-

Octavia E. Butler was the author of more than fourteen novels and short-story collections. She received the MacArthur Foundation "genius" grant, the Hugo Award, the Nebula Award, and a lifetime achievement award in writing from PEN, as well as many other recognitions. She died in 2006 at the age of fifty-eight.

ble, looking for survivors and salvaging what she can. Shori feels a connection to the burned rubble but has no idea why and cannot remember anything of her past, including her name.

In her state of confusion, Shori is picked up by Wright Hamlin, who believes she is an abused child, as she appears to be about eleven years old. In his car, Shori is overwhelmed by his scent and bites his hand to suck his blood before she realizes what she is doing. Wright is taken aback at first but quickly succumbs to Shori and begs her not to stop. This is the first glimpse Butler offers the reader into Shori's true identity; through her recovery, Shori will discover she is not human.

Wright takes her home and realizes that although Shori looks like a child, she is much older than she appears. The two begin a sexual relationship. Shori instinctively knows how much of Wright's blood she can take to stave off her hunger without causing him harm. She realizes, however, that he alone will not be able to sustain her, and she searches the neighboring houses for her next meal. She finds it in a lonely older woman, Theodora Harden.

During the day, Shori surfs the Internet, researching vampires and the burned village, hoping to glean insight into the life she has lost. She is unable to learn anything about who or what she is. Butler cleverly inserts modern technology and products throughout *Fledgling* to keep the novel and characters realistic and nonsupernatural. Shori feels compelled to revisit the fire scene, and Wright agrees to take her to the rubble. Once there, the two are assaulted by a young man, Raleigh Curtis, who is guarding the site. Shori bites him and begins to question him, intuitively knowing that biting humans places them at her mercy. She discovers that Curtis has been bitten by another of her kind. She instructs the man to tell his master that she will return to the ruins on a specified date, in hope of meeting him and learning what she is and what has become of her family.

Shori and Wright return to the designated meeting place and are met by a very tall, thin, pale man who is overcome by happiness when he sees Shori. He explains that he is her father, Iosif Petrescu. He begs her to return with him to his village, where she will live until she reaches maturity. Shori is fifty-three years old, still a child among their community in which people typically live for hundreds of years.

Shori and Wright accompany Iosif to his home, which is a compound filled with houses and people. Although Shori has no recollection of the community, everyone there is happy to see her and relieved that she is alive. Iosif immediately begins to answer Shori's questions of who and what she is. He explains that she is Ina, an ancient race, and explains, "We have our own traditions—our own folklore, our own religions." Similar to vampires of folklore, Ina must feed on human blood to survive, but they do not harm the human. They are taller and thinner than humans, with advanced senses. Ina live for hundreds of years and awaken only at night.

Iosif goes on to explain that each Ina selects specific people to feed on, and a human who agrees to live with an Ina will become that Ina's symbiont. Once the symbiosis is formed, the symbiont can only be fed upon by his or her Ina, for another Ina's venom would cause both Ina and human pain and sickness. The human provides the Ina with life-sustaining blood, and the Ina's venom, in return, is not only pleasurable but also fortifies the human's immune and circulatory systems, allowing the human to live four times as long as he or she normally would. Symbionts feel lucky to have been chosen; their Ina protect them, increase their lifespan, and shelter them and their families. Symbionts are free to carry on normal lives, but they must live with their Ina, for without Ina venom the symbiont will die. The symbiotic relationship between the highly developed Ina and humans is analogous to humankind's relationship with the environment: Neither can live without the other, a warning Butler frequently issues in her novels.

Shori also learns from Iosif that she is a living Ina experiment. In her, her grandmothers mixed Ina DNA with human, African American DNA, giving Shori dark skin which allows her limited exposure to the sun and enables her to stay awake during the day. Iosif believes that the human DNA saved her life during the attack on the village. He informs Shori that the burned-out village was the home of her female relatives and their symbionts; adult Ina males and females live separately and come together only to mate. Iosif theorizes that Shori's mother and grandmothers were killed in order to stop the experiments and to keep the Ina lines pure. Because Shori has lost her female family, she is permitted to live with Iosif and her male relatives until she is fully mature. She agrees and arranges for Wright and Theodora to join them. Iosif gives Wright driving instructions, and they agree to see one another in a week's time.

When they return to the compound, they find smoldering rubble. Again, an Ina community has been burned and its inhabitants killed, and once again, the victims are relatives of Shori. As Shori and Wright sort through the ashes, Brooke and Celia, symbionts of Iosif and Shori's brother Stefen, return home to find their community and families destroyed. Devastated and afraid, Shori, Wright, Brooke, and Celia head to a remote cabin Iosif owned in order to plan their next move in safety. Upon their arrival, however, the house is attacked and burned. This time the four fight off their attackers, killing a few, and flee. This third attack proves the theory that the murderers are after Shori.

Unaware of any other Ina, Shori questions Brooke and Celia, who tell her of another Ina clan, the Gordons, in Northern California. Shori befriends the Gordon family and learns more of her heritage and that of other Ina families. The Gordons invite her and her symbionts to live with them, and Shori sends for Theodora. Shori and the symbionts begin keeping watch during the day, when the Ina must sleep. As Shori is settling into her new home, the community is attacked. Her advanced senses of hearing and smell give the symbionts on guard plenty of warning, and they kill all but three of the attackers before any Ina or symbionts suffer serious harm. Shori and the elders bite and question the surviving attackers and learn that the Ina family responsible for the attacks is the Silk family from Pasadena, California. As suspected, they have attacked Shori and her families in an attempt to kill her and prevent any further experimentation, revealing that even an advanced society can be susceptible to ignorance and fear.

Once it is determined that the Silks have committed the murders, the Gordons organize a Council of Judgment meeting among members of seven ancient families, including both the Silks and the Gordons (Shori's representatives). The meeting will determine the Silks' fate should they be deemed guilty. As the families arrive at the compound, Shori learns more of her heritage as she meets distant relatives. During the council meetings, Theodora is found dead, an attack intended to harm Shori further. It is determined that Theodora was last seen with one of the council members, Katherine Dahlman's symbiont Jack Roan, who has since escaped the grounds. Katherine, a Silk, is removed from the hearings and is placed on trial herself. During the trials, Ina prejudice is revealed when Milo Silk tells Shori, "You are not Ina . . . and you have no more business at this council than would a clever dog!"

Shori is able to continue with the relentless questioning, accusations, and insults made against her and her ancestors, while coping with the overwhelming guilt, grief, and physical pain of losing a symbiont, after a council member tells her to "remember your dead. Keep them around you." The trials uncover a prejudice certain Ina have not only against mixing their DNA with that of humans but also against ethnic diversity and scientific progress. Through Shori's strength, she is able to counter the bigotry and vows "to stop them from hunting me. To stop them from killing anyone else." As the trial is ending, Shori finally receives the answers she has searched for and the acceptance and belonging she has craved; she declares in front of the council: "I am Ina."

With *Fledgling*, Butler again produced a strong African American protagonist, a woman who is forced to take on more than any one person should have to bear. As in her other novels, Butler creates multilayered histories around her characters. In *Fledgling* she creates an entire race of people. Typical of Butler's style, the author uses the race of Ina to explore racism and relationships and, in doing so, to make social commentaries. In general, Butler's works serve to illuminate how some people misspend their lives and the effects of one's choices on future generations. *Fledgling* is no exception, with Butler warning that not only is modern society susceptible to fear and prejudice born of ignorance, but also that it must work on improving and appreciating its symbiotic relationship with nature and the environment if the human race is to survive. Butler's groundbreaking career was cut short when she died in early 2006 following a stroke.

Sara Vidar

Review Sources

Booklist 102, no. 4 (October 15, 2005): 37.
Entertainment Weekly, October 21, 2005, p. 80.
Essence 35, no. 6 (October, 2005): 96.
Kirkus Reviews 73, no. 16 (August 15, 2005): 867-868.
Library Journal 130, no. 13 (August 1, 2005): 66.
Publishers Weekly 252, no. 33 (August 22, 2005): 36.

FLESHMARKET ALLEY

Author: Ian Rankin (1960-   )
First published: Fleshmarket Close, 2004, in Great Britain
Publisher: Little, Brown (New York). 421 pp. $23.00
Type of work: Novel
Time: Around 2003
Locale: Edinburgh, Scotland

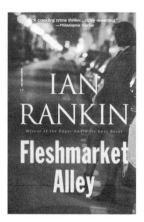

*Scotland's best-known policeman confronts new chal-
lenges following the murder of an asylum seeker*

> *Principal characters:*
> JOHN REBUS, a detective inspector in the
>   Lothian and Borders Police
> SIOBHAN CLARKE, a detective sergeant who
>   often works with Rebus
> MORRIS GERALD CAFFERTY, called BIG
>   GER, an Edinburgh gangster and Rebus's longtime nemesis
> STEF YURGII, a murdered Turkish Kurd asylum seeker
> FELIX STOREY, an immigration officer
> CARO QUINN, a painter and human rights protester
> RAY MANGOLD, the landlord of the pub The Warlock
> MR. AND MRS. JARDINE, the parents of Tracy and Ishbel
> TRACY JARDINE, rape victim and suicide
> ISHBEL JARDINE, the Jardines' missing daughter
> DONNY CRUIKSHANK, a convicted rapist
> STUART BULLEN, the owner of The Nook, a lap-dancing bar
> MR. TRAYNOR, the governor of Whitemire Detention Centre
> MO DIRWAN, a Glasgow-based human rights lawyer
> KWAME MANA, called KATE, a Sengalese student at the University of
>   Edinburgh and dancer at The Nook
> CHANTAL RENDILLE, a Sengalese student who witnessed Yurgii's
>   murder
> PETER HILL, Yurgii's murderer

Genre fiction has often had to pay for its popularity by being looked upon as subliterary, especially in the United States where cultural arbiters tend to be overly scrupulous in distinguishing "real" (or "high") art from mass entertainments such as science fiction, romance, and mystery. Since the 1960's, popular culture has been treated with increasing seriousness, within the academy and without. As a result, the boundary between the literary novel and genre fiction has become increasingly porous. Nowhere is this change more evident than in the detective novel, especially in its Scottish branch, which has come to house a distinctive and often quite literary subgenre of it own: tartan noir.

Tartan noir's roots reach back to William McIlvanney's Laidlaw series (begun in 1978), arguably earlier still to the Sherlock Holmes stories of Arthur Conan Doyle (trained at Edinburgh University) and even the *Private Confessions of a Justified Sinner* (1824) by James Hogg, an influence on Edgar Allan Poe, originator of the American detective story. Recent novels by Louise Welsh, Val McDiarmid, and Denise Mina have greatly extended tartan noir's range, but it is Ian Rankin who not only serves as the bridge between then (McIlvanney) and now (Mina et al.) but who is also the person most responsible for putting tartan noir on the global literary map.

Rankin published his first novel in 1986 and his first detective fiction the following year. With few exceptions, he has stayed with the form and the same detective ever since. Genre fiction depends, as genres in general do, on repetition to create a sense of sameness, ringing its variations on a theme, while maintaining a high degree of stylistic and structural uniformity. Rankin's John Rebus novels are no exception. What distinguishes Rankin's detective novels (or, more accurately, "police procedurals") is the way in which, and the degree to which, Rankin incorporates these differences within one novel and

Since winning the Crime Writers' Association's Gold Dagger Award in 1997, Ian Rankin has become both internationally renowned and Britain's best-selling crime writer. He was awarded an Order of the British Empire in 2002 and the Crime Writers Association Cartier Diamond Dagger for lifetime achievement in 2005, the same year that Fleshmarket Close *was selected the Crime Thriller of the Year at the British Book Awards.*

from novel to novel. His still unfinished series is now nearly two decades old. Rankin's breakthrough came in 1997, when he won the Crime Writers' Association's prestigious Gold Dagger Award for *Black and Blue*, his eighth Rebus novel (and ninth Rebus book, including a collection of Rebus short stories). His novels shot to the tops of Scottish best-sellers lists, gaining a worldwide audience.

Along the way, the Edinburgh in which all but one of the Rebus books are set became known as "the crime capital of the world"—or more accurately, the crime fiction capital. This labeling of Scotland's capital city is a bit odd. The real Edinburgh, which has a very low homicide rate, seems better suited to novels about history such as James Robertson's *The Fanatic* (2000) or, given its reputation for class-bound propriety and Calvinist repression, Muriel Spark's *The Prime of Miss Jean Brodie* (1961)—at least until Irvine Welsh's *Trainspotting* appeared on the scene in 1993. Larger, newer, more urban-industrial Glasgow, with its history of gang violence, seems a more likely setting for crime fiction, as McIlvanney's, Mina's, and Louise Welsh's novels demonstrate.

Part of Rankin's achievement, therefore, is the way he capitalizes on Edinburgh's dramatic Dr. Jekyll and Mr. Hyde-like topography, making the setting both physically real and thematically revealing of the nation no less than the characters. More a collection of villages than a monolithic urban center, Edinburgh's divisions are dramatically apparent in the contrast between Old and New Towns. The New Town's rectilinear layout embodies the ideals of the eighteenth century Enlightenment, and its street names (Rose, George, King, Queen, and so on) evidence the wedding of Scotland's economic, sociocultural, and political destiny to England's following the 1707 Act of Union. The medieval Old Town looms above, with its subterranean depths and mazelike streets whose very names imply a not quite vanished past: its Tollgates and Canongates, its Lawnmarkets, Grassmarkets, Fishmarkets and, yes, Fleshmarkets.

Rebus's name is highly evocative as well as appropriate, referring to a kind of picture puzzle. Rebus is himself a puzzle within the puzzle that is each novel. Because the novels take place in real time, starting in the mid-1980's, the Rebus of *Fleshmarket Alley* is seventeen years older than when the series began. He is a year older and a bit slower and a year closer to mandatory retirement with each novel. In *Fleshmarket Alley* he is also a bit more mellow, less haunted by his past, especially his past failings as husband and father, and less desperate in his drinking and smoking and what previously seemed an almost suicidal pursuit of wrongdoers. This time around, Rankin has him do nothing more physical than carry a bottle of single malt to his Arden Street flat, lift a pint of India Pale Ale at his favorite hangout, the Oxford Bar, and accidentally fall a few feet through an open trapdoor.

Rebus is still a loner, however. Unlike Doyle's Sherlock Holmes, he has no learned amanuensis, and unlike Agatha Christie's character Hercule Poirot, no comic sidekick. Rebus did take a fatherly interest in Brian Holmes, but Holmes left the police force several novels ago. Rebus has at times taken a more than fatherly interest in Siobhan Clarke, his former partner, sole confidant (to the degree he confides in anyone) and heir apparent. After twenty years, Rebus's Arden Street flat still looks more occupied than lived in. When he wants company, he either calls Clarke or goes to the Oxford Bar (whose back room is impervious to cell phone signals). He makes even less effort than usual to pursue this novel's love interest. Rebus lives to work, but as knight errant; no joining the Masons, that favorite institution of the Scottish police, for him.

Now even his work is threatened. The Crime Investigation Division (CID) office in his "old hunting ground," St. Leonard's police station, has been shut down, and Rebus and Clarke have been reassigned to Gayfield, where Clarke has been given a desk and he has not. "'I'm not supposed to be here,' Detective Inspector John Rebus said. Not that anybody was listening," the novel begins.

"Here" might as well be Gayfield or, less synechdochically, Lothian and Borders police, but in fact "here" is Knoxland, a housing scheme, as they are called in Scotland (housing estates in England, housing projects in the United States). Although Knoxland is fictional—and therefore highly unusual because Rankin almost always uses real places: Gayfield, St. Leonard's, Arden Street, Fleshmarket Close (changed to "Alley" for the American market)—it is typical of the housing constructed in Scotland in the 1960's: places where real needs, high ideals, good intentions, inadequate planning, and worse materials came together too soon become breeding grounds for the disaffection, drug addiction, violence, and social decay that Irvine Welsh depicts so well.

In *Set in Darkness* (2000), Rebus bitterly notes that one such scheme will soon be razed and its residents dispersed, not to improve their lot but because this particular scheme, located so close to the new Scottish parliament, occupies land suddenly too valuable to leave to the underclass. In *Fleshmarket Alley*, Knoxland (named for Scotland's founding Calvinist, John Knox, its individual buildings named for the nation's most famous writers: Sir Walter Scott, Robert Burns, James Barrie, and Robert Louis Stevenson) is located too far from the city center to be of any value except to the government as a human warehouse. It is also where the novel begins and the first murder occurs.

The victim is an unidentified "tan-skinned," "Asian-looking" male. Tabloid journalist Steve Holly believes the murder is a hate crime, Edinburgh's first in what promises to be a growth area. Rebus is not so sure; he knows that Knoxland is rife with possibilities, race being one, drugs another, casual violence a third. One of the reasons Rankin's novels are so interesting is that they are often so topical, as in his treatment of asylum seekers in *Fleshmarket Alley*. Much criticized for supposedly exploiting the case of an immigrant murdered in Glasgow, Rankin in fact uses the novel to expose and explore in detail and with no less sympathy an issue which has not received much attention and which, when it does, is often seen as an a Glaswegian problem.

In Scotland, and especially in Edinburgh, immigration issues—along with the immigrant population—remain largely invisible. The declining birth rate combined with continued emigration make the influx of foreigners, including asylum seekers, increasingly necessary to Scotland's future. Rankin makes clear how dependent economically depressed villages such as the novel's fictional Banehall are on the existence of detention (or "removal") centers such as Whitemire, run for the government by a private American contractor, where conditions are deplorable, despair the norm, suicide attempts not infrequent, and opportunities for exploitation and corruption plentiful. As Rebus notes, there is "more than one kind of fleshmarket."

There is also more than one kind of mystery in *Fleshmarket Alley*. A few pages after Rebus visits the Knoxland murder scene, the parents of Tracy Jardine, whose rapist, Donnie Cruikshank, Clarke helped convict but who later was released, request help with a new problem. Their younger daughter, Ishbel, has disappeared. Shortly thereafter, two skeletons are discovered in the cellar of a pub on Fleshmarket Alley, just off the touristy Royal Mile in the heart of Edinburgh's old town. The novel traces the course of the subsequent investigations, plus one more—midway through the novel Cruikshank is bludgeoned to death.

More than thirty-two chapters plus epilogue cover ten days, Monday through the Wednesday of the following week. In almost any other writer's hands, this plot would seem impossibly contrived. Its many implausible coincidences are not, however, distracting in *Fleshmarket Alley*, or in most of the other Rebus novels. Building suspense through crosscutting from one investigation to another, and building momentum through equally deft pacing, Rankin makes the confluence of so many diverse narrative strands and characters seem entirely believable. He accomplishes this without introducing a single red herring, as is fitting given the novel's two conceits: the jigsaw puzzle and the spider's web—both hoary clichés yet, again, utterly convincing.

Rankin weaves together housing schemes and housing scams, drug peddling and paramilitaries, asylum seekers and lap dancers, human rights and human slavery, the influx of immigrants and the outsourcing of services, sexual predators and human rights activists, good cops and bad, missing daughters and Senglaese students, and much more in a web of contingencies which takes on an aura of inevitability that Rebus tries to control, but with only limited success. At novel's end, mysteries are solved, some of the villains caught, but the one pulling the strings remains at large, known to Rebus but beyond his power. With four years and perhaps as many as four novels to go before he must retire, Rebus will have more chances to do what he can within the limits Rankin has established for him.

Robert A. Morace

Review Sources

Booklist 101, no. 7 (December 1, 2004): 619.
Entertainment Weekly, February 4, 2005, pp. 137-139.
Kirkus Reviews 72, no. 24 (December 15, 2004): 1169.
Library Journal 130, no. 1 (January, 2005): 85-86.
New Statesman, 133 (October 4, 2004): 54-55.
The New York Times Book Review 154 (February 6, 2005): 25.
Publishers Weekly 252, no. 2 (January 10, 2005): 41-42.
The Times Literary Supplement, October 1, 2004, p. 22.

FOLLIES
New Stories

Author: Ann Beattie (1947-   )
Publisher: Scribner (New York). 305 pp. $25.00
Type of work: Short fiction

In a novella and nine stories, the spokeswoman for the passive and uncommitted takes a largely comic look at baby boomers growing older

Often labeled the spokeswoman of the yuppie generation of the 1960's and 1970's, Ann Beattie has been alternately praised for her satiric view of that era's notorious passivity and criticized for presenting sophisticated, *New Yorker*-magazine versions of characters unable to understand themselves and unwilling to understand others. In the collection *Follies*, Beattie departs from her so-called minimalism and plays with a variety of literary parodies and comic voices. Instead of being tight-lipped, she is downright voluble. Instead of writing in an impassive monotone, she skips about her characters with self-conscious authorial glee. For the first time, she seems to be having a good time in her writing.

The longest story in the book, taking up over one-third of it, is the novella *Fléchette Follies*. The title is a sly joke about the tone and structure of the novella itself, for "flechette" is a type of ammunition used in cluster bombs and "follies" is a kind of slapstick comic romp; both terms describe the narrative style of the story very well. The main characters are a man named George Wissone, who gets in a minor traffic accident one morning with a woman named Nancy Gregerson in Charlottesville, Virginia (where Beattie is an English professor at the University of Virginia). Because Gregerson is worried about her son, Nick, who has disappeared in London—a victim, she supposes, of drug traffic and street life—she is curt and rude to Wissone, accusing him of having too much to drink. Later, she regrets her behavior, and when she runs into him at a coffee shop, she apologizes and they have a chat.

Puzzled by his reluctance to talk about his own life, she jokes that he is probably a Central Intelligence Agency (CIA) operative and asks if he would go to London and try to find her son. As it turns out—in true follies, almost slapstick, fashion—Wissone is indeed a CIA agent; furthermore, as he is not involved in a serious assignment at the time, he is quite happy to search for Gregerson's son, not because he is attracted to Gregerson or eager to do a good turn for her but merely because he wants to see if he can be a responsive human being, willing to do someone a favor when the goal is not money, sex, or danger. He wants to do something he thinks a normal person with a normal life would do.

However, again in true follies fashion, Wissone's task is anything but normal, and Beattie's story is anything but realistic or minimalistic. When Wissone gets to En-

Ann Beattie has had four short stories included in The O. Henry Prize Stories *(1980, 1985, 1988, and 2002); one of her stories, "Janus," was also included in* The Best American Short Stories of the Century *(1999), edited by John Updike. She has received the PEN/Bernard Malamud Award for excellence in the short story, as well as the REA Award for the Short Story.*

gland, he makes inquiries, and then abruptly, as if Beattie has no other purpose than to get him out of the way so she can hurry on to the end of the story, George Wissone steps out into the street and is run down by a cab hurriedly taking a pregnant woman to a doctor's appointment. He dies immediately, trapped under the cab. The remainder of the novella deals with Wissone's best friend and colleague trying to find out what happened to him, pursuing an investigation that includes an annoying interview with Nancy Gregerson, who finally orders him and his wife out of her house. *Fléchette Follies* is a curious piece of heavily plotted work for the previously laconic Beattie. Although it is a pleasure to read because of the author's clever narrative style, it is mostly a bit of writerly fun, a playful parody combining light comedy and intrigue.

The collection's other long story, "That Last Odd Day in L.A.," is more like some of Beattie's previous short pieces, for it focuses on one of her baby boomer characters now grown older. The protagonist has made a lot of money by investing early in Microsoft; now he is divorced and dating a woman, but the relationship is desultory at best. He recalls a day in Los Angeles when he rescued a baby possum from a swimming pool and seemed to receive a benediction or blessing from a deer. The story ends when the son of the woman he is dating shoots him, and he winds up in the emergency room, where he has an epiphany of sorts about how he has undermined his past relationships with his wife and his children.

In the contributors' notes to the 2002 edition of *The O. Henry Prize Stories*, Beattie says "That Last Odd Day in L.A." began when, enduring cold weather in Rome, she tried to think of warmer places and Los Angeles came to mind. Like *Fléchette Follies*, the story does not seem to have any purposeful direction but rather meanders along like a pleasant Beattie riff, filled with multiple popular and high culture references: to a song made famous by Jimmy Durante, a film with Robert DeNiro, a novel by Robert Penn Warren, and the ending of James Joyce's *Ulysses* (1922). The seemingly random way the story rambles about aimlessly is suggested by Beattie's remark that she hardly knew where the story was going until she reached the part when the protagonist fishes what he thinks is a dead possum out of a swimming pool and then watches it scamper away. She says then she suddenly saw the underlying intention of the story but was unprepared herself for the violence of the ending. Although the theme of "playing possum" may indeed be here, the story is mostly a bit of stylistic fun that Beattie is having with one of her characters growing older.

Several other stories in the collection are light experiments with various academic and literary conventions. In "Duchais," a graduate student fills in for his sick roommate, taking a job as a professor's research assistant. However, he is actually made to do a variety of household chores—going to the dry cleaners, mixing drinks, serving as a butler and houseboy at the professor's home. Years later, after he has become a lawyer and has returned to Virginia for a twentieth class reunion, he stands in front of the old professor's house and remembers himself as a young man who had tried to prove he could face difficult things but instead had felt like a helpless child.

"Apology for a Journey Not Taken," subtitled "How to Write a Story," is a playful literary game in which a woman has to postpone a planned trip over and over again because of a series of unexpected events. The story begins with the narrator saying she could explain why she was not where she should have been, but that perhaps the story should unfold by itself. In fact, the story—perhaps an illustrative exercise for one of Beattie's creative writing classes—is about the basic narrative truth that stories are, by their very nature, postponements of completion, for if there were no postponements, the story would end immediately.

"Find and Replace" is based on the metaphor of the word processing function by which a novelist can immediately change the name of a character by searching on all instances of the name and immediately replacing it with another. After the death of her father, the protagonist returns to her childhood home in Florida to be with her mother. However, she finds that, in a seemingly immediate "find and replace" fashion, the mother is planning to marry another man. The story is energized by the flippant voice of the daughter narrator, who at first is distressed by her mother's precipitous action, but, because of a serendipitous encounter with a young man at a car rental agency, realizes how things change, even in a very short time.

"The Rabbit Hole as Likely Explanation," another mother/daughter piece, is one of the most affecting stories in the collection. Taking its title from Lewis Carroll's *Alice's Adventures in Wonderland* (1865), the story focuses on a woman visiting her mother in a nursing home in Virginia. Trying to deal with her fear that her mother may be losing her mind, her banter with her mother illustrates Beattie's facility at creating clever repartee and quick-paced dialogue. One of the mother's verbal characteristics is to use the word "desperate" at inappropriate and unexpected times. However, often there is more truth in the mother's use of the word than absurdity. The story ends with the daughter beginning to cite the old Eastern conundrum about a man waking up one morning having dreamt he was a butterfly and then not being sure whether he is not really a butterfly, now dreaming he is a man. Instead, she seizes on the mother's verbal idiosyncrasy and says perhaps the man is dreaming that he is desperate.

In "The Garden Game," one of the shortest but most interesting narrative games in the collection, a woman remembers the summers she spent during her youth with her aunt and uncle in Maine. She particularly recalls a game her uncle played with her, hiding things in the garden for her to find the following year, pretending that the hiding and the subsequent finding were accidents. When she became a teenager, she had lost all interest in the game. As an adult, she wonders about all the metaphoric significance of all the treasures her uncle buried, for which she did not even care to hunt.

In "Just Going Out," the one truly chilling story in the collection, two cousins raised by their uncle and his various lady friends, become involved via e-mail with a young filmmaker from New York who tries to draw them into an exploitative relationship. Even in this story, Beattie cannot resist writerly reflections about how stories proceed and reach a conclusion. At the end, the narrator recalls a story about an explorer at the South Pole who got frostbite and knew he was going to die. Not wanting to be a burden to the others, he simply leaves the party with the famous line that he is going out and may be gone some time. A writer's interest, says the Beattie narrator, would be on the thoughts of the explorer as the snow hit his face, for the wind was in the hands of the writer, and as long as he made the story credible, the reader would feel what the explorer felt.

Follies is definitely a shift in style for Beattie's short fiction. It may be that as she has gotten older, she has grown tired of the fictional milieu she has developed over the years and now wants to play various literary games—parodying familiar genres, exploring metaphors, fooling around with the many narrative conventions she has mastered. The result is a lot of self-conscious, self-indulgent fun for both Beattie and the reader.

Charles E. May

Review Sources

Atlanta Journal and Constitution, June 12, 2005, p. 8L.
Booklist 101, no. 11 (February 1, 2005): 916.
Kirkus Reviews 73, no. 4 (February 15, 2005): 188.
Library Journal 130, no. 5 (March 15, 2005): 77-78.
Los Angeles Times, May 16, 2005, p. E9.
The New York Times 154 (April 26, 2005): E1-E8.
The New York Times Book Review 154 (May 22, 2005): 16.
Pittsburgh Post-Gazette, June 19, 2005, p. J4.
Publishers Weekly 252, no. 11 (March 14, 2005): 43-44.
St. Louis Post-Dispatch, May 15, 2005, p. C10.
The Washington Post, June 19, 2005, p. T03.

FOUCAULT AND THE IRANIAN REVOLUTION
Gender and the Seductions of Islamism

Authors: Janet Afary and Kevin B. Anderson (1948-   )
Publisher: University of Chicago Press (Chicago). 346 pp. $60.00; paperback
$24.00
Type of work: History, literary criticism, and philosophy
Time: 1978-1979
Locale: Iran and France

> *This critical analysis of French philosopher Michel Foucault's journalistic writings on the Iranian Revolution connects them to his better-known philosophical works*

Principal personages:
    MICHEL FOUCAULT (1926-1984), a French philosopher and professor of
    "The History of Systems of Thought" at the Collège de France
    MOHAMMAD REZA PAHLAVI (1919-1980), the shah of Iran's constitutional monarchy
    AYATOLLAH RUHOLLAH KHOMEINI (1900-1989), a Shiite Muslim cleric
    and supreme leader of the Islamic Republic of Iran

In the fall of 1978, the leading Italian newspaper *Corriere della sera* sent French philosopher Michel Foucault on two trips to Iran in order to report on the growing political unrest that would eventually develop into the Iranian Revolution of 1979. Foucault wrote eight brief articles for *Corriere della sera* as well as a number of others for French publications, all of which grew out of his two visits to Iran.

Only three of these articles have been available in English translations until Janet Afary and Kevin B. Anderson's book *Foucault and the Iranian Revolution: Gender and the Seductions of Islamism*. The authors reprint as an appendix to their book all of Foucault's writings on Iran, along with some of the attacks his reports generated in the French press. This alone is a valuable contribution to Foucault studies in the United States, yet Afary and Anderson's book is also certain to spark controversy and debate, because the bulk of the volume consists of a critical reading of Foucault's Iranian writings, which the writers use to question the theories presented in Foucault's better-known writings.

Before 1978, opposition to the government of Shah Mohammad Reza Pahlavi came from a variety of sources: liberal, secular groups that objected to the shah's human rights violations and the widespread corruption of the regime; Marxist groups that identified the shah with Western imperialism; and Islamic groups that were opposed to the shah's efforts to reduce the role of Islam in Iran, along with the country's growing modernization and Westernization. The trigger for more widespread revolt against the shah was a protest against an official press story that libeled the Ayatollah Ruhollah Khomeini in January, 1978, when several students were killed by the Iranian Army.

～

*Janet Afary is an associate professor
of history and women's studies at
Purdue University and the author
of* The Iranian Constitutional
Revolution: Grassroots Democracy,
Social Democracy, and the Origins
of Feminism *(1996). Kevin B.
Anderson is an associate professor
of political science and sociology at
Purdue University and the author
of* Lenin, Hegel, and Marxism: A
Critical Study *(1995).*

～

Traditions of Shiite Islam dictate that mourn-
ers memorialize a person forty days after his or
her death, so in February Shiite groups across
Iran organized marches to honor the fallen students and to protest the shah's regime. More
demonstrators were killed, and a continued cycle of protest and violence developed, organized around the Shiite forty-day tradition of
mourning. Eventually, as these protests gained
in strength and scope, the shah was forced to
flee the country in January, 1979.

Khomeini returned to Iran in February, and
the Islamic Republic that took power turned out
to be perhaps even more brutal and more repressive than the shah's monarchy. In the aftermath
of the revolution, there were numerous summary trials and executions; women's
rights, which had been expanded under the shah's Westernist regime, were curtailed;
and political opposition was quashed.

At the time he visited Iran, Michel Foucault held the position of professor of the
history of systems of thought at the Collège de France, a very prestigious post, and he
was one of France's most prominent intellectuals. He had risen through the ranks of
the French educational system on the strength of a number of controversial, groundbreaking books. One of Foucault's central contributions was a far-reaching critique of
the progressive notion of history. Modern people typically imagine that they are
better off than their forebears and that modern societies give greater individual autonomy to a greater number of people than premodern societies, yet Foucault questioned
the idea that human society—especially in the West—is generally advancing and that
the growth and extension of rationality has necessarily led to greater human freedoms.

For example, in *Discipline and Punish: The Birth of the Prison* (1977), one of
Foucault's most influential works, he examines the changes that have taken place in
philosophies of punishment over the last several hundred years. If most readers were
to look at this history, they might conclude that what they have seen is improvement:
Cruel corporal punishment has been replaced by a more humane system that emphasizes instead the rehabilitation of the prisoner. Foucault rejects this simple narrative.
He begins his book with two examples that are designed to illustrate the shift in approaches to punishment and criminality that took place between the eighteenth and
nineteenth centuries.

The first is a rather graphic, shocking description of a public execution that took
place in France in 1757: Robert Damiens, who had been convicted of the attempted
regicide of Louis XV, was drawn and quartered, in dramatic and brutal fashion, in
front of a large crowd. Foucault's second example is a description of the timetable of a
prisoner's day in a juvenile facility in Paris in 1837. The details in this document are
mundane—outlining periods of work and instruction—and what is notably absent

from the rules of the latter facility are spectacular bodily punishments. Yet Foucault resists the simple conclusion that this change necessarily represents progress. Instead, he argues, the goal of the latter system is "not to punish less, but to punish better."

The timetable of the institution, while less brutal, has extended its control over every moment and every activity of the prisoner's day; rather than attacking the criminal's body directly, the body is controlled from within by what Foucault calls discipline. The various techniques of the prison—most crucially, observation and examination—are designed to encourage prisoners to internalize the normalizing judgments of society and to monitor themselves. The modern prison may not exhibit the same obvious displays of power as the earlier, more spectacular public executions, but according to Foucault, power is more effectively wielded in this system. Most strikingly, Foucault argues that these "mechanisms of discipline" developed in the prison have "spread throughout the whole social body," into factories, hospitals, schools, and beyond. Thus, Foucault suggests that all of society is affected, in the modern West, by this disciplinary control: It have become "the disciplinary society."

In *Discipline and Punish*, Foucault therefore suggests that obvious forms of domination in the premodern period have been replaced by more insidious forms of domination in the modern period. Several of Foucault's other books follow a similar trajectory, likewise rejecting the progressive narrative of Western history. *Madness and Civilization* (1965) examines changes in attitudes toward and treatments of the mentally ill. *The Birth of the Clinic* (1973) looks at the development of the medical profession. *The History of Sexuality* (1978) analyzes shifting practices of and ideas about sexuality.

In each case, Foucault resists the conclusion that modern social practices—what philosophers typically call modernity—should be understood as necessarily more liberatory than past practices. Foucault's analysis of modernity therefore raised important questions which he continued to examine until his death in 1984. Some of the most crucial questions involved the possibilities for resistance and revolt. If one does live in a disciplinary society, in which power is so widespread and effective, how can individuals and oppressed groups effectively resist?

It was this concern with the possibilities of resistance to modern power that took Foucault to Iran in the first place. As he recounts in an interview republished in the book's appendix, what interested Foucault about the Iranian situation was that the revolutionaries managed to craft an effective resistance even under the repressiveness of the shah's regime, which was unafraid to use all the elements of modern power. "Yet, despite all this," Foucault said, "a people rose up in revolt." The explanation Foucault offers is that Shiite Islam was the force that allowed the people to resist the strength of modern state power.

Afary and Anderson's most basic criticism of Foucault's writings on Iran is fairly simple: They believe Foucault's portrait of the developing Iranian revolution was too enthusiastic and too uncritical, and he was therefore blind to the socially regressive tendencies of the Islamist revolutionaries (following common usage among scholars of Islam and the Middle East, Afary and Anderson use "Islamist" for the fundamentalist interpretation of Islam, in order to distinguish it from more liberal Islamic traditions). They see Foucault as far too eager to praise the resistance of the revolutionaries and, especially, to praise the role that Islam played in supporting the revolution. As Khomeini took power, and Islamism began to be used to support repressive violence and to curtail human rights, it cast suspicion on any earlier, more positive assessments of Islam as a political and social force.

Afary and Anderson's most significant line of argumentation is their analysis of the underlying attraction Islam might have had for Foucault. According to Afary and Anderson, the "deep flaws that marked [Foucault's] writings on Iran" cannot simply be dismissed "as aberrant or the product of a political mistake." Rather, his Iranian writings "accentuate some of the problematic consequences of his overall theoretical enterprise." The central problem in Foucault's theory, Afary and Anderson argue, is his unrelenting opposition to modernity, which led him into a dangerous sympathy with the Islamist protesters and their religious leaders. Because he rejected many of the achievements of modernity—for example, the expansion of civil rights for women and minorities through modern legal structures—Foucault was particularly susceptible to what the writers call, in the book's subtitle, "the seductions of Islamism."

The authors sketch what they call a perplexing affinity between Foucault, "this post-structuralist philosopher," and "the antimodernist Islamist radicals on the streets of Iran." Afary and Anderson emphasize several characteristics that they claim Foucault and the Islamists had in common: Both were "searching for a new form of political spirituality"; both "clung to idealized notions of premodern social orders"; both "were disdainful of modern liberal judicial systems"; and both were enamored of martyrdom, of "individuals who risked death in attempts to reach a more authentic existence." For Afary and Anderson, the similarities between Foucault and the Islamist radicals suggest the limits and dangers of the critique of modernity.

Foucault was certainly disappointed by the turn the Iranian Revolution took, and his final two writings on Iran expressed his "horror" at the violations of human rights that were becoming widespread. Foucault never returned publicly to the Iranian Revolution. Nonetheless, Afary and Anderson suggest that his disappointment over the turn of events may have led him to rethink aspects of his critique of modernity. However, the authors spend much less time developing this idea than in documenting what they see as Foucault's failure to respond appropriately to the Iranian Revolution.

The project Afary and Anderson undertake—to reread Foucault's Iranian writings in the light of his other works—is admirable. So is their choice to present Foucault's writings in their entirety. Yet there are two central weaknesses in the book's analysis. The first is Afary and Anderson's claim that Foucault's major writings "privileged premodern social relations over modern ones." It is true that Foucault questioned the obvious superiority of modernity, but this is not to say that he wished to replace a progressive narrative with a regressive one. His comparisons with premodern periods were designed, polemically at times, to challenge readers to recognize the hidden dominations of the modern age. He wished not to valorize traditional sources of authority but to critique "the disciplinary society" of modernity.

The second weakness is that Afary and Anderson have flattened somewhat the complexity of Foucault's thinking about the Iranian Revolution, which is more nuanced and less simplistically enthusiastic than their representation suggests. Foucault's writing, as presented in the appendix, demonstrates that he was less interested in the final outcome of the revolution—which he freely admitted he could not predict—than in "the revolutionary experience itself." When he analyzed the role of Islam, then, he was less interested in how the content of Islam would be translated into a practice of government than in the resources it provided for the people's resistance.

In any case, Afary and Anderson's book will certainly reopen debate on a very interesting moment in Foucault's life and work, and should lead to reconsiderations of some of the most difficult, yet most important, political and social questions of this time.

Eric A. Wolfe

Review Sources

Library Journal 130, no. 7 (April 15, 2005): 90.
Middle East Journal 59, no. 4 (Autumn, 2005): 701-702.
The Nation 281, no. 5 (August 15, 2005): 31-34.
The New York Review of Books 52, no. 18 (November 17, 2005): 15-18.

THE FOUNDERS ON RELIGION
A Book of Quotations

Editor: James H. Hutson (1937-)
Introduction by Hutson
Publisher: Princeton University Press (Princeton, N.J.).
   235 pp. $20.00
Type of work: History, philosophy, and religion
Time: The 1730's to the 1830's
Locale: The American colonies, before and after independence from Great Britain

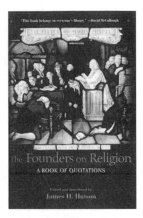

These quotations on more than seventy topics, organized alphabetically, express the religious views of seventeen members of the founding generation of the American republic

Americans have debated the relationship of religion and government since before the birth of their nation. Americans often use the words of the Founders to support their position on the relationship of church and state. Hutson's book provides ample evidence that the views of the Founders are complex, and that it is problematic to use quotes from them as proof texts for any particular position. A study of this book makes it clear that there is little consensus among the Founders when it comes to the topic of religion.

This book is valuable to specialists and nonspecialists alike who want to form an accurate picture of the religious convictions of the Founders. The views of the Founders provide food for thought for historians and all who want to reflect on the role of religion in American society in the light of their thinking.

James H. Hutson presents the religious views of the Founders on a wide range of themes in their own words. This collection of quotations provides a comprehensive picture of what the Founders thought about religion. In contrast to books on the Founders' religious views that quote them selectively in order to support a particular agenda, Hutson provides a large collection of complete quotes that illustrate the depth and diversity of the Founders' religious beliefs.

Hutson presents material that has not been seen by many specialists. He has found new sources that allow for an improved understanding of the Founders' religious views on a variety of topics.

Hutson has already established himself as the foremost authority on the religious views of the American Founders. He wrote or edited three other books on religion and America's founding generation prior to the appearance of *The Founders on Religion*. In *Forgotten Features of the Founding: The Recovery of Religious Themes in the Early American Republic* (2003), Hutson challenges assumptions long held by many American historians about the importance of religion in early American history. He argues that the percentage of the population who regularly attended church services at the time of the American Revolution was approximately 70 percent, not 10 percent, as other historians have claimed. In *Religion and the New Republic: Faith in the Founding of America* (2000) and *Religion and the Founding of the American Republic* (1998), Hutson discusses the role of religion in the American colonies' fight for independence and in the Founders' understanding of the role and limits of religion for the well-being of the American republic.

In *The Founders on Religion*, Hutson quotes both the famous members of America's founding generation as well as those whose renown has diminished with time. Hutson includes, in addition to those of the first four presidents, George Washington, John Adams, Thomas Jefferson and James Madison, statements from other well-known Founders, such as Benjamin Franklin, scientist and first American ambassador to France; Alexander Hamilton, aide-de-camp to

James H. Hutson has been chief of the Manuscript Division of the Library of Congress since 1982. In addition to the books he has written or edited about the role of religion in early American history, his more important contributions to the study of American history include John Adams and the Diplomacy of the American Revolution *(1980), winner of the Gilbert Chinard Prize;* To Make All Laws: The Congress of the United States, 1789-1989 *(1989); and* The Sister Republics: Switzerland and the United States from 1776 to the Present *(1991).*

Washington and principal author with Madison of the *Federalist* papers; Patrick Henry, governor of Virginia during the Revolutionary War; and John Jay, first chief justice of the United States. Figures quoted who have become lesser known over time include: Elias Boudinot, president of the Confederation Congress and director of the United States Mint; Henry Laurens, president of the Continental Congress; Benjamin Rush, influential physician and social reformer; and John Witherspoon, president of Princeton University and member of the Continental Congress. Hutson also includes quotes from two prominent women: Abigail Adams, wife of John Adams, and Martha Washington, wife of George Washington.

The quotes are presented alphabetically by topic and are arranged alphabetically within each topic by the Founders' last names. Although many of the topics are not obviously religious in character, the Founders' strong interest in the spiritual and philosophical dimension of life inspired spiritual reflection in them. The quotes present the Founders' religious perspectives on subjects as diverse as addiction, animals, children, crime and punishment, death, education, marriage, patriotism, reason, republicanism, slavery, and women. Other topics have more obvious religious implications and include such themes as the afterlife, atheism, the Bible, Christianity, Communion, ecumenism, faith, God, hell, Islam, Jews, miracles, morality, prayer, profanity, prophecy, and religion.

Hutson's choice to organize the topics alphabetically allows the reader to see with ease in what ways the Founders tend to agree or disagree on any given topic. The Founders represent the full range of attitudes toward religion. Some, such as Boudinot and Witherspoon, were very pious Christians. Others expressed skepticism about religion. Jefferson is found on this end of the spectrum. Hutson presents the more mature and definitive views of the Founders, as some changed their opinions over time. For example, Madison was very pious in his youth, but in his mature years his fervor diminished. Jefferson, on the other hand, a staunch skeptic for most of his life, seemed to soften his views toward religion at the end of his life. Other Founders, such as Roger Sherman, were acknowledged to be religious specialists. Many Founders devoted themselves to the study of religious treatises. Adams and Jay are but two examples.

Many Founders were quite religious in their personal lives. They advised their children to live and understand their lives according to religious principles. Abigail Adams urged her grandson John Quincy Adams to live by the religious principles he learned as a child. Charles Carroll reminded his son that wisdom begins with fear of the Lord. Jay told his son that the Bible is the best book of all. He told his daughters that virtue and religion should be the foundations of their life.

Most Founders regularly attended church services. The quotations in *The Founders on Religion* often demonstrate their great familiarity with biblical texts. Nonetheless, they advocated freedom of conscience. Washington's assertion that citizens should answer to God alone for their religious beliefs represents the thinking of many of the Founders.

The Founders are almost unanimous in their advocacy of the separation of church and state. The existence of an official government church destroys religious liberty, according to Jefferson. John Dickinson asserted that the separation of church and state ensures the peace and well-being of society. He noted that when they are mixed, persecution results.

Although the Founders supported separation of church and state, they valued religion's influence on society. The Founders viewed religion as a useful ally of government because it taught people to be law-abiding and morally upstanding citizens. John Adams maintained that religion and virtue are the foundations of a republican form of government. Carroll, the only Roman Catholic to sign the Declaration of Independence, asserted that attacks against Christianity undermine morality and the security of government. Even Jefferson observed that Christianity, albeit only in its original purity, is the religion that best serves the cause of liberty.

The Founders did not put much stock in claims of religious belief or creeds. Most held that a person's conduct matters much more than any statement of belief. Abigail Adams insisted that true religion comes from the heart and cannot be imposed by forcing adherence to any belief. For Franklin, virtue is more important than the acceptance of any statement of belief. Jefferson asserted that he never judged people by what they believed; he judged them by how they lived their lives.

The Founders also agreed that intervention by Divine Providence brought success to the American colonies' fight for independence. Jefferson included an appeal for the protection of Divine Providence in the Declaration of Independence. One of the more pious Founders, Boudinot, likened the freedom that God bestowed on the Israelites when he led them out of Egypt to the freedom that came with independence from Great Britain. Franklin, who was not a churchgoer most of his adult life, also saw the providential action of the Supreme Being behind the American colonists' success in their struggle for independence.

Although the Founders agreed on the importance of Divine Providence, their views on the nature of God differ. Both John Adams and Jefferson believed God to be beyond comprehension. In addition, John Adams rejected the notion of a God who predestines humans to eternal damnation, a view embraced by the Calvinists of the time. Franklin's meditations on the nature of God reflect his scientific orientation. He marveled at how God structures creation to meet the needs of its creatures. Rush thought it inappropriate to ascribe human passions to the Supreme Being.

The Founders do not agree on the identity of Jesus. Adams and Jefferson did not believe Jesus is God. Franklin also doubted the divinity of Jesus but believed his moral teaching to be superior to all others. Sherman, on the other hand, believed Jesus to be both human and divine, as traditional Christian teaching maintains.

On the issue of morality, the Founders differ as well. Adams and Witherspoon considered religion to be the key to morality. Franklin held that morality is everyone's duty, regardless of their religion or lack thereof, and claimed that a virtuous heretic finds salvation before an evil Christian.

On the topic of crime and punishment, Hutson provides two quotations. In the first, Jay bases his support for capital punishment and war on passages in the Bible that describe God commanding the Israelites to wage war and put criminals to death. In the second, Rush appeals to incidents in the life of Jesus to argue the exact opposite: that war and capital punishment are contrary to the will of God.

This brief survey of the Founders' views gives some idea of how difficult it is to fashion generalizations about their thinking on religion. It is even more difficult to surmise what were the attitudes of the general population about religion at the time of the birth of the United States. In the introduction to *The Founders on Religion*, Hutson observes that the Founders probably do not represent the mainstream of the thinking of their day. Adams and Jefferson both indicated that they were aware that their views were not shared by most. Hutson concludes that Boudinot's views were probably the closest of any of the Founders to the beliefs of most of the population.

The Founders were prosperous politicians and military leaders. They were among the elite of their day. Even though it is difficult to know what the religious views of ordinary people were, the statements of the Founders do shed light on the thinking of some of the religious denominations active at the time of the birth of the United States and the tensions between them as they vied for influence in the new nation. For the reader interested in the debates about the relationship of church and state, this book provides ample material to further the discussion.

Evelyn Toft

Review Source

Library Journal 130, no. 18 (November 1, 2005): 82.

1491
New Revelations of the Americas Before Columbus

Author: Charles C. Mann (1955-   )
Publisher: Alfred A. Knopf (New York). 465 pp. $30.00
Type of work: Anthropology and history
Time: Prehistoric times to 1492
Locale: North, Central, and South America

Archaelogical and paleontological discoveries in the last centuries changed theories of Native American life in the pre-Columbian Americas. Evidence discovered in the last few decades have produced even more radically altered theories of American populations, culture, and practices prior to European contact

Journalist Charles C. Mann's interest in the pre-Columbian people of the Americas began in 1983 while he was on an assignment in Mexico covering a National Aeronautics and Space Administration program to monitor atmospheric ozone. On the scientists' day off, Mann tagged along with them to the ancient Mayan ruins of Chichén Itzá. His interest developed over the subsequent decades, as he visited various other Mesoamerican ruins, both on vacation and on assignment. This curiosity and examination of facts and theories, past and present, has led to a remarkable book about what might have been going on in the Americas before the Europeans arrived.

In the introduction in *1491*, titled "Holmberg's Mistake," Mann describes a visit to the Beni, a Bolivian province "about the size of Illinois and Indiana put together." During the early 1940's, Allan R. Holmberg, a doctoral student, lived among the Sirionó tribe in the Beni. Holmberg reported them to be "among the most culturally backward peoples of the world." The mistake Holmberg made was to assume that these people had always lived this way, that their way of life had remained unchanged from primitive times, and that they were essentially a people who had "no real history."

In reality, the Sirionó of the Beni were the remnants of a tribe that had flourished in this region before smallpox and influenza arrived in their villages in the 1920's. More interesting, their ancestors were not only much more numerous but had left evidence of a highly developed culture that built cities and developed the lands of the Beni for agriculture. Mann was shown the traces of massive earthworks in a flyover of the region and then examined them on the ground. The seasonal flooding of the Beni was managed by these structures, allowing the Indians to trap fish during the wet seasons.

Unfortunately, this view of primitive Indians was already widespread. When people think of the Indians of Amazonia, they are likely to picture small bands of highly mobile hunters and gatherers, often extremely violent and warlike, living in a natural harmony in the jungle depths. The idea of the noble savage still colors many people's view of Indians as innocent, childlike, and totally natural beings.

Holmberg's mistake also includes the belief that the native peoples of the Americas had little impact on the land, that they did not change it in any lasting, purposeful way. Choosing three areas of the Americas and the cultures that occupied them, Mann examines what is known about these peoples, including some of the most recent discoveries. The Mayans in Mesoamerica, the eastern tribes of North America, and the Inca of Peru, have left physical traces of their cultures. In many cases, close examination of written accounts from the time of contact with Europeans reveals truths about the cultures that have been missed by those operating under the same assumptions as Holmberg did.

Charles C. Mann is a journalist who works as a correspondent for The Atlantic Monthly *and* Science. *He has written four previous books and been a finalist for the National Magazine Award three times. He has won awards from the American Bar Association, the Margaret Sanger Foundation, the American Institute of Physics, and the Alfred P. Sloan Foundation. His work was included in* The Best American Science Writing, 2003 *and* The Best American Science and Nature Writing, 2003.

Mann also mentions the neolithic revolution, which is the invention of farming. Considering that the Middle East, where farming began, is known as the cradle of civilization, the neolithic revolution was a defining event in human history. What is not widely known is that another, completely independent neolithic revolution also took place, in Mesoamerica. Archaeologists currently estimate that it occurred about ten thousand years ago, which puts it slightly later than the Middle Eastern version. However, as recently as 2003, the seeds of cultivated squashes were found in coastal Ecuador that predate the ancient Sumerian accomplishment.

Mann alternates between intense, in-depth examination of what is known or believed about a particular culture and his general theory of misapprehension about what was occurring in the Americas when the first Europeans arrived. Sometimes this is annoying, especially when he jumps abruptly from Andean culture to eastern North American cultures. However, he weaves the common threads together skillfully, and the evidence mounts until it seems that not only did the arrival of the Europeans ruin everything but that the conquests and assumptions of inferiority also robbed the world of the Americas' cultural richness.

The book is divided into three sections. Part 1 discusses the belief that the Americas were empty country, waiting to be populated by those who could put it to better use. Mann shows how estimates of the number of people living in the Americas are faulty, colored by preexisting beliefs. Taking into account the vast numbers of fatalities caused by European diseases against which Indians had no immunities, he revises the numbers upward until he posits a land fairly teeming with people engaged in all sorts of enterprises. Not all scholars and scientists of this period agree with the revised estimates, and Mann explains why this is so. He again examines the reports of famous explorers such as Hernando de Soto, Francisco Pizarro, and Hernán Cortés, gleaning from their records population sizes and numbers of villages that do not support the idea of an empty America. Yet, a century after de Soto traveled through the southeastern part of North America, Europeans indeed found a land emptied of its former inhabitants.

Mann looks to genetics to explain why the diseases of the Europeans had such a terrible impact on the Indians. He points out that the peoples of the American continents seem to have an unusually homogeneous biochemistry. Although the "timing and manner of Indians' arrival in the Americas," is in dispute, "almost all researchers believe that the initial number of newcomers must have been small." The differences in the human leukocyte antigens (HLAs) present in this population from the HLAs of the arriving Europeans made them unusually vulnerable to diseases that had adapted to human hosts long before but to which the Indians had no immunity. Mann hesitates to assign blame for the calamity of extermination, however, pointing out that neither the Indians nor the Europeans of first contact times understood the mechanisms of infection and disease. The first Europeans unwittingly unleashed epidemics, although centuries later disease was sometimes knowingly spread.

Part 2 looks at cultural achievements in the Americas. Mann solves the puzzle of why the wheel was not employed in Andean cultures beyond use in children's toys. The Andeans had no large beasts of burden such as were available in other parts of the world, and the steep mountain paths were unsuited to such vehicles. The sure feet of the relatively small llamas were perfectly adapted to travel in the mountain reaches. Until the coming of Europeans, nowhere throughout the Americas were animals large enough or suitable for riding, but it did not take long for Indians to become mounted once horses were available.

Mann looks at such cultural developments as the growth and use of cotton and the development of maize. The latter was a particularly amazing feat. Grain-bearing grasses of the New World needed only some adaptation to agriculture to produce bountiful harvests. Wild forms of these plants can still be found. However, no clear ancestor of maize has been identified. The closest similar plant is so much smaller and bears so many fewer edible seeds that if it was an ancestor of modern maize, there must have been some genius in breeding it and incredible foresight for what it could become. Maize is one of the most prolific food sources available in the world, producing more edible food per acre than any other grain. Combined with the beans and squash also available in the New World, it provides a complete, nutritious diet for human beings.

Some of Mann's most fascinating material, found in chapter 5, "Pleistocene Wars" (part 2), concerns the stubbornness of scientists who refuse to acknowledge new evidence that upsets the currently held theories. This is an ongoing occurrence, and for every new theory Mann describes, he cites the opinions of its detractors. Scientists are accused of everything from wishful thinking to political correctness to dismiss their ideas.

In part 3, Mann examines the ways in which Indians formed the land into usable acreage, despite often daunting natural conditions. Not only did the Indians practice agriculture extensively, but they also managed the lands in ways that were vastly superior to the methods Europeans practiced at the time, and in many cases to what is known and practiced today. They apparently solved the problem of the infamous soil of Amazonia, which proves to be little suited to agriculture once the forest has been cleared. Areas of human habitation still exist that are founded on a rich, dark soil (called *terra preta do Índio*—rich, fertile "Indian dark earth") that was deliberately produced by humans. Broken ceramics are found in this earth, along with a high percentage of charcoal, nutrients, and microbial organisms necessary to break up organic matter so that it is readily available to plants. The northeastern Indians practiced land management by burning off underbrush. The amazing number of fruit trees that the European colonists found had probably been deliberately planted by a population that was now much diminished and driven from their lands.

The book also contains a coda and several appendixes. In the coda, Mann makes the startling but convincing case that the ideas of personal liberty that Americans hold so dear can be traced directly to the Indian societies encountered by the English colonists. He compares the proscribed lives of Europeans of that time with the freedom of the Indians, which were often annoying to the former. The colonists found that even an Indian child reared among them would, upon but one visit with his relations, never be persuaded to return. When one looks at the difference between the societies, it is not hard to imagine why.

Mann relates the story of Deganawidah and the Great Law of Peace that became the Haudenosaunee constitution and established a league of tribes and great council to settle disputes. This council of Northeastern seaboard tribes was limited strictly to relations between member nations and outside groups; "internal affairs were the province of the individual nations." Mann points out that although Indian leaders of the eastern seaboards were absolute rulers theoretically, in actuality they required the consent of the governed in all matters.

In appendix A, "Loaded Words," Mann explains his reasons for using the word "Indian" rather than "Native American." Appendix B, "Talking Knots," describes an Inca form of writing in which knotted strings are read by the *khipukamayuq*—"knot keepers." This is a unique system that was mostly lost when the Spanish sought to repress alternate versions of events. Appendix C, "the Syphilis Exception," considers whether there was at least one infectious disease that traveled from the Americas back to Europe. Appendix D, "Calendar Math," describes the calendar systems of the Maya, which consisted of a sacred calendar, a secular calendar, and "the Long Count," a system for tracking the days "that . . . linked the other two." The book also contains an extensive notes section, bibliography, and index.

Patricia Masserman

Review Sources

Booklist 101, no. 22 (August 1, 2005): 1986.
Business Week, September 5, 2005, pp. 108-109.
Esquire 144, no. 2 (August, 2005): 46.
Kirkus Reviews 73, no. 11 (June 1, 2005): 625-626.
Library Journal 130, no. 13 (August 15, 2005): 96.
The New York Times Book Review 155 (October 9, 2005): 21.
Publishers Weekly 252, no. 25 (June 20, 2005): 69.
Science News 168, no. 8 (August 20, 2005): 127.
The Washington Post Book World 35, no. 31 (August 7, 2005): 5.

FREAKONOMICS
A Rogue Economist Explores the Hidden Side of Everything

Authors: Steven D. Levitt (1967-   ) and Stephen J.
  Dubner (1963-   )
Publisher: William Morrow (New York). 242 pp. $26.00
Type of work: Current affairs, economics, and sociology
Time: The 1990's to the 2000's
Locale: Primarily the United States

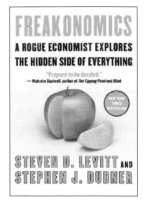

*An award-winning economist explores topics usually
considered outside the realm of his specialty, presenting
theories regarding issues that often are considered moral
rather than economic or scientific*

Steven Levitt obviously overstates the breadth of his
work in the subtitle of *Freakonomics: A Rogue Economist
Explores the Hidden Side of Everything*, but he can be forgiven in his zealousness. He
claims to be founding "freakonomics" as a new field of study, one that asks unusual
questions that others fail to see or to embrace. Within that context, a claim that
freakonomics explores "the hidden side of everything" is not so exaggerated, and social scientists within many disciplines—political science, sociology, and economics
among them—have attempted to construct overarching theories that capture most of
what they see as the important dimensions of the world. Within this volume, however,
Levitt explores only a few topics to illustrate the kinds of issues that can be addressed
using his approach.

In stepping outside what are commonly accepted as the boundaries of the field of
economics, Levitt actually steps back a century or two into the past. Before economics was recognized as a discipline in its own right, it was part of what was called political economy, which encompassed both politics and economics, among other areas.
Even further back, the types of questions Levitt studies were considered part of
"moral theory"; Adam Smith, now recognized as one of the key figures in early economics, also wrote on what he called the theory of moral sentiments. Levitt seems to
acknowledge this history, at least subtly: The table of contents for *Freakonomics* recalls a nineteenth century work. After each chapter title is a brief statement of the
chapter's contents, then several phrases indicating key points made in the chapter.
There are no subheadings within chapters, and in fact the material within each chapter
blurs together, sometimes leaving the reader wondering how Levitt makes the leap
from one topic to another.

In fact, it is not always clear who is writing and whose research is being reported.
Before each chapter appears a short excerpt from an article about Levitt written by co-
author Stephen Dubner for the August 3, 2003, issue of *The New York Times Magazine*. The chapters themselves report Levitt's research results and theories both from
his and from an outsider's (Dubner's) perspective. Much of the time, data sources are

not attributed in the text, so it is not always clear if research is Levitt's (rarely), is coauthored by Levitt (commonly), or, in the case of some minor results, is someone else's entirely (acknowledged in the source notes at the back of the book).

Steven D. Levitt teaches economics at the University of Chicago and is the 2003 recipient of the John Bates Clark Medal, awarded every two years to the best American economist under the age of forty. Stephen J. Dubner is the author of the books Turbulent Souls: A Catholic Son's Return to His Jewish Family *(1998) and* Confessions of a Hero-Worshiper *(2003). He has written for major publications, including* The New York Times *and* The New Yorker.

What, then, is Levitt attempting to do with his new field of freakonomics? He states that he is taking economics back to its basics, as a study of incentives and the ways in which people attempt to get what they want, given that scarcity and competition exist. Levitt stresses that he is exploring how the world really works, rather than examining issues of morality or how people would like the world to work. The text is markedly nontechnical, with no equations and only a few summaries of data. Levitt seems to ask the reader simply to trust him that the data actually show what he claims, although the extensive notes to the book do provide citations to academic papers (his and others') containing more complete analyses. Levitt thereby both invites nonspecialists into his field of study and opens his analysis to scrutiny by those who wish to delve deeper.

Chapter 1 begins with a brief discourse on incentives. Levitt believes that most incentives do not arise organically; instead, someone had to invent them, with some goal in mind. This opens the question of whether such artificial incentives actually do achieve their goals. He gives an example of a day-care center faced with the problem that some parents were late picking up their children. The center decided to levy a small fine each time a child was picked up late. The result was that parental tardiness increased; apparently, parents balanced the small fine against their own inconvenience in being on time and decided that the cost was worth it. The fine also may have converted a social or "moral" issue ("I should pick my child up on time because it's the right thing to do") into an economic one ("How much will it cost if I am not on time?"). Throughout the book, Levitt stresses that types of incentives—economic, social, and moral—often play off or replace one another.

The example raises the issue that when rules are set, cheating often follows. Levitt expands on this concept in an examination of high-stakes testing, using the Chicago public schools as a source of data. Educational reforms in the 1990's raised the stakes of testing, making it the basis for student promotion to the next grade as well as for teacher salaries and bonuses and for school budgets. With those kinds of incentives, Levitt expected to find cheating, and he did. He looked at the ways in which cheating could be accomplished and which classrooms had the highest incentives to cheat. Analysis of student answer sheets indeed showed widespread cheating in the form predicted—teachers in the lowest-achieving classrooms changing the answer sheets turned in by their students. Furthermore, the year after some cheating teachers were fired, cheating fell by 30 percent.

Cheating can take myriad forms, and Levitt provides several illustrative examples. He found that sumo wrestlers manipulated their performance to enhance their rankings, and thus their salaries. As another example, Levitt interviewed former economist Paul Feldman, who sold bagels in office buildings on an "honors system" of payment. Feldman found that several factors influenced the rate of honest payment, including the type of collection receptacle (open basket, coffee can with slot in the lid, or wooden box with slot), the size of the office, the weather, and the nearness of a major holiday (which corresponded with increased theft).

From cheating, Levitt moves in chapter 2 to discrimination and the use of information. He describes how the Ku Klux Klan was weakened considerably when its secrets were made public and how the Klan relied on its "credible threat" of violence rather than actual violence. Levitt uses real estate brokers to illustrate the value of information and people's interests in revealing it, finding that brokers make much better deals when negotiating for their own properties rather than for the properties of their clients. Levitt examines contestant behavior on the television quiz show *The Weakest Link*, in which contestants can vote against other contestants. In evaluating participants' responses to questions and their voting behavior, he finds consistent biases against Hispanic and older contestants but not against African Americans, possibly because the contestants did not want to appear biased. Hispanics were perceived as being worse players than they in fact were. Older contestants faced a different bias: Whether it was to players' advantage or not, they tended to vote older contestants off the show in disproportionately larger numbers.

Chapter 3 examines the economics of crime, specifically incentives facing American street gangs dealing in crack cocaine. Financial records for one gang revealed a heavily skewed organizational chart, likened to that of McDonald's restaurant chain: The few gang members at the top made a very good living, but the vast majority could not live on what they earned and stayed in the business only in the hope of rising to the top.

The discussion raises the wider issue of increased crime rates which accompanied the introduction of crack cocaine. Once crime rates rose, the conventional wisdom continued to predict further increases. When crime rates fell unexpectedly in the 1990's, most analysts were stumped. Chapter 4 discusses various theories proposed in hindsight, and Levitt finds that some had merit but most did not. His surprising answer, and the most controversial of his research results discussed in the book, is that crime rates fell as a delayed result of the 1973 *Roe v. Wade* Supreme Court decision, which legalized abortion. In short, his theory, which he backs up with data, is that pregnant women who had had abortions tended to live in conditions associated with later criminality in their children, including low levels of education, single parenthood, and poverty. Thus, abortion rights, more than any other factor, prevented criminals from being born. Levitt states clearly that proposing abortion as a means of (future) crime prevention would have huge moral implications; his intent is merely to provide data and thereby illustrate the unintended consequences of a change in public policy.

The final two chapters are more amusing, if somewhat troubling. In both, Levitt discusses measures that parents take to improve their children's lives. He finds so-called conventional wisdom to be largely wrong, as well as sometimes contradictory. According to Levitt's analysis of child rearing, very little of what parents do matters in terms of their children's later attainment of education and income. What matters, instead, is what the parents are. Choice of school was found not to matter significantly: Students who did well when they switched to "better" schools would have been predicted to do well at their old schools. Similarly, Levitt found no difference in measured educational attainment in connection with whether a child's mother worked outside the home between the child's birth and kindergarten, or with whether parents regularly took the child to museums, or with whether the child watched television frequently. What mattered were the parents' attributes, such as their own education and income; there was little that parents could do that would make a difference.

Chapter 6 takes the question of "perfect parenting" to an amusing extreme by examining the names parents give to their children and questioning whether those names predict the children's later life outcomes. Examination of data from California showed that unusual names were more common for the children of women who were unmarried, low income, and less educated, as well as for those of teen mothers. Levitt constructed lists of names associated with worse outcomes (lower education, lower income) for those who had them. Rather than the names somehow causing those outcomes (perhaps as a result of discrimination against those with names perceived as being "low income" or "black" or something else), however, the train of causation runs further back: Mothers whose own characteristics made it likely that their children would be underachievers were more likely to give their children these names. An interesting result is that high-achieving names tend to filter down over time, with lower achievers starting to use them for their children and higher achievers then abandoning use of them.

Levitt surveys a broad range of topics in *Freakonomics*, seemingly linked by little more than his own curious mind and the places it has taken him in his research. He provides a valuable service by indicating the kinds of questions that can be both asked and answered with some relatively simple analysis. The book is both insightful and entertaining, and it is encouraging in showing how the tools and the worldview of economics need not be confined to obvious matters of dollars and cents but instead can extend to examinations of the conventional wisdom and common sense.

A. J. Sobczak

Review Sources

America 193, no. 6 (September 12, 2005): 25.
Booklist 101, no. 18 (May 15, 2005): 1622.
Commentary 120, no. 1 (July/August, 2005): 67-69.
The Economist 375 (May 14, 2005): 85-86.
Kirkus Reviews 73, no. 6 (March 15, 2005): 337-338.
Library Journal 130, no. 8 (May 1, 2005): 98.
The New York Times Book Review 154 (May 15, 2005): 12.
Publishers Weekly 252, no. 11 (March 14, 2005): 53-54.

THE GLASS CASTLE

Author: Jeannette Walls (1960-   )
Publisher: Scribner (New York). 288 pp. $25.00
Type of work: Autobiography
Time: The 1960's to 2005
Locale: Arizona, California, Nevada, West Virginia, and
New York City

Walls describes growing up with an alcoholic father and a blithely negligent mother, her family's struggle to survive after moving to West Virginia, and her eventual escape to New York City and a successful life

Principal personages:
JEANNETTE WALLS, the author
REX WALLS, her alcoholic father
ROSE MARY WALLS, her artist mother, who chooses to live in poverty
rather than embrace a conventional lifestyle
LORI WALLS, her older sister, the first of the Walls children to escape
Appalachian poverty
BRIAN WALLS, her younger brother, who follows Lori and Jeannette to
New York
MAUREEN WALLS, the youngest of the Walls children, whose childhood
beauty proves to be a survival tool

In *The Glass Castle*, Jeannette Walls describes her life in clear, meticulous, extremely readable prose. Her tough childhood makes some others' claims of survival seem self-indulgent. Walls's writing portrays the difficult circumstances of her family without a trace of self-pity. Despite the inability of her parents to provide a stable home, Jeannette's love for her entire family is unmistakable.

Although the book is divided into five sections, the chapters within each section are not numbered. The first part is called "Woman on the Street," followed by the longest section, "The Desert." Then comes "Welch," "New York City," and finally, "Thanksgiving."

In the opening chapter, Walls describes seeing her mother on the streets of New York City. Through the window of a taxi, just as she is wondering whether she is overdressed for a party, she glimpses her mother rooting through trash barrels in the East Village. Not wanting to risk being seen with her, Jeannette orders the taxi driver to take her back home, to her Park Avenue address, while her mother goes about her life on the street like so many homeless New Yorkers.

From this scene, Jeannette takes the reader back to her earliest memory. She is three years old. As she stands on a chair at the stove boiling hot dogs in a pot, her dress catches fire. A reader cannot help but be struck by the inappropriateness of a child this young preparing her own meals. During the time Jeannette is hospitalized for her burns, she enjoys her stay within quiet, snug walls, experiencing regular meals for the first time and discovering such marvels as chewing gum.

Jeannette and her older sister, Lori, have a brother, Brian, and another sister, Maureen. The resourceful children eat whatever they are given and forage for food or collect scraps and bottles that they can sell for cash. Despite their circum-

Jeannette Walls is a journalist who contributes regularly to to the MSNBC.com Web site. She lives in New York and is married to John Taylor, a fellow writer. The Glass Castle *is her first book.*

stances, Jeannette's memories of her young days seem to be happy ones. The children are not particularly "bad," occupied as they are with the problem of basic survival. Their parents do give them lots of practical advice and encourage their independence.

Rather than being neglectful and uncaring during their children's younger years, Walls's parents, in this portrayal, possess offbeat practicality and a liberal philosophy. Walls's mother, Rose Mary Walls, considers herself an artist and spends as much time as possible painting, writing, and sculpting. She wishes her children to be self-reliant, and the Walls children are forced to look out for themselves and one another in daily life. Rex Walls, Jeanette's father, is a dreamer, always working on some invention guaranteed to make the family rich, if only he can get the funding to complete his plans.

The family is rootless and highly mobile, masters of "the skedaddle," usually accomplished late at night. Whenever the family's unpaid bills have piled up, the Wallses pile a few possessions in whichever old car they have and hit the road. Walls's childhood passes this way in a series of small, dusty mining towns in the deserts of Arizona, California, and Nevada. When the family settles long enough for the children to attend school, they are made aware of their relative poverty. Though not the only ones who are needy, they are often the poorest family in their community.

Rex Walls can talk himself into jobs at nearby mines, digging the minerals or sometimes working as an electrician, but the jobs never last. In these days, Rex has two distinct states to his alcoholism. The family prefers his "beer phase"; they can handle his fast driving and loud singing. When he brings home a bottle of "the hard stuff," however, he inevitably turns into "an angry-eyed stranger who threw around furniture and threatened to beat up" anyone within reach. Times of little money have their bright side, in that Rex cannot buy hard liquor.

In between the births of their first and second daughters, the Walls had lost a child to sudden infant death syndrome, and Rose Mary claimed that Rex had changed because of it. As the narrative goes on, however, it grows more apparent that Rex Walls is a fairly classic alcoholic, with enough charm and plenty of excuses to cruise through life. Neither parent seems to want a comfortable life for themselves and their children. Although Rex is always full of big dreams, he does little to realize them, and Rose Mary's art never seems to earn attention. The biggest of Rex's dreams is to build an enormous mansion of glass for his family, out in the desert and equipped with solar panels so that they will never lack for power. He draws up elaborate, detailed plans for the Glass Castle, inventing a fabulous life they will all live someday.

Rose Mary insists on looking at the family's life as "one long and incredibly fun adventure," and the children rarely break the "unspoken rule" against voicing discontent. On one occasion, when Jeannette eats the only remaining bit of food in the house, half a stick of margarine, her mother shows her irrationality by calling the child selfish. The confrontation leads to one of many instances when Rose Mary defends herself by blaming the failings of her husband—but does nothing to change her and her children's lifestyle.

As the family drifts through one desert town after another, Rex's alcoholism worsens. He demands that his wife obtain cash from her well-off mother, a retired rancher in Texas, to finance his latest scheme, the "Prospector," a machine designed to draw gold from ore. When Rose Mary refuses, Rex goes into a rage which culminates in a violent physical fight. Not long after this, Rose Mary takes a job as a teacher, although she resents leaving her art.

Apart from such bouts of drunken violence and her obvious disappointment in her husband, Rose Mary maintains a cheery, laissez-faire outlook on life. She has so few conventional social ideas that she does not even inform the children when their grandmother dies. The family inherits a large adobe house in Phoenix, Rex finds a job as an electrician, and the family prospers for a time. At his daughter's request, Rex even quits drinking, an agonizing withdrawal he endures alone in his room. Despite a steady income, however, the Wallses cannot seem to keep their new house in good repair. Eventually Rex loses his job, word gets around, and he is back to full-time drinking.

Rose Mary decides that the family will move to Welch, West Virginia, the town where Rex grew up. His family still lives there, and Rose Mary hopes their Walls relatives can help keep Rex in line. Their time in West Virginia turns into a dark period in the Walls family history. Rex's parents do not appreciate him and his family moving in with them and grudgingly share their meager resources. The Appalachian coal community cannot offer many jobs, and Rex soon becomes known as the town drunk.

Although Jeannette does not report any sexual abuse from her parents, a groping incident between her grandmother and her brother causes her to wonder whether her father was abused by his mother. She speculates that this may be why he is so angry and had resisted returning to West Virginia. Eventually the family is asked to leave the elder Wallses' home. Rex and Rose Mary buy a rickety old house whose only saving grace is that it is perched so high up in the hills that they are spared the flooding the town below receives.

The family's situation continues to deteriorate. No repairs are made to the house, and it slowly deteriorates around them. The facilities are so primitive that the children rarely bathe or wash their clothes. Jeannette feeds herself by furtively retrieving the leftover lunches her classmates throw away in the bathroom trash. The Walls children find a two-carat diamond ring on their property, but instead of selling it to feed her children, Rose Mary insists on keeping it to replace the wedding ring her husband pawned to buy liquor. When she is twelve, Jeannette visits the library to do some research and approaches her mother with the idea of leaving her father. Rose Mary refuses angrily.

At thirteen years of age, Jeannette passes herself off as seventeen and starts working in a store. She begins to save her money for an "escape fund." Lori and Brian pitch in when they learn of her plan, and together the children begin amassing money to allow Lori to move to New York City after she graduates from high school. Unfortunately, Rex breaks open the piggy bank and unapologetically spends all the money on drink. Lori does escape, however; when Jeannette is offered an opportunity to leave Welch, she insists that Lori go in her place.

Jeannette works hard on her high school paper and leaves Welch for New York City after completing her junior year. Through school, she lands an internship at a small newspaper. Brian follows after completing his junior year. These three children of poverty, not averse to working hard, find jobs to support themselves. Jeannette's editor convinces her to go to college, and she is accepted at Barnard.

Three years after Jeannette moves to New York, her parents call to tell her they have followed. Their lives have not changed, however. They are thrown out of boardinghouses and flophouses and end up living with Lori until she throws them out. Rex and Rose Mary become homeless people, but they seem to enjoy their freedom, finding a community in the city's streets. Ashamed of them, Jeannette hides her history from friends, but she feels deep guilt at the material success for which she has worked. She offers her parents help on numerous occasions.

Rex contracts tuberculosis. He gives up drinking while he is in the hospital but resumes once he leaves. Her parents become squatters in an abandoned building and appear to be happy with their lives. Her mother even chides Jeannette for her lack of values, worrying aloud that "Next thing I know, you'll become a Republican."

The most heartbreaking revelation comes near the end of the New York section. After Rose Mary's brother dies, she approaches Jeannette for a loan to buy his half of the Texas land she inherited from her parents. The oil leases on this land have yielded an occasional payment over the years, but Rose Mary had always been vague about details. When the sum her mother asks for proves to be large, Jeanette is astonished: All those years, while the family suffered without food, heat, or plumbing, her mother was sitting on land worth a million dollars.

The only Walls child who does not benefit from the move to New York City is the youngest, Maureen. She drifts from one boyfriend to another, seeking someone to take care of her. She exhibits signs of mental illness, and after moving into her parents' squatters apartment, eventually spends all day sleeping. She is sent to a mental hospital for stabbing her mother after Rose Mary suggests that Maureen become self-sufficient like her siblings. Maureen eventually makes her way to California, the warm land she always dreamed about, and Jeannette expresses hope that she will find peace.

The last section of the book briefly describes a Thanksgiving family reunion. Rex has died, but Rose Mary still lives in the squatters apartment and maintains her cheerful enthusiasm. The Walls children are grown, but as they look at the wonderful Thanksgiving dinner spread on the table before them, Brian cannot help but remark, "You know, it's really not that hard to put food on the table if that's what you decide to do."

Patricia Masserman

Review Sources

Booklist 101, no. 11 (February 1, 2005): 923.
Entertainment Weekly, March 11, 2005, p. 107.
Kirkus Reviews 72, no. 24 (December 15, 2004): 1195.
Library Journal 130, no. 3 (February 15, 2005): 141.
The New York Times Book Review 154 (March 13, 2005): 1-13.
Publishers Weekly 252, no. 3 (January 17, 2005): 41.
The Spectator 297 (April 30, 2005): 38-39.

GOD'S GYM

Author: John Edgar Wideman (1941-   )
Publisher: Houghton Mifflin (Boston). 175 pp. $23.00
Type of work: Short fiction

These ten new stories examine race, family, spiritual fathers, and the relationship between fiction and reality

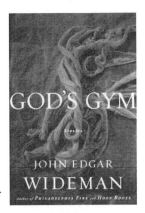

John Edgar Wideman once told an interviewer that for a long time he did not respect the short story. He thought the form too gimmicky, that is, he added, until he began to see how a short story has its own kind of logic and beauty. Most of these ten stories, as in Wideman's earlier collections, *Damballah* (1981), *Fever* (1989), and *The Stories of John Edgar Wideman* (1992), explore the logic and beauty of the short story by rejecting linear narrative for a lyrical form of meditation and improvisation characteristic of jazz riff, a form that derives from the repetitive call-and-response patterns of West African music.

God's Gym takes its title from the opening story "Weight," chosen as the first prizewinner in the 2000 edition of the *O. Henry Awards Prize Stories*. In the contributors' notes to that collection, Wideman says that the opening line of the story, "My mother is a weightlifter," came to him first and that he wrote the story in order to discover what the sentence meant—only to realize that it was about his whole life, specifically about his relationship with his mother. The story is a touching extended eulogy which, both lyrically and lightheartedly, explores a metaphor of the mother as a weightlifter, who should wear a T-shirt with the words "God's Gym," for she bears the burdens of her family and neighbors. It ends with the son twisting his fingers into the brass handles of her coffin and lifting.

Because he is always so concerned with the relationship of fiction to reality, Wideman explores here the process by which he wrote the story, recounting how his mother initially objected to the levity of the metaphor, complaining that he should be ashamed of himself for taking the Lord's name in vain by using the phrase "God's T-shirt." Admitting that events in the story may not have happened exactly the way he describes them, Wideman knows that what actually happened is sometimes less important than finding a good way to tell it. In "Weight," Wideman's way of telling the story of his mother is to explore the implications of a metaphor as he practices for her death, trying on for size a world without her.

"Are Dreams Faster than the Speed of Light" is another exploration of the parent/child relationship, in this case a son's responsibility to his father. When a man is told he has only a few months left to live, he realizes that the most important task on his "must do" list is to kill his own father, a fiercely independent old man who can no longer care for himself and is confined to a hospital like a fatally wounded animal. Wideman identifies the central character of the story as himself, referring to the fact

John Edgar Wideman won the PEN/ Faulkner Award in 1984 for Sent for You Yesterday *and in 1990 for* Philadelphia Fire. *He was named a MacArthur Fellow in 1993 and won the prestigious REA Award for accomplishment in the short story in 1998.*

that he takes his middle name, Edgar, from his father. He extends his meditation (or what he calls a riff) by comparing his relationship with his father with spiritual fathers and sons of the past—Socrates and Plato, Aristotle and Vergil.

Wideman also includes meditations, or jazz riffs, on some of his spiritual ancestors. "The Silence of Thelonious Monk" celebrates artists before Wideman who have tried to go beyond the referentiality of language and the temporality of time to achieve some transcendent state or quality. As the narrator of the story recalls listening to the music of the great jazz musician Thelonious Monk, he identifies with Monk's enigmatic silences of speech and the transcendent wordlessness of his music. Trying to find a way to express his inexpressible sense of loneliness after the loss of a lover, the narrator says that love is as close to music as one can get and that he hears his loved one's comings and goings in the music of Monk. In the early morning hours he lies awake, lamenting that his story is about not holding on to the woman tightly enough and that, like Monk, he has retreated to silence. However, the great musician upbraids him in a dream, arguing that he never retreated but rather attacked in a different direction.

In addition to his paean to the music he loves, Wideman, who was an all-Ivy basketball player, pays tribute to the sport at which he once excelled. "Who Invented the Jump Shot" an excerpt from his 2001 memoir *Hoop Roots*, ostensibly a fanciful satiric exploration of a basketball mystery, is actually an opportunity for Wideman to put himself inside the characters of others, including a young basketball player, and to examine the complexity of the artist role-playing another character who turns out to be based on himself. In this story Wideman also creates a modern version of a folkloric figure named Rastus who speaks in the dialect of the fictional Southern slave, as the story reenacts the horrible history of that hateful institution.

Even the lightest story in the collection, "Who Weeps When One of Us Goes Down Blues," which riffs on that lamentable moment in a basketball game when a player falls or "goes down," Wideman is not content with creating a mere finger exercise but rather uses the act of falling as a metaphor for the trials of his ancestors, dating back to his great grandfather's slave days and even further to those tribal days of his distant African ancestors, only to end with the fear that "going down" may signify the loss of the old traditions, the old language, the old ways.

"Fanon" is an excerpt from Wideman's *The Island: Martinique* (2003). In it, a man writing a book on the famous revolutionary writer Frantz Fanon struggles with the duality of black and white developed in Fanon's *Les Damnés de la terre* (1961; *The*

Wretched of the Earth, 1965). The story ends with a meditation that links Fanon's death in a hospital room in Bethesda, Maryland, with the death of Marilyn Monroe in Los Angeles, as the narrator imagines that Fanon's black body and Monroe's white one are chained together in the hold of a slave ship crossing the Atlantic Ocean.

The binary opposition of black and white is also explored in "Sharing," perhaps the most conventional narrative in this largely lyrical collection, in which a black man comes to a white female neighbor's house to borrow mayonnaise. A conversation fraught with fears and suspicions ends with a reminder of the straightforward, yet complex, idea that underlies much of Wideman's fiction: Whether black or white, beneath their skins people are the same. This story is unlike others in the collection in its presentation of a relatively straightforward dramatic situation. Because the circumstances of the story seem so pat, Wideman remains relatively detached from it, content merely to set up and play out a minor domestic drama predictable in its conclusion.

The only story in the book weaker than "Sharing" is the self-indulgent "Hunters," which begins with a stereotypical attack on a young African American couple by racist white hunters who rape the woman and kill them both. The attack is so extreme and the language so grotesque that the story seems like a risky parody of the horrors of racism. When one discovers that, indeed, the story has been invented by the young African American male narrator to exact a sort of revenge on an old girlfriend, his explanation that the blood was only ketchup, that it was all his own jealousy and anger, seems trivial in the light of the horrible truths of African American history. Wideman is best when he steers away from conventional polemical examinations of race and sticks closer to those themes that most concern him—the mystery of identity, the loss of self, the power of family, and the complex relationship between reality and fantasy.

Many of Wideman's recurrent themes coalesce in the longest and most memorable story in the collection, "What We Cannot Speak About We Must Pass Over in Silence." The title, a quote from philosopher Ludwig Wittgenstein, reflects Wideman's recognition of the complexity of human experience, which so often resists being captured by language.

The story, chosen for 2004's *Best American Short Stories*, begins with a fifty-seven-year-old man learning of the death of a casual friend whose son is in an Arizona prison. Although the death does not move the man, he grieves to the point of tears for the man's son he has never seen, empathizing with him as one who has suddenly been cut off from his last living contact with the world outside prison walls. The story focuses on the central character's obsessive quest for the young man—which becomes a search for his own identity, for he realizes that when he looks in the mirror he sees a stranger, and he wonders how long he has been losing track of himself.

Tackling the labyrinthine bureaucratic prison system in an effort to locate the boy, the central character enlists the help of a young paralegal assistant named Suh Jung, with whom he begins a love affair. Finally locating the son, he writes to him to express his condolences. The young man's only reply is that all he knew about his father until receiving the letter is that some man must have had sex with his mother. Still the man pursues his quest to meet the son. Pretending to be the father, he makes the trip to the Arizona prison, is searched, goes through various checkpoints, and finally arrives at the door to the visiting room, only to be told in the story's final paragraph that because of a computer error his visit has been canceled. Such an ending is not as pessimistic as it sounds, for an actual meeting with the son would have been an inevitable disappointment, whereas the search has been a testimony to the human need to find both family and self.

C. S. Lewis once remarked that although stories must contain series of events, it must be understood that such series are only nets in which to catch something that has no sequence but is rather something more like a state or quality. Wideman has always struggled with this hard truth—that the means of fiction always seem to be at war with its ends. He once insisted that events in human experience do not take place in an orderly chronological sequence but in "tangled skeins" of necessity and chance. Stories, insists Wideman, break down the usual ways of conceptualizing reality. At any given moment, he has noted, one may be conscious of only a few things which make up that moment. In writing, however, one can reexamine the moment and discover things that one had no notion were there. In these ten stories, Wideman examines the many layers of even the simplest moments. His are not easy works to read, but they are worth the effort. In Wideman's case, the difficulty of his fiction is evidence of the integrity of his art.

Charles E. May

Review Sources

Booklist 101, no. 7 (December 1, 2004): 619.
The Boston Globe, February 22, 2005, p. D2.
Kirkus Reviews 72, no. 23 (December 1, 2004): 1115.
Library Journal 130, no. 1 (January, 2005): 104.
The New York Times, March 20, 2005, section 7, p. 20.
Pittsburgh Post-Gazette, February 13, 2005, p. J4.
Publishers Weekly 252, no. 2 (January 10, 2005): 36.
The Seattle Times, February 27, 2005, p. J10.
The Washington Post, February 8, 2005, p. CO4.

THE GOLDEN WEST
Hollywood Stories

Author: Daniel Fuchs (1909-1993)
Publisher: Black Sparrow (Boston). 256 pp. $24.95
Type of work: Memoir, novella, and short fiction
Time: 1937-1989
Locale: Hollywood, primarily, and Brooklyn, New York

*Fuchs sympathetically describes the Hollywood milieu
in which he worked as a screenwriter, and his fiction concerns the fates of his Hollywood characters*

Principal characters:
> ROSENGARTEN, Daniel Fuchs's screenwriter
> alter ego
> F_____, a prominent film director
> ROGERS HAMMET, a down-and-out film pro-
> ducer
> ADELE HOGUE, a temperamental Hollywood star
> BURT CLARIS, a talent agency employee working with Hogue
> HARRY CASE, one of Hogue's former lovers
> FANNIE CASE, the owner of the Palm Springs hotel where Hogue hides
> ROBERT WIGLER, a film producer
> DICK PRESCOTT, Claris's boss at the talent agency

In his introduction to Daniel Fuchs's *The Golden West*, John Updike points out that, unlike so many eastern writers who went to Hollywood to write for films, Fuchs was an anomaly. It was fashionable for eastern writers to attribute their declining literary powers to their stints in Hollywood. Fuchs, who wrote mostly screenplays after he went to Hollywood in 1937, never criticized the Hollywood moguls who paid him. Abandoning a promising future as a novelist—his Williamsburg Trilogy had won him critical acclaim—did result in criticism from other writers, particularly Mordecai Richler. However, Fuchs liked writing for the masses and enjoyed the collaborative nature of screenwriting, which was the opposite of the individualistic process of writing fiction.

In the memoirs included in this collection, Fuchs provides anecdotes about his work with William Faulkner, Billy Wilder, and some unnamed producers and directors. For Fuchs, filmmaking involves wizardry and mystery, and the difference between hits and failures depends upon the writer's success in finding the story that already exists, one "touched with grace and blessed." Fuchs also has tremendous admiration for the collaborators who work tirelessly to put together films, "striving to get it right, to run down the answers to realize and secure the picture." Fuchs maintains that the films produced in the latter half of the twentieth century were the product of the "best, most solid creative effort of our decades." Almost all the Hollywood

*Before becoming a Hollywood
screenwriter, Daniel Fuchs was an
elementary school teacher in
Brooklyn, New York. He published
four novels, many short stories and
essays, and more than a dozen film
scripts—one of which,* Love Me or
Leave Me, *won an Academy Award
in 1955.*

denizens, even notorious studio bosses such as Harry Cohen and Louis B. Mayer, are treated sympathetically in this book.

In his stories and sketches Fuchs describes his initial reaction to the Hollywood scene. In "Dream City: Or, The Drugged Lake," the narrator is so frustrated by his inability to be productive that his only consolation is the fact that the date that his contract ends is not that far away. In "Hollywood Diary," the entries are also bleak. He waits in vain for a script on which to work and then encounters the rigid hierarchy that exists at the studio commissary. Although "Florida" does not concern a screenwriter, it does reflect the uncertainty, whimsicality, and fragility of people of who are barely surviving. Ready to leave Hollywood after his pitch for an idea falls on deaf ears, Johnny Mantle is ironically and inexplicably saved, just as the down-and-out William Drice is miraculously restored to power. Chronic optimism is the face of bleak reality is the order of the day for the Hollywooders who attend Curtis Spogel's party. Aside from Spogel, an accountant and hence not in the film business, no one wants to admit that film, partly because of television, is in decline and that the Golden Age is almost over.

In "Triplicate" Rosengarten, the protagonist, is Fuchs's alter ago, a screenwriter from the East Coast who is an outsider at the Hollywood party where the story's action occurs. The short story is essentially a collection of character sketches with no real plot. Rogers Hammet, one of the guests, is a stage producer whose career is on the wane. Fuchs then proceeds to describe the relationship between Hammet and Rosengarten, when Hammet was a success and Rosengarten an aspiring writer. Hammet doles out advice, denigrates filmmaking, and then criticizes Rosengarten for writing for films. Hammet, however, is at the party to salvage his career: He has an idea for a film script for an adaptation of *Life on the Mississippi* and needs Rosengarten's help. When he realizes that Rosengarten is tied up in another project, Hammet turns ugly and begins verbally to attack F_____, a prominent director who is also at the party. In the course of his tirade Hammet tells a salacious story about actress Louisa Lissak, another guest whom Garrison, the host, plans to wed. The "duplicate" is F_____, whose insecurities lead him into a fear of failure and self-destructive behavior. Hammet's and F_____'s stories are parallel, but the identity of the "triplicate" is uncertain. It could be Garrison, intent on making it in Hollywood through connections, the jealous academic critic who resents Rosengarten's success, or it could be Rosengarten himself, perhaps in the uncertain future. Rosengarten is nagged by dissatisfaction and worry and is aware of his problem of reconciling expectations and reality. The story ends with Hammet mourning his loss: "no more, no more, no more."

West of the Rockies, which Fuchs described as a "failure," is a novella about an actress, Adele Hogue, whose refusal to report to the set bankrupts the film, destroys the director, and leads to her marriage to a hanger-on who will manage her career. Hogue closely resembles Marilyn Monroe, Elizabeth Taylor, and Judy Garland, whose emotional traumas, physical problems, and absences from sets were legendary. Hogue's afflictions (the neuritis which causes her scalp to burn, the severe pain in her left arm) and paranoia increase as she ages and feels more vulnerable. She is also guilt-ridden, convinced that she has not deserved the fame and fortune she possesses, and dependent on others, especially men, to control her life. Multiple marriages and affairs are a result of her insecurity. As Fuchs portrays her, she is a sympathetic figure rather than a selfish, narcissistic star.

While Hogue is ostensibly the focus of the book, Fuchs narrates through Burt Claris. Claris is, as Fuchs describes him, a "grifter"—a con man who has used his past career as a football player to court and wed the daughter of a wealthy family, which has used their connections to get Claris a public relations job with a prestigious talent agency. Claris's only talent is in socializing with the firm's clients, including Hogue, with whom he has drifted into an affair. At the beginning of the novella Hogue and her three children are staying at Fannie Case's hotel, and Hogue's refusal to report to the set is causing major problems. Dick Prescott, Claris's boss and the person who should be responsible for Hogue's return to the set, has shunted the responsibility to Claris, who is caught in the middle and fears that his wife will learn of his affair. When he realizes that Hogue needs him near her, that he is to be the "boon companion" she needs, he gains a different perspective on his situation. The grifter, the user, discovers that "he was the one who was getting taken, not the other way around."

Two minor characters resemble Claris. While he hangs around the hotel, Claris learns that Pepi Straeger has been killed in an automobile crash. Fuchs describes Pepi as a once-popular Viennese singer now out of favor, a "hanger-on," adept at "making himself handy"—terms that describe a possible future for Claris, who is also a bit of a parasite. Louis, the steward who provides a room where Claris and Hogue can have sex, risks his job in so doing because he knows that he will benefit if Claris is successful. Similarly, Claris risks his job by having the affair with Hogue and comes to realize that he can also benefit if he can marry her and manage her career. So develops the theme of using others despite the inherent risks. Wigler, the producer whose picture is eventually ruined, apparently cannot avoid making sexual advances to a woman in the midst of the turmoil.

The best example of mutual use is the complex relationship between Hogue and Harry Case, whose brief but torrid affair resulted in the breakup of his marriage to Fannie. Even though Hogue broke off the affair, she continues to depend upon Harry, who is likewise addicted to her. Plagued by guilt, she requires the kind of recriminations that only Harry, with his elephantine memory, can provide; and he similarly needs her insults and criticisms. When Hogue isolates herself in Fannie's hotel, Harry's appearance is inevitable, but on this occasion he cannot prevail. The stage is thus set for another male presence, Claris, to assume Harry's role. Adding to this sick relationship is Hogue's friendship with and dependence on Fannie, who aids and abets the couple's quarrels. In fact, Hogue takes refuge at Fannie's because she knows that Harry will appear, and she can then fall back on their relationship.

At the same time that Hogue and Harry's relationship unravels, Claris phones his wife in New York and gets a cool reception. Concerned that she may have learned of his affair with Hogue, he returns home and finds letters indicating that his wife also has been unfaithful. He consults a lawyer about a divorce, hoping that the letters will result in his getting a financial settlement from his wife; but the lawyer informs him that he will get nothing. Claris's mercenary motives, hitherto subtly cast, are now evident. When he learns that he has also lost his job at the talent agency, he realizes that he wants Hogue's money. Claris admits that "he had lived by small larcenies all his life" and now wants a "working partnership" with Hogue. Before that can happen, he has to turn on her, confront her, as Harry had, with her behavior, and she has to respond in kind. Claris, who has come to see her as "one of them," rather than as an individual, has no illusions about the nature of their "deal." Her words to Harry about the identity of her new lover are equally flat: "A man. What the hell. Another husband, another marriage—marriage two hundred and twelve." Despite the lack of love, before the cameras Hogue can mouth "I love you" to Claris. Despite the downbeat ending, Fuch's last sentence manages to convey a wistful quality about the times, before television was established and before the demise of the studio system, in which the story occurs, the only time perhaps that the story could have taken place.

Thomas L. Erskine

Review Sources

The Atlantic Monthly 295, no. 5 (June, 2005): 101-102.
Library Journal 130, no. 8 (May 1, 2005): 129.
The Nation 281, no. 8 (September 19, 2005): 28-32.
The New Republic 232, nos. 21/22 (June 6, 2005): 42-46.
The New York Times Book Review 154 (July 10, 2005): 13-14.
The Wall Street Journal 245, no. 111 (June 8, 2005): D14.

THE GOOD WIFE

Author: Stewart O'Nan (1961-   )
Publisher: Farrar, Straus and Giroux (New York). 312
   pp. $24.00
Type of work: Novel
Time: The 1970's to 2005
Locale: Owego and other parts of upstate New York

An account of spousal love in the face of betrayal, hardship, and the exigencies of life for a woman faithful for nearly thirty years to a husband in jail for murder

> *Principal characters:*
> PATTY DICKENSON, the constant "good wife" through whose eyes the story is revealed
> TOMMY DICKENSON, her thoughtless husband whose choices change not only his but also her life
> GARY ROOKER, Tommy's fair-weather friend and partner in crime
> CASEY, the only son of Patty and Tommy, who grows from birth to adulthood during the novel
> DONNA, Gary's wife and a friend to Patty
> EILEEN, Patty's savvy younger sister and sympathetic ear—the "wild" one of the family
> SHANNON, Patty's older sister, the "success"

The Other Side of Midnight is the title of both the first chapter of Stewart O'Nan's ninth novel, *The Good Wife*, and the 1973 book by Sidney Sheldon that Patty Dickenson is reading on the early winter night that changes her life. Her pregnant body snuggled into bed, she waits for her husband. She waits, too, for their first child, whom she is convinced is a boy. Tonight she anticipates something else. She waits in bed, wrapped in a sexy black peignoir. Life is good and hopeful. She cannot know that the seemingly smooth trajectory of her life will be interrupted forever by a phone call. The phone rings. For her and for her growing family, the dark and desolate "other side of midnight" has just begun.

The call is from her husband, Tommy. He tells Patty that he and his good friend and drinking buddy, Gary, have gotten into "a little spot." He assures her that, although the pair have been arrested and the phone call is coming from jail, things are not so bad. There is a "bunch of stuff," but without detailing its content he assures her that everything will be fine. The bubble of his assurance is burst by a second phone call. This time the caller is Donna, Gary's wife. The "bunch of stuff" turns out to be a very serious situation. The men have been arrested after attempting to rob the home of an old woman, Mrs. Wagner, not unknown to Patty's family, who is now dead. The charges are robbery and murder.

A native of Pittsburgh, Stewart
O'Nan gave up a productive career
in engineering to write. His works
include A Prayer for the Dying
(1999), Snow Angels *(1994), and*
The Speed Queen *(1997). In 1996,*
Granta *named O'Nan one of the*
Twenty Best Young American
Novelists. He collaborated with
author Stephen King to write about
their favorite team in Faithful: Two
Diehard Boston Red Sox Fans
Chronicle the Historic 2004 Season
(2004).

Served poorly by his lawyer and unable to rise above the damning evidence and the betrayal by his friend Gary, Tommy is sentenced to the maximum term for second-degree murder. Gary gets off with the equivalent of a slap on the wrist. Tommy's legal appeals fail. The damning consequence of one night of poor judgment is lived out in the dismal routine of twenty-eight years in prison. Patty and the reader face the experience with him: the quotidian ugliness, hopelessness, and degradation of a spirit-suppressing life.

Through the lengthy ordeal, Patty not only keeps her marital commitment but tries to smooth the course of the long years in prison for her husband. She bears their son, Casey, raises him to respect his father, and endures whatever it takes to cobble a precarious life for herself and her child. Desperate for money, she does whatever work will pay the bills, steeled to the exigencies of life as a single mother with few resources or skills. She juggles her work life, family obligations, and her episodic contacts with her husband. She endures the loss of her own residence as she moves in with her mother, the taunting of reporters as she leaves the courtroom, and the judgment of those around her. Whenever she can, she visits Tommy and submits to everything the system requires, from the indignity of personal searches as she enters the prison to the guards' arbitrary exercises of authority.

She tries to make Tommy's life in prison as carefree as possible, baking him lasagna and taking advantage of periodic conjugal visits under the worst of conditions. Through these recurrent waves of difficulty Patty remains afloat, a constant wife and resilient heroine. She emerges as a much stronger person than the naïve young wife anticipating a sexual evening with the husband she adores. The world may self-destruct around her, but she remains focused on what she believes must be done.

The reader is drawn into Patty Dickenson's bleak experience in a way that lingers in memory and mood even after the book is done. O'Nan has a writing style that burrows its way into the consciousness of the reader and refuses to dislodge. He frames his story with care. The opening scene of the book, set in the chill of a winter night, speaks of Patty confined within "black mirror" windows that enclose her within the "walls of a box," her bedroom. At the end of the book, set likewise in the marital bedroom, the windows no longer box her in. Rather, they are open to the strong beam of the full moon and the calming sounds of a warm summer night.

As the book concludes, Patty seems no longer to have romantic illusions about who her husband is; she lies in bed at peace, optimistic that the future will be fine. The reader may be uneasy, sensing that maybe Patty's contentment will be short-lived. Is this not the same optimistic tone that pervades the opening lines of the story? Has Patty ever really faced the irresponsibility of the person to whom she is married, preoccupied as he is with body building, acquisition of adult toys such as a dirt bike and an eight-track player and with little regard for her well-being? The title of the concluding chapter is "In the Dark." Perhaps she still is.

In the final analysis, it is only Patty whom the reader gets to know well. One feels not only the emotions of O'Nan's singular character but also sweats in the heat and shivers in the cold with her. One is drawn into the humdrum tasks of Patty's life, the constant desperation as money and hope become increasingly threadbare, the submission to those things which appear to beat her down. The dust of Patty's daily living is difficult to shake from one's psyche. Other characters in the book seem almost two-dimensional by comparison. It is difficult to flesh out the husband or son, the mother or coworkers, even though they linger in the book's fabric. Only hints are dropped, and they are dropped only to delineate the situation and perceptions of the central figure, Patty. Rather than being a fault of the book, this lack of definition brings the reader even deeper into the experience O'Nan has crafted. This technique is very similar to the author's haunting and successful portrayal in *A Prayer for the Dying* (1999), where the major character moves among a cardboard supporting cast.

Some will see *The Good Wife* as a poignant love story: a tale of the persistent devotion of a woman smitten with a less-than-perfect husband, even when he falls short of being even that. Embracing Patty sympathetically as a realist with no illusions about Tommy's perfection or his resolve to be better, they will praise and admire Patty for her ability to make sweet the proverbial lemonade from the sour fruit she is given. They will champion her devotion to the permanency of marriage and willingness to carry on through surmounting obstacles.

Others, however, will find in Patty the epitome of a victim. She is one who is willing to "stand by her man," even in the face of his adolescent and careless disregard for her needs. Never does she challenge his "take-not-give" approach to their relationship and to life in general. She remains, or chooses to remain, "in the dark." More jaundiced readers likely will judge her as a person who enables the indolence and lack of responsibility in her spouse by an overwhelming courage to do what must be done, in truth to do it all herself. They will see this courage and generosity to be misplaced. In the nearly thirty years from the time of the arrest to the final scene of the novel, Tommy shows not a hint of growth or change. He does not verbalize his poor judgment or a commitment to change for the better.

Patty neither recriminates nor withdraws from him. She continues, instead, to prop him up and hope. For some readers this passivity in the face of systemic injustice will produce an anger, not only at Tommy but also at Patty for not simply getting out of the bad situation. Where is the intervention of a women's shelter and assertiveness counseling when it is clearly needed? Where are the more insightful members of her family, who might name the situation more clearly for her? Does she simply not want to see and hear?

Some will see the novel as subtle social commentary about the unfairness of the prison system to those without means, and of treatment approaching abuse which is inflicted on the innocent relatives and friends of prisoners. Without proper counsel, Tommy seems to be given a sentence disproportionate to his part in the crime. Demeaned by the rules and frustrated by the reality of the penal system, Patty, representative of many whose loved ones are in prison, continues to endure what is necessary to sustain contact with them. Those who linger on these layers of social commentary in the book will be outraged at the systemic injustice or simply affirmed in what they already believe about it. The reader may or may not easily lay aside the book and the indictment of social institutions such as welfare money and the prison system.

A novel that can evoke such strong and varied reaction in the reader is a very good novel. As noted above, O'Nan again achieves the lingering effect in the reader that he did in his earlier work *A Prayer for the Dying*. *The Good Wife* likewise gets under one's skin, provoking thoughtful reflection. Is Patty a "good wife," or merely a victim in denial of the real Tommy. Does the book really have a happy ending, or is this promise only in the mind of its protagonist? To read *The Good Wife* is to be open to think deeply, to experience a gripping story in such a way that the book will never really close again. This book is highly recommended for book clubs and any other forum which seeks lively discussion.

Dolores L. Christie

Review Sources

The Atlantic Monthly 295, no. 4 (May, 2005): 128.
Booklist 101, no. 12 (February 15, 2005): 1036-1037.
Kirkus Reviews 73, no. 2 (January 15, 2005): 79.
Library Journal 130, no. 4 (March 1, 2005): 80.
The New York Times Book Review 154 (May 8, 2005): 7.
People 63, no. 16 (April 25, 2005): 44.
Publishers Weekly 252, no. 9 (February 28, 2005): 40.

A GREAT IMPROVISATION
Franklin, France, and the Birth of America

Author: Stacy Schiff (1960-   )
Publisher: Henry Holt (New York). 489 pp. $30.00
Type of work: Biography and history
Time: 1776-1785
Locale: Paris, France

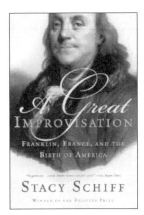

This biography narrates Benjamin Franklin's success-ful mission to secure a French alliance and French money for the newly proclaimed United States of America and de-scribes his contributions when negotiating the 1783 peace treaty with Great Britain

Principal personages:

BENJAMIN FRANKLIN (1706-1790), the leading American diplomat in France, 1776-1785

WILLIAM TEMPLE FRANKLIN (1760-1823), his grandson, his secretary in France

JOHN ADAMS (1735-1826), a peace commissioner in the 1780's, later the second president of the United States

JOHN JAY (1745-1829), a peace commissioner in the 1780's, later the first chief justice of the United States

THOMAS JEFFERSON (1743-1826), Franklin's successor as minister to France, later the third president of the United States

CHARLES GRAVIER, COMTE DE VERGENNES, (1717-1787), the French minister of foreign affairs

PIERRE-AUGUSTIN CARON DE BEAUMARCHAIS (1732-1799), a play-wright, the conduit of secret military supplies from France to the United States

MARQUIS DE LAFAYETTE (1757-1834), a French volunteer who com-manded American troops during the Revolutionary War

LOUIS XVI (1754-1793), the king of France

DAVID MURRAY, VISCOUNT STORMONT (1727-1796), the British ambas-sador to France

On October 26, 1776, Benjamin Franklin sailed from Philadelphia charged with representing the United States in Paris, securing formal recognition by the French government, and obtaining increased French aid for the new nation. He would not see the city again until September 14, 1785, nearly nine years later. Seventy-year-old Franklin had no diplomatic experience, his spoken French was hard to understand, and his written French crude and ungrammatical. Yet in *A Great Improvisation: Franklin, France, and the Birth of America*, author Stacy Schiff claims that he was the best possible choice for the position. No revolutionary leader had more European ex-

~

Stacy Schiff published Saint-
Exupéry: A Biography *(1994) and*
won the Pulitzer Prize in biography
for Véra (Mrs. Vladimir Nabokov):
Portrait of a Marriage *(1999). She*
has contributed book reviews to
The New Yorker, The New York
Times Book Review, The
Washington Post, *and* The Times
Literary Supplement. *She lives in*
New York City.

~

perience or better French. Schiff cites Thomas Jefferson's admission that even after five years in Paris, he was never certain he understood what was said to him or whether his spoken and written French conveyed his actual meaning.

Franklin's tumultuous welcome when he arrived in France in December demonstrated the wisdom of the congressional choice. He was not merely the best-known American but also one of the most widely admired men in the world, acclaimed throughout Europe as the scientist who tamed lightning, the successor to Isaac Newton and Galileo. Intellectuals and aristocrats (in eighteenth century France often one and the same) clamored for his attention. The Parisian public eagerly purchased matchboxes, teacups, candy dishes, fabrics, and canes decorated with likenesses of Franklin. Recognizing the value of public enthusiasm for things American in encouraging the government's willingness to support the revolution, Franklin deliberately played to the crowd. Schiff notes that when hailed as a frontiersman and backwoods philosopher, Franklin, who had never lived anywhere but in cities during his seventy years, adopted a fur hat and plain suits as his distinctive costume in glittering eighteenth century Paris.

Schiff calls Franklin a natural diplomat. Aspects of Franklin's personality, his reserve and reluctance to commit himself until absolutely necessary, and his pragmatic willingness to compromise—attitudes that led some of his American colleagues to accuse him of being duplicitous and insufficiently devoted to the American cause—were characteristics well attuned to life at the Court of Versailles. Despite getting little guidance from Congress, he improvised an effective foreign policy for the United States, successfully negotiated a treaty of alliance with France, and joined with John Jay and John Adams in securing a very advantageous peace treaty with Great Britain.

Franklin's task was eased by decisions and actions already taken by Louis XVI and his minister for foreign affairs Charles Gravier, Comte de Vergennes. The French resented the draconian peace treaty Britain had imposed in 1763 and hoped for revenge. When antagonism grew between the American colonies and their mother country, the French eagerly sent agents to Philadelphia to assess the possibility of embarrassing Britain. Even before the colonies declared independence, Vergennes urged sending aid. On May 2, 1776, the king of France provided one million livres (matched by the king of Spain a month later) to pay for military supplies. To permit deniability when the British ambassador, David Murray, Viscount Stormont, protested, Vergennes had Pierre-Augustin Caron de Beaumarchais, a playwright famous for his subversive *Barber of Seville* (1772), claim he had purchased guns and powder from French arsenals and shipped them to America on his own account.

Always interpreting events in Franklin's favor, Schiff insists that colleagues and friends gave Franklin greater difficulty than official enemies. Using polite evasions,

Vergennes easily ignored Lord Stormont's complaints that welcoming Franklin and providing not-very-secret aid violated French protestations of neutrality. Rivalry and quarrels among French and Americans involved in expediting military aid to America had more to do with slowing movement of supplies to America than British opposition.

Franklin pretended to have no secrets, which was true in a sense he did not intend— many helpers aiding the American mission, including some Franklin considered his best friends, were in fact spies who sent copies of documents and detailed reports of American activity to their British and French employers. Aristocratic Virginians, certain they were better qualified than bourgeois Franklin to conduct diplomacy, bombarded Congress with vicious letters accusing him of various misdemeanors and dereliction of duty. Although Adams worked effectively with Franklin in negotiating the peace treaty with Britain, he developed a visceral dislike of Franklin that spilled over into open criticism, accusing him of being too subservient to Vergennes in politely requesting loans. Adams claimed American success was so clearly in the French interest that Vergennes should immediately provide more money and arrange more effective naval aid. His remarks irritated Vergennes, who had Franklin forward to Congress his denunciation of Adams.

Constant backbiting from his colleagues poisoned Franklin's relations with Congress, which often ignored his requests and never praised his successes. Many members were unimpressed with Franklin's French celebrity and suspicious that it proved assertions by his enemies that he was overly pro-French. Early in his tenure in Paris, Franklin requested appointment of a consul to relieve him of the burden of managing maritime affairs and helping Americans engaged in commerce. Congress failed to do so until 1782, when Franklin expected to soon be relieved of his post.

Franklin wanted Congress formally to select his grandson, William Temple Franklin, as mission secretary, a position he had effectively filled from 1776. Fluent in French, Temple, as he was called, performed many vital functions for the diplomats, including correcting his grandfather's formal correspondence. When Franklin put Temple on the payroll, critics called it nepotism. Congress did not provide a secretary until Jefferson replaced Franklin in 1785, and then it ignored Franklin's plea to choose Temple in favor of someone with better political connections but no knowledge of French.

Schiff describes how Franklin's inadequacies as an administrator were exacerbated by his need to fulfill personally so many roles. Despite his later reputation as a penny-pinching businessman, Franklin had little interest in bookkeeping, or the patience to keep accurate account books. Adams complained bitterly when he undertook the almost impossible task of straightening out the mission's financial records. When called upon to adjudicate naval matters, Franklin's decisions earned him the enmity of American privateers operating in European waters. He had difficult dealing with the flood of aristocrats volunteering to serve as generals in the American army, most of whom discovered on arrival in America that their services were neither desired nor rewarded.

One of the few successes was Marie-Joseph-Paul-Yves-Roche-Gilbert du Motier, Marquis de Lafayette, who sailed for America in 1777 in a ship carrying arms and ammunition for which he paid himself. Lafayette soon won the friendship of General George Washington and a general's commission commanding American troops. Returning to France several times during the war, Lafayette usefully supported Franklin's requests by providing the French government with firsthand accounts of the desperate American need for war supplies.

Franklin's handling of Vergennes when achieving an overt French alliance and in soothing the foreign minister's irritation at the way the American delegation conducted peace negotiations with Great Britain, demonstrated how well he had mastered the art of diplomacy. Schiff terms these his supreme triumphs as a diplomat. News that the Americans had captured an entire British army on October 17, 1777, at the Battle of Saratoga did not reach Paris until December 4. Franklin immediately used the success to advance his drive for formal recognition of the United States, trumpeting the American success to everyone and suggesting that a similar fate would soon overtake all British forces in the New World.

When the British government sent unofficial emissaries to sound out Franklin on whether the Americans would settle for something short of complete independence, Franklin played off the British against the French, stimulating Vergennes's fear that the United States would abandon the war and render French aid a waste of money. Franklin kept Vergennes voluminously informed of the barrage of peace feelers from London, leading Vergennes to overcome his reluctance to risk war with Britain and offer formal recognition of the new nation. On February 6, 1778, Franklin and Vergennes signed two documents. An open treaty of amity and commerce recognized the United States and granted its exports most-favored-nation status. A secret pact established a military alliance which would go into effect in the event of war between France and Britain and guaranteed that neither country would abandon the war before American independence was established.

The surrender of the British army at Yorktown on October 19, 1781, marked the high point of Franco-American military cooperation arranged by Vergennes and Franklin. The land forces, half French and half American soldiers, were all armed, clothed, and fed by France, the artillery and ammunition came from France, and a French fleet successfully held off the British navy. The victory provided the occasion for America's greatest diplomatic success.

On July 20, 1782, Franklin gave the British his ideas on a peace treaty. Necessary articles were complete independence, evacuation of all British troops, access to Newfoundland fisheries, and a Great Lakes and Mississippi boundary which doubled the size of the thirteen colonies. Among possible conditions, Franklin suggested that Britain cede Canada to the United States as a gesture of goodwill. When Franklin was incapacitated by painful kidney stones, actual negotiations fell to John Jay, who successfully insisted that Britain formally acknowledge American independence before discussing other terms and got Franklin to agree to ignore Congressional instructions to consult the French at every step. With a last-minute assist from Adams, who had been held up in Holland negotiating a Dutch loan, the three peace commissioners signed a preliminary peace treaty (including Franklin's entire list of necessary articles) on November 30, 1782.

Franklin had the task of informing Vergennes of the agreement. Vergennes censured the Americans for ignoring him during the negotiations, but he could hardly have been surprised at the news, given how thoroughly the American mission was infested with spies. Franklin demonstrated his diplomatic skill with an inspired response: "The English, I just now learn, flatter themselves that they have already divided us. I hope this little misunderstanding will therefore be kept a perfect secret; and that they will find themselves totally mistaken."

Schiff is a gifted storyteller and literary stylist. Her colorful narrative of Franklin's Paris years, based on extensive use of archival and documentary primary sources, is fascinating reading. At times she provides too much detail, as in repetitious descriptions of the endless infighting between Americans assigned, or who attached themselves, to the Paris mission. The same accusations repeat as various self-important political figures discover that Franklin ignored their advice. Schiff is stronger on narrative than on analysis and could have used more explanation of why the French were so willing to give Franklin what he asked, why monarchists chose to support a rebellious republic to the point of bankrupting their own government.

The strongest part of the book is Schiff's demonstration of how much the American Revolution owed to French support. She convincingly shows that Washington's military victory over the British would not have been possible without the aid of French arms and ammunition, soldiers, and navy.

Milton Berman

Review Sources

Booklist 101, no. 13 (March 1, 2005): 1121.
The Economist 375 (April 30, 2005): 78-79.
Harper's Magazine 311 (October, 2005): 88-94.
Kirkus Reviews 73, no. 2 (January 15, 2005): 111.
Los Angeles Times, April 1, 2005, p. E28.
The New York Times Book Review 154 (April 3, 2005): 8.
Publishers Weekly 252, no. 6 (February 7, 2005): 50.
The Washington Post, April 3, 2005, p. T4.

THE HA-HA

Author: Dave King (1955-   )
Publisher: Little, Brown (New York). 340 pp. $24.00
Type of work: Novel
Time: The early twenty-first century
Locale: A midwestern town

A veteran, rendered speechless in the Vietnam War, struggles to reconnect with life through his relationship with a nine-year-old boy

> *Principal characters:*
> HOWARD (HOWIE) KAPOSTASH, a middle-aged Vietnam veteran
> SYLVIA MOHR, his high-school sweetheart, now a cocaine addict
> RYAN MOHR, her nine-year-old son
> LAUREL CAO, Howie's Vietnamese housemate from Texas
> STEVE (NIT) and HARRISON (NAT), Howie's housemates, house
>   painters
> SISTER AMITY BRIDGE, Howie's employer at Mercy Convent
> TIMOTHY, a homeless veteran

The inability to communicate is one of the most dreaded losses to confront an intelligent person, as Howard Kapostash, the protagonist of Dave King's debut novel, *The Ha-Ha*, well knows. This remarkable book is a tour de force given that it is narrated entirely by a character who cannot speak. Thirty years ago Howie was wounded in Vietnam when a land mine exploded, causing a hematoma in his left temporal lobe and leaving him with a dented skull and a puffy scar. His doctors say that he has anomia, an inability to recall names, but Howie believes that he is physically incapable of forming words (his one dependable syllable is "Not!"), although he fully understands the speech of others. He can read a few words sporadically, but he cannot write at all and is understandably frustrated when he is unable to respond to a complex question. Speech-impaired but mentally alert, he carries a card informing strangers that he is "of normal intelligence!"

Howie lives in the four-story Victorian house that belonged to his parents and still sleeps in his boyhood room. To help with expenses, he shares his home with three housemates, all in their thirties. Laurel Cao, originally from Vietnam, has a broad Texas accent from growing up in Austin. She has her own business, Soupe Toujours, which supplies gourmet soups to local businesses. Instead of paying rent, she handles Howie's paperwork. The two men, Steve and Harrison (whom Howie has silently nicknamed Nit and Nat), paint houses and are "younger than they deserve." Immature and irresponsible, they do not share in the daily work of the household, and Howie's opinion of them is not high.

Currently Howie is a part-time maintenance worker at Mercy Convent under the watchful eye of Sister Amity, where his favorite job is mowing the Long Field. He likes to ride the John Deere mower to the very edge of the ha-ha, a deep ditch which conceals the boundary wall and creates an illusion of continuity in the landscape. Ascending the slope of the ha-ha and sharply turning back down reminds Howie of his sixteenth and final day in Vietnam when, slightly stoned, he and two other men walked through the jungle on patrol. Their lieutenant, distracted by an orchid, accidentally stepped on a mine and was killed, but the others survived. Howie's indelible memory is of "the floating feeling as the ground fell away. The orange dust grew warm around me and filled recognizably with bits of life: the lieutenant's netted helmet, a few leaves clinging to its brim; a spray of pebbles, like an asteroid belt." He tries to recover the sensation of becoming airborne and falling through the orange air; he savors the weightlessness, the risk.

Dave King earned a B.F.A. from the Cooper Union in painting and film and an M.F.A. in writing from Columbia University. He teaches English at Baruch College and cultural studies and poetry at the School of Visual Arts. King has published poetry in The Paris Review. *This is his first novel.*

Living on wages and disability insurance payments, Howie appears to have adapted well to his changed life. Occasionally he feels a sudden rage but is usually able to control himself; otherwise, he remains disengaged. His interior monologue is coherent, and there is nothing wrong with his intellect or judgment, except when it comes to his high school sweetheart, Sylvia Mohr. When he left for Vietnam at eighteen, Sylvia saw him off. His love for her has never wavered, yet she contacts him only when she needs help with errands or repairs—and he allows it. Once an art student, Sylvia ultimately gave up that lifestyle for temporary jobs and a cocaine addiction. She has a nine-year-old biracial son, Ryan. Currently, strung out on cocaine and at her sister's urging, an unfocused Sylvia is entering a drug rehabilitation program for "a tune-up" and at the last moment asks Howie to be Ryan's temporary guardian while she is in treatment.

The problem for Howie, then, is how to care for, communicate, and cope with a nine-year-old boy in a household of independent adults who barely speak to one another. Howie, who has had few close relationships, says of himself and Ryan, "We don't go beyond neutral." Although he has accepted responsibility for Sylvia's son, he believes that the boy's "happiness is his own business." Still, in an awkward attempt to bond, Howie takes Ryan to a Golden Gloves championship boxing match. In real fights, Howie has always tried not to get hurt. His response to problems has been a self-protective withdrawal, habitually tucking his hands inside the bib of his overalls in an attempt to disappear. That tactic does not work with Ryan, who uses withdrawal too, punishing his foolish mother by refusing to speak to her in spite of her repeated phone calls.

Tensions and arguments inevitably develop. When a mysterious after-school activity leaves Ryan with scratches and bruises, Howie discovers that some older boys have built a little go-cart track and are taking turns driving around it. He rescues the sulky Ryan, a youngster who is permanently attached to his Cleveland Indians cap, from this risky activity and enrolls him in Little League baseball instead. Ryan responds by uprooting some petunias and knocking over a barbecue grill because he has no baseball glove and is afraid of ridicule. Howie, who had forgotten what it was like to be a boy, begins to see himself in Ryan and to identify with him.

From Laurel's delicious soups to Howie's home-cooked meals, food helps to bring these characters together. When Howie prepares breakfast for himself and Ryan, Laurel soon leaves her kettles to join them. Companionship slowly blossoms at breakfast, as everyone grows accustomed to eating and working together. Housemates Steve and Harrison buy a lunch box for Ryan and even accept clean-up duties, although Howie turns jealous when they try to connect further with the boy by treating him like an equal.

The baseball team finally unites Ryan and Howie; it is at the center of their relationship. Ryan excels at baseball, and a startled Howie is quickly named as a batting coach and umpire. Even Harrison, who likes to play catch with the boy (both are left-handed), is drafted as the team's first-rate pitching coach, while Steve and Laurel cheer. From an onerous duty and a favor to Sylvia, Ryan is transformed into an important member of the household, blending them all into a functioning family.

Then Howie takes Ryan on the John Deere mower to the edge of the ha-ha. He wants to share with him the thrill of the ha-ha, to explain to Ryan how he is haunted by his memory of the explosion and the transcendence of rising, floating in the orange air, in "those last minutes when life was good." For him, the ha-ha represents "a compression of that day in the jungle, and of my whole eighteen years of freedom before, into one or two moments of breathless grace." When Ryan accidentally falls from the mower, Sister Amity is furious at the risk they have taken and suspends Howie, who resents being scolded like a child and angrily determines not to return. He cannot sense her empathy, the kindness underneath her starched exterior.

At a café where Howie and his father used to eat, he and Ryan accidentally encounter Sylvia and have a brief, unsatisfactory reunion. Howie notices how Sylvia deliberately excludes her female companion, a fellow addict, from the conversation; nevertheless he is hopelessly, helplessly, in love again and planning their future even as he is running out of money. He continues to avoid Sister Amity's phone messages, although she sounds conciliatory and he needs the income. He turns impulsive and willful, charging more purchases although he knows he cannot afford them. When after three weeks Howie does return to the convent, he has already exhausted his bank account and is drawing from the money market fund that his parents left him.

Howie is like the John Deere mower, teetering on the edge of the ha-ha, knowing that he can easily plunge into anger or madness. The ragged veteran Timothy is the shadow that he has tried so hard to resist. Howie's interaction with this homeless man mirrors his own internal struggle as he moves from a wary distance through stages of fury, guilt, and compassion. In their first encounter, Howie wonders whether Timothy might be a former school friend, but filthy, mad, drugged Timothy promptly salutes him as "Bro." After Howie encounters Sylvia with a new boyfriend, he gives Timothy a vicious beating, almost as if he is trying to destroy some part of himself; yet later he accepts the veteran and tries to help him.

Howie's contact with Ryan has forced him to reexamine his past—his own impairment, his relationships, his anger, his grief. He has been blinded by his feelings for Sylvia and his fear of losing Ryan, whom he has truly learned to love, because he has already lost so much and knows too well how easily things can change. Howie is able to access the sensitive part of himself, the part that he has buried deep within; he allows himself to become vulnerable and experience fully the pain and frustration that are so much a part of his life. He can finally form a clear picture of Sylvia, who cannot complete her sentences even when she is sober and who blames others for the consequences of her own behavior. Wanting her is a bad habit, and he learns to see her whole—the inconsistency, the manipulation, the fact that she does not care for him as he does for her. When she returns from eight weeks in the drug program, Howie realizes that he does not really like the new, brittle, determined Sylvia. She is an illusion, like the ha-ha.

Author King's life with an autistic brother doubtless enabled him to create a successful, multifaceted character who is unable to communicate except through looks and gestures. Howie, who hates bullies, does not know how to handle his anger or that of others, yet Laurel tells him he is a kind man. Lonely, withdrawn, he has good friends but for a long time fails to recognize them: Ryan, Laurel, Steve and Harrison, even Sister Amity (who materializes in the middle of the night in a rumpled nightgown and pink sweatpants). Howie is not a perfect person and sometimes not entirely likable, perhaps because he tries so hard to be honest with himself. He has done things of which he is ashamed, things he regrets, but within him there is an innate decency, a wistful lyricism, that makes the reader glad to know him.

Joanne McCarthy

Review Sources

Booklist 101, no. 16 (April 15, 2005): 1475.
The Christian Science Monitor, January 4, 2005, p. 14.
Kirkus Reviews 72, no. 17 (September 1, 2004): 825.
Los Angeles Times, January 9, 2005, p. R10.
The New York Times Book Review 154 (January 23, 2005): 25.
Publishers Weekly 251, no. 46 (November 15, 2004): 37-38.
Time 165, no. 5 (January 31, 2005): 70.
The Washington Post, February 6, 2005, p. T04.

HARRY POTTER AND THE HALF-BLOOD PRINCE

Author: J. K. Rowling (1965-   )
Publisher: Scholastic (New York). 652 pp. $30.00
Type of work: Novel
Time: The late 1990's
Locale: England

In the sixth novel in Rowling's best-selling series, the wizarding community is thrown into chaos as Harry's archenemy, Lord Voldemort, steps up his evil campaign to eliminate Harry and rule the world

Principal characters:
> HARRY POTTER, a sixteen-year-old student at Hogwarts School of Witchcraft and Wizardry
> RONALD WEASLEY, his best friend and fellow student
> HERMIONE GRANGER, his close friend and fellow student
> ALBUS DUMBLEDORE, the headmaster of Hogwarts and Harry's mentor
> SEVERUS SNAPE, the professor of Defense Against the Dark Arts at Hogwarts
> DRACO MALFOY, Snape's favorite student and Harry's foe
> RUBEUS HAGRID, the teacher of the Care of Magical Creatures at Hogwarts
> GINNY WEASLEY, Ron's younger sister
> HORACE SLUGHORN, the professor of Potions at Hogwarts
> PETUNIA and VERNON DURSLEY, Harry's muggle aunt and uncle
> DUDLEY DURSLEY, Harry's repugnant cousin

On July 15, 2005, one minute before midnight, millions of people around the world were lined up at their local bookstores to purchase *Harry Potter and the Half-Blood Prince.* Why did the penultimate book in Rowling's best-selling series soar to the top of the best-seller lists before it even hit the shelves?

One possible reason is that J. K. Rowling is a consummate storyteller. From *Harry Potter and the Philosopher's Stone* (1997; published in the United States as *Harry Potter and the Sorcerer's Stone,* 1998), the first book in the series, to the newest volume, her spellbinding plots are compelling, suspenseful, and multilayered. Although each book follows a similar story line—Harry and his friends fight the powers of evil personified in Lord Voldemort, a renegade wizard—Rowling makes each tale fresh by adding new and often quirky characters, unexpected plot twists, and cliffhanger endings. She also explores philosophical issues such as good and evil and right and wrong, although rarely are these categories sharply drawn. Ambiguity is more often the rule in Rowling's work than the exception.

Another reason Rowling's Harry Potter novels keep fans reading is that the enchanting world she creates is imaginative and original, even though she borrows freely from classical literature, mythology, and folklore. While her work sometimes echoes masters of fantasy such as C. S. Lewis and J. R. R. Tolkien, as well as Roman and Greek myth, she puts her own unique spin on these influences. In Rowling's wizarding world not only do witches and wizards fly on broomsticks, they also use them to play a dangerous, fast-paced game called Quidditch. Photographs and pictures of people on walls and in newspapers wave and talk. Centaurs teach divination classes. Bestial werewolves are not all bad, and subservient house-elves are not all good.

Finally, she creates a host of engaging characters that readers love—and love to hate. Harry and Albus Dumbledore, Ron Weasley and Hermione Granger, Tom Riddle and Severus Snape, Ginny Weasley and Sirius Black, Peeves and Headless Nick, Dobby and Kreacher, Luna Lovegood and Neville Longbottom, Rubeus Hagrid and Grawp, Dolores Umbridge and Cornelius Fudge, and many other intriguing individuals with oddly appropriate names people the pages of Rowling's novels. Although she bestows magical powers on her characters, they have the same flaws and foibles that muggles—or nonwizards—possess, making them attractive and accessible to readers.

J. K. Rowling has published six best-selling Harry Potter books, which have captured the imaginations of adults and children alike. She has won the Hugo Award, the Bram Stoker Award, and the Whitbread Award for Best Children's Book, as well as many other honors. Her books have been translated into sixty-one languages. Rowling lives in Scotland with her husband and three children.

Many of the above-named characters appear in *Harry Potter and the Half-Blood Prince*. The sixth book of the series opens in the office of an unnamed prime minister of England, who is awaiting a telephone call from the equally anonymous president of a "far off country"—"a wretched man" in the prime minister's view. While he waits, he ruminates on a series of catastrophic events which have been plaguing his country—a freak hurricane, a bridge collapse, and two high-profile murders. Suddenly Cornelius Fudge, the inept minister of magic who favors lime-green bowler hats, arrives in the prime minister's office via the flames in the fireplace. Fudge informs the prime minister that what seem to be random disasters are actually carefully planned attacks on the muggle domain by dementors, sinister specters. The scene in the prime minister's office is both ominous and humorous as Rowling sets the stage for the tragic conflict to come and has a bit of fun at the expense of politicians who are more concerned about their public images than governing their countries.

Meanwhile, as the dementors wreak havoc and Voldemort's followers, known as Death Eaters, plan their strategy to dominate both the muggle and the wizarding worlds, Harry and his best friends Ron and Hermione return to Hogwarts for their sixth year of study. The school is not the same place they left two months previously, when they went on summer vacation. Horace Slughorn, a name-dropping elitist, has been lured out of retirement to become the new Potions teacher, and slimy, snarling Severus Snape has finally secured his dream job as professor of Defense Against the Dark Arts.

Dumbledore, Hogwarts's beloved headmaster, is often absent from the school on mysterious errands, one of which has resulted in his right hand being burned black. Because of Voldemort's rise to power, security at the school has been tightened. Hogwarts's ill-tempered caretaker, Argus Filch, conducts searches at the door of the castle, strong enchantments protect the entrances and grounds surrounding the school, and aurors keep watch to repel any surprise attacks. The omnipresent threat of terrorism in Rowling's novel is chillingly familiar to those living in a post-September 11, 2001, world, and readers no doubt will identify with the apprehension that Hogwarts students feel.

Despite the grim situation outside the walls of the school, the young witches- and wizards-in-training are nonetheless portrayed as typical teens. They study at all hours, wait anxiously to see if they have made the Quidditch team, flirt with members of the opposite sex, and make out in the hallways. Teenage hormones are unleashed, but so is genuine romance. After Harry overcomes his reluctance to date his best friend's sister, he and Ginny Weasley finally become a couple. Ron and Hermione's constant bickering masks their growing attraction for each other. Ron even dates the clinging Lavender Brown in order to spite Hermione—and it works. Rowling's chronicles of the characters' dating dilemmas make it clear that she has not forgotten what it is like to be a teenager. There is a special poignancy in her descriptions of adolescent love, heightened by the shadow of darker days to come.

Darker days are indeed on the horizon. Although this is the first book in the series in which Voldemort does not appear in person, his pernicious presence pervades the novel. His Death Eaters are everywhere. Harry even suspects his fellow student and adversary Draco Malfoy of joining their ranks. Although Voldemort has been a primary character in all six books of the series, Rowling has not explained the reasons behind his penchant for evil.

In *Harry Potter and the Half-Blood Prince*, the author finally reveals Voldemort's back story. Through Pensieve sessions with Dumbledore, Harry discovers his history is similar to that of Tom Riddle, the future Lord Voldemort. Both are orphans and both possess unusual powers. The difference between them, Dumbledore points out, is that Harry has been surrounded by people who love him, with the possible exception of the Dursleys, Harry's despicable muggle relatives. When Voldemort tried to murder Harry and his mother fifteen years before, her love protected her son even as she sacrificed her life for him. Tom Riddle, on the other hand, never knew love. Abandoned by his muggle father, Tom's witch mother, a direct descendent of the villainous Slytherin, died shortly after Tom was born. He was placed in an orphanage, where he terrorized his fellow boarders. A compassionate Dumbledore found him and brought him to Hogwarts. Dumbledore's kindness, however, was not sufficient to rehabilitate or redeem him.

Dumbledore's willingness to extend second chances to those who seem to least deserve them is puzzling, especially in regard to Severus Snape. As head of Slytherin

House at Hogwarts and a former Death Eater, Snape's behavior and motivation have been suspect throughout the series. In the fifth book, *Harry Potter and the Order of the Phoenix* (2003), Harry, using the Pensieve, discovers that Snape and Harry's father, James, were classmates. An outsider who was as repugnant as a teenager as he is as an adult, Snape was mercilessly taunted and humiliated by James and Sirius Black, Harry's godfather. James's cruelty toward Snape goes a long way in explaining Snape's apparent dislike of Harry. The conflict between Snape and Harry is not the only problem, however. Snape's attraction to the dark arts and his malicious personality make him a poor choice to be part of the Order of the Phoenix, a group opposed to Voldemort. Because of Dumbledore's faith in him, however, he is welcomed into the fold by the other members.

In *Harry Potter and the Half-Blood Prince*, Snape's character comes under more intense scrutiny. At the beginning of the book, Draco Malfoy's mother, Narcissa, and her sister, Bellatrix, both Death Eaters, visit Snape at his home to beg him to help Draco fulfill a mission assigned to him by Voldemort. Bellatrix takes Snape to task for not killing Harry when he had numerous chances to do so. Snape ably defends his inaction and affirms his commitment to the Dark Lord. His declaration of loyalty to Voldemort is not entirely convincing, however, considering that he has helped Harry in the past when he was vulnerable. At the end of the book, an incapacitated Harry watches, horrified, as Snape murders a beloved character. It does, indeed, seem that Snape has been acting as a double agent all along. A nagging questions remains: How could Dumbledore have been so wrong about Severus Snape? Was he really that naïve, or was there something he knew about Snape that others did not?

Rowling's exploration of the psychology of evil does not end with Voldemort and Snape. Some of Harry's responses to his circumstances also raise disturbing questions. Voldemort's attack on the infant Harry left him with more than a scar on his forehead. A deep link was forged between the maleficent wizard and the child, a connection that eventually led to a frightening conjunction of psyches in the preceding book. In spite of the Dark Lord's repeated attacks, Harry remains on the side of good, but he does not reject evil entirely if he finds it useful.

One of the final scenes in *Harry Potter and the Half-Blood Prince* finds Harry and Snape engaged in a pitched battle against each other. Harry tries to defend himself against Snape's magical attacks by employing the "Sectumsempra" curse, a jinx used by dark wizards to eviscerate their foes, but he fails to execute the curse. Snape sneers that Harry does not have the will or the heart to kill. Later Harry vows to do away with Voldemort using whatever means are at his disposal, including, one would assume, weapons associated with the dark arts. Does his willingness to use the same type of magic as Voldemort mean that he has lost faith in the strength of good? Is Rowling saying that only darkness is strong enough to defeat darkness?

In the world of myth and magic, seven is a powerful number that symbolizes completeness and wholeness. In *Harry Potter and the Half-Blood Prince*, Harry finishes his education at Hogwarts, says goodbye to adolescence, and stands at the brink of adulthood. The troubling questions raised in book six will no doubt be answered in book seven, as Harry completes his mission to exterminate the Dark Lord. It remains to be seen how the war between good and evil will be played out in the wizarding world, which is, after all, a reflection of the everyday one.

Pegge Bochynski

Review Sources

Booklist 101, no. 22 (August 1, 2005): 1948.
Books and Culture 11, no. 6 (November/December, 2005): 22-24.
Kirkus Reviews 73, no. 15 (August 1, 2005): 800.
National Review 57, no. 16 (September 12, 2005): 48-49.
The New York Times Book Review 154 (July 31, 2005): 12.
People 64, no. 5 (August 1, 2005): 43.
Publishers Weekly 252, no. 29 (July 25, 2005): 77.
School Library Journal 51, no. 9 (September, 2005): 212-213.
Time 166, no. 4 (July 25, 2005): 60-65.

HENRY ADAMS AND THE MAKING OF AMERICA

Author: Garry Wills (1934-   )
Publisher: Houghton Mifflin (Boston). 467 pp. $24.00
Type of work: History and literary criticism

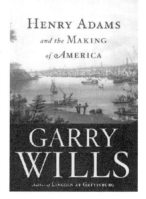

Wills examines Adams's History of the United States of America *(1889-1891), sometimes subtitled* During the Administrations of Presidents Thomas Jefferson and James Madison*, as a misunderstood masterpiece*

> *Principal personages:*
> HENRY ADAMS (1838-1918), a historian and writer
> JOHN ADAMS (1735-1826), his great-grandfather, the second president of the United States
> ABIGAIL ADAMS (1744-1818), his great-grandmother
> JOHN QUINCY ADAMS (1767-1848), his grandfather, the sixth president of the United States
> THOMAS JEFFERSON (1743-1826), the third president of the United States
> JAMES MADISON (1751-1836), the fourth president of the United States

In the twelve years between 1879 and 1891, Henry Adams published fifteen books, including his two novels *Democracy* (1880) and *Esther* (1884), lives of two then-famous Virginians, Albert Gallatin and John Randolph, collections of Gallatin's writings and his own historical essays, and his nine-volume *History of the United States of America* (1889-1891). As Garry Wills rightly observes, however, while Adams is a writer "deeply esteemed and widely studied," his reputation is based not on these works of the most productive period of his life but on his last book, *The Education of Henry Adams*, which he wrote in his sixties and which appeared in a trade edition in 1918, shortly after his death.

Henry Adams and the Making of America, the latest volume in Wills's distinguished series of studies in American history, tries to shift this balance: to recover Adams's *History* from neglect and previous misreadings and to prove that it is both "the non-fiction prose masterpiece of the nineteenth century in America" and the beginning of modern historical writing in the United States.

In his polemical introduction, Wills argues that the *History* has been either unread of misread by previous commentators. When it is discussed at all, it is described as a critique of the administrations of the Jeffersonians, written by a descendant of their leading Federalist opponents. This reading, Wills insists, is not supported by the *History* but is imposed upon it by historians and critics who have either read only parts of it or been misled by "the family feud" thesis and "the *Education* effect." He charges (but never proves) that historians seem to have written about the *History* on the basis of reading only the opening six chapters of its first volume—a survey of the state of

∽

Garry Wills is the author of A
Necessary Evil: A History of
American Distrust of
Government *(1999). He has also
written books on Saint Augustine
and on Abraham Lincoln; his*
Lincoln at Gettysburg *(1992) won
the Pulitzer Prize for general
nonfiction. Wills is an adjunct
professor of history at
Northwestern University.*

∽

America in 1800, before Thomas Jefferson's presidency began—which they treat as Adams's judgment on the state of America after the Jeffersonians. The family feud thesis views Henry Adams as an avenger, setting out to restore the Adams family's place in history by demonstrating the failures of those who defeated his great-grandfather and undermined his grandfather. The *Education* effect is the result of "reading Adams backward" from *The Education of Henry Adams* and finding its pessimism and sense of failure in something written twenty years before.

Wills sets out to correct and reverse these trends, to "read forward toward the *History*," in a book that is divided into two parts. In part 1, "The Making of an Historian," he examines Adams's biography, focusing on the experiences and works that led him to the attitudes and historical method that shaped the *History*. In part 2, "The Making of a Nation," he presents a volume by volume analysis of the *History*, arguing that during the four terms of Jefferson and James Madison the United States moved from being fragmented to having a national identity. In a provocative epilogue, he argues that Adams has much to teach in the present, where opposing sides in various political and constitutional conflicts lay claim to the "original intent" of the Founders as benediction for their positions.

"The Making of an Historian" is a masterful performance, full of original insights, previously overlooked materials, valuable context, apt quotations, and intellectual range. It succeeds brilliantly in both demolishing the family feud thesis and explaining how Henry Adams evolved into the author of the *History*. Drawing on the diaries and letters of Adams's grandmother, Maryland-born Louisa Johnson Adams, which Adams read and organized, as well as statements from Adams's own letters and works, Wills shows that he was always more drawn to the South than the North, to Washington and Virginia rather than Massachusetts, and was, in fact, not an admirer but a critic of the Adams family and his presidential forebears.

Adams told his Harvard students that "John Adams was a demagogue." He also saw his great-grandfather as a political failure, pointedly saying that George Washington and Jefferson—not John Adams—"doubtless stand pre-eminent as the representatives of what is best in our national character or its aspirations." He demonstrated his anti-Federalism in comments such as his observation that "everyone admitted that Jefferson's opinions, in one form or another, were shared by the majority of the American people." In his biography of Gallatin, he praised the "triumvirate" of President Jefferson, Secretary of State Madison, and Secretary of Treasury Gallatin, asserting that "no statesman has ever appeared with the strength to bend their bow," (praise and hyperbole that he would temper when he later wrote his *History*).

The kindly grandfather who appears in the opening pages of *The Education of Henry Adams* could not be further from the John Quincy Adams he found in his grandmother's private papers or described in his own. The elder Adams's letters to his wife show him to be cold, priggish, humorless, overbearing, emotionally abusive, and cruelly insensitive. (In her letters to her daughter-in-law, Abigail Adams appears almost as bad.) In an eighty-page critique of his brother Brooks's proposed biography of their grandfather, Henry unleashes a litany of invective. He writes that his grandfather had "an astonishing faculty for self-deception"; that for much of his career he was "a tool of the slave oligarchy"; that he was "abominably selfish," "incapable of feeling his duty to others," "indifferent to art," "demonic"; that he "must have lived a life of pure void." Henry Adams was so critical of both his great-grandfather and his grandfather in his first major work, *The Life of Albert Gallatin* (1879), that his brother Charles attacked him and the book anonymously in a review in *The Nation*.

Wills then provides a fascinating intellectual biography that traces the emergence of Henry Adams as a leader in the development of historical method in the nineteenth century. Newly opened archives created the opportunity to draw on new source materials, but the archives were unorganized, uncataloged, and geographically dispersed. In America, and especially in Boston, Wills explains, this led to the rise of "gentlemen historians"—writers such as Francis Parkman, George Bancroft, Edwin Everett, and Adams, who had the connections, leisure, and financial independence to visit widespread archives, hire copyists, and gain diplomatic appointments that allowed them to spend time in the collections in other countries. Adams's own historical debut at twenty-three, for example, an examination of the various claims John Smith made about his relationship with Pocahontas, was made possible by his gaining access to archives in England while he was a part of his father's diplomatic mission there during the Civil War.

In 1870, Adams accepted an appointment to teach history at Harvard, began offering one of the first graduate seminars in history in America, and became the editor of the *North American Review*. In the early 1870's, Adams focused his energies both on trying to create political reform through muckraking reports on the political scene and developing and teaching the new methods of historical scholarship. Research for his biography of Gallatin gave him access to "the inner councils of the Jeffersonians." Work on subsequent biographies of Randolph and Aaron Burr (unpublished) and his two novels were experiments in prose forms through which he evolved from "a chronicler" into the historian and literary stylist of the *History*.

In "The Making of a Nation," Wills traces Adams's examination of the major events, arguments, and figures of the period from 1801 through 1817 as they unfold in the *History*. He generously quotes Adams, thereby indisputably demonstrating that the book is a prose masterpiece. As Wills summarizes and discusses each volume, Adams emerges as an extraordinary combination of political, diplomatic, military, intellectual, cultural, financial, economic, geographic, demographic, legal, and religious historian. His portraits of figure after figure—of Jefferson, Madison, James Monroe, Gallatin, John Marshall, Samuel Chase, Burr, Andrew Jackson, Randolph, Tecumseh, and hundreds of lesser-known Americans; and of an international cast headed by Napoleon and Talleyrand, George Canning and William Pitt, Manuel de

Godoy, Toussaint Louverture—sparkle with insight, wit, and style. One of the great achievement of Wills's book is that throughout his more than two hundred pages of summary and analysis of the *History*, the reader's interest almost never flags. On the contrary, he is offered a fascinating review of the history and characters of the times, as well as of Adams's treatment of them. This summary is enlivened by Wills's wit and style.

The ultimate irony of the nine volumes of Adams's *History* is that it is, as Wills acknowledges, "a comedy of errors, not a tragedy." Adams's description of Jefferson's two presidential terms is, finally, a catalog of failures of practice and principle in both foreign and domestic terms. Aside from the Tripolitan War and the Louisiana Purchase, his foreign policy record consisted of courting Napoleon—who repeatedly outfoxed him—failing to support the struggle for liberty in Haiti and Spain, attempting to negotiate agreements that never materialized, weakening the national defense on both land and sea, and establishing an embargo that was internally divisive and externally ineffectual.

Domestically, Jefferson created a national political party, but he also expanded the patronage system, suppressed dissent, abused the powers of the executive, sought to undermine the judiciary, so alienated the New England states that they seriously considered secession, supported slavery and its expansion in both the South and the West, regularly neglected his duties in favor of extended vacations each summer at Monticello, and imposed an embargo that seriously hurt the domestic economy without accomplishing its purposes.

The five volumes devoted to Madison's two terms describe most of the same weaknesses, without the saving grace of Jefferson's strength or literary style. Adams labels Madison's cabinet "the least satisfactory that any president had known" up to that point. His negotiations with foreign governments were similarly unsuccessful, nearly farcical, and his conduct of the War of 1812-1817, which he began, was an almost total disaster. His commitment to the Non-Intercourse Act that succeeded the embargo resulted in a general disrespect and disregard for the law that would not be equaled until Prohibition. Wills says that Madison "was an amateur in foreign policy and economics." He was also an amateur in military strategy (as was Jefferson), which did not stop him from ignoring those who better understood the country's lack of preparedness on the eve of war, the need for regular army forces, or the potential power of the various enemies his navy and troops would face.

Madison's popularity and moral authority plummeted, even before his administration negotiated a peace treaty that achieved none of the five aims for which he had brought the country to war. His reputation was saved at the end of his second term by a conjunction of events that he did not shape—especially Jackson's victory at the Battle of New Orleans.

It is hardly surprising, then, that many have seen the *History* as the story of the failures of these two administrations. One need not subscribe to either the family feud thesis or the *Education* effect to read it this way. Wills is certainly right, however, in his essential assertion: As Adams tells the story, both in spite of and in the process of these failures, Jefferson and Madison's administrations succeeded because they "almost inadvertently" created a sense of national identity. The comedy of errors ends happily because of unintended consequences.

Wills chooses to read Adams forward to the *History*. If one reads forward from the *History* to the *Education*, what Adams learned in writing the *History* becomes even more apparent. In a wonderful essay on Adams included in his *An American Procession* (1984), Alfred Kazin makes the connection, stating that Adams's "subtle purpose" was to show how political leaders were "swept by a force, national destiny, that they could not control. It was not science but force that was, already in Adams's *History*, the great motif and interest of his work." The theme of the *History*, he wrote "is the submission of principle to power." In this conflict between force and will, chaos and order, and reality and principle, failure leads to success.

Kazin also perfectly captures the impression that the *History* cannot help but make on its readers. The most striking literary characteristic of the *History*, he writes, is "its easiness, its intellectual address, that magisterial command over the materials that is associated with the historian's natural confidence in himself as a judge of history." This description applies to *Henry Adams and the Making of America* as well.

Bernard F. Rodgers, Jr.

Review Sources

Booklist 101, no. 22 (August 1, 2005): 1988.
Foreign Affairs 85, no. 1 (January/February, 2006): 152-154.
Kirkus Reviews 73, no. 14 (July 15, 2005): 784.
Library Journal 130, no. 13 (August 15, 2005): 103.
The New Republic 233, no. 16 (October 17, 2005): 30-35.
The New York Review of Books 52, no. 18 (November 17, 2005): 19-20.
The New York Times Book Review 154 (September 11, 2005): 17.
Publishers Weekly 252, no. 28 (July 18, 2005): 201.

THE HISTORIAN

Author: Elizabeth Kostova (1964-   )
Publisher: Little, Brown (New York). 647 pp. $26.00
Type of work: Novel
Time: 2008, the 1930's, the 1970's, the 1950's, and the 1400's
Locale: Amsterdam; Budapest; Istanbul; Les Bains, France; and Sophia, Bulgaria

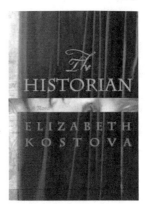

After finding a mysterious book and reading a series of letters dating from the 1930's, a sixteen-year-old girl joins her family's terrible quest to kill Dracula

Principal characters:
> THE NARRATOR, an historian
> HELEN ROSSI, the narrator's mother, the illegitimate daughter of Professor Bartholomew Rossi
> PAUL, the narrator's father and Helen's husband
> PROFESSOR BARTHOLOMEW ROSSI, Paul's mentor and Helen's father
> BARLEY, a young Oxford student who accompanies the narrator on her quest to find her father
> DRACULA, the fifteenth century Wallachian prince, still alive and creating minions

Elizabeth Kostova's debut novel, *The Historian*, begins with a false introduction set three years in the future, suggesting that the work is not a fictional tale but rather the true events of the writer's life. This introduction further deceives in that it contains the basic components of nonfiction, including a discussion of the writer's scope and method and concluding with a list of those persons the author thanks. Though she does not give away the story line in this introduction, Kostova's narrator hints at her personal investment in the themes: "This is the story of how as a girl of sixteen I went in search of my father and his past, and of how he went in search of his beloved mentor and his mentor's own history, and of how we all found ourselves on one of the darkest pathways into history."

This misleading beginning gives primacy to the narrator's point of view, allowing her voice to serve as the central thread of the text, despite the fact that the events in *The Historian* are told through multiple voices in a variety of media, over the course of many decades from several different countries.

Though the narrator's role in conveying the events of the novel is important, her main function in the first half of the book is to serve as a conduit through which the reader learns the basic premises of the tale. Intrigued by an ancient book on her father's shelf, she takes it down, only to discover it is blank except for a central woodcut of a large, imposing dragon. When she asks Paul, her father, the story of this unusual book, he tells her of finding it in his stack of books at the library. As a graduate student studying history, he quite naturally asks his mentor, Bartholomew Rossi, about the origins of such an obviously old book and learns that Rossi possesses a similar tome. The story behind Rossi's book, however, turns tragic when he disappears soon after he gives Paul a packet of letters related to the book and its dark, secret history. Eventually, Paul tells his daughter about the books as he provides her with Rossi's letters that he read years before. The letters indicate that by possessing the books, both Rossi and Paul are part of a dreadful history with ties to Vlad Tepes, known as Dracula—a real fifteenth century prince who is still very much alive as a vampire.

Elizabeth Kostova graduated from Yale University, where she won the Wallace Prize for fiction. She earned an M.F.A. from the University of Michigan, where she was honored with the Hopwood Award for the Novel-in-Progress. The Historian is her first novel.

Shortly afterward, Paul disappears. The narrator, suspecting the worst, finds another series of letters from her father. From these she learns about her father's involvement with Dracula after Rossi disappeared. Her father, intent on finding him and uncovering the truth of the books and the vampire, arms himself against Dracula by researching him. While researching, he discovers another person intent on the same subject—a young woman he finds reading Bram Stoker's *Dracula* (1897) in the college library. Paul soon learns that the young woman, Helen, is actually Rossi's illegitimate Romanian daughter. After tracking Dracula through a variety of historical sources, Paul and Helen travel all over communist Eastern Europe to uncover Dracula's lair, eventually finding Rossi, but only after he has become a vampire.

The narrator reads her father's letters while she and Barley, an Oxford student, take the train to Les Bains, France, a place indicated as a possible tomb location for Dracula which he purportedly visits only at certain times. Eventually, the three narrative quests from three different periods of history—Paul and Helen's to find Rossi, the narrator and Barley's to find her father, and the family's to find Dracula—culminate in a showdown with Dracula himself.

As the narrator learns about her family's involvement with this historic and dangerous person, Kostova provides the reader with both a real and an imagined history of Vlad Tepes, the fifteenth century Wallachian prince whose historically grotesque torture techniques earned him a gruesome spot in the real history of Central Europe. The characters' research into the prince's escapades highlight Kostova's brand of revisionist history concerning the real Vlad, making him into someone almost admirable in his desire to defeat the Turks in his homeland. Kostova places Dracula's real-life cruelty in its historical context, suggesting that his impaling of thousands might have been common for a warlord intent on protecting his borders. What emerges from her depiction of the historical Dracula is a more balanced portrait of the real person, a man who was probably no more bloodthirsty than other fifteenth century princes from that region.

Even when Kostova brings in the mythic materials of vampire legend, she keeps the focus on Dracula's personal history, downplaying his literal bloodthirstiness. The most vicious of his minions—a librarian who follows Paul and Helen on their odyssey to find Rossi—is vicious because he wants to be a vampire. Even with his dark powers, Dracula's main focus is not on turning others into vampires but on furthering his own research agenda. When he attempts to enlist scholars to aid him, he follows a fair method. First, he plants a dragon book among a recognized scholar's books. The scholar does what a scholar does best: He or she researches its origins. Dracula anticipates this action and, in fact, collects the various documents these scholars unearth for his own private library about himself.

If the scholar happens to get too close to discovering Dracula's tomb—the secret of all secrets which could lead to his extinction—things change. The scholar receives a warning—typically a creepy visit by a minion or the sudden death of someone or something close to the scholar. If, after the warning, the scholar continues on the search, then his or her life is threatened. If Dracula, or a subordinate, feeds on the scholar three times, then the scholar becomes a vampire as well but a vampire enlisted to recruit other scholars. The Dracula who emerges from Kostova's text is a scholar himself—someone trying to find the most pertinent primary historical documents across time by forcing others to build up his collection.

The historians who receive these books, then, must use their academic skills toward a purpose other than their primary research work. Beginning with the various histories of Dracula—real and mythic—they must use these to find his tomb and destroy him. In doing so, they interview other scholars, read primary and secondary texts, examine maps, and get firsthand information about folk culture, topographical variants, and museum artifacts in a variety of locales. Kostova weaves these quests with other components to present other histories and regions accurately. For example, Helen and Paul travel during the 1950's to communist Eastern Europe. Not only do they have to learn more about Dracula in a world that denies his existence but they must do so under tightly guarded totalitarian regimes. The many travel sequences in *The Historian* also emphasize Kostova's interest in depicting international cultures. Her descriptions of Istanbul and Budapest take on the resonance of a travelogue, catapulting the reader into these distinct cultural milieus.

In addition to its reflections on history, *The Historian* is also a vampire tale, in part an homage to Stoker's *Dracula*. Like Stoker, Kostova uses a variety of textual media to relay the story line. Just as Stoker relied on letters and the characters' personal journals to forward the plot, Kostova makes use of letters and storytelling as her primary organizing methods. Kostova's Helen is also reminiscent of the heroines of Stoker's text—notably Lucy Westenra and Mina Harker—two women who are bitten by Dracula. The subtext of the biting and transformation of Lucy into a vampire has a lurid sensuality which one also sees as Kostava's Helen describes her longing for Dracula, communicated in a postcard she writes for her daughter: "I cannot understand why this fiend has not come down the centuries to find me yet. I am his for the taking already, polluted already, longing slightly for him. Why does he not make his move and put me out of this misery?" Helen, however, successfully thwarts Dracula, primarily because of her intelligence and verve.

Despite the successes of Kostova's text, the novel does strain credulity at times. Kostova's prince is not the shadowy count of Stoker's text or any of the countless Hollywood incarnations of Dracula but a real Vlad Tepes, taken from accurate historical research. The vampire veneer and its focus on bats, wolves, and the two puncture wounds on Helen's fair neck suggest that an appreciation of the mythic vampire remains critical to an appreciation of the book. Kostova expects the reader to become a believer, to allow the superstitious mind to supersede the rational mind. Bartholomew Rossi addresses this issue when he finds Paul scoffing at his assertions that Dracula is alive: "I can joke about the legend, which has been monstrously commercialized, but not about what my research has turned up. In fact, I felt unable to publish it, partly because of the presence of that legend. I thought the very subject matter wouldn't be taken seriously." Though Kostova runs this risk as well, the lushness of her prose style, coupled with the use of historical myth and truth make it easier to see Kostova's work as a document which might not be entirely fictional.

Rebecca Hendrick Flannagan

Review Sources

Booklist 101, no. 18 (May 15, 2005): 1646.
Entertainment Weekly, June 24, 2005, pp. 166-169.
Kirkus Reviews 73, no. 9 (May 1, 2005): 499.
Library Journal 130, no. 11 (June 15, 2005): 58-59.
The National Post, July 9, 2005, p. WP13.
The New York Times 154 (June 13, 2005): E9.
The New York Times Book Review 154 (July 10, 2005): 16.
Newsweek 145, no. 24 (June 13, 2005): 74.
Publishers Weekly 252, no. 35 (September 5, 2005): 58.
The Washington Post Book World 35 (June 15, 2005): 15.

THE HISTORY OF LOVE

Author: Nicole Krauss (1975-   )
Publisher: W. W. Norton (New York). 255 pp. $24.00
Type of work: Novel
Time: Post-World War II
Locale: Mostly New York

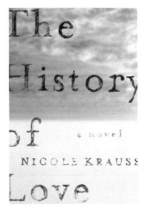

Krauss's sophomore novel concerns survivors of the Holocaust and the impact of a book about true love on the lives of people connected beyond time and space

Principal characters:
> Leo Gursky, a retired locksmith and reclusive octogenarian writer, survivor of the Holocaust
> Alma Mereminski-Moritz, his love since childhood, mother of two sons, one of whom is Leo's
> Isaac Moritz, Leo and Alma's son, a renowned writer
> Alma Singer, a teenage girl named for Alma as Leo wrote about her in *The History of Love*
> Charlotte Singer, a widowed translator, young Alma's mother
> Bird, Charlotte's seven-year-old son, who believes he may be a messiah
> Zvi Litvinoff, Leo's childhood friend, exiled in Chile, who published Leo's manuscript as his own

Nicole Krauss, an acclaimed poet who has worked with Joseph Brodsky, negotiated a six-figure deal to write two books after rave reviews acclaimed her first novel, *A Man Walks into a Room* (2002). An excerpt from *The History of Love*, called "The Last Words on Earth," was published in *The New Yorker* in February, 2004; subsequently Krauss sold the book rights to *The History of Love* in almost twenty countries and the film rights to Warner Brothers.

The History of Love is the title of a book within a book around which some people's lives have been wrapped, shaping their destinies. The reader enters that magic world, and it opens views to other worlds. The novel is about reading and writing, the way a book can change lives, love, and loss. Witty and emotional, it is also about nostalgia for the places one cannot revisit because they are lost forever. In the end, however, it is about living and surviving, often creatively accomplished.

This ambitious and remarkable work depicts unconventional life journeys; its themes include love lost but never forgotten, human destiny charted by the atrocities of war, and loneliness of the "invisible" people. Leo Gursky survives the massacre of the Jews in his native village of Slonim, in Poland, by hiding in the woods for three-and-a-half years. His girlfriend Alma Mereminski, the love of his life, escapes to the United States. Leo follows and finds her, but he arrives too late. Because his letters

did not reach her, she thought he was dead, like
many others. Now she is married, with two sons.
One is Leo's.

A locksmith and a writer, Leo lives in Manhattan, not far from Alma and her family but
without any physical contact with them. After
having lost his parents, his native land, his only
love, his son, and the book he wrote while a
young man—inspired by his first and only love—
he is now retired. The book opens with him, at

~

*Upon publication of her first book,
Nicole Krauss became the focus of
both public and critical attention.
An avid reader from an early age,
her influences include Henry Miller,
Ayn Rand, Philip Roth, and Gabriel
García Márquez.*

~

eighty, brooding over his wasted life and approaching death. He often wonders who
will be the last to see him alive. He makes a point of being "seen" and sits as a model
in a nude drawing class. Most of the time, though, he is alone and philosophizing:
"Put even a fool in front of a window and you'll get a Spinoza."

Leo and Alma's son, Isaac Moritz, a famous writer, dies at sixty from Hodgkin's
disease. Until Isaac's death, Leo wonders if Isaac knew who his father was. Once, in
order to attend his son's book reading, Leo had obtained tickets months in advance.
He joined Isaac's fans in lining up to meet the writer. Once eye-to-eye with Isaac,
however, he could not say a word. Isaac was kind and patient, but a security guard
firmly grasped Leo's elbow and escorted him out. Only after Isaac's death does Leo
find himself in his son's home, touching and sniffing his clothes, trying on his shoes,
larger than his own.

There are two major, and several minor, life stories flowing, like blood, through
this book. Unknown to one another, and Leo, the characters all meet in the heart, symbolized by his book. Leo had given his old manuscript to his childhood friend, Zvi
Litvinoff, in Minsk. Since then, Litvinoff has lived a refugee's life in Chile. A young
woman, Rosa, falls in love with him and marries "her dark crow." He reads the manuscript to her, and she helps him translate it into Spanish, assuming it is his. After it is
published, the book takes on its own life, touching people with its powerful energy of
love. Litvinoff gains notoriety, which improves his life. He lives with his secret, never
finding a suitable moment to tell Rosa, unaware that she had found out and deliberately destroyed the evidence. She even informed Gursky that the manuscript had been
lost when their home flooded.

In addition to Leo's first-person, earthy, eccentrically witty narration, there is another voice, that of another Alma, the teenage Alma Singer, named for the book's heroine. Her voice is counterpointed with Leo's, bringing with it youthful imagination, curiosity, and wonder with life. Her journal successfully portrays the lives of all of her
family members. The book *History of Love* has great significance for the family
Singer: Her father gave it to her mother at the time of their courting. Now he is dead, her
mother a widow faithfully dedicated to his memory. She is stacking books and dictionaries between her and the outside world. Unexpectedly, she receives a commission
from a Jacob Markus, wanting her to translate *The History of Love* from Spanish.

With the book to aid in her secret quest, young Alma Singer looks for a man who
could change her mother's solitary life. Alma also helps her dreamy, out-of-touch

mother in raising Bird, Alma's younger brother, another dreamer. He believes he is a Lamed Vovnik (one of thirty-six anonymous saints in Yiddish folklore) who can fly. He jumps from the second floor (at age six), breaking his arm and earning his nickname. In accordance with Jewish tradition, he avoids writing God's name and spells it G-d. He believes he just may be a messiah. Secretly, he reads his sister's writing and gets into the mystery of the lost book, unknowingly adding to its resolution. While recording the "real" but awkward exchange of kisses with her first love, Misha, Alma is secretly but strongly dedicated to finding out more about her namesake.

Numerous supporting characters are lush and picturesque: Bruno, born out of Leo's loneliness and undying love; Litvinoff's wife, Rosa; Alma's Uncle Julian (with his lopsided smile and a passion for Alberto Giacometti). All of them are intelligent and unusual but vibrantly true to life. Just as one sympathizes with Leo Tolstoy's character Anna Karenina in spite of her transgression, one cannot harshly judge Litvinoff and Rosa for stealing Leo's book. The circumstances of their lives make it understandable. Love is brimming in the book as a motivating force behind human actions, spilling into the world through the readers.

In an interview, Krauss admitted she had decided to write a book based on her knowledge, not research. She enjoyed writing it and therefore expects the readers to enjoy it too. Many of her favorite writers are given homage within the work, for example, Antoine de Saint-Exupéry, Pablo Neruda, Miguel de Cervantes, Jorge Luis Borges, and Franz Kafka). So are composers, painters, and numerous others great, gifted, and famous. The creative spirit, with the message, resonates in the reader.

Through her devoted, passionate search, young Alma finds out that Jacob Markus is only a character from the book her mother is translating. The real man behind the commission is Isaac Moritz, son of the original Alma. It is too late to meet Alma or Isaac in person, Alma soon finds; instead, she connects with Leo. His years of longing end when the two of them meet. Ready to join his loved ones, Leo sees young Alma as the embodiment of his long-awaited love, young and beautiful as he has always remembered her from their blissful youth. Their separate voices now unite in a powerful duet in an Ode to Joy of life and love (*Amor omnia vincit*). It is a happy ending that life gives, as a well deserved gift, to Leo, gentle and touching as a mother's lullaby or a last kiss.

The History of Love defies a thorough summary. The work examines the place of love in human lives, the invisible golden thread connecting all people through the most powerful energy in the universe. It celebrates the magic of life and love through some extraordinary episodes in the lives of remarkable people. Perhaps all people are remarkable when their most intimate stories are known. Of these, most often the words are not spoken—although there are words for everything in life, Krauss tells the reader through Leo.

At almost fifteen, Alma seems to embody what is known about the young Nicole Krauss, yet the character confesses to feeling more comfortable expressing Leo's point of view. Dedicated to Krauss's grandparents, who taught her "the opposite of disappearing," this novel is an immigrant story, teaching empathy with the "invisible" people around the world and around the corner—one's neighbors, one's sisters and brothers.

It is worth noting the author's diction: almost scientific precision coupled with sensitivity, emotion, and gentleness. Her sense of wonder turns her story into a roller coaster ride of excitement, revealing the unknown sides of human lives. She uses many stories within the novel and many characters of all ages, from an earthy old man or a dreamy middle-aged widow to her idiosyncratic son and curious, level-headed teenage daughter. Krauss employs letters, journals, diagrams, different languages and orthographies, even the words that stay unsaid, with images and almost-blank pages that speak louder than the busy ones.

Mira N. Mataric

Review Sources

Booklist 101, no. 14 (March 15, 2005): 1265.
Kirkus Reviews 73, no. 4 (February 15, 2005): 191.
Library Journal 130, no. 7 (April 15, 2005): 74.
The New Republic 232, no. 18 (May 16, 2005): 39-42.
New York 38, no. 17 (May 16, 2005): 76-78.
The New York Review of Books 52, no. 11 (June 23, 2005): 49-51.
The New York Times 154 (April 25, 2005): E1-E7.
The New York Times Book Review 154 (May 1, 2005): 19.
Publishers Weekly 252, no. 8 (February 21, 2005): 154.

THE HOT KID

Author: Elmore Leonard (1925-   )
Publisher: William Morrow (New York). 312 pp. $26.00
Type of work: Novel
Time: The 1920's and 1930's
Locale: Oklahoma and Kansas City

A United States marshal and a bank robber, both sons of rich fathers, clash in Depression-era Oklahoma

Principal characters:
    CARLOS (CARL) WEBSTER, a United States marshal
    JACK BELMONT, a would-be bank robber
    LOUISE (LOULY) BROWN, a young woman infatuated with the criminal type
    TONY ANTONELLI, a crime journalist
    VIRGIL WEBSTER, Carl's father, a rancher and oilman
    NARCISSA RAINCROW, Virgil's housekeeper and lover
    ORIS BELMONT, Jack's father, an oil baron
    NANCY POLIS, Oris's mistress
    NORM DILWORTH, Jack's partner in crime
    HEIDI WINSTON DILWORTH, Norm's wife and Jack's mistress
    EMMETT LONG, a bank robber
    CRYSTAL DAVIDSON, Long's gun moll
    CHARLES ARTHUR (PRETTY BOY) FLOYD, a bank robber
    NESTOR LOTT, a former special agent for the U.S. Justice Department
    JOE YOUNG, a member of Floyd's gang
    TEDDY RITZ, a Kansas City gangster

Elmore Leonard began his writing career in the 1950's, turning out Western novels and stories. Not until the demand for Westerns abated did he begin writing the crime fiction for which authorities as disparate as Martin Amis, Stephen King, Quentin Tarantino, and George Will have proclaimed Leonard a genius. Leonard, who has also written such historical fiction as *Cuba Libre* (1998), set during the Spanish-American War, returned to the Western with *The Tonto Woman, and Other Western Stories* (1998). *The Hot Kid* combines Leonard's interests in crime, Westerns, and historical fiction and represents his best work since *Out of Sight* (1996).

The Hot Kid opens in Okmulgee, Oklahoma, in 1921, when fifteen-year-old Carlos Webster witnesses Emmett Long kill an Indian policeman while stealing thirty dollars from a drugstore. Impressed by how the United States marshals track down and arrest Emmett, Carlos decides he wants to be a lawman. Shortly afterward, the boy shoots and kills a cattle thief. At this, Carlos's half-Cheyenne father, Virgil, who raised him, realizes, "My lord, but this boy's got a hard bark on him." Carlos's Cuban mother died when the boy was born. Virgil raises cattle and pecans but is wealthy from the oil dis-

covered on his property. The other member of
the Webster household is Narcissa Raincrow,
whose job description has evolved from nanny to
housekeeper to Virgil's lover.

Jack Belmont is the same age as Carlos but his
moral opposite. As a youngster, he had let his
younger sister drown, leaving her brain-damaged.
As an eighteen-year-old in 1925, he decides to
blackmail his father, the oil millionaire Oris. The
"good-looking, useless boy" wants ten thousand
dollars a month, or he will tell his mother about
Nancy Polis, Oris's mistress who runs a board-
inghouse Oris bought her. Jack has been arrested
numerous times, including once for rape. "Everything I got into," he says, "either I didn't start
it or it was a misunderstanding." Nonetheless, he
does what he wants, when he wants, because he
has never been held accountable for his actions.
After Oris refuses to pay, Jack enlists the ex-
convict Norm Dilworth in a bungled plot to kid-
nap Nancy. Jack is so despicable his mother plans
to shoot him the next time she sees him. His only
goal is to become "public enemy number one."

*Elmore Leonard was born in New
Orleans, and his family moved to
Detroit when he was nine. He
served in the Navy Seabees during
World War II and graduated from
the University of Detroit. Leonard
began writing fiction in the 1950's
while working as an advertising
copywriter. His many awards
include being named a Grand
Master by the Mystery Writers of
America in 1992.*

By 1927, Carlos, now known as Carl, is a U.S.
marshal on the trail of Emmett Long's gang of
bank robbers—whose newest member is Jack, just out of prison. Carl, a ladies' man,
becomes friendly with Crystal, Emmett's moll, during his pursuit of the gang. Carl
kills Emmett, having said, "If I have to pull my weapon I shoot to kill," and journalist
Tony Antonelli begins making Carl famous for using that line. In the world of *The Hot
Kid*, the number of men someone has killed is very important, with Carl keeping track
of how many both he and certain criminals have shot. One criminal's wife tells Carl
he is more frightening than any outlaw because he enjoys shooting bad guys. Carl
says, "I can shoot at 'em, but not lie to 'em." Of such contradictions are born memorable characters.

Tony, the journalist, continues chronicling Carl's exploits in *True Detective Mystery* magazine. Leonard depicts Carl much like a gunman of the Old West, and Tony
resembles the legendary Ned Buntline, who wrote about the exploits of outlaws, gun-
fighters, and lawmen for the dime novels of the nineteenth century. Tony, who always
seems to have more details than do the police, sees the movie-star-handsome Carl as
his own means to success, dubbing him "the hot kid." Tony thanks the marshal for
providing him something to write about, as if his writing is just as important as keeping the peace.

The other major character in the story is Louly Brown. In 1924, when Louly is
twelve, she attends the wedding of her cousin Ruby to Charles Arthur Floyd. A year

later, Floyd is notorious as an outlaw whom the newspapers call Pretty Boy, and Louly develops a crush on him. She thinks of him as Choc, his chosen nickname, short for Choctaw. Louly enters Floyd's sphere by becoming pen pals with the convict Joe Young, who joins Floyd's gang upon being released from prison. After having sex with the moronic Joe, Louly "saw how this being a gun moll wasn't all a bed of roses." She begins slowly to shift her focus after Carl questions her about Floyd. "She liked the way he shook her hand and thanked her, and the way he touched his hat, so polite for a U.S. marshal."

An especially colorful interlude finds Jack, his girlfriend Heidi, and Louly in 1930's Kansas City as Leonard revels in the details of the era during which the city was known as the "playground of criminals." Louly and Heidi go to work for the enigmatic Teddy Ritz, a gangster who passes himself off as a political operative. Carl arrives to rescue Jack from Teddy's clutches. The lawman wants Jack on his turf and wants to deal with him only on his terms. Impressed by the marshal's resolve, Teddy tries to tempt him to crime.

Indicative of Leonard's style is the way he opens *The Hot Kid*. Carlos is telling the local police chief about the shooting at the drugstore. The boy, however, leaves out pertinent details, as is shown when this interrogation is followed by a flashback to Carlos's confrontation with Emmett Long. Leonard helps establish Carlos's independent character by revealing the information the boy withholds from the police, such as Emmett's taking Carlos's peach ice-cream cone. Later, Tony reveals that Louly had shot someone in Floyd's gang before her character has been introduced; in this way Leonard alerts his readers that Louly is not just another female.

Leonard is known for his distinctively realistic dialogue, which makes use of the twisted syntax of ordinary folks: "I see these two men come in wearing suits and hats I thought at first were salesmen"; "I'm here to put Emmett Long under arrest or in the ground, one"; "News accounts describe Carl as must be one of the world's deadliest shots." Leonard also displays a colorful, profane American vernacular. The racist Nestor Lott recruits Ku Klux Klan members to attack Italian Americans by saying, "You know these dagos are all Socialists, enemies of our American way. We run 'em out now or they'll be after your jobs, your farms, and they'll lure your Christian women as Eyetalians know how to do." Carl impresses Jack by talking like a real person, without the "official way of speaking" of other lawmen. "You can be a mean bugger, huh?" Carl asks Jack.

Leonard's dialogue, falling midway between the naturalistic styles of Quentin Tarantino and David Mamet, is effortlessly graceful, lacking the strained self-consciousness of most writers who attempt to emulate the likes of Dashiell Hammett and Raymond Chandler. Leonard is, however, self-conscious in another sense. Tony, paid by the word, is a partial self-portrait, and the crime journalist prides himself on writing "the way people actually spoke."

Even in his narrative, when Leonard filters an experience through the consciousness of a character, he uses that character's verbal style: "She thought she had to go to the bathroom, the urge coming over her in her groin and then gone, Louly took a few moments to compose herself and act like the mention of Choc didn't mean anything special, Joe Young's grin in her face, giving her the feeling he was dumb as dirt." Leonard has fun with Tony's elevated descriptive writing: "The sky hung as a shroud over the Bald Mountain Club, gray and unforgiving, a day that dawned with an indifferent beginning, but would end in violent deaths for twelve victims of the massacre."

The Hot Kid is full of small touches typical of Leonard. Floyd's family gathers to watch him rob a bank. The criminals consciously ape the behavior of the film gangsters played by James Cagney. A marshal taps cigarette ash into the cuff of his pants to ward off moths. Lott is given a medal during the Great War after forcing his men at gunpoint to advance against fatal enemy fire. Jack's lawyer refuses to visit him in jail because prisons are unsanitary. John Dillinger thinks Bonnie Parker and Clyde Barrow are giving bank robbery a bad name by stealing only small amounts. Heidi tries to explain Kansas City jazz to Jack: "You're not supposed to understand it . . . you feel it."

The climax of *The Hot Kid* has Carl teaming with his enemy to protect Jack's roadhouse from Lott and his "Christian avengers." Carl and Jack repel the attack while Jack plots to kill Norm so that he can have his friend's wife, Heidi. All this is observed by Tony, who cannot believe Carl is helping Jack. Tony calmly takes notes during the gun battle, even as Lott plows a Packard into the roadhouse. Jack flees the scene by stealing Tony's car, the first of two times he takes it. Lott is doomed to failure in Leonard's world because "He was so serious about being stupid." Because Leonard usually emphasizes character and mood at the expense of plot, such a tour de force as Lott's attack is rare. It is one of the most compelling sequences in Leonard's fiction.

Recent Leonard novels such as *Tishomingo Blues* (2002) and *Mr. Paradise* (2004) have offered colorful characters, brilliant individual scenes, and the usual splendid style but have lurched awkwardly from scene to scene at times, finally lacking the usual spark of fun. With his consistent themes of the vagaries of American racism, the pervasiveness of greed, and the stupidity of the criminal class, all smoothly submerged within his storytelling and all on display in *The Hot Kid*, Leonard is an entertainer with an edge. *The Hot Kid* is Leonard at his very best, with period details, characters, and style operating at full throttle from first page to last.

Michael Adams

Review Sources

The Atlantic Monthly 296 (November, 2005): 153.
Booklist 101, no. 14 (March 15, 2005): 1246-1247.
Kirkus Reviews 73, no. 4 (February 15, 2005): 192.
Library Journal 130, no. 7 (April 15, 2005): 74-76.
Los Angeles Times Book Review, May 8, 2005, p. 3.
The New York Times 154 (May 2, 2005): E1-E6.
The New York Times Book Review 154 (May 8, 2005): 1-11.
Publishers Weekly 252, no. 13 (March 28, 2005): 55.
The Washington Post Book World, May 15, 2005, p. 6.

THE HUMMINGBIRD'S DAUGHTER

Author: Luis Alberto Urrea (1955-   )
Publisher: Little, Brown (New York). 499 pp. $25.00
Type of work: Novel
Time: The late nineteenth century
Locale: The states of Sinaloa and Sonora, in Mexico

This novel is based on the life of the author's great-aunt Teresita, who was believed by the people of Mexico to be a saint and was believed by the corrupt government of Mexico's dictator, President Porfirio Díaz, to be a dangerous revolutionary

Principal characters:
> DON TOMÁS URREA, a wealthy rancher in Mexico
> TERESITA, the illegitimate daughter of Don Tomás by a fourteen-year-old Indian servant
> DON LAURO AGUIRRE, an engineer and Don Tomás's best friend
> HUILA, an elderly Indian midwife and healer, or *curandera*
> SEGUNDO, Don Tomás's ranch foreman
> BUENAVENTURA, Don Tomás's illegitimate son and Teresita's half brother
> LORETO, Don Tomás's wife
> GABRIELA, Don Tomás's mistress
> JUAN FRANCISCO, Don Tomás and Loreto's oldest son

The Hummingbird's Daughter is the result of twenty years' research by award-winning author Luis Alberto Urrea, who became fascinated by a family folktale about his great-aunt Teresita, known as the Saint of Cabora. Urrea bases his novel on facts gleaned from travel, interviews, fieldwork, and a series of newspaper articles from the 1930's which ran in such publications as *The New York Times*, the *Los Angeles Times*, and the *San Francisco Daily Examiner*.

According to Urrea's research, Teresita was born Niña García Nona María Rebecca Chávez on October 15, 1873, near Ocoroni, Sinaloa, in Mexico. Her mother, Cayetana Chávez, was a desperately poor, fourteen-year-old Indian girl. Her father, Don Tomás Urrea, was a wealthy rancher. Cayetana eventually abandoned her young daughter to the care of Cayetana's abusive sister, who beat the girl with a wooden spoon. Don Tomás would not find out until years later that Teresita was his daughter.

As the story opens, Don Tomás's backing of the opposition candidate for governor of Sinaloa angers Mexico's dictator, President Porfirio Díaz, who invalidates the election results. To avoid possible imprisonment or even death, Don Tomás leaves Sinaloa, uprooting his entire household and moving everyone to another ranch owned by his family farther north, at Cabora, in Sonora. The six-year-old Teresita rides a donkey during the migration, just as her real-life counterpart was said to do.

Once in Cabora, Don Tomás discovers that Teresita is his illegitimate daughter and takes her into his household. Because Teresita is obviously gifted, Don Tomás and his friend Lauro Aguirre teach her to read. (Most women at that time were illiterate.) She also becomes an excellent horsewoman and learns to play the guitar. However, when Teresita is a teenager, an obsessed ranch hand attacks her and leaves her for dead. As her body is being prepared for burial, she rises, as if from the dead, and thereafter has the miraculous ability to heal others. Teresita also reportedly has the ability to fly to distant places while in the dream state—attested to in real life by a half sister who supposedly accompanied her on at least one of these dream flights. She exudes the fragrance of roses. News of her miracles spreads far and wide, and thousands of pilgrims travel to the ranch to see her.

Besides healing the sick, Teresita also sends a political message: She urges her fellow Indians not to allow the Mexican government to run them off their lands. This message angers President Díaz, who orders her arrest. Both she and her father are captured and imprisoned. Because Díaz fears open revolt by the Indians if Teresita is executed, he instead exiles her to the United States. Here ends the novel, although Teresita apparently continued to heal the sick and write articles for Aguirre's Texas newspaper urging Mexican independence until her untimely death at age thirty-three.

Luis Alberto Urrea was born in Tijuana, Mexico, but grew up in San Diego. He teaches at the University of Illinois, Chicago. His novels and poetry have won numerous awards, including an American Book Award, a Western States Book Award, a Christopher Award, and a Colorado Book Award. He has been inducted Into the Latino Literary Hall of Fame.

Urrea's novel is much more than just bare fact. The author uses the historical information he gathered to form the framework for a beautiful and lyrical story of a young girl's coming-of-age and self-discovery during the politically unstable period in Mexican history preceding the revolution of 1910. Urrea fleshes out the characters, the period, the locations, and the trials and tribulations of daily life. He vividly depicts a time and place that is probably unfamiliar to his American readers. Several reviewers noted the work's beautiful lyricism, particularly in the first half of the novel, as in this passage describing the journey from Sinaloa to Sonora:

> And in the trunks of the oldest trees, among the stones in the creek beds, buried in the soil, lying among the chips of stone kicked aside by the horses, the arrowheads of long-forgotten hunters, arrowheads misshot on a hot morning, arrowheads that passed through the breast of a raiding Guasave, gone to dust now like the bowman and scattered, arrowheads that brought down deer that fed wives and children and all of them gone, into the dirt, blowing into the eyes and raising tears that tumbled down the cheeks of Teresita.

346 *Magill's Literary Annual 2006*

Passages such as this one reveals Urrea's background as a poet, as well as the extent of his research. The narrative abounds with descriptions of scenery and plant life: "Desert marigold. Threadleaf groundsel. Paleface flower. Texas silverleaf. Sage. Desert calico. Purple mat." Food figures prominently; many meals are described in full, such as the following: "[Don Tomás] ate chorizo and eggs, calabaza and papaya, a bowl of arroz cooked in tomato sauce with red onions sprinkled over it, coffee and boiled milk, and three sweet rolls." To enhance the ambiance, Urrea throws in a mix of Spanish words and phrases: Don Tomás calls the men such uncomplimentary names as *pinches cabrones* and *pendejos*. There are exclamations of *Por Dios!* and lamentations such as *Qué barbaridad!* When a swarm of bees descends on a local cantina, the people cry *Muchas abejas!* When Don Tomás flirts with a local girl, he utters *piropos*, or compliments to flatter her. Because these expressions flow naturally through the text, they should not impede the non-Spanish-speaking reader's comprehension.

The story's setting at the end of the nineteenth century allows an interesting blend of the traditional ways of the native population and the scientific innovations of the invading Europeans. Throughout the book, Don Tomás shares with Teresita protagonist status. He represents the modern, scientific, educated white male, and Urrea seems to identify most with him. Huila, a servant in Don Tomás's house and the ranch's *curandera* or midwife, represents the native population, whose members call themselves the People. Teresita—half Indian, half white—becomes the medium between the two worlds. In matters of faith, the People seem to embrace Catholicism more fanatically than do the Spanish, who introduced it.

Through Teresita's eyes, the simple, traditional lifestyle of the Indians is contrasted with the more modern lifestyle of the wealthy whites. As a little girl, she is amazed by the grandeur of Don Tomás's house; she gingerly climbs the steps—something she has never seen before—leading up to the front door, then she tries the porcelain doorknob that allows her to enter into the equally amazing interior: the floors of polished wood (not dirt), the beautiful furnishings, a library full of books that only the educated white men (Don Tomás and Aguirre) can read, the grandfather clock, which she thinks is a tree with a heartbeat. This unauthorized first venture, like Alice's into Wonderland, is what leads her aunt to beat her. Nevertheless, Teresita is eventually welcomed into the house permanently once her father realizes that she is his daughter.

Teresita, who adopted the name because she admired the Catholic Saint Teresa, blossoms into a beautiful young woman, sympathetic, kind, and with a unique sensibility which is the result of her dual upbringing. Don Tomás allows her to continue her apprenticeship with Huila as a *curandera* at the same time that he indoctrinates her in the ways of the Europeans. What Teresita learns about plants and other natural cures is combined with a peculiar dose of Catholicism as practiced by Huila and the rest of the native population, who still offer up a glass of tequila or a *bolillo* to God as their ancestors had done for their native gods. As with Saint Teresa, Teresita wishes to "ease suffering." Hence, even before her miraculous arising from the dead, she has entered onto the pathway of her life's work.

To the People, Teresita's gifts are no more miraculous than the wonders that Don Tomás has already introduced. With his friend Aguirre, they have developed the indoor flush toilet and plumbing, a primitive refrigeration system, and other miracles of modern science; it is an age of miracles, and the People are willing to believe. Not only do the People look to Teresita to heal their physical ailments but their emotional ones as well. Many see Teresita as a prophet, urging the People to stand strong against the invading Spanish—although she maintained a strict pacifism throughout her life.

The narrative is an intriguing mix of horrific tragedy and Magical Realism. The brutality of the era figures constantly in the background, where whites slaughter Indians and Indians slaughter whites. There are mutilations, tortures, kidnappings. The People are starving, working under grueling conditions for their white masters, yet there is hope.

Urrea plays up the idea that amid the worst brutalities, mercy and understanding can still prevail, and both Teresita and Don Tomás do their parts. For example, when Don Tomás learns that Indians have burned down the ranch at Cabora just before their arrival, that they have brutally murdered some of the servants and have stolen livestock and women, rather than seek revenge he seeks peace. He forms a pact with them: He will protect them from starvation and the Mexican government, and they, in turn, will protect the people of the ranch from other Indian invaders. Teresita, too, offers up her own brand of mercy through her power to heal—and her refusal to do harm, even to her enemies. After an incident involving her half brother, Buenaventura, when his teasing leads to her putting him into a catatonic fit, she vows never to harm another soul.

To counter the novel's weighty subject matter, Urrea introduces a fair amount of humor as well. One of the best examples is the juxtaposition of a scene in which Don Tomás calmly deals with a swarm of bees at a local cantina—drugging them with marijuana smoke and capturing them in a portable hive on the back of one of his wagons—with a scene in which his angry wife, Loreto, arrives at the ranch, furious over Tomás's philandering. A huge and heated argument ensues, which ends with their son Juan Francisco taking off in one buggy, Loreto following in another, stranding the poor priest who had accompanied them and leading to the priest's hijacking the bee wagon to follow after them. Ironically, this is also the moment Don Tomás learns that Teresita is his daughter.

The book's title derives from a nickname for Teresita's mother. Cayetana was known as the hummingbird. The hummingbird was believed by the People to be a messenger of God. As with other messengers of God, Teresita is persecuted and driven from her home. The initial move of Don Tomás from Sinaloa to Sonora foreshadows their last and final move, from Mexico to the United States. Yet Teresita's persecution only serves to enhance her image as a martyr and a saint. Tragedy continued to plague Teresita, however, in the United States. Perhaps Urrea is saving that for another novel.

C. K. Breckenridge

Review Sources

Kirkus Reviews 73, no. 8 (April 15, 2005): 450.
Library Journal 130, no. 9 (May 15, 2005): 109.
Los Angeles Times, July 30, 2005, p. E1.
The New York Times Book Review 154 (July 3, 2005): 9.
The New Yorker 81, no. 19 (July 4, 2005): 81.
Publishers Weekly 252, no. 16 (April 18, 2005): 44.

THE HUNGRY TIDE

Author: Amitav Ghosh (1956-   )
Publisher: Houghton Mifflin (Boston). 333 pp. $25.00
Type of work: Novel
Time: 1950-2000
Locale: The Sundarban Islands, off the eastern coast of
    India

*In a beautiful but hostile island world, three people
from very different backgrounds share adventures, learn to
love, and make discoveries about the past and about themselves*

Principal characters:
> PIYALI (PIYA) ROY, an young American
> woman of Indian descent and a marine
> biologist specializing in dolphins
> FOKIRCHAND (FOKIR) MANDOL, an illiterate fisherman but a keen
> observer of nature
> KANAI DUTT, an urbane, forty-two-year-old New Delhi businessman,
> owner of a translating and interpreting business
> NILIMA BOSE, Kanai's energetic, seventy-six-year-old aunt, founder of
> the Lusibari hospital and the foundation that supports it
> NIRMAL BOSE, her husband, a retired headmaster and an outspoken
> opponent of the government's policies in Morichjhapi
> KUSUM MANDOL, Fokir's mother, one of the victims of the Morichjhapi
> massacre
> MOYNA MANDOL, Fokir's wife
> TUTUL MANDOL, their young son

The Hungry Tide is the fifth English-language novel by Amitav Ghosh and, like
his earlier works, it reflects the author's expertise as a sociologist with a Ph.D. from
Oxford University, his broad general knowledge, and his insight into the colonial
past. English and American writers would find it difficult to surpass Ghosh's elegant
style. Although in his early works he has sometimes lost control of the narrative, he
handles the intricate structure of *The Hungry Tide* as effectively as he does the book's
various themes.

As one of Ghosh's recurring themes is the presence of the past, it follows that the
action in his novels typically takes place over long periods of time. In *The Shadow
Lines* (1988), he follows two families through three generations and more than half a
century. His novel *The Glass Palace* (2000) spans 115 years. By contrast, *The Hungry
Tide* involves just a few weeks in the lives of a few characters. The time frame is
greatly expanded, however, through accounts of past events, sometimes presented by
the characters and at other times by the narrator through a journal written thirty years
before and through a myth which originated in a far distant past.

Amitav Ghosh won France's Prix Medici Étranger for The Circle of Reason *(1986), India's Sahitya Akademi Award for* The Shadow Lines, *an Arthur C. Clarke Award for* The Calcutta Chromosome *(1995), the Grand Prize for Fiction at Frankfurt's International e-Book Awards for* The Glass Palace, *and a Pushcart Prize for one of his essays. Ghosh is a visiting professor at Harvard University.*

At the beginning of the novel, Kanai Dutt, a middle-aged businessman from New Delhi, encounters Piyali Roy, or Piya, a young marine biologist from Seattle. They are on a train to Canning, in southeastern India, from where they will go by boat to the Sundarban Islands, an archipelago in the Ganges Delta made up of a number of small, mangrove-covered islands. Piya has a grant to study a rare species of river dolphin, while Kanai has been asked by his aunt to peruse a notebook left by his uncle Nirmal Bose, who died under mysterious circumstances during a rebellion thirty years earlier. Before they separate at Canning, Kanai politely invites Piya to visit his aunt at her home on Lusibari, one of the Sundarbans' most remote islands.

Piya makes arrangements for her studies, hiring the required forest guides and a boat, and heads out. However, almost immediately she begins to have misgivings, and after falling into the water and being rescued by a fisherman named Fokir, she decides to stay with him on his small boat rather than return to the guides, who seem excessively interested in her money and her equipment. Her decision proves to be a wise one. Although Fokir speaks no English and cannot read or write, he is so intelligent that Piya has no difficulty communicating with him. She has only to show him her equipment and several pictures of dolphins for him to grasp her reason for being in the Sundarbans and to understand that she wishes to hire him and his boat. Fokir and his young son Tutul make room for Piya on their boat, and they proceed.

While Piya explores the present, Kanai ventures into the area's past. First his aunt, Nilima Bose, delivers a lecture about the early history of the Sundarbans, and then Kanai begins reading the notebook of Nirmal, his late uncle. From that point on, the narrator will periodically insert into the story a separate, italicized chapter representing a section of the notebook. Kanai will not read the final entry until about two-thirds of the way through the novel.

Fokir knows the area so well that he is soon finding dolphins for Piya to study. He also makes sure that, in her enthusiasm, she does not forget that they are in crocodile-infested waters and that there are tigers in the mangroves. The narrative now begins switching back and forth, with one chapter devoted to the adventures of Piya and Fokir in the fishing boat and the next to Kanai on Lusibari, and the past. Some of the Lusibari chapters are notebook entries. In other chapters, the narration offers background information. For example, in a chapter titled "Nirmal and Nilima," the reader learns that the couple came to the Sundarbans in 1950, less than a year after they were married, because Nirmal's political activities had attracted the attention of the authorities and he needed to "disappear" for a while. His notebook was written in 1979, at the time of the Morichjhapi rebellion, and it reveals the fact that Nirmal never changed; he was just as idealistic at the end of his life as he had been in the beginning. Kanai begins to suspect exactly what Nilima would rather not know: that her husband's idealism may indeed have cost him his life.

In other chapters, Kanai relives an earlier period when, having been suspended from school, he was sent to Lusibari to contemplate his misdeeds and prepare himself for reentry into the educational system. He remembers his first meeting with a strong-willed teenager named Kusum, with whom he was halfway in love. At a performance honoring Bon Bibi, the legendary protectress of the island people, Kusum had told Kanai about watching her father being dragged off by a tiger and her own sense of betrayal when Bon Bibi ignored her calls for help. After the play, Kanai saw Kusum being spirited away so that she would be safe from the villainous man who sold her mother into prostitution and had been pursuing the daughter ever since. Kanai never saw Kusum again. However, during this visit he learns about her later life, which ended in martyrdom at Morichjhapi. Kusum, as it turns out, is Fokir's mother.

In the first part of *The Hungry Tide*, Ghosh maintains the interest of his readers by exploring the past and sustains suspense by keeping Piya in dangerous waters. However, the primary purpose of that section is to prepare for the more dramatic second part of the book. The first section is titled "The Ebb: *Bhata*"; it is followed, inevitably in tidal waters, by "The Flood: *Jowar*," which is the title of the book's second section. Although the work builds toward a cyclone, or hurricane, which floods the mangrove islands, "The Flood" also describes the human condition, for as Ghosh demonstrates, people can be as overwhelmed by internal conflicts as they are by governmental tyranny or by the destructive power of nature.

For example, by the time Piya, Fokir, and Tutul return to Lusibari, Piya knows that she has developed a crush on Fokir. Though Fokir seems unaware of her interest, his wife, Moyna, is not; as a result, she is not as friendly toward Piya as she would ordinarily be toward a guest on the island. Piya, in turn, is unaware of Kanai's interest in her. Although, as Kanai admits, he has never been without women, he takes more than a casual interest in Piya. Evidently she is the first woman since Kusum who has touched his heart.

Nirmal's notebook describes another kind of internal conflict, the struggle between love and duty. When government forces decided to evict a group of squatters from Morichjhapi, which had been declared a nature refuge, Nirmal felt it was his duty to support the squatters. However, he knew that in doing so, he would probably be forfeiting his life, thus deserting the wife who loved him. Kusum, too, had to balance love and duty, for her death left her son an orphan.

Although the barbaric action of the government forces at Morichjhapi was indefensible, Ghosh makes it clear that the issue involved was not a simple one. To Piya, for example, the claims of the environment should come before the needs of people. She makes her position clear when she comes upon villagers torturing a man-eating tiger they have captured. Realizing that they intend to burn it alive, Piya attempts to intervene, and Fokir has to drag her away, explaining that after all, it had killed human beings. His mother, Kusum, would have seconded his comments, for as a nurse trainee, she had been taught that human life, not nature, is of paramount importance.

In *The Hungry Tide*, Ghosh also points out that some of the most serious errors made by colonial overlords arose from their certainty that they could bend nature to their will. Midway through "The Flood," Kanai tells Piya what happened at Canning, the town at which their train journey ended. Having decided that both a new capital for Bengal and a new port were needed, the British set about transforming a little fishing village on the banks of the Matla River into a large metropolis. They would not believe an amateur expert on storms, who warned that within fifteen years a cyclone would drive the ocean into the town and sweep away all of their improvements. It took not fifteen years, but just five, for nature to strike back at those who had defied it. The storm that hit Canning in 1867 was not even a major cyclone, but because the town had been built in an exposed position, where there were no mangrove swamps to protect it, it was devastated by a storm surge. Now the muddy river had taken over where once the town had stood, and only a post office was left to remind travelers of its short-lived glory.

Kanai's story should have warned Piya against ignoring nature. However, she is so excited about the success of her research that when she ventures out again in Fokir's boat, she does not notice how strangely the dolphins are behaving, even though by now she knows them well enough to distinguish one from another. A major storm is moving in, and Piya and Fokir cannot make it back to Lusibari before it hits. They have to take shelter amid the mangrove trees. Fokir positions himself so as to shield Piya, and he is killed by flying debris.

Despite Fokir's death, *The Hungry Tide* ends on an optimistic note. Moyna and Tutul are assured of a secure future, and Nilima's foundation will benefit from the funds Piya has raised for further research. Piya now plans to make Lusibari a permanent base, and Kanai will spend most of his time there, writing the story of Nirmal's notebook. Most important, both Piya and Kanai have discovered who they are and what is important in their lives. Neither of them will again take nature or love for granted. If in the final pages of *The Hungry Tide* Ghosh seems to ignore the issues that he explored earlier in the novel, such as the helplessness of the poor in the face of human tyranny or natural disaster, he can be forgiven, for in the course of his book he has transported his readers to an unfamiliar environment and made it real to them.

Rosemary M. Canfield Reisman

Review Sources

Booklist 101, no. 15 (April 1, 2005): 1341.
The Economist 372 (July 17, 2004): 81.
Far Eastern Economic Review 167, no. 34 (August 26, 2004): 53.
Kirkus Reviews 73, no. 3 (February 1, 2005): 137.
The Nation 280, no. 23 (June 13, 2005): 24-28.
Publishers Weekly 252, no. 7 (February 14, 2005): 50.
The Times Literary Supplement, July 16, 2004, p. 21.
The Washington Post Book World 35 (May 8, 2005): 12.

THE ICARUS GIRL

Author: Helen Oyeyemi (1984-   )
Publisher: Nan A. Talese/Doubleday (New York). 338
    pp. $24.00
Type of work: Novel
Time: 1994-1995
Locale: London and Ibadan, Nigeria

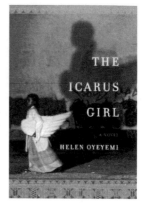

A young girl of mixed race struggles with depression and loneliness until she encounters an unusual playmate who may not be real

Principal characters:
    JESSAMY HARRISON, an eight-year-old girl
    SARAH HARRISON, her Nigerian mother, a
        writer
    DANIEL HARRISON, her English father, an accountant
    GBENGA OYEGBEBI, her highly respected grandfather
    TILLYTILLY (TITIOLA), a remarkable girl who befriends Jess in Nigeria
    DR. COLM MCKENZIE, Jess's psychologist
    SIOBHAN (SHIVS) MCKENZIE, his fearless redheaded daughter, Jess's
        new English friend

The Icarus Girl is a very strange book: an exploration of the clash of two cultures, a study of a child's psychological disintegration, a horror story, and perhaps more. Although it begins in England, the story shifts to Nigeria where, melded with Yoruba custom and folklore, it quickly slides into a mysterious, supernatural realm that the author, Helen Oyeyemi, admits even she does not fully understand. Inhabiting that realm are two girls, Jessamy Harrison, who is English by birth, and Titiola, whom Jess meets in Nigeria and who follows her home.

At first, it is not clear what is wrong with eight-year-old Jess, although something definitely is, because she is constantly screaming. A solitary child, she has no friends. At home in London, she likes to hide in the linen cupboard on the stair landing. She cannot eat in front of other people or meet their eyes; she writes haiku in the dark, lying on her bedroom floor. At school she has been advanced to Year Five but does not like it. She has terrible spells that may well be panic attacks, but otherwise she appears to be depressed. Because her fellow pupils say she is weird, she desperately wants to return to her own Year Four class, but her proud Nigerian mother, Sarah, objects. Sarah, a successful novelist, seems for the most part unmindful of her daughter's problems, but Daniel, her mild English father, is more sensitive, and Jess feels closer to him.

On the Harrisons' flight from London to Ibadan, Nigeria, for their first visit to Sarah's family, Jess hysterically refuses her antimalarial pills, but once there, she becomes calmer. Nigeria is a different world for both her and her father—a land of sun, heat, and vivid color, sharply contrasting with their accustomed English life. There

Jess meets her stately grandfather, Gbenga Oyeg-
bebi, and numerous Nigerian relatives, who live
in separate buildings within the walled family
compound and speak both English and Yoruba.
Gbenga addresses Jess by her Nigerian name,
Wuraola, which no one has ever used, adding to
her sense of alienation.

Helen Oyeyemi was born in Nigeria
and grew up in London. While a
student of social and political
sciences at Cambridge University,
she completed The Icarus Girl, *her*
first novel, just before her
nineteenth birthday. She has also
published two plays.

One night Jess notices an unidentified light in
the compound, in the large, empty house called
the Boys' Quarters, which was once used for servants. The next day, while she explores there,
she finds her name traced on a dusty tabletop. An oddly dressed girl appears and, once
Jess manages to speak with her, they become friends. The girl is Titiola, but because
Jess cannot pronounce her name correctly, she calls her TillyTilly. Mischievous
TillyTilly, who seems somehow out of proportion, "too tall and yet too . . . small at the
same time," encourages Jess to enter her grandfather's forbidden study at night. Afterward, TillyTilly gives Jess a gift—Sarah's childhood copy of Louisa May Alcott's
Little Women (1868). On Sunday she invites Jess to a deserted amusement park,
where the gate mysteriously unlocks and all the rides operate by themselves. Fascinated, Jess decides to be like TillyTilly and learn to do the same things she can do.

Just before she leaves Nigeria, Jess returns to the Boys' Quarters in search of
TillyTilly and stumbles into a room containing a charcoal drawing that her friend has
apparently made of a woman with long, thin arms that reach to her ankles. Before it
burn candles and tea lights, as if it were a shrine. TillyTilly resents Jess's intrusion
into her private place and angrily leads her away, but her mood alters quickly from irritation back to friendship. She promises, "You'll see me again."

Back in England, following another bout of illness and precarious emotions, Jess
reluctantly returns to school. She still has difficulty assimilating. Afraid to show fear,
she is tormented by other pupils and suffers weekly tantrums that send her to the
nurse's office. She has no games, no one to play with, and both her parents are busy,
her mother strict and overprotective. Only her father seems sympathetic. Jess desperately misses her friend until TillyTilly raps on the kitchen door, this time wearing a
proper English dress and announcing that her family has just moved to London. (This
"family" remains unseen.)

When Jess starts to read TillyTilly's gift copy of *Little Women*, she finds the familiar story somewhat changed: Docile Beth, her favorite character, has become jealous
and mean. That night she has her first dream of the strange, long-armed woman of the
drawing, who flies past her, saying, *"We are the same."* The next morning, Jess's
book has returned to its original version. After she dreams again of flying with the
woman with the rubbery arms, she too tries to draw the woman's picture, but
TillyTilly quickly tears it up and draws herself instead.

Because bullying on the school playground compels Jess to fight back, she faces
discipline, but her parents disagree on the proper punishment. Although Daniel, a
gentle man, does not believe in corporal punishment, Sarah does. As a result, Jess is

forced to hold heavy cans of pineapple at arm's length for half an hour. When TillyTilly appears and mocks her, Jess realizes that her playmate can be cruel and unpredictable. She wonders if the TillyTilly in England could be a different person from her talented friend in Nigeria.

Jess's parents have enlisted the aid of a psychologist, Dr. Colm McKenzie, to meet with Jess at his home, where the two can talk informally over hot chocolate and marshmallows in the kitchen. There Jess also encounters his redheaded daughter, Siobhan (Shivs), who is her own age, and the two hit it off immediately. TillyTilly resents the sessions with Dr. McKenzie and becomes even more annoyed when Shivs enters the picture.

Slowly Jess becomes aware that TillyTilly is invisible to others, and that sometimes so is she. She recognizes that TillyTilly is changing her: Her perceptions have begun to alter, her attitudes change, even her memories are subtly modified. When finally she is brave enough to question whether TillyTilly is real, her companion temporarily vanishes.

TillyTilly is clearly unstable, a trickster who can speak without moving her face. She tells Jess not to ask questions because she does not like them. She says she is older than Jess, but she seems to distort time. At one point she pulls Jess down with her through the staircase, through brown earth, into a cramped, dark place. They fall, bump, and awkwardly rise together. TillyTilly's powers are imperfect; she cannot control everything and has made some kind of mistake. Jess is really frightened.

After TillyTilly says that they are both twins, Jess does not know what to believe. She still dreams of the "wise-eyed" flying woman, sensing that TillyTilly and the woman are somehow connected, even though they never appear together. Her visions grow hallucinatory. Feverish, she hears a tiny baby cry underneath her bed, only to be snatched away by TillyTilly. Then, accompanied by an odd, buzzing hum, TillyTilly informs her that the baby, Fern, is Jess's stillborn twin.

When Jess confronts her parents with this story, Sarah cries out that "the spirits tell her things." The parents have kept Fern a secret from Jess, honoring the Nigerian custom of avoiding any talk of death. Sarah explains to Jess the Nigerian belief that twins are able to live in three worlds: the real world, the spirit world, and the Bush ("a sort of wilderness of the mind"). If one twin dies in childhood, the family will make a wooden carving of the child for Ibeji, the god of twins, to ensure that the dead twin is peaceful and will not harm the living. Sarah regrets that an *ibeji* statue was not made at Fern's death, but even now Jess is not fully aware of the danger.

The knowledge of her dead twin shocks her. Almost automatically she cuts out pictures of twins from books at school to show TillyTilly. At this point she knows that something is seriously wrong. Further nightmarish moments follow: She finds herself in intense pain, pressing a burning coal to her lips as TillyTilly encourages her. TillyTilly holds a black chalice, urging Jess to look inside, but she refuses. A shapeshifter, TillyTilly is at one horrific moment "stretched out over the ceiling like a grinning sheet."

TillyTilly is spinning out of control, uttering obscure threats to "get" the babysitter, a teacher, a girl at school, anyone who dares to intimidate Jess. Shortly thereafter, someone at school announces that her teacher is gone, replaced by a substitute. At first Jess is not sure what "get" means, but she ultimately discovers how destructive it can be: "It was as if TillyTilly had a special sharp knife that cut people on the inside so that they collapsed into themselves and couldn't ever get back out." When TillyTilly suggests that they trade bodies and jumps inside her, Jess attempts unsuccessfully to reenter her own body. Both girls are terrified, but they manage to switch back.

The friendship between them is foundering, for both Jess and TillyTilly are too needy. Jess finally understands her grandfather's advice: "Two hungry people should never make friends. If they do, they eat each other up." She knows that TillyTilly is no longer safe for her to be with. Jess finds herself trapped in her bed in a sort of *Exorcist* moment, with TillyTilly's altered voice warning, "Stop looking to belong, half-and-half child . . . there is only me, and I have caught you." Then her father collapses at work.

The Icarus Girl is mostly centered around its complicated plot. Character development is not a strength, except for the bizarre figure of TillyTilly, but who or what she really is remains unclear. Is she some aspect of Jess's dead twin, Fern? Is she a malevolent spirit, the alter ego of the benign long-armed woman who sings, tells stories, yet is never seen at the same time as TillyTilly?

In spite of her otherworldly properties, TillyTilly is certainly not the Icarus Girl of the title. She seeks the shadows, luring Jess to basements, cellars, to darkness under the bed or under the couch. She plummets with Jess through the floor, through the ground, into nothingness. Jess, on the other hand, has had fantasies of flying from the beginning. She often dreams of flying with the long-armed woman. Like the boy Icarus, who would soar to the blazing sun, she longs to fly upward and eventually succeeds. This disturbing, uneven book contains enough dualism to make everyone dizzy, but the roller-coaster ride of a story can be frightening and is definitely not for children.

Joanne McCarthy

Review Sources

Booklist 101, no. 17 (May 1, 2005): 1571.
Kirkus Reviews 73, no. 6 (March 15, 2005): 310.
Library Journal 130, no. 8 (May 1, 2005): 75.
The New York Times 154 (June 21, 2005): E1-E4.
The New York Times Book Review 154 (July 17, 2005): 17.
Publishers Weekly 252, no. 14 (April 4, 2005): 40.

THE ICE QUEEN

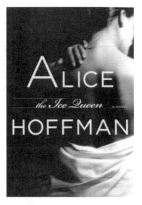

Author: Alice Hoffman (1952-   )
Publisher: Little, Brown (New York). 211 pp. $23.95
Type of work: Novel
Time: The early twenty-first century
Locale: New Jersey and Florida

A woman, after wishing bad things in anger, experiences setbacks such as being struck by lightning—and then suffers years of confusion and guilt

> *Principal characters:*
> THE NARRATOR, a woman who fears life
> NED, her older brother
> NINA, Ned's wife
> JACK LYONS, a man from whom the narrator wants sex but not love
> LAZARUS JONES, a man who recovered after being "struck dead" by lightning
> RENNY MILLS, a young man whom the narrator meets in a group of lightning survivors

Alice Hoffman seems to have the ability to draw even reluctant readers into her novels. She has a penchant for the bizarre and the supernatural, as overtly displayed in the three generations of witches in *Practical Magic* (1996), a popular novel which was made into a successful feature film. *The Ice Queen* offers plenty of both the bizarre and the supernatural, but Hoffman presents them in such a way that they seem almost natural, so that the reader accepts most of the novel as a realistic psychological character study.

"Be careful what you wish for," the novel opens. The first-person narrator, a New Jersey woman who is never named, has accepted this cliché and personalized it. She is thirty-eight years old, but she vividly remembers—indeed is still obsessed with—what happened when she was eight. Her mother was going out one evening to be with some friends to celebrate her thirtieth birthday. The young narrator resented her leaving and, in a moment of spite, blurted out that she wished her mother would just disappear because she never wanted to see her again. It was an icy night, and her mother died in a car wreck, due in part, officials said, to the balding old tires on the car.

When her grandmother came the next morning to tell the girl and Ned, her twelve-year-old brother, the news, the girl braided her hair for the first time by herself and then cut it off. Already filled with guilt, she was quick to punish herself, firmly believing that her mother's death was her own fault. The children were taken in by their grandmother.

In addition to the death of her mother, the narrator most remembers having Ned read fairy tales to her. She always insisted on hearing the dark and haunting versions of tales by the Brothers Grimm, preferring those to the stories with happy endings by the likes of Hans Christian Andersen. What appealed to her most in the Grimm fairy tales were the inexplicable things that befell the characters and the lack of logic to their fates. Ned always considered himself to be logical and unemotional, but he kept reading her the scary stories.

The narrator thinks that Ned is wise to show little emotion, and she proceeds to emulate his stoicism in most areas of her life. She sees herself as a creature of ice. She does not engage with people around her, except while working at the one job she likes, at the reference desk at the public library. Perhaps she enjoys her capacity there to give factual answers to the patrons' questions. Her special area of expertise is ways to die.

For the most part, aspects of her life are fearful and dreary. An exception is her occasional wild, but depersonalized, backseat sex with Jack Lyons, a local policeman with whom she discusses methods of dying. She does not want to get to know him better. The first time he brings her some flowers, indicating that he has feelings for her, she drops him without explanation.

Alice Hoffman wrote her first book, Property Of *(1977), when she was twenty-one. Her best-selling novels include* Turtle Moon *(1992),* Practical Magic *(1996), and* Here on Earth *(1997). She has also written the highly praised short-story collections* Local Girls *(1999) and* Blackbird House *(2004).*

After the death of their grandmother, Ned insists that his sister move to his home state of Florida, where he is a science professor at the fictional University of Orlon. His field is meteorology, and he specializes in lightning. Annoyed by Ned's enthusiasm, she idly wishes to be struck by lightning—and a ball of lightning rolls right in through the open window. For a while, the left side of her body is paralyzed—half of her wish to be dead, she grumbles. Her inner self is gone, she thinks. Her heart feels frozen. She cannot see the color red; anything red looks pale to her. Her brother enrolls her in a study of lightning-strike victims.

At this point, the book provides a lot of information about the extremely varied effects of being struck by lightning. This is one of the most interesting aspects of the novel. The reader is given facts and statistics, including the datum that people in Florida are killed by lightning more often than in any other state. This material serves as a welcome break from being in the depressed mind of the narrator. Her brush with death has not made her more sympathetic to others, not even with the members of the research group.

One young man in the group, Renny Mills is a student at the university where Ned teaches. Renny tries to befriend the narrator. He wants her to listen to him as he tells about his unrequited love for another student, a young woman who scarcely knows he exists. The narrator is not interested. Renny limps, and his hands have been rendered almost useless by the lightning bolt that hit him. He needs help in constructing a model building for his architecture class. Out of ennui, the narrator does eventually spend some time with Renny working on the project, but on the day that he most crucially needs her help, she is not available. It is revealed that he had to drop the class anyway and that he wanted the model as a present for his dream girlfriend. When the narrator was not there to help him finish it, he went to a hardware store, grabbed a hatchet, and tried to cut off his hand. One of the store workers managed to stop him; Renny was then sent to a hospital. He will go back to his family, which plans to sue the university on the grounds that the research project did not provide adequate psychological attention to the members of the group. The university drops the study.

The reason the narrator failed to meet Renny to finish his project was that she was by then spending all of her time with Lazarus Jones. Jones—or rather, his situation— is virtually the only thing that has captured her attention since she was eight years old. "Lazarus" is a nickname Jones gained because after he was struck by lightning, he was pronounced dead. It was not until forty minutes after the strike, with his body already at the morgue, that he awakened and promptly left. He did not want medical attention and refused to be in the victim research group. Apparently he never leaves his house or speaks to the workers at his orange orchard. When the narrator hears about Jones, she becomes obsessed with finding out what happened to him during the time that he was "dead." She drives to his home in the countryside and demands to talk with him.

Lazarus Jones is as literally overheated as the narrator is metaphorically frozen. When they kiss, she puts ice cubes into her mouth which boil from his fire, or at least quickly melt. They have sexual intercourse in a bathtub filled with extremely cold water. He insists that their trysts occur in the dark, with all the window shades drawn and the lights out. She never sees him without his clothes on. This manic affair seems to overwhelm the novel as the narrator becomes oblivious to other things happening around her.

Such bizarre and supernatural events could also be read as the reflection of the narrator's mental breakdown in her obsessed state. Perhaps the doctors were correct in their diagnosis that the lightning strike left her with neurological damage. Strangely, however, she seems to be not much different from the way she always has been, except that now she has a specific focal point for her interest in death. She fears death, while Jones fears living. She keeps demanding, unsuccessfully, that he tell her what it was like to be dead. Because he will not tell her, she decides she must see his body. She remembers the old fairy tales about women who tricked their husbands and disobeyed their warnings, all of which ended disastrously, but she cannot let it go. She tricks him and views his body. Suddenly, the sexual spell is broken. He is just another man, and one who will soon leave.

Reviewers have commented on the novel as one in which Hoffman takes risks with her dark tale, her oddball characters, her endless descriptions, and her largely unsympathetic narrator. The last section of the novel is even more problematic for many. There are at least two legitimate reasons for the unfavorable response.

One problem is that the last third or fourth of the novel seems barely related to what preceded it. After the abrupt termination of the strange affair between the narrator and Jones, the topic of lightning is dropped. Ned suddenly develops cancer. The narrator has not seen much of him, even after she moved to Florida at his insistence. Now she becomes involved in his sickness and his mortality. She helps Ned's wife, Nina, care for him. Ned changes from being a cynical scientist to being a romantic who says that before he dies, the one thing that he wants to see is the mariposa butterfly migration in California. Nina is pregnant, and she cannot take him, so the narrator does, with the help of innumerable medical assistants. On his stretcher, Ned sees the butterflies and then dies. The narrator lives with her sister-in-law for several months, helping her with the new baby, a girl whom Nina names Mariposa. Then the narrator goes back to New Jersey and works at the reference desk at a library.

Another problem is that the book's ending fits the happy endings of the brighter fairy tales. It certainly is not the ending in the Grimm Brothers stories. The reader may be relieved but may also be dissatisfied by the lack of preparation for the change in the narrator, the reason for which remains unclear. The narrator figures out somehow (or at least convinces herself) that her mother, who never meant to arrive at the celebration with her friends, committed suicide. In the narrator's mind, this makes all the difference in her own life; she did not kill her mother with her rashly uttered wish. At that point, the policeman Jack Lyons shows up again, still wanting to love her. He will accept her however she is, and let her paint every wall or ceiling in their home whatever shade of red she wants. The narrator no longer feels afraid. Why? The best that the novel can suggest is that perhaps it is the magic of fairy tales, the illogic of fate—that anything can happen, bad or good.

Lois A. Marchino

Review Sources

Booklist 101, no. 14 (March 15, 2005): 1246.
Detroit Free Press, April 17, 2005, p. 4L.
Kirkus Reviews 73, no. 5 (March 1, 2005): 249.
Library Journal 130, no. 7 (April 15, 2005): 13.
Ms. 15, no. 1 (Spring, 2005): 90-91.
People 63, no. 18 (May 9, 2005): 51.
Publishers Weekly 252, no. 12 (March 21, 2005): 37-38.
The Times Literary Supplement, November 18, 2005, p. 22.

IF THIS BE TREASON
Translation and Its Dyscontents: A Memoir

Author: Gregory Rabassa (1922-   )
Publisher: New Directions (New York). 189 pp. $22.00
Type of work: Language and memoir
Time: 1942 and 1963-2005
Locale: Hanover and Dartmouth, New Hampshire; New
    York City; Brazil; Puerto Rico; Mexico; Peru

*Scholar Rabassa, writing in his eighty-third year, offers
a cool-headed and humorous defense of translation*

> *Principal personages:*
> JULIO CORTÁZAR, an Argentine writer
> MARIO VARGAS LLOSA, a Peruvian writer
> GABRIEL GARCÍA MÁRQUEZ, a Colombian
>   writer
> JORGE AMADO, a Brazilian writer

If, as George Steiner avers, every act of comprehension is an act of translation, the process by which literature of one language is rendered understandable in another, fully knowable though it can never be, merits respectful attention. *If This Be Treason* is a bold though truncated incursion by a well-known translator into this mysterious realm.

One approaches this surprisingly slim volume at once assured and fearful. Surely, as translator nonpareil of Latin American novelists, Gregory Rabassa has to be the best possible guide. However, as most American-born readers speak only English, will they care to take on a book by a multilingual writer who is disinclined to condescend to his audience? Perhaps the question should be slightly but tellingly restated. Can the nonspecialist take Rabassa? It is the voice of this translator of Gabriel García Márquez, Julio Cortázar, Mario Vargas Llosa, Jorge Amado and some thirty other Latino authors that will win readers or turn them away.

Although Rabassa labels his first original book a memoir, its tone is that of an apology (in the older—the Latinate—sense of a defense, not an expression of regret) for literary translation. Professor Rabassa's tone is doggedly chip-on-shoulder. Early on, the reader is told that a certain "Professor Horrendo," the translator's ugly familiar, will sit in judgment, tossing "the usual occasional brickbats." Here Rabassa is referring to what is arguably his most famous translation, that of García Márquez's *Cien años de soledad* (1967; *One Hundred Years of Solitude*, 1970), an effort that its author, according to the translator, declared better than the original. The twelve-page chapter devoted to the Colombian novelist's masterpiece provides Rabassa's best proof of how inexact yet demanding literary translation can be.

For Rabassa, the problems with *Cien años de soledad* began with the first word, because in Spanish *cien* bears no article, while its English equivalent must be expressed as "one hundred" or "a hundred." Says Rabassa, "I viewed the extent of time involved as something quite specific, as in a prophecy, something definite. A countdown, not just any old hundred years. . . . I am [still] convinced that Gabo [García Márquez] meant it in the sense of *one* as this . . . is closer to the feel of the novel. Also, there was no cavil on his part." *Soledad* is similarly ambiguous, for the word carries the meaning of its English kin—"solitude"—but also the sense of loneliness, thus bearing both the

Gregory Rabassa's English translations of works by Spanish and Latin literary giants have become classics. Rabassa is currently Distinguished Professor of Romance Languages and Comparative Literature at Queens College, New York.

positive and the negative feelings associated with being alone. "I went for *solitude* because it's a touch more inclusive, also carrying the germ of *loneliness*."

Mightily impressed with the English version, Gabo also praised Rabassa for what he assumed was the translator's usual technique of reading a novel through in the original and then rewriting it in English. However, except for *Cien años de soledad*, Rabassa's practice has been just the opposite. He translates as he reads most novels for the first time. In a deft bit of self-justification, Rabassa concludes that being acquainted with *Cien años de soledad* prior to translating it may have been providential. García Márquez has said that the plot "all came together in his mind [beforehand] and he just sat down and strung together the words needed to express it." Was Rabassa "simply translating in a way close to the way" the book was composed? the translator consoles himself by asking.

Readers for whom *The New Yorker* magazine is as much a symbol of elitism as of refinement will warm to Rabassa's fun as he recounts "a beautiful tale of timidity and orthodoxy." García Márquez's *El otoño del patriarca*, (1975; *The Autumn of the Patriarch*, 1975), a novel of dictatorship, of perverted minds and acts, was written without paragraphs and with a minimum of punctuation—García Márquez's way of making time move as if seen from a seat in a passing train. Because the appearance of a chunk of the work in *The New Yorker* would lead readers to the forthcoming book, Rabassa, as well as García Márquez's agent Cass Canfield, agreed to such preliminary exposure, but they stipulated that no semicolons would be allowed.

The translator was upheld with *mierda* (excrement), a word García Márquez used frequently as both expletive and descriptive term and Rabassa translated as the familiar four-letter word. "Since then," writes the author, "I have liked to trumpet the news that in a triumph even greater than his winning the Nobel Prize, García Márquez broke the shit barrier at *The New Yorker.*"

Other than García Márquez, the author to be covered most extensively in Rabassa's book is the late Julio Cortázar, whose *Rayuela* (1963; *Hopscotch*, 1966) carries instructions on how to read the novel in two versions. "When I finished the translation I remembered the instructions at the beginning and realized that I had offered a third reading of the novel by simply barging through from the first page to the last," Rabassa recalls.

Cortázar, the only author covered here whose translator knew him well, maintained that the name for the human species should not have been *homo sapiens* but *homo ludens*. Early critics did not realize that the book *Hopscotch* involves gamesmanship, something to be played. By his instinctive way of letting the words lead him, Rabassa got the drift of what the surreal characters were saying, and his translation won a National Book Award.

In making a work by Cortázar his first translation, Rabassa assumed the proper frame of mind to take on subsequent projects. Spanish and Latino literary surrealism, from Miguel de Cervantes' *El ingenioso hidalgo don Quixote de la Mancha* (1605, 1615; *The History of the Valorous and Wittie Knight-Errant, Don Quixote of the Mancha*, 1612-1620; better known as *Don Quixote de la Mancha*) to *Hopscotch*, 358 years later, seems to Rabassa to be unfinished. Successive translations cannot help but provide new readings, new endings. "In the sense or nonsense of it, every translation I have done since *Hopscotch* has in some way or another been its continuation."

Near the end of Rabassa's memoir, in discussing Oswaldo França, Jr., a little-known Brazilian writer, and his novel *O homem de macacão* (1972; *The Man in the Monkey Suit*, 1986), Rabassa regrets that in letting a flat-talking auto mechanic narrate in first-person voice the story of ordinary people, França, Jr., is unlikely to attract American readers. "It could be that for foreign books to be successful here there has to be some scent of the exotic or strange. . . . What if the mechanic had been the narrator of [F. Scott Fitzgerald's 1925 novel] *The Great Gatsby*?" One wonders how much of the vogue for Latin American Magical Realism can be assigned to translation.

Michael Dirda, the trouble-shooting reviewer for *The Washington Post*, complains that *If This Be Treason* contains nothing really profound and remains more scrapbook than book. Yet Rabassa often answers questions such as the one above about Magical Realism obliquely. "The translator must always listen to the characters' voices as they come over into English and not his or her voice as they are being translated." He wonders what Fyodor Dostoevski would have sounded like had he walked the streets of Rio de Janeiro rather than those of St. Petersburg. If the translator is doing his or her job, the answer is easy: Dostoevskian.

Richard Hauer Costa

Review Sources

Kirkus Reviews 73, no. 4 (February 15, 2005): 219.
Library Journal 130, no. 8 (May 1, 2005): 84-85.
The New York Times Book Review 154 (May 15, 2005): 36.
Newsweek 145, no. 19 (May 9, 2005).

IMAGINED CITIES
Urban Experience and the Language of the Novel

Author: Robert Alter (1935-   )
Publisher: Yale University Press (New Haven, Conn.).
   175 pp. $27.50
Type of work: Literary criticism
Time: 1846-1925

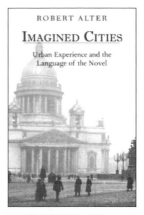

Alter argues that the unprecedented expansion of European cities during the late nineteenth and early twentieth centuries affected the development of the contemporary novel in specific ways, including its alterations in modes of human perception

As a literary critic, the prolific Robert Alter, author of seventeen books of criticism and biblical translation, has been an outspoken advocate of what some might regard as an old-fashioned approach to literature. In *The Pleasure of Reading in an Ideological Age* (1989) he contends that much contemporary criticism is more concerned with advancing a political agenda than it is with the pleasure inherent in the act of reading (that is, interpretation) itself. Alter, however, is no strict formalist. He is acutely aware of the powerful currents of historical change and how novelists register such change at the subtlest levels of perspective and figuration.

In *Imagined Cities* Alter is concerned with the phenomenal growth of European cities during the latter half of the nineteenth century and the first two decades of the twentieth. He argues, as many others have, that the "runaway growth" of the city brought about radical changes in the day-to-day experience of urban dwellers. The experience of a new and crushing urban density, of new modes of transportation, of the vastly quickened pace of daily life, of altered patterns of consumption and financial exchange, of cityscapes poisoned by industrial waste, Alter suggests, brought about a new awareness of the categories of time and space, of "the boundaries of the self and the autonomy of the individual."

What may surprise some readers is that Alter does not include in his study writers such as Émile Zola or Honoré de Balzac, whose novels abound in realistic or naturalistic portrayals of nineteenth century urban life. Alter is more attracted to what he calls the experimental realism of modernists such as James Joyce, Virginia Woolf, and Franz Kafka, writers who are more attuned to "the shifting pulse of experience felt by the individual, how the mind and the senses take in the world, construct it, or on occasion are confounded by it."

The first four chapters of *Imagined Cities* focus on two writers whom Alter perceives as significant forerunners of the modernists: Gustave Flaubert and Charles Dickens. Flaubert's Paris was in many ways the paradigm of explosive growth and change in the nineteenth century. In the first half of the century the city's population

~

Robert Alter is the Class of 1937 Professor of Hebrew and Comparative Literature at the University of California at Berkeley. He has published widely on the modern European and American novel, on modern Hebrew literature, and on literary aspects of the Bible. He is the author of, among other works, Necessary Angels: Tradition and Modernity in Kafka, Benjamin, and Scholem *(1991) and* The Art of Biblical Narrative *(1983).*

~

doubled; by 1860 it had incorporated the surrounding suburbs, and its population had increased by another third. In addition, Paris was, as Alter notes, "the crucible for historical transformation in nineteenth century Europe," having undergone revolutionary upheaval in 1789, 1830, 1848, and 1871. As a result Paris became "increasingly a theater of perplexity, defying summation, lacking social, political, and therefore thematic coherence." In Alter's view, it was Flaubert who first came to terms with this perplexed new urban reality and its impact upon the individual by abandoning the narrative omniscience of his predecessors and replacing it with what Alter calls "narrated monologue"—a variant of limited omniscience in which the unvoiced speech of a character (usually the protagonist) is fused with the voice of the narrator.

According to Alter, "Flaubert's . . . perception is that the individual, caught in the shower of exciting and conflicting stimuli of the urban milieu, can see them only through the distorting medium of his private preoccupations." Thus in Flaubert's great Parisian novel *The Sentimental Education* (1869), the tumultuous and confusing life of the city is rendered exclusively through the eyes of the novel's protagonist, Frederic. As a result, the urban panorama presented so brilliantly by Balzac is here fragmented or dissolved in fleeting perceptions colored by the protagonist's interior life, his fears, hopes, and fantasies. The urban dweller in Flaubert's novelistic vision is no longer part of a dynamic whole but an "isolate individual." His perceptions of time and space become "a maelstrom in which the centrifugal elements of experience are whirled together in dizzying combinations."

In *The Sentimental Education* the coherent world of realist fiction begins to break down even at the levels of syntax and metaphor, powerfully influencing the modernist experimentation that would emerge several decades later. Moreover, the modernists' interest in the nature of consciousness is anticipated in Flaubert. Is consciousness an awareness of thought, or merely the deceptive and superficial awareness of fathomless depths over which the individual has no control? Already in Flaubert's fiction, the answer to that question is ambiguous.

In turning to the later novels of Dickens, Alter readily admits to what appears to be a regression. By contrast to Flaubert, Dickens's novels are consistently narrated in the omniscient manner and, in this respect at least, seem far removed from the stylistic innovations of the modernists. Despite the conventional narrative technique, however, Dickens's fiction is manifestly concerned—more than any other nineteenth century English novelist—with the new and frightening reality of the urban environment. The focus of most of his urban novels is, of course, London, a city whose growth during Dickens's lifetime rivaled that of Paris. Like Flaubert's, Dickens's vision of the city is at times nightmarish, verging on the apocalyptic. If it is true that "the cosiness and cheeriness of the Dickensian world are quite genuine" and that even in his darkest novels he continues to depict a "small, sustaining community of the kindhearted within the urban wasteland," it is also the case that in novels such as *Bleak House* (1853) and *Our Mutual Friend* (1865), this community is beleaguered by a city "sliding into bleak incoherence." If his narrative technique is conventional, Dickens nonetheless may be seen as a stylistic innovator in other respects.

In his fertile use of figurative language and in his uncanny mingling of fairy-tale elements with realistic reportage, for example, Dickens develops what Alter calls an "archaic vision" in which the contemporary cityscape "triggers certain primal fears and fantasies . . . becoming the medium through which we are led to see the troubling meanings of the new urban reality." Alter's readers may also be surprised to find the claim that Dickens anticipates the use of montage, the cinematic technique pioneered by Sergei Eisenstein in the 1920's involving a series of sharp juxtapositions of scenes or images. As Alter makes clear, this is a technique eminently suited to the constantly shifting and confusing urban reality, and he makes a convincing case that Dickens's treatment of urban clutter and disorder does indeed look forward to later filmic innovations and may even have inspired them.

In turning to the modernists Woolf and Joyce, Alter notes that much of the nineteenth century preoccupation with urban disorder and incoherence carries over into the twentieth century novel, but in a different key. He observes that the "dire visions" of the nineteenth century represent, after all, only a "partial view" of what it means to inhabit a great city. People gravitate to metropolitan centers not only out of economic necessity or predatory ambition but often because the pulsating life of the city is an exciting and, at times, even a joyous experience. In Joyce's *Ulysses* (1922) the discontinuity of urban experience is celebrated with great exuberance, especially in the author's use of stream-of-consciousness narration which, Alter suggests, may be the ultimate fulfillment of Flaubert's abandonment of authorial omniscience.

As Leopold Bloom (one of several centers of consciousness in *Ulysses*) moves about the streets of Dublin, the play of interior monologue shifts in bewildering discontinuity of perspectives, from Bloom himself to the briefly glimpsed interior monologues of characters that he passes randomly in the street. The result is what Alter calls a vision of the city as "a prime arena for the clash and interchange of languages, each reflecting the values of the social, professional or ideological subgroup from which it derives." In Flaubert such a discontinuity of perspective induces in his characters (and in the reader) a sense of loss of control. Joyce, by contrast, exults in the discontinuity. Fragmentation in *Ulysses* "becomes a new kind of poetry that affirms simultaneously the inventive energies of the mind and the concrete particularities of everyday experience."

In Woolf's *Mrs. Dalloway* (1923), London becomes the setting for what Alter calls "urban pastoral"—pastoral in the sense that the center of consciousness in the novel, Clarissa Dalloway, achieves a subjective harmony with her surroundings through aesthetic revelation. Unlike Flaubert's Frederic, who is presented as a passive casualty of the fragmentation of the urban environment, Clarissa, like Leopold Bloom, has an "awareness of the mind's constructing the world around it from the materials that the world gives it." Harmony is achieved, but one which is necessarily ephemeral. Clarissa embraces that very ephemerality; the rhythms of the city carry her beyond the awareness of her own mortality and, in the end, beyond the prison of her subjectivity. Even the anonymous crowds of the urban sprawl offer the possibility of existential communion.

Clarissa Dalloway's affirmative embrace of the heterogeneous and fragmented life of the city allows her to overcome isolation, but in Kafka's Prague only radical separation from others is possible. In *The Trial* (1925), "the city for Kafka is above all a place where one is alone." Joseph K., the novel's protagonist, lives in a rooming house, with only superficial and, for the most part, paranoid contact with his neighbors. Even chance encounters on the stairway or a glimpse of the face of a stranger though a window become occasions for suspicion. One would assume that first-person narration would be the natural vehicle for expressing such extreme isolation, but as Alter demonstrates with impressive attention to syntactic detail, Kafka employs instead Flaubert's narrated monologue to exploit "the ambiguity between the seeming authoritativeness of the narrator and the radical, chronically uncertain subjectivity of [Joseph K.]." Joseph K. is "enclosed in a world of suppositions—the very mental activity that finds its perfect habitat in the narrated monologue."

This chronic uncertainty of perception is perhaps best illustrated at the end of the novel when Joseph K., about to be executed at a quarry on the fringes of the city, gazes upward toward a nearby apartment building. There a human figure seems to appear, arms outstretched in what may be a gesture of concern or merely one indifferent and unrelated to Joseph's plight. Kafka's narrated monologue reinforces this essential ambiguity: "Who was it? A friend? A good person? Was it just one person. . . . Was there still help? Were their objections that had been forgotten [since the trial]?" In such a passage it is impossible for the reader to discern whether the questions are the objective speculations of the narrator or the product of Joseph's desperation.

Imagined Cities, though clearly written and, for the most part, a pleasure to read, is a work that assumes a fairly sophisticated knowledge of modernist literature on the part of the reader. Still, it is by no means the sort of jargon-ridden, arcane study that students and lay readers often find so perplexing. If there is a weakness in this study, it is perhaps that Alter's eagerness to avoid ideological criticism sometimes blinds him to the obvious. For example, a strong argument might be made that Clarissa Dalloway's "affirmative" subjective embrace of the fragmentation of urban reality is in part a possibility afforded her by a leisured, upper-middle class status (one shared by Woolf). Unlike most of the denizens of the modern city, she is shielded from the often harsh reality of its fragmentation by an aesthetic distance made possible by affluence. Whether this calls into question her harmonic "communion" with a city of strangers is an issue that Alter, if he had written an even better book, might have at least considered, but does not.

Jack Trotter

Review Sources

The New Leader 88, no. 3 (May/June, 2005): 48.
The New York Times Book Review 154 (June 19, 2005): 8-9.
The Washington Post Book World, July 24, 2005, p. 9.

IMPERIAL GRUNTS
The American Military on the Ground

Author: Robert D. Kaplan (1952-   )
Publisher: Random House (New York). 421 pp. $28.00
Type of work: Current affairs and history
Time: 2002-2004
Locale: Southeast Asia, the Middle East, Central and
    South America

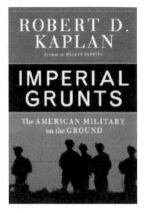

*Kaplan explores the role of the common soldier in help-
ing to establish an American presence and represent American values in countries where political instability is seen as
a threat to U.S. democracy*

In the fall of 2005, as the United States was conducting active combat operations in Iraq and Afghanistan, the
American media carried two stories of operations involv-
ing American military in the mountainous region that forms the border between Pakistan and Afghanistan. In September, American soldiers were seen delivering relief
aid to Pakistanis suffering from the devastation of a major earthquake. Sound bites of
grateful Pakistanis filled the airwaves; many expressed their gratitude toward a country they had hitherto distrusted, or even hated, for its treatment of their fellow Muslims. Less than a month later, however, those same media outlets featured the story of
a group of American soldiers in Afghanistan burning the bodies of two Afghan rebels
and taunting their comrades. Any goodwill built up among Muslims by the relief efforts in Pakistan was sure to evaporate in the face of such an atrocity.

These two scenes highlight the problem discussed at length by veteran journalist
Robert Kaplan in *Imperial Grunts*. While American executives such as President
George Bush may speak passionately about the importance of freedom, and while
members of Congress may debate the necessity of extending the United States' reach
around the globe, the success of U.S. efforts to spread democracy rests on the shoulders of the people who are, to use a common military expression, "in country." The
ways young privates and sergeants behave, Kaplan argues, and the leadership provided by lieutenants, captains, and majors will do more to decide the fate of U.S. efforts than any platitudes spouted by politicians in Washington.

In Kaplan's view, these soldiers, sailors, air personnel, and marines are serving a
political agenda that links the United States with nations of ancient times such as
Greece, Rome, and England: builders of empire. Kaplan sees the United States as an
imperial power spreading its ideology through its military and diplomatic efforts.
Whether fighting to oust insurgents or capture drug traffickers, helping to build wells
or distribute medicines, men and women in uniform are functioning in much the same
way as did their predecessors in regimes that had stamped their ideologies on, and extracted resources from, countries they had conquered by force or entered by treaty.

To determine how successfully the United States has been carrying out its imperial mission, Kaplan embarked on a two-year journey to see how American influence and power worldwide is being maintained by the men and women who work directly with people in other countries around the globe. Kaplan takes as his blueprint for the journey the map of the world fashioned by the U.S. military, which has divided the planet into separate spheres: NORTHCOM, the northern American hemisphere; SOUTHCOM, the southern half of the hemisphere; EUCOM, a region stretching in an arc from the southern tip of Africa up half the continent across the Mediterranean and over Europe and Russia to the Pacific Ocean; CENTCOM, a segment of Africa and Asia including troubled spots such as the Middle East and Afghanistan; and PACOM, the largest area, covering all the Pacific islands, the Asian subcontinent, China, and Mongolia. For each there is a military commander tasked to evaluate and manage conflict and promote American interests; in each there are American military serving either in small, specially trained units or larger, conventional forces representing those interests on the ground.

Robert D. Kaplan is a veteran journalist whose articles in The Atlantic Monthly *have been influential in informing the American public about a number of political issues that have caused the United States to employ its military forces. He is the author of ten books, including* Warrior Politics *(2002),* The Coming Anarchy *(2000), and* Balkan Ghosts *(1993).*

Kaplan's journey took him to faraway locales such as Yemen and Mongolia, to the jungles of Colombia and the Philippines, into the mountains of Afghanistan and to the Horn of Africa, and ended in Iraq, where he participated with U.S. Marines in combat operations that put his life in danger. On trips back to the United States, he visited training sites at Fort Bragg and Camp Lejeune, where soldiers and marines are trained for the tasks they will perform. Wherever he went, he found the troops with whom he came in contact to be dedicated, knowledgeable, and deeply committed to their missions; they are proud to represent their country and eager to talk about the advantages of living in a democratic society. They are realists, though; most recognize that it will take time—years, perhaps even decades—to transform countries such as Yemen and Mongolia into full-fledged democracies, and perhaps even longer in places such as Colombia and Iraq, where civil war prevents ordinary citizens from experiencing that most basic of all rights—not "freedom," the popular mantra of politicians, but "security," the right to live without constant fear of death or dismemberment.

In Kaplan's view, the soldiers, marines, and air personnel with whom he traveled are carrying out heroic tasks, often in the face of strong opposition. Kaplan finds plenty of villains pitted against these heroes. Certainly the drug lords in Colombia, the Taliban in Afghanistan, and the insurgents in Iraq are formidable foes. There are others, however: corrupt politicians who must be bribed before poor people can receive food or medicine, inept laborers or too-eager partisans who are often more hindrance than help in accomplishing humanitarian or military tasks, inscrutable bureaucrats who are more interested in being acknowledged for their supposed importance than in genuinely helping improve their country. The villains most cited by Kaplan, however, wear the same uniforms as his heroes. The generals and colonels in the rear areas seem totally out of touch with activities on the front lines in the countries to which American forces are deployed. Bent on avoiding the debacle of Vietnam, they prize security over every other concern, and as a consequence opportunities to capture or kill the enemy, or to help a friend truly in need, are frequently lost. By contrast, soldiers on the ground are much more willing to risk their lives in a worthy cause than their leaders are to suffer the bad press associated with American casualties.

Because Kaplan tells his tale with the sense of immediacy and suspense associated with the best writers of fiction, it would be easy to get caught up in these accounts of America's front-line ambassadors and miss the larger implications of his argument. Kaplan guards against that happening, however, by constantly reminding readers that this is not simply a book about soldiers in harm's way but also a study of the political philosophy that drives American policy makers to place the troops in such positions. On page after page, Kaplan draws comparisons between American soldiers and those of the Roman legions, or the British in India. Kaplan also writes of what he calls the failure of the Soviet empire in satellite countries that have emerged in the twenty-first century as potential allies or foes of the United States. Kaplan's most frequent comparison, however, is between these twenty-first century warriors and their nineteenth century counterparts: the American cavalry who established a presence in the West. Far away from the prying eyes of Washington, the colonels and captains in command of regiments and companies were required to make decisions that frequently affected the success of U.S. policy in a region.

Whether one agrees that the United States' policy toward Americans Indians was wise, the analogy regarding the need for independent judgment is clear. Kaplan believes that, to be effective in the twenty-first century, the United States will be forced to restructure its military into smaller, more flexible units, with commanders given greater autonomy to deal with situations as they arise. This concept flies in the face of American war-fighting policy since the Vietnam War. As methods of communication and technology have become more sophisticated, command and control has undergone a process of consolidation so that decision-making authority is reserved to those higher in the chain of command, to the point where generals and high-ranking civilians in the Pentagon direct the activities of companies and battalions half a world away. Kaplan argues that, despite the ability for continuous and immediate contact provided by enhanced communications systems, there is no way for those in Washington to understand what is really happening in the jungles of Colombia or the deserts of Iraq. If the United States is to achieve its goal of spreading democracy and removing impediments to democratic rule in faraway states, those in high positions will have to learn to trust the young soldiers and marines who come in direct contact with indigenous populations.

What comes through clearly in *Imperial Grunts* is the genuine respect Kaplan has for soldiers. Such an attitude puts him at odds with many in his profession—a position that has actually worked to his benefit in preparing to write his book. It is true that, since the Vietnam War, journalists have had an adversarial relationship with the American military, and those in uniform have been skeptical of anyone associated with the media. By contrast, Kaplan is one of the few working journalists whose presence is welcomed by the military. He is a reporter in the mold of the legendary Ernie Pyle, who wrote his stories of the American soldiers in Europe and the Pacific while sitting beside them in their foxholes and bunkers. A veteran of the Israeli military, Kaplan has trekked along mountainous trails and across searing deserts with the men and women whose bravery and common sense he celebrates. His riveting accounts of fire fights in the streets of Iraq's cities have the ring of truth to them because he was there beside the marines who were engaged in shootouts with Iraqi insurgents.

No matter how one views the larger political implications of America's foreign policy at the beginning of the twenty-first century, it is hard to dispute Kaplan's major premise: The success or failure of the United States in transforming the world into a planet full of democracies rests squarely on the shoulders of young men and women in uniform whose everyday actions demonstrate to the people of far-flung countries in the Far East, in South America, or in the heartlands of the Caucasus what it means to be an American. The ongoing efforts of such Americans will determine the fate of the American empire. True to the spirit Kaplan finds in the soldiers about whom he reports, in *Imperial Grunts* he offers a realistic, if somewhat sobering, assessment of this work in progress.

Laurence W. Mazzeno

Review Sources

The Atlantic Monthly 296, no. 3 (October, 2005): 84.
Booklist 101, no. 22 (August, 2005): 1987.
Business Week, October 31, 2005, p. 112.
Commentary 120, no. 4 (November, 2005): 89-92.
Kirkus Reviews 73, no. 12 (June 15, 2005): 672.
National Review 57, no. 17 (September 26, 2005): 59-60.
Publishers Weekly 252, no. 25 (June 20, 2005): 70.
Washington Monthly 37, no. 9 (September, 2005): 45-47.

IN A FINE FRENZY
Poets Respond to Shakespeare

Editors: David Starkey (1962-   ) and Paul J. Willis
   (1955-   )
Publisher: University of Iowa Press (Iowa City). 192 pp.
   $40.00; paperback $20.00
Type of work: Poetry

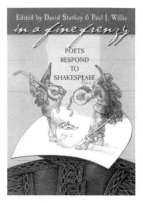

The poems in this collection respond to, comment upon, or are influenced by the works of William Shakespeare

In their clear and useful introduction, the editors of the anthology *In a Fine Frenzy* lay out their criteria for choosing the texts they have included in this collection of poems written in response to William Shakespeare. David Starkey and Paul J. Willis trace the history of such collections, explore the impulses behind them, and explain the reasons they felt that a mainly modern, mainly American anthology could show Shakespeare's effect on the poets of this place and time.

Once they began collecting submissions, they became interested in the characters that were most often covered: Ophelia, Hamlet, Viola, Miranda, Prospero, Desdemona, Iago, Lear, Cordelia, and Horatio. They ponder reasons these characters appeal to the modern sensibility, including the idea that characters such as Ophelia represent the broadly human predicaments of modern lives, a time of disconnection and disengagement. The editors then discuss the wide variety of other ways in which poets were inspired by the bard. There are those who pay homage to the great poet and those who in some way deflate the text. There are quite a few poems that set their text in the classroom, where most people first encounter Shakespeare. Many also are musing upon the relationship between the texts of the sonnets or plays to their own lives.

Following the introduction, the editors organize the poems in a format loosely based on a play. They begin with a poem as prologue, followed by five separate sections divided by interludes, and end with an epilogue. The five sections are titled "The Sonnets," "The Comedies," "The Tragedies (and Histories)," "*Hamlet*," and "The Romances." Within these sections are many surprises; for example, there are tragic poems about the comedies, and there are humorous poems about the tragedies. Some show great reverence for these classics of literature and others are totally irreverent. Two examples of the latter would be "This Is What Happens When You Let Hamlet Play Quarterback" by Jack Conway and "Lear Drives His Rambler Across Laurel Mountain" by Charles Clifton. The collected poems are as diverse in form as recent poetry itself, covering the range from the traditional sonnet and ottava rima to free verse to the prose poem.

In part 1, "The Sonnets," just over half take the traditional sonnet form. Even of those, two by Leonard Nathan are "Ragged Sonnets." Perhaps the most interesting is a teacher's delight titled simply "Shakespearian Sonnet" by R. S. Gwynn. It begins with a note, *"With a first line taken from the tv listings."* That first line is "A man is haunted by his father's ghost," obviously a description of *Hamlet* (pr. c. 1600-1601). The poem is presented in the traditional fourteen lines of rhyming iambic pentameter, with each line an equally mundane summary of one of Shakespeare's great dramas, concluding with the description of *Antony and Cleopatra* (pr. c. 1606-1607) as "A sexy queen is bitten by a snake."

David Starkey teaches at Santa Barbara City College and in the M.F.A. program at Antioch University Los Angeles. He is the author of several collections of poems and a playwright whose work has been produced in New York, Los Angeles, and Seattle. Paul Willis is a professor of English at Westmont College in Santa Barbara, where he teaches Shakespeare and creative writing. He is the author of eco-fantasy novels and chapbooks of poems, and his work has also appeared in several anthologies.

The interlude between this section and part 2, "The Comedies," is one of the surprisingly numerous poems that look at Shakespeare the man, in this case through the mistaken and unenthusiastic eyes of the students of the poet Ron Koertge, appropriately titled "My Students."

Part 2, "The Comedies," begins with songs that Michael B. Stillman wrote to complete the seasons for *Love's Labour's Lost* (pr. c. 1594-1595, rev. 1597), then continues with poems written from the points of view of various characters, including Bottom from *A Midsummer Night's Dream* (pr. c. 1595-1596), Shylock and Portia from *The Merchant of Venice* (pr. c. 1596-1597), and the duke from *As You Like It* (pr. c. 1599-1600). One of the most striking contributions is Mary Makofske's "Viola, to Olivia," which concludes with the insightful comment "Sister, it was not in spite of/ my soft cheek you loved me," emphasizing the homoerotic undertones of that comedy. J. D. Smith rewrites the "Seven Ages of Man" in a poem of the same title, updating it in a comic fashion, but others take a more serious look at characters such as Shylock, who is featured in a powerful and painful poem by J. B. Mulligan.

The second interlude between the "plays" is a quirky look at the bard by B. J. Ward, titled "Shakespeare as a Waiter," in which he shows how an artist, no matter how weary and worn from the menial labor necessary to survive in the world, will find inspiration in constant attention to the life going on all around, just as it is, which might be transformed into the art of tomorrow.

"The Tragedies (and Histories)" section in part 3 is longer and contains some of the more complex poems in the collection. The topics and approaches, as well as style and content, are extremely varied. The editors begin with a look at the seldom performed and lesser-known *Titus Andronicus* (pr., pb. 1594) in a remarkably effective lyric in the voice of Lavinia from that play, calling on the reader to take her loss and dance with it. What follows is an eclectic collection, with some works being commentary on the tragedy or history of choice or on specific characters, while others use one of the plays to reflect on the poet's life or particular circumstances. For example, the poems about *Romeo and Juliet* (pr. c. 1595-1596) include a remembrance of a high school beauty and commentary on a film version, as well as thoughtful reflections on the meaning of suicide.

The greatest number of poems in this section focus on *King Lear* (pr. c. 1605-1606) and *Othello* (pr. 1604, rev. 1623), and a great interest is shown in Iago particularly. The questions of evil, hatred, and destruction of innocence which are explored in these plays are, of course, some of the great questions of life in the twenty-first century; they remain unresolved. Certainly the twentieth century, during which most of these poems were written, saw the horror and yet also the banality of evil which is illustrated in Iago's character, explored in "Iago" by Arthur Powers, "Iago, the Poet" by J. P. Dancing Bear, "Iago to His Torturers," by R. S. Gwynn, and "Iago" by Julian Bernick.

Quite a few of the poems in this section feature women, reminding the reader how many striking women characters the bard created. A very evocative and unusual poem by Jeanne Murray Walker pairs August Strindberg's Mother Courage with Desdemona in "How Mother Courage Saves Desdemona." Others focus on Lady Macbeth, Cleopatra, and Juliet.

"As If" by Jim Peterson continues the motif of interludes focusing on Shakespeare the man. Placed between the tragedies and the particular tragedy of *Hamlet*, the poem imagines the poet in the first-person voice, caring nothing for the carping of critics as he is driven by his passionate yet cold originality.

Part 4 focuses entirely on *Hamlet*, both the play and the character, as this is apparently the most evocative of Shakespeare's dramas for modern writers. The first poem, James Applewhite's "On the Mississippi," begins this section by looking at the play in this new world, as seen by the duke in Mark Twain's *Adventures of Huckleberry Finn* (1884). Applewhite places the bard at the center of the American wilderness and locates him next to one of the great characters of nineteenth century American literature, Ishmael from Herman Melville's *Moby Dick* (1851). In this section the reader hears from Hamlet, Ophelia, Reynaldo, Horatio, Gertrude, and even the first player, each given new voice in their old character. Other poems look at individual poet's reactions to various performances of the play, from the classroom to actor Laurence Olivier. Interestingly, it is Ophelia who receives the greatest attention, perhaps (as the editors speculate) because she is the ultimate marginalized character, robbed of her voice and disregarded by manipulative men. Although there appear many Ophelia poems in the collection, apparently many more were rejected by the editors, to keep the anthology from drowning in them.

The interlude between the great tragedy of *Hamlet* and "The Romances" is appropriately represented by "Shakespeare's Eyebrows," by Sylvia Adams; this poem begins with a reference to the tragedies of modern times, then shifts to the trivial, the discovery of Shakespeare's eyebrows embedded in his death mask, and returns to seriousness at the end with a reference to suicide.

"The Romances" are the focus of part 5, with particular attention paid to *The Tempest* (pr. 1611). Here each of that play's major characters, Prospero, Caliban, Miranda, and Ariel, has his or her poem. Once again, the form and structure of the poems is utterly eclectic, no two in any way echoing the other. Stephen Corey's lovely "The Tempest," which he dedicates to his daughter Miranda, shows profound insight into both the modern young woman and the character in the drama. J. P. Dancing Bear's "Caliban" takes the form of a monologue by the suffering creature, speaking in thought to his long-gone mother, telling his suffering and his truth. Ariel and Prospero both receive free verse attention suitable to their personalities as they appear in the play. *Pericles, Prince of Tyre* (pr. c. 1607-1608) and *Cymbeline* (pr. c. 1609-1610) are also given attention, despite their relative obscurity in present-day theater.

The prologue, like the epilogue, is a single poem by a master poet. The prologue is Marvin Bell's "Shakespeare's Wages," which both mocks and celebrates the bard's overcoming his earlier reputation as a "bad boy" to become utterly respectable. The epilogue is Steven Corey's "Whatever Light," in which Shakespeare dreams the sound of his name. Thus the poems that focus upon specific works are surrounded by the prologue, interludes, and epilogue, which all focus on Shakespeare the man, as well as the artist, rather than the works themselves.

This is a fascinating and eclectic collection of poems which will benefit from further study to examine not only the individual poems but also the interplay of plays, poems, poets, and the modern, to see how writers grow and are enriched through the great literature of the past.

Mary LeDonne Cassidy

Review Source

Comparative Drama 38, no. 4 (Winter, 2004/2005): 471.

IN THE COMPANY OF CHEERFUL LADIES

Author: Alexander McCall Smith (1948-   )
First published: 2004, in Great Britain
Publisher: Pantheon Books (New York). 233 pp. $20.00
Type of work: Novel
Time: The early twenty-first century
Locale: Gaborone, Botswana

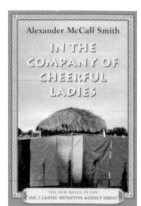

The sixth novel in Alexander McCall Smith's No. 1 Ladies' Detective Agency series tells the story of Mma Ramotswe and the various problems and adventures encountered in her daily life

Principal characters:
  MMA PRECIOUS RAMOTSWE, the
    Botswanian proprietor of her own detective agency
  MR. J. L. B. MATEKONI, Mma Ramotswe's husband of six months
    and the owner of a car repair shop
  MMA GRACE MAKUTSI, an unmarried woman who works in the
    private detective agency
  CHARLIE, a young apprentice at Mr. J. L. B. Matekoni's repair
    shop
  PHUTI RADIPHUTI, a furniture salesman Mma Makutsi meets at a
    dance class
  MMA SILVIA POTOKWANE, the head of an orphanage and friend of
    Mma Ramotswe
  MR. POLOPETSI, a man recently out of prison whose bicycle is hit by
    Mma Ramotswe
  NOTE MOKOTI, Mma Ramotswe's first husband, whom she left
    because he abused her

In the Company of Cheerful Ladies begins with Mma Precious Ramotswe, Botswana's first female private detective, sitting on the open verandah of her favorite café, drinking tea, enjoying her Saturday afternoon. She is thinking about commonplace events which have happened during the week and finding the connections between them and the state of the world. That morning, for example, she had seen a woman who was trying to park her car scrape another car. The woman quickly checked the damage and drove off. Mma Ramotswe knows that behavior such as this is not honest. She reflects that such incidents were less likely to occur in the days when she was growing up in a village and everyone knew one another. Now her beloved African country of Botswana is becoming urbanized, the population is increasing, and people often seem indifferent or uncaring toward others. Still, she thinks, if some things are worse, some other things are better. It is no good just shrugging in despair. One must do what one can.

In the midst of such reflections, Mma Ramotswe (as she is always referred to in the novel) is tested. She witnesses a woman stealing a bangle from a nearby market stall. She tells herself she must not allow this crime. She walks firmly toward the stall to intercept the woman. However, the waitress from the café bounds after Mma Ramotswe and accuses her of trying to leave without paying her bill. The thief walks away.

The waitress does not accept Mma Ramotswe's explanation and not only demands the money for the bill but also says that she will add more money for herself or else she will call the police. When the waitress has gone, a woman at a nearby table leans across and quietly tells Mma Ramotswe that she would have better luck running away from a café at a hotel. Despite these clear examples of how things have changed since her village days, Mma Romotswe retains her philosophical position. To make the world a better place, she believes, one needs to have enough imagination to sympathize with others, to know what it is like to be them and thus not do something which would cause them pain.

Alexander McCall Smith has published scholarly nonfiction, numerous novels and short stories, and several children's books, including the much translated The Perfect Hamburger *(1984).* The No. 1 Ladies' Detective Agency *(1998) brought him international acclaim, and in 2004 he was named Author of the Year in the British Book Awards.*

Throughout the novel, it is this sympathetic and encouraging outlook on life that informs Mma Romotswe's actions as she encounters problems, whether they are connected with the business she founded, the No. 1 Ladies' Detective Agency, or with family and friends, or even with difficult "non-friends." This attitude is also, presumably, one of the main reasons hundreds of thousands of readers were entranced with the first book in the series, *The No. 1 Ladies' Detective Agency* (1998), and have continued to follow Mma Ramotswe's adventures. Author Alexander McCall Smith has said that he did not think of the first book as the beginning of a series, but he became so fond of Mma Ramotswe that he did not want to let her go. *The No. 1 Ladies' Detective Agency* received two Booker Judge's Special Recommendations and was selected for numerous book club groups, such as the *Today Show* Club. McCall Smith was named 2004 author of the year in the British Book Awards. The series is widely available internationally, and it continues to be enthusiastically received.

Although McCall Smith has published more than fifty works on a variety of topics, including children's books and many novels, this series marked his first venture into mystery writing. McCall Smith has said in interviews that he does not think of these novels as mysteries but as novels about a woman who happens to be a private detective. *In the Company of Cheerful Ladies* includes only one case that Mma Ramotswe's agency is paid to investigate, which is to find the location of a suspected criminal. That case is worked largely through a few letters and telephone calls. There are no violent murders, no wild shootouts, no organized crime or political corruption. The "mysteries" that make up most of the story are more problems of daily life.

The various problems that appear can be listed as questions needing answers. Who was hiding in Mma Ramotswe's house and ran away without his trousers? Who left a beautiful big pumpkin as a present? Why does Charlie, an apprentice mechanic at Mr. J. L. B. Matekoni's shop, suddenly have money and say he does not need his job? Could a man who has just been released from prison be trustworthy? What should Mma Ramotswe do when someone from her past reappears and demands blackmail money? Who stole her tiny white van that she loved to drive? The reader is treated to Mma Ramotswe's thoughtful insights into the characters of others as she resolves these situations.

In addition to Mma Ramotswe, another major appeal of the novel is the continuing cast of characters surrounding her. Mma Ramotswe became engaged to Mr. J. L. B. Matekoni at the end of the first novel in the series. Now they have been married for six months. He lives in her house on Zebra Drive, along with the two children he rescued from an orphanage. Among his possessions is a velvet painting. Mma Ramotswe smiles to herself that she is sure that if her house were burglarized the velvet painting would not be taken. Matekoni's house has been rented to tenants, but he is busy with his car repair business and does not check on what is happening with his renters. There is, in fact, a problem, but it is handled smoothly by Mma Grace Makutsi, who works at the detective agency, located conveniently at the same address as his garage.

Mr. J. L. B. Matekoni (as he is always referred to, even by his wife), prides himself on providing honest and expert service at Tlokweng Road Speedy Motors. He worries that his two apprentices do not sufficiently understand and appreciate cars and trucks and the need to care for them as individuals each with its own ways. He has always loved his profession, but he is beginning to be concerned that the new automobiles have sophisticated computerized systems that both reduce the intuitive role of the mechanic and make it much more difficult to service and maintain the vehicles. He has many of the same good qualities that Mma Ramotswe admired in her father.

The likeable Mma Grace Makutsi, now promoted to first assistant detective in the agency made up only of her and Mma Ramotswe, still thinks proudly of her high rating of 97 percent in the final examinations at the Botswana Secretarial College. She runs the Kalahari Typing School for Men, teaching an evening class, but she also feels the need to enlarge her circle of acquaintances, particularly in regard to meeting interesting men. To this end, she splurges on new red shoes, so that now she has three pairs, and she enrolls in an evening dance class which promises its lessons can teach anyone to dance and learn the social graces associated with dancing. In dancing school, she is introduced to Phuti Radiphuti, clearly the worst dancer in the class.

Mma Grace Makutsi and Mma Ramotswe have a solid friendship as well as an excellent working relationship. Each, however, remains aware of her need to be understanding of the other. The two retain a level of politeness and formality that enables them to negotiate differences without offense to either one. An example of this is the considerable thought and time that goes into Mma Makutsi letting Mma Ramotswe know that she would prefer to make traditional tea for herself for her morning break rather than continue to drink the bush tea which Mma Ramotswe enjoys. By the time the discussion concludes, both women are feeling that they have been successful in the handling of the situation.

The emphasis on finding win-win solutions for all parties involved is seen throughout the novel. It works for Mma Makutsi in her talks with a minister of religion who has spoken with the man for whom the agency is looking. The minister finds a way to respond to Mma Makutsi questions without feeling that he has betrayed a confidence.

It works in Mma Ramotswe's discussions with her longtime friend Mma Silvia Potokwane, matron at a home for orphaned children. Mma Potokwane mentions, with purposeful casualness, that she has heard that Note Mokoti is currently in Gaborone. She knows that this will be disturbing news to Mma Ramotswe, but she does not make an issue of it. Mma Ramotswe does not play up the issue either, but it is an important one for her nonetheless. Note Mokoti was her first husband, an abusive man. He soon shows up and demands blackmail money from her, trying to exploit the fact that they did not get a legal divorce before she married Mr. J. L. B. Matakoni. It is a tense situation for Mma Ramotswe. She carefully considers what to do, and her solution is one that, typically, employs efforts to understand the other person and to create a situation that will be satisfactory for all, or will at least end the problem.

The detectives at the No. 1 Ladies' Detective Agency particularly excel at detecting ways to solve the problems of ordinary people, including themselves. By the end of the novel, Mma Ramotswe has added an "assistant to the assistant," another person who will work part-time at the agency and part-time at Tlokweng Road Speedy Motors. This is yet another instance of finding happy solutions that are beneficial to all.

Mma Ramotswe is fond of quoting a manual titled *The Principles of Private Detection* by Clovis Andersen. She considers its advice when she encounters problems. She does not necessarily agree with everything the author says, however. In fact, she thinks perhaps she should write her own book, or that she and Mma Makutsi should write it together. It could be called, she says, *Private Detection for Ladies. In the Company of Cheerful Ladies*, like the other novels in the series, vividly dramatizes Mma Ramotswe's theories of detection and the thinking that precedes her actions. Still, even though they constitute her methodology and her advice, readers would no doubt also be delighted to have the book she would write, Mma Ramotswe's *Private Detection for Ladies*.

Lois A. Marchino

Review Sources

Booklist 101, no. 11 (February 1, 2005): 917.
Geographical 76, no. 10 (October, 2004): 80.
The New York Times 154 (April 24, 2005): 16-17.
Publishers Weekly 252, no. 7 (February 14, 2005): 51.
School Library Journal 51, no. 9 (September, 2005): 244.

IN THE PROVINCE OF SAINTS

Author: Thomas O'Malley (1967-   )
Publisher: Little, Brown (New York). 306 pp. $24.00
Type of work: Novel
Time: April, 1976, to September, 1981
Locale: New Rowan and Dublin, Ireland

Nine-year-old Michael McDonagh comes of age in a rural Irish village, uncovering rumors and secrets about his family and himself that alter his life forever

> *Principal characters:*
> MICHAEL MCDONAGH, a sensitive boy who matures into a reflective young adult
> JOHN MCDONAGH, Michael's father, who works in the United States and returns occasionally to Ireland
> MOIRA MCDONAGH, Michael's terminally ill mother, who lives a life of shame and resentment
> CAIT DELACEY, schoolmate of Michael and object of his adolescent affection
> MAG DELACEY, Cait's mother, whose death sets in motion a series of revelations
> BRENDAN DOLAN, Michael's drink-addled uncle, who hides dark secrets
> LUGH MCCONNAHUE, a day laborer on a neighbor's farm, who gives young Michael the attention and affection he craves

In the Province of Saints opens abruptly with the death of a village woman, Mag Delacey, in the middle of a particularly harsh winter that destroys crops and livestock. Events of that fateful season make a permanent impression on nine-year-old Michael McDonagh, as he watches the carcasses of sheep hauled away. His father, John, home from America, has to work off a debt caused when Michael's dog kills a neighbor's sheep. Michael is stricken to hear his parents constantly quarrel and one day finds his father weeping over the grave of the recently deceased Mag Delacey.

John McDonagh comes and goes three times over the next five years, departures that are more acts of abandonment than the results of financial necessity. Each time Michael mourns the absence and yearns for his next meeting. The novel then charts the doomed fortunes of the ruptured McDonagh family, as mother Moira slips further into illness and emotional isolation. Young Michael's closest attachments are to his Uncle Oweny, who dies suddenly in his car, Lugh McConnahue, a simple farm laborer who nurtures the boy and offers paternal wisdom and acceptance, and Cait Delacey, a classmate with whom Michael has a budding, innocent relationship.

As the novel moves chronologically from one episode to another, Michael is repeatedly confronted with death and sinister rumors. He watches his father grieve when the man's brother dies, he finds Lugh's battered body in a river, his mother contracts what is certainly terminal cancer, and he learns that Cait's mother was likely murdered by her father. The young boy is confused initially by the insults and stray remarks of fellow villagers until he eventually discovers that his father and Mag Delacey were once lovers, that John Delacey slowly poisoned his wife as a result of the betrayal, that Cait may very likely be his half-sister, and that his Uncle Brendan is either a sympathizer or member of the Irish Republican Army (IRA).

As the boy struggles with revelations and emotions that scald his heart, the reader encounters a bleak portrait of claustrophobia and hopelessness. O'Malley is clearly concerned with exploring the dynamics of small-town life, in this case the village world of rural County Wexford. O'Malley avoids the cliche of conflating rural life exclusively with Western Ireland, thus the inhabitants of New Rowan, less than one hundred miles from Dublin, are not hopelessly isolated yet live far apart from the modern world. With so little outside stimulation, they are left with rumors, gossip, and generations-old resentments. Thus, Moira McDonagh is as embarrassed by her husband's fecklessness as she is by her impoverished condition. More embarrassing still is the fact that the whole town knows her business, "Oh, and they'll have a grand old time of it when I sign up for the dole and the child allowance. Moira McDonagh this and Moira McDonagh that . . . and they call themselves Christians, all of them bloody hypocrites."

In this world of inbred hatreds and grievances, which explode into the open at consistently inopportune moments, one would expect people who are forthright and loquacious, yet Michael aches over the fact that truths are either overheard surreptitiously or intuited. No one, apart from Lugh, can articulate exactly what they feel or what is most important to them. Michael yearns for a confidant, yet each time he tries to share intimacies, he is stifled by "the timeless silence that bound us all." Similarly, when Michael and Cait wait out a storm in an abandoned cottage, the boy mixes comforting intimacy with painful distance, "Listening to the rain and to Cait's breathing, feeling her body wrapped within my own, I stared up through the slats and raindrops shimmering there at the edge of the roof and the gutter, at the edge of night, and felt all the things we could not say pressing down upon us." Perhaps the most devastating silence comes after the boy sees the bottle of poison that killed Cait's mother on display in the family kitchen and insists she destroy it; once accomplished, she is so angry she never speaks to him again. The people in New Rowan live among but rarely with one another, each isolated in his or her own thoughts and hurts.

Closely linked with the idea of provincial village life is O'Malley's portrait of Ireland at the end of the twentieth century, a place barely recognizable today given Ireland's position as an economic tiger in the European Union. Indeed, part of the novel's power is its ability to capture the last vestiges of Old Ireland as it is trans-

◇

Thomas O'Malley was born in Ireland. He lived there and in England in his youth and came to the United States at age sixteen. O'Malley received a B.A. from the University of Massachusetts and studied at the Iowa Writers' Workshop. He has been a Returning Writing Fellow and a recipient of the Grace Paley Endowed Fellowship at the Fine Arts Work Center in Provincetown, Massachusetts. He lives in Rhinebeck, New York, with the poet Caroline Crumpacker and their daughter. In the Province of Saints is his first novel.

◇

formed into a markedly different place in the twenty-first century. O'Malley deftly reveals the cultural beliefs and superstitions that have informed and animated Irish life for centuries.

For instance, Moira's problems are never explained in terms of modern psychology but instead through the lens of Irish mythology and folklore. Her sister Una confidently proclaims that Moira has broken a *geis*, "a magical prohibition placed upon you, and you should never never break it. Once broken it was like a weapon, a bag of arrows cast at you but that might do injury to another if evoked." When her sister's mood lifts, Una is just as quick to announce that the *geis* has been lifted and normalcy restored.

Stories of witches abound and quickly invade the perceptions of young Michael. At ten the boy believes he has seen the spirit of a widow long believed to have been a witch haunting the countryside. "It was said that she killed her husband and children. Her love had been so great, so possessive of them, it had poisoned and consumed them, and they died with the fever of it. Now she wandered the glen and could never know love again." Soon, he believes his own mother has become a witch, wandering the fields at night after her children have gone to bed. "My mother spoke with the dead. After the doctors declared her cancer free, she could feel and hear their ghosts, see them clear as day."

The traditional Irish belief in the "little people," or *sidhe*, also defines the tortured conditions of these people. The Irish, especially those living in rural areas, have long believed in a spirit world that exists coterminously with the physical one, thus legends are rife with stories of ordinary people who mix with the spirit world and are either empowered or undone by their exposure. Fears of abduction are particularly strong.

> In the country, ghosts, spirits, and faeries could take hold of one at any time. One always had to be aware walking the long unlit road from the town, or in the winter, after leading the cows to pasture after milking, of the Host who would at any moment take unwitting souls for their own. All they had to do was call to you, and if you listened—just once— you were gone.

Tied to ideas of Old Ireland are the powers of memory and history, concerns that have defined the Irish since their Celtic roots, when poets were keepers of the tribes' genealogies and exploits. Even the stunted people of New Rowan have a reverence for the past, as Michael notes when recounting the talk of bar flies who rehearse the indignities of Ireland's colonial occupation by the British. Young Cait has no tokens of her mother's life except the bottle of poison, which for the girl is a grim memorial but a personal remembrance nonetheless. The town's recollection of the McDonagh-Delacey infidelity is a memory that follows and defines young Michael as surely as anything else in his life. The rumor that Michael's family is connected to the IRA initially seems absurd but later proves prescient.

The omnipresence of death acts as a grim reminder of Ireland's tragic history, where countless leaders and common people passed violently or before their time. Not surprisingly, the Irish often exhibit a far greater reverence for the dead than the living, and nowhere is this more evident than with the periodic announcements of the deaths of Bobby Sands and the other hunger strikers in Long Kesh prison. The suggestion throughout is that Michael is being tutored in the ways of death rather than life.

In the Province of Saints is a classic coming-of-age story, in which Michael's physical maturation is symbolic of his emotional and psychological development. Protagonists in such stories typically endure some type of spiritual crisis, and Michael is no exception. Loss becomes the only constant in his otherwise turbulent and sorrowful existence. He loses Uncle Oweny and Lugh to death, Uncle Brendan to capture and incarceration, his mother to near-death and emotional dislocation, and his father to a pattern of abandonment. The most wrenching loss, however, may involve Cait, the girl he pines for, appears to have won, only to lose her when he thinks he is offering help and solicitude. As if her absence were not enough, he ultimately discovers she may be his sister, and thus everything he has felt and done with her becomes suddenly illicit.

Another pattern in the *Bildungsroman*, however, is the protagonist's acquisition of a philosophy of life, and for Michael that lesson comes from his greatest pain. At one point he mourns the loss that comes with love, feeling one is always betrayed for loving and "wishing you had never loved in the first place." Nevertheless, Michael does love, He loves those who are unloved, such as Lugh, those who would seem not to deserve love, his father, and those who are simply difficult to love, his mother. As he is leaving Ireland, in another snow storm as powerful as the one eight years earlier, he sees "All boundary and geography were gone"; he is, in effect, open to something vast and redefining. He develops beyond his own sorrows to become, as his mother tells him, "a fine man."

At this point the meaning of the novel's title becomes most evident. In his determination to understand and hold his family together, in his devotion to others, in his love for those who appear beyond or unworthy of his affection, Michael approaches a selfless condition akin to sainthood. To all appearances New Rowan is a God-abandoned place, but the divine surrounds him in unexpected places—huddled in his father's overcoat as they walk in the rain or in a day made magical by simply laboring beside Lugh and enjoying the weather. His mother gives him a hint about the nature of the divine when she explains why she shuns churches, "'I meet God in other places.'" Indeed, the same is ultimately true for Michael, who comes to understand that sainthood emerges from an openness to a flawed humanity and from a submission to something higher and more radiant than oneself.

In one of the novel's most beautiful passages, Michael has his own mystical vision when he sees the play of light on a dark street, "a warm circle in the center of the road leading people home to their beds, like what the soul must look like when one gives it up to God." O'Malley has written a painful yet lyrical and open-hearted novel that asserts the power of people to transcend their own limitations. *In the Province of Saints* is a masterful accomplishment by any standard but especially considering it is a debut effort. It is unfair to compare young Irish writers to James Joyce, and while O'Malley is no Joyce, he is another in a cavalcade of exemplary literary talents that seem to flow ceaselessly from a tiny island.

David W. Madden

Review Sources

America 193, no. 19 (December 12, 2005): 25-26.
Booklist 101 (July, 2005): 1900.
The Hartford Courant, September 11, 2005, p. G2.
Library Journal 130, no. 12 (July 1, 2005): 70.
The New York Times Book Review, September 4, 2005, p. 16.
Publishers Weekly 252, no. 28 (July 18, 2005): 186.
The Washington Post, August 21, 2005, p. T07.

ISTANBUL
Memories and the City

Author: Orhan Pamuk (1952-   )
First published: Istanbul Hatiralar ve şehir, 2003, in Turkey
Translated from the Turkish by Maureen Freely
Publisher: Alfred A. Knopf (New York). 385 pp.
   $27.00
Type of work: History, literary history, and memoir
Time: The second half of the twentieth century
Locale: Istanbul, Turkey

Turkey's most famous modern writer mingles recollections of his childhood and youth with reflections on the past and present of his beloved Istanbul

> *Principal personages:*
> ORHAN PAMUK, a Turkish author and a lifelong resident of
>   Istanbul
> GÜNDÜZ PAMUK, his father, to whom *Istanbul* is dedicated
> MRS. PAMUK, his mother, a beautiful woman
> ŞEVKET PAMUK, his older brother
> ANTOINE-IGNACE MELLING, a German painter
> REŞAT EKREM KOÇU, a Turkish researcher and writer, author of the
>   Istanbul encyclopedia

Although Orhan Pamuk began publishing novels in his native Turkey when he was twenty-six, the first three of them have not yet been translated into English. His fourth, which appeared in England in 1990 under the title *The White Castle*, established his reputation among Western readers as a brilliant postmodern novelist who juggles time and place, perspectives, identities, and narrative techniques so deftly that his readers are left breathless but oddly satisfied.

Istanbul: Memories and the City is classified as a memoir, but it is as complex as any of Pamuk's novels. In a sense, it is many books in one. Some of the sections are intimate recollections reminiscent of Marcel Proust, while others are reflections inspired by Pamuk's observations, much like some of the walking poems of eighteenth century England. There are also character sketches, some of them about family members such as his grandmother, others describing the lives of writers and painters whom Pamuk never met. At times *Istanbul* resembles a travel book, at other times, a history of the Ottoman Empire and the days that followed it, and at still other times, a collection of essays in art or literary criticism. These various strands have been woven into a single unified narrative, which is enhanced by more than two hundred photographs and illustrations which range as widely in subject matter as does the text. The result is a truly marvelous book, which is at once a portrait of the author, of his city, and of his society, present and past.

Among the many awards that Orhan Pamuk has won are the Independent *award for foreign fiction (1990), the International IMPAC Dublin Literary Award for* My Name Is Red *(2003), and the German Publishers and Booksellers Association's Peace Prize, presented at the Frankfort Book Fair in 2005. In 2005, Pamuk was inducted into the American Academy of Arts and Letters as an honorary member.*

Other authors might have divided such a book into sections, devoting one segment to personal history, another to geographical and historical observations, and a third to portrayals of the city by various writers and painters. Pamuk chose a far more original approach. The thirty-seven chapters into which his book is divided are not grouped according to subject matter. Instead, he moves back and forth between his memories, his observations, his reading, and his speculations. Thus after beginning with three chapters about himself and the rooms in which he grew up, Pamuk moves to descriptions of the streets, reflections on the dominant colors of Istanbul, comments on the unique atmosphere in the areas adjacent to the Bosphorus, and an account of the life and works of Antoine-Ignace Melling, who published a book of Bosphorus landscapes almost a hundred and fifty years before Pamuk was born.

In chapters scattered throughout the book, Pamuk refers to the impression his city made on a number of other Western visitors. A half century after Melling painted Istanbul, the French poet Gérard de Nerval described his walk through a section of the city that Pamuk well knows, though as he points out, it is now greatly changed. In Istanbul, the author notes, Nerval did not sense the gloom that Pamuk believes came to characterize the city after the fall of the Ottoman Empire. In fact, in the Istanbul of 1843 Nerval had a brief respite from the depression that would drive him to madness and finally to suicide.

When the French writer Gustave Flaubert made his visit to Istanbul seven years later, he was less captivated with the city than Nerval had been, but then, as Pamuk notes, Flaubert was not at his best, having picked up syphilis in Beirut; moreover, he had spent all of his enthusiasm on Egypt and was already planning the books he would write as soon as he returned home. Two years after Flaubert left, Théophile Gautier, another French writer and a friend of Nerval, spent seventy days in Istanbul. In his newspaper columns and and in his book *Constantinople* (1853), Gautier captured what he saw as only an artist-turned-art critic could do. Pamuk credits Gautier with recognizing the essence of the city: its melancholic beauty.

As Pamuk admits, it is perhaps odd that the most thoughtful of his fellow Turks are so interested in what the West thinks about them. In fact, Pamuk devotes an entire chapter, "Under Western Eyes," to this very issue. On one hand, he explains, what Western observers say matters a great deal to a people whose goal is to become more Westernized; on the other hand, the increase in nationalism has made Turks understandably sensitive to criticism they feel is unfair, particularly when it is based on Western visitors' exotic expectations and on their consistent misinterpretations of what they see. Ironically, Pamuk adds, the very features that most delighted outsiders have now vanished, victims of the Westernizing process. Gone are the Janissaries, the dervishes, the harems, the colorful Ottoman garb, and even Arabic calligraphy; only the dog packs that every visitor has noted still remain.

Some of the most interesting segments of *Istanbul*, however, are those that Pamuk provides as a counterbalance to the accounts of Western writers. In the chapter "Four Lonely Melancholic Writers," he notes the fact that all four of the writers he mentions lived near his home, and in his early years he may well have passed them in the street. While all of them were influenced by Western writers, especially by the French, each believed, according to Pamuk, that he would find his authentic voice in his relationship to his own city and his own traditions. That idea is illustrated in a chapter devoted to one of the four writers, Reş at Ekrem Koçu, whose monumental work, the *Istanbul ansiklopedisi* (1958-1971; Istanbul encyclopedia), began appearing in 1958 but was never completed. According to Pamuk, this compendium of odd stories and little-known historical facts not only reflects the writer's melancholy personality but also reinforces the notion that is the basis of Pamuk's memoir: that Istanbul is a city pervaded by the memories of past glories, a city that, as Gautier said, is as melancholy as it is beautiful.

During his childhood, Pamuk became aware of the fact that his family, too, was not as glorious as it once had been. His grandfather made a large fortune but died young, leaving his factory to his two sons, the author's uncle and the author's father, Gündüz Pamuk. Though the head of the family was now the author's grandmother, she could not steer her sons away from unwise projects or foolish investments, which kept eating away at the family assets.

Pamuk makes it clear that he dearly loved both his handsome father and his beautiful mother. Although the two often quarreled, they did not draw the children into their disputes. However, periodically either Orhan's mother or his father would disappear for weeks at a time, leaving Orhan and his older brother, Şevket, with other family members. Orhan was just as happy when he was separated from Şevket, for as he explains, the two competed for their mother's love, and often the rivalry led to fights that the younger boy could not win. Certainly his brother's jealousy and his parents' quarrels could have made Pamuk's childhood an unhappy one. However, the author makes it clear that it was not. The two boys did have good times together, and all in all, they probably got along as well as any brothers that close in age. The quarrels between their parents and the absences that often followed merely meant that another member of the extended family, all of whom lived in the Pamuk apartments, would take in one of the boys and probably spoil him a little.

The fact that Pamuk's childhood was punctuated with exciting events is reflected in the chapter "On the Ships That Passed Through the Bosphorus, Famous Fires, Moving House, and Other Disasters." Their home in the Pamuk apartments was a wonderful vantage point from which the boys could observe dramatic events such as collisions between ships and the subsequent explosions. Another amusement was watching the mansions where the pashas once lived burn brightly and then tumble into ruin—set afire, it is thought, for the insurance money.

Upon reflection, of course, the burned-out mansions are another reminder of a vanished past. What the future will bring to the city Pamuk loves so much is an open question, which the author discusses in the nineteenth chapter, titled "Conquest or Decline? The Turkification of Constantinople." Though in 1955 Pamuk was too young to be aware of what was happening, members of his family told him about the state-sponsored riots that year, when in the name of nationalism mobs attacked every non-Muslim they could find, destroying the shops and the homes of Greeks, Armenians, Jews, and Christians. They even turned on wealthy Turkish Muslims such as the Pamuks, but fortunately Orhan's family had secured for themselves a number of small Turkish flags, and as a result of displaying them they were spared. Pamuk mentions the fact that it became customary to reprimand anyone who spoke French, Greek, or Armenian in public. As a result of this nationalistic frenzy, a large segment of the middle-class trading community moved elsewhere. Moreover, a city whose cosmopolitan atmosphere had attracted visitors over the centuries dwindled into provincialism.

The loss of cosmopolitanism has made the once-glorious Istanbul, which attracted so many foreign visitors, merely an optional stop on a standard tour of the Middle East. Pamuk himself would become a victim of this destructive nationalism. After he referred in an interview to the well-established fact that early in the twentieth century, the Turks undertook a campaign of cultural cleansing, killing some thirty thousand Kurds and a million Armenians, Pamuk was branded a traitor by the local press. He was charged in 2005 with an offense against the Turkish identity. Amid protests from the world community, the charges were soon dropped.

If reason were allowed into such a courtroom, *Istanbul* would be the only defense that Pamuk would need. His love of his country and, even more markedly, of the city where he has chosen to spend his entire life is reflected on every page of his memoir. The melancholy that so many writers, including Pamuk, see as characterizing present-day Istanbul is based on their recognition that much has been lost. However, as the epigraph to *Istanbul* suggests, these remnants of the past, these reminders of loss, make the city even more beautiful. If Istanbul is not as wealthy or as glamorous as it once was, Pamuk believes, there is no reason that it cannot once again become one of the most interesting cities in the world. That objective cannot be achieved by replacing charming old houses beside the Bosphorus with huge, ugly apartment blocks nor by replacing a cosmopolitan culture with narrow nationalism. However, Pamuk insists in this fascinating book, there is a way for Istanbul to build on the memory of its glorious past a new and unique identity within the global community. One hopes that future will include appropriate recognition for Turkey's great writer and for one of the country's greatest patriots.

Rosemary M. Canfield Reisman

Review Sources

Booklist 101, no. 18 (May 15, 2005): 1633.
Contemporary Review 287 (August, 2005): 126.
Kirkus Reviews 73, no. 7 (April 1, 2005): 405.
Library Journal 130, no. 9 (May 15, 2005): 137.
New Statesman 134 (April 11, 2005): 52-53.
The New York Times Book Review 154 (June 12, 2005): 10.
Publishers Weekly 252, no. 16 (April 18, 2005): 54.
The Spectator 298 (May 14, 2005): 68.
The Times Literary Supplement, May 13, 2005, p. 36.

IVAN THE TERRIBLE
First Tsar of Russia

Author: Isabel de Madariaga (1919-   )
Publisher: Yale University Press (New Haven, Conn.).
   Illustrated. 484 pp. $35.00
Type of work: Biography
Time: 1530-1584
Locale: Russia

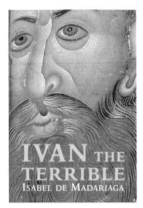

The life, accomplishments, and brutalities of Russia's first czar are skillfully reconstructed from published sources and historical works

Principal personages:
   IVAN THE TERRIBLE, born VASILY
      VASILEVICH, the ruler of Russia from
      1547 until 1584 as Ivan IV
   ALEKSEI FEDEROVICH ADASHEV, a close adviser to Ivan
   PRINCE ANDREI MIKHAILOVICH KURBSKY, an influential friend of Ivan
      who defected in 1564
   SIGISMUND II AUGUSTUS, the king of Poland-Lithuania
   STEPHEN BATHORY, the prince of Transylvania, later the king of Poland-
      Lithuania
   SYLVESTER, the archpriest in the Annunciation Cathedral
   VLADIMIR ANDREEVICH, the prince of Staritsa

According to the publisher, Isabel de Madariaga's biography of Ivan the Terrible is the first to cover the events of the czar's life from his birth to his death, to describe his policies, his marriages, and the atrocities he committed. Most readers associate Ivan's name with his cruelty; he is noted for his reign of terror and for killing his own son. Fewer readers are acquainted with the specifics of his reign. In 1626, fire destroyed much of Ivan's archive, but he also remains an obscure figure to Western readers because of his remoteness from Western Europe.

De Madariaga, a professor of Russian studies, examines in her first chapter medieval Russia, split by the Mongol conquest of 1238-1242, before taking the reader to the sixteenth century and the reign of Vasily III, Ivan's father. Such historical background goes a long way to tie together details vaguely recalled from history courses and whets the appetite of the reader.

In her third chapter, de Madariaga presents the circumstances immediately preceding Ivan's rule. Before Vasily III died in February, 1533, he provided for a Regency Council to eliminate rivals of his son, the three-year-old Grand Prince Ivan. On the council were Ivan's mother, the Grand Princess Elena Glinskaia, and Elena's uncle Mikhail Lvovich Glinsky. The death of Elena enabled one Prince Vasily Vasilevich

Shuisky to dominate the council, and his mis-
treatment of young Ivan ended only with the
Shuisky brothers' deaths.

At Ivan's coronation in the Church of the
Metropolitan in January, 1547, he took the titles
not only of Grand Duke of Vladimir, Novgorod,
and Moscow but also of czar, meaning either a
king or an emperor. As de Madariaga relates,
while the customary understanding of the czar's
functions was covered by legal ordinance, "in
Russia they were accepted as the manifestation

*Isabel de Madariaga is emeritus
professor of Russian studies at the
University of London and a fellow
of the British Academy. She is the
author of* Russia in the Age of
Catherine the Great *(1981) and*
Catherine the Great: A Short
History *(1990).*

of a specific charisma, the charisma of power." Even before his coronation, Ivan demonstrated his charisma by arranging for a bride show, and in February, 1547, he married Anastasia Romanovna Iurieva Zakharina and moved into the Kremlin residence
with her.

Ivan's tendency to cruelty is thought to have been controlled somewhat in his early
years through the influence of his personal servant Aleksei Adashev and the priest
Sylvester. Adashev, especially, mediated the struggle for land between the aristocratic boyars and their descendents, the service gentry. In the Assembly of 1549, a
large public gathering, Ivan admonished the boyars about oppressing the service gentry and the peasants, and he removed the service gentry from the jurisdiction of provincial governors, making them subject to officials in the capital.

A year later Ivan revised the law code of Ivan III, trying to abolish the rampant
maladministration and corruption. The new code dealt with brigandage and peasants'
rights but also instituted harsher punishments for crimes against the Crown. One important new article established the provisions for the repurchase of free land. "For the
first time in Russia," says de Madariaga, "law (*pravo*) in the sense of the norms to be
followed in obtaining and dispensing justice was declared to proceed solely from law
in the sense of legislation."

In 1550 Ivan began reshaping the military and expanding his frontiers. One thou-
sand cavalrymen from his three thousand private followers were given estates on
which to live, generally near Moscow, where they could be mustered on short notice.
He also formed a corps of infantry armed with muskets who, with the cavalrymen,
became his personal guard. The young czar found his territories landlocked by the
Polish-Lithuanian Commonwealth on the southwest, while to the north the Livonian
Knights virtually blocked him from the Baltic Sea. The khanate of Crimea cramped
Russia in the south, and along the Volga River to the east lay the khanates of Kazan
and Astrakhan and the Tatars of Kabarda, all remnants of the Mongol Golden Horde
that broke up in 1502. When the khan of Kazan died in 1549, Ivan saw his chance to
avenge the Russian people on their longtime oppressors, and in August, 1552, a
seven-week siege of Kazan began that ended with a brutal Russian victory. Conquest
of Astrakhan soon followed.

In March, 1553, Ivan fell gravely—and suspiciously—ill, precipitating a crisis
over his anticipated succession. The czarina's family, the Iurev Zakharins, wanted

Ivan's six-month-old son, Dmitri, to inherit the rule, but a group of powerful boyars pushed Ivan's first cousin, Vladimir of Staritsa, as a candidate. The crisis passed when the czar recovered, but Dmitri's accidental drowning soon afterward raised fears that were calmed only upon the birth of another son, Ivan Ivanovich, in March, 1554.

In the summer of 1553, an English sea captain, Richard Chancellor, landed unexpectedly on the shores of the White Sea, enabling a degree of Anglo-Russian trade. Four years later, when Livonia signed a treaty with Poland-Lithuania to defend against Russia, Ivan sent a large Tatar force into Livonia under the command of the former khan of Kazan, whose conquest of the Baltic city of Narva gave Ivan his much-desired opening to the West. Events turned against the czar in 1559, as the czarina became fatally ill and Russia suffered a crushing loss in a battle at Dorpat in Livonia. Moreover, Adashev and Sylvester's opposition to the war may have created a rift between them and Ivan and produced a turnover in the men closest to the czar, but the whole story of their relationship is clouded by unreliable sources.

The czarina's death in 1560 worked a terrible effect on Ivan. Says de Madariaga, "He had always been cruel and sadistic, but the loss of control, the extent and precipitate nature of the operations he began now to embark upon were new, and the degree of sadism unprecedented." The letters of Ivan's intimate friend, Prince Andrei Mikhailovich Kurbsky, reproved the czar for his dissipation, fornication, and sodomy, and when Prince Dmitri Obolensky Ovchinin complained about Fedor Basmanov, "the Tsar's new catamite," Ivan poured boiling water on Obolensky Ovchinin and stabbed him. In 1561, Ivan took as his second wife Princess Maria Kucheny, daughter of the khan of Kabarda, but his brutality continued unabated.

Ivan's closeness to Prince Kurbsky faded when Ivan banished the prince to Dorpat as commander. When Kurbsky became more alarmed by Ivan's heartless persecution of the boyars, he fled to Livonia in April, 1564. His departure was followed by further, lesser desertions, fueling Ivan's paranoia and leading to his demand that his courtiers put up financial sureties to guarantee the loyalty of individuals.

In December, 1564, Ivan stripped the monasteries and churches of their valuables and packed them off with him and the new czarina to Aleksandrovskaia Sloboda, his hunting lodge northeast of Moscow. He accompanied this move with the bewildering proclamation that because the people were hostile to him, he was transferring rule to them. A year later he declared his willingness to return but only if he were given absolute power to punish the boyars and any other traitors as he pleased. The people of Moscow, completely dependent on the czar for their civil and religious protection, joined a large deputation imploring Ivan to return. Acceding to their request, he astonished everyone with the news that he was establishing for himself a large *oprichnina*, or body of land, leaving the remaining territory, the *zemshchina*, to the rule of the boyars. In shaping the boundaries of his *oprichnina*, Ivan chose the most prosperous areas; and in assembling a group of *oprichniki*, or dedicated followers, he temporarily favored men from the lower classes over the boyars. The expansion of the *oprichnina* led to evictions and "a veritable orgy of arrests and killings, in which it is difficult to detect a specific policy."

The czar's campaign in Livonia dragged on in 1565 and 1566, with both Denmark and Sweden, as well as Poland-Lithuania, making claims on Livonia. Further problems came from the boyars, who presented Ivan with a "collective remonstrance" against the many executions conducted under the *oprichnina*. A large Lithuanian embassy arrived in Moscow in May, 1566, prompting Ivan to hold an "Assembly of the Land," or *Zemskii sobor*, as such gatherings were to be called in the nineteenth century.

During this meeting, three hundred boyars joined with the service gentry to plead for abolition of the *oprichnina*, a move that set Ivan off on "one of the most awful periods of terror the Tsar launched against his people." A murky period—1567-1572— followed, with what may have been an effort by Poland's King Sigismund to stir up trouble for Ivan by urging a group of boyars under Ivan Petrovich Federov to replace Ivan by his cousin Vladimir of Staritsa. The czar's retribution was swift: He killed Federov and massacred several hundred of his family and followers before executing the Metropolitan Filipp and Vladimir.

In a chapter titled "Armageddon," de Madariaga recounts Ivan's senseless torture and butchery: "Throughout 1567, 1568 and 1569 executions followed each other in Moscow, or wherever the Tsar was. There was no formal procedure. The Tsar simply gave orders wherever he was, on horseback, in church or in his chamber." Thousands died at the hands of the *oprichniki* in towns such as Novgorod and Pskov. The climax to these horrors came on July 25, 1570, when "116 victims were [publicly] dispatched in various ingenious ways."

The years 1571-1572 were difficult for Ivan. His foreign policy undertakings with Poland-Lithuania, Sweden, and England proved frustrating, and many of his soldiers deserted to join the Crimean army. The Tatar leader Devlet Girey surprised the czar by marching right to Moscow and burning it flat, with a great loss of lives, livestock, and food. The *oprichnina* leaders became the scapegoats for this catastrophe, as up to one hundred of them were poisoned. By late 1572, Ivan had recovered enough to mount raids against Sweden, but he remained worried about another attack by the Crimeans.

After the death of his second wife in 1569, he married Marfa Sobakina who died of poisoning in November, 1571, just days after the wedding. The Church allowed him to marry a fourth time in May, 1572, but five months later he dispatched his new wife, Anna Koltovskaia, to a convent and in "some kind of wedding ceremony" married Anna Vasilchikova in January, 1575. He was eventually to have two more wives.

The failure of the *oprichnina* as a military force led to its dissolution in 1572. When King Sigismund II Augustus of Poland-Lithuania died in the same year, Ivan mustered an effort to be elected in his place but with no success. Good news came with the seizure of a Swedish-held fort in Livonia, but the victory cost Ivan one of his most reliable henchmen, the ruthless Maliuta Skuratov Belsky. The death by torture of three prominent boyars in spring, 1573, is attributed by Kurbsky to the malign influence of the mysterious astrologer Dr. Eliseus Bomelius, whose presence at Ivan's court failed to save him from the usual horrible death.

Ivan startled his people in 1575 by appointing the khan of Kasimov, Simeon Bekbulatovich, grand prince of Russia while he remained prince of Moscow. A year later, Ivan rescinded this puzzling move and occupied himself with plans for renewed war with Livonia and the problem of finding a new king for Poland-Lithuania after Henri of Anjou's abrupt departure. His influence, however, proved minimal as the Poles chose the "typical Renaissance figure" Stephen Bathory, prince of Transylvania. The czar's campaign against Livonia in 1576 achieved only partial success, and his frustration prompted a brutal looting of the Livonian quarter of Moscow in winter, 1578.

Shocking battlefield losses to Stephen Bathory in 1579 depressed the ambitious czar, and his attempts to bring in Pope Gregory XIII to mediate with Bathory eventually collapsed because Bathory knew that Ivan would never accommodate the pope in a campaign against the Ottomans. The aggressive Bathory's capture of Pskov was matched by Sweden's brutal conquests of Narva and three other towns in September-October, 1581. These seemingly endless conflicts were finally settled on January 15, 1582, with a ten-year truce negotiated by the pope's ambassador to Russia, Antonio Possevino. Ivan ceded that of Livonia which he held, and Bathory returned the Russian forts occupied by the Commonwealth.

The czar's mood at the time may be gauged by his sudden outburst of anger against his son, Ivan Ivanovich, hitting the heir in the head with a staff and killing him. This sad event broke the czar's spirit, and he soon became ill. He died on March 18, 1584. Various accounts of his death have been given, but de Madariaga believes "the balance of the evidence is that the Tsar died of choking, or of a sudden heart attack after some months of illness." The final chapter of the book explores "Ivan's legacy to Russia."

Frank Day

Review Sources

Booklist 101, no. 17 (May 1, 2005): 1562.
Foreign Affairs 84, no. 3 (May/June, 2005): 145.
Library Journal 130, no. 10 (June 1, 2005): 141.
London Review of Books 27, no. 23 (December 1, 2005): 17-18.
The New York Review of Books 52, no. 14 (September 22, 2005): 34-36.
Publishers Weekly 252, no. 15 (April 11, 2005): 40.
The Times Literary Supplement, May 6, 2005, pp. 6-7.

JOHN KENNETH GALBRAITH
His Life, His Politics, His Economics

Author: Richard Parker (1946-   )
Publisher: Farrar, Straus and Giroux (New York).
820 pp. $35.00
Type of work: Biography, economics, and history
Time: 1908-2003
Locale: The United States, India, and Europe

This biography of economist Galbraith describes his ideas and his history of political involvement as well as the events in his life

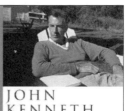

JOHN KENNETH GALBRAITH
HIS LIFE,
HIS POLITICS,
HIS ECONOMICS
RICHARD PARKER

Principal personages:
JOHN KENNETH GALBRAITH (b. 1908), an American economist, author, political commentator, and diplomat
CATHERINE (KITTY) ATWATER GALBRAITH (b. 1913), his wife
JOHN MAYNARD KEYNES (1883-1946), an influential British economist
JOHN D. BLACK (1883-1960), a Harvard agricultural economist and early mentor of Galbraith
ADLAI E. STEVENSON (1900-1965), an unsuccessful Democratic candidate for president of the United States in 1952 and 1956, supported by Galbraith
JOHN F. KENNEDY (1917-1963), the president of the United States, who appointed Galbraith U.S. ambassador to India
JACQUELINE B. KENNEDY (later ONASSIS; 1929-1994), the First Lady of the United States and a friend of Galbraith
LYNDON B. JOHNSON (1908-1973), the president of the United States, whose domestic policies Galbraith supported

John Kenneth Galbraith is a monumental figure. Nearly seven feet tall, he served in major offices in the administrations of Presidents Franklin D. Roosevelt and John F. Kennedy. He was a tireless campaigner for Democratic presidential candidates and an outspoken critic of the Vietnam War. Born in 1908, Galbraith received international attention for his editorials and comments on the economic difficulties of the United States in late 2001. During his long life, the Harvard University professor produced a long series of influential books, including such widely known, best-selling works as *American Capitalism* (1952), *The Affluent Society* (1958), and *The New Industrial State* (1967). A worthy biography of Galbraith must also contain a political history of the United States from the Depression to the twenty-first century and a summary of modern economic theory and practice. With *John Kenneth Galbraith: His Life, His Politics, His Economics*, Richard Parker has produced a worthy biography.

The political economist and representative of the U.S. East Coast intellectual elite did not receive his education in political economy and grew up far from the East Coast

∼

*Richard Parker teaches at Harvard's
Kennedy School of Government,
where he is a lecturer in Public
Policy and a senior fellow at the
Shorenstein Institute. Trained as an
economist, Parker cofounded* Mother
Jones *magazine. His previous books
include* The Myth of the Middle
Class *(1972) and* Mixed Signals:
The Future of Global Television
News *(1995).*

∼

and centers of intellectual life. Galbraith, in fact, was not even born in the United States, but in Canada, on a farm in Ontario. There, as Parker points out, the future Harvard professor did have early exposure to his lifelong liberalism. Galbraith's father was active in Canada's Liberal Party, breaking with it over the party's support for the military draft of Canadians into the trenches of World War I.

The later world-renowned academic began his own academic career studying animal husbandry at the Ontario Agricultural College. A fellowship enabled him to take up graduate study in agricultural economics at the University of California at Berkeley. While his doctorate was in agricultural economics, Galbraith took advantage of his time at Berkeley to study economics more broadly. One of his early influences there came from the writings of Thorstein Veblen, some of whose thoughts would later resonate in *The Affluent Society*.

In the fall of 1934, the semester after receiving his Ph.D., Galbraith managed to get a one-year job as a junior researcher in agricultural economics at Harvard. This tenuous foothold at America's oldest and most prestigious university put Galbraith in contact with Professor John D. Black, an agricultural economist who arranged for Galbraith to stay on at Harvard after the single year. For the rest of his career, as Parker shows, Galbraith's ascent owed as much to his gift for making influential friends who recognized his abilities as to the abilities themselves.

While at Harvard, Galbraith began writing on the agricultural economics of Roosevelt's New Deal, and the young scholar took a summer job with the New Deal's Agricultural Adjustment Administration. At this time, also, Galbraith became familiar with the work of John Maynard Keynes, whose *General Theory of Employment, Interest, and Money* (1936) revolutionized economic thinking and became the most important influence on Galbraith's own views of economics.

A fellowship to study for a year in Cambridge confirmed Galbraith's commitment to Keynesian economics, although Keynes himself was unavailable due to illness. For the rest of his life, Parker maintains, Galbraith would take Keynes as a model. In addition to following the British economist's economic ideas, Galbraith pursued the older man's commitment to public service and political engagement. Even in writing for a wide, nonacademic readership, Galbraith echoed Keynes.

In his discussion of Keynes and the role of Keynes in Galbraith's work, Parker displays an impressive ability to explain complex economic theories for general readers, without oversimplification. Parts of the biography offer a good introduction to economic ideas, although it is an introduction that is clearly on Galbraith's side in all controversies. Whether describing the Keynesian analysis of advanced market societies or contrasting Keynesian accounts with classical microeconomics or the later monetarist, New Classical, and rational expectations schools of economics, Parker leaves no doubt that he thinks of the Keynesian approach as the best foundation for economic theory and policy, and Galbraith's interpretation of Keynes as the right one.

Refused consideration for renewal at Harvard, Galbraith taught briefly at Princeton University before his interest in public life, and the need for a job, drew him back to government work. With the entry of the United States into World War II, the young man took charge of managing the nation's price controls at the Office of Price Administration (OPA). This put him in one of the most controversial positions in the wartime Roosevelt administration. As the individual most visibly in charge of setting wage and price limits, Galbraith became a target for conservative critics of government control over the economy. By 1943, he was forced out of the OPA and found himself once again out of work.

Galbraith's knack for catching the attention of powerful people rescued him from unemployment after losing his job at the OPA and broadened his career experience. The famous publisher Henry R. Luce hired Galbraith to write for *Fortune* magazine for the rest of the war. At *Fortune*, the economist helped to make Keynesian ideas familiar and acceptable to segments of the American business elite, helping to prepare the nation for the predominance of those ideas after the middle of the twentieth century.

Following the war in Europe, Galbraith went back to public service, as part of a team surveying the effectiveness of strategic bombing in Germany. Galbraith and his team concluded that aerial bombing had not had much of an impact on Germany. Later, after the end of the war with Japan, the survey team concluded that naval warfare in the Pacific region had been more important to the U.S. victory than the bombing of Japan, and that Japan probably would have surrendered even without the dropping of atomic bombs. With the surveys, Galbraith stirred up controversy once again. The exposure to American military effort also led him to think about the possibility that American economic expansion would be driven by "military Keynesianism," by government spending on arms and defense, rather than by government investment in the domestic economy. As World War II turned into the Cold War, Galbraith became a critic of heavy reliance on military spending and an advocate of direct spending on public welfare.

After the war, Galbraith returned to Harvard. His old mentor John D. Black arranged for him to be hired as a lecturer, a position that would later turn into a tenured job. Once again, Galbraith was at the center of controversy, as enemies he had made during his OPA and bombing survey days attempted to block the appointment. However, he remained and would continue to be a Harvard professor, although often not in residence, until his retirement.

The question of public spending became one of the key issues in Galbraith's best-known book, *The Affluent Society*. In this, he argued that in the highly productive American economy, the key problem was no longer how to produce enough goods but how to create enough demand for all the goods produced. This led to a heavy emphasis on corporate spending on advertising and to an unbalanced tendency toward expenditures on private consumer goods. Public goods, such as clean air and recreational facilities, were continually overlooked as ever-increasing effort went into cranking out more needless luxuries and creating the desire for those luxuries.

Galbraith's liberalism led him to support Democratic candidate Adlai E. Stevenson in two unsuccessful runs for president. Through his involvement with the Stevenson campaign, Galbraith became a high-level political adviser. This led to his close connection with another, more successful Democratic candidate, John F. Kennedy, who was elected president in 1960. His closeness to Kennedy and Kennedy's wife, Jackie, resulted in Galbraith's appointment as U.S. ambassador to India, where Galbraith played an important part during the brief war that broke out between India and China. During the early 1960's, also, Galbraith began warning Kennedy against involving U.S. troops in Vietnam.

The Vietnam War pushed Galbraith's relations with Kennedy's successor, President Lyndon B. Johnson, to the breaking point. Galbraith had approved of Johnson's Great Society program of domestic spending, which seemed to be moving the nation away from its pursuit of military Keynesianism. However, as Johnson stepped up American involvement in Vietnam, Galbraith became one of the war's most visible and outspoken critics.

During the years that followed the 1960's, Galbraith became an outsider. Especially as the United States turned toward conservative political and economic policies after the election of President Ronald Reagan, Galbraith seemed to be out of touch with the times. However, Parker argues that Galbraith continued to be an insightful critic of the trends of the last part of the twentieth century. The deregulation of banking and other industries, the Reagan era tax cuts, and the cutbacks in domestic spending benefited the wealthiest Americans at the expense of all others, Galbraith maintained, and helped make the United States a nation in which wealth was increasingly concentrated. At the very end of the twentieth century, Galbraith criticized the New Economy, based heavily on private speculation in high technology. After the market downturn of 2001, Galbraith, now over ninety years old, began appearing prominently on editorial pages once again.

It is often said that biographers tend either to love or hate their subjects. Parker's admiration for his subject shows throughout the book, and the book is a testimonial to a man Parker clearly regards as an important public intellectual. The author agrees with Galbraith on nearly every point of politics and economics. Occasionally, readers may wonder whether any human being, however wise, could be so consistently right about almost everything during the course of more than sixty years of thinking and public action.

It is difficult to probe the personal life of a still-living subject. Accordingly, Parker touches only occasionally on Galbraith's relations with his family members, his friends, and other aspects of his personal life. This gives readers a good picture of the thinker and political actor, but the man behind the picture remains a distant and somewhat idealized figure.

While this is clearly a book that takes sides on economics and politics, it is a comprehensive and authoritative account of the life of one who seemed to be almost everywhere and doing almost everything for seven decades. Those who are already familiar with Galbraith's writings will gain insight into the life behind them. Those who have not yet read Galbraith's major works will be encouraged to do so by this fascinating biography.

Carl L. Bankston III

Review Sources

Booklist 101, no. 12 (February 15, 2005): 1040.
The Economist 375 (April 9 2005): 72-73.
Kirkus Reviews 72, no. 24 (December 15, 2004): 1190.
Library Journal 130, no. 7 (April 15, 2005): 100.
Maclean's 118, no. 5 (January 31, 2005): 42-44.
National Review 57, no. 4 (March 14, 2005):. 47-48.
The New York Review of Books 52, no. 9 (May 26, 2005): 15-18.
The Wilson Quarterly 29, no. 2 (Spring, 2005): 126-127.

JOSEPH SMITH
Rough Stone Rolling

Author: Richard Lyman Bushman (1931-   )
Publisher: Alfred A. Knopf (New York). 740 pp. $35.00
Type of work: Biography
Time: 1805-1844
Locale: New York, Ohio, Missouri, and Illinois

*This biography of the founder of the Church of Jesus
Christ of Latter-day Saints, by a distinguished professional
historian who is also a practicing member of that church,
is detailed and massively documented*

Principal personage:
JOSEPH SMITH (1805-1844), founder of the
Church of Jesus Christ of Latter-day
Saints

Born into a modest New England farming family in 1805, Joseph Smith lived barely thirty-eight and one-half years before his life was abruptly ended by an angry mob in Illinois. His was a brief life span, even by the standards of his time. Nevertheless, despite the brevity of his life, he must be regarded as one of the most significant Americans of the nineteenth century. His crowning achievement was the creation of the Church of Jesus Christ of Latter-day Saints—better known as the Mormon Church. His church, in turn, played major roles in promoting European immigration and in the settlement of the western United States, particularly what became the state of Utah.

Without Smith, there would have been no Mormon Church, and the map of the western United States might have developed quite differently. Smith's achievement went beyond merely creating an entirely new church. He gave the church a structure and institutions that ensured its survival and growth long after his death. By the turn of the twenty-first century, his church claimed more than twelve million members worldwide and claimed to be the fastest-growing religion in the United States. Although these specific claims have been challenged, it remains clear that the Mormon Church and its members represent a powerful force in modern American society and one that continues to grow stronger.

Richard Lyman Bushman's *Joseph Smith: Rough Stone Rolling* is a richly detailed, beautifully written, and impressively documented biography of Smith that probes almost every aspect of Smith's remarkably complex and almost always fascinating life. This book has been acclaimed as one of the finest studies of Smith yet written, and the word "definitive" has frequently been used to describe it. Such praise raises the question of what constitutes a definitive biography. Although Bushman himself makes no claim to have written one, his book helps demonstrate why a definitive biography of the founder of the Mormon Church may be impossible.

As the concept is generally understood, a definitive study is one that answers all important questions about its subject in ways that satisfy readers who consider its evidence and arguments carefully. Many people, however, would argue that the very notion of definitive biography is a chimera. The most common obstacle to achieving such a work is limited source material. For example, it is unlikely that enough evidence will ever be found to write a definitive account of the assassination of President John F. Kennedy.

In the case of Joseph Smith's biography, the problem is not so much a matter of source materials—although that is part of the problem—as one of opposing personal beliefs. Faithful Mormons believe that Smith was a true prophet of God, most of whose actions were divinely inspired. They believe that Smith saw God, Jesus Christ, and angels in the flesh; spoke with them;

A Harvard-trained historian, Richard Lyman Bushman is Gouverneur Morris Professor of History, emeritus, at Columbia University. His other works include From Puritan to Yankee: Character and Social Order in Connecticut, 1690-1765, *which won the Bancroft Prize in 1967;* Joseph Smith and the Beginnings of Mormonism *(1984);* King and People in Provincial Massachusetts *(1985);* The Refinement of America: Persons, Houses, Cities *(1992); and, with wife Claudia Lauper Bushman,* Building the Kingdom: A History of Mormons in America *(2d ed., 2002).*

and was instructed by God to reestablish the true Christian church on Earth. A central step in that process was the revelation to Smith of a set of ancient records that he translated with the benefit of divine guidance and published as the Book of Mormon. That book purports to be a history of the peopling of the New World by ancient Middle Eastern migrants known as the Jaredites and Nephites, who brought with them a religion based on the Christianity of the New Testament era.

Shortly after Smith published the Book of Mormon in early 1830, he and a handful of his followers founded the Church of Christ—which was later renamed the Church of Jesus Christ of Latter-day Saints—in New York State. A central feature of the Book of Mormon is its account of the appearance of Jesus Christ himself in the New World after his resurrection. Smith's church was thus not only an entirely original American sect but one that claimed a relationship between the Scriptures and America that no other Christian sect offered. Modern editions of the book emphasize the church's Christian roots by adding a subtitle: "Another Testament of Jesus Christ." In the Book of Mormon and other writings, Smith went even further, claiming that the Garden of Eden was located in Missouri and that the gathering of Zion would occur in North America. Mormonism may thus be the most American of religions.

These and other revelations, on which Smith built his church, represent rather large claims, and they naturally have an impact on the way that Smith's life is written. Indeed, the field of Smith biography is notoriously controversial, with no biography satisfying everyone. Leaving aside biographies that are clearly meant to discredit Smith and his church, there is a fundamental rift between Mormon believers and nonbelievers. Mormons are certain that Smith was a prophet and that the Book of Mormon is a divinely inspired and true history of the Americas. To them, anyone who challenges those assumptions is anti-Mormon.

A case in point is the distinguished biographer Fawn M. Brodie, whose *No Man Knows My History: The Life of Joseph Smith* (1944; rev. ed., 1971) was the first critical biography of Smith that attempted to interpret his life without reference to divine guidance. Brodie saw the Book of Mormon as a work of fiction and attempted to explain how Smith wrote it. Because Brodie was a former Mormon who had rejected the church's teachings, many Mormons dismissed her book as something in the nature of a personal vendetta and refused to consider the arguments that she advanced to make her case.

Richard Bushman appears to be an ideal person to write a biography of Smith. Like Brodie, he is a distinguished scholar. However, whereas Brodie began her career with her study of Smith, Bushman has already carved out an impressive career as a historian and has devoted several decades to studying Smith's life. *Joseph Smith: Rough Stone Rolling* is, in fact, an expansion of his 1984 book, *Joseph Smith and the Beginnings of Mormonism.* Moreover, Bushman is a self-professed practicing Mormon. In one person, therefore, he combines the sensitivity to his subject of a believing Mormon with the credentials of an established secular scholar. However, even that combination might not produce a satisfactory biography of Smith. The problem lies in the unusual nature of the subject, as Bushman himself recognizes in his preface:

> Yet, it is unlikely there will ever be consensus on Joseph Smith's character or his achievements. The multiplication of scholarly studies and the discovery of new sources have only heightened the controversies surrounding his life. The central difficulty is that Joseph Smith lives in the faith of the Mormons, like Abraham in Judaism or Muhammad in Islam. Everything about Smith matters to people who have built their lives on his teachings.

Bushman goes on to admit that a

> believing historian like myself cannot hope to rise above these battles or pretend nothing personal is a stake. For a character as controversial as Smith, pure objectivity is impossible. What I can do is to look frankly at all sides of Joseph Smith, facing up to his mistakes and flaws. Covering up errors makes no sense in any cases. Most readers do not believe in, nor are they interested in, perfection. Flawless characters are neither attractive nor useful. We want to meet a real person.

Bushman clearly believes that Smith was divinely inspired but does not push that view on his readers. Instead, when he discusses a revelation of Smith's, he takes it as a given either that Smith had such a revelation or at least believed that he had one. Mormon readers are likely to assume the former, while others are left wondering where Smith actually got his ideas. The Joseph Smith whom one meets in Bushman's book is, indeed, a real person with flaws, and this seems to be a primary reason Mormons like this book. Mormons consider Smith a prophet but do not officially regard him as a saint. By moving away from pious Sunday school depictions of Smith, Bushman satisfies the Mormon need for a real, flesh-and-blood man without challenging their faith in his role as a prophet.

In fact, Bushman depicts Smith as having so many flaws and making so many mistakes that one wonders why his followers took him seriously. Smith repeatedly showed poor judgment in important business decisions, he relied on followers who turned against him, and he constantly revised his failed schemes for building a new Zion in the Midwest. Although he possessed a great deal of warmth and could easily win over people, including enemies, with his charm, he was not a good public speaker and left important sermons and addresses to others. Bushman argues that one of Smith's greatest strengths was creating a successful organizational structure that involved most of his church's male members, so that the work of the church could be carried on in his absences—which were frequent and sometimes prolonged. Although Smith was always the central figure in his church, it carried on quite well without him. Indeed, Smith may have done the church a favor by dying when he did. His death provided a compelling martyr figure, while allowing Brigham Young, a vastly more effective leader, to take control of the church and lead it to a safe haven in the West.

Smith's many flaws extended deeply into his personal life. By surreptitiously entering into plural marriages—often with women who already had husbands—he threatened his marriage to Emma Hale Smith, who bore him eight children and to whom he was apparently devoted. It is significant that after Smith was killed in Illinois, and Brigham Young led the bulk of his followers west, into the Great Salt Lake Valley, Emma remained behind. It might thus be said that this man whom Mormons credit with raising family values to the highest plain was a failure in his own family.

As the founder of the Mormon Church, Smith naturally occupies a special place in church history. The so-called Joseph Smith story serves as something akin to a foundation myth. It is taught to children in Sunday school classes and provides the subject of the first lesson that church missionaries present to prospective converts. According to this story, when Smith was about fourteen years old, he grew concerned about the diverse and often contradictory religious beliefs among the Christian sects he observed in upstate New York. Being a sober and reflective youth, he took to heart the following passage, which he found in the New Testament:

> If any of you lack wisdom, let him ask of God, that giveth to all men liberally, and upbraideth not; and it shall be given him. (Jas. 1:5)

Alone, Smith went into a nearby woods, where he found a clearing and got down on his knees to pray for guidance. Which church, he asked, was the correct one? To his amazement, the heavens opened, God appeared before him and introduced his son, Jesus Christ, and advised him that as no church was correct, he should join none of them. He was further advised that he would be visited by an angel. Three years after that astounding event, Smith began receiving visits from an angel named Moroni, who eventually revealed to him a buried cache of golden plates, on which an ancient history of the settlement of the Americas was inscribed. In early 1828, Smith began "translating" the plates with the aid of magical implements. He worked from behind a curtain, dictating his translation to a scribe who never saw what he was doing. In mid-1829, he completed the translation. The following year, he published it as the Book of Mormon. By then, Moroni had taken the golden plates back to Heaven after only a handful of people other than Smith had even glimpsed them. It is not even clear in what language they were written. All that remained was Smith's dictations and occasionally contradictory stories about the origins of the plates that Smith later recorded.

To a nonbeliever, the Smith story is implausible on a number of levels. First, one might wonder why God would choose a poorly educated American boy with no evident history of interest in religion to serve as his instrument to reestablish the true church on earth. Is it possible that no other equally sincere person asked him the same question during nearly two millennia of Christian history? To the Mormon faithful, this issue confirms the Smith story because they see Smith as having been too young and too poorly educated to have written the Book of Mormon on his own. Brodie challenged that view in her biography, but Bushman does not address the question.

The story of the golden plates, and their convenient disappearance, poses even more difficult questions. The fact that God saw fit to remove the plates from the earth made it necessary for Smith's followers to accept their existence on faith. Accepting that story, and many others, on faith has become a tenet of Mormonism, which shuns critical analyses of sensitive issues. Believers are expected to resolve their doubts through prayer and reflection, not through investigations.

The implausibility of the Joseph Smith story goes beyond simple distinctions between belief and nonbelief in divine inspiration. Even if one were to accept the Book of Mormon as an authentic history of the Americas, the book's contents pose many difficult problems, the most obvious being the complete lack of a Book of Mormon geography. Apart from the Hill Cumorah, where Smith claimed to have found the plates, not a single place mentioned in the book can be connected to an actual site in the New World. The Book of Mormon is also filled with obvious anachronisms: horses, sheep, cattle, wheat, barley, silk, wheeled chariots, iron and even steel-working, and many other things not known to have existed in the New World during the period in which the book's narrative is set. Mormons believe that some—if not all—American Indians are descended from the Book of Mormon's fallen Lamanite people. However, no linguistic or biological traces, in the form of DNA, of Middle Easterners have been found among modern American Indians.

Textual analyses of the Book of Mormon also raise difficult questions about its authenticity. Large portions of the book appear to be taken directly from the Bible, but some passages contain significant differences. According to the teachings of the Mormon Church, the versions in the Book of Mormon should be the more correct, as the Bible has suffered from errors in translation. After the Dead Sea Scrolls were discovered in the mid-twentieth century, church leaders hoped that analysis of the previously unknown ancient manuscripts would confirm the authenticity of the Book of Mormon texts. However, the opposite has occurred. Some passages in the King James Version of the Bible that the scrolls showed to contain translation errors contained the same errors in the Book of Mormon version. This fact alone suggests that Smith's source for these passages was not divinely inspired plates but the King James Bible, whose florid language the Book of Mormon mimics.

While questions such as these go beyond the scope of a biography of Joseph Smith, one must question the objectivity of any scholar who writes on Smith and fails to address them. If the Book of Mormon is, in fact, a true history of the early Americas, the discrepancies between its contents and what historians, archaeologists, linguists, biotechnicians, and other scholars can discern about early history must be resolved.

There is an insurmountable gulf between the views of Mormon believers and those of nonbelievers. Either Smith was a true prophet of God, or he was not. There can be no middle ground. If he was a true prophet, then his remarkable life can be explained as a series of events guided by divine intervention, and many of those events cannot be explained by the ordinary tools of secular scholarship. On the other hand, if Smith was not a true prophet, then other explanations for his actions must be sought.

R. Kent Rasmussen

Review Sources

Booklist 102, no. 1 (September 1, 2005): 26.
Foreign Affairs 84, no. 6 (November/December, 2005): 143-143.
Kirkus Reviews 73, no. 14 (July 15, 2005): 773.
Library Journal 130, no. 12 (July 1, 2005): 86.
The New York Review of Books 52, no. 18 (November 17, 2005): 35-37.
The New York Times Book Review 155 (January 15, 2006): 14-15.
Publishers Weekly 252, no. 29 (July 25, 2005): 70.

THE JOURNALS
Volume I, 1949-1965

Author: John Fowles (1926-2005)
Edited, with an introduction and notes, by Charles Drazin
First published: 2003, in England
Publisher: Alfred A. Knopf (New York). Illustrated.
668 pp. $35.00
Type of work: Autobiography
Time: 1949-1965
Locale: Spetsei, Greece; London, England

Fowles records his emotional and intellectual life, his reading, travels, loves, and friendships, from his last undergraduate days through his development as a teacher, husband, and writer

Principal personages:
JOHN FOWLES, the writer
ELIZABETH FOWLES, his wife
ROY CHRISTY, Elizabeth's first husband

This extraordinary volume chronicles the life-in-progress of a young man whose principal ambition is to become a writer, an ambition that, after years of struggle, poverty, and unrewarding work as a teacher, is finally realized with the success of his first novel, *The Collector* (1963). In the great tradition of literary autobiography, this work contains a frankness and spontaneity, especially about the doubts, misgivings, false starts, and failures, that remove it from the usual fables of identity a retrospective work might create.

Instead, John Fowles writes of his present as it passes, vents his reactions to people, critiques films and stage performances, and lists his thoughts about his readings, his love affairs, and his anxieties, all from his own immediate perspective. Charles Drazin, as editor, provides extensive but not obtrusive notes on Fowles's friends and associates, the locales and institutions he visited, the books he reads and authors he mentions. These useful notes are also accompanied by a first-rate index which is invaluable for scholars using the book as a research tool for cross-referencing the writer's literary works with his journals. Yet the scholarship is not essential for general readers to appreciate the work; in that regard the editor has struck a balance serving a wide readership.

The editor has divided the journals into ten parts, the first two of which, dealing with Fowles's last year at Oxford and his first year teaching at Poitiers in France, present a portrait of the artist as a very young man, filled with youthful prejudices, opinions, and judgments which range from the incredibly naïve and petulant to the remarkably profound. At times Fowles seems intent upon criticizing all, including

himself, in a manner that betrays arrogant prig-
gishness; at other times he seems lost in admiration for those very things he criticizes. This is especially true of his uneasiness at the home of his
parents and of his uneasy romance with Ginette
Marcailloux in Poitiers, which was marred by
her tension and bad temper as well as his own
bad temper and bouts of depression. Apart from
the personal roller coaster he describes, the entries are also of inestimable value for literary
critics of the later Fowles, to mine for clues
about sources, analogues, and allusions in his
fiction as he mentions the works he is reading
and offers concise evaluations of their merits.

〜
*Born in England, John Fowles was
educated at Oxford University and
taught in France, Greece, and
England while writing poetry,
drama, and fiction. His initial
literary success came in the 1960's
with the publication of* The
Collector *(1963),* The Aristos
(1964), and The Magus *(1965). He
died at his home in Lyme Regis in
2005 after battling a long illness.*
〜

Part 3, "An Island and Greece," introduces a magical place which transformed his
life and his writing. Having secured a teaching post at the Anargyros and Korgia-
leneios School on the island of Spetsei, Fowles began a fascination with the genius of
the place that would inform his major novel, *The Magus* (1965). In retrospect, the editor of the journals mentions in a note, Fowles looks upon the journal entry for January 6, 1952, as the genesis of that novel. Clearly some of the language he uses to
describe his early impressions of the island's topography and its allure for him anticipates several of the lush descriptions he would write more than a decade later. Additionally, although he remains critical of his colleagues, forgiving some and begrudg-
ing others, and makes acerbic notes on the personalities and appearances of some of
his students, his tone in this era shows mature and certain growth. Other significant elements of his first few months in Greece include his travels to Mycenae, Delphi, and
Mount Parnassus, which he climbed in homage to its literary inspiration and, in turn,
found inspiring in him a new belief in himself as a writer.

After that first half-year in Greece, his sojourns in England paled. Nothing was to
prepare him for the next school year's mad, passionate, moonstruck love he found
with Elizabeth Christy, the wife of a newly arrived colleague, Roy Christy, at the
school on Spetsei. The journals recount Fowles and Elizabeth's initial attraction, his
conscious avoidance of intimacy though they were increasingly thrown together by
circumstance, and, ultimately, their passionate love affair which got both Fowles and
Christy fired from the school. As in every section of the journals, Fowles casts a cold
eye upon himself, his situation, his colleagues, and his students—and also upon Elizabeth, noting her faults, failings, and inadequacies but persisting in his infatuation with
her. The journal entries show a progressive euphoria with Elizabeth, recounting the
joys of new love amid the dangers of their affair.

Part 6, "Return to England," illustrates the period beginning in July, 1952, and the
homecoming in England. Despite Fowles and Elizabeth's elopement, the process of
separation from Roy seemed interminable, as did the myriad problems with the relationship, not least of which was Roy's insistence that his and Elizabeth's daughter remain in Roy's sole custody. Fowles documents his teaching in Ashridge, a suburban

finishing school for women, and its attendant problems, including amorous liaisons with students. He dwells upon Elizabeth's problems, reveals the pair's quarrels and inevitable reconciliations, his struggles with writing and disaffection with work. Most of all, he documents a period of grinding poverty, surviving on a small weekly salary with most of it going toward rent. Ultimately, the domestic, if not the financial, situation improved slightly in 1954 when Fowles found employment at St Godric's, a secretarial and language school in Hampstead, London, providing him with steady work for the following decade and allowing him to be closer to Elizabeth. This stormy period of alternating quarrels and reconciliations took on a different, public face in April 2, 1957, when the pair married.

Fowles's attempts at composing various projects, especially *The Aristos* (1964), were stymied during the period covered in part 7, "Married Life in London," 1957 through October, 1960, but the journals have less to do with still-present domestic unhappiness than with his reflections upon the literature he read, the films he saw, thumbnail sketches of his students, and a lengthy dialogue of self-analysis at the end of the section. The next section of the journals, covering a little more than a year, mainly concerns the inability of John and Elizabeth to have children, her visits to a fertility clinic, and unsuccessful treatments. Fowles's notes on his reading during this period and on contemporary Italian cinema provide a counterpoint to the troubled time of Elizabeth's medical ordeals and his reactions to them. One minor note in early December of 1960 describes his writing *The Collector*, a project he had begun in late November and was to finish, without further commentary in the journals, in another three weeks' time.

After such prolonged periods of darkness and economic uncertainty, the sea change in Fowles's personal and literary fortunes that the ninth section of the journals demonstrates is, indeed, a new climbing of Parnassus, as the editor calls it. Like many of Fowles's manuscripts, the book he had written in a few weeks two years previously had lain neglected until Fred "Podge" Porter, a friend, read some of it and found it publishable. The manuscript was professionally typed, and Elizabeth took it to a literary agent whom the typist had recommended; this marked a turning point for Fowles. The chronicle of how the book got into the hands of Jonathan Cape, a first-rate publishing house, its revisions, and the windfall of financial prosperity it brought has a Dickensian, fairy-tale quality about it without the attendant sentimentality Fowles often observes in the journals of Charles Dickens's work.

His literary and financial success also led Fowles and Elizabeth to spend a long summer holiday in Italy in 1963 and to submit other works of his for publication, although little came of the latter effort for some time except for in the case of *The Magus*, then incomplete, which Cape had already agreed to publish . On the strength of his newly found financial independence, Fowles also left employment at St. Godric's in April of 1963 and, in addition to his omnivorous reading, began working on *The Magus* with renewed vigor as well as undertaking lengthy and frustrating negotiations on the screenplay of *The Collector*, for which Columbia Pictures had bought film rights.

In autumn of 1963 Fowles began his stint as a literary lion, traveling to the United States to promote his book, which was published there by Little, Brown of Boston and giving a round of interviews in New York City. The writer of the journal entries of this period is much the same as that of earlier times, except that he has much in which to rejoice despite his hard-bitten view of the world and of himself. One notable experience he details is his meeting with Gloria Vanderbilt in her New York home, her warmth toward him and her complete understanding of his book.

The volume concludes with part 10, written between September, 1963 and November, 1965, and contains accounts of Fowles's newfound fame and literary associations in England as well as of his time in Hollywood while *The Collector* was being filmed. Replete with Hollywood gossip, descriptions of the painstaking and sometimes painful reading process by the actors, conversations about simplifying the language of the book for film audiences, the entries reflect the bustle of his days and nights in Los Angeles. His breezy reports of meetings and conversations with Terence Stamp and of his attempts to get Samantha Eggar to liven up her performance add immeasurably to the immediacy of the telling. He details the difficulties and obstacles to shooting the film, from the wrong electrical set-ups to the wrong set and costuming to the maddening process in which power overshadows intelligence in decision making, in such a way as to add a distinct sense of the unreality of the American film world.

Meanwhile, Fowles was still working hard on *The Magus*, rewriting, adding, deleting some segments. His comments on the creative process, the recursive hovering over sections, the cutting of large portions, the blocks and stumbles in writing and the question of writing in the first-person or the third-person voice illuminate Fowles's work habits and the problems attendant upon completing a long narrative. Having completed the work, he negotiated publication on both sides of the Atlantic Ocean as well as the film rights and agreed to write the screenplay for Twentieth Century Fox—for a production that would never be released commercially in the United States, as it happened. Fowles's wealth, however, grew to the extent that he could leave London and move to Lyme Regis, a seaside resort town.

Ironically but typically, the last entry in this volume of the journals describes Fowles's love of the new residence on the seaside, still with worry over money. His house in Highgate remained unsold, the expenses of the new house accumulated, and he faced an overdraft of five thousand pounds while waiting for payment on the deal with Fox.

John J. Conlon

Review Sources

Booklist 101, no. 17 (May 1, 2005): 1560.
Contemporary Review 284 (April, 2004): 246.
The Economist 369 (November 1, 2003): 82.
Kirkus Reviews 73, no. 6 (March 15, 2005): 331.
London Review of Books 26, no. 9 (May 6, 2004): 32-33.
Publishers Weekly 252, no. 13 (March 28, 2005): 67.
The Spectator 293 (October 25, 2003): 66.
The Times Literary Supplement, November 14, 2003, pp. 12-13.

JUICED
Wild Times, Rampant 'Roids, Smash Hits, and How Baseball Got Big

Author: José Canseco (1964-   )
Publisher: Houghton Mifflin (Boston). 361 pp. $26.00
Type of work: Memoir
Time: 1980-1999
Locale: Miami; Oakland, California; and other locations in North America

This unflinching tell-all by a controversial former professional athlete recounts the impact of steroids on Major League Baseball during the 1980's and 1990's

Principal personages:
JOSÉ CANSECO, one-half of the Oakland Athletics' "Bash Brothers" (so called because he "bashed" the baseball), a professional athlete who claims credit for introducing steroids to the major leagues
MARK MCGWIRE, the other half of the "Bash Brothers," who allegedly benefited from Canseco's knowledge of steroids
JASON GIAMBI, a baseball player who—in Canseco's view—abused steroids while part of the Oakland Athletics baseball franchise and who payed the price because he could not control his love of partying
JOSÉ CANSECO, SR., José's father, a stern and demanding man

José Canseco played professional baseball for seventeen years and during the late 1980's and early 1990's was among the game's most popular and controversial players. Canseco demonstrated a rare combination of speed and power; he was the first player in Major League Baseball to hit forty home runs and steal forty bases in the same year. Throughout his career he won many awards, set a few records, and made a lot of money. A fitness enthusiast and weightlifter, Canseco helped set improved standards of physical fitness in baseball. Before he broke into the major leagues, teams discouraged players from lifting weights during the season, fearing they would become muscle-bound and lose flexibility. Following Canseco's lead, baseball players became stronger, faster, and more powerful. Off the field, Canseco was controversial as well, partly for his brushes with the law in California and Florida and partly for a brief relationship with pop singer Madonna.

Out of baseball, Canseco has demonstrated a talent for remaining controversial with the publication of his tell-all book *Juiced: Wild Times, Rampant 'Roids, Smash Hits, and How Baseball Got Big.* In this work, Canseco claims that almost every successful baseball player since 1990 has used steroids, and not just the mediocre players willing to try anything to remain in the big leagues. The superstars were using steroids, breaking records on the baseball diamond, and reaping multimillion-dollar contracts in return. Canseco names names.

According to Canseco, Mark McGwire, his former teammate on the Oakland Athletics franchise, used steroids; so did Barry Bonds, a baseball superstar on the San Francisco Giants franchise. So did Sammy Sosa, a star player for the Chicago Cubs; so did many other stars. "The challenge is not to find a top player who has used steroids." Canseco claims, "The challenge is to find a top player who *hasn't*."

A "juicer," as Canseco explains, is a person who uses steroids; to be juiced is to be developed by steroids. In this way, the title of the book refers not only to Canseco but also to baseball as a sport. Just as many baseball players benefited from using steroids, Canseco claims, franchise owners benefited because more athletic players exhibited a more exciting brand of baseball, which lead directly to more fans in the stands, more media coverage, and more television and advertising revenue.

~

José Canseco played professional baseball for seven different teams in a career that spanned seventeen years. He won awards ranging from Rookie of the Year in 1986 to Most Valuable Player in 1988. Throughout the 1990's, he remained popular as much for his exploits off the field as on it. Juiced *is his first book.*

~

Predictably, sportswriters who reviewed advanced copies of this book howled in protest. None of the other professional sports leagues is as obsessed with its own history as is Major League Baseball. A hard-core baseball fan cherishes the singular history of his or her favorite team, if not the league as a whole. To such fans, Canseco's brash claims seem to taint the record-breaking achievements of modern superstars. Many reviewers considered Canseco's book mean-spirited because it seems to call into question the achievements of other athletes, including Canseco's teammate McGwire.

The national sports media and other book reviewers, however, seem to have missed the point. *Juiced* is not primarily a book about baseball; it is not simply about Canseco's love for the sport that made him famous and wealthy. It is about Canseco's love for steroids, about his claim that they enabled him to compete at the highest levels for far longer than anyone could have expected. *Juiced* is offered as proof of his claim that combinations of steroids and human growth hormone can turn almost anyone into superman or superwoman. Considered in that light, there is no reason for Canseco not to offer McGwire, Bonds, Sosa, and other athletes as evidence for his claim.

Juiced begins with an account of Canseco's childhood in Cuba and Miami. The early chapters are dominated by José Canseco, Sr., a Cuban patriarch who demands excellence of his two sons, Ozzie and José. As José describes him, the elder Canseco is a faultfinder, a blamer, and a loudmouth, the sort of father who shouts at his son for making a mistake in a little league game. Apparently, the elder Canseco had a lot to yell about because José was not a very good player. Although he could hit the ball, he was thin and prone to back injuries. As he reached high school and his body filled out, Canseco demonstrated enough promise to attract the attention of major league scouts, one of whom convinced the Oakland Athletics to draft Canseco in 1982.

From 1982 to 1984, Canseco struggled at a number of minor league stops, from Medford, Oregon, to Madison, Wisconsin, getting more and more frustrated with his few home runs and low batting average. He was on a team in Modesto, California, when he learned that his mother back in Miami was dying. At her bedside, Canseco vowed to become the best. To Canseco, combinations of various steroids and human growth hormone enabled him to fulfill that vow.

To be clear, Canseco's book is an encomium to anabolic androgenic steroids, or artificial chemical analogues to testosterone. These were originally designed to treat men who produced unusually low levels of testosterone or for people who experienced tissue wasting as the result of disease. For such patients, the compounds helped build muscle mass and helped make possible a higher quality of life. Taken too frequently or in excessive doses, however, steroids have been linked to a variety of problems, including infertility, liver tumors, cancer, high blood pressure, and neurologic problems. To his credit, Canseco points out that he did not simply start injecting himself haphazardly but developed a fairly sophisticated program of anabolic steroid use. As he puts it:

> I was educating myself on all aspects of steroids—from why they were invented, to their chemical makeup, how to use them properly, what dosages, how to cycle off, how to cycle on, which steroids did what for the body, which one was good for strength, or for quick-muscle-twitch fiber, or for foot speed. I wanted to keep getting better and better every year, and I was seeing that the steroids could help me do that.

Besides increased strength and reflex speed, hormones gave him more confidence, says Canseco. He believed he was doing something good for his career, and that belief contributed to the overall picture. "I was training the way no other baseball player had ever trained," Canseco writes, "And the results were starting to show." By the beginning of 1986, Canseco was called up to the major leagues and was being heralded as the newest star of the Athletics.

The middle chapters of *Juiced* are more diffuse than the first part of the work, as Canseco's narrative wanders from steroid use into descriptions of the seamy side of professional sports, including the groupies who had sex with their favorite baseball players whenever the team came to town. By spending several chapters on the major league lifestyle, *Juiced* emulates Jim Bouton's book *Ball Four* (1980). In that book, Bouton, a pitcher with several baseball teams in the 1970's, describes life in baseball as he lived it during the 1960's and 1970's. The players of Bouton's era drank hard and used amphetamines to perk themselves up afterward. In *Juiced*, Canseco gives himself credit for helping change baseball for the better; the heavy drinkers and drug users just could not compete on the field with the bulked-up, faster, stronger steroid users. For players, the choice became change with the times or get out of baseball.

As a case in point, Canseco describes the attempts of one player, Jason Giambi, to combine a hard-partying lifestyle with steroid use, with ugly results. In Canseco's opinion, using steroids wisely requires a healthy lifestyle. In his career, Canseco hardly lived a monastic life, but he rarely drank, got plenty of rest, and spent all of his time in the gym, at the park, or at home with his family. Giambi, according to

Canseco, used steroids to excess and partied to excess. As a result, although he bulked up, he looked terrible: "You could see the retention of liquids, especially in his neck and face; to those in the know, that was a sure sign of steroid overload, plus drinking a lot and having a bad diet." Put in more common terms, "You could literally put your finger on his skin and see the water under there as it indented and then filled in."

After this cautionary tale, Canseco spends the final part of *Juiced* on an extended diatribe against the nonplayers in Major League Baseball. He variously casts aspersions on the franchise owners, the player's union chiefs, the umpires, sportswriters, and other personages in the sport and on its margins. Throughout the middle part of the book and into its final chapters, Canseco complains that ingrained bias against Hispanic players caused his team, and the league as a whole, to push him into the background and to promote white players such as Cal Ripken.

It is at this point in the narrative that *Juiced* loses direction and interest. A book full of complaints about how unfair life is has limited market appeal. On the other hand, there is clearly a market for books which point out the various ways athletes try to bend the rules in order to compete and earn more money. Overall, Canseco makes a good point: bigger, faster, more powerful athletes make for faster, more exciting games. More excitement brings more fans to the games, as well as more television coverage, more publicity, and more advertising revenue. By bulking up, Canseco and other "juicers" helped make a lot more money for franchise owners and reaped personal fortunes in return.

Michael R. Meyers

Review Sources

Newsweek 145, no. 9 (February 28, 2005): 57.
People 63, no. 9 (March 7, 2005): 54.
Reason 37, no. 2 (June, 2005): 55-58.

JUICING THE GAME
Drugs, Power, and the Fight for the Soul of
Major League Baseball

Author: Howard Bryant (1968-   )

Publisher: Viking Press (New York). 432 pp. $24.95

Type of work: Current affairs

Time: The 1990's

Locale: Major League Baseball sites, especially New
York, Oakland, San Francisco, San Diego, St. Louis,
Chicago, Milwaukee, Atlanta, Boston, Baltimore; also
Washington, D.C., and the Dominican Republic

*Sportswriter Howard Bryant takes a deep look at how
steroids crept into baseball and why they went unchecked
for a decade*

Principal personages:
> BUD SELIG, the embattled baseball commissioner during the steroids
> scandal
> SANDY ALDERSON, the Oakland A's general manager who became a
> voice for ethical reform
> FAY VINCENT, Selig's predecessor as commissioner
> MARVIN MILLER, the founder and respected former head of the players'
> union (MLPA)
> TONY LA RUSSA, the Oakland A's manager who kept silent about known
> dopers on the team
> RICHARD MELLONI, GARY WADLER, and CHARLES YESALIS, among the
> "crusaders," prominent voices raised against steroids
> BARRY BONDS,
> JOSÉ CANSECO,
> JASON GIAMBI,
> MARK MCGWIRE,
> KEN CAMINITI,
> SAMMY SOSA,
> TONY GWYNN, and
> REGGIE JACKSON, famous baseball players

Howard Bryant's chronicle of Major League Baseball's "juiced" era was not
2005's only book with a long title that plays on that word. Several months before
Bryant's *Juicing the Game: Drugs, Power, and the Fight for the Soul of Major
League Baseball* was released, José Canseco published *Juiced: Wild Times, Rampant
'Roids, Smash Hits, and How Baseball Got Big*. In language that might be taken as
Bryant's contra-theme, Canseco glorifies steroids as baseball's game-saving enablers
after 1994's devastating 232-day players' strike. Says Canseco:

[Mark] McGwire and [Sammy] Sosa brought base-ball back to life [in 1998]. People were as excited about baseball as they had ever been. And why? Because the owners had been smart enough not to chase steroid use out of the game, allowing guys like McGwire to make the most of steroids and growth hormone, turning themselves into larger than life heroes in more ways than one.

What Canseco, who admitted using anabolic ste-roids to anyone who would listen, views as base-ball's savior looms for Bryant as the game's de-stroyer. For him, echoing baseball purists such as perennial batting champ Tony Gwynn, the enhance-ment of the home run, baseball's prime crowd-pleaser, by bulked-up sluggers Barry Bonds, Mc-Gwire, and Sosa, was "engineered by design."

McGwire and Sosa's stirring race in 1998 to eclipse Roger Maris's long-standing home run re-cord, which transformed them into larger-than-life heroes, was followed three years later by Bonds's hitting of seventy-three homers. In November, 2005, baseball fi-nally, after a decade of inaction, mandated penalties severe enough to stamp out ana-bolic steroid use. For first and second offenders, the penalty is now fifty- and one-hundred game suspensions, respectively. A third infraction will ban the offender for life. Meanwhile, the larger-than-life heroes noted above have all been brought down to size by life itself, as this book demonstrates.

In *Juicing the Game*, Bryant, a sports columnist for the *Boston Herald*, offers a so-phisticated yet passionate assessment of the steroid flap that rocked the game to its foundations—performance on the field and governance in the commissioner's office. Bryant asks why baseball's chieftains—notably Commissioner Bud Selig—did so lit-tle for so long. He charges that baseball turned a blind eye to even known strength-enhancing drugs, so long as their effects induced fans to pay soaring prices to watch the boys of summer hit homers in far greater numbers than ever before.

Bryant's book is encyclopedic and scholarly. Rather than draw on the recycled col-umns of the baseball-beat reporter he was in San Jose, California, and Bergen, New Jersey, for the Oakland A's and New York Yankees respectively, the author abets his profound knowledge of baseball history with in-depth interviews with players, execu-tives, team managers, and journalists. Tracing the roots of the steroid scandal, Bryant points out that weight training began to become popular in the late 1960's and early 1970's. By the mid-1990's, he writes, creatine—a dietary supplement that helps an athlete work out harder and longer—was "as ubiquitous in major league clubhouses as tobacco."

It was not long before creatine gave way to androstenedione ("a dietary supple-ment whose creation was designed to mimic a steroid"). "Andro" gave way to testos-terone and a host of powerful anabolic substances. For struggling players, such drugs

Howard Bryant is the author of Shut Out: A Story of Race and Baseball in Boston, *which won the Casey Award for the Best Baseball Book of 2002 and was a finalist for the Society for American Baseball Research's Seymour Award. He writes a sports column for the* Boston Herald *and previously covered the New York Yankees for* The (Bergen, N.J.) Record *and the Oakland A's for the* San Jose Mercury News. *He lives in Boston with his wife and son.*

and supplements could mean the difference between riding buses in the minor leagues and team jets in the majors—and the difference between celebrity and immortality.

For all the fame of sluggers like Babe Ruth and Mickey Mantle, baseball is a game of finesse that calls for multiple skills, unlike football and basketball, where size and strength dominate. This is a traditionalist's view that grubbers for multiyear, million-dollar contracts forgot. "For the man once considered," according to Bryant, "the best player in the game," Canseco bulked up so much on steroids that during his last years he could not run down a fly ball or steal a base. He performed as one of the game's flawed, a designated hitter, and was washed up at thirty-five. Mark McGwire's may be the saddest case. An icon of rectitude until he disgraced himself on national television in March, 2005, "collapsing in tears" under questioning before a House of Representatives hearing on steroids in baseball. "With the ultimate chance for redemption . . . he intimates he will invoke the [Fifth Amendment, against self-recrimination]." He had answers for nothing, not andro, even though seven years earlier—in 1998, his 70-homer year—he had discussed the then-legal drug openly. A six-foot-five, 190-pounder before joining his A's "Bash Brother" Canseco for locker-room injections, a larger McGwire spent parts of eight seasons disabled with chronic back agonies, probably due to the strain of carrying 250 pounds on his once-slim frame.

Of all the steroid-era iconic players—"icon" and "iconic" seem to be Bryant's favorite words—Sammy Sosa is the most revealing. "Already vulnerable to suspicion, though never directly accused of anything, Sosa . . . had become officially tainted and forever difficult to evaluate." At thirty-three, after four spectacular seasons—243 homers and strong play in right field—Sosa's decline has been almost as sharp as Canseco's. During those four seasons, Sosa became the "new face" of the Chicago Cubs and of Latin baseball, a player with flair who embodied something baseball had lost. Sosa made baseball fun. His downside, according to Bryant, was his self-absorption at the expense of his teammates. "The boom box that sat near Sosa's locker had become a symbol for the divisiveness he engendered. Sammy was bigger than anyone." When the Cubs blew a sure playoff slot the final two weeks of 2004, Sosa walked out before the season's last game. His statistics down, he signed with Baltimore for 2005 and played badly on a team of underachievers.

The finest of the player profiles—that of the only individual to whom Bryant devotes a chapter—is of Barry Bonds, who four times declined Bryant's requests for an interview. A mini-biography without a trace of rancor, his essay demonstrates a complexity in the relationship of this superstar to the game that may be unrivaled in baseball history. Yet when Bryant writes that Bonds has rejected the rituals of the legendary—Joe DiMaggio, Ted Williams, and Willie Mays are cited—how can he be sure, since this superstar labored himself back into shape to hit homers during the final days of 2005? Jason Giambi, seven years Bonds's junior and an admitted steroids user—Canseco called him their "prime mis-user"—made 2005's greatest comeback. Surely Bonds, a much finer athlete, would be better equipped to defy time. "He became invincible," Bryant writes.

Bonds had seemingly mastered the game. He was no longer merely a great player, but a phenomenon. . . . His enormity overshadowed every other player and forced the game to look at itself in a way no other player of his stature had. . . . And yet the greatest player. . . maybe of all time, had accomplished so much while leaving the sport itself with too many questions to answer.

In 2007, McGwire will be eligible to be considered for membership in baseball's Hall of Fame. Even as more severe penalties for detected steroid users were ratified, there was an announcement that the name of legendary player but admitted gambler Pete Rose would not appear on the Hall of Fame ballots in 2006.

Richard Hauer Costa

Review Sources

Booklist 101, no. 21 (July 1, 2005): 1874.
Library Journal 130, no. 12 (July 1, 2005): 89.
The New York Times 154 (July 5, 2005): E1-E8.
The New Yorker, November 21, 2005, p. 56.
Publishers Weekly 252, no. 24 (June 13, 2005): 46-47.

K.

Author: Roberto Calasso (1941-   )
First published: 2002, in Italy
Translated from the Italian by Geoffrey Brock
Publisher: Alfred A. Knopf (New York). 327 pp. $25.00
Type of work: Literary criticism
Time: 1912-1924
Locale: Prague, Bohemia, Austro-Hungarian Empire
    (now the Czech Republic)

Franz Kafka's stories and novels, like his letters and diaries, were studies in alienation and "foreignness," creating for readers the experience of being a stranger in a world that is strangely familiar

Principal personages:
FRANZ KAFKA (1883-1924), an author
HERMANN KAFKA (1852-1931), his domineering father
FELICE BAUER (1887-1960), his fiancé in 1914 and 1917
MILENA JESENSK-POLLAK (1896-1944), his mistress in 1920-1921
MAX BROD (1884-1968), his friend and publisher
JOSEF K., the protagonist of Kafka's unfinished novel *The Trial*
    (1914)
K., the protagonist of Kafka's unfinished novel *The Castle* (1922)

Roberto Calasso burst onto the American literary scene with *Le nozze di Cado e Armonia* (1993; *The Marriage of Cadmus and Harmony*, 1998), a brilliant retelling of Greek and Roman myths which recalls Ovid's *Metamorphoses* (c. 8 C.E.; English translation, 1567). With *The Marriage of Cadmus and Harmony*, the Italian editor and publisher established a writing pattern which would remain his own: a wide intellectual sweep made in a series of episodes and punctuated by frequent breaks and asides, a detached scholarly voice enlivened by quotations and paraphrases from many sources, and a sense of complete familiarity with the whole of Indo-European literature in the original languages. He also announced an overarching concern with myth and its main subject, the gods.

Calasso expanded his reach into modern European culture with *La rovina di Kasch* (1983; *The Ruin of Kasch*, 1994), on the Napoleonic age and its Romantic aftermath. Then he turned to Hindu mythology with *Ka* (1996; *Ka: Stories of the Mind and Gods of India*, 1998), which did for the Indian subcontinent what *The Marriage of Cadmus and Harmony* had done for the Mediterranean region.

Subsequently, he published two surveys of literary modernism, concentrating on Europe in the late nineteenth century: *I Quarantanove gradini* (1991; *The Forty-nine Steps*, 2001) and *La lettertura e gli dei*, (2001; *Literature and the Gods*, 2002), where he found the "absolute" verse of the Hindu Vedas culminating in the Symbolist poetry of Stéphane Mallarmé. *K.*, however, is the real successor to the earlier trilogy of studies in myth.

That Calasso has devoted a book to Franz Kafka suggests he has found a whole world of mythology in the Bohemian author's works. The book is as ambitious within the study of Kafka as the earlier books were in the worlds of ancient Greece and India. However, it seems less successful in re-creating a world for readers not already familiar with it. To reinforce one's familiarity with the facts of Kafka's life and world, one is far better off with an illustrated biography

Born and educated in Italy, Roberto Calasso has been associated with Adelphi Edizione since he was a graduate student. He has written dozens of introductions, some of them reissued in The Forty-nine Steps *(1991), and has received many awards. In 2001, he held the Weidenfeld Chair at Oxford.*

such as Jeremy Adler's *Franz Kafka* (2001). Calasso writes for insiders who know their Kafka, or think they do. He has gone deep inside the Kafka lode. He has consulted the surviving manuscripts as well as the standard German editions, from which he translates passages into Italian and to which he often refers in twenty-one pages of endnotes. He writes with an assurance that seems well earned.

K. begins with five chapters on *The Trial* and *The Castle*, Kafka's fragmentary novels of 1914 and 1922, respectively. Two chapters offer insights into the roles that women play in those works. Calasso continues with five chapters on Kafka's major short stories—"The Hunter Gracchus," "The Judgment," "The Burrow," "The Metamorphosis," and "Amerika," the last of which Calasso discusses in his chapter "The Missing Person." These chapters move into the story of Kafka's life as a writer. He concludes with four more chapters on *The Trial* and *The Castle*, which turn out to be fragments of a still larger story which Kafka did not live to complete, and a final chapter on the aphorisms Kafka wrote on a holiday in 1921, three years before he died of tuberculosis. Only then, in a temporary reprieve from his demons, did Kafka perceive that paradise is "a perennial hidden presence" (Calasso's words). Then Kafka did glimpse, "on the garden path, the goddess of happiness" (Kafka's words).

Given Calasso's fascination with myth, one might expect *K.* to be all about mythical patterns in the fiction, but that is not so: Calasso takes pains to show that Kafka's unique style of storytelling grew out of nineteenth century realism, as Kafka found it in the works of Charles Dickens and Fyodor Dostoevski. *The Castle's* "newness" comes, says Calasso, from "its *not* being a fable." What makes the worlds of Kafka's castle and court compelling, for Calasso, is the minimalism: the choice of a few commonplace details, elaborated and juxtaposed in a new kind of phantasmagoria. Although other fictions, such as "The Burrow," must be considered apologues, or moral fables, Kafka's novels only touch on the world of legend and fable.

Calasso's chief insight is that *The Castle* can be read as a gloss on *The Trial*. He argues that the experience of being accused and brought to trial is essentially the same as that of being recognized and recommended for a promotion. Condemnation is almost undistinguishable from election, he suggests, and both concepts are basic to the Judaeo-Christian tradition. In either circumstance, one's individuality is placed under scrutiny and thus threatened. The court and the castle are both branches of government—the one judicial, the other administrative—and both are aspects of the Law. This Law (with a capital *l*) is all pervasive: religious, political, and psychological. The father in Kafka is thus a literal father and a metaphor for the paternal authority in religion (the father confessor or God the Father), in politics (the patriot or the patriarch), and in the individual (Sigmund Freud's concept of the superego). Only at this point does Calasso find something like a Kafka myth, and even then the myth is riddled with ambiguities.

The ambiguities arise from this continual mingling of the literal and the metaphorical. They demand close and careful reading—the sort of reading, notes Calasso, that Jews typically give to the Torah and Talmud. It is with reading the law, rather than with the law itself, that Calasso finds Kafka a most Jewish writer, even something of a Kabbalist. Calasso is a careful reader himself, as one instance may indicate. In *The Trial*, any evidence can be used against the accused, even legends. To Josef K., and perhaps to most readers of his story, this seems an extreme form of case law. Calasso teases out a deeper significance and persuasively suggests it was part of Kafka's design. As Western society prides itself on becoming more rational, and its legends are relegated to the dustbin of past ideas, there remain some who realize that there is a core of legend in the rational code of law and that the legends have their endings from which one can learn about the future, endings that often have moral implications such as the metamorphoses in Ovid. Hence the passion that a few members of Kafka's court show for the "final verdicts" found in legend. Hence the passion that Calasso shows for Kafka.

Calasso has taken literally the critical dicta that books are made out of other books (Northrop Frye), if not indeed out of quotations (Walter Benjamin). This latest book draws on many of Kafka's best critics, from Elias Canetti to Robert Musil and Vladimir Nabokov. It also draws upon much of Calasso's previous work. In *K.* one finds Odysseus from *The Marriage of Cadmus and Harmony*, Talleyrand from *The Ruin of Kasch*, Krishna from *Ka*, Lautréamont from *Literature and the Gods*, and Freud from *The Forty-nine Steps*. If *K.* is less successful than the earlier surveys of Greek and Hindu lore, it may simply be that it has been made from books that are far more accessible to modern readers. If someone does not know the Greek or Hindu myths, Calasso is a good instructor. If someone has not read Kafka, the best option is to read Kafka in a recent translation. No critical study can substitute for the experience itself.

Reviewers have seldom questioned Calasso's erudition but have sometimes doubted his ability to tell a story or to develop an argument without distracting digressions. Reviews of *K.* have largely been favorable, perhaps because Calasso is clearly writing criticism rather than literature and because Kafka's stories are readily available. Reviews say that Calasso's language blends perfectly with Kafka's (*Booklist*), that his interpretations are broadly intellectual rather than narrowly academic (*Los Angeles Times*), and that the book establishes him as Kafka's "ideal" critic (*The New Yorker*). One of the fullest and most favorable reviews finds the interpretations so natural that readers may feel they possess Calasso's brilliance (*The New York Times*). It cautions, however, that *K.* is for those who know their Kafka and that even they will want to read Kafka all over again after sampling Calasso. It also suggests that he has missed Kafka's humor.

Much of that humor comes from the ambiguity, mentioned earlier, when a statement is open to both literal and figurative interpretation. In *The Trial*, for example, the reader is told that the makeshift legal chambers double as a launderette. The literal explanation is that people live here and must keep their clothing clean. The metaphorical explanation is that the law court is a place where people's dirty laundry is aired. The humor is part of Kafka's genre, usually said to be satire, but the laughter it provokes is just as common in the fables and legends that he loved to imitate.

The book was translated by Geoffrey Brock, an American poet who has already translated Italian literature by the poet Cesare Pavese (1908-1950) and the novelist Umberto Eco (b. 1932). Brock has newly translated all quotations from Kafka, rather than relying on older translations, and has closely followed the nuances in Calasso's translations. In preserving Calasso's often gnomic utterances, Brock has made some good word choices. For example, he uses "foreignness" for *estraneit* when the cognate "strangeness" fails to capture the sense of displacement that Calasso finds in Kafka. Very occasionally, he retains an Italian word even though it does appear in English dictionaries. For example, he has Calasso say that Kafka moves "from *chiaso* to *scuro*" rather than "from the clear to the obscure." Poetic touches such as these are reminders that Calasso has written something more than straight criticism or appreciation, that he has attempted once more to enter the world of the gods. Thus far Calasso has been blessed with good translators, including Tim Parks and William Weaver. Brock has proven a worthy successor.

Thomas Willard

Review Sources

Booklist 101, no. 11 (February 1, 2005): 929.
Library Journal 130, no. 4 (March 1, 2005): 84.
Los Angeles Times, January 16, 2005, p. R8.
The New Republic 232, no. 15 (April 25, 2005): 31-35.
The New York Review of Books 52 (Febrary 10, 2005): 4-7.
The New York Times Book Review 154 (May 1, 2005): 16-17.
The New Yorker 81, no. 3 (March 7, 2005): 81.
Publishers Weekly 252, no. 2 (January 10, 2005): 53.
Review of Contemporary Fiction 25, no. 2 (Summer, 2005): 136.
The Village Voice, January 18, 2005, p. 70.

KAFKA ON THE SHORE

Author: Haruki Murakami (1949-   )
First published: Umibe no Kafuka, 2002, in Japan
Translated from the Japanese by Philip Gabriel
Publisher: Alfred A. Knopf (New York). 436 pp. $26.00
Type of work: Novel
Time: 1944-2002
Locale: Japan

A teenage boy and an elderly man go on separate odys-
seys to discover their destinies

Principal characters:

KAFKA TAMURA, a fifteen-year-old boy
     from Tokyo
SATORU NAKATA, an elderly man who talks
     to cats
MISS SAEKI, the administrator of a private library
OSHIMA, a library assistant
HOSHINO, a truck driver
KOICHI TAMURA (JOHNNIE WALKER), Kafka's deranged father, a
     sculptor
SAKURA, a hairdresser
COLONEL SANDERS, a metaphysical concept

Haruki Murakami is often described as the most popular novelist in Japan and the most popular Japanese novelist in the world. Murakami takes elements of popular fiction genres, such as detective stories, and bends them into new shapes, often with surreal results. He has said that he read American novels such as those by Ernest Hemingway and Kurt Vonnegut, Jr., before reading Japanese novels, and this influence shows. His books are crammed with references to American and European literature, music, films, and brand names. His best-known work, the epic *Nejimaki-dori kuronikuru* (1995; *The Wind-Up Bird Chronicle,* 1997), was inspired by David Lynch's quirky television series *Twin Peaks* (1990-1991). As with Lynch's, Murakami's postmodern universe is one where nothing is as it seems, where anything can happen at any time. While most Murakami protagonists are men in their thirties, *Kafka on the Shore* centers on a teenager and an elderly man.

Dissatisfied with his life in Tokyo, fifteen-year-old Kafka Tamura runs away from home. Kafka has had a bad relationship with his father, Koichi, a famous sculptor, and has not seen his mother since he was four, when she left with his older, adopted sister. Koichi predicts that Kafka will kill him and sleep with his mother and sister, a prophecy which haunts him.

Satoru Nakata, in his late sixties, lives in the same neighborhood, though he and Kafka have never met. When Nakata was a schoolboy in 1944, a mysterious accident led to the loss of his memory and his ability to read and write. As with Kafka, Nakata has been neglected by his family. Telling their stories in alternating chapters, these two characters recall the structure of Murakami's *Sekai no owari to h do-boirudo wand rando* (1985; *Hard-Boiled Wonderland and the End of the World*, 1991).

Kafka spends most of his time reading, listening to popular music, working out, and thinking about sex. He has no friends and no close attachments. He longs to find his mother and sister. After working most of his adult life as a furniture maker, Nakata lives on a government subsidy and from the money he earns by finding lost cats. He can speak to and understand cats; these felines, who appear throughout Murakami's fiction, are the closest Nakata comes to having

The son of high-school literature teachers, Haruki Murakami majored in drama at Waseda University. He and his wife, Yoko Takahashi, managed Peter Cat, a Tokyo jazz club, for seven years until he began writing full time in 1981. Murakami has translated into Japanese the works of such writers as Truman Capote, Raymond Carver, F. Scott Fitzgerald, John Irving, Ursula K. Le Guin, Tim O'Brien, and Paul Theroux. He has taught at Princeton and Tufts Universities.

friends. Murakami presents Nakata's world, in which money and politics are abstractions, as being less limited than it appears. Nakata simply enjoys whatever comes along.

Kafka's travels take him to Takamutsu in Shikoku, the smallest of Japan's four major islands. His need to seek solace in a library leads him to the Komura Memorial Library, the repository of a wealthy man's personal collection. Kafka becomes friends with the sympathetic library assistant, the androgynous Oshima, and learns that the library director, Miss Saeki, was in love with the Komura family's son, who died years earlier. Just before his death, Miss Saeki became famous for composing and singing a popular song, "Kafka on the Shore." After losing her lover, she retreated from the world, only recently taking the position at the library.

Miss Saeki agrees to let Kafka work as Oshima's assistant in exchange for room and board. Kafka lives in the former room of Miss Saeki's lover, where he finds an alluring painting of a young man on a beach. The spirit of Miss Saeki's fifteen-year-old self visits nightly to gaze forlornly upon the painting. Kafka finds himself falling in love with both the spirit and the flesh of the woman whom he suspects may be his mother. Kafka and Oshima discuss the Oedipal implications of this attachment. Kafka meets Sakura, a young hairdresser, on the bus to Takamutsu and is torn between sexual desire for her and wanting her to be his long-lost sister.

Meanwhile, Nakata discovers that a psychopath who calls himself Johnnie Walker, and dresses like the liquor trademark, is killing neighborhood cats. After Johnnie Walker, actually Kafka's father, forces Nakata to kill him, the old man journeys to Takamutsu, the site of his childhood accident. He is accompanied by Hoshino, a young truck driver who abandons his job to help Nakata find his destiny.

Kafka on the Shore is an ironic quest novel because neither Kafka nor Nakata understands what he is seeking, only that he will recognize it when he sees it. Their method is much like that of Murakami, who has said in interviews that he rarely knows where his characters will lead him. Kafka has conversations with an alter ego named Crow (roughly the translation for Bohemian writer Franz Kafka), who warns him, "Sometimes fate is like a small sandstorm that keeps changing directions." In quite different ways, Kafka and Nakata struggle to overcome the pull of fate.

Libraries, important in several Murakami novels, offer Kafka a refuge from his life without friends or parental affection: "no entrance fee, nobody getting all hot and bothered if a kid comes in. You just sit down and read whatever you want." Libraries are better than his real home, and he is always treated with respect in them. The Komura Memorial Library "makes me feel like I'm in some friend's home." It is "exactly the place I've been looking for forever."

What unites Kafka, Nakata, Oshima, Miss Saeki, and Hoshino is that each is incomplete. Oshima explains how the ancient Greeks believed all people are searching for their missing halves. It is important that the friendless Kafka and Nakata develop relationships during their quests because, in Oshima's words, "it's really hard for people to live their lives alone." Murakami suggests the necessity of both individual freedom and responsibility to a larger good.

Another theme is the Western influence on Japan, the intermingling of cultures. In the library, one parlor or reading room is furnished in the Japanese style, while another parlor is Western. Kafka employs an Eastern discipline to maintain his workout routine while listening to Western artists Prince, Radiohead, and John Coltrane in order to maintain his sanity. Kafka and Nakata retreat into habit, repeating daily tasks, to establish order in a disorderly world.

Literature is extremely important to Kafka. When he feels tense, he tries to relax by thinking about all the books waiting for him to read them. Literature provides an order missing elsewhere. Oshima uses *Genji monogatari* (c. 1004; *The Tale of Genji*, 1925-1933) by Murasaki Shikibu to explain how Miss Saeki's younger spirit can exist. When Kafka first goes to the library, he reads a rare edition of Richard Burton's 1885-1888 translation of *The Arabian Nights' Entertainments*: "Compared to those faceless hordes of people rushing through the train station, these crazy, preposterous stories of a thousand years ago are, at least to me, much more real." When he reads, "Slowly, like a movie fadeout, the real world evaporates. I'm alone, inside the world of the story. My favorite feeling in the world." He renames himself after Franz Kafka because of his admiration for the writer's ability, in such works as "In a Penal Colony," to create not metaphors or allegories but a greater reality. In discussing *Kofu* (1908; *The Miner*, 1988) by Sōseki Natsume, however, Oshima suggests that literature provides metaphors onto which people can cling.

Nakata describes his intellectual emptiness as being "like a library without a single book." He dreams about being able to read, and Murakami constantly suggests that the dream world is as vital as reality.

Murakami has translated J. D. Salinger's *The Catcher in the Rye* (1951), and Kafka, especially early in the novel, resembles a less neurotic Holden Caulfield: "Maybe I should tell Oshima everything. I'm pretty sure he won't put me down, give me a lecture, or try to force some common sense on me." Both novels romanticize the anguish of adolescence. Before meeting Oshima, Miss Saeki, and Sakura, Kafka has had difficulties communicating with people, making his feelings known. Nakata has had the same problem, except with cats. One cat, Mimi, tells him "it's a breath of fresh air to be able to communicate with a sensible human being such as yourself." Hoshino struggles to understand Nakata but concludes that unusual people are more interesting than the ordinary.

On two occasions, to avoid discovery by the police, Kafka retreats to a remote mountain cabin owned by Oshima's brother. The solitude he finds there corresponds to that which Nakata has known all of his life, though Kafka's is much more reflective. This setting allows Murakami to engage in the descriptive writing at which he excels, and he turns the mysterious forest surrounding the cabin into another major character.

Oshima uses Franz Schubert's *Sonata in D Major* to make the point that sometimes imperfect art is more satisfying that perfection: "You discover something about that work that tugs at your heart—or maybe we should say the work discovers *you*." Hoshino is a pony-tailed slacker but becomes transformed by his experiences with Nakata and through hearing classical music in a coffee bar. Ludwig van Beethoven's *Archduke Trio* discovers and changes him. The ways in which art comforts and transforms is a major Murakami theme.

Many of Murakami's works have elements of science fiction and fantasy. Losing some of his mental abilities results in Nakata's possessing other powers he cannot understand, so he causes the skies to rain down sardines, mackerel, and leeches. Miss Saeki's "Kafka on the Shore" refers to fish raining from the sky, and she thinks she recognizes Nakata as a figure in the background of the painting. Nakata discovers he is looking for the entrance stone mentioned in her song. Hoshino is helped in finding the stone by a metaphysical concept taking the form of Colonel Sanders, the Kentucky Fried Chicken icon. Two soldiers who disappeared during World War II lead Kafka to a secret world within the woods. Hoshino battles a creature like something out of the 1979 film *Alien*. By placing such incidents within the context of everyday life, Murakami makes them seem both startling and melancholy, recalling the Magical Realism of Latin American fiction. In Murakami's universe, emotional truth outweighs literal truth: "It's hard to tell the difference between sea and sky. Between voyager and sea. Between reality and the workings of the heart."

All of Murakami's novels deal in some way with the power of the imagination. Kafka finds a note Oshima has written in a biography of Adolf Eichmann: "Our responsibility begins with the power to imagine." Alone in the remote cabin, Kafka discovers he is afraid of imagination, responsibilities, and dreams. Once Kafka understands the difference between letting things happen and trying to exert some control, he is on his way to discovering his identity. With its insights into the elusiveness and intangibility of life, *Kafka on the Shore* is about much more than its protagonists' personal quests.

Michael Adams

Review Sources

The Atlantic Monthly 295 (June, 2005): 124.
Booklist 101, no. 6 (November 15, 2004): 532.
Kirkus Reviews 72, no. 23 (December 1, 2004): 1110.
Library Journal 130, no. 1 (January, 2005): 99.
Los Angeles Times Book Review, January 23, 2005, p. 3.
The New Leader 88, no. 1 (January/February, 2005): 28-29.
New Statesman 134 (January 24, 2005): 52-53.
The New York Times 154 (January 31, 2005): E10.
The New York Times Book Review 154 (February 6, 2005): 1-10.
The New Yorker 80 (January 24, 2005): 91.
Newsweek 145, no. 4 (January 24, 2005): 67.
People 63, no. 2 (January 17, 2005): 55.
Publishers Weekly 251, no. 49 (December 6, 2004): 42.
The Times Literary Supplement, January 7, 2005, pp. 19-20.

KREMLIN RISING
Vladimir Putin's Russia and the End of Revolution

Authors: Peter Baker (1967-   ) and Susan Glasser
(1969-   )
Publisher: Scribner (New York). 453 pp. $27.50
Type of work: Current affairs
Time: 2000-2005
Locale: Russia

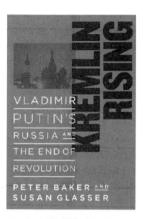

The reemergence of authoritarian rule in Russia discourages committed democrats even as the public accepts it

Principal personages:
VLADIMIR PUTIN, the president of Russia
starting on January 1, 2000
BORIS YELTSIN, the Russian leader most
responsible for ending Communist Party
rule
VLADIMIR GUSINSKY, a former theater director who in 1989 opened the
first independent bank, then developed a media empire
BORIS BEREZOVSKY, a Yeltsin adviser who became immensely wealthy
from investments in transportation, oil, and television
MIKHAIL KHODORKOVSKY, an oil entrepreneur who became the sixteenth
richest man in the world in 2000, then lost everything

As *Kremlin Rising* opens, Vladimir Putin is a minor KGB agent working in obscurity in Dresden, East Germany, where his only notable achievement is becoming fluent in German and English. This depiction is somewhat misleading; he had been an outstanding athlete, winning competitions in judo and dance; moreover, his grandfather had been Joseph Stalin's cook, a position of considerable responsibility for one of proletarian background. Lastly, Putin's dour mien and lack of spontaneity made many otherwise astute men underestimate his ambitions and abilities—and even think of him as a friend.

When the Soviet Republic began to crumble in 1989, Putin left the KGB to work for Anatoly Sobchak, the mayor of Leningrad (soon renamed St. Petersburg), a liberal reformer whom Putin had known from his student days. Under Sobchak, Putin was first responsible for press relations, then in 1994 became deputy mayor. In this office he began to master the skills necessary to advance in rough-and-tumble post-Soviet political cirlces. His experiences made him disdainful of democratic ideals and practices. In 1996, after Sobchak's defeat in the election, another liberal friend, Deputy Prime Minister Anatoly Chubais, recommended Putin to President Boris Yeltsin, for whom Putin became deputy chief-of-staff. Then, in July, 1998, he became head of the Federal Security Bureau (the successor to the KGB) and the Security Council. He made these into efficient organizations—in fact, almost the only organizations in

∽

Susan B. Glasser and Peter Baker were Moscow bureau chiefs for The Washington Post *from 2000 to 2004. A married team, they covered Russia and fourteen former Soviet republics. Both have also served in the newspaper's Washington, D.C., bureau.*

∽

Russia that were not mired in corruption and incompetence. In August, 1999, the increasingly erratic Boris Yeltsin named Putin prime minister, appreciating Putin's steadfast loyalty; on December 31, 1999, Yeltsin resigned, leaving Putin as acting president. In the election of March 26, 2000, Putin became president of Russia. It was perhaps the swiftest and most unexpected rise to power in modern history.

Putin moved immediately to consolidate his power. His most important step was to crush the independent press and television empires of Vladimir Gusinsky and Boris Berezovsky—who had assisted him previously—using intimidation, manipulation of the criminal justice system, and demagoguery. Both men fled the country quickly, Gusinsky to Israel, Berezovsky to Britain. In time, most of their assets were seized. Such was the retribution for their willingness to sacrifice the independence of the press to the reelection of Boris Yeltsin, who was not only ill or drunk through most of the late 1990's but who also ignored criminality and corruption in the government and in Russian society at large, including the excesses of the oligarchs who took advantage of the chaos to amass huge fortunes. As several of the newly rich media lords were Jews, Putin's takeover of their stations met with popular approval.

Because the press was now under Putin's control, when the Chechen war resumed later in 2000, he could restrict news coverage to his version of events. For example, when atrocities committed by Russian troops captured the world's attention, he could explain away the outrage as anti-Russian propaganda. The war, unfortunately, instead of lasting a few weeks, as Putin had predicted, dragged on, with no signs of either victory or a peace settlement. The public, nevertheless, came to see in Putin the strong leader that Russians have long venerated. Whether Ivan the Great or Ivan the Terrible, Peter the Great or Joseph Stalin, such a man could show the Chechens and the world that Russia is still a great power.

The terrorist attacks in the United States on September 11, 2001, provided an opportunity for Putin to deflect world attention from the war in Chechnya. By phoning George Bush to offer Russian support (and as the first foreign leader to do so), Putin changed the Chechan War into a part of the war on terror. There was some truth to this spin, but there was also Putin's manipulation of the American president's naïve desire to believe that a change had taken place in the relationship between Russia and the United States. To the contrary, anti-American feelings and disgust with Russia's experiments in democracy and capitalism were spreading widely. Such attitudes had never vanished in the KGB circles from which Putin was drawing more and more government officials.

Putin replaced elected governors with officials of his own choosing. This, Putin believed, was the most effective way to curb both the oligarchs and the Communist Party; it would also bring stability to a nation in chaos. Stability was Putin's justification for almost everything.

However, there were limits to his authority. Efforts to reform the army—to end the brutal treatment of recruits and to provide better training—failed miserably. Russian generals could only think in terms of World War III—that is, war against the United States. Their record in Chechnya boasted few successes, but they continued employing the same strategies as before; and, as before, they were constantly being caught flat-footed by daring, if self-defeating, Chechen terrorist tactics.

In 2003, armed Chechens took control of a popular Moscow theater, holding nine hundred people hostage and warning that unless Russian troops pulled out of Chechnya, the terrorists would blow up the building and kill everyone in it. A rescue operation was successful, to an extent, but such was the Russian habit of secrecy that doctors were not told what type of gas had been used on the hostages, nor were enough medical personnel summoned. More than one hundred victims died unnecessarily. Putin, unhappy with the press reports, moved to take over the remaining independent television stations.

The loss of lives in the hostage rescue operation was small compared to the number of people suffering every day from acquired immunodeficiency syndrome (AIDS), tuberculosis, and the effects of overindulgence in alcohol, tobacco, and drugs, the degradation of the environment, and an inadequate health care system. Russia was the only advanced country in the world to see a decline in life expectancy, and the birth rate fell well below the replacement level. Putin, apparently believing that only a strong government could tackle such problems, made these low priority. Perhaps, once power was consolidated, he would do something.

Putin used the public's desire for strong and stable government to manipulate the election process in 2003, reducing the Communist Party's share of the vote to 13 percent. The ultra-nationalist party of Vladimir Zhirinovsky's share grew to 12 percent, while the democratic parties' votes almost vanished. The election was, as foreign observers noted, "free but not fair." Not only was Putin's United Russia almost the only party to receive attention from the media, but it also manipulated the vote counting—sometimes downward, to avoid the election's appearing to be a farce. United Russia controlled two-thirds of the seats in the Duma, thereby preventing the Communists from troubling the government as they had done through the Yeltsin years.

Not every indicator was negative. The flat tax ended widespread tax evasion, and Russia became the world's second largest exporter of oil. Putin ignored public opinion concerning the American invasion of Iraq, sacrificing one of Russia's main trading partners after Saddam Hussein ignored his advice to resign from office.

Putin had other matters with which to contend, matters that required American friendship. He moved against the last oligarch from the Yeltsin period, Mikhail Khodorkovsky, a business genius who had taken a failing state oil concern and made it into a major producer of petroleum at a moment when oil prices were skyrocketing. Khodorkovsky's money made him a major player in Russian politics—and Putin owed much to him in the first election campaign. However, when Khodorkovsky began to support democratic parties in 2003, his friends and aides warned him that he was courting disaster. Khodorkovsky ignored them, saying that someone had to step forward eventually, because without democratic procedures and the rule of law, they would all lose everything. His was either a dire mistake or that moment in which a courageous man chooses between self-preservation and moral behavior—in this case, to defend the long-term interests of his nation. Khodorkovsky was arrested, subjected to a highly arbitrary and unfair trial for tax evasion, then stripped of his companies by tactics very similar to those he was on trial for having used to obtain them. He remains in prison, a willing example of civil courage.

The elections of 2004 secured the United Russia Party's hold on power. Putin then introduced reform measures long advocated by democrats: eliminating popular subsidies, investigating police corruption, introducing trial by jury, reducing crime and extortion. He also pursued his few remaining political opponents. The process resembled nothing as much as a process of putting a new privileged class in the place of the old.

Of course, there is much precedent in Russian history for this happening. It did not begin with Vladimir Ilich Lenin, much less with Putin. Not surprisingly, Putin became deeply interested in the way that history was being taught. After 1991 there had been a massive rewriting of the school texts, but in the Yeltsin years the public became so disillusioned with the shortcomings of Russian democracy and capitalism that people began to look back favorably even on the years under Stalin. Thousands had been tortured and murdered then, in Siberia or before firing squads, but the average citizen heard little about it. At a time when the public was being told of starvation in Europe and America, Russians had guaranteed jobs, medical care, and enough to eat. The Soviet Union was powerful and respected.

As the public moved toward believing that Russia needed a strong leader, Putin encouraged such thinking. Students were already saying, "Lenin Was Right After All" and "Communism is the better system for Russia." There was an inevitable confrontation between Putin's desire to make Russians feel good about themselves and their country and those educators who wrote that Stalin was a tyrant and that communism had been an economic and moral failure. Today the textbooks are being rewritten to emphasize patriotic and unifying themes, concepts inherent in the name of Putin's party, United Russia.

By 2005, ordinary Russians had lost interest in politics. They saw the process as little more than a corrupt struggle between unappealing gangs. If even the most powerful players in Russia could be easily destroyed, what chance was there for the average citizen? The most basic problems remained unchanged and were considered perhaps unchangeable—disease, drugs, divorce, the declining life-expectancy rate, the low birthrate, environmental degradation, and, above all, the war in Chechyna—which was brought home in the summer of 2004 when Chechen rebels seized a school in Beslan and hundreds died. Yet, slowly life was getting better in many ways. Perhaps Putin was not a totalitarian but merely an authoritarian—that is, a ruler who would allow common people to attend church, to read what they wanted, to start their own businesses, maybe even to say quietly what they thought, so long as they did not aspire to change the government or challenge the clique that ran it.

Then, there is that nagging doubt: Is Putin merely a KGB colonel in a modern suit? If so, when will he throw off the disguise?

William L. Urban

Review Sources

Booklist 101, no. 21 (July 1, 2005): 1892.
Business Week, July 11, 2005, p. 92.
Foreign Affairs 84, no. 5 (September/October, 2005): 181-183.
The New York Times 154 (July 1, 2005): E39.
The New York Times Book Review 154 (July 17, 2005): 26.
The Philadelphia Inquirer, July 17, 2005, H14.
The Wall Street Journal 245, no. 115 (June 14, 2005): D8.

LAST CALL FOR BLACKFORD OAKES

Author: William F. Buckley, Jr. (1925-   )
Publisher: Harcourt (Orlando, Fla.). 349 pp. $26.00
Type of work: Novel
Time: 1986-1987
Locale: Washington, D.C., Moscow, Leningrad, and Vienna

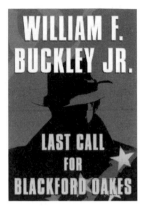

In the eleventh and final novel of Buckley's Blackford Oakes Cold War spy series, old hatreds end new loves as Oakes matches wits with his old nemesis, master spy Kim Philby, in a final deadly game

Principal characters:

BLACKFORD OAKES, a charming, semi-retired Cold War master spy

HAROLD ADRIAN RUSSELL (KIM) PHILBY, also known as ANDREI FYODOROVICH MARTINS, historically the most notorious and perhaps the highest ranking defector to the Soviet Union, a senior officer in the British Secret Service (SIS) and SIS liaison with the Central Intelligence Agency (CIA) and Federal Bureau of Investigation (FBI), an unapologetic traitor

GUS WINDELS, a naturalized Ukranian Sovietologist, CIA agent undercover in Moscow, Oakes's special ops partner, past and present

URSINA CHADINOV, a urologist and Moscow State University professor, Oakes's fiancé

TONY OAKES, Blackford's son by his beloved and not-long-deceased wife, Sally Partridge, and through her, heir to an established business in Mexico

DR. VLADIMIR "VOLODYA" SPIRIDONOVICH KIROV, a senior professor of urology at Moscow State University, Ursina's mentor, and friend to both Ursina and Titov

RUFINA IVANOVNA PAKHOV, Ursina's apartment-mate and friend

DR. LINDBERGH "LINBECK" VISSARIONOVICH TITOV, a new-style Russian scientist

NIKOLAI DMITRIEV, IVAN PLETNEV, and GENERAL LEONID BARANOV, three suspected anti-Gorbachev conspirators

Last Call for Blackford Oakes is the final book in a Cold War spy series begun in 1975 as a response to the conspiracy premises of the film *Three Days of the Condor* (1975). William F. Buckley, Jr., wanted the lines between good and bad clearly drawn to confirm that the Central Intelligence Agency (CIA) acted on the side of right for good ends against an unquestionably amoral empire, Stalinist and Soviet tyranny. Thus, where John le Carré, Len Deighton, Graham Greene, and other writers of Cold War conflicts delineate the murky morality of all modern spy organizations, East and West, with the individual an expendable pawn in a larger, amoral game, Buckley sticks to an older tradition of Western honor, loyalty, and patriotism.

In the first book in the series, the handsome, debonair Blackford Oakes, a bright and witty Yale graduate and daring former fighter pilot, saves the queen of England. In other volumes, he travels to Cold War hot spots such as Havana, East Germany, and the Gulf of Tonkin; flies a U-2 plane over Soviet territory; and restores broken church windows. While Oakes foils the plans of Fidel Castro during the Cuban Missile Crisis or plugs a security leak in the Eisenhower administration (turning the tables on the KGB in *Marco Polo, If You Can*, 1982), Buckley comments on national and international politics, always with a deeply conservative Republican twist.

As the last in the series, *Last Call for Blackford Oakes* echoes back to Oakes's past exploits and past encounters, especially in *High Jinx* (1986) where the 1950's exposure of Cambridge spies Sir Anthony Blunt, Guy Burgess, Donald Maclean, and Kim Philby sets the stage for Oakes's present adventure. It also continues the tradition of being more concerned with ideologi-

Yale University alumnus William F. Buckley, Jr., has been the moral voice of conservatism since he published God and Man at Yale *(1951). He has founded* The National Review, *hosted the long-running television program* Firing Line, *written more than forty books (including thirteen novels), and received numerous awards, including thirty-five honorary degrees and the Presidential Medal of Freedom (1991).*

cal differences and the debate of ideas than with high adventure. Thus, dinner conversations and friendly cocktail party exchanges loom large as speakers consider the future of perestroika and glasnost.

Whether he is describing sailing, a secret high-tech telescope, or the intricate movements of a Bach concerto, author Buckley, who is himself a concert harpsichordist, a transatlantic sailor, a former CIA agent, and a political pundit, employs urbane diction that is both precise and erudite, reflecting the clarity of a careful technician but also the depth of education and style of a Yale graduate who continues to revel in the arts. The shift in point of view as a means to provide a well-rounded debate grows out of his experience on television's *Firing Line*. His characters, in the main, are an elite set, well educated, financially comfortable, at home in the drawing room, and quite capable—although sometimes ruthlessly so.

The novel is broken into three books. The longest, book 1 (chapters 1-28), establishes the background situation, finds Oakes investigating briefly in Moscow, and then switches focus to his autumn romance (he is seventy, she forty) and subsequent engagement to Dr. Ursina Chadinov, a beautiful and successful Russian urologist, despite looming political repercussions. Having foiled a 1986 plot on Mikhail Gorbachev's life in *A Very Private Plot* (1993), Oakes seeks President Ronald Reagan's permission to investigate rumors of a second such plot, as Reagan can override the stricture that prevents former CIA section heads from entering the foreign territory whose espionage security secrets they hold. His intelligence feedback comes from Gus Windels, the Ukrainian-born, Iowa-raised CIA operative who in 1986 had posed as his son as they traveled together in Russia.

In fact, it is Windels, not Oakes, who does most of the spying and detecting, tracking the plotters through his informant Galina, a prostitute who uses her unique position to exchange underground information between both sides. Through his meetings with Galina, Windels learns that the plot is being masterminded by Nikolai Dmitriev and General Leonid Baranov, both snubbed for government positions, and Ivan Pletnev, whose brother Viktor was killed during interrogations for his involvement in the previous assassination plot. Though all the pieces are now in place for a gripping spy adventure, the conspiracy actually fizzles out quickly; Dmitriev disappears, most likely to Lubyanka prison, Baranov is demoted and sent abroad, and Pletnev backs out in fear.

With the conspiracy out of the way and Oakes still in Moscow, the narrative turns to his social life. Still attractive, witty, and charming, Oakes moves easily in international circles. Oakes's meeting and flirtations with Ursina soon lead to a passionate affair and her eventual pregnancy. Then, at a dinner party celebrating the engagement of Ursina's roommate, Rufina, Oakes discovers that the groom-to-be, "Andrei Martins," is none other than the infamous Soviet master spy Kim Philby. Book 1 ends with Ursina under heavy suspicion after she is pulled from the roster of the upcoming International Peace Forum for writing an incendiary, anticommunist speech. Though inspired by Oakes, she has kept this tract hidden from him.

Book 2 (chapters 29-38) begins with Buckley's political counterpart, fellow Catholic and leftist critic of American policy Graham Greene, advising Kim Philby to check out Ursula's new American lover. Philby soon discovers Oakes's true identity and is infuriated at his insolent intrusion on Philby's home territory and his seduction of a loyal communist mind. Philby confers regularly with Colonel Mikhail Bykov of the KGB, and the two mull over options to eliminate Ursina without risking bad publicity. The solution arrives when Philby learns from Rufina that Ursina suffers complications with her pregnancy and requires immediate surgery. Seizing this opportunity, Bykov and Philby, acting in the mind-set that they are protecting the reputation of an innocent Russian and punishing an arrogant American manipulator, enlist the aid of Dr. Kirill Olegyevich Shumberg, a renowned obstetrician and surgeon who has worked secretly for the KGB in the past. Shumberg takes over Ursina's operation at the last moment and ensures she never recovers.

Book 3 (chapters 39-64) traces the devastating psychological effect Ursina's death has on Oakes, who retreats from life and drowns his sorrows in reclusion and alcohol until his son Tony and gloating, taunting letters from a vengeful Philby snap him out of his malaise and drive him to a revenge only he can take. Meanwhile, Dr. Vladimir Kirov, Ursina's colleague and mentor, and his friend, Dr. Lindbergh Titov, one of the top Soviet scientists, begin to suspect foul play in her death. Titov confronts Shumberg, who has conveniently had Ursina cremated before an autopsy could be performed and refuses to allow Titov access to any of her medical records. Finally fed up with the bureaucratic restrictions on accessing information, Titov leaves for Vienna, arranging for his wife Nina and son Aleksei to join him later. However, the Russians capture Nina and Aleksei en route to their checkpoint in Helsinki, and Titov demands negotiations arbitrated by the Austrian government with two delegates present from each side.

Oakes and Windels represent the American side, suggesting that Titov defect to the West. Philby and Kirov represent the Russians. Kirov, while disgusted with the injustices Titov has suffered, nonetheless asks his friend to return to his homeland, and Philby threatens that his wife and son will not be released unless he does so. Oakes convinces Titov to stand his ground, and the Russians do indeed crack under the pressure of appearing as tyrants to the rest of the world. After the Titovs' safe passage is ensured, Oakes tells Gus that he has resigned from the CIA and plans to murder Philby and flee. Oakes shoots Philby in the throat the following day and is immediately shot down himself by a Soviet guard. The novel ends with Gus peering over the corpse of his partner and Kirov whispering to Philby, "I hope he has killed you."

The real-life Philby died in 1988 at age seventy-one; as his title telegraphs, Buckley makes that death a vital part of his book. The ending is abrupt, but it signals the end of an age and of a genre. With the Cold War over, there is no longer a place for master spies. Not all has changed in the former Soviet Union, but Buckley captures the Russians on the verge of transformation, with international negotiations far more important to their national image than ever before. Lindbergh Titov and Ursina Chadinov represent the good that Russia offers the West, the hope is for a more peaceful, cooperative future in which the old guard must yield to modern realities and international pressures.

Buckley fuses historical realities with speculative fiction as to what might have been, including, among others, such real personalities as former CIA director Richard Helms, Canadian prime minister Pierre Trudeau, Mexican novelist Carlos Fuentes, American actors Kris Kristofferson and Gregory Peck, American authors Norman Mailer and Gore Vidal, Russian scientist Dr. Andrei Sakharov (photographed with Dr. Edward Teller), and British novelist Graham Greene. Greene, whose role is pivotal, served alongside Philby during World War II, wrote the forward to Philby's autobiography, *My Silent War* (1968), and reputedly depicted Philby as the Harry Lime character in *The Third Man* (1949). Ronald Reagan reads Greene's spy spoof *Our Man in Havana* (1958) with pleasure. Such real-world connections allow Buckley to suggest that the fascination of Western liberals with Soviet rhetoric was misplaced and that Buckley's fictive version of events is a plausible alternative version of behind-the-scenes diplomacy. The novel, in fact, builds in part on Rufina Philby's memoirs, *The Private Life of Kim Philby: The Moscow Years* (2004).

Scott Fremin and Gina Macdonald

Review Sources

Booklist 101, no. 14 (March 15, 2005): 1246.
Books & Culture 11 (January/February, 2005): 30.
Kirkus Reviews 73, no. 6 (March 15, 2005): 302.
National Review 57, no. 9 (May 23, 2005): 48-49.
The New York Times Book Review 154 (July 17, 2005): 10.
Publishers Weekly 252, no. 14 (April 4, 2005): 42.

LAST NIGHT

Author: James Salter (1925-   )
Publisher: Alfred A. Knopf (New York). 132 pp. $20.00
Type of work: Short fiction
Time: Around 2003
Locale: Arlington, Virginia; Hollywood, California;
Long Island, New York, and New York City

*These ten stories of modern American life focus upon
the intense, flawed inner lives of the characters*

    Principal characters:
        PHILIP ARDET, a writer for a business publi-
          cation
        ARDIS, a suburban Long Island housewife
        JANE, a young single woman ill with cancer
        BRIAN WOODRA, a young man in love with his father-in-law's mistress
        ARTHUR, a middle-aged New York stockbroker who reencounters an old
          love
        CHRIS HOLLIS, a married bookseller who is accosted by a former lover
        NEWELL, a West Point graduate who sacrifices his Army career for a
          wife who deserts him
        WALTER SUCH, a translator who participates in his wife's suicide

The short story is perhaps the most peculiarly American of all the literary forms, one that seemingly sprang into existence not long after the United States' inception. Most literary historians credit Edgar Allan Poe with creation of the form in the 1840's, and it proved to be the ideal vehicle for miniaturists who wished to relate a brief tale with a limited number of characters for the growing periodical market. Such is the flexibility of the form that it can accommodate works as diverse as Poe's tales of horror or the ironic humor of O. Henry. A common denominator in most short fiction, both past and present, is that it is primarily an entertainment medium for the masses. In the limited space of a few pages, a writer may tease with humor and irony, pummel the reader with the violence of his or her characters, or gently reach a moment of in-sight—but the writer's chief goal is to leave the reader wanting more. This is some-what problematic in the career of James Salter, an author who seems to be far more dedicated to the quality of his art than in increasing his readership and thus his in-come. While someone such as Richard Ford will delight his readers with his tales of infidelity in upper-middle-class America, Salter deals with the same theme and the same milieu but in more muted tones. This is evident in *Last Night*, a brief compila-tion of ten stories, many of which were previously published in magazines.

    The opening work in the collection, "Comet," is a representative example of Salter's skill in character development and use of language. The story concerns Philip and Adele Ardet, middle-aged survivors of previous relationships who have appar-

∾

James Salter's published work includes the memoirs Burning the Days *(1997) and* Gods of Tin *(2004), as well as such novels as* A Sport and a Pastime *(1967),* Light Years *(1975), and* Solo Faces *(1979). He won the PEN/Faulkner Award for* Dusk, and Other Stories *(1988).*

∾

ently found happiness in their marriage to each other. Any good storyteller can give a satisfactory account of a relationship that is destined for dissolution, and in a short story the source of the conflict is often an act of infidelity. Salter, on the other hand, takes a far more subtle approach, using Adele's drunken revelation of her husband's affair in his first marriage as the turning point in the story. Philip's growing disenchantment is accentuated and anticipated by the seasonal imagery, where the commencement of their marriage on a June day is followed by Adele's outburst at an autumn dinner party. Though executed with great subtlety, Salter's message is clear: The Ardets' marriage—following the same cycle as their prior relationships—is strained and probably destined to end.

Such is Salter's skill that even the title suggests the eventual outcome of their marriage. The comet that appears on the evening of the fateful dinner party is a kind of heavenly flare, one that will blaze in its close approach to the sun and then quickly fade from view. On a deeper level, the comet—whose cyclical appearance mirrors that of the seasons—symbolizes the flash and expiration of the Ardets' once sexually charged relationship. What makes this tale of disenchantment so absorbing is Salter's efficacious use of language, something that has endeared him to his fellow authors as a kind of writer's writer. Rather than simply state that Philip loved his wife on their wedding day, Salter declares: "He could have licked her palms like a calf does salt." This superb simile suggests that Philip's desire for his wife is mere animal appetite, one that will cease once it has been satisfied.

One of the recurring themes in Salter's fiction is sexual longing, especially the kind of desire that takes its own perverse course, complicating his characters' lives as surely as it enriches his fiction. This compulsion can range from Walter Such's blatant unfaithfulness to his dying wife in the title story, "Last Night," to the fantasies of Ardis, the troubled young wife in "My Lord You." Michael Brennen, the object of Ardis's weirdly deflected desires, is a poet whose sole appearance in the story consists of a drunken pass at Ardis at a dinner party. Although she is initially offended by his advances, she is clearly fascinated by this man and spends the rest of the story trying to meet him again.

Why would this attractive, upper-middle-class Long Island wife risk her comfortable existence for a man who pawed her breasts without a trace of compunction? As in "Comet," Salter's use of language provides a clue to Ardis's behavior. Unlike the respectable Ardis, Brennan's life as a poet enables him freely to satiate his animal appetites with impunity. It is an aspect of human behavior that Sigmund Freud characterized as the id: untrammeled desire. Indeed, it is said of Brennan that "the irrational flickered from him." Despite the fact that Brennan's attentions were unwelcome, this disturbing experience sends shock waves through Ardis's life, prompting her to read his verse and attempt to encounter him again.

What makes this and the other tales so convincing is the fact that Salter adheres to his characters' emotional integrity, even as their actions threaten to shatter their lives. Salter is no moralist. If his characters receive any sort of comeuppance, it is the result of their own flawed natures. Thus, one can only marvel at the delicious irony of Ardis's stalking of the alcoholic poet, even as one pities her self-destructive behavior. Salter's skill is also evident in that Brennan's starving dog, who follows her with the same determination with which she pursues Brennan, perfectly captures the essence of her misplaced longing. Again, as in the case of Philip Ardet, this is an instance where the author quite purposefully juxtaposes human and animal behavior. With one small push this approach could easily transform the tale into a satire in the manner of Jonathan Swift. To his credit, however, Salter wisely restrains himself and allows his characters' actions to speak for themselves.

If many of Salter's characters fail to lead their lives with a suitable degree of restraint, his stories are no less affecting when his characters needlessly repress their feelings, something that is poignantly evident in "Such Fun." Jane, the reticent central character in the tale, forms an effective contrast to the loquacious Kathrin, who fearlessly boasts of her sexual exploits and failed marriage. Given what has transpired in the preceding tales in *Last Night*, one would expect that Kathrin and her impending divorce would be the focus of the story. Indeed, much space is devoted to her adventures, both past and present. However, what drives the story toward its climax is Jane's shattering revelation of her terminal illness to a taxi driver, something she could not bring herself to confide to her closest friends. Obviously, it would have been more therapeutic for Jane to have unburdened herself to her friends. Had Salter adopted this more straightforward course, as many other writers would do, the unfortunate result would be pure bathos. Ironically, it is through artistic restraint, what remains unsaid, that the author achieves a more affecting ending. Salter is one of the few writers talented enough to explore a well-worn theme with such fresh insights.

Given the fact that he invariably deals with comfortable middle-class people whose lives are compromised by infidelity, it is astonishing how remarkably original these stories strike the reader. This even proves to be true in a tale such as "Platinum," where Brian Woodra's affair develops into an obsession that jeopardizes his marriage. Again, this is achieved, in part, by the high quality of the writing. When Brian begins his affair with Pamela, Salter appropriately notes that "he felt a thrilling, natural complicity." That is, Brian is aware that his desire is largely fed by the fact that he is violating his marriage vows. It is what follows, though, that captures the nature of this feckless character: "His heart filled with excitement, like a sail." On one level one can read this as a direct description by the author of what Brian is experiencing; however, what makes the simile so effective is that it is just the sort of thing that Brian himself would probably say to Pamela. This is language that is so apt that it transcends mere description and actually embodies the character.

Salter's sophisticated use of language is also evident when his writing is free of tropes, such as his characterization of Brian's wife, Sally. On her wedding day, the text relates, she had "a lovely face with only the barest hint of smallness behind it and you instantly saw the expense of her upbringing." What makes this particular moment so effective is the fact that Salter simultaneously achieves two goals. He informs the reader of the elevated nature of Sally's social status and then supplies the telling detail that provides the key to her character. By indicating the "smallness" that lies behind Sally's face, Salter reveals a crucial character trait, one that would prove to be Brian's undoing if his affair were to come to light. This underscores the inherent difficulty in writing good short fiction. While a novelist may devote hundreds of pages of text to a character's physical appearance and motives, the short-story writer is compelled to achieve the same task in much less space. Given the density and quality of Salter's writing, it is clear that he consistently produces prose that rivals poetry in its depth.

Perhaps the most lasting impression of Salter's writing—whether it be his novels or his short fiction—is its elegiac tone, a quality that is enhanced by his deft use of memory. This is especially true of "Palm Court," where a New York stockbroker named Arthur is about to be reunited with a woman he passionately loved long ago. A surprise phone call from Noreen triggers Arthur's memories of their three-year relationship, which ended long ago when she married someone else. Interestingly, Salter devotes most of the text to Arthur's replaying of their past relationship—a strategy suggesting that Arthur's memory of their relationship is ultimately more satisfying than the thing itself. Inexplicably, the story reveals that Arthur let slip an opportunity to wed Noreen in the past, and he decides not to renew the relationship after her divorce.

Why would Salter write a story that denies the main character the ultimate happiness he seems to desire? There are no simple answers in this or any of the other tales. In Arthur's case, it is probably because this middle-aged man has worked for the same employer and lived in the same apartment for many years and could not endure the thought of accommodating himself to another person's life—in other words, change. This may not be the sort of story that endears itself to readers seeking a more upbeat ending, such as a flash of insight by Arthur regarding his own motives. Again, Salter proves himself to be a better and more emotionally realistic writer by mirroring the untidiness of life as it is lived. It is for this reason that one can applaud both his talent and his artistic integrity.

Cliff Prewencki

Review Sources

Booklist 101, no. 13 (March 1, 2005): 1142.
Kirkus Reviews 73, no. 4 (February 15, 2005): 195.
The New Leader 88, no. 2 (March/April, 2005): 31-32.
The New York Review of Books 52, no. 12 (July 14, 2005): 30-33.
The New York Times Book Review 154 (June 12, 2005): 13.
Publishers Weekly 252, no. 7 (February 14, 2005): 51.

THE LAST TITAN
A Life of Theodore Dreiser

Author: Jerome Loving (1941-   )
Publisher: University of California Press (Berkeley). Illustrated. 480 pp. $35.00
Type of work: Literary biography
Time: 1871-1945
Locale: Terre Haute, Indiana; St. Louis, Missouri; New York City; Hollywood

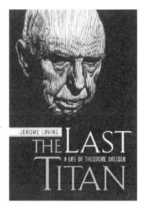

This biographical study of Dreiser traces the sources of many of his plots and demonstrates how he incorporated details from his early life into much of his fiction

Principal personages:
THEODORE DREISER, a novelist
JOHN PAUL DREISER, his father
SARAH SCHANAB DREISER, his mother
PAUL DRESSER, his brother, a musician and composer
SARA OSBORNE DREISER, his first wife
FRANK NORRIS, a fellow American naturalistic novelist

Although Theodore Dreiser has fallen out of favor among many recent literary critics, he certainly has not been ignored. Since the year 2000, five new books about him and his work have been published, and more than a score of full-length critical studies and editions of his work have appeared in print since 1965. The most comprehensive of these, Richard R. Lingeman's two-volume study *Theodore Dreiser* (1986, 1990), is a thorough-going literary biography. In *The Last Titan*, Jerome Loving provides readers with considerable detail about Dreiser's sources for much of his writing, making his book uniquely helpful to Dreiser scholars.

Dreiser did not gain renown as a stylist. His writing style was largely influenced by his work as a journalist in St. Louis early in his career. His greatest contribution to American literature is in his breaking away from the Victorian constraints reflected in the work of many of his predecessors, the so-called Brahmins of American literature. Writers who violated Victorian constraints often were shunned.

Realistic and naturalistic authors such as Stephen Crane and Dreiser paid dearly for their break from Victorian literary standards. Crane's *Maggie: A Girl of the Streets* (1893) so shocked the sensibilities of genteel readers that it was viewed as scandalous and was widely banned. Although Dreiser's first novel, *Sister Carrie*, published seven years after *Maggie*, is often pointed to as a quintessential work of American naturalism, its publication in 1900 brought more acrimony than praise upon its author, even though it was not widely read at that time. Dreiser's Roman Catholic relatives considered the book an embarrassment.

~

Jerome Loving, professor of English at Texas A&M University, is the author of Walt Whitman's Champion: William Douglas O'Connor *(1978),* The Emerson-Whitman Connection *(1982),* Emily Dickinson: The Poet on the Second Story *(1986),* Lost in the Customhouse: Authorship in the American Renaissance *(1993), and* Walt Whitman: The Song of Himself *(1999).*

~

Loving devotes considerable attention to Dreiser's days as a newspaper reporter in St. Louis as well as to details about his childhood in a huge family of twelve children. Theodore was the second youngest. By the time he was born—in fact, long before his birth—Theodore's mother was completely worn out from the demands of her successive confinements and of motherhood. The young Dreiser often felt neglected, and throughout his life he longed for motherly love, which he found in, among others, his two wives and Elaine Hyman, an actress who used the stage name of Kirah Markham and was his mistress for several years. Loving also intimates that Dreiser suffered from bipolar disorder but does not explore this possibility in detail.

Dreiser used some of his siblings as prototypes for characters in his writing. The most notable of these is his sister Emma, who served as a model for Carrie Meeber in *Sister Carrie*. Loving, like most other Dreiser scholars, demonstrates that because the author's writing style was essentially journalistic, some critics ranked it as infraliterary.

Loving also carefully shows correspondences between events in Dreiser's life and incidents in his novels. One of the more telling of these incidents is an account of a trip that Dreiser, working for the St. Louis *Republic*, took in 1893 to accompany twenty outstanding young Missouri schoolteachers to the Chicago World's Fair, all at the newspaper's expense. On this trip, Dreiser first met Sara Osborne White, whom he married five years later. The account of how Charles Drouet first met Carrie Meeber on a train trip is remarkably like Dreiser's account of this trip he made to shepherd a bevy of young, female teachers around the exposition as a reward for their excellence in teaching.

Loving shines in his detailed presentation of the convoluted saga about how the manuscript of *Sister Carrie*, presented to the Doubleday and Page publishing house in April, 1900, finally and after considerable controversy, made it into print in November, 1900. When Doubleday and Page first received the manuscript, copies were distributed to Frank Norris, Hugh Lanier, and Dreiser's close friend Arthur Henry, whose *A Princess of Arcady* (1900) was already under contract to the publisher and scheduled for autumn release.

Dreiser had established a bond with Norris after reacting enthusiastically to Norris's naturalistic novel *McTeague* (1899). The three readers of *Sister Carrie* all recommended that Doubleday and Page publish the novel, and by early summer, 1900, Dreiser had received assurances that the novel would soon be in print. Norris was a particular champion of the book. As the readers' reviews came in, Frank Doubleday, head of the publishing house, was scheduled to leave on an extended trip to Europe with his wife, Neltje, an active feminist. Dreiser subsequently signed a contract which assured publication and established the royalty arrangements.

On Doubleday's return from Europe, however, matters took an ominous turn: Doubleday's wife had read the manuscript and railed against it, presumably because it offended her feminist sensibilities. Doubleday, reacting to his wife's condemnation of the novel, now urged Dreiser to release Doubleday and Page from the contract he had signed, promised to help place the novel with another publisher, and committed his company to publishing Dreiser's next novel.

By this time, however, word was out that Dreiser's first novel was scheduled for publication. Dreiser refused to withdraw from his contract, claiming that a change in the plans for publication would do irreparable damage to his reputation. Finally, on the advice of counsel, Doubleday reluctantly honored the contract and went forward with the publication of *Sister Carrie* but made no concerted effort to promote the book or, indeed, any of the books on its fall list, including Arthur Henry's.

Doubleday and Page obviously considered *Sister Carrie*, which was bound in an unattractive red cover, a sort of orphan publication. It had a press run of a mere 1,008 copies, of which 558 were bound. Norris, now director of publicity at Doubleday and Page, did what he could to promote *Sister Carrie*, sending out 127 review copies. However, no major intellectual or literary journals reviewed the book, although there were a number of newspaper reviews.

Loving explodes the myth that the newspaper reviews were largely negative, stating that "of the handful [of newspaper reviews] that the first edition received between November 20, 1900 and March 9, 1901—fewer than thirty—more than a few hinted that despite the book's colloquial language and seamy plot, it was undeniably a rare example of literary genius." The fact remains, nevertheless, that the public did not clamor to read *Sister Carrie*.

J. F. Taylor, a publisher who had bought the plates of *Sister Carrie* from Doubleday for five hundred dollars, placed Dreiser on a hundred-dollar-a-month retainer in November, 1901, with the understanding that he would finish his new novel, *The Transgressor*, and that if it sold well, Taylor would then publish a new edition of *Sister Carrie*. Dreiser, however, was unable to live up to the conditions of this contract and finally withdrew from it.

It is not surprising, therefore, that in 1903, Dreiser, living outside Philadelphia, was so destitute that he contemplated suicide. His wife, Sara, nicknamed "Jug," had returned to her parents' home in Missouri. Having drifted from place to place—Virginia, West Virginia, Missouri—Dreiser now moved to New York City and, living on pennies a day, finally found employment on a railroad maintenance crew.

Although *Sister Carrie* enjoyed considerable success in Britain, American publishers shied away from Dreiser and his writing in the early years of the twentieth century, viewing his naturalistic presentation of life as too depressing and hopeless. With the publication of *Jennie Gerhardt* in 1911, Dreiser produced his last female leading character. Although his novels that focus on women are neither profane nor sexually explicit, he turned from writing about women of questionable reputation by the end of the century's first decade and began to write about American enterprises in such novels as *The Financier* in 1912 and *The Titan* in 1914, both parts of a trilogy. The last volume of this trilogy, *The Stoic*, was not published until 1947, two years after Dreiser's death. His fifth novel, *The "Genius,"* was published in 1915.

What Walt Whitman had done for poetry, Dreiser succeeded in doing for prose. He viewed people as they really were and demonstrated how little actual control they have over their destinies, which are constantly being subjected to the various determinants that direct their lives. Much of his thinking was shaped by his early exposure to Herbert Spencer's *First Principles* (1862), a book that the young Dreiser devoured; by his exposure to Charles Darwin's theories of evolution; and by Sigmund Freud's theories regarding the sexual makeup of humans.

Dreiser felt the losses in his life very keenly. The death of his mother in 1890 almost undid him. When his ever-dependable brother Paul Dresser and his father died within a short time of each other, Dreiser was again devastated. He had a number of close friends, but his relationships were sufficiently intense that they often collapsed utterly. He had an early falling out with Arthur Henry, who was not only a friend but a resident for some time in the home of Dreiser and his wife. Henry Mencken came into Dreiser's life at a time when the author very much needed a friend. Their association, which continued for several years, waned following a quarrel they had in 1925, shortly before *An American Tragedy* was published.

In one of Dreiser's public encounters with Sinclair Lewis, who in 1931 became the first American Nobel laureate in literature, Dreiser slapped Lewis in the face for accusing him of plagiarism. He was also known to have thrown a cup of coffee in the face of publisher Horace Liveright. Despite his fondness and frequent dependence upon his brother Paul, Dreiser was jealous of Paul's success as a composer. Loving presents extremely interesting details about Dreiser's often fractured personal relationships. Like many creative people, Dreiser harbored within him demons which had a devastating effect on such relationships.

Besides *Sister Carrie*, which reflects much of the social Darwinism that had infused the writing of Honoré de Balzac and Émile Zola in France during the late eighteenth century, Dreiser's most lasting contribution to American literature was in another of his naturalistic novels, *An American Tragedy* (1925), which remains a classic. The book was also Dreiser's greatest commercial success. It was widely read and discussed and was made into a film. The work was the major justification for Dreiser's being nominated for a Nobel Prize in Literature. His writing was still controversial enough that the Nobel Committee derailed this bid for him to receive this highest of all literary honors, but the nomination alone was a singular acknowledgment of his international recognition.

R. Baird Shuman

Review Sources

Kirkus Reviews 72, no. 24 (December 15, 2004): 1186.
Library Journal 130, no. 2 (February 1, 2005): 80.
Publishers Weekly 252, no. 8 (February 21, 2005): 171.

LEE MILLER
A Life

Author: Carolyn Burke (1940-   )
Publisher: Alfred A. Knopf (New York). 426 pp. $35.00
Type of work: Biography
Time: 1907-1977
Locale: Poughkeepsie, New York; New York City; Paris;
England

*This carefully researched and ruminative life of the im-
portant twentieth century photographer was written with
the full cooperation of her family*

Principal personages:
    LEE MILLER, a photographer
    THEODORE MILLER, her father
    FLORENCE MILLER, her mother
    ERIK MILLER, her brother
    MAN RAY, the distinguished artist and photographer who became her
        lover and mentor
    AZIZ ELOUI BEY, her first husband
    ROLAND PENROSE, her second husband

Lee Miller was brought up in Poughkeepsie, New York. The daughter of a highly successful engineer with a penchant for photography, she served as a model at a young age, posing for many of her father's photographs. His shots of his young daughter in the nude, however, raise disturbing questions—ones that author Carolyn Burke explores but cannot answer. Miller remained close to her father, who continued to photograph her in the nude even after she was raped, at the age of seven, while staying with family friends in Brooklyn, New York. Years later, Theodore continued to photograph his daughter in the nude when she became Man Ray's lover and model.

Miller's mother, Florence, remains something of a mystery in this biography. Apparently she condoned her husband's exploitation of their daughter as part of his "art," but what else she may have thought of this quasi-incestuous relationship eludes the biographer's research. Florence, trained as a nurse, gave her daughter painful treatments for the gonorrhea Lee suffered as a consequence of the rape. The whole family, including Lee's brother Erik, could hear Lee's screams coming from the white-tiled bathroom where Florence administered the excruciating douches required then to eradicate the disease.

Miller broke away from her family to study stage design in Paris for nine months. There she began a surprisingly active and apparently untroubled sex life. Although she returned to Poughkeepsie to study at Vassar College, her eventual move to New York City and to some kind of career in the arts was inevitable. Her first success came as a model for *Vogue* magazine. She was photographed in haute couture, but she

～

Carolyn Burke, a biographer, art critic, and translator, met Lee Miller while conducting research for her biography Becoming Modern: The Life of Mina Loy *(1996). Burke has taught at universities in the United States, Australia, and France. She has published articles and translations from the French in* Art in America, The New Yorker, Heat, Sulfur, *and* Critical Inquiry. *Born in Australia, she now lives in Santa Cruz, California.*

～

showed her versatility in poses that were both sophisticated and virginal. It was, however, as a photojournalist and war correspondent that she would make her mark. By 1934, *Vanity Fair* magazine deemed her one of the seven most distinguished living photographers in the world.

Miller's life in some ways resembles those of other famous women of her period. Like the writer Martha Gellhorn, who left St. Louis for Paris, Miller checked into a *maison de passe*, a hotel for prostitutes. Gellhorn also modeled clothes in Paris and developed a taste for European life. Gellhorn sought out older male writers (including H. G. Wells and Ernest Hemingway) who mentored her writing, just as Miller sought out Man Ray, who not only put her in front of his camera but also taught her how to use the camera to photograph herself and others. Both women went beyond their mentors in seeking out history-making events that led to their fame as war correspondents.

Miller seems even more heroic than Gellhorn. Not only did Miller overcome a feeling that her life was irrevocably blighted by her childhood rape, she also achieved distinction as a pioneering photojournalist, taking some of the most arresting photographs of the Blitz (turning it into a "theater of war," Burke suggests), the liberation of Paris, and the concentration camps (especially Dachau, where her contemporary Gellhorn alighted and set what is perhaps her most important novel, *Point of No Return*, 1989).

Unlike Rebecca West, who did so much to open the world's eyes to fascism and communism, or Lillian Hellman, who rivaled Miller in the culinary arts and shared a knack for self-dramatization, or Gellhorn who grew bored when she could no longer live for adventure, Miller found a way to come to terms with her own theatricality— that is, her desire to put herself at the center of history.

Burke focuses, for example, on the revealing shot taken of Miller in Adolf Hitler's bathtub, taken in the last days of the war. She sits in the tub, a grimy Aryan goddess, making a mockery of Nazi racial ideology, to be sure, but also suggesting how she is implicated in the evil of adoration—caught between the photograph of the führer on one edge of the tub and a small statue of Venus on the other.

Burke shows her brilliance as a biographer by incorporating Miller's history into an understanding of this photograph. Miller knew that her posing for *Vogue* created a certain kind of standard for beauty, a figure others were meant to idolize. She understood, in other words, what the costs of charisma can be when it narrows the world to a typology of the ideal, especially when that ideal is revved up by the modern media of photography and film.

In the same vein, Miller took a stunning photograph of Gellhorn, which Burke analyzes too briefly. The writer sits in front of a mirror, pen in hand, watching herself write while above her a photograph of Hemingway hovers. Unlike Miller, Gellhorn, Hellman, and West never acknowledged just how self-conscious they were about writing themselves into the world's consciousness. Miller is their superior in understanding what it means to model oneself after other charismatics in order to make oneself the model.

Only Jill Craigie, a documentary filmmaker who, like Miller, later in life settled into a long marriage (Labour leader Michael Foot was her third husband) understood the devastating toll charisma-building could take. Craigie's name does not appear in Burke's biography, but it should, as Craigie was the director of *Out of Chaos*, a documentary about wartime artists filmed in London in 1943. Miller visited the set and was photographed with Craigie and Henry Moore.

Miller made sure *Vogue* wrote about the film because she understood that Craigie was doing something new: breaking down the barrier between modern artists and the general public. Craigie's footage of Moore drawing and describing how he did his tube shelter drawings is one of the primary documents of self-revelation in twentieth century art—a piece of film that has been used repeatedly in documentaries about Moore and modern art. That Miller was the only major journalist to visit the set of the film and to interview Moore and Craigie testifies to her intense interest in the nexus between artists and their art.

Miller's photographs do much the same thing as Craigie's film: They theatricalize art and history, making both more accessible. As Burke shows, when famous photographer Margaret Bourke-White photographed the suicide scene of a Nazi official, she "shot the scene from above, at a distance." Then Miller arrived on the scene.

> The treasurer and his family still lay on their deathbeds when Lee reached the site hours later. She photographed them not from above but on the same level, the macabre scene formed by the women in the background and the man in the foreground, his allegiance signaled by the portrait of Hitler opposite his desk. "On the same level"—history brought home, in other words. In Lee Miller, we are in presence of an exceptionally honest artist-observer, one who knows just how deeply implicated she is in the scenes that become, in effect, her set designs.

The reader thus learns not only about the scene but also about the scenic eye.

Miller, as talented as her male counterparts, found herself after World War II confined to what Gellhorn called "the kitchen of life." Miller made the most of her role as "Lady Penrose" when married to Pablo Picasso biographer Roland Penrose, discovering the joy of cookery and establishing a reputation as, among other things, "the sandwich queen." This was a second marriage for her—the first was to Aziz Eloui Bey, an Egyptian, exiled her to Alexandria, Egypt, where she flourished briefly but ultimately chafed at the rarefied atmosphere that provided little stimulation for her genius. The sensitive Bey understood Miller's ambition and her need to forsake the kind of stability that appealed to her but which ultimately could not pacify her restless spirit.

Miller's later years, like Gellhorn's, were often difficult. She drank too much and apparently missed her life of adventure. She did not dwell on it, however, and many who knew her in these years did not realize how important a figure she had been in the

1930's and 1940's. Miller sought to make the most of her domestic life, making a study of the art of cooking. Her marriage to Penrose was often under strain, but it endured.

Burke is fortunate to have secured complete access to her subject's archives and to have received the cooperation of Miller's family. Evidently, the biographer has also been able to preserve her independence—not an easy feat when the subject's family controls much of the material on which the biographer depends to tell her story. This handsomely produced and impeccably written and researched book (which includes many of Miller's most important photographs) is surely a state-of-the-art biography.

Carl Rollyson

Review Sources

Booklist 102, no. 8 (December 15, 2005): 11.
The Economist 377 (December 3, 2005): 81.
Kirkus Reviews 73, no. 20 (October 15, 2005): 1120.
Library Journal 131, no. 1 (January 15, 2006): 108-109.
New Statesman 134 (December 5, 2005): 51-52.
The New York Times Book Review 155 (January 8, 2006): 7.
Publishers Weekly 252, no. 39 (October 3, 2005): 61.
The Washington Post Book World. November 27, 2005, p. 8.